FOURTH EDITION

Learning and Teaching

Research-Based Methods

Donald P. Kauchak

University of Utah

Paul D. Eggen

University of North Florida

Boston   New York   San Francisco
Mexico City   Montreal   Toronto   London   Madrid   Munich   Paris
Hong Kong   Singapore   Tokyo   Cape Town   Sydney

VP/Editor-in-Chief: Paul Smith
Series Editor: Traci Mueller
Series Editorial Assistant: Erica Tromblay
Marketing Manager: Amy Cronin
Production Editor: Susan Brown
Editorial-Production Service: Matrix Productions Inc.
Composition and Prepress Buyer: Linda Cox
Manufacturing Buyer: JoAnne Sweeney
Cover Administrator: Linda Knowles

For related titles and support materials, visit our online catalog at www.ablongman.com.

Library of Congress Cataloging-in-Publication Data

Kauchak, Donald P.
    Learning and teaching : research-based methods / Donald P. Kauchak, Paul D. Eggen.—
4th ed.
      p. cm.
    Includes bibliographical references (p.) and index.
    ISBN 0-205-33757-0
    1. Teaching. 2. Effective teaching. I. Eggen, Paul D. II. Title.

LB1025.3 .K38 2003
371.102—dc21

                                                  2002020210

Photo credit: All photos by Will Hart.

Printed in the United States of America

10 9 8 7 6 5 4 3   05 04 03

Contents

Chapter 4   Effective Teaching: The Research Base   119

Chapter 9 Capitalizing on Social Interaction   284

Chapter 10 Problem-Based Instruction   326

Chapter 11 Teacher-Centered Instruction   357

Preface

Research continues to highlight the central role teachers play in determining the quality of learning in classrooms. Teachers *do* make a difference in how much students learn, and this difference depends on how they teach. The influence of teachers on both student achievement and motivation is even more convincingly documented in the research literature than it was in 1989, when the first edition of this text was published. Knowledge of research continues to be the primary way teachers become effective professionals. The goal of this text is to translate the results of research into methods that preservice and in-service teachers use to increase learning and student motivation.

This book brings together two areas of the educational literature. One is the research on how teaching influences learning, which includes a wide range of studies conducted since the early 1970s. While originally grounded in the research on effective teaching, this literature has expanded to include topics such as teacher and student cognition, constructivism, teaching for understanding, and the importance of social interaction in learning.

Teaching methodology is the second area addressed in this book. Methods texts typically stress teaching procedures viewed as desirable, based on the state of the art at the time. The emphasis in these texts is on classroom application, with less emphasis on research.

This edition attempts to combine the best of these two areas. We apply the research on teaching to strategies that are theoretically sound, yet practical and usable.

This interpretation of the literature has been enriched by our work in the schools; as we've used this book in our classes, teachers and students have helped us ensure that our applications are effective and true to the complexities of today's schools and students.

GOALS OF THIS TEXT

We have two goals in combining these areas:

- To change how teachers think about teaching
- To change how they actually teach

Researchers studying the way people learn to teach focus on two areas: (1) teacher thinking, and (2) teacher knowledge (Borko & Putnam, 1996). The way teachers think and what they know are the two major factors that influence how they actually teach. And the way teachers think depends on what they know; in other words, teacher thinking and teacher knowledge are interdependent. So, to meet our goals, we attempt to help teachers acquire the background knowledge that will influence both their thinking and the way they actually work in classrooms. This knowledge is grounded in the rapidly expanding research base that is making teaching increasingly professional.

Without the research to provide a conceptual foundation, methods become mechanical applications of rules implemented without understanding. On the other hand, without practical suggestions for teaching practice, the research literature remains abstract and irrelevant. In this edition we again try to avoid both pitfalls by emphasizing the conceptual underpinnings of the research and the implications of this research for actual classroom practice.

PORTFOLIOS AND PROFESSIONAL GROWTH

As we've moved into the twenty-first century, increased emphasis is being placed on teacher professionalism (Cochran-Smith, 2001). Professionals are not only knowledgeable and skilled but are also able to reflect on their growth as educators. This emphasis is reflected in the increased use of teacher portfolios—collections of work over time—to document their professional growth.

We have added two features in this text to assist you in using portfolios. A section in Chapter 1, Developing a Professional Portfolio, describes what portfolios are and how you can use this text to begin developing a portfolio. Portfolio Activities at the end of each chapter provide concrete suggestions for portfolio entries as well as questions for reflection. The combination of portfolio activities and questions are designed to help you integrate and personalize text content as you grow professionally.

TEXT THEMES

Today's schools are changing and these changes present both opportunities and challenges. To address these changes, we have organized the fourth edition around three powerful and pervasive forces in education. These forces provide the basis for three themes that are integrated and applied throughout the text. They are:

- The *diversity* of our learners
- Ways of enhancing learner *motivation*
- The use of *technology* for increasing learning

The diversity of our learners reflects the growing diversity of our country. This diversity has important implications for the way we teach. In addition to an entire chapter on diversity (Chapter 2), we also address the topic of diversity in the following chapters:

CHAPTER	DIVERSITY SECTION
3	Planning for Diversity: Individualized Instruction
4	Teacher Attitudes, Learner Diversity, and Motivation
5	Effective Questioning: Involving Diverse Learners
6	Learner Diversity: Challenges to Home-School Communication
9	Using Cooperative Learning to Capitalize on Diversity
12	Accommodating Diversity: Reducing Bias in Assessment

Learner motivation is receiving increased attention both in the schools and in the research literature. The development of motivated and self-regulated learners is becoming ever more important to both teachers and researchers. We describe different perspectives on motivation in the following chapters:

CHAPTER	MOTIVATION SECTION
2	Motivation: The Need for Challenge
3	Motivation: An Integral Part of Planning
4	Teacher Attitudes, Learner Diversity, and Motivation
5	Effective Questioning: Increasing Student Motivation
7	Constructivist Learning Activities and Student Motivation
10	Motivation and Problem-Based Instruction
11	The Motivational Benefits of Effective Feedback

Technology is the third theme of this edition. Technology is changing the way we live as well as the way we learn and teach. Various forms of technology, including computers, the Internet, videodiscs, videotape, and educational television are all influencing the ways we teach. Tomorrow's teachers need to know how to integrate technology into their teaching. We address applications of technology in the following chapters:

CHAPTER	TECHNOLOGY SECTION
2	Technology as a Tool for Inclusion
3	Technology as a Tool for Individualizing Instruction
7	Using Technology to Represent Content: Databases and Construct Knowledge
8	Utilizing Technology in Concept Learning
9	Computer-Mediated Communication: Using Technology to Facilitate Cooperative Learning
10	Anchored Instruction: Technology as a Tool to Teach Problem Solving
12	Using Technology in Assessment

As we used this text in our classrooms and listened to the suggestions of our colleagues, we have made the following pedagogical additions to the fourth edition:

- Developing a Professional Portfolio
- Portfolio Activities
- Outcomes-Based Education
- National Reforms
- Standards-Based Professional Development
- INTASC Standards
- National Board Certification
- Assistive Technology
- Working with ESL Students
- Expanded Coverage of Project-Based Learning

These changes reflect the changing realities of modern classrooms as well as the new responsibilities that today's teachers carry.

We sincerely thank our colleagues who reviewed the previous editions as well as new manuscript; their experience, insights, criticisms, and suggestions assisted our decisions concerning diversity, motivation, and technology: Alan A. Block, University of Wisconsin–Stout; John-Michael Bodi, Bridgewater State College; Randy Brown, University of Central Oklahoma; Greg Bryant, Towson State University; Marjorie Checkoway, Madonna University; Thomas A. Drazdowski, King's College; Mary Dean Dumais, Kean University; Margaret Ferrara, Central Connecticut State University; Dee Ann Holmes, Emporia State University; Susan Johnson, Northwestern College; Daniel Kain, Northern Arizona University; James Koper, Western Kentucky University; Robert Locatelli, University of Nevada–Las Vegas; Marc Mahlios, University of Kansas; Mary E. Outlaw, Berry College; Laura M. Stough, Texas A&M University; Suzanne M. Tochterman, Colorado State University. We hope our new and revised edition helps you prepare for the challenges of teaching in the twenty-first century.

D. K.

P. E.

1

Research and Teaching

■

*T*his book is about teaching and the different ways teachers help students learn. Next to the students themselves, teachers are the most important influence on school learning. This chapter begins by examining the concept of effective teaching, briefly outlining its history, and illustrating how research can be used to improve the way you teach and how students learn. In this chapter we also describe the different components of learning to teach. *Pedagogical content knowledge* enables teachers to present topics in understandable ways. *Knowledge of basic principles of teaching and learning* helps teachers understand connections between their actions and student achievement. *Teaching strategies* translate research into classroom-oriented plans for action. These three components are tied together by teacher decision making, which integrates them into purposeful teacher actions.

Finally, in this chapter we introduce the themes that run through this text. These themes remind us of the *diversity of our learners,* why *learner motivation* is critical, and how *technology* can be used to increase achievement.

When you've completed your study of this chapter, you should be able to meet the following objectives:

- Explain how research contributes to the process of learning to teach.
- Describe different views of learning and explain how they influence teaching.
- Describe the process of learning to teach in terms of pedagogical content knowledge, knowledge of teaching and learning, teaching strategies, and teacher decision making.
- Implement lessons that accommodate learner diversity, increase motivation, and capitalize on the benefits of technology.

Three middle school teachers were eating lunch together on their 40-minute break between classes. After weather and local politics, the conversation turned to teaching, or, more specifically, to students.

"How are your seventh graders this year?" Paul Escobar asked. "I can't seem to get them motivated."

Stan Williams replied with a frown, "I've got three basic math classes, and I've spent the first two months reviewing stuff they're supposed to know already. They don't seem to want to think," he concluded, turning to the others with an exasperated look.

"Mine aren't so bad," Leona Foster replied. "In fact, the other day we had a great discussion on individual rights. We were discussing the Bill of Rights, and some of them actually got excited about it. And it was even one of my slower classes. I was impressed with some of their comments."

"But how am I going to get them to think if they don't even know how to multiply or divide?" Stan answered in frustration.

"I know what you're talking about, Stan," Paul Escabar interjected. "I'm supposed to teach them to write, but they don't even know basic grammar. How am I supposed to teach them subject-verb agreement when they don't know what a noun or verb is?"

"Exactly!" Stan answered. "We've got to teach them basics before we can teach them all the other stuff, like problem solving and thinking skills."

"I'm not so sure about that," Paul replied. "I had a real eye opener the other day. . . . Let me tell you about it. I've been going to workshops on using writing teams to teach composition. I tried it out, putting high- and low-ability students on the same team. They were supposed to write a critical review of a short story we had read, using television movie critics as a model. We talked a little about basic concepts like plot and action, watched a short clip of two movie critics arguing about a movie, then I turned them loose. I couldn't believe it—some of the kids that never participate actually got excited."

"That's all fine and good for English classes, but I'm a math teacher. What am I supposed to do, have them critique math problems? 'Oh, I give this math problem two thumbs up!' Besides, these are supposed to be middle school students. I shouldn't have to sugar coat the content. They should come ready to learn. My job is to teach; theirs is to learn. It's as simple as that."

DEFINING GOOD TEACHING

"It's as simple as that" . . . Or is it? Teaching has always been a challenging profession, but changes both within and outside classrooms have made it even more challenging. Schools are being asked to teach thinking and problem-solving skills at the same time that students come from increasingly diverse backgrounds. Definitions of good or effective teaching are becoming not only more crucial but also more complex.

But, what is effective teaching? How does effective teaching relate to learning? What responsibilities do teachers have to motivate their students? What are the implications of student diversity on the teaching/learning process? How can teachers use new technologies to promote learning? Are "basics" the best path to thinking skills, or should thinking skills be used as a vehicle to teach basics?

These are important questions for anyone in education because they center around the question "What is good teaching?" These concerns are particularly important to developing teachers because your answers to these questions will influence the kind of teacher you become. As you ponder these questions, thinking about yourself and the classrooms you've experienced, each of you will form a personal definition of effective teaching. This individual response is as it should be: Each teacher is as unique as each student. But beyond this individual uniqueness, some strands exist that pull these questions together.

Let's consider commonalities a bit further. Does your definition of effective teaching apply to all levels? For example, do effective kindergarten and high school teachers teach in similar ways? What about students? Would your definition of good teaching apply equally well to low- and high-ability learners? And how about subject matter? Does an effective history teacher teach the same way as effective English or art teachers?

Finally, how does time influence your definition? Do effective teachers teach the same way at the beginning of the school year as at its close, at the beginning of a unit as at the end, or even at the beginning of a lesson and at its completion?

Each of you will wrestle with these questions, either implicitly or explicitly, as you begin and continue with your teaching career. The purpose of this book is to help you resolve these questions based on the best information available to the profession.

The field of teaching is at a particularly exciting time in its history. Education has always been one of the most rewarding professions, but at the same time it continues to be one of the most challenging. An effective teacher combines the best of human relations, intuition, sound judgment, knowledge of subject matter, and knowledge of how people learn—all in one simultaneous act. This task is extremely complex, and one of the factors making it particularly difficult has been the lack of a clear and documented body of knowledge on which to base professional decisions.

The situation has changed. Education now has a significant and rapidly expanding body of research that can guide teaching practice and the training of teachers. That's what this text is all about; it is a book about teaching practice that is founded in and based on research. As you study the chapters, you will be exposed to a detailed body of research, and you will learn how this research can be applied in your classroom.

We developed this text around a series of themes that will be introduced in this chapter. As your study continues, you will see how research helps teachers as they make their professional decisions. This research, as with all research, is not perfect, but having it as a foundation is a giant step forward. Despite some weaknesses and even some controversy, this research marks a major advance in education. It is already finding its way into tests used to certify teachers (Darling-Hammond & Cobbe, 1996) and into both preservice and in-service programs for teachers (Sikula, 1996). Your study of this text will provide you with the best information available to the profession at this time.

RESEARCH IN TEACHING: AN HISTORICAL PERSPECTIVE

Historically, teaching has been a profession in search of a body of knowledge that could inform classroom practice. In the past, educational practice and educational reforms were often based on the views and intuition of prominent thinkers rather than on research evidence (Slavin, 1989). Because of the stature of these people and the power and eloquence of their positions, their assertions often were translated into practice despite the lack of evidence to support the practice.

For example, the post-Sputnik years spawned a national wave of curriculum revision in math and science during the 1960s and early 1970s. The view held by prominent scientists and mathematicians was that the content in those areas was inappropriate because it did not accurately reflect the "structure" and research methods of different disciplines. Curriculum revision was aimed at correcting these deficiencies. The changes sounded good, and enormous amounts of money, time, and effort were pumped into the revision efforts. While the programs enjoyed modest popularity, they were clearly not as successful as the original developers had hoped for nor as effective as the millions of dollars poured into them promised (Fensham, 1992).

One of the reasons for this lack of success was that programs were developed without a coherent body of knowledge on which to base curricular decisions, such as considerations of the intellectual development of the learners who would study the materials, the extent to which the materials would be motivating for students, and whether they were usable by teachers. Many of the strategies required skills teachers didn't have and materials not readily found in classrooms. A lack of information about the realities of teaching and learning in classrooms was a primary reason these projects were only marginally successful.

Studies of Teacher Characteristics

As researchers began to seek connections between teaching and learning, they initially focused on teacher characteristics, such as neatness, sense of humor, or cognitive flexibility (Rosenshine, 1979). Initial research asked whether or not teachers having these desirable traits resulted in increased learning. For example, do students taught by a teacher with a good sense of humor learn more and/or have better attitudes than those taught by a more serious teacher? In hindsight, we see that the question was oversimplified; magnificent teachers of many different personalities can be found.

In addition to problems with focus, the research also had problems with methodology. Researchers seldom spent time in classrooms to see if a teacher rated high in a certain trait taught any differently from those rated low in the trait. They merely assumed that a difference existed. For example, if a teacher scored high on a test of cognitive flexibility, researchers failed to determine whether this trait influenced how the teacher taught or interacted with students. Unfortunately, this line of research led nowhere. Gage, a prominent researcher in the field, reviewed over 10,000 studies in this area and concluded in 1960 that few, if any, generalizations could be made about the results.

In hindsight, the research on teacher characteristics was not completely misguided. Two teacher characteristics—teacher experience and understanding of subject matter—have proved to be powerful variables influencing how teachers understand events in the classroom and explain content (Berliner, 1994; Shulman, 1987). Veteran teachers are able to use their experience to interpret the complex events that occur in classrooms and to make the many split-second decisions that are needed every day. Similarly, subject-matter expertise allows effective teachers to frame and explain ideas in ways that make sense to students. We will return to both of these ideas later in the chapter.

The Search for the Right Method

During the 1960s, the next wave of research focused on global methods and attempted to link certain teaching strategies, like inquiry instruction or discovery learning, with student outcomes, such as scores on standardized achievement tests (Dunkin and Biddle, 1974; Medley, 1979). This research was characterized by a belief that a particular type of teaching, such as discussion, was better than an alternative, such as lecture. To investigate this question, teachers were trained in a particular technique and then asked to teach their students by this method. The performance of their students was compared to the performance of students taught by an alternate method.

Like research on teacher characteristics, this line of research was also flawed. The methods were often poorly defined and poorly taught to teachers, few classroom observations were made to determine if the methods were actually used, and often no sound relationship existed between the methods and the tests used to measure outcomes. For instance, a research study might ask if discussion was superior to lecture, but a paper-and-pencil recall test was used to measure student learning. A paper-and-pencil test ignores many of the benefits of discussions, such as improved communication skills or the development of critical thinking. In addition, the strengths of discussions are their ability to get students to think critically about ideas, something best measured by an essay test. As might be expected, this line of research also proved unproductive.

School-Level Research

A third line of research focused on variables such as school size, training level of teachers, and aptitude or socioeconomic status of the students. These studies tried to determine the effects of these variables on student achievement and attitude. The most notable study of this type was the famous Coleman Report (1966), which involved 4,000 schools and 654,000 students. The study analyzed data at the school rather than the classroom level—thereby masking individual teacher differences—and concluded that teachers made little difference in how much students learned. Understandably, this research had a dampening effect on efforts to identify effective teaching practices; the study concluded that factors outside teachers' influence, such as the background of the students and the curriculum, were more important than the teacher.

Subsequent researchers questioned some assumptions and procedures involved in these schoolwide studies and, as a consequence, their results as well. For example, in these studies, standardized test scores of student achievement for each individual class were averaged with those of the other classes in a school to get a school-wide score. These averages masked results that would provide valuable information about *individual* teachers. As we all know, individual teachers within a school vary considerably in their teaching effectiveness. Prominent researchers pointed out these problems (Alexander and McDill, 1976; Good, Biddle, and Brophy, 1975), and a new wave of research was launched.

Teacher Effectiveness Research: Teachers Do Make a Difference

As a consequence of the results or, more accurately, the nonresults of earlier efforts, research on teaching finally focused on teachers' actions in classrooms, attempting to find links between these actions and student learning (Good, 1996). These studies marked a new way of thinking about research in education. Unlike previous work, this research focused on the teacher and the kinds of interactions teachers had with students (Shulman, 1986). Researchers identified teachers whose students scored higher than would be expected on standardized tests and other teachers whose students scored as expected or below for their age and ability level. They then went into classrooms, videotaped literally thousands of hours of instruction and tried to determine what differences existed in the instructional patterns of the teachers in the two samples. These studies were labeled *process-product research* because they attempted to find a link between teacher actions or behaviors (processes) and student learning outcomes—primarily scores on standardized achievement tests (products) (Gage, 1985). Finally, researchers were focusing on what teachers actually did that made a difference in what students learned.

Initially, the process-product research was correlational; that is, teacher actions and student outcomes were related, but the researchers did not know if the results were actually caused by the teacher actions. The complexities of attributing causal relationships with correlational research are illustrated with the problem of teacher disapproval (Gage and Giaconia, 1981). Researchers found an inverse relationship between teacher disapproval and student achievement; teachers who were more negative in their classroom had students who achieved at lower levels than teachers who were more positive (see Figure 1.1). However, it was unclear whether disapproval caused or was the result of low achievement, or whether it was related to a completely different variable such as classroom management problems. For example, one way to explain this inverse relationship is that teachers, frustrated over their students' lack of learning, resorted to disapprovals more often. An alternate explanation is that poor classroom management led to more disapprovals by teachers trying to survive a chaotic classroom, which also led to decreased learning. Note that none of these possible explanations directly or causally linked disapprovals to lowered achievement. The point here is that correlational findings may suggest cause-and-effect relationships but do not in themselves prove them. To address this problem directly, the next wave of research was experimentally designed to find causal links, if they existed (Gage and Giaconia, 1981).

These experimental studies trained teachers to use the specific behaviors identified in the correlational studies (e.g., waiting a period of time after asking a question before calling on a student to respond). In addition, investigators observed the trained teachers' classes to determine whether the teachers were actually implementing the desired behavior in the classroom. Finally, classes of trained and untrained teachers were compared. Because these efforts focused on *differences between less and more effective teachers, it became known as the* **teacher effectiveness research.** A number of significant differences were found, many of which we'll describe in later chapters.

Beyond Effective Teaching: A Focus on Student Learning

The literature on effective teaching made an invaluable contribution to education because it both confirmed the critical role teachers play in student learning and provided

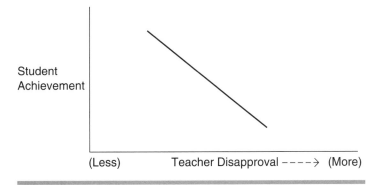

Figure 1.1 Teacher Disapproval and Student Learning

"education with a knowledge base capable of moving the field beyond testimonials and unsupported claims toward scientific statements based on credible data" (Brophy, 1992, p. 5). It provides, however, only a threshold or a baseline above which all teachers should be. Expert teachers go beyond this threshold to construct lessons that help students learn content in a meaningful way.

Despite impressive results, critics also identified shortcomings in the teacher effectiveness research. Critics charged that it focused too much on lower-level learning and tended to break knowledge into small pieces, thus reinforcing students for overt performance at the expense of meaningful learning (Marshall, 1992; Stoddart et al., 1993). In addition, critics contended that the research was decontextualized and failed to take students, their backgrounds, and the classroom environment into account (Goodenow, 1992). In essence, the critics were reminding us that students and student learning should be our primary focus in discussions about teaching. These criticisms resulted in fundamental changes in views of effective teaching methods with major shifts from teacher-centered to learner-centered approaches.

CONTEMPORARY VIEWS OF TEACHING AND LEARNING

At the same time that perspectives on teaching were changing, similar changes were occurring in the way researchers viewed learners and learning. Behaviorist views of learning, which emphasized external influences in the form of rewards and punishment, gradually gave way to more cognitive perspectives. These cognitive perspectives emphasized active internal processes that students used to organize, store, and retrieve information (Bruning, Shraw, and Ronning, 1999). More recently, research has emphasized the critical role that learners play in constructing new knowledge (Eggen and Kauchak, 2001). We analyze these changes in the sections that follow.

From Behaviorist to Cognitive Perspectives

For the first half of the twentieth century behaviorist views of learning predominated in education (Mayer, 1996; Reynolds, Sinatra, and Jelton, 1996). **Behaviorism** *emphasized the importance of observable, external events on learning and the role of reinforcers in influencing those events.* The goal of behaviorist research was to determine how external instructional manipulations affected changes in student behavior. The role of the teacher was to control the environment through stimuli in the form of cues and reinforcement for appropriate student behavior. Students were viewed as empty receptacles, responding passively to stimuli from the teacher and the classroom environment.

Over time, researchers found this perspective on learning to be oversimplified and perhaps misdirected. While learners do indeed react to stimuli from the environment, research revealed that students were not passive recipients but instead actively changed and altered stimuli from the environment as they attempted to make sense of their environments. Student characteristics such as background knowledge, motivation, and the use of learning strategies all influenced learning (Bruning et al., 1999). The role of the teacher also changed from dispenser of rewards and punishment to someone who helped students organize and make sense of information. These differences between behaviorism and **cognitive psychology,** *which focuses on thought processes within learners,* are summarized in Table 1.1.

Table 1.1 COMPARISON OF BEHAVIORIST AND COGNITIVE VIEW
OF LEARNING

	View of Learning	View of Learner	View of Teacher
Behaviorism	Accumulation of responses through selective reinforcement	Passive recipient of stimuli from environment	Controller of stimuli and shaper of behaviors through reinforcement
Cognitive	Development of strategies to encode and retrieve information	Active meaning maker through strategy use	Partner in the process of meaning making; teacher of organizational and retrieval strategies

Constructivism: Students as Creators of Understanding

In about the last twenty years, constructivism—a recent development in cognitive psychology—has focused our attention on the central role that learners play in constructing new knowledge. Influenced by the work of Jean Piaget and Lev Vygotsky as well as linguistics and anthropology, **constructivism** *is an eclectic view of learning that emphasizes four key components:*

1. Learners construct their own understanding rather than having it delivered or transmitted to them.
2. New learning depends on prior understanding and knowledge.
3. Learning is enhanced by social interaction.
4. Authentic learning tasks promote meaningful learning.

Constructivism has fundamentally changed the way we view teaching and learning. As opposed to passive recipients of information, learners become active meaning makers, building upon current knowledge. To facilitate the process, teachers design learning situations in which learners can work with others on meaningful learning tasks. Many of the teaching strategies that you'll learn about in this text are based upon constructivist views of learners and learning.

Learner-Centered Psychological Principles

In an attempt to summarize these recent changes in perspectives on learning, the American Psychological Association published *Learner-Centered Psychological Principles: Guidelines for School Redesign and Reform* (Presidential Task Force on Psychology in Education, 1993). As the title implies, these principles are designed to provide guidance to teachers and administrators working to reshape learning in the schools. A summary of these principles can be found in Figure 1.2

These generalizations remind us as teachers of the centrality of our students in the learning process. We need to consider our students' background knowledge, development, and motivation as we plan for instruction. In addition, we need to actively encourage students to think about their own learning and make our classrooms comfortable and stimulating places to learn—places where students feel part of a community of learners.

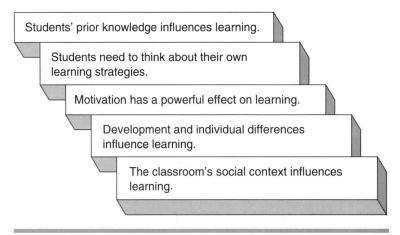

Students' prior knowledge influences learning.

Students need to think about their own learning strategies.

Motivation has a powerful effect on learning.

Development and individual differences influence learning.

The classroom's social context influences learning.

Figure 1.2 Generalizations about Learning and Teaching

In addition to these broad, general changes in views about teaching and learning, content-specific ones have also arisen. The National Council for the Teaching of Mathematics has developed new guidelines that stress student involvement in meaningful problem-solving activities (NCTM, 1989, 1991). The field of science has also published guidelines that call for deeper, more thoughtful and intensive study of science topics (American Association for the Advancement of Science, 1993). In the language arts, moves toward literature-based approaches to reading and process-oriented writing emphasize the need for active student involvement and learning (McCarthy, 1994). Common to all of these is refocused attention on the learner and what teachers can do to help students learn.

The combination of all these lines of research is what make this an exciting time to study education. Researchers are uncovering a number of links between teacher actions and student achievement. Because of this and other related research, our views of exemplary teaching practice and the professional development of teachers have changed. Our goal in preparing this text is to communicate these findings and their implications to prospective teachers and practicing teachers in the classroom.

TEXT THEMES

In response to recent developments in education, three themes appear throughout the text:

- The *diversity* of our learners
- Ways of enhancing learner *motivation*
- The use of *technology* for increasing learning

Because these topics influence so many different aspects of teaching, they are integrated throughout the text. Let's examine them briefly.

The Diversity of Our Learners

The students attending America's schools are becoming increasingly diverse. For example, teachers will encounter students with a wide range of learning abilities. The practice of inclusion, which attempts to accommodate the learning needs of all students in as regular an educational setting as possible, results in the presence of more students with exceptionalities in regular classrooms. About 10 percent of the student population is included in this group, and exceptionalities range from mild learning disabilities to physical disabilities such as deafness and blindness (U.S. Department of Education, 2001).

Ethnicity and culture also contribute to diversity. More than 7 million people immigrated to the United States during the 1970s, and another 7 million came during the 1980s. Between 1980 and 1994, the African-American student population grew by 25 percent, the Hispanic student population by 46 percent, and the Asian-American student population grew by 100 percent (U.S. Census Bureau, 1996).

More than 100 ethnic groups and 170 Native American groups live in the United States. Experts estimate that by the year 2020 our country will see considerable increases in the numbers of Hispanic and African-American students, and a dramatic increase in Asian/Pacific Islander and American Indian/Alaskan Native populations will occur (U.S. Census Bureau, 1998b; Young and Smith, 1999). Each of these groups brings a distinct set of values and traditions that influence student learning.

This growth in immigration is also resulting in an increase in language diversity. Currently there are approximately 3.2 million children in U.S. schools whose home language is other than English. California has 1.4 million of these English as a Second Language (ESL) students, comprising nearly 40 percent of the student population in that state (U.S. Department of Education, 1998; Stoddart, 1999). In the Los Angeles School District, more than 81 languages are represented, with as many as 20 found in some classrooms. Nationwide, the number of students whose primary language is not English is expected to triple during the next 30 years. The most common language groups for these students are Spanish (73%), Vietnamese (4%), Hmong (1.8%), Cantonese (1.7%), and Cambodian (1.6%).

Poverty and student differences in socioeconomic status also present challenges to teachers. Consider these statistics:

- Seven out of ten women with children are in the workforce.
- The divorce rate has quadrupled in the past 20 years; the number of single-parent families is estimated at 25 percent and is expected to increase.
- Sixty-eight percent of all births to teenagers occur out of wedlock.
- The incidence of poverty among single-parent families is between seven and eight times higher than in families headed by married couples.
- Sixty percent of teenage families live in poverty as compared to 14 percent of the total population.
- Children, while only 27 percent of the total population, constitute 40 percent of the poor.
- Poverty is more prevalent among minorities than nonminorities
(More Families in Poverty, 1993; U.S. Census Bureau, 1998b).

These conditions create challenges for both teachers and students. Teachers need to be prepared for this diversity when they enter tomorrow's classrooms.

Ways of Enhancing Learner Motivation

Motivation, the second theme of the text, is a challenge for beginning and veteran teachers alike. In a review of over 83 studies involving beginning teachers from nine countries, Veenman (1984) found that only classroom management ranked ahead of motivation as a beginning teacher concern. Experienced teachers usually come to grips with classroom management, but they continue to wrestle with the problem of motivation. In his classic study of classrooms, Jackson (1968) found that a teacher's greatest source of satisfaction or joy in teaching came from seeing an individual child make progress, especially one who was initially unresponsive or unmotivated.

Motivation *is a force that energizes and directs student behavior toward a goal.* Our challenge as teachers is to increase student motivation and direct it toward the school-related tasks that students need to learn.

Student motivation is critical for learning (Wang, Haertel, and Walberg, 1993; Weinstein, 1998). In addition, increased motivation results in improved student attitudes about learning, fewer classroom management problems, and greater satisfaction with school for both teachers and students. It is a powerful factor influencing the total learning environment.

The Use of Technology for Increasing Learning

The third theme for this text is technology. Technology has changed the way we live and has also changed the way we learn and teach. Some examples of the dramatic growth of technology in schools include:

- Currently, there are over 9 million computers in American schools—about one for every 5.7 students.
- Seventy-five percent of public schools have access to some kind of telecommunications.
- More than 50 percent of public schools are linked to the Internet.
- Almost every school in the country has at least one television and videocassette recorder.
- 41 percent of teachers have a TV in their classroom.
  (Teachers and Technology, 1995; Schrum and Fitzgerald, 1996; Fatemi, 1999)

Probably the most dramatic growth has occurred in the area of computer technology. Initially, computer literacy, or preparing students for life in the age of computers, was the focus of most computer use in the schools. Over time, instructional uses of computers have expanded to include:

- Computer-assisted instruction, including simulations, multimedia instruction, drill and practice, and tutorials
- Information tools for students, including spreadsheets, databases, and other capabilities for information retrieval, processing and multimedia learning
- Computer-managed instruction, including student record keeping, diagnostic and prescriptive testing, and test scoring and analysis
- Design of instructional materials, including text and graphics

Technology in general, and computers in particular, are being viewed as essential parts of instruction to help students develop critical thinking skills (Roblyer and Edwards, 2000). Today's teachers need to know how to use these technologies to help students learn.

LEARNING TO TEACH

This book is written to assist you in the lifelong process of learning to teach. Becoming an expert teacher is a complex, multifaceted process that continues throughout an individual's professional lifetime. It requires intelligence, sensitivity, experience, and hard work. It also requires several different kinds of knowledge—knowledge of subject matter, such as history, literature, or algebra; knowledge of how to illustrate and represent abstract ideas in understandable ways; knowledge of learners and how they learn, and an understanding of how teachers can help in this process.

Let's turn now to a closer look at the different kinds of knowledge it takes to become an expert teacher.

Knowledge of Subject Matter

We can't teach what we don't understand ourselves. This simple statement is self-evident, and it is well documented by research examining the relationships between what teachers know and how they teach (Shulman, 1986; Wilson, Shulman, and Richert, 1987). To teach effectively about the American Revolution, for example, a social studies teacher must know not only basic facts about the event but also how it relates to other aspects of history, such as the French and Indian Wars, our relationship with England prior to the Revolution, and the characteristics of the individual colonies. The same is true for any topic in any other content area.

Pedagogical Content Knowledge

Knowledge of content—no matter how complete—is not enough, however; it is a necessary but not sufficient condition for effective instruction. An effective teacher must also *represent that information in ways that learners will understand. The ability to do this is called* **pedagogical content knowledge** (Shulman, 1986). For example, consider the concept of *mammal,* which is typically taught in different ways to students at different levels. At the elementary level, the teacher might use pictures and concrete examples (e.g., a gerbil or guinea pig) to emphasize characteristics like "covered with hair" and "warm blooded." At the junior high level, teachers build on this foundation by emphasizing additional characteristics like "live birth" and "four-chambered heart." Finally, at the high school level, biology teachers discuss characteristics like mammals' ability to adapt to their surroundings, different classes of mammals, and what it means to be a primitive (e.g. the duck-billed platypus) compared to an advanced mammal. The same concept is taught in different ways at each of these levels to accommodate the background, interests, and capabilities of students.

When teachers plan, one of their greatest challenges is to figure out ways of making abstract topics understandable. To illustrate this idea, let's examine one teacher's thinking as he wrestles with teaching the concept of *theme* to a high school English class. As he plans, he first defines it for himself as "an idea or thought that a story explores or treats." He realizes that this definition is abstract; if students are to understand it, he will need to illustrate it with concrete examples.

> I'm trying to think of an everyday example so as to "get into it," with the students. . . . What things are repeated in your life—but are never the same each time?

> Seasons, school, sunrises, meals, etc. . . . for example: A baseball game has a pattern that we can anticipate—9, 3-out innings. However, it is how that pattern is varied in each of its nine repetitions that gives a game meaning; that tells us who wins or loses. We know that a school year has a planned pattern of 2 semesters and four grading periods. But it is the variation within that pattern that gives the school year meaning for you or for me. *(Wilson et al., 1987, pp. 115–116)*

He unsuccessfully teaches the lesson; students don't grasp the parallels between his examples and a theme, nor are they able to identify one in a piece of literature. His examples of a baseball game and school semesters don't work, so he plans again.

> My frustrations led me to look for a better image, a better metaphor that I could give . . . for tracing and understanding theme. What I came up with was the trailing of a wounded animal by a hunter. Here the hunter discards all or most of the information the scene before him presents. He concentrates only on that which pertains to the animal he is searching for. Now some of the clues might be from the animal itself—blood or hair—just as the word or words of a theme appear outright in any given passage. But also a hunter must see the broken grass, the hoofprint, the things that are indicators.
>
> *(Wilson et al., 1987, pp. 116–117)*

Throughout the transformation of content from an abstract idea to the analogy of trailing a wounded animal, the teacher tries to help his students understand the process of finding a theme in literature. Effective teachers use their knowledge of content and their pedagogical content knowledge to help students make connections like this every day.

Knowledge of Teaching and Learning

Learning to teach not only involves understanding content and how to translate that subject matter into an understandable form, it also requires knowledge about the process of teaching and learning themselves. **Knowledge of teaching and learning** *involves a general understanding of instruction and management that transcends individual topics or subject matter areas* (Borko and Putnam, 1996). To understand how knowledge of teaching and learning is a central component of learning to teach, let's look at a teacher who has taught her students the process for adding fractions and is now reviewing with them.

"Class, look at this fraction on the board. What do we call the number on the bottom? Celena?"

"Uh . . . denominator."

"Good, Celena. And what do we call the number on the top, Carl?"

" . . . "

"We talked about this yesterday, Carl. Remember, it tells us the number of parts in the fraction. Think about the term that it is derived from, number."

"Oh yeah, numerator."

"Excellent, Carl. Now, look closely at this addition problem. It says to add $1/2$ and $1/3$. What do we have to do first? Think for a moment, because this is important. Look up at the pies that I've drawn on the board to represent these different fractions."

This teacher was trying to help her students do several things in her review. First, she wanted them to remember the names for the top and bottom numbers in a fraction—two concepts that she had already taught. When Carl could not answer, the teacher provided a prompt that helped him respond correctly. After students recalled the terms numerator and denominator, the teacher referred them to a problem on the board. She illustrated the abstract problem with a concrete example to promote their understanding of the process. Finally, she told them to pause for a moment—an idea called "wait time"—encouraging them to take some time to think about why changing the denominator was important.

Review, concept, prompting, concrete example, and *wait time* are all pedagogical concepts—concepts about teaching and learning. As such, they are part of a professional body of knowledge that helps us analyze and understand the teaching process. Your teacher education program is designed to help you understand these and many other pedagogical concepts, which will help you recognize and appreciate effective teaching when you observe it and ultimately help you plan and implement effective lessons in your own classroom. Each of the chapters in this text includes information about connections between teaching and learning.

Teaching Strategies

Research on effective teaching has established links between teacher actions or behaviors and student learning. Research on wait time, for example, indicates that giving students time to think about a question both increases the quality of their immediate responses and increases long-term achievement (Tobin, 1987). Research also tells us that providing students with concrete examples to illustrate abstract ideas improves students' ability to understand those ideas (Eggen and Kauchak, 2001). An expert teacher is one who understands the relationships between teacher actions and student learning and can implement these actions with students.

In our work with teachers, we have found that sharing research with them is not enough. Research results must be translated into teaching strategies directly related to classroom practice, and teachers must be given opportunities to practice the strategies and receive feedback about their efforts. Teaching strategies are a third component of learning to teach. A **teaching strategy** *is an interconnected set of teaching actions designed to accomplish specific goals.* Teaching strategies can be thought of as research translated into integrated teacher actions.

To illustrate the idea of a teaching strategy, let's return to the teacher wrestling with the concept of theme and look at one way to teach this abstract idea.

"Class, today we're going to learn about the idea of *theme.* It's an idea that will help us understand and appreciate the literature we read. Look up at the overhead and read the definition there.

A theme is an idea that reoccurs or repeats itself throughout a story.

"Let's see if we can understand how theme relates to a story, Hemingway's *The Old Man and the Sea,* which we've just finished. One of the major themes in that book was the struggle of man against nature. Hemingway introduced this theme at the beginning when he told us about the old man's struggles to make a living catching fish. He worked hard every day but went for weeks without catching a decent fish. That's one place where the theme—man struggling against nature—occurred. The fisherman represented man, and the sea that wouldn't let him catch fish was nature. Who can give me a second example of this theme where man struggled with nature? Deena?"

"Well, like when the old man hooked the fish and had to fight with it for a long time."

"Good, Deena. Go ahead and explain how that illustrates the idea of this theme."

"I . . . I'm not sure . . . but I'll try. The theme . . . the theme is man's struggle against nature and the fish is nature, so he's struggling with it."

"Good thinking, Deena. Note, everyone, how the same idea—man against nature—is repeated in the story. That's why it's a theme. Who can think of another place where this theme reoccurred or repeated itself? Eddie?"

" . . . How about the shark attack?"

"Go on."

" . . . Well, after he caught the fish, he tried to bring it back to sell it, but the sharks wouldn't let him. So he . . . "

"What was he struggling with—besides the sharks?"

"Oh, okay, nature. He was struggling with nature."

How does this illustrate a teaching strategy? A teaching strategy consists of coordinated teacher actions designed to reach a particular goal—in this case, helping students understand the concept of *theme*. The teaching strategy used by this teacher involved three basic steps.

- Defining the concept
- Illustrating the abstract idea with specific examples taken from the story
- Questioning to promote students' active involvement in learning and to help them connect the examples to the concept

Research indicates that this is an effective strategy when we want students to understand abstract concepts (Eggen and Kauchak, 2001). Defining the idea provides a frame of reference for the rest of the lesson, the examples illustrate the concept and give it meaning, and questioning involves students in the learning process. In Chapters 7 through 11, we describe a number of teaching strategies ranging from learner-centered constructivist strategies that capitalize on social interaction to teacher-centered approaches, such as direct instruction and lecture-discussions. Each has a specific set of research-based procedures designed to accomplish specific goals.

Teacher Decision Making

Teachers must know the content they teach and know how to transform this content into a form students can understand. They must also understand how teachers can help students learn and how to translate this knowledge into teaching strategies. We call these four components of learning to teach knowledge of subject matter, pedagogical content knowledge, knowledge of teaching and learning, and teaching strategies. But learning to teach involves even more than a thorough understanding of these components. Expert teachers not only have a repertoire of knowledge and strategies, but they also understand when specific teacher actions are appropriate and why. For example, the teacher-centered approach to teaching concepts described earlier, which results in increased understanding of concepts, may not be appropriate for teaching other important goals, such as social interaction skills like active listening and building on others' ideas or attitudes, and values, such as openness to alternate points of view. These goals need different approaches that require student-student interaction and encourage learner initiative (Slavin, 1995). Understanding how to implement knowledge of teaching and learning and when and how different teacher strategies are appropriate is an important dimension of effective teaching, requiring a great deal of expertise. This dimension is called professional decision making, a process that governs and guides the other four components.

Decision making *involves the application of professional judgment in deciding when, where, how, and why to use the other components of teaching.* As shown in Figure 1.3, decision making is an executive function that governs the application of the other teaching components.

Professional decision making can be thought of as a filter that helps determine when and where research findings should be used. Educational research needs to be applied selectively and strategically, with the goals of teaching and with students' well-being continually in mind; this is the essence of professional decision making. Let's see how decision making influences teaching in the classroom.

A kindergarten teacher has just distributed materials for an art project and is now surveying the room to see if everyone has started. She notices that Jimmy is staring out the window with his thumb in his mouth and tears in his eyes. It is the beginning of the school year, and Jimmy still isn't used to the idea of being away from home. Should the teacher wait a minute and see if the art materials will do the trick, or should she intervene?

A middle school teacher is getting more and more frustrated. Mary is obviously more interested in her friends than in English, and the teacher can't keep her from talking. He calls on her; she doesn't hear the question. Should he reprimand her, repeat the question, or go on to another student?

A high school teacher has just distributed an assignment. She goes over the work in some depth, explaining its importance and how it should be done. She concludes by reminding the class that the grade for the assignment counts as one-fourth of the semester grade. A barely audible "Who cares?" follows. Should the teacher ignore it and go on, or should she respond?

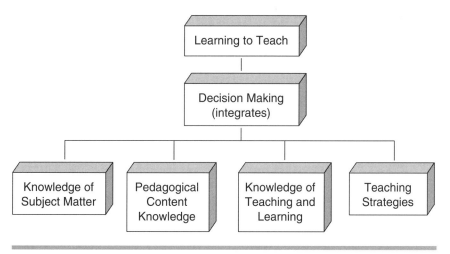

Figure 1.3 Components of Learning to Teach

We all remember our educational psychology texts' admonitions about the effects of reinforcement and punishment on behavior. These are documented research findings. But what do the findings tell the classroom teacher in the preceding examples? In each case, direct intervention might cause as many problems as it solves. Ignoring the problem raises similar issues. To make the situation more complex, these decisions must be made immediately.

The number of decisions—conscious or otherwise—that teachers must make every day is staggering. Jackson (1968) suggested that more than 800 decisions per day are made in elementary classrooms. Murray (1986) estimated the number at 1,500. Even using the more conservative figure, that translates into more than 130 decisions per hour in a 6-hour teaching day!

Before you get discouraged, remember that effective teachers not only make these decisions but also make them well. Research also shows that expert teachers structure their classrooms to run efficiently, so more time and energy can be devoted to important decisions—decisions that affect learning (Doyle, 1986; Leinhardt and Greeno, 1986).

Learning to Teach in an Era of Reform

You are becoming a teacher in one of the most tumultuous periods in the history of American education. Critics, both inside and outside the profession, are calling for **reforms,** *which are suggested changes in teaching and teacher preparation intended to increase the amount students learn.* To implement these reforms, teachers must be well prepared, and leaders in education are saying that we need to professionalize teaching (Blair, 2000). We examine the implications of these reform efforts for your professional development as a teacher in this section.

Reform: What Does It Mean? To place recent reform efforts in perspective, we should point out that the process of change and reform has been a part of education throughout its history. From colonial times to the present, schools and the teachers in them have been fair game for outside critics.

The modern reform movement is often traced to 1983, when the National Commission on Excellence in Education published *A Nation at Risk: The Imperative for Education Reform.* This widely read document suggested that America was "at risk" of being unable to compete in the world economic marketplace because our system of education was inadequate. The terms *at-risk students* and more recently *students placed at risk* can also be traced back to this document; these students were at risk of not acquiring the knowledge and skills needed for success in our modern society. Since 1983, a great many suggestions have been made for improving our nation's schools and the teachers who work in them.

Changes in Teacher Preparation. Reforms in teacher education focus on upgrading the knowledge and skills of teachers. These reforms include:

- Raising standards for acceptance into teacher-training programs
- Requiring teachers to take more rigorous courses than they have in the past
- Requiring higher standards for licensure, including teacher tests
- Expanding teacher-preparation programs from four years to five

- Requiring experienced teachers to take more rigorous professional development courses
(Blair, 2000)

Some of these suggestions are almost certainly going to affect you. We'll describe two as examples. First, you will likely be required to take more courses in English, math, science, history, and geography than have been required of teachers in the past. In addition, there is a movement to require all teachers, elementary and secondary, to major in a content area for their undergraduate degree. The rationale behind this push is related to both knowledge of content and pedagogical content knowledge—that teachers can't teach what they don't know themselves.

Second, you probably will be required to pass a test before you're awarded your teaching license. At the present time:

- Thirty-nine states require prospective teachers to pass a basic skills test.
- Twenty-nine states require high school teachers to pass tests in the subjects they plan to teach.
- Twenty-seven states require principals to evaluate new teachers.
(Olson, 2000)

The American Federation of Teachers, the second largest professional organization for teachers in the U.S., recently proposed that prospective teachers pass both tests aimed at basic content, such as math and English, as well as tests designed to measure teachers' knowledge of teaching principles (Blair, 2000). This proposal signals a change in policy from the past and suggests that teacher testing is not only here to stay, but likely to increase.

The National Teachers Examination (NTE), also called the *Core Battery of the Praxis II* (Educational Testing Service, 1999) is the most commonly used teacher test. The Praxis Series (*praxis* means putting theory into practice) is currently being used in 35 states and consists of three components (Educational Testing Service, 1999):

- Praxis I: Academic Skills Assessments—designed to measure basic or "enabling" skills in reading, writing, and math that all teachers need.
- Praxis II: Subject Assessments—designed to measure teachers' knowledge of the subjects they will teach. In addition to 70 content-specific tests, Praxis II also includes the Principles of Learning and Teaching (PLT) test and the Professional Knowledge test.
- Praxis III: Classroom Performance Assessments—use classroom observations and work samples to assess teachers' ability to plan, instruct, manage, and understand professional responsibilities. In addition, Praxis III assesses the teacher's sensitivity to learners' developmental and cultural differences.

You are most likely to encounter Praxis I during your teacher preparation, Praxis II after its completion, and Praxis III during your first year of teaching.

Standards-Based Professional Development

One important outcome of the reform movement in education is the increased use of standards to focus curriculum and instruction on important learning goals. Standards-based education is changing K–12 education, as you'll read about in Chapter 3 when we discuss teacher planning. It also is changing the kinds of experiences you'll have in your teacher education programs.

Beginning Professional Development: INTASC Standards. In the past, learning to teach was easier and the demands on beginning teachers were not as great. This situation has changed (Berliner, 2000). A rapidly expanding body of literature consistently demonstrates that teaching now requires professionals who are highly knowledgeable and skilled.

The profession is responding. Created in 1987, the *Interstate New Teacher Assessment and Support Consortium* (INTASC, 1993) was designed to help states develop better teachers through coordinated efforts of support and assessment. INTASC has raised the bar by setting rigorous standards for new teachers in important areas such as planning, instruction, and motivation. These standards describe what you should know and be able to do when you first walk into a classroom.

At this point general standards organized around 10 principles have been prepared, and subject area standards and a Test for Teaching Knowledge (TTK) are being developed. These principles are outlined in Table 1.2.

The principles are expanded by describing the knowledge, dispositions, and performances teachers are expected to demonstrate. For instance, with respect to the first principle, teachers should understand how students' misconceptions in an area—such as believing that the earth is closer to the sun in the summer (in the Northern Hemisphere) can influence their learning (knowledge of the subject matter and how it influences student learning). In terms of dispositions, teachers should be committed to continuous learning (disposition to continually grow as a professional). Finally, teachers should be able to use a variety of ways to illustrate ideas to make them understandable to students, such as using demonstrations, pictures, technology, and classroom discussion to illustrate the seasons (performance-using the knowledge and dispositions to increase student learning). Similar knowledge, dispositions, and performances exist for each principle.

The INTASC standards are demanding, but this is as it should be. If you expect to be treated as a professional, you should have the knowledge and skills that allow you to make the decisions expected of a professional. Being able to meet the INTASC standards is a good beginning.

Advanced Professional Standards: National Board Certification. Licensure is the process states use to ensure that teachers meet minimal professional standards. In comparison, national board certification by the *National Board for Professional Teaching Standards (NBPTS)* seeks to strengthen teaching as a profession and raise the quality of education by recognizing the contributions of exemplary teachers, compensate them financially, give them increased responsibility, and increase their role in decision making. National Board Certification is directed by five core propositions which are outlined and described in Table 1.3.

National board certification has five important characteristics:

- It is designed for experienced teachers. Applicants must have graduated from an accredited college or university and must have taught at least three years.
- Applying for national board certification is strictly voluntary and independent of any state's licensure. It is intended to indicate a high level of achievement and professionalism.

Table 1.2 **THE INTASC PRINCIPLES**

Principle	Description
1. Knowledge of subject	The teacher understands the central concepts, tools of inquiry, and structures of the discipline(s) he or she teaches and can create learning experiences that make these aspects of subject matter meaningful for students.
2. Learning and human development	The teacher understands how children learn and develop and can provide learning opportunities that support their intellectual, social, and personal development.
3. Adapting instruction	The teacher understands how students differ in their approaches to learning and creates instructional opportunities that are adapted to diverse learners.
4. Strategies	The teacher understands and uses a variety of instructional strategies to encourage students' development of critical thinking, problem solving, and performance skills.
5. Motivation and management	The teacher uses an understanding of individual and group motivation and behavior to create a learning environment that encourages positive social interaction, active engagement in learning, and self-motivation.
6. Communication skills	The teacher uses knowledge of effective verbal, nonverbal, and media communication techniques to foster active inquiry, collaboration, and supportive interaction in the classroom.
7. Planning	The teacher plans instruction based upon knowledge of subject matter, students, the community, and curriculum goals.
8. Assessment	The teacher understands and uses formal and informal assessment strategies to evaluate and ensure the continuous intellectual, social, and physical development of the learner.
9. Commitment	The teacher is a reflective practitioner who continually evaluates the effects of his/her choices and actions on others (students, parents, and other professionals in the learning community) and who actively seeks out opportunities to grow professionally.
10. Partnership	The teacher fosters relationships with school colleagues, parents, and agencies in the larger community to support students' learning and well-being.

Source: From Interstate New Teacher Assessment and Support Consortium. (1993). *Model standards for beginning teacher licensing and development: A resource for state dialogues.* Washington, D.C., Council of Chief State School Officers. Reprinted by permission.

Table 1.3 **PROPOSITIONS OF THE NATIONAL BOARD FOR PROFESSIONAL TEACHING STANDARDS**

Proposition	Description
1. Teachers are committed to students and their learning.	■ Accomplished teachers believe that all students can learn, and they treat students equitably. ■ Accomplished teachers understand how students develop, and they use accepted learning theory as the basis for their teaching. ■ Accomplished teachers are aware of the influence of context and culture on behavior, and they foster students' self-esteem, motivation, and character.
2. Teachers know the subjects they teach and how to teach those subjects to students.	■ Accomplished teachers have a rich understanding of the subject(s) they teach, and they appreciate how knowledge in their subject is linked to other disciplines and applied to real-world settings. ■ Accomplished teachers know how to make subject matter understandable to students, and they are able to modify their instruction when difficulties arise. ■ Accomplished teachers demonstrate critical and analytic capacities in their teaching, and they develop those capacities in their students.
3. Teachers are responsible for managing and monitoring student learning.	■ Accomplished teachers capture and sustain the interest of their students and use their time effectively. ■ Accomplished teachers are able to use a variety of effective instructional techniques, and they use the techniques appropriately. ■ Accomplished teachers can use multiple methods to assess the progress of students, and they effectively communicate this progress to parents.
4. Teachers think systematically about their practice and learn from experience.	■ Accomplished teachers are models for intellectual curiosity, and they display virtues—honesty, fairness, and respect for diversity—that they seek to inspire in their students. ■ Accomplished teachers use their understanding of students, learning, and instruction to make principled judgments about sound practice, and they are lifelong learners. ■ Accomplished teachers critically examine their practice, and they seek continual professional growth.
5. Teachers are members of learning communities.	■ Accomplished teachers contribute to the effectiveness of the school, and they work collaboratively with their colleagues. ■ Accomplished teachers evaluate school progress, and they utilize community resources. ■ Accomplished teachers work collaboratively with parents, and they involve parents in school activities.

Source: Reprinted with permission from the National Board for Professional Teaching Standards. *What Teachers Should Know and Be Able to Do, 1994.* All rights reserved.

■ Acquiring national board certification requires that teachers pass a set of exams in their area of specialty, such as math, science, early childhood, or physical education and health.
■ Additional evidence, such as videotapes of teaching and a personal portfolio, are used in the assessment process.

- The primary control of the NBPTS is in the hands of practicing teachers, which increases the professionalism of teaching.

Since the NBPTS is for veterans, why are we providing this information in this book—one studied by preservice teachers early in their programs? There are four reasons. First, national board certification can provide a long-term career goal combined with financial incentives for you as a new teacher. Thirty-nine states and nearly 200 school districts have spent millions of dollars to reward teachers who successfully complete the process; by late 2000 nearly 5,000 teachers had done so, with another nearly 10,000 awaiting word on whether or not they had passed (Blair, 2000). California teachers who successfully complete this certification process receive a $10,000 bonus; in North Carolina, the state pays the entire $2,000 application fee and rewards successful applicants with a 12 percent increase in the state's portion of salaries paid to teachers (Feldman, 2000).

Second, the criteria in Table 1.3 emphasize the pedagogical content knowledge, general pedagogical knowledge, and knowledge of learners and learning that we discussed earlier in the chapter. The NBPTS recognizes that increasing professionalism requires teachers who are both highly knowledgeable and skilled in their areas of specialization.

Finally, evidence indicates that national board certification makes a difference. A study comparing teachers who had successfully completed the process to those who had attempted but failed to achieve national board certification found that the nationally certified teachers scored higher on nearly all measures of teaching expertise. The study involved at least 75 hours of observation of each teacher, together with interviews and samples of student work (Blair, 2000). National board certification is a long-term goal that is well worth pursuing and one we're encouraging you to keep in mind as you begin your career.

Developing a Professional Portfolio

The interview was going okay, but I was uneasy. The principal I was interviewing with was cordial, but she certainly wasn't enthusiastic. "I've had it," I thought to myself. She even quit asking me questions after about 20 minutes. I really wanted the job, too.

As I was about to leave, I happened to mention, "Would you like to see my portfolio?" She looked at it for a couple minutes, and then she started asking some probing questions. When she stuck my CD-ROM in her computer and saw me teaching, she really lit up. I got the job! (Shannon, a recent graduate and new teacher)

As you begin this section you might wonder, "Why are they talking about interviews and portfolios now, in the middle of my teacher education program? Jobs and interviews may be months, even years, away. The answers are simple. The sooner you start assembling your professional portfolio, the better, and professional portfolios are one of the best ways to document and reflect on your growth as a teacher. A **professional portfolio** *is a collection of work produced by a prospective teacher.* Just as artists use portfolios of produced work to illustrate their talents and accomplishments, teachers use portfolios to document their knowledge and skills.

The reason you should start now in thinking about your portfolio is that you may want to include products that you complete throughout your program, including assignments for the course you're in now. For instance, suppose you teach a particularly good lesson for one of your methods classes. You may want to include a copy of the lesson plan, a videotape of you teaching the lesson, and student work samples to document the lesson's effectiveness and your growth as a developing teacher. Though this experience will have occurred long before you actively seek a job, it can be a valuable entry nevertheless. The sooner you start thinking about what to include in your portfolio, the less likely you are to omit valuable or important entries.

Portfolios also provide tangible benchmarks that you can use for reflection; and reflection, or thinking about your actions and beliefs, can accelerate your growth as a professional. For instance, suppose you have yourself videotaped teaching a lesson for one of your teaching methods courses. The videotape is a concrete indicator of your skills at that point and provides a tangible basis for your reflection. Later, you may complete another videotaped lesson during an internship experience or student teaching. A comparison of your performance in the two lessons provides a concrete measure of your progress.

Possible Portfolio Entries. The contents of a professional portfolio can take many forms. Some possible suggestions are included in Table 1.4.

These types of portfolio entries provide different perspectives on your growth as a professional.

Preparing a Portfolio. Preparing a portfolio typically involves five steps (Martin, 1999):

1. *Specify a goal.* For example, you're probably taking this course because you've either decided that you want to teach, or you're at least considering teaching. Finding a satisfying job would be a likely goal.
2. *Determine how both past and future experiences relate to the goal.* You might choose to tutor a student with a reading problem, for example, to get professional experience that will make you more marketable.
3. *Strategically collect items that provide evidence of your developing knowledge and skill.* A video clip of you working with the student would be a excellent entry, for instance.

Table 1.4 POTENTIAL PROFESSIONAL PORTFOLIO ENTRIES

Lesson plans	Community involvement
Unit plans	Grading policies
Videotapes of lessons taught	Transcripts
Student work samples	Volunteer work
Student projects	Technology competence
Action research projects	As a teacher:
Classroom management plan	Principal evaluations
Classroom rules	Supervisor evaluations
Communications with parents	

Source: Adapted from Bullock and Hawk (2001).

4. *Decide what items among your collection best illustrate your knowledge and skills.* For example, since a prospective employer is unlikely to view a bulky collection or series of videotapes, a videotaped lesson is likely a better entry than is a clip from a tutoring session.

5. *Determine how to best present the items to the person or people connected to your goal,* such as the personnel director of a school district in which you want to teach.

In addition to planning for your professional portfolio, you also need to construct one. All professional portfolios have four components:

- *Purpose:* To document a particular aspect of your growth as a teacher, such as your ability to plan or implement a specific type of lesson.
- *Audience:* This can vary from a professor or instructor to a prospective employer.
- *Evidence:* Consists of work samples that document accomplishments and growth.
- *Reflections:* Thoughts about the evidence and how they document professional growth.

(Bullock and Hawk, 2001)

Just as professional portfolios have different components, they also have different purposes (Bullock and Hawk, 2001). **Process portfolios** *are designed to showcase a teacher's growth over a period of time.* For example, a process portfolio on assessment would contain student assessments and work samples that document your developing ability to assess student learning progress in a number of different ways.

A second type of portfolio, a **product portfolio,** *contains a specific set of evidence developed over a short period of time to meet a desired outcome.* For example, a product portfolio on planning might include a unit plan integrating several content areas around a common theme. A product portfolio documents professional growth through a final product.

A third type of portfolio, a **showcase portfolio,** *contains collections of a person's best work as chosen by that person.* For example, a showcase portfolio on teaching writing would document your ability to use different approaches to writing instruction together with work samples of students. Showcase portfolios are often used for job interviews and may contain elements of the other portfolio types.

As we said earlier, the sooner you start making these decisions, the more complete and effective your portfolio will be. As you begin, we offer three suggestions:

- Initially, err on the side of including too much in the portfolio. If you think you might use it, include it now. You can always remove an item, but including an item you've discarded is difficult, if not impossible.
- Always date the entry. If you want to organize your portfolio chronologically, the dated items will make organizing the information simpler.
- Make all entries and supporting information with clear communication in mind. You're trying to convince a potential employer that you're knowledgeable and skilled, and you want to make his or her decision as easy as possible. A well-organized portfolio creates a positive impression; the opposite occurs with a disorganized one.

ELECTRONIC PORTFOLIOS. As we move farther into the information age, the development of electronic portfolios is becoming more commonplace. They include everything a paper-based product includes, but they do it more efficiently. For example, one CD-ROM disk can hold the equivalent of 300,000 text pages (Lankes, 1995). Typed documents can be scanned into word processing files and stored on floppy disks or CD-ROMs, and video can be digitized and also stored on CD-ROMs. This saves both time and energy. People who want to view a video episode in a paper-based portfolio must find a VCR, review the tape and put it back into the correct portfolio container. In contrast, video footage in an electronic portfolio can be augmented with text and graphics and accessed with the click of a mouse. This is what got Shannon her job. The principal was impressed with both her teaching and the fact that the information in her portfolio was so easy to access.

Electronic portfolios require sophisticated computer equipment and software as well as skilled users. In spite of these obstacles, however, it is likely that the expansion of technology will eventually make paper-based portfolios obsolete, so the sooner you develop your technology skills in these areas the more effective your portfolio will be.

ORGANIZING YOUR PORTFOLIO. You will want to organize your portfolio to make it accessible to an evaluator. As an organizational guide, put yourself in evaluators' shoes. Remember, they don't know much about you, you want them to, and you want to make it as easy for them as possible. Let communication and ease of access be your guide for organizing the information in your portfolio.

Regardless of whether your portfolio is paper based or electronic, you will want to start with a title page followed by a table of contents. Then you'll want to include the most impressive entries, followed by those less significant. Work samples and evidence of performance, such as video clips, are always treated more significantly than testimonial letters, which are often essentially disregarded.

USING THIS BOOK TO LEARN TO TEACH

This book can help you in your efforts to become an expert teacher in several ways. Perhaps most importantly, it describes research findings that connect teacher actions to student learning. Some of this research is described as concepts that are highlighted in **boldface** type and *defined in italics* to identify them as important ideas. These important concepts, with page numbers, are also found at the end of each chapter to aid you in your study. Other research findings appear as teaching strategies designed to accomplish specific goals. Our intent in presenting this information is to provide you with the conceptual tools you need to analyze your own and others' teaching and to plan and implement effective lessons in your own classroom.

Case studies are used throughout this book in an attempt to bridge theory and practice. We begin each chapter with a case that frames important concepts and major issues in the chapter, and we end each chapter with an additional case for you to analyze called "Reflecting on Teaching and Learning." These case studies serve several functions. First, they illustrate abstract ideas, attempting to help you understand what these ideas look like in classrooms. We used brief case studies in the previous section to illustrate *teacher decision making*—an abstract and potentially difficult to understand concept. In addition to being useful illustrations, case studies show how important ideas can be applied in classrooms. You should know that the Praxis II series, described previously, uses case studies such as these to test beginning teachers' knowledge. Your familiarity with the use of cases to illustrate complex ideas will assist you on this test. These cases are based on our experiences in the real world of schools and are an attempt to provide you with a realistic slice of classroom life.

Discussion questions are also found at the end of each chapter. They invite you to go beyond the content, to look for relationships in the material, and to integrate the material in a personal way. The answers to some of these questions can be found within the text, while others are more open ended, asking you to use your own experience and judgment. Hopefully, they will stimulate your growth in professional decision making.

The third set of exercises, Portfolio Activities, is designed to assist you in developing your own professional portfolio by applying research findings in actual classrooms through assignments that demonstrate the implications of research findings for classroom practice. These portfolio activities appear in three forms. Some ask you to interview teachers, to discover how expert teachers think about and solve real-world problems. Research suggests that studying the thoughts and actions of expert teachers is a productive way to learn about teaching (Berliner, 1994) and reflecting on the thoughts and actions of others provides you with a concrete frame of reference to construct your own developing personal philosophy of good teaching. A second kind of activity asks you to observe teachers in action, based on information you've studied in this book. You'll watch teachers teach, analyze the strategies they use to help students learn, and reflect on their effectiveness, not only for these students, but for the students you'll be teaching. The third kind of activity invites you to try these ideas for yourself. It involves structured teaching experiences designed to help you apply concepts and strategies in real classrooms with real students and reflect on their effectiveness. If at all possible, we recommend that you use all of these to make the content of this text personally meaningful and document your growth as a teacher.

Summary

Defining Good Teaching. The central role of research in informing teaching practice has changed the way we think about teaching and learning. Research now provides us with ways to analyze teaching to maximize learning.

Research in Teaching: A Historical Perspective. Initially, research on teaching focused on teacher characteristics and later moved to a search for one effective method. Both lines of research failed to link teacher actions to student learning. School-level research, focusing on out-of-classroom variables, also ignored the role of teacher actions in promoting student learning. The teacher effectiveness research established that teachers do indeed make a difference in students' learning.

Contemporary Views of Teaching and Learning. As research has shifted from behaviorist to cognitive views of learning, teaching has focused on active ways to involve students in learning. Constructivism and learner-centered approaches to instruction both stress the central importance of student's active involvement in learning.

Text Themes. Recent developments in education influenced three major content themes for this text—diversity, motivation and technology. A focus on diversity explores ways to capitalize on student differences in the classroom. Motivation reminds us of the importance of energizing and directing student learning. Technology provides us with electronic tools to enhance student learning.

Learning to Teach. Learning to teach is a complex process involving many components. Teachers need to know their subject matter but also need pedagogical content knowledge—knowledge of how to translate this content into forms that are understandable by students. Knowledge of teaching and learning, which addresses the relationship between teachers' actions and student learning, needs to be combined with teaching strategies aimed at specific goals. Teacher decision making combines all of these components in effective teaching. Learning to teach in an era of reform will require teachers to demonstrate their competence to teach throughout their professional careers.

Using This Book to Learn to Teach. A number of features in this book are designed to help you learn to teach. Important concepts are highlighted in bold and listed at the end of each chapter. Cases provide access to classrooms and encourage you to connect important ideas to students and learning. Discussion questions invite you to go beyond the content in the book and link this content to your own experiences. Finally, portfolio activities suggest ways that you can use chapter concepts to observe, analyze, and implement ideas in classrooms.

Important Concepts

Discussion Questions

1. Rank order the following teaching strategies on a continuum of learner centered to teacher centered. Explain how each involves students in the learning processes.

   Cooperative learning groups
   Discussion
   Drill and practice
   Homework
   Lecturing
   Student projects

2. Reexamine the information in Table 1.1, comparing behaviorist and cognitive views of learning. Which view do you think is more motivating for students? Why? Which view is more demanding for teachers? Why?

3. Think about your own experiences in schools. How would those experiences have been different if the learner-centered principles in Table 1.2 were being used? Try to be as specific as possible.

4. In terms of effective teaching, research suggests that content mastery is an essential component. Is this component equally important at all grade levels? In all subject-matter areas?

5. How does your definition of good teaching vary in terms of high- and low-ability students? Are there more similarities or differences between the two groups? What would you do with one group that would be different from what you would do with the other?

6. What kinds of diversity did you encounter in the schools that you attended? What types of diversity do you anticipate encountering in the classrooms you'll teach in? How can student diversity be both an asset and a challenge to your teaching?

7. Reread the case study at the beginning of this chapter. What *is* the teacher's responsibility in terms of motivation? Do you agree with Stan Williams? What about the question regarding basic skills versus thinking strategies: Do basic skills need to precede thinking skills? What are the advantages and disadvantages of this approach?

8. What forms of technology did you encounter in the schools that you attended? How was it used to promote learning? What types of technology are you encountering in your teacher education program? What is the biggest challenge involved in using technology in your teaching?

9. Research has shown a correlation between teacher enthusiasm and student learning. Explain this correlation in two ways, then design an experiment to test one of these explanations.

10. One of the problems in learning to teach is that good teaching often appears effortless. Think back to some of the good teachers that you've had. What specific things did they do that made them effective? Compare these behaviors with other, less effective teachers.

Portfolio Activities

1. *Effective Teaching: The Teacher's Perspective.* How do experienced teachers think about effective teaching? Interview two teachers and ask the following questions:

   What is effective teaching?
   How do they know when it is occurring in their classroom?
   What are some ways to measure effective teaching?
   What factors (e.g. students, content area) influence the definition of good teaching?

   Compare the response of the two teachers with your own ideas about effective teaching.

2. *Effective Teaching: The District's Perspective.* How does the district evaluate its teachers? In your interview with the teachers in Exercise 1, find out how they are evaluated. If a form or instrument is used, ask to see it.

   What criteria are used?
   How is the form used? That is, how many times is the teacher observed with it?
   What does the teacher think of the process?

How will the process of being evaluated as a teacher influence your professional development?

3. *Effective Teaching: The Student's Perspective.* The bottom line in our teaching is its effect on students. This exercise is designed to make you more sensitive to the learning process from a student's perspective.

Identify six students to observe; three should be male and three should be female. Also, one should be a high achiever in the class, one a medium achiever, and one a low acheiver. If you are using another teacher's classroom, an ideal way to do this is to have the teacher select the students but not identify their status. This provides you with an opportunity to infer classifications from behavior and responses.

Position yourself at the side of the classroom and toward the front so that you can see the students' faces. Observe the six students as they enter the class, at the beginning of the lesson, during the major part of the lesson, and during any seatwork.

Which students are most attentive?

Which students take notes?

Which students participate the most in the lesson?

Is there any relationship between teacher behaviors (e.g., questioning) and student engagement rates?

If possible, interview the students and ask them what kinds of things the teacher does to help them learn.

What implications do the students' perspectives have for you as a teacher?

4. *Diversity.* Observe a classroom and note the diversity you find there. How do students in the class differ in terms of:

   a. gender
   b. ability
   c. culture and ethnicity?

   Do all students participate equally in the class? Interview the teacher and ask him or her how diversity influences their teaching. What opportunities and challenges will student diversity provide you as a developing teacher?

5. *Motivation.* Observe a classroom and try to determine:

   a. Students' level of motivation during the lesson. (How can you tell?) Does it seem to vary during the lesson?
   b. Different students' levels of motivation. Is there any pattern? How does location in the room influence this?
   c. The teacher's strategies to influence student motivation.

   If possible, discuss your observations with the teacher afterward. How do you plan to motivate students in your own classroom?

6. *Technology.* What kinds of technologies are being used in the classroom you are in? What other types of technologies are available in the school? Interview the teacher and ask:

   a. How does technology enhance learning and teaching?
   b. What influence does it have on student motivation?
   c. What obstacles are there to the teacher's greater use of technology?
   d. How did the teacher learn to use this technology?
   e. How will you use technology in your classroom?

2

Student Diversity

*W*hen we walk into classrooms across the country, one fact is obvious—there is amazing diversity in the students we teach. This diversity appears in a variety of forms, ranging from obvious differences in physical appearance to the ways different students respond to instruction. In a single grade we have learners who are mature for their age and others who are slower in developing. Some will be poised and self-confident while others will be shy and hesitant. A number will have traveled extensively and still others will have spent most or all of their lives in one small neighborhood. All of these differences influence our students' ability to profit from our teaching.

In this chapter we examine different aspects of student diversity and discuss ways that teachers can adapt their instruction to best meet the needs of all their students. In the process we look at the influence that culture, language diversity, learning ability and learning styles, socioeconomic status, and learner exceptionalities have on learning. When you have completed your study of this chapter, you should be able to meet the following goals.

- Define the concept of culture and explain how it influences learning.
- Explain how language influences learning.
- Describe how different teaching strategies can be used to accommodate differences in learning ability.
- Identify factors that influence at-risk students and describe effective teaching practices for these students.
- Explain how students with exceptionalities can be integrated into the regular classroom.

Shanda Jackson watched as her first graders streamed into the room on the first day of school. Though she had read the class rolls, she couldn't believe the different shapes, colors, and sizes before her eyes. Some were tall—looking almost like second graders—while others were tiny. A few were husky and well developed; others were short and skinny.

"I wonder if all their parents know about the free breakfast program?" she silently asked herself. And the names—she hoped she'd be able to remember them and pronounce them all correctly. There were Jones and Lees and Wongs and Hassads and Trangs and Jamals. This was going to be an interesting class.

As she learned about her students, she also noticed differences in the way they acted and learned. Some came to class bright and eager, while others looked like they hadn't gotten enough sleep. Several knew how to print and read their names; others acted as if they had never held a book before. A few used their fingers to count and even add, and others began sucking on them when they became tired or discouraged.

"They're lovable," Shanda thought as she smiled to herself, "but how am I ever going to get them all to learn?"

How indeed? One of the facts of modern teaching is the increasing diversity of our students. They not only come in different sizes and levels of maturity, as they always have, but now more than ever they come to our classes speaking different languages and bringing with them different cultural and background experiences.

As we saw in Chapter 1, research is a powerful tool to help teachers teach more effectively, and it can also help us capitalize on these differences in our students. Research can identify general teaching strategies that are effective with *all* learners and suggest ways to modify our teaching to meet the needs of different learners. One of the most important dimensions of diversity that teachers deal with is culture, which we discuss in the next section.

CAPITALIZING ON CULTURAL DIVERSITY

To begin this section, let's look in on Shanda again as she works with her students.

Shanda sat back on the bus and breathed a sigh of relief—twenty-six students there and twenty-six students back. Success! There were moments at the zoo when she had wondered if she would get them all back on the bus, but now that the head counting was over she could relax.

Was it worth all the trouble, she wondered? It *was* a fun trip and many of her first graders had never been to the zoo. It also gave Shanda a chance to see her students in action in a different setting. She couldn't believe how different they were.

It wasn't just how different they looked. Shanda knew when she signed her contract to teach in this large inner-city school district that her students would be diverse, but she wasn't prepared for this—eleven different cultures and six different languages. She jokingly referred to her class as her "Little United Nations." They not only responded differently in class but also on this field trip. Some were active and assertive and led the way in exploring the zoo; others hung back, clinging to her for moral and physical support. Some eagerly asked questions while others listened shyly. She knew some of these differences came from what they were used to at home, but she hadn't quite figured out how to capitalize on these differences in the classroom.

The cultural backgrounds of our students is an ever-increasing source of diversity. The United States has always been a nation of immigrants, and this immigration has produced a country of many cultures. Over 14 million people immigrated to the United States during the 1970s and 1980s. Between 1980 and 1994, America's classrooms saw the following changes:

- An increase in Asian-American students of almost 100%
- An increase in Hispanic-American students of 46%
- An increase in African-American students of 25%
- An increase in Caucasian students of 10%

(U.S. Census Bureau, 1996)

Experts estimate that by the year 2020 our country will see considerable increases in the number of Hispanic and African-American students, and a dramatic increase in Asian/Pacific Islander and American Indian/Alaskan Native populations will occur. At the same time, the white student population will decrease by 9 percent (U.S. Census Bureau, 1998b; Young and Smith, 1999). Each of these groups brings a distinct set of values and traditions that influences student learning.

This diversity has been hailed as one of our country's strengths, bringing new ideas and energy to the country. But it also poses challenges to teachers as they attempt to teach children with different attitudes, values, and languages. In this section we discuss cultural diversity and examine ways that culture can be used to enhance classroom learning.

Multicultural Education: The Challenge

Culture *refers to the attitudes, values, beliefs, and ways of acting and interacting that characterize a social group.* It includes the foods we eat, the clothes we wear, how we play, the music we listen to and the kinds of churches we attend. It also includes the attitudes and beliefs we have about learning and the beliefs we have about schools and classrooms.

Multicultural education *examines ways that culture influences learning and attempts to find ways that students' cultures can be used to complement and enhance learning.* It attempts to help teachers become more aware of and sensitive to the subtle and not so subtle ways that students' cultures can affect the way they approach learning.

Economic changes in our country also underscore the need for effective multicultural education. In the past, immigrants and members of minority groups easily found jobs in factories, farms, and other areas requiring little formal education. In our technological society these jobs are rapidly declining, and reading, writing, computing, problem solving, and decision making are becoming increasingly important for economic survival. Students who exit our schools without these skills are considered *at risk,* a topic we'll return to later in this chapter.

Theories of Minority Achievement

The data on minority student achievement indicate that schools are not doing an effective job of educating and integrating minority students into the mainstream of American life. Whether the measures are achievement test scores or dropout rates, statistics indicate that minority students underperform in schools (Macionis, 2000). Why is this so?

The Cultural Deficit Theory. According to the **cultural deficit theory** *the linguistic, social and cultural backgrounds of minority children prevent them from performing well in the classroom* (Villegas, 1991b). Minority children come to school lacking *cultural capital,* the accumulation of common experiences in the early years that schools use and build upon. According to the cultural deficit theory, minority students do poorly in school because what they bring to school is inadequate compared to what the majority population brings.

Critics charge that there are two major problems with this theory (Villegas, 1991b). The first is that it points the finger of blame at minority children, absolving the schools from responsibility for their success. In one sense it's as foolish as saying, "I taught them, they just didn't learn." If they don't learn, then we didn't teach them. In the same way, it is our professional responsibility to take students, regardless of their backgrounds, and teach them as much as possible.

The second problem with the deficit theory is that—theoretically—once students get to school, the school should be able to "reduce" the deficit, filling in areas where the students are deficient. By spending increased periods of time in the schools, minority students should gradually "catch up." However, just the opposite occurs; as the number of years in school increases, the gap in achievement grows wider and wider.

The Teacher Expectations Theory. A second theory used to explain underachievement in minority students focuses on lowered teacher expectations. **Teacher expectations** *include the attitudes and beliefs that teachers hold about students' abilities to learn which influence student achievement.* As we will see in Chapter 4, positive teacher expectations form a powerful foundation for learning. Teachers' beliefs that all students can learn exert a powerful and positive influence on learning. Unfortunately, the opposite is also true.

Negative expectations impact learning in both explicit and implicit ways. Explicitly, they influence minorities through tracking and grouping practices that diminish learning. Research indicates that a disproportionately higher percentage of minorities are found in lower groups and tracks (Good and Brophy, 2000). When cultural minorities find themselves in low-ability groups in the elementary grades, they are often headed down a one-way street to an inferior education throughout their school lives.

Teachers must be aware of the expectations that they have for students and must continually monitor their actions to ensure that positive expectations are communicated to all students. We examine ways to do this in Chapter 4. But what else can teachers do to increase learning for students from different cultures?

The Cultural Difference Theory

A second-grade class in Albuquerque, New Mexico, was reading *The Box Car Children* and was about to start a new chapter. The teacher said, "Look at the illustration at the beginning of the chapter and tell me what you think is going to happen."

A few students raised their hands. The teacher called on a boy in the back row.

He said, "I think the boy is going to meet his grandfather."

The teacher asked, "Based on what you know, how does the boy feel about meeting his grandfather?"

Trying to involve the whole class, the teacher called on another student—one of four Native Americans in the group—even though she had not raised her hand. When she didn't answer, the teacher tried rephrasing the question, but again the student sat in silence.

Feeling exasperated, the teacher wondered if there was something in the way the lesson was being conducted that made it difficult for the student to respond. She sensed that the student she had called on understood the story and was enjoying it. Why, then, wouldn't she answer what appeared to be a simple question?

The teacher recalled that this was not the first time this had happened, and that, in fact, the other Native American students in the class rarely answered questions in class discussions. She wanted to involve them, wanted them to participate in class, but could not think of ways to get them to talk. (Villegas, 1991b, p. 3)

Why don't Native Americans eagerly respond to teacher questions? Are they interested in the same kinds of topics and issues as other students? Do they feel that answering questions in class is important? Could the questions have been asked differently to encourage their participation? The cultural difference theory provides answers to these and other related questions about the influences of culture on learning.

The **cultural difference theory** *of learning attributes academic problems of minority students to cultural differences or discontinuities between home and school.* Probably the most important of these is in the way that language is used. When home language patterns, are congruent with school patterns, learning is enhanced; when they aren't, conflict occurs. Let's see how this works by analyzing the language patterns in two different "cultures"—school and Native American families.

Language use patterns in schools are amazingly homogeneous, not only over time but across grade levels and different parts of the country (Cazden, 1986; Cuban, 1984).

> . . . the dominant form of interaction is the teacher-directed lesson in which the instructor is in control, determining the topics of discussion, allocating turns at speaking, and deciding what qualifies as a correct response. Verbal participation is required of students. Implicitly, teaching and learning are equated with talking, and silence is interpreted as the absence of knowledge. Students are questioned in public and bid for the floor by raising their hands. They are expected to wait until the teacher awards the floor to one of them before answering. Speaking in turn is the rule, unless the teacher specifically asks for choral responses. Display questions prevail. Individual competition is preferred to group cooperation. Topics are normally introduced in small and carefully sequenced steps, with the overall picture emerging only at the end of the teaching sequence. *(Villegas, 1991a, p. 20)*

Contrast this pattern with one uncovered by an anthropologist working in the Warm Springs Indian Reservation in Oregon. Philips (1972) found that Native American children grew up being supervised by older children rather than adults. Learning from adults was more through observation rather than direct verbal instruction. Question-and-answer sessions between adults and children seldom, if ever, occurred. Children would observe adults and then try things out on their own, receiving praise and feedback not from adults but from other children.

When we contrast the culture of the classroom with that of their home, we can see why these students were reluctant to ask and answer questions in front of the whole class. Over time they became less and less involved in classroom activities and fell further and further behind in achievement. Sensitized to these differences, teachers found that when these students were placed in peer learning situations, like group projects or peer tutoring, they spoke freely with their peers and participated in classroom activities; this was something they were used to doing.

A similar problem of cultural language discontinuity was discovered by Shirley Heath (1983) in her study of rural African-American students in the Piedmont area of the Carolinas. Like the Native Americans from Oregon, these children also struggled with the teacher-centered question-and-answer format found in most classrooms. Both teachers and parents were perplexed and frustrated about these students' failure to participate in school. As Heath studied the language patterns found in African-American homes in her study, she discovered why.

Heath found that their parents did not regard children as legitimate conversational partners until they were older, instead tending to give directives rather than questions. When questions were used, they were "real" questions asking for "real" information (e.g., "Where you been?") rather than designed to test the child's knowledge. Or they were more the "open-ended story-starter" type (e.g., "What you been doin' today?") that did not have a single, convergent answer. These patterns contrasted with those found in schools, where teachers asked many convergent questions, testing students' knowledge and providing specific practice and feedback. When these students went to school, they were unprepared to participate in the active give and take of convergent question-and-answer sessions.

When teachers were made aware of these differences, they incorporated more open-ended questions in their lessons. For example, in an elementary social studies unit on "our community," teachers would show the class photographs of different aspects of local communities and ask questions like, "What's happening here?" "Have you ever been here?" and "Tell me what you did when you were here." This not only fit African-American students' home language patterns more closely but also provided safe, nonrestrictive opportunities for students to tell what they knew about a topic. Teachers also helped these children become more comfortable and competent with answering factual questions. Effective bridges were built between students' natural, culturally learned interaction styles and the schools.

Culturally Responsive Teaching

What does this suggest to us about our teaching? Should minority students be made to fit in with schools as they exist today? It hasn't happened to this point, and it isn't likely to occur in the near future. Should schools be completely overhauled to match the learning patterns of a particular cultural group? Probably an impractical idea, since most classrooms contain several different cultural groups. Logistics alone preclude the use of any *one* particular strategy or adaptation.

What *is* required is a general approach of acceptance and valuing, which can create a positive classroom climate that invites all students to learn. In addition, teachers in multicultural classrooms need to *understand the cultures of the students they teach, communicate positive attitudes about cultural diversity, and employ a variety of instructional approaches that build upon students' cultural diversity.* These strategies, which comprise **culturally responsive teaching** (Gay, 2000, Villegas, 1991a) are listed in Table 2.1 and discussed in the next section.

Learning about the Cultures of Our Students. Culture affects learning, and one of the most effective ways of capitalizing on this factor is to find out about the cultures that your students bring to school. One principal did this by attending a special ceremony at a local church to honor Pacific Islander students, a significant minority population in her school. She arrived a few minutes early and was seated on the stage as a guest of honor. She settled down and waited for the ceremony to begin—and waited and waited—until it finally began nearly an hour late. She didn't quite know what to make of this.

The ceremony itself was warm and loving, showcasing each child, who was applauded by the group. After the ceremony the kids returned to their seats for the

Table 2.1 STRATEGIES FOR WORKING IN
MULTICULTURAL CLASSROOMS

Strategy	Examples
Learn about the cultural resources in your classroom.	▪ Visit homes and talk to parents. ▪ Observe students both in and out of school. ▪ Read literature by writers who are members of other cultures. ▪ Talk to teachers of other cultures.
Accept and value student diversity.	▪ Emphasize mutual respect for all types of diversity. ▪ Encourage students to share cultural patterns and norms with each other.
Build on students' cultural backgrounds.	▪ Teach about different cultures. ▪ Use different strategies (e.g., peer tutoring or cooperative learning) to accommodate different cultural styles. ▪ Eliminate grading practices that emphasize competition and differences among students.

remainder of the meeting, which involved adult concerns. For a while, they were fine; then they got bored and started fidgeting. The principal describes the rest:

> Fidgeting and whispering turned into poking, prodding, and open chatting. I became a little anxious at the disruption, but none of the other adults appeared to even notice, so I ignored it, too. Pretty soon several of the children were up and out of their seats, strolling about the back and sides of the auditorium. All adult faces continued looking serenely up at the speaker on the stage. Then the kids started playing tag, running circles around the seating area and yelling gleefully. No adult response—I was amazed, and struggled to resist the urge to quiet the children. Then some of the kids got up onto the stage, running around the speaker, flicking the lights on and off, and opening and closing the curtain! Still nothing from the Islander parents! It was not my place, and I shouldn't have done it, but I was so beyond my comfort zone that with eye contact and a pantomimed shush, I got the kids to settle down.
>
> I suddenly realized then that when these children, say, come to school late, it doesn't mean that they or their parents don't care about learning or that they're a little bit lazy—that's just how all the adults in their world operate. When they squirm under desks and run around the classroom, they aren't trying to be disrespectful or defiant, they're just doing what they do everywhere else. (Winitzky, 1998, p. 123)

Our students bring with them sets of attitudes, values, and ways of acting that may or may not be conducive to learning in traditional unidimensional classrooms. We saw this in the examples of language conflict and we can see it in the example of the Pacific Island students. Teachers in multicultural classrooms need to make an active effort to enter into students' lives to understand their values and ways of acting and behaving. Some effective ways to do this include the following (Peregoy and Boyle, 2001):

▪ Take time at the beginning of your class to introduce yourself, and ask students to do the same.

- Make yourself available before and after school to help students with assignments as well as talk with them about their lives.
- Use dialogue journals to encourage students to share facts about themselves. Set aside a given time every day and provide journal starters like "favorite foods" or "favorite hobbies." Collect these periodically and respond to them.
- Begin the school year with a unit on family origins, supplemented with a world map with string connecting each child's name and birthplace to your city and school.

Activities such as these can redefine your classroom from a place where students come to learn content to one in which they are all part of a learning community.

Accepting and Valuing Student Diversity

In one third-grade classroom with a predominantly Central American student population, youngsters are greeted most mornings with the sound of salsa music in the background, instruction takes place in both English and Spanish, magazines and games in both languages are available throughout the classroom . . . and every afternoon there is a Spanish reading lesson to ensure that students learn to read and write in Spanish as well as English. (Shields and Shaver, 1990, p. 9)

Our students need to know that we understand their home cultures and that we value the diversity that they bring to our classrooms. We do this by openly discussing cultural differences, emphasizing its positive aspects both in classrooms and in society as a whole. We also communicate positive attitudes about diversity by encouraging students to bring their cultures into the classroom, including their music, dress, and different foods. In addition, recognizing and celebrating different holidays like Martin Luther King Day, Muslim holy days, Mexican Independence Day, and the Jewish holidays communicates that students' cultures are important and valued. We also teach positive attitudes by emphasizing mutual respect for all cultures and ensuring that all cultural groups are treated with respect.

Building on Students' Cultural Backgrounds

Maria Sanchez, a fifth-grade teacher in a large urban elementary school, walked around her classroom, helping her students with their social studies projects, which they were working on in small groups. Maria's class was preparing for Parents' Day, an afternoon in which parents and other guardians would join in the class's celebration of the different countries that students came from. Student projects, focusing on these different countries, were designed to provide information about the countries' history, geography, and cultures. The class had been studying these countries in social studies all year long, and a large world map with pins and yarn on it marked students' country of origin with a picture of each student. While many of the pins were clustered in Mexico and Central and South America, there were also many students from all over the world. Each student had been encouraged to invite someone from their family to come and share a part of their native culture. Some were bringing food, while others were bringing music or native dress from their different homelands.

Effective teachers also learn about their students' cultures and use this information to promote personal pride and motivation in their students. The benefits of building on students' cultural backgrounds are felt in both the classroom and the home. In addition to increased student achievement, parents become more positive about school, which in turn enhances student motivation (Shumow and Harris, 1998). Maria recognized this when she invited parents and other caretakers to share their cultural heritage with her class. Students bring to school a wealth of experiences embedded in their home cultures. Sensitive teachers build on these experiences, and all students benefit.

LANGUAGE DIVERSITY

In addition to cultural differences, increased immigration has resulted in increasing numbers of students with limited backgrounds in English entering our classrooms. The number of non–English-speaking and limited-English-proficient (LEP) students increased by more than 50 percent between 1985 and 1991, and between 1991 and 1993 the language minority population increased 12.6 percent compared to an increase of only 1.02 percent in the general population (Weaver and Padron, 1997).

The diversity in language is staggering. Currently, there are over 3.2 million students in U.S. schools whose first language is not English. California has 1.4 million of these English as a Second Language (ESL) students, comprising nearly 40 percent of the student population in that state (U.S. Department of Education, 1998; Office of Bilingual Education and Minority Language Affairs, 1999; Stoddart, 1999). Nationwide, the number of students whose primary language is not English is expected to triple during the next 30 years. The most common language groups for these students are Spanish (73%), Vietnamese (4%), Hmong (1.8%), Cantonese (1.7%), and Cambodian (1.6%). This language diversity poses a challenge to teachers because most instruction is verbal. How should schools respond to this linguistic challenge? Let's examine this question, beginning with the topic of dialects.

English Dialects

Mrs. Caplow says, "Let's write a story about our school tour."

Andrea says, "I write no story."

"I no want to," Mike adds.

Mrs. Caplow responds, "I know you do not want to, but we must learn how to read and write."

Joe says, "I want to make horseshoe."

Mrs. Caplow says, "Not now, Joe."

She then writes on the top of the chalkboard, "Our School Tour," and continues, "Okay boys and girls, what did we do on our school tour?"

"Went outside," Laura responds.

"Did we take a tour?"

After hearing no response she continues, "What is a tour?"

Laura says, "A trip."

"Okay. Let's write, 'We took a trip and we met our school helpers.' " (Actually they met no one.)

She then says, "That is a short story."

Susan calls out, "I ain't got no paper."

Mrs. Caplow responds, "Oh no, Susan, let's not say 'ain't.' Let's say, I haven't any paper.'"

Susan says, "I haven't no paper." (Rist, 1973, pp. 79–80)

Anyone who has traveled in the United States can confirm the fact that our country has many regional and ethnic dialects. A **dialect** is a *variation of standard English that is distinct in vocabulary, grammar, or pronunciation.* Everyone in the United States speaks a dialect; people merely react to those different from their own (Banks, 2001). Some dialects are accepted more than others, however, and language plays a central role in what Delpit (1995) calls "codes of power," the cultural and linguistic conventions that control access to opportunity in our society. What does research say about these dialects?

Research indicates that students' use of nonstandard English results in lowered teacher expectations for their performance (Bowie and Bond, 1994), lowered assessments of students' work, and lowered self-assessments by the students themselves (Taylor, 1983). Teachers often confuse nonstandard English with mistakes during oral reading (Washington and Miller-Jones, 1989), and some critics argue that dialects, such as Black English, are substandard. Linguists, however, argue that these variations are just as rich and semantically complex as Standard English (Labov, 1972; Rickford, 1997).

So, what should a teacher do when a student says, "I ain't got no pencil," bringing a nonstandard dialect into the classroom? Opinions vary from "rejection and correction" to complete acceptance. The approach most consistent with culturally responsive teaching is to accept the dialect and build on it (Speidel, 1987). For example, when the student says, "I ain't got no pencil,' the teacher (or adult) might say, "Oh, you don't have a pencil. What should you do then?" Although results won't be apparent immediately, the long-range benefits make the effort worth it.

Language differences don't have to form barriers between home and school. **Bidialecticism,** *the ability to switch back and forth between a dialect and Standard English, allows access to both* (Gollnick and Chinn, 2002). For example, one teacher explicitly taught differences between Standard and Black English, analyzing the strengths of each and specifying respective places for their use. The teacher read a series of poems by Langston Hughes, the African-American poet, focusing on the ability of Black English to create vivid images. The class discussed contrasts with Standard English and ways in which differences between the two languages could be used to accomplish different communication goals (Shields and Shaver, 1990). In this way students were made aware of differences in dialects, the strengths of each, and when different dialects should be used.

English Language Development Programs

In many instances our students come to us speaking a language other than English. There are many terms used to describe students whose first language isn't English (Peregoy and Boyle, 2001). *English learners, English language learners, nonnative English speakers,* and *second language learners* are all used to refer to students learning English as a second language. The term *limited English proficient* (LEP) is also used to refer to students who range from beginners to intermediates in learning English. There are also several terms given to educational programs for these students, with English as a Second Language (ESL) and English Language Development (ELD) the most common.

There are numerous approaches to teaching English as a second language. Though all are designed to teach English, they differ in how fast English is introduced and to what extent the first language is used and maintained. True bilingual programs offer instruction to nonnative English speakers in two languages: English and their primary language. They attempt to maintain and enhance the native language while building on it to teach English. Other programs place more emphasis on English acquisition. We look at three of these English language development programs: maintenance bilingual programs, transitional bilingual programs, and English as a second language (ESL) programs.

Maintenance Bilingual Programs. **Maintenance bilingual programs** *teach in both the native language and English, maintaining and building on the students' native language* (Banks, 2001; Gollnick and Chinn, 2002). These programs are found primarily at the elementary level and occur in areas where there are large numbers of students who speak the same language, like the southwest United States. Their purpose is to develop students who are truly bilingual—that is, who can speak, read, and write in two languages. While maintenance programs help maintain and build students' language, and culture, they are difficult to implement because they require groups of students with the same native language and bilingual teachers who speak this language. They are also controversial, with critics claiming they fail to teach English quickly enough. This criticism led voters in California to pass Proposition 227, which drastically curtailed the use of maintenance bilingual programs in that state (Schnaiberg, 1999b).

Transitional Bilingual Programs. **Transitional bilingual programs** *use the native language as an instructional aid until English is proficient.* In transitional programs, instruction begins in the native language and English is gradually introduced. However, the transition period is sometimes too short, leaving some learners ill prepared for instruction in English (Gersten and Woodward, 1995; Spencer, 1988).

English as a Second Language (ESL) Programs. *Since they focus ultimately on the mastery of English,* all bilingual programs are actually **English as a second language (ESL) programs.** ESL programs differ from the other programs in their emphasis on teaching students English and mainstreaming them into regular classrooms. Often ESL programs place students in regular classes for most of the day and pull them out for separate instruction in ESL classrooms for the remainder. These ESL classes are often called **sheltered instruction** and *are designed to provide students with content instruction along with English language development.* ESL programs are common when classes contain different students who speak a variety of languages, thus making maintenance or transitional programs difficult to implement. They are also common at the high school level, where the logistical problems of students going from one content classroom to the next make other alternatives impossible.

Teachers can assist LEP students in bilingual programs through sensitivity and awareness and by taking advantage of opportunities to facilitate language development. Research indicates that a surprising number of teachers are unaware of the home languages that students bring to school; one study found that teachers recognized only 27 percent of the nonnative English speakers in one sample of Asian students (Schmidt, 1992). Teachers can't adjust their teaching to meet the needs of LEP students if they aren't aware that these students exist.

Table 2.2 EFFECTIVE INSTRUCTION FOR ESL STUDENTS

1. Use examples and learning activities to provide a concrete frame of reference.

2. Write key concepts and terms on the board and refer to them during discussions.

3. Use interactive questioning strategies.

4. Use groupwork to provide opportunities for linguistic and academic development.

A second way to help LEP students is through the use of instructional strategies that encourage student language use and development (Fitzgerald, 1995; Ravetta and Brunn, 1995). These are outlined in Table 2.2 and described in the following paragraphs.

When teaching ESL students teachers need to provide concrete examples of the ideas they are presenting. For example, a lesson on ecosystems in science becomes much more meaningful when it begins with pictures of different ecosystems. In a similar way, a first-grade story on hats becomes more meaningful when the teacher brings in several hats to share during the lesson. These concrete examples and pictures can then serve as a frame of reference for key concepts and terms that the teacher writes on the board to provide both focus and information about how important words are spelled. Interactive questioning provides opportunities to actively involve students while assessing their understanding of new vocabulary. Groupwork provides further opportunities for students to practice their language skills of listening and speaking while also learning new content. All of these strategies have proven effective for learners in general (Eggen and Kauchak, 2001); for ESL students they are essential (Peregoy and Boyle, 2001).

STUDENTS PLACED AT RISK: TEACHING THE CHILDREN OF POVERTY

Today's students are different in yet another way. Never before have schools attempted to teach so many students who are physically and mentally ill-prepared to learn. A combination of economic and social forces threaten the ability of many students to profit from their educational opportunities.

Consider these statistics:

- Seven out of 10 women with children are in the workforce.
- The divorce rate has quadrupled in the past 20 years; the number of single-parent families is estimated at 25 percent and is expected to increase.
- Sixty-eight percent of all births to teenagers occur out of wedlock.
- The incidence of poverty among single-parent families is between seven and eight times higher than families headed by married couples.
- Sixty percent of teenage families live in poverty as compared to 14 percent of the total population.
- Children, while only 27 percent of the total population, constitute 40 percent of the poor.
- Poverty is most common in families headed by single mothers.
- Poverty is more prevalent among minorities than nonminorities.

(More Families in Poverty, 1993; U.S. Census Bureau, 1998a)

When we compare these figures with life in middle-class America, they paint a picture of a different kind of diversity—a diversity in terms of economic and social opportunity.

Students placed at risk *are those in danger of failing to complete their education with the skills necessary to survive in modern society* (Slavin, Karweit, and Madden, 1989). The term is borrowed from medicine, where it refers to individuals who don't have a specific disease but are likely to develop it, such as an overweight person with high blood pressure being at risk for a heart attack. It became widely used after 1983 when the National Commission on Excellence in Education proclaimed the United States a "nation at risk" (National Commission on Excellence in Education, 1983), emphasizing the growing link between education and economic well-being in today's technological society. For example, between 1979 and 1996 the real earnings of 25–34 year old male dropouts fell by 28 percent (Murnane and Tyler, 2000). Compounding the problem is the fact that the percentage of 18–24 year olds who left school without a diploma increased from 21.2 percent in 1994 to 25.3 percent in 1998.

Economic and social ills combine to produce the following educational problems:

- Poor attendance
- High dropout rates
- Low achievement
- Low motivation
- Management problems
- Dissatisfaction with and disinterest in school
- Low involvement in extracurricular activities
- High rates of drug use
- High criminal activity rates

(Barr and Parett, 2001)

Children placed at risk often come to school underfed and without proper care. They may not be eager to learn because their emotional needs for safety and security have not been met. At-risk students can be difficult to teach and can pose serious educational problems for teachers. To deal with these challenges, we need to understand how economic and social factors interact to impact learning.

Students Placed At Risk: Understanding the Problem

How does poverty, and the myriad of ills that go with it, result in decreased learning and motivation? Sociologists offer us one way to understand the connection. They use **socioeconomic status (SES)** as a concept to describe a family's relative position in the community. *SES is determined by a combination of parents' income, occupation, and level of education.* SES consistently predicts not only performance on intelligence tests but also classroom performance, achievement test scores, grades, truancy, and dropout and suspension rates (Macionis, 2000). Children of wealthier parents, parents who have white-collar jobs, and parents with higher levels of education generally perform better on all of these school-related measures. Of the three, the best predictor of a student's academic performance is the level of schooling attained by the parents. We'll see why shortly.

SES influences learning in a number of ways. First, SES impacts learning at a basic needs level; students who don't receive adequate nutrition and medical and dental care, for example, come to school physically unprepared to learn. Free breakfast and school lunch programs for low-income families are one government response to this problem. Many teachers in low-income neighborhoods keep a box of crackers in the desk for students who come to school without breakfast.

SES also influences the kinds of experiences students bring with them to school. High-SES students are more likely to travel extensively, to visit museums and zoos, and to talk about these experiences with their parents. When they come to school, they are more likely to know concepts like *big* and *small, up* and *down,* and *left* and *right.* Why are these concepts important? Think for a moment about teaching the differences between *d* and *b, p* and *q,* and a capital *C* and a small *c* without these concepts. All learning builds on prior experiences. Low-SES students' early years often fail to provide the experiences needed to help them succeed in school.

The impact of SES is also transmitted through parental attitudes and values. Is learning important? Are schools essential for learning? How do hard work and effort contribute to learning? Why is homework important? These attitudes and values are learned in subtle and not-so-subtle ways.

Learning to read is a classic example. High-SES homes have books, magazines, and newspapers around the house, and parents model the importance of reading by reading themselves and reading to their children. They develop "print awareness" in their young children by holding up cereal boxes, pointing to stop signs, and putting the child's name on the door to his bedroom. When their children enter school, they not only know about the power of the printed word, they are eager to read.

The opposite is also true. The homes of poverty are less likely to have books and magazines lying around. The television set plays continually, competing with quiet reading and homework time. The parents are less likely to read, and when the young child comes to school, reading is more a mystery than an exciting challenge.

In reviewing differences between high- and low-SES students, one researcher reached these conclusions:

High socioeconomic status students are likely to be confident, eager to participate, and responsive to challenge. They typically want respect and require feedback, but do not require a great deal of encouragement or praise. They tend to thrive in an atmosphere that is academically stimulating and somewhat demanding. In contrast, low socioeconomic status students are more likely to require warmth and support in addition to good instruction from their teachers, and to need more encouragement for their efforts and more praise for their successes. It appears to be especially important to teach them to respond overtly rather than to remain passive when asked a question, and to be accepting of their relevant call-outs and other academic initiations when they do occur. (Brophy, 1986, IV-146)

As with working with culturally different students, these instructional modifications adapt instruction to build on students' needs and strengths.

Resiliency: Capitalizing on Student Strengths

Recent research on students placed at risk has focused on the concept of resilience. **Resilience** *results in a heightened likelihood of success in school and in other aspects of life despite environmental adversities* (Wang, Haertel, and Walberg, 1995). The idea of resilience focuses on young people who thrive in spite of the obstacles encountered with students placed at risk. Resilient children set and meet goals, they expect to succeed, they feel as if they're in control of their own lives, and they have well developed interpersonal skills (Bernard, 1993; Wang et al., 1995).

Resilient children acquire these abilities from families that are caring while holding high moral and academic expectations for their children. Schools that are both demanding and supportive also help promote resilience; in many instances, these schools serve as homes away from home (Haynes and Comer, 1995). Let's look more closely at what schools can do.

Teaching Students Placed At Risk

Research offers some suggestions for helping students placed at risk. These students need greater structure and support both in their instruction and for motivation. They need to experience success and need to understand that effort results in achievement. Let's see how this works in a first-grade classroom.

Instructional Adaptations for Students Placed At Risk. To examine instruction that is effective with students placed at risk, let's return again to Shanda Jackson's classroom and see how she works with her first graders.

Shanda began her math lesson by having students from each row come up to distribute the baggies of beans. When all the students had these, she began.

"Class, I need to have everyone's eyes up here. Good. Today we're going to learn a new idea in math. It's called subtraction. Can everyone say subtraction? Good! Subtraction is when you take away. Let's look up here at the overhead and the felt board.

"Kareem had four cookies in his lunch. He sat down next to his friend, Jared. Jared didn't have any, so Kareem gave him two of his. How many are left?

"Let's do that up here on the felt board. Hmm, four cookies—see how they're round—take away two cookies, leaves how many cookies? Let's count them. Four minus two equals two. That's subtraction."

"Now I want each of you to take out four beans from your bag and do the same."

As the students did this, Shanda moved around the room to make sure they were doing it correctly.

"Excellent, everyone. Now I have another problem for you. Let's pretend the beans are pieces of candy. Who likes candy? (All hands go up.) Cassie had three pieces of candy. Everyone take out the right number of beans to show how much candy she had."

Shanda circulated again to make sure every student had three beans out.

"Now Cassie's two friends came along and each of them wanted a piece, so Cassie gave one to each. Can you take away two beans, one for each of her friends? Now who can tell me how many pieces of candy Cassie had left?"

Teaching students placed at risk is not fundamentally different from teaching students in general. It utilizes general principles of effective teaching and refines them to provide high structure and strong support for learning. The increased structure and support appear in several forms, as we see in Table 2.3 (Brophy, 1986; Peterson, 1986).

Table 2.3 **EFFECTIVE INSTRUCTION FOR STUDENTS PLACED AT RISK**

Strategy	Description
Active teaching	The teacher explains concepts and skills through interactive teaching.
Use of concrete examples	Abstract ideas are illustrated with examples and concrete manipulatives.
Interactive teaching	Teachers use questioning to actively involve students in learning activities.
Practice and feedback	Students have opportunities to practice the concept or skill they're learning.
High success rates	Students are successful as they practice skills and concepts.

Let's look again at Shanda's lesson in the context of these elements. **Active teaching** *means that the teacher assumes responsibility for explaining and modeling the idea to be learned.* Shanda did this when she called the class together and told them that they were learning a new skill today and then explained the skill at the feltboard.

She then used manipulatives and questioning to help her first graders learn the process of subtraction. Note that she didn't just write numbers on the board like 4 − 2 = 2. Instead, she illustrated the process with real-life examples using cookies and candy—examples that 6 year olds could understand and identify with. In addition, she actively involved students, having all students do the physical operation at their own desks.

Interactive teaching also involves all students through questioning. This not only allows all students to participate but also provides the teacher with an opportunity to informally check students' comprehension. Shanda used interactive teaching in at least three ways. For example,

- She asked students to say *subtraction*.
- She asked who liked candy.
- She asked how many pieces of candy Cassie had left.

These questions both encouraged student involvement and helped Shanda diagnose her students' attention and developing understanding.

Interactive teaching methods are essential. In a comparison of more and less effective urban elementary teachers, researchers found that less effective teachers interacted with students only 47 percent of the time versus 70 percent of the time for their more effective counterparts (Waxman et al., 1997). Interactive teaching is characteristic of good instruction in general; its importance with students place at risk is crucial (Gladney and Greene, 1997; Hudley, 1998; Wang et al., 1995).

Effective teaching also allows students opportunities to actively try out their developing ideas. To be effective, opportunities for practice and feedback should be available to all students. For example, all of Shanda's students had beans to add and subtract with, and she moved around the room to make sure all students were involved and on task.

Student success is critical in the process. Because they may not have a history of successful school experiences, lack of success can result in frustration for students placed at risk and can further detract from motivation that may already be low. Shanda ensured high success rates by taking small instructional steps and monitoring learning progress as the lesson proceeded.

By now you might be saying to yourself, "Wait a minute. Aren't these procedures for students placed at risk just good teaching?" If you did, you're absolutely correct. Effective instructional practices for students placed at risk are not qualitatively different from those for regular students. The same principles of good teaching that work in the regular classroom also work with students placed at risk. It is, however, all the more critical that they be applied conscientiously and thoroughly with students place at risk. Collectively, these practices provide an instructional safety net that minimizes the possibility for frustration and failure, two factors that are especially damaging for students placed at risk.

Motivation: The Need for Challenge

While increased structure and support are important when teaching these students, additional research has highlighted the importance of challenge. A study of at-risk high school students in one blue-collar community found that many characteristics of effective practices were being implemented (Miller, Leinhardt, and Zigmond, 1988). However, researchers also found that academic expectations for students were lowered, little emphasis was placed on higher-order thinking and problem solving, students spent an inordinate amount of time on worksheets, and boredom and apathy were common. The increased structure and support had resulted in a program that lacked rigor and excitement.

Several programs have been developed to provide challenge for students placed at risk. The *Accelerated Schools Program* builds on student strengths by combining high expectations with an enriched curriculum focusing on a language-based approach in all academic areas (Levin, 1988; Rothman, 1991). The *Higher Order Thinking Skills Program* (HOTS) focuses on teaching students skills such as inferencing and generalizing to help them realize the importance of critical thinking in learning (Pogrow, 1990).

Results from both programs have been encouraging. One Accelerated Schools site in San Francisco registered the highest achievement gains on standardized test scores in the city, and spring-to-spring comparisons of achievement gains in one HOTS program showed students were 67 percent above the national average in reading and 123 percent higher in math (Rothman, 1991).

Common to both programs are high expectations, emphasis on enrichment versus remediation, and the teaching of higher-order thinking and learning strategies. These strategies are integrated into the regular curriculum so that students can see their usefulness in different content areas (Means and Knapp, 1991).

What does this suggest for teachers? First, it reminds us that high expectations and emphasis on higher-order thinking are as important for at-risk students as for other students. Second, it makes teachers' ability to use challenging teaching strategies all the more important. We examine these strategies in detail in Chapters 4 through 10 of the text.

TEACHING STUDENTS WITH DIFFERENT LEARNING ABILITIES

Melanie Parker, an intern from a nearby university, was ready to teach her first math lesson in Mrs. Jenkins's middle school math class. The topic was the decimal system, and she had preplanned with Mrs. Jenkins, who had suggested a review of place value, such as identifying three 10s and two 1s in a number like 32. Though she was nervous at the beginning, everything went smoothly as she explained the concept and used interlocking cubes to illustrate it. As she passed out practice worksheets, Mrs. Jenkins walked over to Melanie and whispered, "You're doing great. I need to run down to the office. I'll be right back." The students quickly went to work, since they were accustomed to having interns and preinterns in the class and didn't react when Mrs. Jenkins left.

Melanie's nervousness calmed as she circulated among the students, periodically making comments. She noticed that some were galloping through the assignment, others needed minor help, and a few were totally confused. As she worked with the students, she noticed that the quiet of the classroom was turning into a low buzz.

"Joel, why aren't you working?" Melanie asked as she turned to a student near her.

"I'm done."

"Hmm?" she thought as she looked around the room.

"Beth, finish your assignment and stop talking," Melanie said, turning to another student visiting with her neighbor.

"I can't do this stuff!"

Melanie looked at the clock and saw that there were still 10 minutes to the bell. From the fidgeting and talking, it appeared that several of the students had completed their assignment, while others had barely begun. Panic! What to do?

Just then Mrs. Jenkins walked in the room, surveyed the class and looked at the clock as she walked over to Melanie.

"How is it going?"

"Fine, but half of them are done and the other half need extra help."

Mrs. Jenkins then turned to the class and said in an authoritative voice. "Class, if you're done with your work, put it away in your homework file for tomorrow. Then you can either do the math exercises on the computer in the back of the room or find a partner for one of the math games. Let's get busy now."

As Melanie quickly learned, the students we teach differ in their ability to profit from our instruction. As one of our colleagues jokingly estimates, "In any lesson, probably a third already know it, another third are really learning it, and the rest don't know what you're talking about." While probably overstated, there is some truth in what she says. The students in most classes vary considerably in their ability to learn, and this has important implications for instruction.

What does this variability look like in the classroom? In a typical second-grade classroom, for example, students will range from below first grade to beyond the fourth in reading ability, meaning that some will still be working on beginning reading skills, such as sounding out words, whereas others will be ready to focus on complex comprehension abilities (Elwall and Shanker, 1989). In higher grades the range of abilities is even greater.

The amount of time it takes students to master new content is another way of thinking about the variability in student learning ability. Melanie's experience illustrates this idea; some students understood the topic quickly, while others struggled to understand it at all. In many classes it can take slower students more than five times longer to master a topic than their faster peers (Bloom, 1981).

While reading grade levels and time required for learning are alternate ways of describing learner variations in learning ability, it is still most commonly expressed in terms of *intelligence* or intellectual ability. For example, estimates suggest that you're likely to have students with intelligence test scores ranging from 60 or 70 (IQ) to 130 or 140 in an average, heterogeneously grouped classroom (Hardman et al., 1999). This range is so great that students at the lower end would be classified as mildly handicapped and would be eligible for special help, while students at the upper end might be considered gifted and/or talented. In the next section we examine the concept of intelligence and discuss how it influences teaching.

Intelligence: What Does It Mean?

We all have an intuitive idea about intelligence. In everyday language it's how "smart" or "sharp" people are, how quickly they learn, the insights they have, or even the wide range of—sometimes trivial—knowledge they possess. More formally, intelligence is measured by standardized tests that produce the well-known IQ or intelligence test score. The two most popular intelligence tests used today are the Weschler Intelligence Scale for Children (WISC) and the Stanford-Binet.

What do these tests actually measure, or perhaps more appropriately, what is intelligence? When a thousand experts were asked the second question, they identified **intelligence** *as having three components:*

- *Abstract thinking and reasoning*
- *Problem solving ability*
- *Capacity to acquire knowledge (aptitude)*
  (Snyderman and Rothman, 1987)

When we examine these dimensions, we can see why intelligence is an important concept for educators and why scores on intelligence tests correlate moderately well (.50 to .70) with school performance (Sattler, 1992).

Despite this correlation, the concept of intelligence is controversial, with controversies focusing on three issues. First is the "nature-nurture" controversy, with some authorities arguing that intelligence is genetically determined and essentially fixed at birth (Jensen, 1987)—the *nature* position. Others take the *nurture* position, contending that intelligence can be influenced both indirectly (e.g., through diet and access to medical care) and directly through educational interventions (Sternberg, 1986). This issue has important implications for how we view our students. Do they come to us with their intellectual ability fixed and unchangeable, or are there things that teachers can do to improve intelligence? An optimistic view of education, called the *interactionist* position, holds that students come to our classrooms with genetic potential and that we as teachers can do much to help learners reach that potential.

A second controversy focuses on the issue of cultural bias. Some experts argue that intelligence tests *are* culturally embedded and influenced by both language and a learner's past experiences (Anastasi, 1988). This issue has important implications for the use of these tests with minority populations. Research has found that an overreliance on intelligence tests with non–English-speaking populations resulted in the classification of a disproportionate number of these students as mentally retarded (Mercer, 1973; Fine, 2001)

Multiple Intelligences: The Work of Howard Gardner

The third controversy relates to the concept of single versus multiple dimensions of intelligence. Historically, intelligence tests produced a single score that indicated a general measure of intellectual functioning; later, tests such as the WISC provided two scores, one verbal and the other performance; now there is considerable interest in the concept of multiple intelligences (Gardner, 1983; Sternberg, 1986). Theories of multiple intelligences suggest that there are several kinds of "smarts" rather than just one. For example, **Gardner's theory of multiple intelligences** *breaks intelligence into eight different areas: linguistic, logical-mathematical, musical, and spatial, bodily-kinesthetic, interpersonal, intrapersonal, and naturalist.*

Gardner's work is intuitively sensible. We all know people, for example, who don't seem particularly sharp at school tasks but have a special ability to get along well with others, or they appear to have insights into their own strengths and weaknesses. Gardner would describe these people as being high in interpersonal and intrapersonal intelligence, respectively. In other cases we see people who excel in English but do less well in math—linguistic versus logical-mathematical intelligence—and we've all seen examples of gifted musicians and gifted athletes who don't excel in the other areas. These different dimensions are summarized in Table 2.4.

Viewing intelligence as multidimensional suggests that teachers should create learning environments in which different kinds of students can excel. Giving learners choices is consistent with this view. For example, a middle school English teacher breaks assignments down into required and optional. Seventy percent of the assignments are required for everyone; the other 30 percent provide students with choices about what to read and do and they negotiate with the teacher on the specific assignments. Other ways of providing students with learning options are discussed in the next section.

Intellectual Diversity: Implications for Teaching

Intellectual diversity is a fact of teaching life. You will encounter a range of learning abilities in your classrooms. In responding to this diversity a teacher has a number of options, some of which are the following:

1. Create multidimensional classrooms. Design learning tasks that encourage and capitalize on intellectual diversity.
2. Make time requirements flexible. Adjusting time requirements allows slower students more time to complete assignments.
3. Group students according to their ability. This allows teachers to teach to a particular ability level but carries with it other problems.
4. Provide strategy instruction for slower students. Strategy instruction increases students' ability to learn by teaching them more efficient ways of performing academic tasks.
5. Use peer tutoring and cooperative learning. These strategies use students as resources and capitalize on the benefits that social interaction in learning can provide.

Let's examine these options more closely.

Table 2.4 GARDNER'S DIMENSIONS OF INTELLIGENCE

Dimension	Example	Application
Linguistic intelligence and effectiveness: Sensitivity to the varied uses of language	Poet, journalist	How can I get students to talk or write about an idea?
Logical–mathematical intelligence: The ability to reason and to recognize patterns in the world	Scientist, mathematician	How can I bring in number, logic, and classification to encourage students to quantify or clarify the idea?
Musical intelligence: Sensitivity to pitch, melody, and tone	Composer, violinist	How can I help students use environmental sounds, or set ideas into rhythm or melody?
Spatial intelligence: The ability to perceive the visual world accurately, and creatively modify the world perceptively	Sculptor, navigator	What can I do to help students visualize, draw, or conceptualize the idea spatially?
Bodily-kinesthetic intelligence: A fine-tuned ability to use the body effectively and creatively	Dancer, athlete	What can I do to help students involve the whole body or to use hands-on experience?
Interpersonal intelligence: A sensitivity to others' thoughts and feelings	Therapist, salesperson	How can peer, cross-age, or co-operative learning be used to help students develop their interactive skills?
Intrapersonal intelligence: An understanding of self	Self-aware individual	How can I get students to think about their capacities and feelings to make them more aware of themselves as persons and learners?
Naturalist intelligence: Recognizing similarities and differences in the physical world	Naturalist, biologist, anthropologist	How can I encourage students to observe and think about the world around them?

Adapted from Armstrong (1994); Gardner and Hatch (1989); Chekles (1997).

Creating Multidimensional Classrooms. To capitalize on students' strengths, learning tasks need to be adapted so that all members of the group can participate and succeed. For example, in one social studies project that focused on ways that historians learn about our past, students had a number of learning options.

> [D]ifferent groups of students study castle floor plans and pictures of ruins, listen to recordings of Crusade songs, analyze the text of a speech by Pope Urban, and examine half-human pictures of infidels in the Crusaders' Handbook. To grasp the deeper concepts of how historians learn, students spend several days on this project so they can experience each of the media in turn: text, music, and spatial-visual material (Cohen, 1991, p. 5).

In addition, students were also provided with options about how they could demonstrate what they learned.

Each group presents products which require a variety of creative intellectual abilities. Students create their own version of a Crusader castle and show how it can be defended, write a song about current events that echoes the purpose of the music of the Crusades, and perform a skit illustrating how the Crusader Handbook was used to recruit naive villagers. As students present these products, the teacher stimulates a general discussion on the different sources used by historians. (Cohen, 1991, p. 5)

Multi-ability classrooms like this allow all students to contribute to the group. As opposed to narrow, convergent tasks that have only one right answer, **multi-ability tasks:**

- *Are open-ended, involving general answers or several ways to solve problems.*
- *Provide opportunities for different students to make different kinds of contributions.*
- *Use a variety of skills and call on a wide range of knowledge.*
- *Incorporate reading, writing, constructing, and designing skills.*
- *Incorporate the use of multimedia.*
(Cohen, 1986)

Multi-ability classrooms promote learning for all students. In a comparison of a multi-ability approach to learning high school social studies, students who used these strategies learned more than students who merely discussed the same content (Bowers, 1990). The advantages were more apparent for lower-ability students, who often have problems with tasks, such as lectures, that focus primarily on passive verbal instructional strategies.

Flexible Time Requirements. When the amount of time available for learning is the same for all students, the gap between faster and slower students grows wider and wider (Bloom, 1981). One way to accommodate these differences in learning ability is to provide extra time for slower students. For this strategy to work, the classroom needs enrichment activities available to students who complete their assignments quickly. Mrs. Jenkins did this by making computers and math games available when students completed their assignments early. Alternate enrichment options are described in Table 2.5.

Table 2.5 ENRICHMENT OPTIONS FOR FASTER STUDENTS

Enrichment Option	Description
Free reading	A shelf of books or magazines, (e.g. *Ranger Rick, National Geographic World*) are kept in the back of the room for students to use.
Games	A part of the room is sectioned off for students to play academic games on the floor.
Computers	A menu of computer software games and simulations provides student choice.
Learning centers	Learning materials with objectives, directions, and learning activities guide students.
Individual research projects	Students choose long-term projects to investigate; teachers assist by helping to gather individual books and other resources.
Peer tutoring	Structured learning activities help students assist each other.

Ability Grouping

Adrienne Foster sat back and thought as she finished checking her third-grade students' math quiz. The scores were bimodal; half of her class understood multiplication with carrying and half were still struggling. If she continued with multiplication, half the class would be bored; if she went ahead with division, the other half would be lost. What to do?

The next day she began her math class by explaining that some students were ready for division and some needed some more work on multiplication. She gathered the students still working on multiplication around her in one corner of the room and gave them a sheet with additional problems on it. She told them that they would get back together as soon as she introduced division to the other group. As she worked with the division group, she kept one eye on them and the other on the group doing their multiplication. Some hands went up, but she had to tell them to wait a few minutes until she was done with the division group. It wasn't an easy juggling act, but she didn't know what her alternatives were.

Grouping is a common instructional response to student diversity, especially at the elementary level, and it can take several forms (Good and Brophy, 2000). **Between-class ability grouping** *divides a class of 75 third graders, for example, into three groups: one high, one medium, and one low. Grouping across grade levels, also called the* **Joplin Plan,** mixes, for example, third-, fourth- and fifth-grade students of similar reading ability in the same reading class. These students then return to their own classrooms for the other subjects. **Within-class grouping** *breaks students in an individual class into different groups for specific subjects.* Adrienne Foster did this in her third-grade class.

Despite its popularity, grouping has several problems:

- Teachers have inappropriately lowered expectations for students in lower groups, and instruction in these groups is often poorer than that for high-ability groups (Good and Brophy, 2000). As a result, low groups fall farther and farther behind.
- Students in low groups often develop problems with lowered self-concept and motivation.
- Ability tracks tend to stabilize, which permanently labels students as "slow" not only within a grade level but also from year to year (Oakes, 1992).
- Teaching multiple groups is very demanding, and off-task behavior is a common problem for students who are not in direct contact with the teacher.

Sometimes, however, as Adrienne concluded, groups are necessary. This often occurs in subjects that are hierarchically organized such as reading and math, where later skills build on prerequisite ones. When grouping is used, experts recommend the following precautions:

1. Only use grouping when necessary; avoid grouping in subjects that are not hierarchical (e.g. music, art, science, social studies).
2. Assess frequently, keep groups flexible, and reassign students when their learning progress warrants it.
3. Make sure that the quality of instruction to low-ability students is comparable to that provided for high-ability students.
4. Constantly be aware of the potential negative consequences of grouping.
   (Hallinan, 1984)

Strategy Instruction. Research indicates that a major difference between high- and low-ability students is their knowledge and use of learning strategies (Turnbull et al., 1999). In addition to richer content backgrounds, high-ability students use this knowledge more efficiently in learning new information than do their lower-ability peers. For example, consider the thinking of a high-ability student faced with the task of learning a list of 10 spelling words for a quiz.

> Okay . . . 10 words for the quiz on Friday. That shouldn't be too hard. I have two days to learn them.
>
> Let's see. These are all about airports. Which of these do I already know—*airplane, taxi, apron,* and *jet?* No problem. Hmm. . . . Some of these aren't so easy, like *causeway* and *tarmac.* I don't even know what a tarmac is. I'll look it up. . . . Oh, that makes sense. It's the runway. I'd better spend more time on these words. I'll cover them up and try to write them down and then check 'em. Tonight, I can get Mom to give me a quiz and then I'll know which ones to study extra tomorrow. (Eggen and Kauchak, 2001, p. 200)

This student's actions were strategic in several ways. She assessed the task and adapted her studying to match it; she spent more time and effort on the words she didn't know; and she monitored her progress through quizlike exercises. Low-ability students, by contrast, passively approach the task, reading the list with little thought to what they know or ways of improving. They spend time on words they already know and make little effort to test themselves in order to receive feedback to direct their future efforts.

Research suggests efforts to teach learning strategies to our students are productive (Turnbull et al., 1999). This instruction should include talking about the strategy, modeling it while thinking out loud, and providing opportunities for practice. For example, a teacher trying to teach the spelling strategy could have all students take a pretest and talk about the importance of the differences between words they know and don't know. Then she might suggest different ways of practicing, such as self-quizzes, peer quizzes, and flash cards. Finally, she could do long-term follow-up by reminding students from time to time when strategies are appropriate. Some examples of strategies in different areas are found in Table 2.6.

Table 2.6 LEARNING STRATEGIES IN DIFFERENT CONTENT AREAS

Strategy Area	Examples
General memorization tasks	Selectively rehearsing important information; categorizing; grouping; imaging
All content areas	Note taking, outlining, selectively underlining, self-quizzing
Reading	Summarizing; outlining; underlining
Math	Identifying givens in word problems; selectively rehearsing math facts
Writing	Outlining; considering the audience; illustrating ideas with facts; making coherent transitions

Peer Tutoring and Cooperative Learning. A final way to deal with learning diversity in your classroom is to use students themselves to help each other. Peer tutoring places students in one-to-one pairs and supplies them with structured learning materials for practice and feedback. Cooperative learning strategies place students of differing abilities on the same team and uses group rewards to encourage cooperative learning. The research on both of these practices is so positive (Top and Osguthorpe, 1987; Slavin, 1995) that we'll return to them in Chapter 8 and provide a detailed discussion of ways to implement them in your classroom.

LEARNING STYLES

One thing Nate Crowder remembered from his methods classes was the need for variety. He had been primarily using large-group discussions in his junior high social studies class, and most of the students seemed to respond OK. But others seemed disinterested, and their attention often drifted.

Today, Nate decided to try a small-group activity involving problem solving. They had been studying the growth of big cities' problems.

As he watched the small groups interact, he was amazed at what he saw. Some of the quietest, most withdrawn students were leaders in the groups.

"Great!" he thought. But at the same time, he noted that some of his more active students were sitting back and not getting involved.

The differences Nate encountered in his class may be the result of learning styles. **Learning styles,** *also called* cognitive styles, *are the different approaches students have for learning, problem solving, and processing information* (Snow, Corno, and Jackson, 1996). Students with different learning styles perceive, understand, and try to solve learning tasks in different, relatively stable ways. The stability of learning styles is important; it allows the teacher to identify them and adapt instruction accordingly.

Field Dependence/Independence

Field dependence/independence is *the ability of an individual to select relevant from irrelevant information in a complex and potentially confusing background* (Witkin, Moore, Goodenough, and Cox, 1977). For example, when encountering math word problems, a field-independent person is more likely than a field-dependent individual to extract and use relevant information—while ignoring irrelevant information—in solving the problem. Field dependence/independence is typically measured by presenting people with geometric figures embedded within other figures to see if they can pick out the disguised form in the larger context. Field-independent students are able to break the complex display down into its subcomponents; field-dependent students experience more difficulty and are more influenced by surface features.

Field dependence/independence is influenced by development (Farr and Moon, 1988); older children are less dependent on surface appearances, for example. Some research suggests that because of this analytical ability field-independent students have an advantage in math and science courses that require the ability to distinguish between relevant and irrelevant information (Davis and Williams, 1992).

Differences in field dependence/independence influence classroom performance. For example, researchers have found that field independent students take notes that are better organized and had more key ideas than those taken by field-dependent students (Frank, 1984). Field-independent students were also better at restructuring problems to fit end goals. They typically prefer to work alone and do well in individualized systems.

Field-dependent students, by contrast, are more sensitive to context cues and attack problems more globally (Saracho, 1990). They are more socially dependent and look to others for cues. As a result, they work better in groups and are more responsive to teacher praise and other forms of social reinforcement. They also benefit more from teacher efforts to structure new content and experience more difficulty with inductive or open-ended activities (Meng and Patty, 1991).

Conceptual Tempo: Impulsive and Reflective Learners

Students also differ in the rate at which they respond to questions and problems. This is called **conceptual tempo** (Kagan, Pearson, and Welch, 1966; Messick, 1994). *Impulsive* students rush to blurt out answers, and *reflective* students analyze and deliberate before answering. Error rates correspond to these differences. Reflective students think more before they answer; impulsive students take more chances and make more mistakes. Impulsive students perform better in speed games in which the target is low-level factual information; reflective students have an advantage when high-level problem solving is the task. Research in reading shows that reflective students are better at identifying inconsistencies in text; their more impulsive counterparts are more likely to read past or skip over them (Walczyk and Hall, 1989).

Self-instruction training is one strategy that can be used to help students understand the impact of conceptual tempo on their learning (Meichenbaum, 1986). Self-instruction training teaches students to monitor their thinking by talking themselves through a problem solution, such as "Now, let's see . . . the problem asks for the distance around the circle. That's the circumference. Now, what's the formula for circumference?" By making students aware of their own thought processes, we reduce their tendency to be impulsive and also improve their general problem-solving skills. Research on self-instructional training suggests that one of its limitations is its inability to generalize to other learning situations. To address this problem, we should actively involve students in learning about the process, making them aware of when, why and how the process will help them learn (Diaz and Berk, 1992).

Classroom Learning Styles: The Work of Dunn and Dunn

One of the most popular approaches to applying learning styles in classrooms was formulated by Rita and Kenneth Dunn (1978, 1987). These researchers identified a number of preferred learning style dimensions, including the following:

- *Modality*—does the student learn better through listening or reading?
- *Structure/support*—does the learner need high structure or is he or she an independent learner?
- *Individual/group*—does the learner work best independently or in groups?

- *Motivation*—is the student self-motivated, or does he or she require external rewards?
- *Environment*—how do light, temperature, noise, and time of day influence learning?

(Dunn and Dunn, 1978)

The existence of these different preferences or styles makes intuitive sense. We've all heard people say, "I'm a morning person" or "Don't try to talk to me until I've had my cup of coffee." In terms of learning modalities, we've also heard, "I'm a visual person. I need to be able to 'see' it," meaning someone who learns most effectively through visual representation of concepts and other ideas. Other people tend to be more auditory, learning best through oral presentations. A few are tactile; they have to "feel" it.

To identify students' different learning styles, these researchers developed the *Learning Style Inventory* (Dunn, Dunn, and Price, 1985). This inventory asks students to respond to statements such as "I study best when it is quiet" and "I can ignore sound when I study" with a Likert scale (i.e., strongly agree, agree sometimes, disagree, strongly disagree). The instrument provides both individual and class profiles, which can be used to accomplish the following:

- Create special learning environments for individual students.
- Group students on the basis of similar learning styles.
- Design optimal learning environments for a particular class.

Learning Styles: Implications for Teachers

Teachers encountering these learning styles for the first time often ask, "How can I possibly adapt my teaching to fit every learning style?" You probably can't for every one, but Dunn and Dunn (1987) offer suggestions about different ways to change the regular box-crate classroom into a more flexible environment, designed to meet the needs of different students. For example, if a teacher finds that noise is a significant factor in a student's learning, she or he might move the student away from traffic and high-activity areas, put carpeting in study areas to minimize classroom noise, recommend cotton or soft rubber earplugs or nonfunctioning earphones to limit distractions, or allow earphones for a student who prefers music when learning. Probably as important as the actual changes is the message that the teacher is sensitive to students as individuals.

Research on the effectiveness of matching classroom environments to students' learning styles is mixed. Some research suggests that the match enhances learning (Dunn and Dunn, 1987), while other research finds either no effect (Snider, 1990) or negative effects (Knight, Halpen, and Halpen, 1992).

Unquestionably, individual students come to us with different ways of attacking the tasks of learning and solving problems. The key question is, "What should we as teachers do in response to these differences?" and perhaps a more realistic question might be, "What *can* we do about these differences?"

One position would take all instruction and tailor it to the distinctive needs and predispositions of individual students (Witkin et al., 1977). Field-independent students, for example, would be allowed to work on independent projects, while field-dependent students would be allowed to work in small groups. The opposite position (Shipman and Shipman, 1985) strives for balance and would attempt to make impulsive students more reflective and vice versa (e.g., "Now think a minute before you answer. Don't just blurt out the answer!"). Unfortunately, neither of these positions is realistic in a class of 30 students.

So where does this leave us? Is there no value in considering learning style as one element of pupil individuality? Probably not. We believe the concept of learning styles has two important implications for teaching. The first, and perhaps most important, suggests the need to vary our instruction. We have often heard that teachers who vary the way they teach are more effective than those who instruct the same way all the time. Instructional alternatives such as individual projects, small group discussions, cooperative learning, and learning centers provide flexibility in meeting individual learning styles. The importance of instructional variety is supported by research (Rosenshine, 1971). The existence of different learning styles helps us understand why.

The second implication is that the concept of learning style reminds us that our students are indeed different and helps us become more sensitive to differences in their behavior. In turn, we are less apt to interpret the differences as unimportant or inappropriate. The classroom becomes a model of tolerance, and the learning climate improves. Teachers need to use a variety of learning strategies while still remaining sensitive to individual students. A challenge, yes, but something that good teachers do on a daily basis.

STUDENTS WITH EXCEPTIONALITIES

Jim Kessler circulated around the room while his sixth-grade students worked on their unit test. Most were working smoothly, writing an answer and then looking up to think. Others were obviously struggling and Jim could only shake his head in both understanding and frustration. It was like this during regular class time.

There was quiet Samantha—barely said a word in class—shy, slow, she seemed to struggle in every subject. She was a sweet girl; never complained, tried her hardest. Next to her was Jake. Even now his feet were shuffling and his pencil beat a rhythm on the desk. He was energy looking for a destination. Though he did all right in math, he struggled in any subject in which he had to read. Jim had to cajole and coerce him just to pick up a book. Next to Jake was Steven, the playground terror. Steven did all right in the classroom, when other students left him alone, but he had a temper with a short fuse that seemed to ignite at just the slightest provocation. Once Jim got him settled down again, he'd do fine, but it took some doing.

What a collection! If he didn't have the resource teacher to help him he didn't know what he'd do.

Samantha, Jake, and Steven are students with exceptionalities. **Students with exceptionalities** *are those who require special help to reach their full potential,* and you will almost certainly have some of them in your classes (Heward, 1996). This is the result of Public Law 94-142, the Individuals with Disabilities in Education Act (IDEA), which was passed in 1975 with the goal of ensuring a high-quality, free public education for all students with exceptionalities.

Inclusion. In the past, students with exceptionalities were often placed in separate classrooms and facilities. As educators realized that segregated classes and services were not meeting the needs of students with exceptionalities, they wrestled with alternatives. One of the first was **mainstreaming,** *the practice of moving students with exceptionalities from segregated settings into regular classrooms.* Popular in the 1970s, mainstreaming had advantages and disadvantages (Hardman et al., 1999). Mainstreaming began the move away from segregated services and allowed students with exceptionalities and other students to interact. However, students with exceptionalities were often placed into classrooms without the necessary support to help them succeed.

As educators grappled with these problems, they developed the concept of the **least restrictive environment (LRE),** *one that places students in as normal an educational setting as possible while still meeting their special academic, social, and physical needs.* Broader than the concept of *mainstreaming,* the LRE can consist of a continuum of services ranging from mainstreaming to placement in separate facilities. Mainstreaming into a regular classroom occurs only if parents and educators decide it best meets the child's needs.

Central to the LRE is the concept of **adaptive fit,** *which is the degree to which a student is able to cope with the requirements of a school setting and the extent to which the school accommodates the student's special needs* (Hardman et al., 1999). Adaptive fit implies an individualized approach to dealing with students having exceptionalities; it can only be determined after an analysis of a student's specific learning needs. As educators considered mainstreaming, the LRE, and adaptive fit, they gradually developed the concept of inclusion.

Inclusion is a comprehensive approach to educating students with exceptionalities that advocates a total, systematic, and coordinated web of services (Heward, 1996; Turnbull et al., 1999). The inclusion movement has three components:

1. Placing students with special needs in a regular school campus
2. Creating appropriate support and services to guarantee an adaptive fit
3. Coordinating general and special education services

Inclusion is both proactive and comprehensive; it makes all educators responsible for creating supportive learning environments and leaves open the possibility of services being delivered in places other than the regular classroom. Its basic thrust is to include students with exceptionalities in regular classrooms whenever possible, but it also allows for delivering services in other places (Bradley and Switlick, 1997; Larrivee, Semmel, and Gerber, 1997).

Working with Students with Exceptionalities: Support for Classroom Teachers

The practice of inclusion often places students with exceptionalities in regular classrooms, and teachers are expected to help in meeting the needs of these students. They are not alone, however. While school districts are sometimes short of funds and teachers don't always receive all the help called for, support systems such as the following can assist the regular classroom teacher in adapting instruction to meet the learning needs of students with exceptionalities:

1. Specially trained special educators and school psychologists meet with the classroom teachers to help adapt instruction.
2. If warranted, students with exceptionalities receive extra assistance in pullout resource rooms.

3. Assistance or collaborative consultation teams (Heward, 1996) bring special educators into the regular classroom to help the classroom teacher in the following ways:

   a. Meet with the classroom teacher to identify and define any learning problems.

   b. Observe a student's classroom behavior.

   c. Collect work samples from the classroom.

   d. Cooperatively design specific instructional changes with the teacher.

   e. Team teach with the regular teacher.

A major outcome of these meetings is the construction of an Individualized Education Program (IEP). Mandated by law, the **IEP** *outlines an individualized plan of action for each exceptional student.* Each IEP must contain the following components:

- The child's present levels of educational performance
- Annual goals and short-term instructional objectives
- Specific educational services to be provided
- The extent to which the child will participate in regular education
- Projected date for initiation of services
- Expected duration of those services
- Objective criteria and evaluation procedures

(Smith and Luckason, 1992)

The classroom teacher's input during both planning and implementation is essential to the program's success.

The Exceptional Student Population

How common are students with exceptionalities in the classroom? Approximately 11 percent of the school age population is classified as exceptional, and the majority of these (about 70 percent) are taught either in the regular classroom or in a regular classroom with assistance from a resource room (U.S. Department of Education, 2000). If your class is typical, you will have two or three students with exceptionalities needing extra help. We describe characteristics of these students in this section.

Students with Mild–Moderate Disabilities. The vast majority of students with exceptionalities are students with mild-moderate disabilities. **Students with mild-moderate disabilities** *learn well enough to remain in the regular classroom but have enough problems with learning to warrant special help.* The three major subcategories of mild-moderate disabilities are *mental retardation, learning disability,* and *behavioral disorder.* Let's look at them.

Students with mental retardation *have limited intellectual ability, resulting in problems in adapting to classroom tasks.* The majority of these students are mildly or educable mentally retarded and have IQs ranging from 50 to 70 (an average IQ is around 100). This lower level of intellectual functioning requires that classroom requirements need to be adapted to match the learner's capabilities.

In contrast, **students with learning disabilities** *have normal intellectual capabilities but have problems with specific classroom tasks such as listening, reading, writing, spelling, or math operations.* This category is the largest group of handicapped students, constituting almost 45 percent of the total exceptional student population (Heward, 1996). Behavior patterns include hyperactivity and fidgeting, problems with attention, disorganization, and lack of follow-through and uneven performance in different school subjects.

The third category—**behaviorally disordered, emotionally disturbed,** or **emotionally handicapped**—*display persistent behaviors that interfere with their classroom work and interpersonal relations.* Students with behavioral disorders fall into two general categories—the acting out child, (externalizing) and the quiet, withdrawn child (internalizing). (Hallahan and Kauffman, 2000). The acting out child can be physically aggressive and display uncooperative, defiant, and even cruel behaviors. The quiet, withdrawn child is much less visible and is often timid, shy, and depressed, and lacks self-confidence. Experts warn that virtually all students act like behaviorally disordered students sometime in their school years; the key characteristic is that the behavior pattern is chronic and persistent.

In addition to the students we have just discussed, you may have learners in your classes with impaired sight, hearing, or speech. If you see indicators of these disabilities in any of your students, immediately bring them to the attention of your principal, school nurse, school psychologist, or guidance counselor, who can have the student tested.

Teachers' Roles in Working with Students Having Exceptionalities

Toni Morrison had been working with her class of second graders for a week trying to get them into reading and math groups that matched their abilities. Marisse, a transfer student, was hard to place. She seemed to understand the material but lost attention during different parts of lessons. When Toni worked with her one on one, Marisse did fine, but Toni often noticed her staring out the window.

One day as Toni watched the class work in small groups, she noticed that Marisse held her head to one side when she talked to the other side of the classroom. Toni wondered. . . . She spoke to the principal, who recommended that Marisse be referred to the school psychologist for possible testing.

Two weeks later, the school psychologist came by to discuss her findings. Marisse had a hearing problem in one ear that would require a hearing aid as well as special help from Toni.

In a few days, Marisse came to school with her hearing aid. She obviously felt funny about it and wasn't sure if this was a good idea. Toni moved her to the front of the room so she could hear better, made sure to give directions while standing in front of Marisse's desk, and double-checked after an assignment was given to ensure that the directions were clear to her.

After a couple of days, Toni took Marisse aside to talk about her new hearing aid. Marisse *could* hear better, but she still felt a little strange with it. Some of the kids looked at her funny, and that made her uneasy. Toni had an inspiration: Why not discuss the hearing aid in class and let the others try it? This was a risky strategy, but Marisse reluctantly agreed to it.

It worked. During show-and-tell, Marisse explained about her new hearing aid and gave the class a chance to try it out themselves. The strange and different became understandable, and Marisse's hearing aid became a normal part of the classroom. (Eggen and Kauchak, 1992, pp. 204–205)

In working with students with exceptionalities, teachers have three major roles—*identification, fostering acceptance,* and *modifying instruction.* Because they are able to observe students on a day-to-day basis, teachers are in the best position to identify learning problems in their students. If instructional modifications aren't proving successful, the teacher can then refer the student to a special educator or school psychologist for formal evaluation.

A second role that teachers perform in working with exceptional children is fostering acceptance. Perhaps the most difficult obstacles students with exceptionalities face are the negative attitudes of other students and the impact these attitudes have on their own confidence and self esteem (Hardman, et al., 1999). Having a disability and being different is often not well understood or accepted by other students, and just placing students together in inclusive classrooms is often not sufficient to bring about attitude change and acceptance. The teacher's active efforts are necessary to change attitudes and bring about acceptance.

Teachers can help by modeling acceptance, by actively teaching about diversity, and by making every possible effort to ensure that these students experience success and feel needed and wanted. Toni Morrison did this by adapting her classroom to meet Marisse's special learning needs and by emphasizing that Marisse was a valued and integral part of the classroom learning community. This may be the most important contribution a classroom teacher makes for these students. Teachers also help by helping other students understand the nature of the learning problem. Toni did this when she had Marisse explain her hearing aid to other students.

Adapting Instruction for Students with Exceptionalities

Many classroom teachers are apprehensive when faced with adapting instruction for students with exceptionalities. Probably the term *exceptional* has much to do with this apprehension. This is unfortunate because research shows that many of the basic approaches that work with regular students also work with mainstreamed students (Hardman et al., 1999; Heward, 1996). These include:

- Warm academic climate
- Effective use of time
- Effective classroom management
- High success rates
- Effective feedback

The biggest challenge teachers face in working with students with exceptionalities is adapting instruction to ensure success. Teaching topics at a slower pace, providing more opportunities for practice and feedback, giving shorter assignments (e.g., 10 versus 15 problems), and breaking assignments into smaller parts (e.g., 20 problems into four groups of five) all can help in this process.

Reading assignments pose special problems for mainstreamed students because available texts are often inappropriate for their reading level. Some ways of adapting regular reading materials include:

- Setting goals at the beginning of an assignment
- Using advance organizers that structure or summarize the passage
- Introducing key concepts and terms before students read the text

- Creating study guides with questions that focus attention on important information
- Asking students to summarize information in the text
  (Graham and Johnson, 1989)

These adaptations also work with regular students; their use with students with exceptionalities provides extra structure and support to help ensure success.

Technology as a Tool for Inclusion

Technology can be a valuable aid in teaching students with exceptionalities, but the same problem encountered with mainstreaming also applies (Hativa, 1988; Male, 1994). Simply placing students with exceptionalities in front of computers will not automatically solve their learning problems. Computers need to be integrated into the regular instructional program and used when they are more effective than other forms of instruction. Three areas, though, appear promising.

Computers: One Avenue to Automaticity. Computer-assisted instruction (CAI) can help develop automaticity—the ability to perform routine operations, such as multiplying whole numbers or adding suffixes to words, with little mental effort—in basic skill areas (Roblyer and Edwards, 2000). For example, research indicates that students with mild learning disabilities depend heavily on finger-counting strategies in computing math problems, which then becomes a bottleneck when they move to more complex skills. Work with computers can help students overcome this tendency.

Effective computer programs begin by pretesting to determine students' entry skills. They then build on the skills by introducing new math facts at a pace that ensures high success rates. When students fail to answer correctly, the program provides the answer and retests that fact. To develop automaticity (and discourage finger counting), presentation rates are timed, and students' response times are shortened as their proficiency increases.

Computers have also been used to provide practice and feedback during reading lessons (Golden, Gersten, and Woodward, 1990). Middle school students in remedial reading classes who used computers to practice inferencing skills in reading comprehension lessons scored higher than comparable control students on both immediate and maintenance tests of inference skills.

Assistive Technology

Jaleena is partially sighted, with a visual acuity of less than 20/80 even after corrective glasses. Despite this disability, she was doing well in her new fourth-grade class. Tera Banks, her teacher, had placed Jaleena in the front of the room so that she could better see the chalkboard and overhead and had assigned several students to work with her on her projects. Using a magnifying device, she was able to read most written material, but the computer was giving her special problems. The small letters and punctuation on things like website addresses made it very difficult for her to learn to use the computer as an information source. Tera worked with the special education consultant in her district to get a special monitor that magnified content several times. She knew it was working when she saw Jaleena quietly working alone at her computer on the report due next Friday.

Assistive technology, *which includes adaptive tools that help students with disabilities learn and perform better in daily life tasks,* is affecting the ways students with exceptionalities learn. These adaptive tools include motorized chairs, remote control devices that turn machines on and off through a nod of the head or other muscle action, and machines that amplify sights and sounds. Probably the most widespread contribution of assistive technology is in the area of computer adaptations. These adaptations include either alternative input or output devices (Lewis and Doorlag, 1999).

Adaptations to Computer Input Devices. To use computers effectively, students must be able to input their words and ideas. This can be difficult if not impossible for those with visual or other physical disabilities that don't allow standard keyboarding. One adaptation includes devices that enhance the keyboard, such as making it larger and easier to see, arranging the letters alphabetically to make them easier to find, or using pictures for nonreaders. Additional adaptations completely bypass the keyboard. For example, students with physical disabilities that don't allow them to use their hands to input information, use switches activated by a body movement, such as a head nod, to interact with the computer. Touch screens allow students to go directly to the monitor screen to indicate their responses.

Adaptations to Output Devices. Adaptations to the standard computer monitor either bypass visual displays or increase their size. Size enhancement can be accomplished by using a special large screen monitor, such as the one Jaleena used, or by using a magnification device that increases screen size. For students who are blind, speech synthesizers can read words and translate them into sounds. In addition, special printers can convert words into Braille and Braille into words.

Speech/voice recognition technologies are rapidly developing and can assist students with exceptionalities in several ways (Newby et al., 2000). Speech recognition systems can translate speech into text on the computer screen, bypassing the need for keyboard inputting. These systems can be invaluable for students with physical disabilities that affect hand and finger movement. Other devices translate printed words into speech, allowing nonspeaking students to communicate verbally.

These technologies are important because they prevent disabilities from becoming obstacles to learning. Their importance to students with exceptionalities is likely to increase as technology becomes a more integral part of classroom instruction.

Computers: Tracking the Progress of Students with Exceptionalities. A third way that technology has proven useful in working with students with exceptionalities is in monitoring and improving student IEPs (Mercer and Mercer, 1993). Because they are able to store and update information, computers can:

- Modify existing IEPs
- Track learning progress
- Analyze and interpret test data

A number of firms presently market software programs that perform these functions (see Mercer and Mercer, 1993).

Summary

Capitalizing on Cultural Diversity. Students in today's classroom are more diverse than they have ever been, and this diversity poses special challenges and opportunities for teachers. Diversity appears as differences in cultural and language backgrounds, socioeconomic status, and learning abilities and style.

The cultural backgrounds of our students influence their ability to profit from instruction. Cultural deficit, teacher expectations, and cultural differences are three prominent theories that attempt to explain differences in achievement among cultural groups. Teachers can capitalize on cultural diversity by using the cultural resources of their students, communicating positive attitudes about diversity, and employing teaching strategies that build upon diversity.

Language Diversity. Language diversity results from large numbers of students immigrating to this country and from dialect differences in different sections of the United States. In dealing with a dialect, the most effective strategy is to accept and build on it.

Different language development programs emphasize retaining native languages to differing degrees. Maintenance bilingual programs attempt to nurture and retain the native language; transitional bilingual programs use the native language as an instructional aid until English is proficient. ESL programs focus primarily on the mastery of English.

Students Placed at Risk: Teaching the Children of Poverty. Students placed at risk are in danger of failing to complete their education with the skills necessary to survive in a modern technological society. Economic and social problems combine to produce conditions that detract from learning. These include nutritional and health problems and experiential differences that fail to provide a firm foundation for learning. Effective teaching for students placed at risk is not fundamentally different from good teaching in general. Teachers are also becoming increasingly aware of the need for high expectations and challenge.

Teaching Students with Different Learning Abilities. Current views hold that intelligence is alterable, culture embedded and multifaceted. Flexible time frames, grouping, strategy instruction, and peer tutoring and cooperative learning activities are all ways teachers adapt their instruction for students of different abilities.

Learning Styles. Field dependence/independence describes differences in students' ability to focus on detail and separate relevant and irrelevant information. Conceptual tempo describes some students as impulsive and others as reflective. Other work focuses on preferred modes of learning. Research on learning styles reminds us to treat all students as individuals and teach with a variety of instructional strategies.

Students with Exceptionalities. Students with exceptionalities require special help to reach their full potential. Teachers help these students through identification, fostering acceptance, and modifying instruction to meet their special needs.

Important Concepts

Reflecting on Teaching and Learning

Sharon Beasley didn't know what to expect. Though she had been teaching for several years, enrollment shifts in her district resulted in her being transferred from a wealthy, virtually all Caucasian school in the district to the central part of the city. She looked forward to the change with both enthusiasm and apprehension. She had confidence in herself as a teacher and believed she had been doing a good job with the second graders in her classes but she didn't quite know what to expect at Webster Elementary.

She started the school year as she always did—with pretesting. She used the same pretests that she had used previously and was eager to see how her new class performed. As she graded the pretests, her face took on a concerned, if not bewildered, look. Some of her students were right where she thought they should be. However, a large part of her class was well below grade level, needing work on basic skills that they should have learned last year in first grade. "There is no way I'll be able to teach them all the same way," she thought to herself, "so I better break them into groups to match their abilities."

The next day she formed four reading and math groups. Interestingly, they consisted of just about the same students, even though the content areas were different. She decided to go very slow with her two lowest groups so as not to lose them. Many of them were struggling with English as a second language, and this posed problems for them in language arts. The two top groups she pushed hard and was pleased with the results. For logistical and practical reasons, she decided not to group for the other subjects. Instead she utilized whole group lessons that gave her a breather from the complexities of running four groups at a time. Most of the lessons went well, but she noticed that the same students who did well in math and reading also excelled in subjects like science and social studies. Her A students seemed to have answers for all of her questions, but the students in her lower groups seemed bored and unengaged. When she graded her quizzes and homework, she noticed that many of her students handed in partial work or didn't hand in any at all. She sent a letter home to all students explaining her grading system and asking parents to help their children but received replies from only half of the parents. When she asked students why their parents didn't respond, she only received shrugs. This was discouraging.

She thought that perhaps motivation was a problem, so she decided to design a thematic unit with learning activities around Christmas, a holiday that she believed all students were excited about. She wrote some math story problems around Christmas shopping, made a crossword puzzle using Christmas terms, and designed a social studies unit around Christmas around the world. This seemed to make some difference, but still there were students who she felt were on the fringe of the class.

Sharon talked to her principal and some other teachers, and they suggested that perhaps she needed some outside help with her slower students. After consulting with the special education specialist in her school, they decided to have five of her students tested. As Sharon had suspected, each of the five had some type of learning problem. Interestingly, four of the five came from homes where English wasn't spoken at home.

With the help of the specialist, she designed learning activities for these five that could be reinforced in the resource room, where the five went for special help for one half hour every day. At the suggestion of the specialist, she designed lessons that began with concrete examples and were more interactive for her entire lower group. Sharon asked many more questions and made sure that students had plenty of time to answer. When students didn't seem to understand her question, she'd rephrase it or have one of the other students ask it in Spanish. She also did more groupwork, with the students helping each other.

Sharon's class was working better, but still she wondered if there was more she could do.

Questions for Analysis

1. Analyze Sharon's use of grouping. Which grouping practices were supported by research? Which weren't? What could she have done to make her grouping more effective?

2. How well did Sharon use interactive questioning strategies to involve her students? What alternatives might she have tried?

3. How effective was Sharon's communication with her students' parents? What might she have done to improve her communication?

4. Comment on the choice of Christmas as the focal point for her thematic unit.

5. Provide an alternate explanation for the composition of her five resource students. How well did Sharon do in adapting her instruction for these students?

6. What other suggestions do you have to improve student learning in Sharon's class?

Discussion Questions

1. What cultural groups live in the areas where you will be teaching? What do you know about these cultures? How do their cultural beliefs and attitudes influence learning?

2. What important differences exist between the cultural difference theory and the other two theories? Why are these differences important for teachers and students?

3. How were the interaction patterns of the Warm Springs Native Americans similar to those of rural African Americans in the Carolinas? Different? What implications do these similarities and differences have for instruction?

4. How are the different instructional approaches to teaching English similar? Different? What are the advantages and disadvantages of each?

5. How are students placed at risk similar to culturally different students? Different? What implications does this have for instruction?

6. Students placed at risk used to be called underachievers or potential dropouts. Why is *at risk* a more appropriate term, and how does the use of this term signal changes in society?

7. What is the SES of the students you will likely be teaching? What indicators did you use to reach this conclusion? How will this influence your teaching?

8. Which of Gardner's multiple intelligences is most emphasized in school's today? Least? Which do you think should be emphasized more? Why?

9. What are the pros and cons of teachers attempting to change students' learning styles? Which learning style difference is most important to you? Why?

10. How do learning styles relate to Gardner's multiple intelligences? Do you think these differences are genetically or environmentally influenced? Explain.

11. Think about the dimensions of intelligence identified by experts: (a) abstract thinking and reasoning, (b) problem-solving ability, and (c) capacity to acquire knowledge. Which do you think is more important in today's world? Least? Why?

12. Of the four strategies listed to accommodate diversity—creating multidimensional classrooms, flexible time, grouping, and strategy instruction—which have the most positive long-term potential for students? Least? Why?

13. How are the three categories of mild-moderate disabilities—intellectual disability, learning disability, and behavioral disorder—similar? Different?

Portfolio Activities

1. *Teaching Multicultural Students.* Observe a class using interactive teaching. In observing this classroom, analyze the class for any differential participation rates by minority students. To do this, identify a comparable number of minority and nonminority students to observe (three or four of each is optimal). Observe them during the lesson noting the following:

   a. How do their attending rates compare—that is, are they participating in the lesson and listening to the interaction?

b. How often do students from each group raise their hands to answer a teacher question?

c. How often do students from each group get called on?

What implications do your results have for your teaching?

2. *Teaching Students Placed At Risk.* Identify a class with considerable numbers of students placed at risk. Observe a lesson in that class and analyze it in terms of the following strategies:

a. active teaching
b. use of manipulatives and examples
c. active student involvement
d. interactive teaching
e. practice and feedback
f. high success rates

What else does the teacher do to teach these students effectively? What implications do your findings have for you as a teacher?

3. *Differences in Learning Ability: Student Perspectives.* Observe a class working on an in-class assignment. As you do this, circulate around the room so you can observe the work progress of different students. As you do so, note the following:

a. Beginning times—Do all students get immediately to work, or do some take more time starting?

b. On-task behaviors—What percentage of the class stays on task throughout the assignment?

c. Completion times—When do the first students complete the assignment? When do the last students finish?

d. Teacher monitoring—What does the teacher do during the seatwork? How do students signal that they need help?

e. Options—What options are there for students who complete their assignments early?

What strategies can teachers use to accommodate students with different learning abilities?

4. *Differences in Learning Ability: Teacher Perspectives.* Interview a teacher to investigate the teacher's use of the following strategies to deal with differences in learning ability: (a) flexible time requirements, (b) grouping, (c) strategy instruction, (d) peer tutoring and cooperative learning. Ask these questions:

a. Are differences in learning ability a problem for the teacher? Why or how?

b. Does the teacher use any of the strategies mentioned in this book? Which ones work and why? Have any been tried that didn't work?

c. Does the teacher employ any other strategies for dealing with differences in learning ability?

How do you plan to deal with differences in learning ability in your classroom?

5. *Students with Exceptionalities.* Interview a teacher about students with exceptionalities in the classroom. Ask the following questions:

a. Which students are classified as exceptional? What behaviors led to this classification? What role did the teacher play in identification?

b. In working with students with exceptionalities, what assistance does the classroom teacher receive from the following people?
  (1) special education teacher
  (2) school psychologist or school counselor
  (3) principal
c. What does an IEP look like? How helpful is it in working with exceptional students in the classroom?
e. What strategies does the teacher use to help these students in the classroom?

What implications do the teacher's responses have for you as a teacher?

3

Teacher Planning: Research and Reality

The intercom breaks into the middle of a teacher's class and blares, "Teachers, don't forget to turn in your plans for next week before you leave this afternoon."

A teacher, responding to another's question about her summer, replies, "I'm going to be writing curriculum for the district the first two weeks, and then I'm going to rest, rest, rest!"

Two friends discuss their plans for the weekend.

In the broadest sense, each of these examples involves some element of planning. Planning is a human endeavor that spans a broad spectrum of activities; its basic function is to simplify the environment and allow for strategic, goal-oriented activity. The importance of planning in teaching cannot be overemphasized.

Why do teachers plan? How do they actually plan for their instruction? How does it help them in their professional decision making? How important is planning for effective teaching?

We try to answer these questions in this chapter. We discuss traditional approaches to planning, including topics such as preparing year-long, unit, and lesson plans and the historically revered linear rational planning model. We also discuss planning for integrated units, and the chapter concludes with research examining teacher planning, its effects on effective instruction, and planning for diversity. When you have completed your study of this chapter, you should be able to meet the following goals:

- Identify major variables that influence instructional planning.
- Describe similarities and differences between taxonomies in the three domains.
- Explain how long term, unit, and lesson planning relate to each other and fulfill different planning needs.
- Identify advantages and disadvantages of integrated and thematic units.
- Describe research that has examined teacher planning and its effects on instruction.
- Describe different planning strategies for individualization.

To introduce the topic of teacher planning, consider the following teachers involved in classroom planning.

Peggy Stone, a student intern in a large middle school, was scheduled to be observed by her university supervisor. While understandably a bit apprehensive at the prospect of being evaluated, she eagerly anticipated the experience because she had carefully planned her lesson the night before.

As the students filed in the room, she handed her supervisor the following copy of her lesson plan.

Unit Title: Mathematical Operations

Goal: To have students understand the order of mathematical operations and how they are used.

Objective: Students will understand the order of arithmetic operations, so when given a series of problems involving the four operations, they will solve each correctly.

Rationale: Students need to understand the order of operations so they can accurately simplify and solve algebraic expressions.

Content: Arithmetic operations are completed in the following sequence:

1. Multiply and divide (left to right).
2. Add and subtract (left to right).

Procedures:

1. Show the students the following problem:

$14/7 \times 2 + 5 - 6$

Ask what the right answer is. Encourage multiple answers.

2. Explain to the students that we're beginning the topic "Order of Operations."
3. Ask the students to explain what operation means. Clarify if necessary.
4. Present the rules for order of operations. Write on board.
5. Demonstrate a solution to the problem, referring students to rules for order of operations as the demonstration proceeds.
6. Show students the following problem:

$6 + 9 \times 4/3 - 7$

7. Solve the problem with the help of students, calling on individuals to verbally describe each step.
8. Present several other problems and solve them as a group.
9. Present students with the attached worksheet and guide them through the first two problems.
10. Have students work the remaining problems on the sheet as I monitor the class.
11. Give homework assignment, all odd-numbered problems on page 194 of their text.

Assessment: Present students with problems involving order of operations. Have them solve the problems.

Materials and Aids: Sample problems, worksheet, text.

Now, let's look at a second teacher.

Jim Hartley, a veteran of 10 years experience teaching secondary American history, walked into his room early, as he always did, and pulled out his plan book. He looked to see what he had written in anticipation of the day's work, nodded to himself, and headed off to the media center. His plan appeared as follows:

British Exploration

Religious freedom, secular, nongovernment sponsored

Spanish Exploration

3 Gs—gold, God, glory

More integration with natives, slave labor

(Film on Spanish and Mexican fiesta)

Were these two teachers' lessons well planned? Was Peggy Stone's class better planned than Jim Hartley's? Do their plans alone or together represent the scope of teacher planning? What does teacher *planning* mean? We attempt to answer these questions in the paragraphs that follow.

We answer the last question first. Definitions of instructional planning range from the simple products that appear on paper or in a planning book, such as those of Peggy and Jim, to complex psychological processes in which a teacher "visualizes the future, inventories means and ends, and constructs a framework to guide his or her future action" (Clark and Peterson, 1986, p. 260). The future might be as long away as a year or as near as the next day. In both cases, teachers consider how content, goals, materials, and activities will influence student learning. With year-long planning, this thinking is more general and abstract, while daily lesson planning involves more specific and concrete thinking.

Beginning education students often think of planning simply as writing an objective and preparing a lesson plan. It is much more than that, however, and it is also much more than the information that appeared in either Peggy's or Jim's respective plans. For example, Jim planned to use a film to encourage a comparison of Spanish and Mexican fiestas and ultimately lead to questions about cultural similarities and differences. He wanted his students to think about why there were differences, in spite of the fact that the two groups had many similar origins. He then planned to compare the Spanish with English settlers in terms of their interactions with the Native Americans. Jim had much more in mind in terms of content, sequence, and method than appeared on paper. Typical of veteran teachers, his actual plans were much more complex than what appeared on paper (Morine-Dershimer, 1979). In contrast, Peggy was much more detailed in her written plans. This is typical of beginning teachers; because of inexperience and anxiety they structure their lessons in greater detail and write more things down (Neale, Pace, and Case, 1983).

Planning *includes all the instructional decisions teachers make prior to actually teaching.* Content, activities, learner motivation, grouping of students, projects, grading practices, and classroom management are all considered in this process. We discuss planning for classroom management in greater detail in Chapter 6, and we examine the role of planning for assessment in Chapter 12.

PLANNING: A FUNCTIONAL ANALYSIS

Why do teachers plan? The answers to this question are the focus of this section. No two teachers teach in the same way; similarly, no two teachers plan in exactly the same way. Teaching is a highly personal and idiosyncratic process, and planning allows teachers to personalize the curriculum—in a sense, to make it their own. In this regard planning serves three important functions:

- It allows teachers to anticipate instructional needs in advance so materials can be gathered and organized.

- It provides a "script" that directs interactions with students.
- It provides a form of emotional or psychological security, which bolsters teachers' confidence and helps reduce the normal anxiety associated with teaching.
  (Clark and Yinger, 1979; McCutcheon, 1982)

Let's look at these functions in practice.

Janet Evans is a new faculty member in a math department at a magnet school designed to attract diverse high-ability students throughout the city. Because her transcript revealed a few computer courses, she was assigned to teach a second-year programming course for which she has little background. She is experiencing considerable anxiety, both because she is new and because she lacks confidence in her understanding of the content. She spends hours every day studying but is quite dissatisfied with her plans as she enters the classroom each day.

One day she enters the teachers' lounge with an extra bounce in her step; her conversation is more animated, and she is more enthusiastic.

"You're in a good mood today," remarks another rookie who has become her confidant.

"I've found the secret," she replies. "It's transparencies. When I have to present new material, I just write my outline down on the transparency with questions or problems for students. I use them to remind me where I am, and then I can keep the flow of my presentation going."

She added with a grin, "It takes seven transparencies to make it through a whole class."

Consider another example.

Trina Arnold is an elementary teacher planning a lesson on invertebrates.
"The kids don't like science," she thinks to herself. "I even heard two of them saying how boring it is. What am I going to do?"

As she tried to think of ways to make her unit more motivating, she seized on the idea of bringing in some real animals to class. On her way home from school that evening, she stopped in at a fish market and bought a crab, a clam, and a small fish. The next day she took all three, plus her daughter's hamster, into class. During the lesson, students examined and compared the four animals, analyzing their similarities and differences and, using the chart shown in Figure 3.1, compared vertebrates and invertebrates. As they worked, she noticed a level of energy and excitement that she hadn't seen in them before.

	Examples	Similarities	Differences
Vertebrates			
Invertebrates			

Figure 3.1 Matrix Comparing Vertebrates and Invertebrates

"That's the best science lesson I ever did," she concluded to herself afterward. After that experience, Trina tried to bring something interesting to class and involve students actively in each science lesson.

Consider how each of the planning functions manifested themselves in these two scenarios. We said that planning organizes instruction and helps teachers feel more confident and secure. Janet Evans's experience illustrates these functions. By structuring content on her transparencies, she was able to organize and personalize it, emphasizing some topics and deleting others. In addition, the transparencies provided a script for her interactions with students; she no longer had to keep all the information in her head. Finally, the transparencies bolstered her confidence and helped ease her anxiety because she felt well prepared.

We have all been in situations where we feel nervous or uncertain in anticipating a teaching challenge. The content may be unfamiliar, we are unsure of our audience, or we have had a bad experience in the past. The tendency in these cases is to plan in more detail and to write more information on paper. This also helps explain why Peggy Stone had more extensive written plans than did Jim Hartley; she was an intern, in contrast to his 10 years of experience.

Our second example is quite different from the first. While Janet used her planning time to identify and organize topics that helped her feel more secure, Trina Arnold used her planning time to consider the motivation and involvement of her students.

Does planning actually affect the way teachers teach? Research results suggests that it does. Researchers have found a positive correlation between the number of planning statements teachers made about content and their tendency to remain focused on the topic they were teaching (Peterson, Marx, and Clark, 1978). They further found that written statements about teaching procedures were related to the way teachers interacted with their students. Planning is functional, influencing the ways teachers carry out their plans once they are made.

What factors influence the shape teacher plans take? This question is the focus of the next section.

VARIABLES IN INSTRUCTIONAL PLANNING

A number of variables—teachers and their personalities, the learners we teach, content, the instructional context, resources, and available time—affect the planning process. These are illustrated in Figure 3.2 and in the sections that follow.

The Teacher

The most significant variable in the planning process is the teacher. Teachers' beliefs about the role of schools and what children should learn, their own capacity to help students, and their general philosophical approach to teaching and learning all affect the decisions they make (White and Williams, 1996). A teacher's philosophical position, while seemingly remote and abstract, is important for learning. Teachers who feel a sense of mission and believe all students can and will learn are more active in their role, have higher expectations, and work harder to help students achieve (Ross, 1995). Teachers with philosophical commitments to excellence take more personal responsibility for student failures

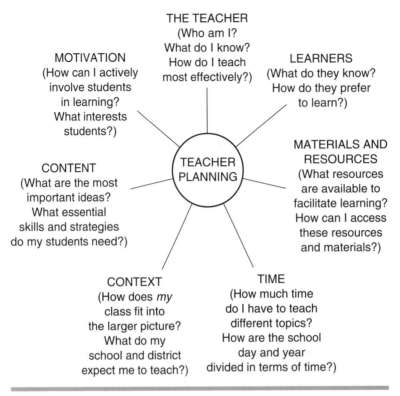

Figure 3.2 Factors Influencing Teacher Planning

and increase their efforts to help underachieving students. Less committed teachers are more likely to attribute lack of achievement to student shortcomings (Pintrich and Schunk, 1996).

Teachers' understanding of the content they teach also affects the planning process. Research indicates that teachers unfamiliar with lesson content ask lower-level questions, stick closer to the text, and discourage students from asking questions (Carlsen, 1987; Dykstra, 1996; Shulman, 1987). The implications of this research are clear: Developing your understanding of the content you teach is an essential part of planning. When you are teaching unfamiliar content, you need to spend extra time studying to ensure that the lessons you develop will be effective.

Learners

Karen Passey, a kindergarten teacher, sat down to plan her next week's lessons. "Hmm, let's see, figures and shapes. I better plan on something active for my afternoon group, or they'll go bonkers after 5 minutes of sitting quietly."

Pam Shepard looked at her planning book to refresh her memory about the topics for her next semester. "Hmm. Shakespeare. My honors classes should be able to handle it without any problems, but I'll have to really plan carefully with my third period class."

As we saw in Chapter 2, learners exert a powerful influence on our instructional decisions, and many of these decisions occur during the planning process. The age of our students, their background knowledge, motivation, and interests all affect decisions we make as we plan for instruction.

Learners' ages are among the most powerful variables affecting planning. Age is closely related to attention span, which determines—at least in part—how long an activity within an individual lesson can be (Berk, 1997). One teaching adage recommends, "Don't plan any single learning activity longer than the age of your students." Karen Passey, in planning for her kindergartners, made sure that any quiet listening time wouldn't exceed 5 minutes. A middle school teacher might be able to stretch this to 12 or 15 minutes, but beyond that would probably be pushing it.

Students' background knowledge is another powerful factor influencing planning. All new learning builds upon current understanding (Eggen and Kauchak, 2001). For example, a lesson on writing paragraphs depends on skills such as writing grammatically correct sentences, organizing ideas, and presenting information succinctly and accurately. In a later section, we'll describe how task analysis can be used to determine prerequisite knowledge.

Motivation: An Integral Part of Planning

Learner motivation is another important variable influencing planning. Motivation is the second greatest concern of beginning teachers, exceeded only by management (Veenman, 1984). For experienced teachers, motivation is often their greatest concern; they continue to wrestle with it long after management concerns are resolved (Zahorik, 1996).

Student motivation occurs at two levels—global and lesson specific. At a global level, student motivation represents the cumulative effects of past learning experiences. If they have been successful, students come to us confident, alert, and eager for new learning. Unfortunately, the opposite is also true.

The second type of motivation—lesson specific—is more malleable and more subject to the immediate influence of the teacher. Lesson-specific motivation can be increased in many ways. We look at three ways teachers can increase motivation through their planning here.

First, teachers can plan to capitalize on students' interests (Zahorik, 1996). Teachers describe the importance of student interest in this way:

> Student interest is a major interest to me in planning sessions. I don't think kids have to love everything I'm teaching, but if they are "sleeping" before I even get into the lesson, they don't get a chance to see where the lesson was going. (Elementary teacher)

> Student interest is the major concern after the mandated curriculum. I try to take each thing I have to do and find some way to relate it to the students, or find an aspect of it which will really grab their attention. (Secondary history teacher) (Zahorik, 1996, p. 559)

Effective teachers use student interest as a springboard to pull them into lessons. For example, elementary teachers use children's fascination with Halloween to teach writing, poetry, art, and music. In a similar way, effective middle school and high school science teachers capitalize on teenagers' fascination with their changing bodies to teach biology and health concepts. Strategic planning integrates motivation into every lesson.

A second way to plan for student motivation is to design activities that arouse students' curiosity, draw them into lessons, and keep them there (Eggen and Kauchak, 2001). One researcher called these motivational strategies "catch factors" because they capture students' attention and increase their interest in the topic (Mitchell, 1993). Asking open-ended or rhetorical questions is one strategy for capitalizing on curiosity and increasing motivation. For example, a lesson on dinosaurs might begin with, "Consider the dinosaur—the largest and most fearsome of all land animals, some as big as a house. Suddenly they became extinct. Why?" In a similar way, a lesson might begin with a discrepant event—an event that is puzzling to students. For example, a home economics lesson on baking might begin with two loaves of bread, one perfect and the other flat. The teacher would begin the lesson by saying, "These two loaves started out the same way and had the same ingredients. One turned out like this; the other this way. Why do you suppose? . . . We'll find out in this lesson."

A third strategy for increasing motivation is to design lessons that actively involve students (Zahorik, 1996). Using manipulatives, games, simulations, role playing and drama projects, problems, and puzzles are all techniques used to increase involvement. In planning motivating lessons, effective teachers consciously avoid activities that place students in passive roles.

Content

The type of content we're teaching also influences the planning process. For example, if we're planning to teach a concept, we'll need to gather positive and negative examples to illustrate it. If we're teaching a skill, such as solving math word problems involving addition, we'll need to find or construct a number of these problems so students can practice on them. If we're teaching integrated bodies of knowledge with interconnected ideas, we need to organize them in a way that is meaningful to students. We'll return to this idea in Chapters 7 through 11, when we discuss different teaching strategies.

Teaching Context

Another powerful factor influencing planning is the context in which teaching and learning occur. **Teaching context** *includes state and district guidelines, school policy, and leadership.* For instance, McCutcheon (1982) described two school districts in Virginia; both had adopted the same basic text, but the first encouraged teachers to adapt freely, and the second required teachers to cover all the content in the book before turning to supplementary materials. Teacher autonomy and initiative had different meanings in the two districts.

The school principal also affects the planning process. In her study of elementary teachers' planning, McCutcheon (1982) found that even though all the principals she studied required written plans, their definition of plans varied greatly in detail, format, and length of time. Some inspected plans every week, others monthly, and still others at random intervals.

One principal sent out the following memo:

Each teacher is expected to keep *daily* lesson plans of classroom activities. Good teacher planning is essential for effective teaching. In case of teacher absence, lesson plans are to be available in the top desk drawer for the substitute teacher. This is a must. Detailed lesson plans should be kept a week in advance.

Lesson plans should be kept in a looseleaf notebook. These notebooks will be checked from time to time by the principal. (McCutcheon, 1982, p. 263)

Clearly, the plans written at this principal's school will be quite different from those in a school where planning is considered to be an individual, professional activity.

Standards-Based Education. Planning is also influenced by national, state, and district guidelines where teachers are held accountable for their students' achievement on standardized tests (Darling-Hammond and Snyder, 1992). When teachers feel pressured to cover certain content and topics because the information will appear on a standardized test, their planning and teaching are affected. **Standards-based education,** *which is the process of focusing curriculum and instruction on predetermined standards,* is presently exerting a powerful influence on teacher planning both through the goals or standards they suggest as well as the tests that follow from them. The following are examples of national standards for middle school math students created by the National Council of Teachers of Mathematics.

Number and Operations Standard for Grades 6–8: Instructional programs from prekindergarten through grade 12 should enable all students to compute fluently and make reasonable estimates.

In grades 6–8 all students should:

- Select appropriate methods and tools for computing with fractions and decimals from among mental computation, estimation, calculators or computers, and paper and pencil, depending on the situation, and apply the selected methods;
- Develop and analyze algorithms for computing with fractions, decimals, and integers and develop fluency in their use;
- Develop and use strategies to estimate the results of rational-number computations and judge the reasonableness of the results;
- Develop, analyze, and explain methods for solving problems involving proportions, such as scaling and finding equivalent ratios. (National Council of Teachers of Mathematics, 2000, p. 214)

States also publish standards to guide learning in different content areas:

Science: In Science, students in Missouri public schools will acquire a solid foundation which includes knowledge of . . . properties and principles of force and motion." (Missouri Department of Elementary and Secondary Education, 1995)
Reading: (Grades 6–8) "Demonstrate inferential comprehension of a variety of printed materials." Grade 8 benchmark: "Identify relationships, images, patterns or symbols and draw conclusions about their meaning." (Oregon Department of Education, 1996)

Social Studies: (Grade 5) "The student will describe colonial America, with emphasis on . . . the principal economic and political connections between the colonies and England."
(Virginia Board of Education, 1995)

As you can see, these standards are often general and vague. Not until they are translated into specific learning activities or test items do teachers or students have a clear idea of what should be learned or how it will be measured. This is another reason why teacher planning is so important.

The standards movement is widespread; virtually all states have specified standards for at least some of the content areas, and students as well as teachers are being held accountable for meeting these standards.

Testing. As you begin reading this section, you might wonder, "What does testing have to do with teacher planning?" The answer is, a great deal. A powerful way that states and districts attempt to influence what is taught is through the tests they give. One elementary teacher, reassigned to a different grade level, found out about her new curriculum in this way:

When I came up to fifth grade, I really didn't know everything that would be covered in the fifth grade, so one of the teachers said, "Well, this skill will be on the achievement test, and you'll find this on the achievement test, and you'll find this on the test." And I know to teach my children survival skills that I had to teach those. Let's just face it, that's just the way it is. You know, I tell them, "This may be on the achievement test and this is something that I really want to stick." (Brown, 1991, pp. 102–103)

Tests provide concrete guidelines about what should be taught, and principals and other teachers often pressure teachers to "cover" all of the knowledge and skills that will be tested sometime during the year.

As enthusiasm for accountability has increased around the country, all but two states have adopted statewide testing systems (Olson, 1999). It is virtually certain that the curriculum in your school will be influenced by a standardized test developed or adopted at the state or local level. As a beginning teacher, you need to be aware of the different kinds of tests your students will be required to take. Armed with this information, you can make wise professional planning decisions about what curriculum is best for your students.

Outcomes-Based Education. An additional way that states and districts attempt to influence curriculum is by specifying and testing for specific objectives. **Outcomes-based education (OBE)** *attempts to describe curriculum in terms of objectives or results.* OBE attempts to go beyond the listing of topics to be learned by specifying specific outcomes for a course of study. OBE tries to put teeth in these outcomes by testing whether students have attained these goals.

Proponents claim that OBE makes sense; if we want students to attain certain knowledge or skills, we should specify exactly what these are, teach them, and test for them (Manno, 1995). Critics contend that many of the most important skills (like critical thinking or communicating with others) can't be specified in behavioral terms and trying to do so promotes minimal academic standards and "dumbing down" of the curriculum. As you can imagine, working in an outcomes-based environment will radically affect the way you plan and teach.

Materials and Resources

Materials and other resources also have a major impact on teacher planning. Textbooks are first among them. Beginning teachers depend heavily on text materials to help them decide the topics to be taught, sequencing, depth, and even the test items they give their students (Blumenfeld, Hicks, and Krajcik, 1996). As teachers acquire experience, they become more independent, adding and deleting topics and generally personalizing their curriculum. However, even veterans rely heavily on available materials and often voice frustration when topics covered by district or state objectives do not appear in their textbooks (Clark and Elmore, 1981).

While textbooks will strongly influence your planning decisions, you shouldn't depend on them completely. The following are some reasons why.

- *Needs.* The topics presented in textbooks may not be consistent with the specific needs of your students, school, or district. Following a textbook too closely then fails to meet these needs as effectively as possible.
- *Scope.* To appeal to a wide market, textbook publishers include a huge number of topics, more than you can possibly teach in the time available. So you will need to be selective in the topics you teach. Curriculum experts advise, "Schools [and teachers] should pick out the most important concepts and skills to emphasize so that they can concentrate on the quality of understanding rather than on the quantity of information presented" (Rutherford and Algren, 1990, p. 185).
- *Quality.* Textbooks are sometimes poorly written, lack adequate examples, or even contain errors of fact. One study of history textbooks, for example, found that "Content is thinner and thinner, and what there is, increasingly deformed by identity politics and group pieties" (Sewall, 2000). One analysis of middle school science texts concluded, "It's a credit to science teachers that their students are learning anything at all" (Bradley, 1999, p. 5). Similar problems have been found in other areas (Manzo, 2000). Following a textbook too closely can lead to shallow understanding or even faulty ideas that detract from learning.

What does this information suggest for you as a teacher? Nowhere in teaching is professionalism more important than in teacher planning. This is particularly true regarding textbooks. It's easy to allow textbooks to make professional decisions for you, such as teaching the next chapter because it's there, and this is what many teachers unfortunately do.

Textbooks can be a valuable resource, and they will certainly influence your decisions. However, don't be afraid to deemphasize, or even eliminate, topics and chapters in the text and include other topics that aren't in it. Curriculum decision making such as this requires professional understanding, effort, and energy. Teachers report that the process of curriculum planning can be one of the most creative and satisfying aspects of teaching (Clandinin and Connelly, 1996).

The availability of other materials also influence planning. If the film had not existed, for example, Jim Hartley's approach to his lesson comparing Mexican and Spanish customs would necessarily have been quite different. Reaching his goal would have been difficult; the goal might even have been revised. In fact, some research indicates that teachers first consider activities when they plan (Clark and Peterson, 1986), and their activities are usually based on available materials.

Time

Finally, time is an important variable that affects planning (White and Williams, 1996). First, planning can consume a great deal of teacher time—up to 20 hours a week, in some cases (McDaniel-Hine and Willower, 1988)—and beginning teachers, who are learning to survive, usually spend the most time in planning. Time also interacts with other variables; for example, teachers of young children spend much of their planning time gathering and arranging the physical materials that students will use in learning activities (Hill, Yinger, and Robbins, 1981).

Time also serves as a frame of reference, helping teachers structure their planning. The school year is divided into grading periods, the grading periods into weeks, and courses and units are framed in terms of these time periods. Breaking time down into manageable chunks makes the task of planning manageable. We discuss this process in the next section of the chapter.

THE LINEAR RATIONAL MODEL: A SEQUENTIAL PLANNING MODEL

Planning has been heavily influenced by Ralph Tyler and his book, *Basic Principles of Curriculum and Instruction,* first published in 1949. Tyler described the process of planning as a logical and sequential process of starting with goals, processing to teacher actions and learning tasks, and ending with student outcomes. These steps are illustrated in Figure 3.3. Tyler's major contribution to the process of planning was to frame it as a series of logical actions requiring thought and reflection.

In this section of the chapter we will use this logical, sequential framework to consider a comprehensive model of planning that takes us from long term planning, encompassing months and even an entire school year, to specific lesson plans for a particular day. This process begins with goals.

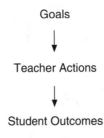

Goals

↓

Teacher Actions

↓

Student Outcomes

Figure 3.3 The Linear-Rational Model of Planning

Goals: A Beginning Point for Teacher Planning

Goals provide a useful starting point in the planning process; they identify what we hope to accomplish in our classrooms in broad, general terms. Some examples of goals that teachers use to guide their instructional planning include:

- Third-grade students should understand plants and how they contribute to our lives.
- Second-grade students will know their math facts.
- Students should develop an appreciation for the rights of others.
- Seventh-grade health should develop in students an understanding of their bodies and how they work.
- Students will understand how to read critically and analytically.

Though different in their focus, each goal gives us a sense of direction for our instruction. In the next section we discuss different kinds of goals, and the implications the differences have for teaching.

Kinds of Goals: The Three Domains

Three physical education teachers were comparing their goals for a unit on exercise. Carol commented, "I'm trying to develop muscle tone, strength, and flexibility so that no matter how they use their bodies in other activities, they'll have a good foundation." "I'm interested in that, too," added Sharon, a second-year teacher, "but I'm more concerned that they know about the different kinds of exercise. They need to know the difference between aerobic and anaerobic exercise and how each affects their bodies." "Both of those are important," Tanya acknowledged, "but I'm concerned about what happens after they leave school. We've got too many couch potatoes out there already. I'm trying to get them turned on to exercise for the rest of their lives."

Which of these goals is most important? What kinds of learning should schools focus on? How will your particular class contribute to the overall growth of your students? Questions like these are not easy to answer. Part of the reason for this difficulty is that schools attempt to accomplish a broad spectrum of goals, and individual teachers must select from this broad array in selecting goals for their classrooms and their students.

Two conceptual tools help teachers think about their goals during the planning process. The first divides goals into areas or domains—cognitive, affective, and psychomotor—that correspond to the kinds of learning that are intended. Each of the physical education teachers had one of these domains in mind when she talked about her goals for the exercise unit. Within each domain, goals can be classified further into levels that correspond to the specific kinds of performance outcome common to different areas of learning in the schools today. Let's look at these domains and levels.

The Cognitive Domain. The **cognitive domain** *deals with the acquisition of knowledge and skills.* Sharon's unit focused on the cognitive domain because it targeted students' knowledge about different kinds of exercise. Presently, other cognitive skills, such as study strategies, problem solving, and higher-order and critical thinking, are receiving increased attention because of their importance in a technological society. One way to

Table 3.1 THE COGNITIVE TAXONOMY

Level	Description
Knowledge	At the knowledge level, the student can recognize, define, or recall specific information. This might include remembering important names, dates, capitals, or even the equation for a formula.
Comprehension	This level targets whether students understand content. Ways of demonstrating comprehension include summarizing, translating, or providing examples of a concept.
Application	The application level focuses on whether students can use information to solve problems. Examples of application-level goals include having students solve math word problems and using punctuation properly in written communication.
Analysis	This level involves asking students to break something down to reveal its organization and structure. Students perform analysis when they discuss why a short story "works" or when they identify the component parts of a science experiment.
Synthesis	Students employ synthesis when they create a unique (for them) product. This might include writing a poem, painting a picture, or creating a computer program.
Evaluation	In the highest level of the taxonomy, students judge the value or worth of something by comparing it to predetermined criteria. We ask students to evaluate when they critique a plan to solve a pollution problem or when we ask students to assess a writing sample.

differentiate these cognitive goals is to use a classification system, called the *cognitive taxonomy* (Bloom et al., 1956), which divides goals into six levels. These levels are outlined in Table 3.1.

The cognitive taxonomy reminds teachers that knowledge is only one of several important goals, it supplies them with alternate goals, and it provides them with a tool to analyze the plans they make. We'll discuss the cognitive taxonomy again when we discuss questioning strategies in Chapter 5.

The Affective Domain. As Tanya suggested, schools exist for more than just making students smarter. We also want them to develop into happy individuals with healthy views about themselves and others (Nucci, 1989). The **affective domain** (Krathwohl, Bloom, and Masia, 1964) *focuses on the development of attitude and values* and divides this process into five levels that correspond to the degree to which attitudes and values are internalized by the individual. A taxonomy for affective goals it outlined in Table 3.2.

As with the cognitive taxonomy, the affective taxonomy provides teachers with a conceptual tool to analyze their planning. If respect for the rights of others is one of our goals, do we just want students to nod when we talk about the importance of respect, or do we want students to respect each other, helping to create a classroom where

Table 3.2 **THE AFFECTIVE TAXONOMY**

Level	Description
Receiving	At this level, the student is willing to listen passively to or attend to some message. Students who listen to a speaker talking about drugs without tuning him out are acting at this level.
Responding	Beyond just receiving a message, students must also react to it. Students react by obeying, discussing, or responding to the attitude or value.
Valuing	When students respond at this level, they show their preference for an idea by voluntarily displaying it. For example, a health class has been talking about nutrition. A student turns to his friend in the cafeteria and says, "Those french fries aren't good for you. They've got too much fat."
Organization	Organization occurs when students take an attitude or value and incorporate it into a larger value system. In the health example, this would occur when the student looks at his own diet and examines implications for himself.
Characterization	At the highest level of the affective domain, students not only reorganize their own thinking but also act consistently with their beliefs. A student who actually changes the way he or she eats over a long period of time would be operating at this level.

everyone feels secure in responding, knowing they won't be interrupted or laughed at? In a larger sense, the affective taxonomy provides some interesting answers to the question, "What are schools for?"

The Psychomotor Domain. A third area that serves as a source of goals for our teaching is the **psychomotor domain,** *which involves the development of coordination and physical skills.* Carol's goal to develop her students' muscle tone, strength, and flexibility would fall into this domain. Though we typically associate the psychomotor domain with physical education, other areas like typing, music, art, and home economics are also involved. In addition, preschool, kindergarten, and the lower elementary grades focus on psychomotor goals through activities like cutting and pasting, coloring, printing, and writing. Like the other areas, the psychomotor taxonomy (Harrow, 1972) shown in Table 3.3 proceeds from simple to complex and from externally to internally controlled.

In the linear rational model goals in the three domains form a logical starting point for the planning process. We discuss this sequential process in the next section.

Long-Term Planning

In previous sections, we discussed the nature of planning, the functions it serves, and how goals in different domains influence instruction. We now want to extend this information to describe a comprehensive model of planning that is practical and complete. This

Table 3.3 **THE PSYCHOMOTOR TAXONOMY**

Level	Description
Reflex movements	Behaviors outside the conscious control of the learner
Basic fundamental movements	Behaviors learned at an early age (e.g., grasping, walking) that form the foundation for later growth
Perceptual abilities	Coordination of muscular movements with the outside world through feedback with the sense organs
Physical abilities	The development of strength, endurance, flexibility, and agility
Skilled movements	Complex physical skills (e.g., skipping rope, shooting a basket) that utilize the first four levels
Nondiscursive communication	The use of our bodies to express feelings or ideas

planning model occurs in three stages—long term, unit, and lesson planning. When doing *long-term planning,* teachers survey available resources, including texts and state and district curriculum guides, and outline a year's or semester's instruction. During *unit planning,* teachers translate these broad outlines into interrelated lessons focused on a central topic or a theme. Finally, during *lesson planning,* specific activities for a given day are considered. Let's see how this works. These different time frames are illustrated in Figure 3.4.

Long-term planning *involves preparing for a year or semester and serves primarily as a framework for later planning efforts.* Long-term planning serves the following purposes:

- It adapts the curriculum to fit the teacher's knowledge and priorities.
- It helps the teacher focus on the structure and content of the new curriculum.
- It develops a practical schedule for instruction. (Clark and Elmore, 1981)

Note how these functions are similar to the general functions of planning discussed earlier.

In addition to framing content issues, long-term planning also serves to establish routines for how the school year will run. The structure provided by routines plays

Long Term Planning (year-long or spanning a semester or term)
---→

Unit Planning (can span 2 weeks to several months)
-------------------------------→

Lesson Planning (addresses daily planning needs)

x x x x x x x x x x
-------------→

September   December   March   June

Figure 3.4 Time Frames in Instructional Planning

"such a major role in the teacher's planning behavior that planning could be character-ized as decision making about the selection, organization, and sequencing of routines" (Yinger, 1977, p. 165). One elementary classroom routine that was effective in produc-ing high math achievement looked like this:

> Monday starts with a longer than usual review to compensate for the long weekend. Each subsequent day begins with homework checking and then proceeds to presentation of new material, and then group and individual practice. Friday's session wraps up the week with further review and a quiz. Students know what to expect each day as math begins, and there is a natural rhythm to the tempo of the classroom during the week. (Good, Grouws, and Ebmeier, 1983, p. 44)

Establishing routines during long-term planning provides a superstructure that helps guide both teacher and student actions for the entire school year.

Much of the initial effort during long-term planning involves covert mental activ-ity, which is often continual, occurring at strange times and places, such as late evening or while driving to school or watching a football game on television (McCutcheon, 1982). As one teacher described it, "The subconscious does a lot of sorting for you. You can think of many things simultaneously. The sorting is rapid, not logical or sequenced, and is different for different reasons" (McCutcheon, 1982, p. 265).

A major focus during long-term planning is selection of content. To aid this process, teachers turn to a number of sources, including curriculum guides, textbooks, teachers' guides, notes from college courses, and other teachers' experiences. They often do a lot of scribbling, sketching, and note taking, making lists of topics, sequenc-ing them, and then adjusting the sequence. Secondary teachers focus primarily on content when they plan, and content decisions are typically the ones made first (Peter-son et al., 1978; Sardo, 1982). Elementary teachers are more likely to rely upon state or district guidelines and think in terms of student activities. Let's see how all this might work.

> Janine Henderson, a third-grade teacher, starts her beginning-of-the-year planning for sci-ence by browsing through materials. She notes that the state curriculum guide has identi-fied plants as one of the topics to be covered during the school year. More specifically, the guide outlines the following goals as desirable learning outcomes:
>
> | PLANTS | GRADE |
> |---|---|
> | 57. Identify the parts of a plant: root, stem, and leaf. | 3 |
> | 58. Identify environmental conditions necessary for plant growth. | 3 |
> | 59. Identify the stages of growth of a plant as seed, seedling, and mature plant. | 3 |
>
> With these goals as a guide, Janine then turns to her third-grade science text and finds that "Seeds and Plants" comprise two chapters in the text. (This is more than coincidence; state curriculum writers relate their goals and objectives to content covered in state-adopted texts, and text writers are sensitive to the kinds of content in state curriculum guides.)

A quick check of the contents of these chapters reveals the following topics:

seeds	roots
embryo	stems
germination	leaves
seedlings	flowers
seed plants	plant life cycle (adapted from Sund, Adams, Hackett, and Moyer, 1985)

The text appears to be a definite resource. Janine then turns to the teacher's edition. Here she finds a number of aids, including:

1. Classroom activities, such as drawing plants at different stages of development
2. Lab activities (e.g., planting seeds, measuring plant growth), including materials needed
3. Duplication masters for worksheets
4. Enrichment activities, including out-of-class projects
5. Test items
6. Additional books to read (for both the teacher and students)

Satisfied with the topic, the direction she is headed, and the availability of resources, Janine jots down, "Plants and Seeds, April and half of May," and moves on to the next general topic.

As we can see from this example, long-term planning is only concrete enough to provide a framework for more specific unit planning. Day-to-day learning activities usually are not considered at this point, nor is extensive study to refresh content background. Too much specificity can be counterproductive, as two teachers observed:

If I plan too far ahead, [the curriculum is] not flexible enough to incorporate children's interests and the needs I see while teaching.

I have to do so much reteaching because kids are absent or gone for band or something that [too much specificity] gets in the way of long-range planning. It interrupts the flow. (McCutcheon, 1982, p. 267)

Products of Long-Term Planning. As teachers proceed with long-term planning, they produce lists in different content areas that are framed in terms of time. These lists are refinements of the scribblings and random thoughts that occur in the beginning of the long-term planning process. For example, the products of a seventh-grade geography teacher's long-term planning might appear as follows:

WORLD GEOGRAPHY (FIRST SEMESTER)
1. Basic concepts (September/October)
   Maps, landforms, water and waterways, elements of climate, population patterns
2. Cultural change and development (November 1–15)
3. Anglo-America (Canada and United States) (November 15–December 15)
4. Latin America (Mexico, Central America, South America) (December 15–January 15)

While brief, the outline simplifies later planning efforts by reducing the number of decisions that must be made. At this point, the teacher thinks of general content, possible goals, and resources, such as ordering films or videos that require advance scheduling. Otherwise, teachers typically wait until the topic approaches before unit planning. Later, the teacher merely refers to these sketchy plans and notes, for example, "Ah, yes. I'll be starting Anglo-America next week, so I need to get ready." The specifics are a function of unit planning.

Unit Planning

Once a general framework is established in long-term planning, teachers find it useful to convert this framework into specific units. A **unit** *is a series of interconnected lessons focusing on a general topic.* It can last anywhere from a week or two to a month or more depending on the topic itself and the age level of the students. Some examples of unit topics in different content areas are shown in Table 3.4.

Unit plans bridge the gap between long-term and day-to-day lesson planning. They help teachers convert broad general topics into specific plans of action. Units are also functional for students because the components—including goals or objectives, content, and activities—are tied together in a logical, coherent manner, providing structure for the new material to be learned.

Unit planning, like all aspects of planning, is a personal process, and no two teachers construct units that are exactly alike. The system shown in Table 3.5 can be used as a starting point for this process. You should experiment, and as you gain experience, adapt and develop a process that works most effectively for you.

Table 3.4 UNIT TOPICS IN DIFFERENT CONTENT AREAS

Art	Home Economics	Physical Education	Music
Watercolors	Nutrition	Aerobic exercise	Rhythm
Perspective	Fabrics	Tennis	Jazz
Pottery	Money management	Body conditioning	Wind instruments
Printmaking	Baking	Swimming	Classical era

Table 3.5 UNIT COMPONENTS

Components	Function
Overview/general goal	Summarizes the general purpose of the unit
Rationale	Answers the question, "Why is this topic important?"
Objectives	Describes the specific outcomes expected from the unit
Content	Identifies and organizes the topics that are included in the unit
Learning activities	Describes the experiences that will be used to help learners reach the unit objectives
Evaluation	Identifies ways that learning will be assessed

Although these components are listed sequentially, the process is not necessarily linear or sequential. Teachers sometimes start with goals, at other times with content or learning activities. The components continually interact in the planning process.

Let's look at a sample elementary language arts unit on library skills.

Overview/Goal

This unit is intended to develop fourth graders' ability to use references files, both in paper form and on computer. This unit will focus on *titles, authors,* and *subjects* files.

The **overview** or **goal** *describes the general purpose of the unit and serves as a starting point for the unit planning process.* If the teacher's ideas about the unit are clear, it can serve as a conceptual organizer for the rest of the process. If the teacher is somewhat unclear, it can serve as a reference point to be returned to later. It can also help communicate instructional intents to students, other teachers, and instructional leaders.

Rationale. The **rationale** in a unit *explains why the unit is important and how it will benefit students.* For example,

Understanding reference systems and how they're organized is necessary for students to use library resources efficiently. The content of this unit will enable them to independently locate desired materials to use in research projects. Since most libraries have both physical and computerized cataloging systems, students should understand how to function in both.

The rationale is important for several reasons. First, simply asking "Why am I teaching this unit?" encourages the teacher to be thoughtful and reflective during the planning process. The rationale can also help connect the new content to other topics in the curriculum. Sharing the rationale with students helps them understand why the topic is important and can help increase motivation to learn.

Objectives. Sooner or later in the planning process teachers need to grapple with the question, "*Specifically,* what do I want my students to learn?" This involves translating general goals into more specific objectives. **Objectives** *are desired educational outcomes stated in specific terms.* Objectives typically have two elements: (1) description of a content area or skill, and (2) a statement of what students will be able to do when they reach the objectives.

When objectives first came into widespread use in education, they were enormously controversial. Proponents suggested that because they translated sometimes vague learning activities into specifically defined learning outcomes, they would become an educational panacea for a host of educational problems. Advocates' zeal further fueled the controversy. Opponents were equally adamant; their complaints centered on the argument that truly meaningful education could not be broken down into a number of specific objectives. For example, how could you put into concrete terms goals like aesthetic appreciation of art or growth in self-concept or self-regulation? While some debate continues today, the issue is insignificant compared to the past, and the use of objectives is widespread in materials such as district curriculum guides and state-level curriculum framework.

Objectives serve a number of important functions:

- They provide focus for instruction.
- They are helpful in communicating our goals to students, parents, and other classroom teachers.
- They provide a first step in thinking about assessing student learning.

In addition, wrestling with objectives often helps teachers clarify their own thinking about what they are trying to accomplish in their classrooms.

The use of objectives in planning was first popularized by Ralph Tyler (1949), who suggested that objectives be expressed in terms that identify both the kind of behavior to be developed in the student and the content or area of life in which this behavior is to operate. Later Robert Mager (1962) published *Preparing Instructional Objectives,* a highly readable book, which suggested that an objective ought to have three parts: (1) an observable behavior, (2) the conditions under which the behavior will occur, and (3) criteria for acceptable performance. The following are examples of objectives written according to Mager's format:

1. Given a ruler and compass, geometry students will construct the bisector of an angle within one degree of error.
2. From a list of sentences, language arts students will identify 90 percent of the prepositional phrases in the sentences.
3. Based on a written argument, the advanced composition student will outline the logic of the presentation, identifying all assumptions and conclusions.

In the examples, the conditions respectively are: (1) "Given a rule and compass"; (2) "from a list of sentences"; and (3) "based on a written argument." The observable performances are: (1) "will construct," (2) "will identify," and (3) "will outline"; the respective criteria are (1) "within one degree of error," (2) "90 percent," and (3) "all assumptions and conclusions."

An alternate and increasingly popular approach to stating objectives was suggested by Norman Gronlund (1995). He believes objectives should first be framed in terms of general goals such as "understand," "appreciate," "know," "evaluate," or "apply," which are then followed by observable behaviors specifying evidence that the learner has met the objective. Using the same content as illustrated in the Mager examples, Gronlund's objectives would appear as follows:

General Objective:	Applies rules of geometric constructions
Specific Behavior:	1. Constructs bisectors
	2. Constructs prescribed shapes
General Objective:	Understands prepositional phrases
Specific Behavior:	1. Provides examples of prepositions
	2. Identifies prepositional phrases in sentences
	3. Writes sentences, including prepositional phrases
General Objective:	Assesses persuasive communications
Specific Behavior:	1. Outlines logic
	2. Identifies assumptions
	3. Identifies conclusions

In comparing the two approaches we see that in addition to including a general goal, Gronlund's objectives do not include conditions and criteria. He asserts that conditions and criteria are useful for programmed instruction and mastery testing in simple training programs. Used for regular classroom instruction, however, they result in long cumbersome lists that restrict the freedom of the teacher. Most teachers agree. Mager's work is significant because of its historical impact, but most of the written curriculum guides you will encounter use Gronlund's approach or a modification of it.

Some examples of objectives for the unit on library skills written according to Gronlund's format are:

General Objective:	Knows differences between title, author, and subject indexes
Specific Behavior:	1. Explains the purpose of each in their own words
	2. Identifies which would be most appropriate with a given goal and amount of information provided
General Objective:	Understands different indexing systems
Specific Behavior:	1. Locates books using the three different indexing systems
	2. Produces a list of references when provided with either a topic, title, or author's name
General Objective:	Understands the Dewey Decimal System
Specific Behavior:	Locates a book using the Dewey Decimal System

Content. The content of the unit describes what students will actually be studying, the information students will know or understand, or the skills they will develop. The way the information is organized is also included in the content section of the unit.

Schematic diagrams, hierarchies, and outlines are all effective ways of organizing and communicating the content organization. The exact type of organizational scheme will depend on the type of content being taught. Outlines are useful in teaching large bodies of interrelated knowledge. Like hierarchies, they help communicate the major ideas of a lesson as well as the relationships among the ideas. For example, an outline for a high school social studies unit covering the causes of the Civil War might appear as follows:

CIVIL WAR
I. Causes of the Civil War
    A. Historical antecedents
        1. Westward expansion
        2. Missouri compromise
        3. Dred Scott decision
        4. John Brown's raid on Harper's Ferry
    B. Conflicting philosophies
        1. Industrial versus agrarian
        2. State's rights versus federal rights
        3. Slavery
    C. Election of 1860
    D. Fort Sumter

The outline helps the teacher clarify his or her own thinking, and it communicates to students the relationship of ideas to be dealt with in the unit.

An outline for the unit on index systems might look like this:

INDEX SYSTEMS
   I. Purposes
      A. To find a specific book
      B. To locate books by an author
      C. To find out about a topic
  II. Types
      A. Title
      B. Author
      C. Subject
 III. Using the index, etc.

A second way of organizing the content of a unit is through conceptual hierarchies. In organizing a content area hierarchically, the teacher is attempting to communicate the relationship between major concepts or ideas. For example, consider the hierarchy in Figure 3.5.

Organizing content in this way raises useful questions for instruction. For example: Should I deal with index systems and the Dewey Decimal System separately, or does it make more sense to integrate them? Or will integrating them overwhelm and confuse the students? What about the alphabetical organization of index systems? Students know how to use a dictionary; should I review that skill before plunging into the alphabetical organization of the index systems?

A third way to organize content is through task analysis. Let's look at this process.

Task Analysis: A Planning Tool to Organize Activities. Through task analysis, the teacher examines content and tries to determine which content or skills are prerequisite to other ideas. It helps answer questions, such as, "How should learning activities be sequenced?" "Which activities come before others?" and "What will students need to know to participate successfully in a lesson?"

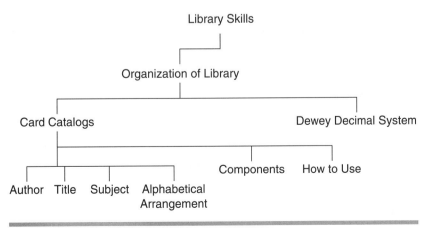

Figure 3.5 Conceptual Hierarchy for Library Skills

Task analysis *is the process of breaking down a topic or skill into its prerequisite skills or parts.* For example, a task analysis for the skill of changing a tire could be broken down into subskills of jacking up the car, loosening the wheel nuts, taking off the flat, replacing it with the spare, replacing the wheel nuts, and lowering the car. Breaking a complex skill into simpler subskills helps teachers plan for instruction.

Task analysis involves the following four steps:

- Specify terminal behavior.
- Identify prerequisite skills.
- Sequence subskills.
- Diagnose students.

Task analysis begins by specifying the terminal behavior or objective that we want students to reach. Objectives stated in behavioral terms are especially valuable here. In identifying prerequisite skills, the teacher is attempting to specify the subskills that lead to the terminal behavior. Sequencing helps the teacher by providing an order for teaching and provides learners with a structure for learning. In the final phase of task analysis, diagnosis, the teacher attempts to find out which of these subskills are already mastered by students. Let's see how these steps help a teacher in the planning process.

Jerilyn McIntire stared at the stack of writing assignments on her desk and didn't know where to begin. Her seventh-grade English students weren't afraid to write, but it seemed like half of them had never heard of punctuation. There were sentence fragments, run-on sentences, sentences without periods, and commas and semicolons were virtually nonexistent. Where should she start?

In considering the problem, Jerilyn came up with one specific starting point—punctuating simple sentences. As she thought about this, she identified the following terminal behavior:

Students will be able to write a simple sentence with correct end-of-sentence punctuation.

Using her terminal goal as a guide, Jerilyn wrote down the skills she felt were prerequisite to the terminal behavior:

- Being able to differentiate between complete sentences and sentence fragments
- Knowing the difference between declarative, interrogatory, and imperative sentences
- Knowing whether periods, question marks, or exclamation marks go with each type of sentence
- Correctly using these marks to punctuate different kinds of sentences

As she wrestled with the problem of ordering these prerequisites, Jerilyn decided that the sequence of subskills as written made sense. First, students had to understand what sentences were. Then she could work on helping them understand the different kinds of sentences and how they were punctuated. Finally, she wanted them to write and punctuate their own sentences.

Jerilyn faced a final problem: How many (and which) students had already mastered the prerequisites? In attempting to diagnose her students, Jerilyn designed a simple quiz that she would administer the next day. In the first part, students would have to differenti-ate between sentences and sentence fragments. In the second, they'd have to punctuate different kinds of sentences, and in the third, they'd have to write their own sentences and punctuate them.

Task analysis works for several reasons. First, it encourages us to examine our goals and state them in specific terms. Like the process of writing objectives in general, this helps clarify our thinking. Task analysis also encourages us to break complex skills into smaller, more teachable subskills. Finally, task analysis shifts our attention from abstract concepts and skills to our students and encourages us to ask, "What do they already know and where should I begin teaching them?" Each of these steps is helpful in preparing and organizing learning activities.

Learning Activities. This component may be the most important part of the whole unit, because it brings students into contact with the important ideas and skills con-tained in the unit. The connection between content and activities is so crucial that Chapters 7, 8, 9, 10, and 11 of this book are devoted to the topic. In those chapters, we will develop the idea that what you are trying to teach (your objectives) should in-fluence how you teach it and how students should learn it. For example, contrast ob-jectives 1 and 3 for the unit on library skills. Objective 1 requires students to *know* something—the three different ways a book can be indexed in a reference system, whereas Objective 3 asks students to be able to *do* something (locate a book using the Dewey Decimal System). Locating a book is a skill and requires modeling by the teacher and practice by students. The first objective, in contrast, requires understand-ing and retention. We discuss these important differences and the implications for in-struction in Chapters 7 through 11.

Evaluation. The final phase of constructing a unit involves evaluating student learning. Evaluation is essential for at least two reasons. First, it provides students with feedback about their learning progress, and feedback facilitates learning (Eggen and Kauchak, 2001). Second, it provides teachers with information about students' learning progress, which allows them to make decisions about what to do next. This might include reteaching, teaching in a different way, or moving on to the next topic. Although it ap-pears at the end of our list of unit components, evaluation is integrally connected to other parts. How you will assess student learning depends on what you want students to learn (your objectives) and the learning activities you involved them in. For example, contrast the following measurement items:

A. What are the three different kinds of reference systems?

_____

_____

_____

_____

_____

_____

_____

B. Go to the card catalog and locate the author's name and call number for each title here.

TITLE	AUTHOR	CALL NUMBER
Ramona the Pest		
Where the Red Fern Grows		
The Little House on the Prairie		

The first type measures knowledge, while the second requires students to apply information. Each evaluation procedure corresponds to a different objective. In the evaluation component of a unit, teachers should test what they have planned for and taught. We will return to this important idea in Chapter 12, when we return to the topic of assessment.

Lesson Planning

Long-term planning helps organize the school year into manageable chunks. Unit planning is a vehicle through which sometimes vague and unconnected ideas are translated into concrete and interconnected learning experiences. **Lesson planning** *focuses teachers' planning efforts on a specific day and class.* At the middle and high school levels, a lesson plan corresponds to a given period; at the elementary levels, lesson length in self-contained classrooms may vary from 15 minutes to an hour or more, depending on the topic, activities, and maturity of students.

As with other dimensions of planning, each teacher approaches lesson planning in unique, personal ways. In addition, the process varies with the topic; if you are familiar with and confident about a subject, you will plan differently than if you are hesitant about it. Experience, too, makes a difference, not only in general terms (i.e., experienced teachers plan differently than beginning teachers) but also in terms of whether you have taught the specific topic before. We saw this in the beginning of the chapter in the different ways that Peggy Stone and Jim Hartley planned for their teaching.

With these ideas in mind, we examine two different models of lesson planning. As you think about them, we encourage you to adapt selectively from them to fit your individual needs.

A Basic Lesson Plan Model. A lesson plan needs to be specific enough to provide structure for the lesson but general enough to provide flexibility when the situation warrants. Few lessons proceed exactly as planned. This fact makes teaching both challenging and potentially bewildering at times.

Writers in this area (Jacobson et al., 2002; Orlich et al., 2001) suggest the lesson plan outlined in Table 3.6 as an optimal blend of structure and flexibility.

As we can see, this lesson plan begins by linking the individual lesson to the unit in which it is embedded. Goals and objectives are then stated, and a rationale is considered. This rationale is more specific than the unit rationale and can be used to introduce the lesson to students (e.g., "This lesson on punctuation will help us write sentences that are clear and understandable"). This is followed by the content, instructional procedures, and assessment procedures for the lesson. Finally, materials and aids are noted to serve as

Table 3.6 ELEMENTS OF A BASIC LESSON PLAN

Component	Function
Unit title	Helps identify the relationship between this lesson and others in the unit.
Instructional goal	Identifies the broad goal for the lesson.
Objective(s)	Identifies specifically what the students should learn.
Rationale	Explains why the lesson is important.
Content	Identifies and organizes the major ideas/skills in the lesson.
Learning activities	Describes the learning experiences that will be used to help the students reach the objective(s).
Assessment procedures	Specifies how student learning will be assessed.
Materials and aids	Identifies the equipment and supplies that will be needed.

last-minute logistical reminders for the teacher. We saw an example of this model at the beginning of this chapter with Peggy Stone and her math lesson.

A shorter variation of the basic lesson plan model is outlined in Table 3.7. This model eliminates the unit component, the goal statement, and the rationale, on the assumption that a teacher keeps these in mind during the planning process.

Lesson Plan Reality. This chapter's title promised research and reality. With respect to reality, our discussion of lesson planning would be incomplete without considering the

Table 3.7 AN ABBREVIATED LESSON PLAN MODEL

Component	Function
Objective(s)	Identifies specifically what students should learn.
Content	Identifies and organizes the major ideas/skills in the lesson.
Learning activities	Describes the learning experiences that will be used to help students reach the objective(s).
Assessment procedures	Specifies how student learning will be measured.
Materials and aids	Identifies the equipment and supplies that will be needed.

Source: Kim and Kellough, 1983.

teacher plan book, a mainstay of classrooms throughout the country. In its basic form, these commercially prepared guides typically appear as follows:

Date	Period 1	Period 2	Period 3
Monday September 24			
Tuesday September 25			
Wednesday September 26			
Thursday September 27			
Friday September 28			

The date on the left identifies the day; the numbers at the top correspond to lessons or periods, depending on whether the form is being used in elementary or secondary classrooms. The boxes are small; typically, they average 1 × 2 inches. There is room only for brief comments, such as:

Homework

Review place value

(Text, pp. 217–222)

Do problems 9–14 on board (p. 228)

Fri. quiz, Chpt. 9

Homework, p. 228, nos. 15–30

Seeing this format raises two questions: (1) Why is this planning form so popular, and (2) how does it relate to the other formats we have discussed? The answer to the first question is simple; the format takes little time and effort, and it's functional. Teachers' days (and nights) are packed with things to do. When they are not actually teaching, teachers plan, grade papers, and do a myriad of other professionally related things. A plan book provides them with a quick and efficient way of recording and keeping track of their planning thoughts. A teacher can plan on Friday, go home and enjoy the weekend, and return on Monday secure in the knowledge that the week is under control.

The answer to the second question isn't quite as straightforward. The brief notes that we see in planning books such as this belie the complexity of teachers' thinking when they plan. We see that this plan is similar to Jim Hartley's at the beginning of the chapter. Because of Jim's 10 years of experience, many of the components of the more detailed lesson plans were implicit and unstated. For example, he—and all effective teachers—could quickly tell what his specific objectives for the lesson were, why they were important, and how he planned to help his students reach them. Because these components were unstated doesn't means that they didn't exist.

However, not all veteran teachers are effective. Would more detailed planning with more specific written information help? This is a question that remains unanswered.

Instructional Alignment: A Key to Learning

Regardless of whether or not teachers' plans are detailed or brief, it is critical for instruction to be *aligned*. **Instructional alignment** *ensures a match between goals, learning activities, and assessment.* Instructional alignment is a simple enough and intuitively sensible idea—it makes sense, for example, to design learning activities that are consistent with goals. As with many other ideas in learning and teaching, however, the idea isn't as simple as it appears on the surface. For example, many teachers say they encourage higher-order and critical thinking in their students, but their primary way of teaching is to lecture. As another example, suppose a teacher wants students to be able to write effectively, but learning activities focus only on punctuation and grammar rules, with no opportunities for students to write and receive feedback. In these cases, the instruction is out of alignment.

Alignment is critical if learning is to be maximized, and teachers should guard against the possibility that their learning activities and goals may be inconsistent. If they are, some adjustment in their planning needs to be made.

INTEGRATING THE CURRICULUM: INTERDISCIPLINARY AND THEMATIC UNITS

Earlier in the chapter we saw how Janine Henderson, a third-grade teacher, did her long-range planning. Let's return now to her work as she moves along in the planning process.

During a weekend Janine was planning for the remainder of the school year. Looking at her long-range plan, she saw that her unit on plants was coming up. The timing was right, spring was on the horizon, and her students often brought her plants and flowers to identify and talk about.

As she looked at her long-range plans in other areas, she noticed that graphing was an upcoming topic in math. "Hmm," she thought, "I wonder if I could combine the two and have students graph something on plants?" She recalled some of the experiments she'd done with bean seeds, investigating the effects of different amounts of water, sun, and fertilizer. She jotted down, "Graph plant growth."

She also noticed that she had listed "State economy" in social studies. She got out a piece of paper and drew the information shown in Figure 3.6.

Much of the school curriculum is divided into separate subject matter areas. At the elementary level, teachers divide the school day into time frames allocated to different areas such as math and reading, and these content divisions are reflected on report cards. At the secondary level, subject matter divisions become even more prominent, with students taking different classes from experts in different content areas.

This division of the curriculum into discrete content areas has both advantages and disadvantages. Advantages include:

- The simplicity of disciplinary boundaries, which makes them understandable and acceptable to parents
- Being able to make efficient use of subject matter "experts"

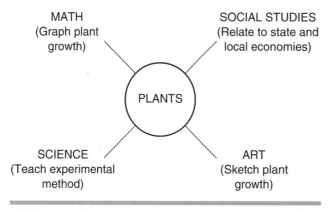

Figure 3.6 Planning for Integration of Content Areas

- Use of content areas to help students understand how different disciplines are structured in terms of major concepts
- Understanding of the processes of inquiry unique to different disciplines

Despite these advantages, dividing the curriculum up into discrete and isolated subject matter areas also has disadvantages:

- Artificial distinctions between disciplines encourage students to see knowledge as fragmented and disconnected.
- Opportunities for inter-disciplinary problem solving are lost.

As students study math and science, for example, they often fail to see connections between the two areas and opportunities to see how one area connects with the other are lost.

An Integrated Continuum

To address this problem, curriculum designers have identified several options that teachers have in organizing their curriculum. These vary from truly separated discipline-oriented units on the left to fully integrated ones on the right (Jacobs, 1989). These are illustrated in Figure 3.7 and discussed in the following paragraphs.

At the far left end of the continuum we have **discipline-based organization.** Much of the instruction in schools is based on disciplines, or separate subject areas. Ja-

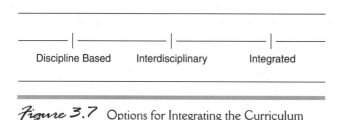

Figure 3.7 Options for Integrating the Curriculum

nine Henderson's initial planning was discipline based as she thought about her planning in terms of separate content areas.

Interdisciplinary planning involves the creation of units in which several subject areas focus their content around a theme. Janine moved to an interdisciplinary approach when she used plants as a focal point and investigated the topic from math, science, and social studies perspectives. Middle school teachers often do this when subject matter teachers maintain their separate disciplines but agree to focus them on a common topic. As we'll see in Chapter 10, this is quite common in project-based instruction and other forms of problem-based learning.

In a truly **integrated approach,** subject matter lines blur and even disappear. Students are encouraged to pursue topics holistically, drawing from different subject matter areas when they prove useful. Here, real-life problems or topics that are meaningful and interesting to students become most prominent and disciplines are called upon only as tools to understand or solve the problem.

Curriculum integration centers the curriculum on life itself rather than on the fragmented information within the boundaries of subject areas. It is rooted in a view of learning as the continuous integration of new knowledge and experience so as to deepen and broaden our understanding of ourselves and our world. (Beane, 1995, p. 622)

Designing and Implementing Integrated Units

In designing thematic or integrated units, the teacher's first task is to identify a focal point for student investigations. Themes or topics can serve as starting points for interdisciplinary or integrated units. Janine Henderson used plants as the theme to structure and organize her planning. Some additional examples of themes include:

Inventors and inventions

Space exploration

Discovery and exploration

Seasons

These broad topics provide a cognitive menu for students, giving them specific options to pursue under the theme's broad umbrella.

Problems can also serve as focal points for thematic units. Some examples include:

What can we do about pollution?

What could be done to increase voter participation and turnout?

How could school lunches be made more appealing and nutritious?

Where did present day popular music come from? What are its origins?

In planning for thematic units, some type of organizing web or network is useful. Teachers typically start in the center, with a topic or problem in the middle, and then branch out from there with additional topics or questions. These topics or questions again provide students with options to pursue in their study. An example of one network can be seen in Figure 3.8.

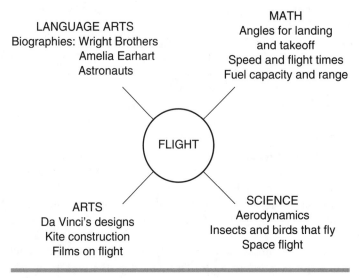

Figure 3.8 Sample Network for Integration

In using interdisciplinary and thematic units, the teacher's role changes dramatically. Instead of being an information provider, the teacher becomes a facilitator, helping students investigate topics of interest. Instruction becomes much less teacher centered.

Student roles also change. Interdisciplinary and thematic units provide opportunities to pursue areas of interest in a coherent and integrated way. Instead of listening, taking notes, and answering questions, students are actively engaged in researching topics. The products that they produce will appear in various forms, including:

- Written research reports
- Posters
- Bulletin boards
- Models
- Dioramas
- Videotapes
- Oral presentations

Research on Integrated Planning

Integrating the curriculum, while intuitively sensible, is controversial. Proponents make the following arguments:

- Integrating curriculum increases the relevance of content by making connections among ideas explicit (Barab and Landa, 1997; Diem, 1996).
- Integrating curriculum improves achievement (Furtado, 1997). Since integrating curriculum is a common feature of block scheduling, it leads to fewer transitions, leaving more time available for instruction (Furtado, 1997).
- Integrating curriculum promotes collaborative planning, which increases communication among teachers (Haschak, 1992).

Opponents of curriculum integration counter with the following arguments:

- Integrating curriculum results in a deemphasis on some important concepts, since teachers don't have a deep understanding of all the content areas that are to be integrated (Carter, 1997; Roth, 1994).
- Planning and instruction for integrating curriculum are inordinately time consuming (Brophy and Alleman, 1991; Beane, 1997).

Integrated curriculum is most popular at the elementary level, where a single teacher can relate several topics, and at the middle school level, where teams of teachers periodically meet to interconnect content areas. It is least common at the high school level, where a disciplinary approach to curriculum is entrenched. National standards driven by subject matter areas, as well as increased emphasis on testing, are likely to encourage this trend at the high school level.

However, one study examining the effects of integrating geometry and art at the high school level found positive results. Teachers integrated these two areas through a unit that culminated in constructing greeting cards that contained elements of both (Schramm, 1997). Comments from students attest to the motivational benefits of interconnected topics: "Geometry has become real to me, not just a subject in school," and, "I took geometry but had a hard time understanding. Now I see how the Pythagorean Theorem relates to a three dimensional work of art" (Schramm, 1997, p. 7).

An important question is, "Is there comprehensive evidence that integrating curriculum increases learning?" At present, the answer is mixed, with research (Portner, 2000) finding both positive and negative results. For example, one study found that elementary teachers who integrated reading with science or social studies produced greater reading comprehension in their students (Portner, 2000). Experts explained the results in terms of students being more motivated to read about interesting topics like pirates and motorboats. Other research is mixed, however, finding either no benefits or negative results (Carter and Mason, 1997; Senftleber and Eggen, 1999). Advocates of curriculum integration counter this negative evidence by arguing that the measures presently available are inadequate, unable to assess the "subtle and difficult-to-measure improvements in student learning" (Vars, 1996, p. 151). The debate is likely to continue.

RESEARCH ON TEACHER PLANNING

The great tragedy of science—the betraying of theory by an ugly fact.

T. H. Huxley

Research on teacher planning highlights an interesting paradox. Time and effort in teacher training programs are spent on processes experienced teachers apparently seldom use. The accumulating evidence suggests that experienced teachers do not prepare written objectives and detailed lesson plans (Morine-Dershimer and Vallance, 1976; Peterson et al., 1978; Zahorik, 1975), and our experience in the schools supports these findings. Further, teachers believe the linear rational model is useful primarily for inexperienced teachers, and student teachers use it only when required to do so by their university supervisors (Neale et al., 1983). Other researchers found that only the least experienced teachers planned according to the linear rational model (Sardo, 1982), and many teachers prepare written plans of any kind only because of administrator demands (McCutcheon, 1982). Finally, researchers found little teacher focus on evaluation during the process of instructional planning (Taylor, 1970). The only elements of the linear rational model that tend to appear in the plans of experienced teachers are brief descriptions of learning activities.

Why don't teachers write out objectives when they plan? Elementary teachers in one study cited several reasons (McCutcheon, 1982). First, objectives already exist in most curriculum guides and texts. To write them again would be redundant and a waste of time. Second, objectives for an activity are often embedded in the activity itself. For example, a kindergarten lesson on geometric shapes would have as an implicit goal the children's ability to identify the different shapes. Similarly, the goal for lessons on single-digit addition could be inferred from the problems used in the activity. Third, objectives are often embedded in criterion-referenced math and reading tests. One teacher commented, "It seems ludicrous to list objectives. They wouldn't be doing the work unless it was aimed at an objective, because the test is all objectives based" (McCutcheon, 1982, p. 263).

Other possible reasons that teachers don't write objectives might simply be that it is just too difficult or it requires too much work. Attempting to write an objective at the beginning of the planning process may be an overwhelming task. It requires teachers to wrestle simultaneously with content and assessment. Juggling both of these components while still trying to articulate a goal or specific outcome for an activity may be overwhelming at this planning juncture.

Finally, considering all the demands on their time and energy, writing out objectives might simply be too much work. If teachers wrote specific objectives for each lesson they taught over the course of a year, the time required could be overwhelming. In this regard, we need to remember that planning is a means to an end, the end being student learning. If teachers can plan and teach effectively without writing out formal objectives, more time and energy are left for other teaching activities such as interacting with students, providing them with feedback, and a myriad of other professional activities.

The research literature also suggests that, contrary to the Tyler model, the planning process is not discrete and linear but rather a continual, nested process. It begins sometime before the school year starts and continues throughout the year. In other words, teachers continually plan, even before the school year starts and at different times during the school year. Planning is a cyclical process in which general ideas undergo progressive elaboration (Yinger, 1977). The germ of an idea for a lesson or unit, encountered in the summer, becomes changed and detailed over time. As the time to teach a particular class grows closer, teachers fill in more and more details, using not only feedback that they have gathered from the present year's students but also information from previous years (Kauchak and Peterson, 1987).

Finally, planning for instruction is not a standard process that is uniform for all teachers. Instead, it is quite variable and subject to influences from a number of sources; the strongest of these is the teacher's experience (Sardo, 1982). Experienced teachers have last year's curriculum to call on, and the planning process may be more adaptation or modification than construction from the ground up. As one teacher put it, "We go with ideas that worked well in the past. We *know* what those are like" (McCutcheon, 1982, p. 264). When we asked a group of experienced elementary teachers to estimate the amount of overlap of this year's curriculum with last year's, they generally agreed it was 70 to 80 percent. Teachers retain the best ideas that worked, adding new ones to replace those that did not. This ability to call on past experiences is a major difference between experienced and beginning teachers (Berliner, 1994). Because experienced teachers have a wealth of past experiences to rely on (not to mention handouts, worksheets, and tests), their workload is reduced. Beginning teachers, in contrast, start from scratch, as attested to by the countless hours spent planning during student teaching and the first year on the job (Bullough, 1989).

Another factor working to make planning a variable process is the content area itself. Elementary teachers report that 85 to 95 percent of the activities in math are adapted from teacher guides (McCutcheon, 1982). This adaption process is not a passive one; teachers screen these instructional activities with dual criteria: (1) Had the activity worked in the past? and (2) Would it work with this particular group? In contrast, planning in other elementary content areas such as science and social studies is much more individualized and teacher centered. Teachers chose isolated units, and interest and availability of materials were primary factors for inclusion of a topic (Zahorik, 1996).

Within the framework of state and county curriculum guidelines, teachers teach what they like and know. The weaker the teacher's content background and the more inexperienced the teacher, the more the published curriculum in the form of text and teachers' guides influences the curriculum. Beginning teachers should not feel guilty about using these aids; as they become more experienced, they will personalize the curriculum, making it their own. Finally, logistical considerations such as the availability of lab materials, videotapes, and books have major influences on how a course is taught.

One major conclusion from this research is that planning is not a uniform process and instead depends on a number of related factors (e.g., teacher experience, content, and the availability of curriculum materials). Also, research underscores the functional nature of teacher planning—teachers plan to get the job done, to maximize student learning given the constraints of the situation.

Because teachers do not write objectives, do not plan according to the linear rational model, and are unlikely to change, should the process be abandoned? Probably not. First, while written objectives are often not the starting point for teacher planning, it does not mean they are ignored. Teachers use objectives, but they come later in the process rather than first, as dictated by the Tyler model (Zahorik, 1975; Peterson et al., 1978). Our experience supports this research finding. Even though objectives are unwritten, effective teachers know exactly what they want their students to know or understand. When asked, they are able to state precisely what their goal is. The issue seems to be more one of *writing the objective down* than it is thinking about objectives. Second, understanding objectives is important because of their widespread use in state and district curriculum materials, textbooks, and achievement tests. Evaluation procedures to assess objectives are also tied directly to them and are designed according to the principles of the linear rational model.

Further, in addition to being users of already prepared objectives, teachers are often asked to participate in curriculum development projects in which goals and objectives are major products. This might be at the grade level, where team planning is involved; at the school level, where intergrade articulation of a curriculum is concerned; or even at the district or state level, where curriculum guides are produced. Also, with the continuing emphasis on educational accountability, teachers are being required to tie learning activities, objectives, and competency tests to performance. Professionals should understand both the strengths and weaknesses of connecting instruction to objectives. In addition, objectives can be a useful communication tool for talking with other teachers as well as students and parents. In sum, knowing how to write and use objectives should be a skill in every professional educator's repertoire.

As teachers plan and record their planning efforts and products, they often do so in a shorthand, cryptic fashion in plan books much like the example with Jim Hartley at the beginning of the chapter. The brevity of these directions belies the thought and energy that goes into the plans. McCutcheon (1982) likened them to shopping lists; the items on a grocery list represent considerable implicit planning and coordination for different menus. This planning and coordination are not evident from a brief inspection of the shopping list. In a similar way, the brief description of activities in a plan book do not do justice to the considerable amount of mental planning that precedes them.

At the beginning of this chapter, we said that planning entails more than the written products of this process. Planning includes all the professional decisions teachers make over a broad time frame. The shortened notes placed in planning books are just summaries of a number of decisions made earlier. When they plan, professional teachers consider things like rationale and objectives, the needs of children, and how a particular lesson relates to others. Because of time and energy, these deliberations do not show up on paper.

One value of lengthier planning models, such as the linear rational model, relates to teachers' development as they first learn to plan; these models provide an initial structure. As teachers become more proficient, many of the processes become essentially automatic, and these concrete reminders are no longer necessary. For example, effective, experienced teachers automatically ask, "Now what do I want them to know? Why is this important? How will I evaluate whether they learned it or not?" Conscious practice as you're learning how to plan helps develop this automaticity.

Finally, from a practical perspective, the ability to put your planning decisions on paper and describe them to others is fast becoming a prerequisite to entrance to the teaching profession. The ability to plan is one of the INTASC standards we discussed in Chapter 1. In short, as you develop as a professional you will be asked to plan and execute lessons and justify your decisions to college professors and supervisors, directing teachers during internships, and administrators supervising you during your first years on the job. The increased emphasis on accountability in education requires beginning teachers to be able to demonstrate their ability to make professional decisions. Effective lesson planning is an important part of professional decision making.

PLANNING FOR DIVERSITY: INDIVIDUALIZED INSTRUCTION

In this chapter we stressed the functional value of planning and how it can be used to organize instruction and promote reflection. The process of planning also provides opportunities for teachers to accommodate diversity through individualization. **Individualized instruction** *adapts instruction to meet the specific learning needs of each student* (Eggen and Kauchak, 2001). In the first part of this section we examine individualization strategies that keep objectives constant for all students and vary either the time or resources available to students. Then we examine strategies that provide different learning options for students. Finally we examine ways that technology can be used to help individualize instruction.

Varying Time

Learners differ in the amount of time needed to master a topic; research indicates that the amount of time needed to master a content area may vary from two to four times as much for slower students (Slavin, 1987). Teachers accommodate this difference in group instruction by giving a common assignment and providing extra time for students who need it. To make this work, teachers provide enrichment activities for students who complete their assignments early. These can include:

- Learning centers
- Computer games and simulations
- Free reading
- Academic games
- Individual research projects

In addition to flexible time requirements embedded in whole group instruction, two other instructional formats—mastery learning and team-assisted individualization—keep objectives constant but vary the time and resources available to students.

Mastery Learning. **Mastery learning** *is a system of instruction that allows students to progress at their own rate through a unit of study* (Guskey and Gates, 1986). Objectives specify the essential learning outcomes for the unit. Formative quizzes are used to provide feedback about learning progress. When students pass the quizzes, they are allowed to continue; when they don't pass, they are moved into alternate learning activities. Summative final exams are used to document final mastery of the content. Individual differences are accommodated by allowing students extra time to master objectives and by providing corrective instruction to remedy learning problems.

Research on mastery learning is generally positive, especially when the criterion measure is specific to the content covered, and these gains are especially positive for low achievers (Slavin, 1987). However, a major obstacle to implementing mastery learning is logistical; finding the extra time to work with students who need it can be a difficult balancing act when large numbers of students are working at different points in the curriculum. Team-assisted individualization addresses this problem.

Team-Assisted Individualization. **Team-assisted individualization** *is a hybrid of mastery learning and cooperative learning* (Slavin, 1985) (We discuss cooperative learning in detail in Chapter 9). In it students work on individualized learning materials in mixed-ability learning teams. These teams provide structure and support through teammates helping with and checking assignments, and team rewards provide motivational incentives for team members. Within this structure the teacher provides direct instruction to small groups of students who are working on the same topic or skill. This teacher-led direct instruction provides quality instruction to all students; the cooperative learning teams provide support and assistance for students pursuing individual objectives.

Research on this instructional strategy has yielded positive results (Slavin, 1985). In six studies involving elementary math, students in team-assisted individualization gained significantly more in computational skills than students in traditional programs.

So far we've looked at strategies that keep objectives constant for students and examined ways that teachers can accommodate different learning rates. In the following sections we look at ways that teachers can individualize not only objectives but also learning materials and activities.

Varying Learning Objectives

Every Friday Carlos Torres gave his class half an hour to confer with him and work on their term papers. He wanted each of his high school English students to read an author in depth, and this semester-long project provided students with an opportunity to learn more about an author and read more of his or her works.

Another way of individualizing instruction is to offer students choices in the learning objectives they pursue. Special projects, term papers, and individual experiments all offer students the opportunity to choose topics that interest them personally. Personalization is an important factor in motivation, and student choice is a way of capitalizing on personalization (Stipek, 1998). Carlos Torres accommodated student interest by designing his course so that 70 percent of the grade was based on core content while the other 30 percent was based on projects. This division allowed him to cover essential content while still providing opportunities for student choice.

Adapting Instructional Materials

When students in Alicia Maxwell's second-grade classroom finished their math assignment, they put it in their folders and went to the back of the room to find a math game. Many of these were on the three computers located in one corner of her room. Some of the other games had dice, others had playing cards, and still others used flash cards. All were designed to reinforce the math skills on which the students were working.

Individual differences can also be accommodated by altering instructional materials, such as using texts written at different levels. If these adapted texts are not available, reading passages can be made more accessible by providing study guides that identify key ideas and conducting prereading discussions focusing on key concepts (Tierney and Readence, 2000). Some teachers even eliminate the text altogether and use high-interest articles from magazines and student periodicals. In other areas, materials such as math games and flashcards can be used to provide learning alternatives for students.

Offering Different Learning Activities

Camille Robertson circulated around the room as her eighth graders discussed their science projects. Each group was responsible for investigating a science project and reporting on it to the rest of the class. Some were doing written reports, others were growing seeds under different kinds of light, and still others were experimenting with batteries and light bulbs.

As we saw in Chapter 2, the way students prefer to learn varies. Some are good listeners and profit from teacher presentations, while others prefer to read or discuss an idea with their peers. The easiest way to address these preferences is to use a variety of teaching strategies. Another is to provide a number of learning options. Camille Robertson did this by allowing a variety of activities to satisfy her science investigation requirement. Other examples of accommodating different learning preferences include typing notes from good note takers and sharing them with others, placing chapters on cassettes and making these available at listening centers, and allowing students to work in teams on group projects. One of the most effective types of alternative learning activities are those that provide corrective instruction, and are specifically designed to help students correct earlier encountered problems (Slavin, 1987). For example, a first-grade teacher who has discovered that several of her students are having problems with letter-sound correspondence might design a learning center with tape recorders and interactive materials to remedy the problem. The center would specifically target the problem content area while providing success experiences for students. Providing learning options makes sense both instructionally and motivationally.

Technology as a Tool for Individualizing Instruction

Technology offers another way to individualize instruction. In the last twenty years the growth of technology has greatly expanded the instructional tools available to teachers (Roblyer and Edwards, 2000). Computers, video discs, integrated learning systems, and video recorders provide teachers with more effective ways to meet the needs of all students. In this section we focus on computers as alternate instructional tools that allow teachers to individualize assignments and provide additional instructional support.

Computers as Reinforcement Tools. Computers have proven to be a valuable resource in providing extra practice and reinforcement for students who need it. Computers' strength lies in their ability to provide adaptive instruction, speeding up when students have mastered basic facts and slowing down when error rates indicate learning problems. Unfortunately, experts estimate that 85 percent to 90 percent of schools' use of computers focuses on drill and practice, a fairly primitive use of computers (Wirth, 1993).

Tutorials: Adaptive Instruction. **Tutorials** are computer programs that introduce new information using text, graphics, and exercises with feedback. Adaptive computer tutorials not only present new information but also provide informative feedback that is specific to learner needs (Forcier, 1996).

A tutorial on high school accounting, for example, might first explain the formula "annual depreciation = cost/expected life" and then ask, "If an electric pasta machine costs $400 and is expected to last four years, what is the annual depreciation?" In response to the answer "$100," the computer would say, "Good," and go on to the next problem or concept. A student who typed $400 might be told, "Sorry, but you're probably not ready to work for H & R Block. $400 is the cost. To find annual depreciation, divide this figure by the expected life (four years). Please type the correct answer."

In providing new information, computer tutorials are adaptive without being re-dundant. So, for example, if students already understood depreciation, the computer could move them to the next concept. This feature allows faster students to move ahead while providing additional help for students who need it.

The most effective tutorials pretest students at the beginning to identify strengths and weaknesses (Forcier, 1996). Using this information, teachers can then use the tuto-rial to remediate background weaknesses or accelerate students past information they al-ready know. Effective tutorials also provide teachers with detailed information about an individual student's learning progress so the teacher can adapt instruction accordingly.

The Apple Learning Series: Early Language is an example of a tutorial software pro-gram that creatively combines a number of technological features to teach beginning reading and writing (Drexler, Harvey, and Kell, 1990; Guthrie and Richardson, 1996). The different components can:

- Provide practice in letter, number, shape, and color recognition and matching of upper and lower case letters.
- Teach the concept of one-to-one correspondence.
- Use voice synthesizers to develop letter/sound correspondence.
- Teach writing and composition skills through word processing and a program that allows children to hear the letters, words, and sentences they've written.

This program appears especially promising for teaching limited-English-proficiency students. One teacher observed:

> The new Spanish-speaking student sat at the computer for a while and stared at it and then at the observer, who finally gave him a few simple directions in Spanish. He took off and with no more help began mastering the games on Muppetville. While working on "Zoo," it was evident that he didn't know all his numbers by sight. The observer showed him how to find the right number by counting on the screen and keyboard. He did this, got the right answer, and clapped his hands with glee. He really enjoyed his successes. He had the same problem during a different game—he could count and add but not always recog-nize the numbers. Without assistance, he transferred the same counting strategy he used at the "Zoo" and got the correct answers. Later, he had no trouble using this strategy again. Each time he was correct, he clapped and smiled. He was one happy boy by the end of his half hour, uninterrupted computer use time. (Drexler, Harvey, and Kell, 1990, p. 9)

By combining a rich instructional menu with opportunities to experiment with new learning in a supportive, nonthreatening way, computers can provide a productive learn-ing environment for students from diverse backgrounds.

Summary

Planning: A Functional Analysis. Planning to teach is more complex than it appears. In addition to the written products that are produced, it involves decisions about con-tent, students, learning activities, and evaluation procedures. Well-planned lessons may be detailed, or they may consist of brief sketches outlining topics and instructional materials. Planning serves a number of functions, ranging from providing security and confidence to simplifying instructional decisions.

Variables in Instructional Planning. A number of factors affect the planning process. Foremost of these is the teacher; who you are, what you know, and your values and beliefs about teaching all influence your planning. The learners you teach also have a central influence on planning; effective teachers consider students' developmental and motivational needs as they plan for instruction. Standards-based education, with its emphasis on accountability, is changing how teachers plan for instruction. Content, teaching context, materials, resources, and time also frame planning decisions.

The Linear Rational Model: A Sequential Planning Model. Long-term planning represents teachers' first attempts to place planning decisions within a time frame, and it usually amounts to lists of topics together with notes and thoughts. Unit planning bridges the gap between long-term planning and lesson planning. A unit plan begins with a general goal that summarizes the general purpose of the unit. A rationale is an explanation of the unit's value and can be shared with students as a motivational tool. Objectives specify the major outcomes of the unit, and the content section outlines and organizes major ideas. Instructional activities translate content and objectives into learning and teaching strategies, and the assessment component describes how learning will be evaluated. Together, these components make up a tangible plan of action for the teacher to follow in the weeks to come.

Lesson planning is the final step in the planning process and generates specific plans of action for a specific class period. The form that specific lesson plans take will vary with the teacher and the situation, but all deal, either explicitly or implicitly, with the fundamental questions of what to teach, how to teach, and why. In this process, instructional alignment, the matching of learning activities and evaluation procedures to goals, is essential. The thoughtful decision making of expert teachers is often masked by the ease with which they produce thoughtful plans for strategic action.

Integrating the Curriculum: Interdisciplinary and Thematic Units. Often the curriculum is presented to students as an array of separate subjects. While separate discipline-based instruction has some advantages, it fails to help students see connections between different subject matter areas. Interdisciplinary planning allows students to see how different disciplines can be focused on a common problem. An integrated approach to planning deemphasizes subject matter boundaries and instead focuses students' attention on a problem or theme.

Research on Teacher Planning. Research on teacher planning reveals a number of interesting findings, many of which question the use of the linear rational model as a primary planning tool for experienced teachers. In addition to discovering that planning was not a discrete, sequential process, researchers found that written objectives often were not the starting point for planning activities, nor was assessment a major concern prior to instruction.

Instead of beginning with objectives, teachers often begin their planning by considering topics or learning activities. Time, effort, and the fact that objectives often exist in curriculum materials or are embedded in learning activities are major reasons that teachers don't explicitly write them.

Planning is not a uniform process and is instead dependent on a number of related contextual factors (e.g., teaching experience, content, and the availability of curriculum materials). Research underscores the functional nature of teacher planning: Teachers plan as they do to get the job done and to maximize student learning, given the constraints of the situation.

Planning for Diversity: Individualized Instruction. Teachers can help accommodate the diversity in their students by individualizing instruction. Instruction can be individualized by varying time available for learning, the materials and resources provided, learning activities, or objectives. Technology can also be a valuable tool for individualization, with adaptive tutorials providing practice and feedback that is geared to each student's individual needs.

Important Concepts

Affective domain
Cognitive domain
Discipline-based planning
Interdisciplinary planning
Lesson planning
Long-term planning
Mastery learning
Objectives
Outcomes-based education
Planning

Psychomotor domain
Rationale
Standards-based education
Task analysis
Teaching context
Team-assisted individualization
Thematic planning
Tutorial Programs
Unit

Reflecting on Teaching and Learning

Angie Becker, a middle-school teacher with a class that is self-contained in the morning but switches in the afternoon, was wrestling with a pile of books on her desk. "Maybe I shouldn't do a unit on nutrition," she thought to herself. "It's not something I'm an expert at and it's going to take a lot of work. But, the kids really need it—I can't believe the stuff they eat for lunch. Oh, well, here goes."

As Angie checked her notes in her planning folder she saw the following:

Food pyramids

Food groups

Analyze lunches

Change eating habits

"Well, this is a start," she continued. "What I need to do is grab their attention. Once I get them into the unit, they'll be okay. It's that first activity that makes or breaks a unit. And since I'm not real solid on this stuff, I'd better make it a good one. Hmm, what I really want them to do is eat healthier but first they need some basic concepts. I'd better write these down or I'll forget them." She continued by writing the following terms on the sheet of paper in front of her:

calories

food groups

vitamins

minerals

carbohydrates

protein

fat

cholesterol

food pyramid

"I think I know where I want them to go, but I'm not sure how to get there. They need to be able to analyze their own diets and come up with positive suggestions for improving it. But first things first. I need to teach them some basic concepts."

As Angie continued to sketch out ideas, her face brightened. "I've got it! I'll talk to the school dietitian and see if she has any ideas. Also, Harvey, the biology teacher, might still have that video on the digestive system. That might be fun."

On the first day of her unit, Angie began the class by writing "Nutrition" on the board and asking students what it meant. After several half-hearted student attempts at defining it, Angie brought out a cafeteria tray with the day's lunch on it. Her students responded immediately.

"Yuck."

"Gross."

"Cafeteria food."

"Smells good to me."

"Okay, class, settle down. Good, Now is this a nutritious meal?" she asked, pointing to the pizza, salad, milk, and jello.

Students looked at the tray and exchanged puzzled looks with each other. Finally, Rashad offered, "Yeah, it's nutritious—else they wouldn't feed it to us. But that doesn't mean it's any good."

"Interesting, class, Do you all agree? Is this a nutritious meal? Most of you are nodding your heads 'yes,' but how do you know? Well, that's what we're going to learn about in our health class for the next couple of weeks."

Angie then had each student write down all the things they had eaten in the last 24 hours and asked them to write a short analysis of this diet. When they had completed this task, she asked them to hand it in so she could read them that evening.

The next couple of days Angie spent talking about different food groups. At the end of the week, she gave the class a quiz that measured whether they knew basic concepts. She began the next week's class with a diary assignment. Students were to write down everything they ate that week and turn their analyses in on the next Monday.

Questions for Analysis

1. What evidence do we have that Angie did any long-term planning? Was her long-term planning congruent with patterns found by researchers?
2. What factors discussed in this chapter influenced Angie's planning behaviors?

3. What goals did Angie have for her unit? How were these written? How could they be rewritten using Gronlund's format?

4. Analyze Angie's objectives in terms of domains and levels.

5. In what ways were Angie's planning behaviors consistent with research?

6. What evidence do we have that Angie considered motivation in her planning?

7. How did Angie assess her students' background knowledge?

8. If Angie had terminated her unit after the quiz on Friday, would her unit have been aligned?

Discussion Questions

1. A colleague of yours claims that teacher planning behaviors are heavily influenced by a teacher's personality. To get at this, he suggests asking two questions: How do you plan for a trip? How are your socks arranged in your drawers? He claims that people who make long travel planning lists and who sort their socks by color tend to be overplanners. How much does personality affect planning? What does your personality say about how you'll approach the planning process?

2. Is including motivation in the planning process becoming more or less important? How important is firsthand knowledge of students in planning for motivation? Why?

3. The chapter mentioned three strategies to increase student motivation—interest, curiosity and motivation. What other ways can teachers plan for student motivation? How is planning for motivation influenced by grade level? Content area?

4. In the text, the potential influence on teachers' planning of curriculum guides and texts, both student and teacher editions, was stressed. What advantages are there in using these? What disadvantages?

5. The following arguments have been raised against the practice of writing objectives in performance terms:
   a. Only trivial objectives can be written in performance terms.
   b. They stifle teacher flexibility and responsiveness to students.
   c. They encourage narrowness; that is, teachers will teach to the objects and students will study the objectives.
   How valid are these criticisms? Are they more valid in some areas of the curriculum (e.g., art or literature) than others? What can teachers do to minimize these potential problems?

6. Are objectives easier to write in some areas of the curriculum than others? What about grade levels? Within a curriculum area, is it easier to write objectives for some types of goals? What can be done in areas where objectives are hard to write?

7. Some people have suggested that education could be improved if the planning process were a centralized process, occurring at the state or district level. Teachers would then be responsible for implementing preplanning units of study. This method would save teachers' time, ensure uniform content, and provide for coordination between teachers at different grade levels. Is this a good idea? What advantages does it have? What disadvantages?

8. You are a substitute teacher who has been called at the last minute to take over a class. How will the following influence your teaching?
    a. The teacher's long-term plans
    b. The teacher's unit plan
    c. The teacher's lesson plan

9. Is interdisciplinary or thematic planning more appropriate at some grade levels than at others? Why? Is interdisciplinary or thematic planning more beneficial for high- or low-ability students? What do your responses to these questions tell you about your view of the relative importance of content in planning and teaching?

10. Of the methods described for individualizing instruction, which are the most labor intensive for teachers? Least? What implications does this have for your teaching?

11. How are tutorial programs different from regular instructional programs? What obstacles do you anticipate in using technology as an individualization tool? What could you do to eliminate or minimize these obstacles?

Portfolio Activities

1. *Teacher Planning.* How do experienced teachers plan? Interview a teacher to find out how he or she plans. Some possible questions might include the following:
    a. Where do you begin?
    b. What help are state and district curriculum guides?
    c. Is there a teacher's edition, and, if so, how is it useful?
    d. Do you coordinate your planning activities with other teachers?
    e. What does your administrator expect of you in terms of lesson plans?
    f. What do the products of the planning process look like?

    How do the teacher's responses compare with the research described in this chapter? What implications do these responses have for you as a teacher?

2. *Teacher Planning: Contextual Factors.* Analyze a teacher's syllabus or outline for a course or a unit within a course. In doing this, compare it with:
    a. State guidelines
    b. District guidelines
    c. The text being used
    d. Your college courses in this area (either subject matter, text, or special methods courses)

    What things are missing? What things are there that you wouldn't do? How would your syllabus look different?

3. *Curriculum Guides.* Analyze either a state or district curriculum guide in one area of the curriculum (or compare two levels).
    a. How recent is it?
    b. Who constructed it?
    c. How is it organized (e.g., chronologically, developmentally, topically, etc.)?
    d. How do the topics covered compare with a text for this area?

    e. How many objectives are listed for a particular course of study?

    f. How many objectives per week are implicitly suggested? Is it a realistic number?

    g. What types of learning (e.g., memory versus higher levels) are targeted?

How could you use a guide like this in your instructional planning?

4. *Teacher's Editions.* Examine a teacher's edition of a text. Does it explain how the text is organized? Does it contain the following aids?

    a. Chapter overview or summary

    b. Objectives

    c. Suggested learning activities

    d. Ditto or overhead masters

    e. Test items

    f. Enrichment activities

    g. Supplementary readings

How helpful would these aids be to you as a teacher? How could you integrate them into your instructional planning?

5. *Objectives.* Write an objective for a lesson you might want to teach. Share it with a fellow student. Is it clear? (Could he or she construct a complete lesson plan based on it?) How could it be made clearer?

6. *Objectives and Measurements.* Take the objective you wrote in exercise 5 and construct a measurement item for it. How else might you evaluate your goal?

7. *Task Analysis.* Using the objective you wrote for exercise 5, do a task analysis on it. This should include the following:

    a. Prerequisite knowledge and skills

    b. A sequence for these prerequisites

    c. Some type of diagnostic instrument to let you find out what students already know

    d. How useful is task analysis for planning instructional activities?

8. *Lesson Planning.* Using one of the models discussed in this chapter, construct a complete lesson plan. Share it with a fellow student and ask him or her to critique it in terms of clarity. (Use the substitute teacher's test—if they had to come in and substitute teach for you, would they know what to do?) What did you learn from this planning exercise?

9. *Planning and Microteaching.* Microteaching is a teaching technique that allows prospective teachers to focus on one aspect of their teaching at a time. This exercise focuses on planning. Take the lesson you constructed in Portfolio Activity 8 and teach it for 10 to 15 minutes to either a small group of your peers or a small group of real students. Audio or videotape the lesson. Listen to or watch the tape and answer these questions:

    a. Were you over- or underprepared?

    b. How well did the planning model you chose fit your personal needs?

    c. In hindsight, what should you have done differently in the planning process to improve your teaching?

4

Effective Teaching: The Research Base

CHAPTER OUTLINE

*I*n Chapter 3 we saw how teachers plan and how planning affects the ways they actually teach. We also looked at different types of planning and how they affect student learning.

We now turn to instruction. As a way of thinking about the content of this chapter, imagine going into a number of classrooms, sitting at the back of the room and watching effective teachers at different grade levels and in different content areas work with their students. They could be at the first, fifth, eighth, tenth, or any other grade level. In some, students will be learning more than would be expected for their age and ability level, whereas in others they will be learning less than would be expected. For years, researchers have looked at differences in the way teachers operate in the high-achieving classes compared to teachers in the low-achieving classes, and they've found significant differences (Shuell, 1996). For instance, as two simple examples, researchers found that teachers of high-achieving students use their time much more efficiently, and they ask many more questions of the students, than do teachers of low-achieving students. *The study of differences in the behaviors of high-achieving students' teachers compared to low-achieving students' teachers* is sometimes called **teacher effectiveness research.** Our goal in writing this chapter is to help you understand this research and assess the extent to which Kathy Johnson, the teacher in the case study that follows, applied it in her work with her fifth graders.

In an effort to make the descriptions of this research more meaningful for you, we have organized them into a general model of instruction that applies to most classroom situations.

When you've completed your study of the chapter, you should be able to meet the following goals:

- Explain how caring, safety, and positive teacher expectations contribute to a positive learning environment.
- Describe teacher characteristics associated with increased learning and motivation.
- Identify ways effective teachers begin lessons to promote learning.
- Describe ways that effective teachers guide learning as lessons are developed.
- Identify ways that effective teachers bring lessons to closure.

Kathy Johnson is a fifth-grade teacher in an urban Midwestern city. About half of her twenty-seven students are considered to be placed at risk, coming from mostly low- to middle-income families. A veteran of six years, she is at her desk working on a unit on the northern and southern states prior to the Civil War.

"Hey, what's up?" her friend Marisse asks as she walks in Kathy's room.

"I'm working on this social studies stuff," Kathy responds. "I know a lot of these kids don't have a lot of background in some ways, but in others, they're actually sharp. I know that if I can get their thinking channeled a little, I can get them to understand a whole lot more than I'm getting out of them now."

"Such as . . . "

"Well, you know that I've been going to this series of workshops to upgrade my certificate, and they are emphasizing student thinking and involvement so much . . . and at first I was skeptical, you know, 'This won't work with my kids' stuff, but I said I'd give it a shot . . . and the kids actually are doing well. . . . That's what I mean when I say that they're actually sharper than we give them credit for.

"Anyway, I've got them working in teams and doing some research on different states in the North and South, and we've put the information in a big chart. We're going to start analyzing it tomorrow to see how it might have affected the Civil War. Some of them are a little uncertain, but most of them are doing really well. . . . Anyway, I'll let you know how it goes."

Marisse waves goodbye and Kathy goes back to her work.

We join Kathy the next morning near the end of her morning break. She typically schedules her day as follows:

8:15–9:15	Math
9:15–10:45	Language Arts
10:45–11:00	Break
11:00–11:30	Social Studies
11:30–12:00	Lunch
12:00–1:25	Reading
1:25–1:35	Break
1:35–2:00	Science
2:00–2:45	(Art, Music, PE, Computers)

Kathy is standing at the door at 10:55 as the students file in from recess. "Nice shirt, Jerome," she smiles. "I didn't notice it before.

"Come up here, Simone," she motions quietly, guiding him to her desk. "You've missed the last two math assignments. . . . I want you to come in tomorrow morning as soon as the bus gets here, and we'll work on them. . . . Okay? Don't forget now."

Kathy smiles as Simone nods shyly, and she watches him as he moves to his desk. Simone has recently come to this country from Haiti, and English is still difficult for him.

The students are in their desks and settled at 11:01, and Kathy says, "I'm pleased to see that you're ready to go. We never have enough time, and I appreciate your help."

"Look over there," she says, referring the students to a large chart taped to the side wall of the room. It appears as follows:

	PEOPLE	LAND AND CLIMATE	ECONOMY
Northern states	Small towns	Many trees	Syrup
	Religious	Remains of glaciers	Rum
	Valued education	Poor soil	Lumber
	Cooperative	Short growing season	Shipbuilding
		Cold winters	Fishing
		Mountains	Small farms

	People	Land and Climate	Economy
Southern states	Aristocratic	Good soil	Large farms
	Isolated	Hot weather	Tobacco
	Social class distinction	Large rivers	Cotton
		Long growing season	Unskilled workers
		Coastal plain	Servants and slaves

Now, as you look at it, let's think about what we've been doing for the last week. Someone go ahead and describe what we've been doing . . . Latisha?"

" . . . We looked up stuff about the different states, and . . . we worked together . . . and we wrote it down, and we turned it in."

"Good," Kathy smiles, "and what were some of the things you found? . . . Michael?"

" . . . We found that in the South, like Mississippi and Georgia they had big farms and grew cotton, and . . . "

"And in New Hampshire and up there, they had little farms," Jason jumps in, pointing to the map of the United States at the front of the room.

"That's good information, Jason, but remember that we don't interrupt our classmates when they're talking."

"What else? . . . Kristi?"

" . . . They had servants and slaves in the South but not so much in the North."

"Good, everyone," Kathy waves. "Now, you heard what Latisha and Michael and Jason and Kristi have said. Keep that in mind as we look at our chart. The information you gathered is all in it, and I added a little of my own. Now, looking at the chart brings up some questions. . . . How are these states different, and why, since all these states are part of the same country—our United States—why are they so different? . . . That's what we're going to try and figure out today. If we work hard, I'll bet we come up with some really important ideas. . . . Everybody ready? . . . Let's go."

Let's stop now and see what research says about effective teaching and effective teachers and how this research can help us understand the actions of Kathy Johnson.

CLASSROOM CLIMATE: A PREREQUISITE TO LEARNING

Think back to some of your own school experiences, and consider classes in which you were comfortable and looked forward to going to compared to those you disliked, in which you were uneasy or perhaps even felt were a waste of time. What were the differences between these two types of classrooms?

One likely and important difference can be explained with the concept **classroom climate,** *which describes the emotional and academic tone in classrooms.* Classrooms with a positive climate are emotionally safe, orderly, and focused on learning. In classrooms with a negative climate students are disruptive, they worry about being criticized or ridiculed, and learning doesn't seem to be emphasized.

A positive classroom climate is crucial if all students are to learn as much as possible. Because classroom climate is so essential, we begin our discussion of the research examining effective teaching with it.

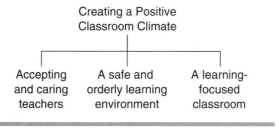

Figure 4.1 Creating a Positive Classroom Climate

A positive climate is created in three ways, which are outlined in Figure 4.1. Let's look at them.

Acceptance and Caring: The Human Dimension of Teaching

Sean Williams surveyed his eighth graders as he passed out his unit exam. The desks were spread apart and there was a feeling of anticipation in the air as they began the test. As Sean moved around the room, he noted with satisfaction that most of his students had plunged into the test and were working diligently. Tony, however, was sitting at his desk and staring out the window.

Sean didn't initially say anything, but when Tony still hadn't started the test after 5 minutes, Sean went over to him, bent down and quietly said, "Tony, you still haven't started the test. Is something wrong?" Tony turned away to avoid looking at Sean and said nothing.

"Please come out in the hall," Sean said to him. When they got there, he could see that Tony was close to crying—something for which rough and tough boys aren't noted. Tony hesitantly described a fight between his parents the night before, which ended with Tony's dad storming out of the house. As Tony described the incident, tears came to his eyes and Sean decided that the test wouldn't do Tony any good at this time.

"Go wash your face," Sean smiled. "Then, come back into the room until the period ends. We'll make the test up tomorrow before school. . . . You okay?"

Tony managed a weak smile and a nod, then headed to the boys' bathroom.

When classroom climate is positive, students know that they are valued as human beings, regardless of their appearance, personality, or achievement. One of the most important ways that teachers communicate that students are valued is through acceptance and caring (Marzano, 1992). **Caring** *refers to teachers' abilities to empathize with and invest in the protection and development of young people* (Chaskin and Rauner, 1995). Sean was empathetic when he listened to Tony describing the fight between his parents, and he invested in Tony's protection.

The most important way teachers invest in the protection of students is with time. For instance, Sean asked Tony to come in to take the test the following morning. Normally, Sean used this time to do some final organization tasks for his day, but he gave Tony the time instead. Everyone has 24 hours a day, and choosing to allocate some of this time to another person communicates caring better than any other way.

Students quickly recognize the differences between teachers who care and those who don't. A fourth grader commented, "If a teacher doesn't care about you, it affects your mind. You feel like you're a nobody, and it makes you want to drop out of school" (Noblit, Rogers, and McCadden, 1995, p. 683).

In addition to spending time with students, caring can be demonstrated in at least four ways:

- Treating students with respect, listening to their comments and questions, and being responsive to legitimate needs for second chances and extra help.
- Treating students as individuals, noticing and commenting on changes in dress, habits, and behavior.
- Being willing to listen to students concerns about personal problems and other nonacademic concerns.
- Going the "extra mile"—being willing to provide extra help with classwork, providing guidance in personal matters, and working on extracurricular activities.

In the introduction to the chapter, we said that we are focusing on the research base for effective teaching, so let's see what research has to say about this somewhat elusive concept called caring.

Since the early 1990s, researchers have been investigating the effects of learners' relationships with teachers and peers on their motivation and learning. They focused on the concept of **relatedness,** *which is students' need to feel connected to others in a social environment and to feel worthy and capable of love and respect.* It is a basic need in all people, they argue (Connell and Wellborn, 1990). Teachers who are available to students and who like, understand, and empathize with them have learners who are more emotionally, cognitively, and behaviorally engaged in classroom activities than teachers rated lower in these areas (McCombs, 1998; Skinner and Belmont, 1993). Also, students who feel like they belong and perceive personal support from their teachers report more interest in their classwork and describe it as more important than students whose teachers are more distant (Goodenow, 1993). These findings suggest that caring teachers—who value all students regardless of academic ability or performance—are essential for both learning and motivation (Stipek, 1996).

A Safe and Orderly Learning Environment

The teacher says, "We have a little filmstrip on weather." And she quickly overviews the content on the filmstrip, which is called "The Weather Is Poetry." As the teacher arranges the filmstrip in the machine, she says, "Before we start this, we're going to turn out the lights, but you can finish your work anyway. We're going to pick it up afterwards." Greg says, "Miss, I can't see to finish." The teacher says, "Yes, you can. Your eyes will adjust." Andrew is yelling, "Lights off, lights off" four times. Finally, the teacher starts the filmstrip, which is a sound filmstrip. Someone turns the lights off. Everyone starts yelling, "I can't see. It's dark in here." The teacher assures everyone that their eyes will adjust. As the film is running, the students talk, move around. Apparently, two of them go outside to work, although the observer did not notice until later. Some move desks. Observer notes that no one can hear the movie. Joe comes in from the hall and stands at the front of the room to watch. The class finally settles a little. About half are watching the film, and half are working on the assignment in the dark. The teacher walks out of the room. And then she walks about the room. She says, "In a few minutes, you're going to see the part about the mud. That's my favorite part. They describe the sound of people walking in the mud." Greg says, "Turn on the lights." The teacher ignores him. During the filmstrip there is a steady exchange of students with restroom passes. Susan comes in, Joe goes out. The teacher goes out. Robert calls after her sarcastically, "You missed the mud." (Carter, 1986, pp. 33–34)

This is a description of an actual middle school classroom. How much learning is likely to occur in this kind of environment?

Positive classroom environments require teachers who care, but caring, while fundamental, isn't enough. Students can't learn if their classmates are disruptive. A safe and orderly learning environment is the second component of a positive classroom climate.

Research indicates that an essential precondition for teaching all kinds of students—bright, slow, white, minority, low SES or high—is an orderly classroom where students know what to expect and what is expected of them (Levine and Lezotte, 1995; Doyle, 1986). This dimension is so crucial to teaching effectiveness that we devote all of Chapter 6 to the topic.

A Learning-Focused Classroom

Effective teachers believe that their most important role is to promote as much learning as possible in their students. While extracurricular activities are important, they don't take precedence over learning. Effective teachers, for example, don't allow students to use class time to discuss club events, and socializing is done out of class, not during time when students should be completing seatwork.

One study investigating the effects of learning-focused classrooms concluded, "Students learn more in schools that set high standards for academic performance, that use their instructional time wisely, and that use student learning as a criterion for making decisions" (Lee and Smith, 1999, intro).

Teachers communicate that *learning* is the primary reason students are in schools in several ways:

- Modeling a belief in the importance of study, effort, and learning
- Clearly communicating learning goals and reasons for the goals
- Using time effectively
- Preventing disruptions that interfere with learning
- Thoroughly and frequently measuring students' understanding with quizzes and alternative assessments
- Providing timely (i.e., the day after they're given) feedback about performance on the assessments

Kathy communicated a learning focus with her students in at least three ways. First, social studies was scheduled to begin at 11, and she began within a minute of that time. Second, she immediately reacted to Jason's disruption by saying, "That's good information, Jason, but remember that we don't interrupt our classmates when they're talking." Third, she said, "Now, looking at the chart brings up some questions. How are these states different, and why, since all these states are part of the same country—our United States—why are they so different? That's what we're going to try and figure out today. If we work hard, I'll bet we come up with some really important ideas." Her comment set an academic tone and provided a clear goal for the lesson.

We've just seen that effective teachers create positive classroom climates and that the way they use their time is a factor in the process. Let's look at the use of time in more detail.

EFFECTIVE TEACHING AND THE CONCEPT OF TIME

Dost thou love life? Then do not squander time, for that is the stuff life is made of.

Benjamin Franklin
Poor Richard's Almanac, 1775

Ben Franklin recognized the importance of time all the way back in 1775, saying it is the stuff of life. It's the stuff of teaching life as well, because it's precious and, unfortunately, often used inefficiently.

In introducing this chapter we suggested that you ask yourself what you would expect if you observed effective teachers at any grade level. One feature they would have in common is that they use their available time efficiently.

That time is critical in learning is suggested by the fact that students in many other industrialized countries typically spend more time in school than do American students, and these students also score higher on standardized tests than do American youngsters. This has led to suggestions that the American school year and school day be lengthened.

These suggestions are simplistic, however, because the length of the school year or day is only one dimension of time. A more complete picture examines *how* teachers use their available time and how this influences learning. In analyzing classroom time use, we'll focus on the four dimensions outlined in Table 4.1. Let's examine them.

Allocated Time: Priorities in the Curriculum

Allocated time *is simply the amount of time teachers assign to different content areas or topics.* If we look back at Kathy's schedule, for instance, we see that she allocates an hour and a half for reading, almost as much for language arts, and an hour for math. By contrast, social studies gets only a half hour and science a mere 25 minutes. These allocations are typical and reflect the fact that elementary teachers emphasize reading, language arts, and math more strongly than social studies and science.

Table 4.1 DIMENSIONS OF CLASSROOM TIME

Allocated time	The amount of time a teacher or school specifies for a content area or topic
Instructional time	The amount of time available for teaching time after routines and administrative tasks are completed
Engaged time	The amount of time students are attending and involved in learning activities
Academic learning time	The amount of time students are involved in learning activities during which they're successful

While it appears that elementary teachers have more control over time allocations than do middle or secondary teachers, this isn't necessarily the case. For instance, a middle school English teacher could choose to emphasize writing by spending a great deal of time on it, while another might devote that time to grammar instead.

Research indicates a positive but weak correlation between allocated time and learning (Karweit, 1989). As a way of thinking about this correlation, imagine that we double the allocated time for a certain subject. While we would expect students to learn more, they would not learn twice as much. In fact, they only learn slightly more than they did with the previous allocation.

Instructional Time: Time from a Teacher's Perspective

The bell had rung and Dennis Orr's eighth graders were filing into his class. Dennis was at the back of the room working on some equipment as the students moved to their seats.

In a few moments he moved to the front of the room and said, "Now, let's see who's here today." He glanced at the top of his desk looking for his roll book and, not seeing it, looked in his desk drawer. "I let some of you look at your averages yesterday," he called out to the class. "Did you return my book?"

"We put it in your file cabinet," one of the boys responded.

"Ah, yes, here it is," Dennis said quietly as he looked in the drawer and saw the book.

Having finished taking roll, he said to the class, "I'm going to show you a demonstration today. Get your books and notebooks out while I finish getting this set up."

The students, basically well behaved, did as he suggested as he began to take equipment from a nearby shelf and assemble it. A few minutes later, he signaled the class.

"Okay, everyone, let's take a look at what we have here." He began the demonstration, having the students make observations of the equipment and the phenomenon taking place. Suddenly he said, "Oh, I almost forgot. All of you in the band will be released 10 minutes early today so you can gather your instruments for the trip to Seaside Junior High."

Now, let's look at another eighth-grade teacher in essentially the same situation.

Steve Weiss, Dennis's colleague across the hall, was sitting at his desk as his students walked in. As they sat down, they got their books and notebooks out of their backpacks and put them on their desks. As they moved toward their seats, Steve checked their names in his roll book.

"I see Jim isn't here. Has he been absent all day?" he asked as the last student was sitting down.

"He's sick," a classmate volunteered, and with that Steve signed the roll and hung it on the clip on his door. As he walked, he pointed to an announcement on the board. "All band students go to the band room immediately after school to get your equipment ready for the trip to Seaside."

Walking back to the center of the room, Steve began, "We studied the concept of pressure yesterday, and today we want to look at how pressure changes under different conditions. I have a demonstration for you. Everyone take a look at the cart."

With that, he rolled a cart to the center of the room with some equipment assembled on it. "What do you notice on the cart, Tony?" he asked as he began the lesson.

In comparing the two teachers we see that Dennis spent several minutes taking roll, searching for his grade book, preparing his demonstration, and making an announcement, whereas Steve took roll as students came in the door, made his announcement as he hung up his roll slip, and had his demonstration prepared in advance. Dennis spent more time on noninstructional activities than did Steve.

Instructional time *is the amount of time available for learning activities.* As Dennis's case illustrates, significant portions of time are frequently lost to noninstructional activities, often more than a third of teachers' allocated time (Karweit, 1989). Further, some teachers seem to be unaware of the value of time as a resource, thinking of it as something to be filled, or even "killed" rather than an opportunity to increase learning (Eggen, 1998; Wiley and Harnischfeger, 1974). With instructional time so important, teachers must do everything they can to maximize the amount they have. Significantly, when noninstructional lapses are decreased, learning increases (Stallings, 1980).

Instructional time is important for another, more subtle reason; disruptions that detract from classroom climate are most likely to occur during noninstructional activities. Well-run classrooms with high rates of instructional time are places with fewer management problems (Emmer, Evertson, Clements, and Worsham, 2000; Evertson, Emmer, Clements, and Worsham, 2000).

Engaged Time: Time from a Learner's Perspective

While instructional time is important, **engaged time,** *the proportion of instructional time that students are focused and on task,* is even more important.

A comparison of high- and low-achieving students demonstrates the importance of engaged time, or "time-on-task." High-achieving students are typically engaged for 75 percent of the time or more, while low achievers often are engaged less than 50 percent of the time (Evertson, 1980; Fredrick, 1977). Further, researchers have found that the engaged time for students of effective teachers is much higher than that for students of less effective teachers (Berliner, 1987; Shuell, 1996). Engaged time is a tangible measure of a teacher's impact on students and, not surprisingly, when principals and other school leaders observe in classrooms, one of the first things they look for is *student engagement rates,* or the extent to which students are paying attention and doing their assigned work.

How can we tell if students are on task? Or, more specifically, what kinds of things would you look for in determining if your students are with you? One of the best indicators is eye contact—are they watching you during a teacher-led discussion, and during individual work do their eye movements suggest that they are reading and actually responding to the materials they're studying?

Interestingly, research indicates that the link between on-task behaviors and achievement is more complex than it appears at first glance. High- and low-ability students differ not only in the *amount* of time they're engaged but also in *when* they're off task (Rusnock and Brandler, 1979; Smyth, 1979). High-ability students finish their academic tasks and *then* go off task; low-ability students go off task before and during their academic tasks.

The issue, then, is not as simple as merely allocating more time to a particular subject, nor does increasing efficiency so that instructional time is maximized solve the problem. If students aren't paying attention during learning activities or doing seatwork when it's assigned, learning won't occur regardless of how well organized and efficient a teacher is. (Because involving students is so essential to learning, we devote all of Chapter 5 to the topic.)

Academic Learning Time: The Role of Success

Research indicates that part of the reason that low achievers go off task relates to frustration (Anderson et al., 1985). The work they're assigned is often beyond their present capability, making it nearly impossible to complete. As a result, they often give up and go off task. This leads us to the concept of **academic learning time,** which we saw in Table 4.1 is *the amount of time students are successfully engaged.*

Student success is important for at least three reasons:

- It indicates that the new learning is building effectively on what students already know (Fisher et al., 1980).
- Success is reinforcing; it is much more rewarding to get questions and problems right than wrong.
- Success builds confidence, preparing students for future learning.

The importance of success is confirmed by the teacher effectiveness research. A study of 250 classrooms showed that students in classes where success was the dominant pattern not only learned more but also felt better about themselves and the material they were learning (Fisher et al., 1980).

How high should success rates be? The answer depends on the situation. Research suggests that students in interactive question and answer sessions should be about 80 percent successful (McGreal, 1985), but in homework assignments, where the potential for confusion and frustration is higher, success rates should be 90 percent or higher (Berliner, 1984, 1987).

As with engaged time, success rates are not as simple as they appear on the surface. Younger students, low achievers, and students from lower socioeconomic backgrounds typically need more success than do their older, higher-achieving, or more advantaged counterparts. These students often lack a robust history of classroom success and tend to become easily frustrated or discouraged.

Content is also a factor. Topics that build on previous knowledge and skills—such as some parts of math and reading—require higher success rates than other less cumulative and structured areas, such as Kathy's social studies lesson.

As we move from allocated time to academic learning time, the correlation with learning becomes stronger and stronger (Nystrand and Gamoran, 1989). Our goal should be a well-organized classroom that has students successfully engaged in meaningful learning activities. While this isn't easy, with effort it is attainable. We begin our discussion of ways to accomplish the goal in the next section.

A GENERAL INSTRUCTIONAL MODEL

In our introduction to the chapter, we said that we would organize the research base for effective teaching into a general instructional model. Our goal in doing so is to make the information more meaningful for you, so it is easier to remember and apply in your own teaching.

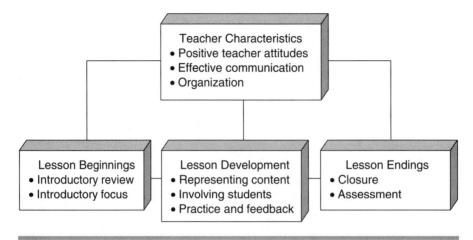

Figure 4.2 A General Instructional Model

Our efforts are represented in Figure 4.2 and discussed in the sections that follow. As you study these sections, remember that the model summarizes research that applies in all classrooms, regardless of grade level, content area, or specific topic.

CHARACTERISTICS OF EFFECTIVE TEACHERS

As we would expect, characteristics of effective teachers such as their attitudes, the way they communicate, and how they organize their learning activities influence the total lesson cycle—its beginning, development, and ending. This is why these characteristics are connected to each phase in the model. In each phase we analyze the specific actions that research indicates are effective. Let's see how these components interact to increase student learning.

Teacher Attitudes

In looking again at Figure 4.2, we see that teachers' attitudes are listed first. We did this on purpose, because teachers' attitudes and beliefs have a powerful impact on their ability to promote student learning (Calderhead, 1996; Good and Brophy, 1997). These attitudes are often demonstrated subtly, but their positive influence on learning is clear. Let's look at an example.

Lorna Davis, a veteran with fourteen years of experience, teaches three sections of Advanced Placement biology and two sections with students of below average to average ability. We look in on one of her average classes.

"We better get moving," Clarice says to Leroy as they approach the door of the classroom. "The bell is going to ring and you know how Davis is about this class."

"Yeh," Leroy smiles wryly. "She thinks all this genetic stuff is sooo important. She thinks she can make scientists out of all of us."

"Did you finish your homework?"

"Are you kidding," Clarice returns. "You miss a homework assignment in this class and you're a dead duck."

"Right," Leroy confirms. "Nobody messes with Davis."

"I didn't know what she wanted on that explanation about attached and detached earlobes, so I went to her help session after school yesterday, and she went over everything again," Clarice continues. "She really tries to help you get it."

From this short episode we can infer a great deal about Lorna and her attitudes about learners and learning. These attitudes and beliefs consist of the following three elements:

- Personal teaching efficacy
- Teacher modeling and enthusiasm
- Teacher expectations

Personal Teaching Efficacy. To begin this section, let's look again at Lorna's teaching. Leroy commented, "She thinks she can make scientists out of all of us." While we can't be sure about her goals based on this short vignette, Leroy's reaction gives us some information about Lorna's attitudes. She is high in **personal teaching efficacy,** *which is the belief that teachers and schools have an important positive effect on students* (Bruning, Shraw, and Ronning, 1999). High-efficacy teachers increase learning more than do low-efficacy teachers. They tend to use praise rather then criticism, to persevere with low achievers, to use their time well, and to accept students and their efforts to answer. Low-efficacy teachers, in contrast, spend less time in learning activities, "write off" low achievers, and criticize students to a greater extent than do their high-efficacy counterparts (Kagan, 1992). High-efficacy teachers also tend to be flexible, more willing to try new curriculum materials and strategies (Poole, Okeafor, and Sloan, 1989).

Kathy Johnson also demonstrated the characteristics of a high-efficacy teacher. Her comment, "I can get them to understand a whole lot more than I'm getting out of them now," suggests that she believes her students *can* learn and she *can* influence it. In addition, her remark, "At first I was skeptical, you know, 'this won't work with my kids' stuff, but I said I'd give it a shot," reflects a willingness to try new ideas. Positive professional beliefs such as these strongly influence the effort teachers make in trying to promote learning.

Teacher Modeling and Enthusiasm

"I see you have David in class too," one teacher said to another. "He sure is a good kid, isn't he?"

"I'm not surprised," the second one responded. "Have you ever met his parents? They're both super people, too—enthusiastic and supportive. David probably picks up his attitude from them."

Modeling *is the display of behaviors that are imitated by others* (Bandura, 1993; Pintrich and Schunk, 1996). The two teachers in our example are suggesting that David is imitating the attitudes and behaviors of his parents, and we see the effects of modeling in a great many other cases. People imitate the hair styles of figure skaters and princesses; the clothing of rock musicians, first ladies and professional athletes; and exercise patterns demonstrated by movie stars. Students pick up attitudes and expressions from the thousands of hours of TV they watch. Observing and imitating the behaviors of others is an important way that all people learn (Bandura, 1986, 1993).

Teachers strongly influence students through their modeling (Good and Brophy, 2000). However, the process is often subtle, and the effects of modeling can be out of a teacher's conscious control. For instance, if a teacher claims to encourage free thinking but disapproves when students offer novel or occasional off-the-wall ideas, they will soon say only what they think she wants to hear. If teachers are inconsistent in what they say and do, children imitate their behavior rather than their spoken words (Bryan and Walbeck, 1970).

Teachers also teach attitudes toward learning through their actions. For example, teachers who modeled persistence in attempting to solve problems had students who strongly persisted in their own efforts, whereas students who saw a teacher persist only minimally actually declined in persistence (Zimmerman and Blotner, 1979). Further, when teachers made statements of confidence about their ability as they persisted, their students had increased estimates of their own ability (Zimmerman and Ringle, 1981).

Clarice's and Leroy's conclusion that "Davis thinks this stuff is sooo important," was the result of Lorna's modeling. It wasn't anything in particular that she said; it was the way she approached her class. Students who see their teachers study and examine—or even struggle with—ideas are acquiring important ideas that they can apply to their own learning. They see that effort, struggle, and persistence, are positive and desirable.

Enthusiasm is one of the most important things that teachers model. This is intuitively sensible. We react well to enthusiastic people, and we find them attractive and enjoy being around them. Research confirms the effects of enthusiasm on learners. Teachers who present information enthusiastically increase learning, self-confidence, and achievement more than do less enthusiastic teachers (Perry, 1985; Perry, Magnusson, Parsonson, and Dickens, 1986).

How do we demonstrate enthusiasm? Teacher enthusiasm shouldn't include pep talks or unnecessary theatrics; rather, teachers should clearly communicate why they find topics interesting and meaningful to them (Good and Brophy, 2000). Teachers communicate enthusiasm both verbally and nonverbally, using body language and exciting language to communicate their genuine interest in a topic.

Teacher Expectations. To introduce the topic of teacher expectations, consider the following scenario, based on an actual classroom incident.

Mary Willis looked around the room as her fourth graders put away their math books and took out their language arts workbooks. When she saw that all books were out, she said, "Class can I have everyone's eyes up here. . . . Good. Today we're going to learn a new skill, how to alphabetize. This is an important skill that you will use again and again, not only this year, but every year of your life. If you don't know the meaning of a word, it will help you find it in the dictionary. I know that all of you will learn how to do this and we'll practice until we're all good at it. Now let's turn to page 47 in our workbooks and see how we begin."

As the class opened their books, Mary noticed Will leaning forward to poke Steve with his pencil. She walked down the aisle, looked Will in the eye, and asked, "Will, have you found the page yet? Quickly now. This is too important for you to be wasting time monkeying around."

The lesson continued with Mary explaining and modeling the skill at the board and then asking students to come to practice with new lists of words. With each she asked for a show of hands to see who was performing the skill correctly. When she was confident that most students understood, she gave an assignment that all students were to complete before free reading. As they worked on the lists, Mary moved around the room checking papers and answering questions.

Effective teachers clearly communicate their expectations for learning. They *tell* students that something is important, and they explain *why* it's important. They openly communicate that they expect *all* students to learn, as Mary did when she said, "I know that all of you will learn how to do this and we'll practice until we're all good at it."

Sometimes teachers' communication efforts are more subtle. They monitor the class for misbehavior, communicating that it is unacceptable because it interferes with learning, as Mary did when she said, "Quickly now. This is too important for you to be wasting time monkeying around." They provide practice that allows all students to practice new skills and receive feedback. Finally, they communicate positive expectations by holding all students accountable for learning.

Teacher expectations *are the inferences teachers make about students' future academic achievement, behavior, or attitudes* (Good and Brophy, 2000), and they strongly influence teachers' behaviors—and ultimately student learning. Unfortunately, teachers tend to treat students they perceive as high achievers much better than those perceived as lower in ability. This differential treatment occurs in four areas: (1) emotional support, (2) teacher effort and demands, (3) questioning, and (4) feedback and evaluation. These differences are outlined in Table 4.2 (Eggen and Kauchak, 2001; Good and Brophy, 2000).

Do students sense this differential treatment? One study concluded: "After 10 seconds of seeing and/or hearing a teacher, even very young students could detect whether the teacher talked about, or to, an excellent or a weak student, and could determine the extent to which that student was loved by the teacher" (Babad et al., 1991, p. 230). Think about the cumulative effects of different teacher expectations over the course of a school year!

Table 4.2 CHARACTERISTICS OF DIFFERENTIAL TEACHER EXPECTATIONS

Characteristic	Teacher Behaviors Favoring Perceived High Achievers
Emotional support	More interactions; interactions more positive; more smiles; more eye contact; stand closer; orient body more directly; seat students closer to teacher
Teacher effort and demands	Clearer and more thorough explanations; more enthusiastic instruction; more follow-up questions; require more complete and accurate student answers
Questioning	Call on more often; more time to answer; more encouragement; more prompting
Feedback and evaluation	More praise; less criticism; more complete and more lengthy feedback; more conceptual evaluations

Teacher Attitudes, Learner Diversity, and Motivation

As we saw in Chapter 2, our learners are becoming more and more diverse and some feel alienated from school and teachers. Teachers' attitudes toward the differences in learners are crucial in making all learners feel welcome and involved in all aspects of school.

The implications for learning and motivation are clear. We need to demonstrate that we care about and value *all* learners in our classrooms, regardless of gender, culture, ethnicity, socioeconomic status, or ability. Further, we want to communicate appropriately positive and high expectations for every student in our classroom.

We saw some specific ways that teachers communicate caring earlier in the chapter. What else might we do? Research offers some suggestions. One program trained teachers to treat students as equally as possible. They learned to call on all students equally, give equivalent feedback, and maintain positive verbal and nonverbal behavior. The results were dramatic. Researchers found that not only did the achievement level of the students go up, but the number of discipline referrals and absentees went down (Kerman, 1979)!

Based on these research results, we make the following suggestions:

- Make an effort to call on all students equally. This means calling on boys and girls, cultural minorities and nonminorities, high and low achievers, and learners from high and low socioeconomic backgrounds all as equally as possible. Calling on all learners communicates that you *believe* all students are capable learners and you *expect* them to participate and learn.
- When students are unable to respond, rather than redirecting questions to others, prompt them until an acceptable answer is given. This also communicates that you expect all learners to be able to answer.
- When girls, cultural minorities, or low achievers give incorrect answers, provide as much information about why answers are incorrect as you would for boys, nonminorities, or high achievers.
- Make eye contact with all the students, and orient your body directly toward all individuals as you talk to them.
- Change seating arrangements of students in your classes so everyone is periodically near the front. Move around so you are physically near all the students as much as possible.
- Use the "two-minute intervention" (Wlodkowski, 1987) with all students. This means taking a minute or two to discuss something personal with them, such as a question about the family, special interest, or recent accomplishment. As people, we all are pleased when someone pays individual attention to us, and school-aged learners are no exception.

Effective Communication

To this point we have discussed time and positive teacher attitudes. Just as they're important for promoting learning, regardless of grade level, content area, or specific teaching method, effective teachers at all levels communicate clearly.

Let's look at an example.

This mathematics lesson will enab . . . will get you to understand number uh, number patterns. Before we get to the main idea of the, main idea of the lesson, you need to review four concepts . . . four prerequisite concepts (Smith and Land, 1981, p. 38).

While this example seems extreme, it is an actual quote from a teacher. False starts, halting speech, redundant words, and phrases that don't make sense all detract from learning.

Now, let's compare that example with the following:

The purpose of this lesson is to help you understand number patterns. Before we begin the number patterns themselves, however, there are four concepts we want to review. They are . . .

Here the purpose of the lesson is stated clearly and precisely, increasing the likelihood that students will know what the lesson is about and where it's going.

Teachers' language is one of the most widely researched variables in the area of teaching (Cazden, 1986; Dunkin and Biddle, 1974). As evidence has accumulated, a clear link between clarity of language and student achievement has been found (Cruickshank, 1985; Snyder et al., 1991), and effective communication is also linked to positive student attitudes (Hines, Cruickshank, and Kennedy, 1985; Snyder et al., 1991).

But what does clear communication mean? Researchers have identified five components:

- Precise terminology
- Connected discourse
- Transition signals
- Emphasis
- Congruent verbal and nonverbal behavior

Precise Terminology. **Precise terminology** *means that teachers eliminate vague and ambiguous words and phrases in their communications with their students.* For example, researchers have found that vague terms such as *might, a little more, some, usually,* and *probably* detract from learning (Smith and Cotten, 1980). Also, teachers who use vague language are perceived by their students as disorganized, unprepared, and nervous (Smith and Land, 1981).

Connected Discourse. **Connected discourse,** a second element of teacher clarity, *means that the teachers' presentation is logically connected and leads to a point.* By contrast, *scrambled discourse* includes loosely connected ideas that occur when a teacher rambles, interrupts the direction of the lesson by including irrelevant material or sequences the presentation inappropriately.

Compare the two following examples:

We've been studying the countries on the Arabian peninsula as part of our unit on the Middle East. As we know, these countries make most of their money on oil; they were the ones who were most responsible for the Arab embargo that pushed our gas prices up in the 1970s. Venezuela and other oil producers were involved too. That contributed to our inflation rate. These countries also have a problem with water. Most of the people live on the coast or near water, although the holy city of Mecca is inland. Three major religions, Islam, Judaism, and Christianity, have their roots there. The people tend to overextend their water supply, and often there isn't enough water to extract and refine the oil.

We've been studying the countries on the Arabian peninsula as part of our unit on the Middle East and have continually stressed the importance of oil in this area of the world. As we know, these countries make most of their money on oil, which they use to buy goods and services from the western economies. However, as precious as oil is, water looms as even a bigger problem. Most of the people live near water and overextend the available supplies, in some cases even extracting and refining the oil has been hampered by the lack of water.

In the first example the point is uncertain; is the theme the water problem, religion, or the oil embargo? With the added information about Venezuela and the inflation rate, it isn't even clear whether or not the focus is on the Middle East. Though essentially free of vague terms, the presentation is still unclear.

In the second example, the discourse is clear, logically connected, and leads to a point, with increased learning as a result (Smith and Cotten, 1980).

Transition Signals. Teachers also contribute to the clarity of their presentations through clear transition signals (Hines et al., 1985). A **transition signal** *communicates that one idea is ending and another is beginning and explains the link between the two.* Using our illustration with the countries of the Arabian peninsula, a teacher might say, "We've been discussing the problems these countries have with water. Now let's talk about the countries of North Africa and see if the situation is similar," or "We're going to stop talking about the countries on the Arabian peninsula for now, and turn to those in North Africa." In either case, the teacher clearly indicates that a shift in the topic is being made. This signal allows students to mentally structure the content as the lesson develops. Our chapter headings serve the same purpose.

Emphasis

"When you're solving equations remember that whatever you do to one side of the equation, you must also do exactly the same thing to the other side."

We said that one of the characteristics of the Jackson era was the rise of the common man."

These two statements are examples of **emphasis,** *which communicates that an idea or topic has special significance.* It is a form of effective communication that helps students determine the relative importance of the topics they're covering.

Emphasis can be accomplished in four different ways, which are often combined. They are illustrated in Table 4.3.

Research indicates that each form of emphasis increases achievement (Maddox and Hoole, 1975; Mayer, 1983). If there is something in the lesson that is essential for students to learn, we ought to tell them it is important! Emphasis does that.

Congruent Verbal and Nonverbal Behavior. "It's not what you say; it's how you say it." We've all heard this maxim, and it refers to **nonverbal communication,** *which is the*

Table 4.3 **FORMS OF EMPHASIS IN THE CLASSROOM**

Type	Example
Verbal statements	"Be sure to get this," "Now remember . . ."
Nonverbal behaviors	Raised or louder voice Gestures or pointing to specific information
Repetition	"What did Heather say about our first example?"
Written signals	"As you'll see on the board, the three functions of the circulatory system . . ."

part of our messages that we convey without spoken words. Nonverbal channels include the tone, pitch, and loudness of our voices, our gestures, body orientations, facial expressions and eye contact. It even includes our use of space, such as moving close to a student.

Nonverbal communication is important because people assess the sincerity of our motives and attitudes through these channels. For example, modeling, enthusiasm, commitment to teaching, expectations for students, and caring are primarily communicated nonverbally. Even young children are capable of reading and judging the nonverbal messages of teachers (Babad et al., 1991).

It's impossible to communicate clearly if our verbal and nonverbal behaviors are inconsistent. Leroy's conviction that Lorna "thinks this genetics stuff is sooo important," and Clarice's conclusion, "She really tries to help you get it," were based more on Lorna's nonverbal behavior than her words. There is little Lorna could have said to convince her students that biology is important if her nonverbal messages were inconsistent with her words.

Nonverbal behavior is also important in classroom management.

David Inez is helping Tyrone with a problem as the class is doing seatwork. Behind him, Steve and Tony are whispering loudly.

"You boys stop talking and get started on your problems," David says glancing at the boys over his shoulder.

The boys slow their whispering briefly, but don't actually stop, and soon they're at it as loudly as ever.

"I thought I told you to stop talking," David repeats again over his shoulder.

This time Tony and Steve barely slow down. David, his back to the boys, doesn't seem to notice.

What message did David send? His words said stop, but his body language said that he didn't really mean it. He spoke over his shoulder, turned his back to them, and didn't follow through to be sure they actually stopped. David's verbal and nonverbal communication were inconsistent, so his words lacked credibility. This pattern is common for teachers who have classroom management problems.

Effective Communication: Implications for Teachers

The research on effective communication has two important implications for teachers. First, we must thoroughly understand our content, and when our understanding is incomplete or uncertain we need to spend more time studying and preparing. Teachers who fully understand the content they teach use clearer language and their discourse is more connected than those with weaker backgrounds (Carlsen, 1987; Cruickshank, 1985). This makes sense. Teachers with a deep understanding of their content are more likely to use precise language, present ideas logically, and emphasize appropriate points. They model enthusiasm and confidence, and their students feel more confident as a result.

Second, we should try to monitor our own communication—literally listen to ourselves talk as we teach—to try to be as clear and concise as possible. Seeing ourselves on videotape can be eye opening. Even veteran teachers are often surprised when they see and hear themselves on tape. Other processes, such as peer coaching, where a colleague observes a portion of a lesson and provides feedback, can be very helpful (Glickman, 1990). Whatever the method, the increase in clarity (and student learning) is worth the effort.

Organization

The term *organization,* as with time, is one that we use in discussing both teaching and our everyday lives: "I've got to get organized," "My new year's resolution is to be better organized this year," "He would be good at the job, but he is so disorganized." These are familiar-sounding statements, and we all struggle to be better organized. We write lists; we arrange elaborate filing systems that we don't use; we pick up the same piece of paper several times before we do anything with it. Each example underscores the fact that organization seems quite simple but in reality can be a major stumbling block to efficiency. This is particularly true in classrooms.

Earlier in the chapter we saw that Steve Weiss, an eighth-grade science teacher, used more of his available time for instruction than his colleague, Dennis Orr. This was primarily the result of more effective organization. A comparison reveals three important differences between the two, which are outlined in Table 4.4.

In examining these differences, we see that each aspect of organization increases instructional time, which both increases learning and reduces classroom management

Table 4.4 CHARACTERISTICS OF EFFECTIVE ORGANIZATION

Aspect of Organization	Example
Starting on time	Steve Weiss began class when the bell stopped ringing. Dennis Orr moved to the front of the room after several minutes.
Materials prepared in advance	Steve's demonstration was prepared in advance. Dennis finished preparing his demonstration while the students waited.
Established routines	Steve's students knew what to do when they came to class. Dennis had to tell his students how to get started.

problems (Emmer et al. 2000; Evertson et al., 2000). Organization is so important that we return to it in Chapter 6 in our discussion of classroom management.

Having looked at the characteristics of effective teachers, let's see what research tells us about the ways effective teachers begin, develop, and end their lessons.

EFFECTIVE LESSON BEGINNINGS

An effective lesson introduction draws students into the lesson, focuses their attention on the topic, and relates the new material to content they already understand. Let's see how this occurs.

Review

Review *examines information that has been covered in earlier lessons, activates learners' background knowledge, and sets the stage for the new topic.* Research examining the way students learn helps us understand the value of reviews. When we learn new information, we interpret it based on what we already know (Eggen and Kauchak, 2001): "People are not recorders of information but builders of knowledge structures. To know something is not just to have received information but also to have interpreted and related it to other knowledge" (Resnick & Klopfer, 1989, p. 4).

Review helps learners determine what they already know, which then provides an anchor for the new information to come. Let's look at an example:

Ken Thomas has begun a unit on the Crusades and wants to examine their effects on the Western World. He begins his lesson by saying, "We've been discussing the Crusades, Let's think for a moment now about what we learned yesterday. First, identify some reasons the Crusades occurred in the first place. David?"

Dorothy Williams's students have studied gerunds and participles and now she wants to move to infinitives. She begins her lesson by saying, "We talked about gerunds and participles yesterday. Give me an example of each. Jeff?"

In both cases, the teachers used the students' existing understanding as the framework for the day's lesson. Students can then connect the new learning to the old—Dorothy's students related infinitives to gerunds and participles, for example—which makes both more meaningful.

Focus

Focus *is the process teachers use to attract and maintain students' attention during a learning activity.* For instance, rather than merely saying, "Today we're going to discuss the northern and southern colonies," Kathy Johnson introduced her lesson by referring to the chart and saying, "Now, that brings up some questions. . . . How are these states different, and why, since all these states are part of the same country—our United States—why are they so different? . . . That's what we're going to try and figure out today. If we work hard, I'll bet we can come up with some really important ideas. . . . Everybody ready? . . . let's go."

By introducing her lesson with her chart and questions to be answered during the lesson, Kathy provided an effective form of focus.

Let's look at some additional examples.

As an introduction to the topic of cities and where they are located, Jim Edwards, a fifth-grade teacher, passed out a map of a fictitious island. On it were physical features such as lakes, rivers, mountains, and bays. The map also included the latitude, prevailing winds, ocean currents, and rainfall for the island. He began, "We have been sent to this island to settle it. Based on the information we have here, we need to decide what would be the best place to start our first settlement."

Susan Wood began a unit on heat and atmospheric pressure with her science students by putting a cup of water in an empty duplicating fluid can, heating the can with a hot plate, and capping it. As the students watched, the can collapsed, almost "magically." Susan then commented, "Now keep what you saw in mind, and we'll be able to figure out why it happened as we study this unit."

Jessie Andrews began his math lesson on percentages by displaying the following question on an overhead: "Who's the best hitter in baseball today?" After a number of opinions had been offered by students, Jessie continued, "Do you want to learn one way to find out? Let's look at percentages and see how they can tell us who is the best hitter."

We see in each of the examples that the teachers provided students with something to see, which helped attract their attention. (While something to see is most powerful, something to hear, feel, smell, or even taste, can also be used effectively.) The need for something sensory to attract attention is based on cognitive learning theory (Eggen and Kauchak, 2001); all learning depends on the extent to which students pay attention to important information in the lesson.

A variety of techniques can be used as forms of focus. For instance, a series of sentences on the chalkboard or equations on an overhead projector would work in an English or algebra class. In addition, outlines, hierarchies, or objectives are also effective.

When visual forms of sensory focus are used, writing the information on the board or displaying it on an overhead projector is more effective than the same information given to students on individual sheets. If students are looking down at their desks, the teacher can't tell if they're looking at the sheet or are looking down because they are not paying attention. When the focus is at the front of the room, the teacher can monitor students' attention through eye contact, which is one of the most effective ways to assess student engagement.

Using Focus to Increase Student Motivation. Researchers have found that *curiosity* can be a powerful source of intrinsic motivation in learners (Lepper and Hodell, 1989). Some of the best forms of focus capitalize on the effects of curiosity to grab and hold students' attention. Teachers can capitalize on the effects of curiosity in at least three different ways:

- Presenting information or ideas that are discrepant from their present understanding or beliefs and that appear surprising or incongruous
(Pintrich and Schunk, 1996)

- Asking paradoxical questions
- Presenting ideas in concrete form

For example, a teacher might have students hold two pieces of paper parallel to each other and blow between them. Because of Bernoulli's principle (the principle that helps us understand how airplanes are able to fly), the papers come together instead of moving apart. This event is surprising and inconsistent with learners' expectations.

In another case, a teacher might ask, "Why have most of the powerful civilizations throughout history eventually collapsed and ceased to remain powerful?" or as Kathy Johnson asked, "Why, since all these states are part of the same country—our United States—why are they so different?" She purposely worded her question in a paradoxical way in an attempt to increase her students' intrinsic motivation.

As another example, imagine the attention-getting power of bringing someone's pet snake, guinea pig, or hamster to class during a science lesson. Each would be much more effective than drawings or even colored pictures in arousing interest.

Planning for increasing learner motivation doesn't have to be difficult or labor intensive. Asking a student to bring a hamster to class is simple, for example, and Kathy's question required nothing more than some thought. Despite this simplicity, many problems with students' inattention and lack of motivation can be traced directly to lack of focus at the beginning of a lesson. Effective focus is not a panacea, of course, but it can make an important contribution to student motivation and, in turn, learning.

DEVELOPING THE LESSON

To begin this section, go back to Kathy's lesson. Recall that she asked her students why the northern and southern states should have been so different, since they were all part of the United States. Let's see how she develops the lesson.

"Now, before we start trying to answer our questions, Where are all these states compared to where we live? . . . Jo?"

" . . . They're over here," Jo answered, motioning to the right with her hand.

"Yes, they're generally east of us," Kathy added, as she walked quickly and pointed to the map at the side of the room, identifying the general location of the states relative to their location with a wave of her hand. "As we look at our chart, keep the map in mind to remind yourselves about where we are and where these states are.

"And about how long ago are we talking about, a few years or a long time? . . . Greg?" she continued.

"A long time. Like when our great-great grandfathers and grandmothers might have lived, I think," Greg responded hesitantly.

"At least," Kathy smiled and nodded. "We're talking about time during the early and middle 1800s."

"We also talked about some important ideas, like 'economy,' " Kathy continued. "What do we mean by economy? . . . Carol?"

" . . . It's . . . the way they make money, like when we said that the economy here is based on manufacturing, like making cars and stuff and stuff for cars," Carol responded haltingly.

"Good idea, Carol," Kathy waved. "You identified auto manufacturing as an important part of our economy, and that's a good example."

"Now, look here," Kathy directed, pointing to the column marked 'Economy.' I want you to work with your partner and I want you to write down at least three things that are different about the economy in the North compared to the economy in the South. . . . You have 4 minutes. Ready? . . . Go ahead."

The students, seated next to their partners, turned to each other and began working. The classroom quickly became a buzz of voices and questions, such as, "How many differences?" "Three differences?" "Is like fishing in the North different from the South? There's no fishing there," "Big farms and small farms is a difference, isn't it?" and many others.

Kathy patiently answered their questions among comments of encouragement and admonitions to work quickly, since they didn't have much time.

At the end of the 4 minutes, Kathy said, "All right everyone, look up here. . . . Let's see what we have. . . . Go ahead. Does some group want to respond? . . . Go ahead, Ann Marie."

" . . . The farms were big in the South but they were little in the North."

"Okay, good observation," Kathy nodded energetically. "Now why might that have been the case? Jim?"

" . . . "

" . . . Would you like me to repeat the question?" Kathy asked, knowing that Jim had not heard her.

"Yes," Jim responded quickly, with a look of relief.

"Why might the farms have been so much bigger in the South than in the North?"

" . . . They . . . had good soil in the South, but poor soil in the North," Jim said slowly, peering intently at the chart.

"Good, Jim," Kathy smiled. "Any other possible reason, anyone?"

" . . . They had mountains in the North," Nataly volunteered after looking at the chart for several seconds. . . .You can't farm the mountains."

"Excellent," Kathy nodded. "Let's look at another difference. . . . Go ahead, Stephanie."

Kathy continued guiding the students' analysis of the information on the chart, in the process finding relationships between the geography, climate, and economy. When students were unable to answer, she rephrased her questions and provided cues to help them along. She then had them consider why the economy of their city might be the way it is.

Now, let's consider this portion of Kathy's lesson and analyze what made it effective. There are three important aspects of lesson development.

- The way content is represented
- The extent to which learners are involved
- The kinds of practice and feedback learners are given

Because these ideas are so essential and interrelated, we devote all of the next chapter to them.

ENDING LESSONS EFFECTIVELY

An effective lesson ending brings closure to the lesson, wrapping up loose threads and preparing students for future learning. To begin this section, let's return once more to Kathy's work with her students.

"You have done very well, everyone," Kathy smiled, pointing her finger in the air for emphasis. "Now, everyone, get with your partner again, take 2 minutes and write three summary statements about what we've learned here today. . . . Quickly now, get started."

As earlier in the lesson, the classroom quickly became a buzz of voices as her students started peering and pointing at the chart, then began writing. In some cases they stopped, crumpled their papers and began again. As they worked, Kathy walked among them offering encouragement and periodic suggestions.

At the end of 2 minutes Kathy announced, "One more minute, and we're going to look at what you've written.

"Okay, let's see what you've got," she continued. "What did you and Linda conclude, David?"

" . . . We said that the weather and the land had a lot to do with the way the different states made their money."

"Excellent! That's good. How about someone else? . . . Danielle, how about you and Tony?"

Kathy had several other pairs offer their summary statements, they further developed the statements as a whole group, and then Kathy collected the papers.

At 11:28 she announced, "Almost lunchtime. Please put away your papers."

The students quickly put their books, papers, and pencils away, glanced around their desks for any waste paper, and were sitting quietly at 11:30.

Just as effective lessons begin by drawing students into the activity and providing a reference frame for new material, effective lessons end by tying the different parts of the lesson together and assessing students' understanding. Closure encourages students to summarize the major ideas in the lesson, and assessment tells both the teacher and students what has been learned and what needs further work.

Closure

"We're near the end of the period, so we'll stop here and pick it up tomorrow."

"That's all for now. Put your stuff away and get ready for lunch."

We have reviewed previous material, have provided an attention-getting lesson beginning, and have carefully developed the lesson with high levels of student involvement and appropriate feedback. The positive effects of these efforts are diminished, however, if we abruptly end the lesson, as we see in the two examples above.

Closure *is the process of summarizing a topic and preparing for future learning.* Closure allows students to leave the class with a sense of the day's content and what they were supposed to have derived from it. It also provides a springboard for their further study at home.

Closure is important because learners instinctively structure information into patterns that make sense to them (Carnine, 1990). If they leave a learning experience with uncertainties, the ideas they intuitively form may be invalid, and because new learning builds on old, these misconceptions can detract from future learning.

The notion of closure is common and intuitively sensible. Perhaps you have even used the term in a conversation, saying something like, "Let's try and get to 'closure' on this."

Let's look at another classroom example.

Mary Eng had developed the process for factoring the difference of two squares in her Algebra I class. She noted, "It's near the end of the period, so let's go over what we've covered so far. First, give me an example that is the difference of two squares. . . . Katilya."

In finishing a lesson on "main idea," Harry Soo said, "Class, I want you now to tell me in your own words what the main idea of a story is. Define it for me."

Teresa Bon had finished a lesson relating the pitch of a sound to the length, thickness, and tension of the object producing the sound. She completed her lesson by saying, "Now let's write a statement that tells us in one sentence what we've found today."

Asking students for additional examples of the ideas they've studied or forming a definition or summary can all be used to tie the different pieces of the lesson together. Research indicates that each of these forms of closure increases learning (Tennyson and Cocciarella, 1986). We will discuss specific forms of closure in more detail in Chapters 7–11, where we present specific teaching strategies.

Assessment

"They seem to be able to solve percent increase problems, but I wonder if they really understand how these are different from percent decrease problems."

"Most of them are getting some ideas down on paper, but they don't seem to elaborate very well. I wonder if I should work more on that, or if I should start having them work a little harder now on the mechanics of their grammar?"

"The homework looked good on solving density problems, but how many of them just put the numbers in the formula without knowing what they were doing?"

These are valid questions. Teachers are constantly asking themselves if their students really "get it." They're determining how fast they can cover the content, identifying problems and misconceptions, and deciding whether or not they should go on to the next topic. Assessment helps teachers answer these questions.

Assessment *is the process of gathering information and making instructional decisions based on the information.* Its purpose is to gauge learner progress and provide feedback for both the teacher and students. It can take several different forms, such as:

- Seatwork and homework exercises
- Observations of student performance
- Answers to teachers' questions
- Samples of student work
- Quizzes and tests

We examine the assessment process in detail in Chapter 12.

This completes our examination of the general instructional model. The model is designed to serve as a framework for the content of Chapters 5 through 11. Our hope is that the information presented here will serve as a foundation for your study of those chapters.

Summary

Classroom Climate: A Prerequisite to Learning. A positive climate invites students into your classroom, communicates that they are valued as individuals, and focuses on learning. Students need to know that they are accepted and that their teachers care for each of them individually.

Positive classroom environments are safe and orderly; students cannot learn as much as possible when their classmates are disruptive.

Classrooms with a positive climate focus on learning. While social development and extracurricular activities are important, they don't take precedent over learning. Teachers who focus on learning provide students with tasks that they find interesting, meaningful, and challenging.

Effective Teaching and the Concept of Time. A major thrust of the chapter is captured with the question: If we watch effective teachers regardless of grade level, content area, or topic, what would we expect to see? One answer to the question lies in their use of time—they allocate their time wisely, they limit the time spent on non-instructional activities, and they design learning activities in which students are engaged and successful.

A General Instructional Model. The general instructional model includes teacher characteristics together with the features of effective lesson beginnings, well-designed lesson development, and clear lesson endings.

Characteristics of Effective Teachers. Effective teachers display personal characteristics that promote student learning. They care about their students, they are high in personal teaching efficacy, they have high expectations for learning, and they are positive and enthusiastic models.

In addition, effective teachers communicate with clear language, logical presentations, appropriate emphasis, and consistent verbal and nonverbal behaviors.

Effective teachers are also well organized. They begin learning activities promptly, have materials prepared in advance, and have well-established, time-saving routines.

Effective Lesson Beginnings. Effective teachers begin their lessons with reviews of previous work; this activates students' background knowledge and helps them connect new topics to content they already know. They also plan for student motivation, hoping to capture and maintain student attention.

Developing the Lesson. As their lessons are developed, effective teachers represent content by using a variety of examples and applications while maintaining high levels of student involvement. They provide students with accurate feedback about their progress and provide practice to reinforce learning.

Ending Lessons Effectively. Effective teachers end their lessons with a thorough review to summarize the topics they've studied, and they have a well developed assessment system to provide information about learning progress.

Important Concepts

Academic learning time
Allocated time
Assessment
Caring
Classroom climate
Closure
Connected discourse
Emphasis
Engaged time
Focus

Instructional time
Modeling
Nonverbal communication
Personal teaching efficacy
Precise terminology
Relatedness
Review
Teacher expectations
Teacher effectiveness research
Transition signal

Reflecting on Teaching and Learning

Dan Kaiser, a veteran with fifteen years of experience teaching social studies, is sitting over a cup of coffee in the teachers' lounge on a Thursday. He is moving into a unit on Ancient Greece and the Age of Pericles in his world history classes, and he is working on his planning.

"You look deep in thought," Ann Stoddard, one of his colleagues, comments, seeing him hunched over his work. "You must be studying the sports page."

"Yeah, right," he nods. "That would be a heck of a lot more fun than what I'm actually doing. . . . Seriously, I'm starting ancient Greece on Monday, and the kids hate it. I want them to understand how Greece has impacted us in modern Western civilization, but they think it's about funny old people wearing sheets. . . . I know it's tough for them, but I think this stuff is important. . . . They always have a hard time with it."

We rejoin Dan on the following Monday. The bell rings at 9:35, signaling the beginning of third period as the last of the students scurry through the door to beat the tardy bell.

"Get to your seats quickly, now," Dan calls over his shoulder. "Andrew, you're just about late. . . . Settle down, and we'll get started."

As the students talk while getting settled, Dan shuffles through the materials on his desk, looking for the transparency he prepared over the weekend.

"All right, settle down," Dan says again to some of the students at the back of the room who are talking, as he adjusts the overhead.

At 9:42 he displays the transparency with an outline of the unit on it. "We're going to be studying ancient Greece during this week," he comments. "We'll look at some of the great thinkers and the great ideas of the age. We'll refer to the outline as we go along. Have paper and pencil ready, because you need to take careful notes on this information."

Dan then begins by identifying and describing some of the main historical figures of the period, such as Socrates, Plato, and Aristotle. As he begins, most of the students are looking at him, but as he continues, several start looking out the window or down at their desks. A few are busily writing notes.

"Did you know," Dan asks with a slight smile, moving over to sit on a stool at the front of the room, "that Socrates in some ways was sort of shiftless? He was often in trouble with his wife because he wouldn't work; he wanted to spend his time talking to his students about whatever."

As he proceeds with his description of Socrates' problems at home, some of the students who were looking away turn back to the front of the room.

Dan continues, telling the class that the Greeks have had a major influence on today's language, thinking, culture and architecture. As he talks, he writes terms on the board, such as "Language influence," "Cultural influence," and "Influence on architecture." Some of the students continue taking notes; others seem somewhat listless.

"Let's slow down for a second," Dan suggests, " . . . and see what you know about Greece. . . . Where is it located? . . . Juanita?"

" . . . Sort of over there," she says, pointing toward the map of Europe Dan has hanging on the side of the room. "Over there, sort of by Italy."

"Okay," Dan responds, stepping down from the stool and moving over to point to the map to confirm the location. "What is its capital? . . . Calvin?"

"Got me," Calvin shrugs.

"Anyone?"

"Athens," Jerome calls out from the side of the room.

Dan continues for a few more minutes, asking questions such as, "What are some famous Greek plays?" "What is the geography of Greece like?" and "What is the name of a famous Greek landmark?"

Some of the students eagerly try to respond, whereas others appear disinterested. The answers to most of the questions come from a relatively small group of students.

Dan then continues presenting additional information about the geography of Greece, pointing out that Athens was a thriving commercial center, which allowed trade with other parts of the known world at the time and which helped it become a center of intellectual activity.

Again, after a few minutes, he notices the inattention of several of the students and comments, "You know, I've given you an awful lot of information. Let's slow down again. Based on what I've told you thus far, what do you personally find most interesting about the ancient Greeks?"

Several students offer comments, although they tend to be the same ones who had answered the earlier questions. Two of them get into a slight argument over whether or not the Greeks had slaves. Dan waves his hand to stop the argument and tells them that the Greeks did indeed have slaves.

Seeing that there are only 10 minutes left in the period, Dan says, "There are just 10 minutes left, so we'll stop here for today. . . . I have your papers here from last week. If you have any questions on the papers, see me."

He then returns papers the students had written for an earlier unit. Each has a letter grade on the front of it. The students quickly scan the papers and put them in their notebooks. He then tells the students to talk quietly among themselves until the bell rings.

Questions for Analysis

Let's analyze Dan's lesson now in the context of the information in the chapter. In completing your analysis, you may want to consider the following questions. In responding to the questions, be specific and take information directly from the case study to document your conclusions.

1. In Chapter 3, we discussed the concept of *instructional alignment.* To what extent was Dan's instruction aligned? Defend your comments with information taken directly from the case study.
2. Analyze Dan's organization. Was it effective? What could he have done to make it more effective? Provide evidence to support your response.
3. Based on the discussion of instruction and motivation in the chapter, how effective were Dan's attempts to motivate the students? What could he have done to make the lesson more motivating?
4. How effective was Dan's lesson beginning? What could he have done to make the beginning more effective?
5. How effectively did Dan develop the content of his lesson? What could he have done to develop it more effectively?
6. How effective was Dan's lesson ending? What could he have done to improve the effectiveness of the lesson ending?
7. Now provide an overall assessment of Dan's lesson. If you believe the lesson could have been made more effective, offer specific suggestions for doing so.

Discussion Questions

1. Some authorities suggest lengthening the school day or school year, supporting their position by citing the relationship between allocated time and achievement. How would you respond to these people? What are some arguments for and against this approach to increasing learning?
2. In research studies, engagement is often inferred from the expressions and actions of students. What are some behaviors that suggest student engagement? Lack of engagement? What are some problems involved in inferring attention from behavior?
3. The ideal engagement rate is, of course, 100 percent. What is a realistic engagement rate for students you work with? (Estimate a percentage.) How does this engagement rate vary with the type of students? Time of day? Different times within the same class period? What can be done to increase engagement rates? What factors outside the teacher's control will affect student engagement rates?
4. This chapter focused on enthusiasm from a teacher perspective. What are some indicators of students enthusiasm? lack of enthusiasm? Are these low- or high-inference behaviors?
5. Are positive teacher attitudes more important at some grade levels than others? Why? In some curriculum areas and/or content areas? Why?
6. Review the findings on teacher expectations with respect to teacher effort and questioning behaviors. What might be some explanations for the reason teachers treat high achievers and low achievers differently in terms of these two categories of behaviors?
7. The model of teaching described in this chapter is teacher centered. For what kinds of goals is a teacher-centered most desirable? Least desirable?

Portfolio Activities

1. *Allocated Time.* Contact several teachers teaching at the same grade level or in the same content areas. If they are elementary teachers, ask them how much time they devote to different subject matter areas, and if they are middle or secondary teachers, to topics within their content area. Ask them why they have decided on these allocations. Bring the information back to class. Compare the rationales these teachers offer to those uncovered by researchers (e.g., how much they like the area or topic, how much preparation it requires, and how difficult they perceive it to be for their students). Finally, describe what you personally believe to be an optimal time allocation plan for the grade or subject, and justify your answer.

2. *Instructional Time.* Observe (or tape) a complete lesson and note the amount of time spent in each of the categories below.

LESSON SEGMENT	AMOUNT OF TIME SPENT
a. Introduction to lesson	
b. Development (main part of lesson)	
c. Summary	
d. Seatwork or practice	
e. Total	

   Analyze the use of instructional time in the lesson. In your analysis, discuss the following factors:

   - Context (type of school, grade level, characteristics of the students)
   - Pace (Did the lesson move too fast or too slow?)
   - Student reactions to the lesson

3. *Student Engagement.* In this exercise, you will be measuring student engagement through a time-sampling technique. Select four students to observe, two high-achieving and two low-achieving (ask the teacher for help in selecting the students), and seat yourself so that you can observe their faces during the lesson. Focus on each student at 15-second intervals and decide whether the student was attending to the lesson. A *Y* indicates yes, an *N* indicates no, and a question mark indicates that you cannot tell. At the end of the 20-minute observation period, compute averages for each student and the group as a whole.

	STUDENT A	STUDENT B	STUDENT C	STUDENT D
Minute 1				
Minute 2				
Minute 3				
. . .				
Minute 20				

   a. Were the engagement rates similar for each student? If they varied, suggest a reason why.

   b. Did the engagement rates vary during the course of the presentation? If so, why?

   c. Were there any specific teacher behaviors that appeared to produce high or low engagement rates? Explain.

d. Were the engagement rates for the high- and low-achieving students different?

e. Observe the same students for three days and see if any patterns emerge.

f. Observe several classes (or subjects) taught by the same teacher and see if engagement rates are similar.

g. Select students who are physically close to where the teacher spends most of his or her time during lessons and compare engagement rates with those of students farther away.

h. Does the type of activity influence student engagement rates? Find out when the teacher is going to be using two different types of lessons and observe students during each.

i. Compare your responses with your classmates. How can you use engagement rates to improve your effectiveness as a teacher?

4. *Success Rates.* Observe (or tape) a lesson during an interactive teaching session and count the number of questions asked, the number answered correctly, the number answered correctly with prompting, and the number answered incorrectly or not at all. Comment on the success rate in terms of what you have learned in this chapter.

5. *Verbal and Nonverbal Behavior.* This exercise investigates the relative amounts of information gained from verbal and nonverbal channels. Have a class first observe a videotape of a teacher teaching a lesson with the sound off; then turn the volume on and watch the tape again. As you listen to and watch the videotape, list the nonverbal behaviors that give you clues about the following characteristics:

a. Teacher warmth and empathy

b. Enthusiasm

c. Modeling

d. Expectations

Were there any instances when the two separate channels produced incongruent messages? How can you use nonverbal communication to improve your effectiveness as a teacher?

6. *Enthusiasm.* Identify an "enthusiastic" college teacher by asking your fellow students. Obtain permission to sit in on a class, situating yourself so that you can also observe students. Analyze the teacher's behavior using Collins's (1978) operational definitions listed here. You will find that you are often inferring some dimension rather than directly observing precise behaviors. This reaction is characteristic of a concept like enthusiasm, which is a high-inference measure.

Varied vocal delivery _____

_____

Animated eyes, eyebrows, eye contact _____

Head, arms, body gestures _____

Body movement, position change _____

Demonstrative facial expressions _____

_____

Descriptive word selection _____

Acceptance of ideas _____

Based on these findings, to what extent should enthusiasm be a concern for you as a teacher?

7. *Effective Communication.* Make a videotape of yourself teaching a lesson. Then watch the tape and note when vague, ambiguous terms; mazes; and other distracting speech mannerisms occur. Is there any pattern to their occurrence? Do more of them occur at the beginning or end of a lesson? Do transitions or interruptions affect these speech mannerisms? If possible, teach another lesson to the same group and try to eliminate these distractors. What did you learn about yourself from analyzing yourself on tape?

8. *Student Involvement.* This exercise examines patterns of interaction in a classroom. Observe a class during an interactive teaching session after sketching a seating chart with boxes large enough to allow you to put numbers in them. Code the teacher's first interaction with a student with a 1 in that student's square. The second student called on gets a 2, the third a 3, and so on. You now have a running tally of who got called on and in what order.

   Is there any pattern to the interactions? Do all students participate? Does location make a difference? Is there any pattern to the sequence of interactions? Discuss your analysis in terms of the teacher expectations research.

9. *Feedback.* Observe a class or make an audiotape of a lesson you have taught. Using the following instrument, note the kind of feedback that follows students' responses to questions for a 10-minute segment of interactive teaching. Then answer the questions that follow.

	QUESTION	STUDENT ANSWER	TEACHER RESPONSE
1.			
2.			
3.			
4.			
5.			
6.			
7.			
8.			
9.			
10.			

   a. What is the most common form of teacher response to a student answer?

   b. Does the teacher verbally acknowledge every response? If not, what effect does this appear to have on students?

   c. How does the teacher deal with either an incomplete or partial response?

   How could the use of feedback be modified to improve student learning?

5

Increasing Learning Through Student Involvement

CHAPTER OUTLINE

*I*n Chapter 4 we summarized the research describing effective teaching in a general model that applies to nearly any teaching situation. In looking back at the model, we see that *student involvement* is an essential part of the lesson development phase.

Research thoroughly documents the relationship between student involvement and learning (Eggen and Kauchak, 2001; Lambert and McCombs, 1998), and your own experiences will corroborate its importance as well. In which do you learn more, classes in which you're asked questions and are actively involved in learning activities, or those in which the teacher gives long lectures as students sit passively? In the latter, many learners—including college students—become inattentive in a matter of minutes.

Because student involvement is so essential for learning, we are devoting this entire chapter to the topic. When you've completed your study, you should be able to meet the following goals:

- Explain why clear goals are essential for student involvement.
- Create representations of content that promote interest and understanding.
- Identify the elements of effective teacher questioning.
- Explain how teacher questioning can be used to increase learner motivation.
- Explain how teacher questioning can be used to accommodate learners with diverse backgrounds.

José Alvarez is a fourth-grade teacher with a class of 30 students ranging widely in ability. The class is labeled average and is composed primarily of lower- to lower-middle-class students. Keith, Tyrone, Latisha, Jason, and Ginny are the five lowest achievers in his group.

José typically teaches science for 30 minutes each day. In this lesson, he wanted his students to understand that heat makes substances expand by increasing the movement of molecules and making the molecules move apart. The students had studied molecules in earlier lessons, so they had a basic understanding of their characteristics.

He began his activity by displaying two soft drink bottles with balloons covering them, and a coffee pot two-thirds full of hot water, as shown in Figure 5.1.

"Now look at these bottles," he began as he held them up. "What can you tell us about them? . . . Keith?"

"You drink out of them."

"Fine, Keith. . . . Beverly?"

"They're sort of green."

"Yes, they are," José smiled. "What else? . . . Lavonia?"

" . . . They look like they're the same size."

"Yes, indeed. They certainly do. Very good, Lavonia."

"What's in the bottles? . . . Nikki?" he went on.

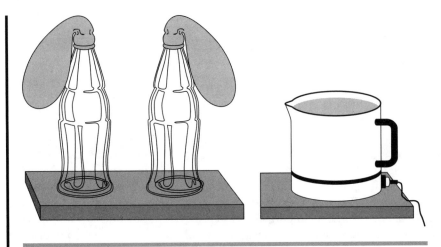

Figure 5.1 Bottles with Balloons on Top

"They're empty."

"Wave your hand in front of your face, Nikki," José prompted. "What do you feel?"

" . . . I . . . feel the air on my face."

"Yes!" he exclaimed. "So what do you think might be in the bottles?"

" . . . Air?"

"Yes indeed. Good conclusion, Nikki. What was one of the characteristics of air that we've discussed? . . . Christy?"

"It's all around us," Jason interjected.

"That's right. Air is all around us. Well done, Jason."

"Now look at the balloons on these bottles," José went on, holding the bottles up again.

"How would you compare the balloons? . . . Leroy?"

"One is red and the other is yellow."

"Yes. Good, Leroy. What else? . . . Rachel?"

"They look like they're made out of rubber."

"Yes, they *are* rubber balloons. How would you compare their sizes? . . . Michael?"

"They look like they're the same size."

"Good, Michael. They are the same size.

"Now look at the balloons and bottles, everyone," he continued. "What did Lavonia say about the bottles themselves? . . . Cliff?"

"We drink out of them."

"Yes, we do," José smiled. "How do the sizes compare? . . . Alfredo?"

"They're the same."

"Good, Alfredo. We said they were the same size. And how about the balloons? . . . Linda?"

"They were the same size, too?"

"And what is in the bottles? . . . Steve?"

"Air."

"So, now what do we know about the amount of air in each system? Kathy?"

" . . . "

"How did the two bottles compare?"

"They're the same size."

"So, what does that suggest about the amount of air in each. "It's the same.""

"And how do we know, Tyrone?"

" . . . "

"What did we say about the sizes of the balloons and bottles? . . . Tyrone?"

" . . . They . . . were . . . equal."

"Good," José nodded. "So how do we know the amount of air in each is the same?"

" . . . The bottles and balloons . . . are the same size."

"Yes, Tyrone. Good thinking."

"Now watch what I do." José said, scanning the room and placing one of the bottles in the coffee pot. Then he asked, "And what did we say about the amount of air in each of the systems, everyone?"

"IT IS THE SAME," everyone shouted in unison.

"Just watch now," he said with anticipation.

As the students watched, the balloon began to slowly rise above the bottle placed in the hot water, as shown in Figure 5.2.

The students began to giggle as they watched. As the balloon popped up, the students were laughing openly, and José laughed with them.

"Now," he said, taking advantage of their interest, "work with your partner, and make as many comparisons as you can of the two bottles. As always, write them down. Work quickly now. You have 3 minutes."

Figure 5.2 Bottles with Expanded Balloon

The students, all of whom were sitting next to their partners, turned to each other and immediately went to work. In seconds, a hum of activity could be heard throughout the room as the students began talking, pointing at the two bottles and balloons, and writing statements on their papers. José walked among them as they worked, periodically stopping to make brief comments to individual pairs.

"Okay, everyone, all eyes up here," José directed at the end of the 3 minutes. He paused a few seconds as the groups stopped their writing and turned their attention to him.

"Good, everyone," he smiled. "Let's see what you came up with. Give us one of your comparisons. Judy?"

"The bottles are the same size."

"Yes, the size of the bottles hasn't changed," José responded, smiling. "And what else? . . . Jim and Latisha?"

"The red balloon is sticking up," Latisha answered for the pair.

"And what else? . . . Stacy and Albert?"

"We think that the amount of the air has increased in the first bottle," Stacy answered.

"Interesting thought," José smiled. "Now, when you mean *amount* of air, do you mean volume or do you mean mass? . . . Think about it for a moment, everyone. . . . Okay, what do you think?"

"We think volume."

"Great! Super thinking," José enthused. "Outstanding work. . . . Now, how do the masses compare? What did you and Leroy come up with there? . . . Robin?"

" . . . We think the masses are still the same."

"Excellent thinking again," José smiled and shook his head. "Boy, you people are sharp today."

"Now, let's look at some other things," he continued. "Jim and Latisha said the red balloon was sticking up. Why do you suppose it is sticking up? Mike?"

"It was heated," Mike responded quickly.

"How do we know it was heated? . . . Ginny?"

" . . . I, er, I didn't hear the question," she answered sheepishly.

"What did I do with this bottle, Ginny?" he asked, holding up the bottle with the red balloon.

"You put it in the coffee pot."

"Yes I did, Ginny. Good. And how do we know the coffee pot was hot? . . . Rosemary?"

"I saw steam coming off from it."

"Very good observation, Rosemary," he smiled. "So what can we say happened to the balloon? . . . Jill?"

"It stuck up."

"What else might we say?" he continued, forming semicircles with his hands and spreading them apart.

Hesitantly, Jill responded, "It got bigger."

"Yes, excellent, Jill. Now, everyone, I'm going to give you another word for gets bigger. It's called *expand*. Everyone say *expand*."

"EXPAND!" they all shouted in unison.

"So what happens when we heat something? . . . Deandra?"

"It expands," Deandra responded instantly.

"And what expanded in this case? . . . Toni?"

"The balloon."

"And what else?"

" . . . "

"What is in the bottles and balloons?"

"Air," Toni blurted out.

"Good. So what is expanding in addition to the balloon?"

"The air!" Toni proclaimed.

"Yes! The air is expanding. And what did we say made that happen? . . . Keith?"

"We heated the bottle?"

"So now let's make a statement about heat and expansion. Give it a try. . . . Gary?"

" . . . "

"What does heat do to things?"

" . . . It makes them expand," Gary answered finally.

"Good! Now let's write that down." With that, José wrote the statement on the board as he had the class repeat it.

José then brought out two drawings (see Figure 5.3). He established with the students that the arrows in the drawings were there to help visualize the direction of movement of the air molecules, and the marks that looked like parentheses around the dots were there to help visualize the motion of the molecules (two sets of parentheses suggesting that the molecules were moving faster than one set of parentheses). He also led students to conclude that the drawing on the left represented the bottle that had been put into the hot water.

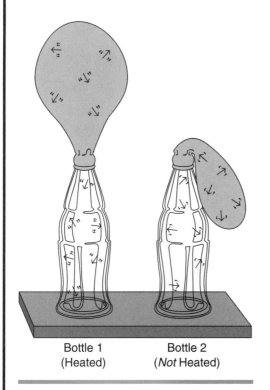

Bottle 1
(Heated)

Bottle 2
(*Not* Heated)

Figure 5.3 Drawings with Molecules

José continued, "Now work again with your partner. As you did with the actual bottles, again make as many comparisons as you can about the two drawings, and write them down. You have 2 minutes. Go ahead right now."

Again, the students quickly began talking, pointing at the drawings, and writing on their papers.

At the end of the 2 minutes, José announced, "Okay, stop. Everyone, eyes on me."

The students quickly stopped working and turned their attention to the front of the room. José began, "Good, now give us a comparison. . . . Roy and Barbara?"

"The molecules in number one are moving faster than the ones in number two."

"Good! And what did we do to the air in number one? . . . Della and Jim?"

"We heated it!" Della nearly shouted.

"Excellent, Della. So now let's make a statement describing heat and the speed of molecules. Go ahead, Jason."

" . . . "

"Do you want me to say that again?" José asked.

"Yes," Jason replied, looking relieved.

"Let's try and make a statement relating heat and the speed of molecules," he repeated.

" . . . "

"Look at these drawings, Jason. What did we say about the molecules in each?"

"They were moving," Jason responded.

"Yes, they were," José smiled patiently. "And which ones were moving faster?"

"Those," Jason responded, pointing to bottle 1.

"Good, Jason," José smiled reassuringly. "And what did we do to the molecules in this one? . . . Vicki?"

" . . . "

"Is this the one we put in the hot water, or is it the one that we left out?"

"Put in the hot water."

"Yes. So what did heating the molecules do?"

"Made them move faster."

"Fine, Vicki. Yes! Heat makes molecules move faster," José said, and he wrote, "Heat makes molecules move faster" immediately below his statement "Heat makes materials expand."

"What else did you notice about the molecules in number one and number two? . . . Steve and Kim?"

"We thought the molecules in number one were farther apart than those in number two."

"Yes! Good, both of you. And why do you suppose they're farther apart?"

" . . . "

"What did we do to these molecules?"

"We heated them," Kim said hesitantly, after conferring briefly with Steve.

"Good. So what does heating molecules do to them? Kelly?"

" . . . It makes them move farther apart."

"Yes! Now here's a tough one. What did we say *expand* meant? Ginny?"

" . . . Gets bigger!" Ginny responded after thinking a few seconds.

"So what actually happens when something expands? Leroy?"

" . . . "

"What happens to the molecules in the material?"

" . . . They move."

"Do they move apart or do they move together?"

"Apart."

"So what does *expand* mean, Leroy?" José encouraged.

"The molecules move apart," Leroy smiled as the realization struck him.

"Yes! Exactly! That's excellent thinking, everyone. Now let's review what we've found out today." He erased the first two statements on the board. He then proceeded to help students make these statements:

"Heat makes materials expand."

"*Expand* means the molecules move apart."

"Heat makes molecules move faster."

Looking at the clock, José saw it was 11:25, so he asked the class to tell him where in the room the air molecules would be moving the fastest. They concluded that over by the window would be the fastest, reasoning that it was the hottest over there. They further decided that the molecules would be farther apart at the ceiling than they would be at the floor. José praised them for their thinking and then finished the lesson.

STUDENT INVOLVEMENT: A KEY TO LEARNING AND MOTIVATION

We know from our own experiences that we are more motivated and we learn more in classes where the instructor involves us in the learning process, and research into the ways students learn supports this contention. Students learn more and retain information longer when they are put in active roles than they do when passively receiving information from others (Eggen and Kauchak, 2001).

You're studying this book because you're involved in a teacher-preparation program. Your purpose in going through the program is to learn how to teach effectively, and your purpose in studying this chapter is to learn how to increase your students' involvement in the lessons you teach.

Research examining the processes you go through in learning to teach focus on two factors: teacher *knowledge* and teacher *thinking* (Borko and Putnam, 1996). Let's look now at the ways expert teachers think as they design lessons intended to involve their students as much as possible. In doing so, we focus on three aspects of instruction:

- The need for clear goals
- The role of high-quality representations of content
- The importance of teacher questioning

These aspects of instruction are strongly interrelated, and we examine them in the sections that follow.

STUDENT INVOLVEMENT: THE NEED FOR CLEAR GOALS

The focus of this chapter is on the need for student *involvement*. However, this idea isn't as simple as it appears on the surface. To illustrate this point, let's look back at José's lesson. His students weren't involved merely for the sake of involvement. Instead, their involvement was directed toward a specific goal. After the topic has been selected and students' needs are considered, this is where the thinking of expert teachers begins.

José's goal was clear and precise; he wanted his students to understand that heat makes substances expand by increasing the movement of molecules and making the molecules move apart. The clarity and specificity of his goal guided his thinking both as he made decisions about how to illustrate the topic and as he conducted the lesson.

As we saw in Chapter 3, effective teaching begins with clear goals. This is particularly true as we work in a standards-based teaching environment. Clear and precise goals are essential for three reasons. First, if teachers aren't sure what they want learners to understand or be able to do, how can they guide their students' developing understanding, and how will they be able to determine what students have accomplished?

Second, clear goals help teachers frame decisions about ways to represent content for learners; the examples teachers use help students understand the abstract ideas they are trying to learn. José Alvarez did this with the Coke bottles and balloons he used. Third, clear goals provide the framework for the interaction that is so essential if students are to learn as much as possible (Eggen, 2001).

So we see that *involvement* is not an end; it is a means to an end. Involvement increases the likelihood that students will reach the goals that have been established by the thinking of expert teachers.

STUDENT INVOLVEMENT: THE ROLE OF CONTENT REPRESENTATIONS

To begin this section, let's think again about both José's lesson and Kathy Johnson's lesson in Chapter 4. The students were very involved in both cases, but this involvement didn't just happen. It occurred in large part *because the teachers represented their topics effectively.* José had his bottles, balloons, and hot water; Kathy had her chart that compared the northern and southern states. In both cases, the teachers were able to involve students because the information students needed to understand the topics was displayed for them. They didn't have to recall important information; *they could see it.*

The emphasis on "seeing" important information captures the essence of effective representations. The ideal that we strive for is: *The information students need to understand the topic exists in the representations.* For instance, José first wanted his students to understand that heat makes substances expand. His students were able to see this relationship by observing the balloon expand when the bottle was put in the hot water. They didn't have to know or remember this relationship; *they could see it.* Then José used his drawings of the bottles, balloons, and molecules to help the students visualize the movement of the molecules in the two bottles. An effective content representation provides students with something to think about and gives the teacher a focal point for dialoguing with students.

Effective representations exist in a variety of forms. Some of them include:

- Examples—the "real thing"
- Demonstrations
- Charts and matrixes
- Models
- Vignettes and case studies

The type of representation depends on the teacher's goal, which illustrates again why goals are so essential. Teachers can't decide what representation to find or create if they haven't thought about what they want the students to understand.

Table 5.1

Type of Representation	Goal	Example
Example	To understand the characteristics of the concept *arthropod*	A real lobster
Demonstration	To understand that heat makes materials expand	José's demonstration with the expanding balloon in the hot water
Charts and matrixes	To understand the differences between the northern and southern states	Kathy Johnson's chart showing the differences between the states
Model	To understand that heat increases the movement of molecules	José's drawings of the bottles, balloons, and molecules
Vignette	To understand the characteristics of the social studies concept *mercantilism*	Vignettes illustrating *mercantilism*

Some sample goals and illustrations of each representation are outlined in Table 5.1.

Let's look at the information in Table 5.1 a bit more closely. For instance, pictures can be effective representations when getting the "real thing" is difficult or impossible. Many young children are very interested in dinosaurs, for example, but using real dinosaurs is obviously impossible, so pictures are a reasonable compromise.

Models *are representations that allow us to visualize what we can't observe directly,* and they're particularly useful in science, where topics such as the structure of the atom and combinations of atoms into molecules are being studied. José's drawings were models because they helped the students visualize the idea that the molecules in the heated bottle were moving faster than the molecules in the bottle not heated.

Vignettes can be effective representations for topics difficult to illustrate in other ways. For instance, consider the following vignettes that illustrate the concept *mercantilism*.

In the mid 1600s the American colonists were encouraged to grow tobacco, since it wasn't grown in England. The colonists wanted to sell tobacco to France and other countries but were told not to. In return, the colonists were allowed to import textiles from England but were forbidden from making their own. All the materials were carried on British ships.

Early French colonists in the New World were avid fur trappers and traders. They got in trouble with the French monarchy, however, when they attempted to make fur garments and sell them to Spain, England, and others. They were told that the produced garments would be sent to them from Paris instead. The monarchy also told them that traps and weapons would be made in France and sent to them as well. Jean Forjea complied with the monarchy's wishes but was fined when he hired a Dutch ship to carry some of the furs back to Nice.

India was a "Jewel in the Crown" of the nineteenth-century British empire. The Indians produced large quantities of materials such as raw linens, foodstuffs, and salt. As the Indians became more nationalistic, however, trouble began. England wanted to produce the cloth-ing from the raw materials in the home islands, and when the Indians tried to establish stronger ties with other countries to increase the scope of possibilities for their trade, this ef-fort was quickly squelched. The British argued that their homeland was more than capable of providing for India's needs, and further, they had a large and efficient fleet. This policy eventually led to Indian protest and ultimately to independence. (Eggen and Kauchak, 2001, p. 24).

In comparing these examples, we see that in each case a relationship between a mother country and a colony existed, and the colony was required to produce raw mate-rials, ship the raw materials to the mother country on the mother country's ships, and buy manufactured goods back from the mother country. These are the characteristics of the concept *mercantilism*. Like a lobster for the concept *arthropod* and José's demonstration for the relationships between heat, expansion, and the movement of molecules, the represen-tations provided students with information that the teacher could use to help students construct new knowledge. This is essential for involving students and increasing learning.

The importance of effective content representations is impossible to overstate, and once clear goals have been established, much of the thinking of expert teachers focuses on ways to represent topics in ways that are understandable for students. This leads us to the use of technology, one vehicle for representing content.

Effective Content Representations: Utilizing Technology

Some of the topics we teach are difficult to represent, and the fact that they're hard to represent is what makes them hard to learn. For instance, it's easy to demonstrate that all objects fall at the same rate regardless of weight—simply drop two objects, such as a pen-cil and a book, to demonstrate that they hit the floor at the same time. It's much more difficult to illustrate the acceleration of an object as it falls, however. In these cases, tech-nology can be a powerful tool. For example, Figure 5.4 illustrates the position of a falling object at uniform intervals of time. We see that the distance between the images is greater and greater, which illustrates the fact that the object is falling faster and faster. This visual representation makes the concept of acceleration much more meaningful than it would be, and without technology it's virtually impossible to represent in a meaningful way.

A similar program, called *Ballistics,* allows physics students to see how initial veloc-ity, angle of projection, and drag medium (such as air) influence the flight of a projec-tile (Forcier, 1996). Because the program is interactive, students can manipulate the different variables and observe their effect on a projectile's path illustrated on a computer monitor. The computer program is able to bring the complexities of the real world into the classroom and make them accessible to students.

Computers, videodiscs, CD-ROMs, videotapes, and films are all forms of technol-ogy that can be used to represent otherwise hard-to-illustrate ideas. As another exam-ple, a film illustrates the concept of dominance by showing the behavior of chickens as a "pecking order" is established.

Simulations provide another opportunity for students to see abstract ideas interact in realistic settings. For example, *Science 2000,* a multimedia science curriculum with a hypertext database tied into videodiscs, allows students to experiment with different variables in the environment. In one unit students focus on ecology by studying an

Figure 5.4 Representation of a Falling Object

ecosystem impacted by a community. As members of the community, students play different roles, such as farmer, developer, and naturalist and use information from a database to study how their actions influence the ecology of a lake.

You have also probably encountered videos of real classrooms in your teacher education program. These videos represent attempts by your instructors to bring the real world of teaching into your college classroom. They allow you to see how abstract concepts related to teaching and learning relate to the real world of classrooms.

Effective Content Representations: Accommodating Learner Diversity

A great deal has been written about the diversity in today's students. However, while this is certainly true, students have always come to classrooms with vast differences in their background knowledge—what they already know. Teachers can best accommodate these differences in the way they represent their topics. For instance, if a teacher brings a real lobster to class, it doesn't matter if a student is African American, Asian American, Hispanic, bright, slow, a boy or a girl, or a student with a special learning need. They can all feel the lobster's cold, hard shell, see the different body parts, and notice the jointed legs. When these are combined with other examples such as a crayfish, beetle, and grasshopper, students can form an accurate concept of *arthropod* despite differences in background knowledge.

Unquestionably, teachers must be sensitive to differences in students' attitudes, values, and motivations, many of which are culturally dependent. However, in terms of the way students learn, effectively representing the topics they teach is a powerful way to accommodate student diversity.

INCREASING STUDENT INVOLVEMENT: TEACHER QUESTIONING

Teacher questioning is the single most effective and most generally applicable strategy teachers have for promoting student involvement. Regardless of grade level, content area, or topic, being able to guide your students with questions is the most important teaching skill that you can possess.

Research supports this assertion (Wang, Haertel, and Walberg, 1993). Effective teachers ask more questions than their less effective colleagues (Hamilton and Brady, 1991; Henderson, Winitzky, and Kauchak, 1996), and large numbers of questions are indicators of effective organization and clear goals (Shuell, 1996; Good and Brophy, 2000).

Because questioning is so essential for involving students, we are devoting the rest of the chapter to this topic.

Functions of Teacher Questions

The effectiveness of questioning can also be explained by the functions they perform. These functions include:

- Assessing current understanding
- Increasing student motivation
- Guiding new learning

Let's look at them.

Assessing Current Understanding. Research examining the ways individuals learn suggests that students' existing knowledge is a powerful factor in how (and whether) new information will be learned. Also, student misconceptions and prior beliefs often interfere with understanding new content (Guzetti and Hynd, 1998). Questioning allows teachers to informally assess students' current grasp of the topics they're studying, because students' answers to the questions reveal their conceptions.

This is an intuitively sensible idea. Even in informal conversations, we assess other people's understanding of a discussion topic by the way they respond to questions and statements. In classrooms, questions can provide teachers with continual feedback about the learning progress of their students.

Increasing Student Motivation. Effective questioning can also increase student curiosity and interest—two important aspects of motivational activities (Pintrich and Schunk, 1996). Effective questions engage students, challenge their thinking, and pose problems for them to consider. For example, Kathy Johnson (in Chapter 4) didn't introduce her lesson with a statement like "Today we're going to discuss the northern and southern colonies." Instead, she used the questions, "How are these states different, and . . . why, since all these states are part of the same country—our United States—why are they so different?" The questions were purposely designed to capitalize on the effects of curiosity in increasing student motivation.

Guiding New Learning. Instruction is the third important function of questioning. Effective questions help students interrelate ideas and integrate new learning with their current understanding.

To illustrate these ideas, think back to Kathy Johnson's lesson in Chapter 4 and José's in this chapter. In both cases the entire lessons were conducted with questioning. Most learning theorists accept the idea that students construct their own understanding rather than recording it as presented by a teacher or some other source. The process of constructing understanding requires careful guidance of expert teachers, and questioning is the most important skill teachers have for providing this guidance. (We introduced constructivism in Chapter 1 and describe it in detail in Chapter 7.)

These functions again demonstrate why clear goals are so important. Teachers assess current understanding so they can best link new learning to what students already know, and they can only guide new learning effectively if they're clear about where the lesson is headed—that is, clear about their goals.

Questioning: The Influence on Student Thinking

To be effective, teachers' questions must have an impact on student thinking. The best planned and executed questioning sequence is worthless if it doesn't cause students to think, relate ideas, and construct new knowledge.

In answering a teacher's question, students should engage in five separate mental operations (Gall, 1984). They're outlined in Figure 5.5 and discussed in the paragraphs that follow.

Learning begins with attention (Eggen and Kauchak, 2001); without attention, the other mental operations can't take place. The most thoroughly planned and well-thought-out lesson becomes ineffective if students aren't paying attention. Questions draw students' attention away from distractions, such as the clock, window, and each other, and invite them into the lesson.

Second, once they're paying attention, students must understand and interpret the meaning of the question. This isn't always easy; the intent of the question may be clear to the teacher, but it may be misperceived by students. This again illustrates the importance of questioning as a way of assessing current understanding. Teachers will know if a student misperceives a question because the answer will be incomplete or inaccurate. Then the teacher can intervene.

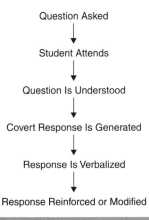

Figure 5.5 Student Mental Operations Elicited by an Effective Question

Third, the question should elicit a *covert response* from each student. Though teachers typically call on one student to answer, our goal should be to have *all* students think about and mentally react to our question. We discuss techniques to promote covert responses later in the chapter.

Fourth, covert responses are put into words when the teacher calls on a student to answer. Research examining ways students learn emphasizes the value of students attempting to put their understanding into words (Bruning, Shraw, and Ronning, 1999). Verbalizing an answer helps clarify the content in students' minds and make connections with other ideas. Verbalizing an answer takes time and effort, especially if the question is a complex or demanding one. Effective teachers provide students with the time to relate interconnected ideas through wait time, which we'll describe later in the chapter.

Finally, based on the teacher's feedback, students conclude that the response was complete and accurate, or they generate a revised response. A correct answer is recognized and reinforced; an incorrect answer is modified. This entire process occurs in a few seconds and is repeated dozens of times a day in many classrooms.

The sequence we just described is the ideal we strive for, but it doesn't always occur. Not all students attend, some don't understand the question, others don't generate a covert response, students don't always listen to the answers of their classmates, and they may not revise their original thinking. When these alternatives occur, learning suffers. Understanding the mental operations questions are intended to elicit, help us see why the elements of effective questioning, which we discuss next, are so important.

ELEMENTS OF EFFECTIVE QUESTIONING

As we saw earlier in the chapter, effective questioning depends on two essential factors. The first is clear and precise goals. The goals may not be written in a plan book, and teachers may have to modify them during lessons if students' current understanding requires it, but effective teachers, nevertheless, begin their lessons knowing what they want their students to accomplish.

The second is effective representations of content, which also depend on clear goals. Expert teachers use content representations that help students reach goals, and they guide their students to the goals through their questioning. Keep these ideas in mind as you study this section.

Effective questioning is a sophisticated set of abilities, and you won't become an expert overnight. However, they can be developed with practice, and if you persevere, research indicates that—just as experts in other areas develop their abilities—you can develop your own questioning expertise (Rowe, 1986).

The research base for effective teaching that we described in Chapter 4 acts as a foundation for effective questioning. For example, effective teachers for all students use their time wisely; display positive personal characteristics; and begin, develop, and end their lessons effectively. Similarly, there are essential questioning strategies that effective teachers, regardless of grade level or topic, demonstrate. They include:

- Questioning frequency
- Equitable distribution
- Prompting
- Repetition for emphasis
- Wait time

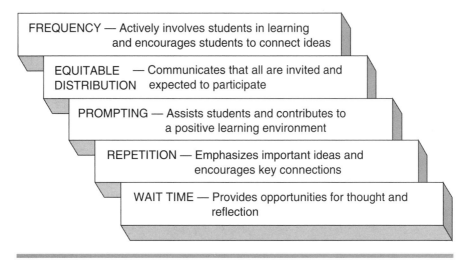

Figure 5.6 Essential Questioning Strategies

These strategies are outlined in Figure 5.6 and discussed in the following sections.

Questioning Frequency

Questioning frequency *refers to the number of questions that teachers ask over a period of time,* and research indicates that effective teachers ask more questions than do those who are less effective (Hamilton and Brady, 1991; Hendersen et al., 1996). Student involvement is essential for learning, and large numbers of questions increase involvement.

We saw the effects of questioning frequency in Kathy Johnson's lesson in Chapter 4 and José's in this chapter. Both asked a large number of questions and guided their students to their goals with their questions.

Equitable Distribution

Equitable distribution *describes a questioning pattern in which all the students in the class are called on as equally as possible* (Kerman, 1979; Good and Brophy, 2000). Equitable distribution runs counter to two common teaching patterns. First, in typical classrooms, about two-thirds of all teacher questions are undirected, meaning that students who volunteer are allowed to answer, and those who don't are allowed to remain passive (McGreal, 1985). This practice detracts from achievement (Shuell, 1996; Good and Brophy, 2000), because the involvement of students who don't volunteer decreases.

Second, we saw in Chapter 4 that teach   treat students differently based on their expectations, and teachers tend to call on students they perceive as having high ability much more frequently than on low-ability students. This is easy to understand. They expect high-ability students to be able to answer, and getting correct answers is reinforcing for teachers, so they fall into patterns of calling primarily on high-ability students (Good and Brophy, 2000).

In contrast to these patterns, José called on all the students in his class as *equally* as possible and *by name*. He had 30 students in the class, and they all responded at least once. (In the actual lesson we observed, each student answered several questions.)

While it's hard to illustrate in a written case study, we want to emphasize that José called on his students whether or not they had their hands up. Students in José's class knew that they were certain to be called on and, as a result, their level of attention was very high. In cases where students "drifted off," José intervened immediately, as was illustrated in the segment with Ginny when she was momentarily inattentive. Let's take another look.

> *José:* How do we know it [the bottle] was heated? . . . Ginny?"
> *Ginny:* I, er, I didn't hear the question [answering sheepishly].
> *José:* What did I do with this bottle, Ginny [holding up the bottle with the red balloon]?
> *Ginny:* You put it in the coffee pot.
> *José:* Yes I did, Ginny. Good. And how do we know the coffee pot was hot? . . . Rosemary?

This simple sequence took less than 5 seconds, but it served two important functions. First, it got Ginny back into the lesson, and second, it contributed to a positive classroom climate. Ginny knew that José had caught her not paying attention, but he didn't admonish or criticize her. Instead, he simply rephrased his original question and went on. This sequence communicated that José was on her side, wanting her to contribute and learn. This helped to create a positive climate in his classroom for all students.

In a review of the literature in this area, experts concluded that teachers should call on volunteers less than ten to fifteen percent of the time (Gage and Berliner, 1988). Think about that figure. The researchers suggested that 85 percent to 90 percent of all teacher questions should be directed to students who do not volunteer! Equitable distribution communicates that the teacher expects all students to attend and that each student will be able to and assisted to answer. If teachers practice equitable distribution as a day-to-day pattern, student involvement and learning can dramatically increase.

While it seems simple, establishing a pattern of calling on all the students in your classes is very demanding; it's easier to merely let volunteers answer. However, the more you practice, the easier it will become and, in time, you'll be able to direct questions to individuals virtually without thinking about it.

Prompting

In the last section we emphasized that all students should be called on as equally as possible. We also know that specific goals are essential, which means that students must supply "right answers" as the lesson moves toward the goal. Student involvement and success are no less important at this point than they are in the beginning, however, so teachers must have a tool for maintaining successful interaction. **Prompting**—*cues teachers provide or other questions they ask when students are unable to correctly answer the original question*—is that tool.

Research indicates that prompting in reaction to a student's inability to give a correct response provides benefits to learning not found in other options (such as turning to another student for the right answer) (Shuell, 1996). Done effectively, prompting can:

- Create a climate of support in the classroom.
- Communicate positive expectations for success.
- Assist students in thinking through and answering a specific question.

Let's take another look at a questioning sequence from José's lesson.

José: What's in the bottles, Nikki?
Nikki: They're empty.
José: Wave your hand in front of your face, Nikki . . . What do you feel?
Nikki: Well, I feel the air on my face.
José: Yes, so what do you think might be in the bottles?
Nikki: . . . Air?

Here, José asked a question for which only one answer—air—was acceptable. However, Nikki said the bottles were empty. José then provided a cue by asking her to wave her hand in front of her face, which led Nikki to conclude that air was in the bottles.

In this example, José prompted with a cue. Now let's look at another segment where he prompted by asking additional questions.

José: So now what do we know about the amount of air in each system? Kathy?
Kathy: It's the same.
José: And how do we know, Tyrone?
Tyrone: . . .
José: What did we say about the sizes of the balloons and bottles, Tyrone?
Tyrone: They . . . were . . . equal.
José: Good. So how do we know the amount of air in each is the same?
Tyrone: The bottles and balloons . . . are the same size.

When Tyrone was unable to answer his original question, José simply rephrased it by asking, "What did we say about the sizes of the balloons and bottles?" This prompt was efficient, since it was established earlier in the lesson that the sizes were the same.

The Alternate Question.   One option a teacher has when a student is unable to give an acceptable response is to ask the original question in a different way, ask another related question that is simpler, or give a directive that leads to a successful response. This is what José did when he told Nikki to wave her hand in front of her face, and this is what he did again when he asked Tyrone what he knew about the sizes of the balloons and bottles.

An alternative question helps in cases where students misunderstand the original question. As teachers, we all know what we want when we ask a question, but our intent may not be obvious to students. The simplest solution to this problem is to rephrase the question in different terms. Additional examples include:

First Question:	How are plot and characterization related in this novel?
Follow-Up:	How does the development of the story line help us understand the major actors in our story?
First Question:	How does the carrying power of a river vary with the speed of its current?
Follow-Up:	Will a fast river carry more or less silt than a slow one?

As in the second example, an effective prompt sometimes rephrases the question in more concrete terms. In addition, effective prompts often narrow the range of response options. For example:

ORIGINAL QUESTION	REFORMULATION
What are these people doing?	What are they planting?
What kind of an elephant is this?	Was he happy or sad?
What else did you see?	Did you see any furniture?
How did they travel?	Did they go by air or water?
What color was it?	Was it a bright or subdued color?

In each of these reformulations, the teacher attempted to help students by not only rephrasing the question but also making the question easier by making the answer more concrete and obvious. This tactic serves two functions. From the individual student's perspective, it takes the pressure off the nonresponding student by making the answering task easier. From a lesson perspective, it not only approaches the content in a slightly different way but also helps to maintain the continuity and momentum of the lesson.

Teachers can also prompt by inserting supplementary information to steer the direction of the lesson. Consider the following excerpt, taken from an actual fifth-grade classroom.

Teacher: What we're going to talk about today is the punctuation that tells when someone is speaking. How do we know, when we are reading, that someone is speaking?
Student: When it is has a . . . um . . . two parentheses around them.
Teacher: All right. [Draws a set of quotation marks on the chalkboard.] "These are called. . . . Does anybody know what these are called?"
Student: Commas.
Teacher: Not commas. Not when they're up in the air like this.
Student: Brackets.
Teacher: Not brackets. These are brackets. [Draws a pair of brackets on the chalkboard.]
Student: Parentheses.
Teacher: Not parentheses. These are up in the air above the words . . . [points to the words within the quotation marks.]
Student: Oooh, ooh, oooh! Quotation marks!
Teacher: Perfect. These are quotation marks. And quotation marks, when you run across them in a story, tell you that someone is speaking directly. (Duffy et al., 1985)

Note how the teacher's response builds on the student's answer, assessing areas of misunderstanding and clarifying areas of understanding. The way in which the teacher responds to a student answer not only provides feedback about the adequacy of the student's reply but can also set the direction for subsequent interactions.

For example, with a correct answer, the teacher not only can affirm the correctness of the answer but also can stress important aspects of the answer:

Teacher: Can anyone give me an example of a mammal?
Student: A dog's a mammal because it gives birth to its young live.
Teacher: Good, Johnny, live birth is one of the essential characteristics of mammals. Let's talk about that one for a while. . . .

In addition to verifying that an answer is correct, the teacher can add more information, explain the response more fully, or frame the response in a larger context. All of these strategies improve the informational quality of the response (Duffy et al., 1986). In a similar way, a teacher's response to an incorrect or partially correct answer provides the teacher with the opportunity to (1) ignore the incorrect part of the answer, (2) emphasize the correct part, and (3) prompt for the part of the answer that was not given.

The point here is that teachers do not need to be afraid of steering the direction of the lesson through the interjection of comments or additional information as they prompt their students. The teacher knows where the lesson should go; responses to student answers provide one opportunity to steer the lesson in that direction.

Effective Questioning: Increasing Student Motivation

Research indicates that *students' beliefs about their capability of accomplishing learning tasks*—a concept called **self-efficacy**—is a powerful factor in increasing motivation to learn (Pintrich and Schunk, 1996). In other words, if students believe that they can succeed on challenging tasks, they develop a sense of self-efficacy, and their motivation is likely to increase.

In developing self-efficacy, student success is crucial. The combination of effective representations of content and open-ended questions is one of the most powerful tools teachers have for assuring success and increasing learner motivation.

Open-Ended Questions. **Open-ended questions** *are questions for which a variety of answers are acceptable,* and José used a number of these in his lesson.

Let's look at some dialogue.

José: Now look at these bottles [holding up the two bottles] What can you tell us about them? . . . Keith?
Keith: You drink out of them.
José: Fine, Keith. . . . Beverly?
Beverly: They're sort of green.
José: Yes, they are. What else? . . . Lavonia?
Lavonia: They look like they're the same size.
José: Yes, indeed they certainly do. Very good, Lavonia.

In this case, José asked a **description question,** *which is an open-ended question that asks students to make an observation.*

In addition to descriptions, **comparison questions,** *open-ended questions that ask students to compare and contrast different items,* can also be used effectively. Let's look at some examples.

José: Now look at the balloons on these bottles [holding up the bottles]. How would you compare the balloons? . . . Leroy?
Leroy: One is red and the other is yellow.
José: Yes. Good, Leroy. What else? . . . Rachel?
Rachel: They look like they're made out of rubber.
José: Yes, they *are* rubber balloons. How would you compare their sizes? . . . Michael?

Michael: They look like they're the same size.
José: Good, Michael. They are the same size.

Open-ended questions are powerful tools for involving students first, because they invite participation in a nonthreatening way. For instance, we saw that José asked one simple question, "What can you tell us about them?" and he was able to get acceptable answers from three students in a matter of seconds. He did virtually the same thing when he asked students to compare the balloons. Because open-ended questions are easy to ask and easy to answer, accomplishing equitable distribution is less demanding. It is very difficult to call on all students in a large class without asking some open-ended questions.

Second, open-ended questions are very effective prompts. For instance, if Tyrone had still been unable to answer when José asked, "What did we say about the sizes of the balloons and bottles?" He could have held up the bottles and asked an open-ended question such as, "Look at these bottles again, Tyrone. What do you notice about them?" In this case it would have been virtually impossible for Tyrone to give an unacceptable answer. This is a powerful technique for involving students, particularly those who don't have a pattern of successfully answering.

Asking questions that don't have specific answers may seem like a waste of time; why don't we merely tell the students or ask more direct questions? In addition to making equitable distribution and prompting easier, open-ended questions are useful for several other reasons:

- Because a variety of answers are acceptable, students are virtually assured of success, which in turn increases motivation. This is particularly important for students who have a history of low achievement and a past history of failing to answer many of the questions teachers commonly ask.
- Because students are assured of success, they learn to feel "safe" in question-and-answer sessions. A sense of safety also contributes to positive classroom climate and student motivation (Eggen and Kauchak, 2001).
- Open-ended questioning—particularly ones requiring comparing and contrasting—promotes critical thinking.
- Open-ended questions are effective in working with cultural minorities, who sometimes lack confidence in fast-paced, convergent question-and-answer sessions (Langer, Bartolome, Vasquez, and Lucas, 1990).
- Open-ended questions allow informal assessment of students' current understanding, which was one of the functions of teacher questions that we discussed earlier in the chapter.

Let's look at this last point in a bit more detail. For example, in a class that has recently studied adjectives, the teacher displays the following sentence:

Teri moved quickly to remove the hot dish from the stove.

and asks, "What can you tell me about the sentence?" If students understand the concept, they will identify *hot* as an adjective in one of the first few responses. If they don't, it suggests that they are less sure of the concept than they should be, and the teacher can provide additional instruction.

The power of open-ended questioning as an instructional tool is confirmed by our experiences in schools. We have seen students who were nearly hostile and openly refusing to respond at the beginning of a class period begin to volunteer responses to questions by the *end of the same class period,* all because they could see that students were able to successfully respond. Open-ended questioning was the strategy used to induce this change. This is a powerful and exciting change in students that occurred very quickly. Imagine the impact of assured success on participation and motivation over an extended period of time!

Finally, open-ended questions address the objections of teachers who are reluctant to call on nonvolunteers, because they are afraid to embarrass students if they're initially unable to answer. Because students are assured of giving an acceptable response, they can be "put on the spot" without danger of embarrassment or anxiety. When students are put in a situation where they know they will be called on and are almost certain of being able to answer, their attention and motivation sharply increase. We have observed the effectiveness of these techniques at all grade levels and curriculum areas.

Using open-ended questions as prompts also illustrates again why effective representations of content are so essential as a tool for promoting student involvement. In Tyrone's case, for example, he could *see* that the bottles were the same size; it wasn't something he had to *know or recall* from a previous lesson. The combination of effective content representations and open-ended questions give teachers tools that help them elicit successful responses from virtually all students under nearly any conditions. They are among the most effective techniques that exist for involving students.

In closing this section, let us share an incident we encountered in a classroom. In an earlier paragraph we stated that open-ended questions are effective because learners are virtually assured of success. Anything can happen in a classroom, however. We were observing a first-grade teacher who was using open-ended questioning with her students. She held a shoe up for the students to observe, and she began, "Tell me about the shoe."

"It's red," Mike responded.

The shoe was black. There was no sign of red on it anywhere! As we all know, young children occasionally give off-the-wall responses, and the teacher handled this one very well. She simply smiled and said, "The shoe is actually black. Now, Mike, tell me something else about it." Quick thinking.

Repetition for Emphasis

In Chapter 4, we discussed the importance of *emphasis* in highlighting important content, and identified repetition as one type. A very effective form of emphasis is a **repetition question,** *which simply asks students to reconsider a question or point that has been made earlier in the lesson.* Repetition questions have an advantage over repetitious statements by the teacher because they provide emphasis and focus, they help maintain interaction between teacher and students, and they give the teacher a quick estimate of whether they "got it" earlier. We have all had the experience of periodically getting lost as a teacher develops a topic, and while this problem is impossible to completely avoid, it can be minimized with strategic repetition questions.

The following segment illustrates José's use of repetition.

José: Now, look at the balloons and bottles, everyone. What did Lavonia say about the bottles themselves? Cliff?

Cliff: We drink out of them.

José: Yes, we do. . . . How do the sizes compare? Alfredo?
Alfredo: They're the same.

At this point José wanted to emphasize that the bottles were the same size, and he asked Cliff what Lavonia had said about them. The need for repetition is illustrated by Cliff's response, "We drink out of them," suggesting that he had wandered, losing the focus of the lesson, which was to establish that the two bottles were the same except for their temperature and the air molecules inside of them. Without the repetition, Cliff, and probably others, would have been uncertain about where the lesson was headed.

José used repetition extensively, and some might even conclude that he used it excessively. This is a matter of judgment, but it is clearly better to refocus students too often than not often enough. Our experience in working with teachers of K–12 students indicates that repetition is not merely a positive teacher action but is, in fact, essential in helping students follow the direction of complex lessons.

Wait Time

What's the square root of 256? Quick! Some of you probably answered the question immediately while others fidgeted with a paper and pencil first. Still others may have seen the "Quick!" and given up immediately.

This problem is analogous to situations that occur in classrooms. Research indicates that teachers, after asking a question, typically wait less than 1 second for students to respond before interrupting, prompting, giving the answer themselves, or calling on another student (Rowe, 1974, 1986). In addition, Rowe found that teachers tend to cut off students' responses rather than letting them think through and construct their answers as fully as possible. Both of these problems are more pronounced when students are perceived as low achievers, and cross-cultural studies also indicate that the phenomenon is not unique to American classrooms (Tobin, 1983; Chewprecha et al., 1980).

In contrast, when teachers pause and give students time to think about their answers, the quality of student responses increases significantly (Rowe, 1974, 1986). *The pause between a question or the pause after a student answer and a teacher interruption or interjection is called* **wait time.**

A number of benefits result from lengthening wait time (Rowe, 1986, 1974). Extending wait times to longer than 3 seconds improves both the teacher's effectiveness and students' performance in the following ways:

- Lessons are smoother and more focused (Rowe, 1986).
- Teachers become more responsive to students by matching the wait time to the difficulty of the question, improving equitable distribution, and increasing participation from minority students (Rowe, 1974, 1975).
- The length and quality of student responses increase, resulting in more higher-order and critical thinking (Rowe, 1986; Anderson, 1978).
- Failures to respond are reduced, the variety of students participating voluntarily increases, and the number of disciplinary interruptions by the teacher decreases (Tobin, 1987).
- Finally, and perhaps most important, achievement increases (Tobin, 1987; Tobin and Capie, 1982).

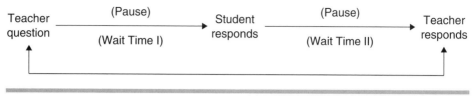

Figure 5.7 Effective Use of Wait Time

Effective wait-times occur at two points in the questioning sequence, as illustrated in Figure 5.7.

The first pause in Figure 5.7, called Wait Time I, gives everyone in the class time to think about the question and generate the *covert response* we described in our discussion of the influence of questioning on student thinking. The second pause, Wait Time II, gives other students time to think about and react to the student's answer. Wait time can be thought of as "think time," providing students with opportunities to think about the content they are learning.

As with any technique, wait time must be implemented with professional judgment. For example, in the cases of drill and practice where overlearning and automaticity are desired (such as multiplication facts), quick answers are desirable (Rosenshine and Stevens, 1986) and wait times should be short. On the other hand, when students are making comparisons, forming conclusions, providing evidence, and demonstrating other higher-order abilities, wait times should be longer.

Effective Questioning: Involving Diverse Students

Questioning is one of the most effective tools teachers have for communicating that they value all students and welcome them in their classrooms. Equitable distribution and prompting, in particular, are essential. Used effectively, they communicate, "I don't care if you're a boy or girl, minority or nonminority, or high or low achiever; I want you in my classroom, I believe you're capable of learning, and I will do whatever it takes to ensure that you're successful." This practice sends a powerful message to students. In addition to conveying positive teacher expectations it also communicates caring and concern for student learning.

Students are sensitive to these practices. They quickly come to interpret your effort to distribute questions to cultural minorities and nonminorities equally, for example, as an indication that both groups are expected to achieve, and the effect on classroom climate is very positive. Prompting all students as equally as possible reinforces this message.

CLASSROOM QUESTIONS: ADDITIONAL ISSUES

Each of the essential questioning skills we've discussed in this chapter—frequency, equitable distribution, prompting, repetition, and wait time—are well documented by research, as are the relationships between questioning, student diversity, and motivation.

Research has examined some additional issues that often surface in discussions of questioning, and we want to consider them in this section. They include:

- High-level versus low-level questions
- Questioning patterns: Selecting students
- Callouts
- Choral responses

Let's look at them.

High-Level versus Low-Level Questions

In our discussion of wait time, we found that the kind of question affects the amount of time a teacher should wait for a response. This observation leads to a related issue. How does the level of teacher question affect student learning? In this section, we want to consider the benefits of low-level questions (e.g., "Who wrote Hamlet?) versus high-level questions ("Why is Shakespeare's *Hamlet* considered a tragedy, in the classical sense of the term?"). Let's see what research says about the issue.

The levels of teacher questions have been widely researched, but the results are surprisingly mixed (Good and Brophy, 2000). Some studies have found a significant, positive correlation between higher-level questions and achievement (Redfield and Rousseau, 1981), others found no relationship (Rosenshine and Furst, 1973; Winne, 1979), and still others identified a negative correlation between the two (Dillon, 1981; Stallings, 1975). What explains these contradictory findings?

The answer again illustrates the importance of clear goals. Goals that are appropriate for the topic, the age of the students, and their backgrounds should determine the level of questions. For instance, if the goal is fact-level learning with young children, such as knowing that $7 \times 9 = 63$, a high percentage of low-level questions is appropriate. For more complex goals, such as understanding the impact of Columbus's discovery of the new world, higher-level questions are more desirable. Students with limited backgrounds about a topic will—at least initially—be asked many low-level questions, and the number of high-level questions will increase as their background improves.

This is the only sensible approach to determining question level. With the complexities of teacher-student interaction, teachers shouldn't consciously decide, "I will now ask a high-level question," or "It is now the time for a low-level question." The solution is to have a clear and precise goal in mind prior to the lesson and to be alert, sensitive, and responsive to students as the lesson develops. The appropriate level of questions will then take care of itself.

This was illustrated in José's work with his students. As we saw earlier in the chapter, his goal was very clear; he knew exactly where he wanted the lesson and students to go. The responses of the students and his goal, rather than preconceived decisions about level, guided his questioning. For example, he began his lesson with simple descriptions and then moved to higher-level questions as he asked the students to make comparisons. However, knowing that he wanted to establish and confirm that the two systems were the same size, he asked a much higher-level question when he asked Tyrone *how they knew* the amount of air was the same in each system? (Note also that José didn't reserve his higher-level questions for his high achievers. All students were treated equally.) When he called on Tyrone, he was not thinking, "I will now ask a high-level question." Instead, he was working toward a goal, which we saw in the segment where José prompted Tyrone. This goal-driven flexibility is the essence of expert teacher questioning.

Bloom's Taxonomy: A Sequential Questioning Strategy

As we saw in Chapter 3, Bloom's taxonomy is a hierarchical classification system based on the cognitive processing demands placed on students. Its value in structuring classroom questions centers on this hierarchical structure. *Hierarchical* means that the upper levels are dependent on and subsume the lower. This characteristic is important for questioning strategies because it suggests that teachers build an informational base at lower levels before proceeding to higher ones.

Let us illustrate these ideas by looking at the six levels in the taxonomy and considering how they function in a classroom setting.

Knowledge. The *knowledge* category, the lowest in Bloom's taxonomy, helps build an informational base for subsequent questions. Processes involved in the Knowledge category include recognition and recall. Some examples of knowledge-level questions include:

Who wrote *Uncle Tom's Cabin*?

What is the chemical symbol for iron?

How many minutes in a basketball game?

Comprehension. *Comprehension* asks students to process information so that the meaning is clear. If the meaning of information being taught isn't clear, then the teacher needs to slow down or even back up to make sure students understand. Students show that they comprehend something when they can translate it into a different form (e.g., verbally describe numerical data presented in graph form), interpret it (e.g., explain why a phenomenon occurs), or extrapolate it (e.g., project a trend beyond the data given). Having students provide examples is another type of comprehension question. Comprehension questions attempt to determine if students understand information in a meaningful way. For example,

Can you tell us, in your own words, the major events in the story so far?

The book says rust occurs when iron is oxidized. What does that mean?

Who can find an example of an oxymoron in our poem?

Application. The third level of Bloom's taxonomy asks students to take information they have learned and apply it to a new situation. Solving new or novel word problems in math would be an example here. The process of *application* actually occurs in two phases. In the first phase, some abstraction, formula, equation, or algorithm is learned; in the second, students encounter a new situation or problem and are asked to apply the previously learned information. Teachers who try to get students to apply information at a later date verify that this second phase is a difficult one. Practice is essential, and classroom questions provide an excellent opportunity for this practice. For example,

Who can apply what we've learned about sonnets and finish this poem?

Now we're trying to find the length of this diagonal line. Any ideas? What formula should we use?

So we want the fish to be crisp on the outside but not overdone on the inside. How should we cook it?

Notice how in each of these examples students are being asked to use or apply information they've acquired previously.

Analysis. *Analysis* questions develop students' ability to take apart some complex phenomena to show how it works. The medium involved in the analysis will vary with the content area involved. In English, it could involve the examination of a speech, a poem, or a book and some type of explanation of how the work holds together and how the different components add to the power of the work. In the area of art, the process of analysis could focus on a painting and show how various components such as color, line, and texture interact to produce an effect. Similar examples occur in every area of the curriculum where student understanding of something is dependent on an understanding of how the interrelated components or parts work together. Some examples of analysis questions include:

Let's write down the major events that have occurred in the Middle East. Then let's ask how these are interrelated and why we are where we are today.

Let's look at this table and try to determine why it's so sturdy and why it has lasted so long.

Who can analyze this paragraph and explain why it is such a powerful way to start this paper?

Synthesis. *Synthesis* questions are different from those in the other levels in several important ways. As opposed to the other levels, which focus more on analytical skills, the synthesis category focuses on creativity. In addition, the synthesis category is product oriented; typically a tangible product results from the synthesis operation. Although most often associated with the fine arts areas of art and literature, synthesis questions also have applications in other areas. For example, creativity can be a central dimension in the design of a science experiment. In the area of home economics, synthesis-level skills can also focus on clothes or food preparation. In other vocational areas creativity can be a central component of woodworking and other vocational classes. Note how each of these questions asks students to be creative in producing some product or plan.

Okay, we know that garbage is a major problem for big cities. What are some creative ways to solve this problem?

Remember, we're on a limited budget for this meal. What are some ways we can stretch our dollars and still produce an exciting menu?

You've viewed the first half of the game on videotape. What would you do differently in the second half to turn your team around? Be creative.

Evaluation. The highest level of Bloom's taxonomy is *evaluation,* which involves judging the merit or worth of some object or work. The process of evaluation occurs in two steps: the first is the establishment of some criteria, and the second is the application of these criteria to some object or idea. For example, in social studies, we can ask students to evaluate a proposed solution to world hunger. This process would involve first some description of the specifics of the problem—givens, resources, and limitations to work with—and then an analysis of the extent to which the proposed solution addressed these parameters. In literature, students can evaluate a written work, describing its strengths and weaknesses. In other areas, such as physical education and home economics, students can evaluate a game plan or a plan of operation such as a menu. Some examples of evaluation questions include the following:

How well did the North use their resources in the Civil War?

Was Hemingway a great American writer? When you answer that, you'll have to define greatness first.

We've read several theories about why the dinosaurs disappeared from the earth. Which makes the most sense? Why?

The Taxonomy: A Classroom Example. The following is an excerpt of a teacher using Bloom's taxonomy to structure a lesson on Shakespeare's *Romeo and Juliet*. Note how the teacher uses lower levels of the taxonomy to serve as a foundation for higher levels. To help you do this, we've labeled the level of the question in brackets.

Lynn Bell's junior English class had been reading Shakespeare's *Romeo and Juliet* for several weeks. Although they had known it was a tragedy, the class was disturbed at the gory ending. Lynn was trying to get them to pull it all together and to view the play in the larger context of a tragedy.

Lynn: Class, it's been a long weekend, so let's review some of the major characters in the play and try to remember some of the major events. [K] Someone? Jack?

Jack: Well, the most important characters were Romeo and Juliet. They fell in love, and that's how all the trouble started.

Lynn: Good, Jack. That's a good starting point. Let's follow up on that. What houses did they belong to? [K] Sandy?

Sandy: Juliet was a Capulet and Romeo was a Montague.

Lynn: Okay, now why is that information important to the play? [C] Anyone? Cassy?

Cassy: Because these two houses had been feuding for a long time.

Lora: And, in terms of Romeo and Juliet, they shouldn't have fallen in love.

Lynn: Good. Now let's return to an idea we discussed briefly earlier. What is a tragedy? [K] Shawn?

Shawn: It's a story that ends unhappily?

Lynn: Anything else? [K] Franco?

Franco: The people in it can't help what's happening.

Lynn: Why is that important? [C] Brad?

Brad: Because the people in the audience can see what's happening but the characters in the play can't. They're just kind of swept along by the events.

Lynn: Any other characteristics of a tragedy? [K] Pam?

Pam: In my notes, it says there is often "growth toward knowledge."

Lynn: Good note taking, Pam. What does that mean? [C]

Pam: Beats me. I just wrote it down.

Lynn: Who can help her out? Did growth toward knowledge occur in this play? [C] Ken?

Ken: Well, at the end the Montagues and Capulets got together and agreed to stop the feuding.

Lynn: Excellent, Ken. Now let's take this one step further. Romeo and Juliet got married. Was it Act II, Scene 5? [K] Scene 6, okay. Now I want each of you to take a few minutes to devise another ending for the story that would still make it a tragedy. [App] When you're done with that, we'll share these with the rest of the class and they'll have to decide if your ending qualifies as a true tragedy. [An]

Let's analyze the lesson. First, note how the teacher began with knowledge-level questions and, after establishing a factual base, proceeded to comprehension questions that checked for understanding. Then, after she felt confident that her students understood the concept of tragedy, she asked them to apply this information to develop a different ending. Finally, the lesson ended with an analysis question, asking students to examine one another's new endings to determine if these were truly tragedies.

Now, a confession. Actual classroom lessons do not proceed this smoothly. They progress instead in fits and starts, and teachers need to exercise that flexibility stressed earlier, adjusting questions to the background of students and the direction and momentum of the lesson. The lesson recorded here was provided as a prototype so that you could see the progression of ideas.

Though somewhat unrealistic, this prototype illustrates several important ideas. One is the value of the taxonomy as a guide to sequencing questions. A second related idea is the importance of using lower-level questions to (1) involve a number of students, (2) establish an informational base, and (3) warm the class up at the beginning of the lesson. Also, note at the end that as the teacher asked an application question requiring more thinking, she provided the class with the necessary wait time (actual minutes) to apply the information they had learned.

Finally, if the lesson had continued, how might the teacher have used the synthesis and evaluation categories to think about the play further? We offer these as possible alternatives but invite you to construct your own.

SYNTHESIS

Write a version of Romeo and Juliet for the twenty-first century. Find a present-day story with the potential to be a tragedy. Flesh out the story in enough detail so that your thinking is evident.

EVALUATION

Some people call *Romeo and Juliet* a love story; others consider the play a tragedy. Which label do you believe is more correct, and why?

Some critics call Shakespeare a master of settings, getting the most from his plays by having the scenes set in dramatic places. Do you agree with this assessment? Defend your answer with examples from *Romeo and Juliet*.

Bloom's taxonomy can provide a useful conceptual tool for asking higher-level questions. It can help us sequence these questions, building on prior knowledge and using previous skills as the foundation for later ones. It can also help us understand why students have problems with questions requiring higher-level questions. Finally, it can serve as a reminder of the breadth and variety of cognitive tasks available to us as we involve our students in the process of thinking through classroom questioning.

Selecting Students

Whom should we call on when we ask a question? As we saw earlier, teachers tend to simply call on students who volunteer, but this is less effective than calling on both volunteers and nonvolunteers.

The most desirable alternative is to call on students randomly, and expert teachers manage this process by mentally monitoring who they've called on as the lesson proceeds. As the activity develops, if you've lost track of who you've called on, simply ask, "Whom have I not called on yet?" When students are in an environment where large numbers of questions are being asked and the teacher supports the students in their efforts to answer, being called on is desirable and they will freely admit it if they haven't been called on (or one of their classmates will point it out). Further, a simple, straightforward question, such as "Who haven't I called on," promotes a comfortable climate of open communication.

An alternative to mentally monitoring who has been called on is to use a deck of cards with all of the students' names and to shuffle them at frequent intervals to prevent sequential patterns from occurring. This cumbersome way of distributing questions can be helpful for beginning teachers, but expert teachers rarely use the technique.

Research has also examined the relative effectiveness of first asking the question and then identifying a student versus first identifying the student and then asking the question. Asking the question first is preferable (Good and Brophy, 2000), and this is the pattern we saw in José's questioning. Asking the question, pausing, and then calling on a specific student communicates that the question is meant for *all* students and everyone is expected to pay attention and think about the answer.

If the teacher selects a student before asking the question, the rest of the students are less likely to generate a *covert response,* an important mental operation elicited by questioning. However, exceptions to this rule can occur for management or motivational reasons. For example, "John, what did we say yesterday about the relationship of Hemingway's early life to his later writing?" can communicate that John ought to refrain from his conversation with a classmate, or that John made a comment yesterday that was especially pertinent to the topic. The fact that this sequence violates the teacher's regular one, as well as the inflection in the teacher's voice, communicates the intent of the message.

Callouts

A **callout** *is an answer given by a student before the student is recognized by the teacher.* We have all been in classes where teachers have said, sometimes pleadingly, "Now, don't shout out answers," or "Don't answer until you're called on." These are efforts to eliminate callouts.

In general, callouts should be prevented. This is most effectively accomplished by establishing and consistently enforcing a rule requiring students to be recognized before answering. Allowing students to respond without being called on is undesirable because callouts usually come from higher-achieving or more aggressive students in the class. These students can dominate the interaction, and slower or more reticent students are forced out of the game. In addition, callouts also increase management problems and decrease the amount of time other students have to think about answers.

However, exceptions to these patterns have been found in studies with minority students and students from low socioeconomic backgrounds. With these students, who sometimes lack confidence and may be reluctant to respond, allowing at least some callouts has been positively linked to increased learning (Good and Brophy, 2000).

We saw this illustrated in José's lesson. Let's take a look.

> *José:* So what do you think might be in the bottles? [after prompting Nikki]
> *Nikki:* Air.
> *José:* Yes indeed. Good conclusion, Nikki. What was one of the characteristics of air that we've discussed? . . . Christy?
> *Jason:* It's all around us.
> *José:* That's right. Air is all around us. Well done, Jason. Now look at the balloons on these bottles. [holding the bottles up again] How would you compare the balloons? . . . Leroy?

In this sequence José allowed Jason to interject a response without admonishing him, because Jason was one of the lowest achievers in his class. With more confident and aggressive students, however, callouts result in shorter thinking times and an unequal distribution of opportunities to respond, both conditions that detract from achievement.

So here, as with many instructional issues, teacher judgment is necessary. The ability and confidence of the student, the goals of the lesson, and the orderliness of the classroom are all factors that need to be considered in deciding whether to allow a student to call out an answer.

Choral Responses

The entire class answering a question at the same time is termed **choral responding.** Choral responses are effective for practicing skills, terms, and facts that should be overlearned and available for immediate recall. It is commonly used in foreign language classes, where students need to repeat words and phrases in the new language, and it's sometimes used in math classes, where automaticity is being developed. José appropriately called for a choral response when he taught his students the term *expand.*

> *José:* Yes, excellent, Jill. Now, everyone, I'm going to give you another word for gets bigger. It's called *expand.* Everyone say *expand.*
> *Class:* EXPAND!

In this case José was teaching a new term and wanted everyone in the class to repeat it.

In contrast, choral responses are inappropriate for open-ended or higher-level questions. Imagine a choral response to a question such as, "Who do you think was our most effective President, and why do you think so?"

The disadvantages of choral responding relate to timing and participation; unless all students answer at the same time, slower students can hesitate and parrot or mouth the answers of the quicker students. A solution to this problem is the use of a standard expression or signal, such as "Class," that follows a question and signals time for participation. Some researchers advocate a blend of choral and individual responding to provide opportunities for both wide participation and diagnosis of individual strengths and weaknesses (Becker, 1977).

As we've seen in this chapter, teacher questioning can be a powerful strategy for encouraging student involvement, accommodating the background diversity of our students, and increasing motivation to learn. It is most effective, however, if the questions direct students to clear goals, and builds upon effective topic representations.

Additional ways to promote involvement also exist, and we discuss them in detail in Chapter 8, where we discuss Peer Interaction Strategies For Teaching.

Summary

Student Involvement: A Key to Learning and Motivation. In Chapter 4 we found that students must be actively involved to learn most effectively. Involving students effectively depends on three factors: clear and precise goals, high-quality representations of content, and skilled questioning by teachers.

Student Involvement: The Need for Clear Goals. Teacher thinking begins with clear and precise goals. The ways teachers choose to represent their content, and the kinds of questions they ask as they guide students through their lessons, depends on their goals. Without clear goals, effective lessons are virtually impossible.

Student Involvement: The Role of Content Representations. High-quality representations of content are essential for involving students, because the information they need to answer teachers' questions and understand the topics is displayed for them. Effective content representations provide a concrete focal point for dialoguing with students.

Effective representations exist in a variety of forms. Some of them include examples (the "real thing"), pictures, demonstrations, charts and matrixes, models, and vignettes and case studies. The type of representation depends on the teacher's goal.

Increasing Student Involvement: Teacher Questioning. One of the most effective tools teachers have for promoting involvement is questioning. Questions can be used to assess students' current understanding, increase motivation to learn, and guide students as their understanding develops. Expert teachers efficiently manage all three functions as they help students reach clear goals. In using questions, it is essential to think about their effect on students' attention and thought processes.

Elements of Effective Questioning. Effective teachers ask many questions, use repetition to emphasize important points and make connections appropriately, direct questions equally to all students in the class—whether or not they volunteer—and give individuals adequate time to think about their answers. They first ask the question, pause briefly, and then call on an individual by name to answer. When students are unable to respond, or respond incorrectly, expert teachers provide cues or other questions that help students give acceptable answers, instead of leaving them in favor of other students. In all cases, questions are designed to help students reach clearly thought out goals.

Distributing questions equally to all students communicates that everyone, regardless of personal characteristics, background, or ability, is welcome in the classroom, should be involved, and is expected to learn. Questioning is one of the most effective ways to accommodate student background differences. Open-ended questions are a particularly effective way of ensuring success, increasing student self-efficacy, and promoting student motivation.

Classroom Questions: Additional Issues. The appropriateness of high- versus low-level questions depends on the teacher's goal. Bloom's taxonomy provides one way to sequence questions so that they build upon students' developing knowledge base. Call-outs generally detract from achievement but in some cases are acceptable, and a mix of choral and individual responses may be desirable. Appropriate use of each depends on the context of the lesson and the teacher's goal.

Important Concepts

Callout	Open-ended questions
Choral responding	Prompting
Comparison questions	Questioning frequency
Description questions	Repetition questions
Equitable distribution	Self-efficacy
Model	Wait time

Reflecting on Teaching and Learning

Carol Woodward, a second-grade teacher, is preparing a unit on place value for her second graders. As she gets ready for the lesson, she takes a box filled with popsicle sticks down from a shelf in her room. Many of the popsicle sticks are gathered in bundles of 10 bound together by a rubber band. Carol counts the bundles and mumbles, "Better make a few more," to herself, as she looks around for additional sticks.

We join Carol in the morning at the beginning of her math class.

"Okay, everyone, we're going to be good thinkers today and try to figure out some important ideas," she begins as she walks around the room putting two bundles of 10 sticks together with a single stick on each student's desk.

After giving her students their materials, she continues, "Okay, tell me what you have in front of you. . . . Just tell me what you see."

" . . . Sticks," Jerome offered.

"Popsicle sticks," Nakisha added.

"They have a rubber band around them," Andy put in, beginning to take the band off.

"Yes, good, Andy," Carol smiled, "but leave the band on for me. It's there for a reason."

"Now, what else?" Carol continued. "Gloria?"

" . . . There's another one," she responded, holding up the single popsicle stick.

"Now, what does this number represent?" Carol queried.

" . . . "

"How many sticks do we have?"

" . . . "

"How many bundles do you have?"

"Two," several students answered at once.

"Good, and how many other sticks do you have?"

"One," they responded again.

"So, how many do we have altogether?"

" . . . Three?" Andrea responded hesitantly with a question in her voice.

"No, not three," Carol shook her head. "Someone try again."

" . . . Thirty," Simone guessed.

"Where did you get that?" Carol wondered with a slight smile on her face.

Simone sat for a few seconds and then shrugged his shoulders in an "I don't know."

"Someone else?" Carol urged. "Come on . . . think about it."

" . . . "

"Let's look at them," Carol said after a few seconds. "How many sticks in this bundle?" she asked, holding up one of the bundles.

" . . . Nine," Kevin answered.

"No, 10," Kathy retorted.

"Good!" Carol responded quickly. "There's 10 here. . . . So there's 10 in the other bundle as well. . . . So, how many do we have altogether?"

" . . . "

" . . . 21," Juanita, one of the highest achievers in the class responded after several seconds.

"Yes, excellent!" said Carol enthusiastically. "We have 21. We have two groups of 10 and we have one more, so we have 21 altogether."

"Now I'm going to give you some more materials, and I want you to tell me how many we have this time."

Carol quickly put another bundle of sticks on student's desks and added two more single sticks. She then repeated the process she had used in the first activity.

Questions for Analysis

1. How was Carol's method of involvement similar and different from the way José Alvarez involved his students? Be specific and concrete in making your comparisons.

2. Teacher questioning is one of the key topics in this chapter. Analyze Carol's questioning in the context of the information in the chapter. In any instances where you believe her questioning could be improved, make specific suggestions for doing so.

3. Assess Carol's activity in terms of student motivation. If you believe that the lesson might have been more motivating, offer specific suggestions for improvement.

4. How effective was Carol's lesson for students with diverse backgrounds? Be specific in your response.

5. In Chapter 3, we discussed the concept of *instructional alignment*. Was Carol's instruction aligned? Explain your answer with information taken directly from the case study.

6. It appeared that the students in Carol's class were having some difficulty understanding what she was trying to accomplish. Offer one or more possible explanations for why they were having a difficult time. Make specific and concrete suggestions for what she might have done to help the students better understand the topic.

Discussion Questions

1. How might the following factors influence the ideal number of questions asked in a class?
   a. Grade level
   b. Content area (e.g., math versus art)
   c. Subject-matter expertise of teacher
   d. Ability level of students
   e. Goals of the lesson
   f. Place of the lesson in a unit (e.g., beginning or end)

2. With respect to using questions to informally assess student understanding, what are the advantages and disadvantages of teacher-centered questioning? What alternatives could you recommend?

3. How would the importance of questioning as a way of assessing student understanding vary with:
   a. Time of school year (e.g., beginning vs. end)
   b. Place in a teaching unit (e.g., beginning or end)
   c. Diversity in terms of student ability
   d. Type of content (e.g., difficult vs. easy)?

4. Why should the success rates for questions be relatively high? Are there times when this should vary?

5. In general, researchers hypothesized that higher-level questions would encourage more learning than lower-level ones. Why might higher-level questions be more effective than lower-level ones? In what circumstances wouldn't they be?

6. Analyze the effects of the following questioning decisions with respect to lesson pace, or the tempo of a lesson.
   a. High-level versus low-level
   b. Calling on volunteers versus calling on students randomly
   c. Wait time
   d. Redirected questions

Portfolio Activities

1. *Questioning Frequency.* Observe or videotape two different lessons. Record the number of questions asked in each minute of each lesson.
   a. How many questions were asked in each lesson (the total number of questions)?

    b. During which time in the lesson (beginning, middle, end) were the most questions asked in each lesson?

    c. In which lesson were the students most attentive and involved?

    d. Which lesson was most briskly paced? How did the number of questions influence the pace of the lesson?

    e. What suggestions do you have for increasing the effectiveness of the questioning in each lesson?

2. *Difficulty Level.* Tape a class in which questioning plays a significant role (this might be your class or someone else's). Listen to the tape and count the number of times:

    a. The original question was answered correctly.

    b. The original question was answered partially correctly.

    c. The original question was answered incorrectly.

    d. The original question elicited no response.

    Add the number of questions in *a through d.* Divide the number in *a* by this total. This gives you the average success rate of questions. Now respond to these questions:

    e. Was the difficulty level appropriate for this type of class?

    f. What do the numbers in *b, c,* and *d* tell you about the effectiveness of the questions? What could be done differently to make the questioning more effective?

3. *Questioning Level.* Tape a lesson in which questions play a major role. Play the tape and jot down the questions in the order they were asked. Now classify these questions in terms of whether they are low level (knowledge) or high level (comprehension and above). What is the ratio of high to low? Is there any pattern in terms of the sequence (e.g., LLLH or LHLH)? How did the teacher use questioning level to reach his or her goals? What might the teacher have done differently to use the level of questions to increase learning?

4. *Choosing a Student to Respond: Volunteers.* Tape a questioning lesson in which volunteers are used to respond. Listen to the tape with a seating chart in front of you and mark the number of times different students are called on. Respond to the following questions:

    a. Were the questions evenly distributed in terms of ability level?

    b. Were the questions evenly distributed in terms of student gender?

    c. How did student location in the classroom affect participation rates?

    d. What suggestions do you have for increasing the effectiveness of the selection process?

5. *Choosing a Student to Respond: Random Selection.* Teach and tape a lesson with a questioning format, and randomly select students by using a deck of cards with the students' names to call on them. (Tell students beforehand what you are doing and why.) Analyze the tape in terms of these questions:

    a. Was this lesson harder or easier to teach than one in which you selected students in some other way?

    b. Did the pace of the lesson differ from the first? How?

    c. Comment on students' attentiveness. Was it higher or lower? How could you tell?

d. What changes in your questioning style did you have to make to adapt to this modification?

e. What are the advantages and disadvantages of using this method to select a student to respond?

6. *Questioning Strategies.* Plan a sequence of questions leading up to some point or conclusion. Record yourself on video or audiotape as you implement this sequence in the classroom. Analyze the tape afterward, and compare the sequence that occurred with the one you planned. What caused you to change this sequence? How helpful is planning a questioning sequence prior to a class?

7. *Wait Time.* Tape yourself (or another teacher) as you use questions in a lesson, and then listen to yourself and try to determine how long you wait after asking a question before calling on a student, how long you wait for a student to answer before intervening, and how long you wait for the student to complete his or her answer. Also, identify the student selected to respond and whether he or she was a high or low achiever. Then respond to the following questions.

a. What was your longest wait time? What type of question did it follow?

b. What was your shortest wait time? What type of question did it follow?

c. What was your average wait time?

d. Did your wait times differ for students of different abilities?

Teach and tape another lesson and consciously try to respond to any problems uncovered answering the above questions. Were you able to do this? What difficulties did you encounter in trying to modify your wait times?

8. *Callouts.* Interview a teacher about the presence of or absence of callouts in their room:

a. How does the teacher feel about callouts?

b. What does the teacher do to encourage or discourage them?

c. Are there ever any situations in which they allow or encourage callouts? How will you deal with callouts in your classroom?

9. *Choral Response.* Interview a teacher about the use of choral response in their room.

a. Does the teacher ever use choral response? When and why?

b. What do they feel are the advantages and disadvantages of choral response?

c. What suggestions do they have for maximizing the instructional benefits of choral responding? How will you use choral responding in your classroom?

_6_

Creating Productive Learning Environments: Classroom Management

*I*f you are uneasy about being in front of students for the first time, you're not alone. This apprehension is common among interns, first-year teachers, and even some veterans. Often the concern results from uncertainty about their ability to prevent disruptions and maintain an orderly learning environment. In this chapter, we examine the topic of classroom management and what teachers can do to create productive learning environments. When you've completed your study of this chapter, you should be able to meet the following objectives:

- Explain how classroom management relates to the goals of student responsibility and self-regulation.
- Describe factors that influence planning for classroom management.
- Describe strategies for implementing management plans.
- Define misbehavior and describe strategies to deal with it.
- Explain how classroom management contributes to instructional goals.

Maria Perez looked around her empty classroom and tried to imagine what it would be like with 27 live first graders. This was "Planning Week," the time teachers had to prepare for the year ahead.

Maria had completed her student teaching internship in a school not far from this one. She had worked all summer on unit and lesson plans and was comfortable with what she wanted to teach.

She wasn't sure about her classroom management plans, however. "How in the world will I get all those rambunctious kids to sit quietly and pay attention?" she wondered. She had watched veteran teachers and saw that they were able to keep the lid on, but she wanted to do more; she wanted to help the children grow—in every sense of the word.

Jeff Thompson, a third-year middle-school teacher, walked around his classroom, trying to burn off some nervous energy.

"The room looks great," he thought. Having survived two years of up-and-down teaching, Jeff wanted this year to be different. Students liked his science classes, but more noise and confusion than appropriate was common. He realized that some noise was inevitable, but his students seemed to be constantly testing him. If only he could get them to willingly cooperate. If only. . . .

THE IMPORTANCE OF CLASSROOM MANAGEMENT

Historically, both teachers and the public at large have believed that creating an orderly classroom is essential for learning. For example, from the 1960s until the end of the twentieth century, national Gallup polls identified classroom management as one of the most important and challenging problems facing teachers (Elam and Rose, 1995; Rose and Gallup, 1999). It's the number one concern of beginning teachers (Rose and Gallup, 1999), and research indicates that disruptive students are an important source of teacher stress (Abel and Sewell, 1999). Nearly half of the teachers who leave the profession during the first three years do so because of problems with managing students (Curwin, 1992).

Classroom management has also been a major concern of school policy makers, parents, and the public at large (Elam and Rose, 1995). Now, as we've moved into the twenty-first century, concerns for safety and order have further increased, in reaction to highly publicized incidents of school violence. Although incidents involving school violence receive enormous press coverage and arouse fear and concern in both parents and students, incidents such as these in schools are rare; it's the day-to-day job of establishing and maintaining orderly, learning-focused classrooms that requires so much teacher effort.

Commonly overlooked in discussions of management and discipline is the role of effective instruction. Research indicates that it is virtually impossible to maintain an orderly classroom in the absence of good teaching and vice versa (Doyle, 1986).

To emphasize this important relationship, in this chapter we'll emphasize teachers' ability to create a **productive learning environment,** *which is a classroom that is orderly and focuses on learning.* In it students feel safe, both physically and emotionally, and the day-to-day routines—including the values, expectations, learning experiences, and spoken and unspoken rules and conventions—are all designed to help students learn as much as possible (Tishman, Perkins, and Jay, 1995).

In productive learning environments, classroom order and effective instruction are interdependent (Jones and Jones, 2001). We discussed effective instruction in Chapters 4 and 5, and now we focus on classroom management, the other component of this relationship.

The importance of classroom management for learning is difficult to overstate. In a comprehensive review of factors influencing learning, researchers concluded, "Effective classroom management has been shown to increase student engagement, decrease disruptive behaviors, and enhance use of instructional time, all of which result in improved student achievement" (Wang, Haertel, and Walberg, 1993, p. 262). Students learn more in an environment that is clean, orderly and safe, and an orderly environment is one of the characteristics of an effective school (Teddlie and Reynolds, 1988).

CLASSROOM MANAGEMENT: A DEFINITION

Classroom management *consists of all the teacher thoughts, plans, and actions that create an orderly learning environment.* As examples of the broad array of teacher actions that fall under this umbrella, consider the following:

Jacinta Cortez has her first graders practice the routines of finishing seatwork and putting it in folders in front of the room. She has them finish a short assignment and then walks them through the process of taking the paper, filing it efficiently, and returning to their desks.

Gary Evans has a list of five rules written on a piece of poster paper in the front of the room. Each morning, he gives his fourth graders an open envelope with three slips of paper in it. When a rule is broken, he first warns the student. The second time the student breaks a rule, he goes to the student's desk and takes one of the slips. Any students who lose all three slips in a day write notes home explaining why they must stay after school. Students who lose no more than two slips during the week are given a free hour Friday afternoon when they can bring treats and play games.

Rose Sosa always carefully prepares each morning for her American history class. "These kids are sharp, and their disagreements are animated," she comments to a colleague in the faculty workroom. "If I'm not prepared, they know it, and their discussions get a little out of hand. They're good kids, though, so all I have to do is tell them to tone it down a little, and they're fine."

Each of these situations is different from the others, but they're all part of the management process. Jacinta teaches small children who need to learn classroom routines; Gary developed a plan for systematically enforcing rules; and Rose spent much of her effort in planning for instruction. Planning and organization, routines and procedures, and systems for handling disruptions are all part of effective classroom management.

Management Goals: Learning and Self-Regulation

We have two goals when we attempt to create productive learning environments. The first is to promote as much learning as possible, and teachers should continually ask themselves if their management system contributes to student learning (Morine-Dersheimer and Reeve, 1994). Our second goal is to develop in students the ability to manage and direct their own learning. The classroom environment becomes "one vehicle for the enhancement of student self-understanding, self-evaluation, and the internalization of self-control" (McCaslin and Good, 1992, p. 8).

To accomplish both of these goals, teachers should try to communicate a *responsibility* rather than an *obedience* orientation (Curwin and Mendler, 1988). An **obedience model of management** *teaches students to follow rules and obey authority, using rewards and punishment.* The goal is conformity. By contrast, a **responsibility model of management** *helps students make appropriate choices and learn from their actions and decisions.* Teachers help students learn to be responsible by explaining the reasons for rules and applying **logical consequences,** *which are effects that are conceptually linked to behaviors.* Let's look at an example.

Jason, a high-energy sixth grader, for some unknown reason decided to spit on the door of his bedroom. His mother, Vicki, wanted to make him wash the door. Matt, his father, wanted to punish him by restricting his freedom.

Washing the door is a logical consequence. Jason spit on it; he washes it. The act and the consequence are conceptually linked. In contrast, restriction isn't related to the action; it's not a logical consequence. Restriction might result in conformity, but it doesn't directly teach Jason that he's accountable for his actions.

Logical consequences communicate to students that the world is a sensible and orderly place, that actions have consequences, and that we are responsible for our actions. Let's look at another example.

The kindergarten boys found a lovely mud puddle in the playground during recess. They had much fun running and splashing and then came back into the room wet and dripping and proceeded to leave muddy footprints all over the room. Their teacher, using logical consequences rather than punishment, called them aside for a conference.

"Boys, we have two problems here. One is that you have made our classroom very dirty and it needs to be fixed so that the other children don't get wet and dirty. What can you do to fix it?" One little boy suggested that they could mop the floor.

"Good idea!" said the teacher. "Let's find our custodian, Mrs. Smith, and you can get a mop from her and mop the floor. Now what about our other problem, your dirty clothes?"

"We could call our mothers and ask them to bring us clean clothes!" suggested one boy.

"Another good idea," said the teacher. "But what if your mothers are not home?" This was a tougher problem.

"I know," one boy finally said, "we could borrow some clean clothes from the lost and found box!"

"Good thinking," said the teacher. "And what can we do so that you don't lose so much time from class again?"

"Stay out of mud puddles!" was the reply in unison. (McCarthy, 1991, p. 19)

By helping students see the relationships between their actions and the problem, the teacher was not only solving the immediate problem but also teaching students how to take responsibility for their actions. Research shows that children who are helped to understand the consequences of their actions on other people become more altruistic and are more likely to take actions to make up for their misbehavior (Berk, 2000).

Creating Responsibility-Oriented Classrooms

Teachers' interactions with students are central to the development of responsibility. Research on parenting styles and their effects on children provide us with some guidelines.

Three distinct parental interaction styles were identified, and these patterns had clear effects on children (Baumrind, 1973, 1991). *Authoritarian* parents valued conformity, were emotionally detached, didn't explain their reasons for rules, and discouraged discussions about issues related to behavior. Their children tended to be withdrawn, and they worried more about pleasing their parents than solving problems.

Permissive parents, by contrast, had few expectations for their children and gave them total freedom. This freedom didn't result in happiness or growth, however. Children of permissive parents were immature, lacked self-control, and were anxious and uncertain.

Authoritative parents were firm but caring. They had high expectations, were consistent, and explained the reason for rules. Their children were more confident and secure, had higher self-esteem, and were more willing to take risks.

Similar styles have been identified in teachers; effective teachers tend to be more authoritative than authoritarian or permissive. They establish rules and procedures and take the time to explain why they're necessary. They have high expectations for their students, and they're supportive as students attempt to meet their expectations. When disruptions occur, effective teachers quickly intervene, solve the problem, and return just as quickly to the learning activity. Like authoritative parents, they are firm but caring, they establish rules and limits, and they expect students to demonstrate self-control. In time, students in their classrooms become self-regulated learners.

Management: An Historical Perspective

Before continuing, let's put classroom management into historical perspective and see how research has affected the views we hold today.

Leaders in the area haven't always focused on the teacher as a manager of classroom activities and creator of productive learning environments. Early research viewed the teacher as either a clinical practitioner or an effective disciplinarian (Doyle, 1986; Jones and Jones, 2001).

The clinical practitioner view stressed the teacher's role as counselor/therapist. According to this view, if the teacher understood the causes of disruptive behavior, they could be solved. This approach proved inadequate for two reasons. First, it considered the teacher's primary management role to be a counselor and therapist. While every teacher needs to be sensitive and responsive to students, and teachers should be caring listeners, counseling is not teachers' primary role. Rather, they are expected to promote learning and responsibility in their students.

The second reason was logistical. It's impossible for elementary teachers with 25 or more students, or secondary teachers with up to 150 students, to spend the time needed to work on each student's individual problems. That's what school counselors and psychologists are hired to do. This doesn't suggest that teachers never deal with management problems on a one-to-one basis. As a general approach, however, it's impractical.

A second perspective viewed classroom managers as disciplinarians. An effective manager, for example, would be one who could quickly quiet a class down when they get too noisy or get kids back in their seats after a disturbance. Research, however, didn't support this view, and the story behind this research is interesting.

Jacob Kounin (1970) is primarily responsible for turning our attention away from discipline or intervention strategies to more preventive management-oriented approaches. But he didn't do so without some fitful starts. He began his inquiry with the hypothesis that effective classroom managers use "desist" strategies that both stop the immediate misbehavior and have a "ripple effect" on other students. In examining these strategies, he focused on teacher variables such as language clarity and the intensity of the desist. For example, "Johnny, please stop talking" is clearer than the statement "Class, pay attention," and "Get to work, *now,*" is firmer than "I think we better get working." Tone of voice and the length of the reprimand were also studied as part of intensity. He then measured the amount of time students were attentive and the number of disruptions in the classroom. However, *no relationship* between the desist strategies of less and more effective classroom managers was found.

Reanalysis of the data provided some interesting information. In a study of 40 first- and second-grade classrooms from both suburban and inner-city classrooms, he identified a variable called "withitness." Teachers exhibit **withitness** *if they are aware of the total classroom environment and can work with a student individually without losing track of the rest of the class.* Kounin described this skill as having "eyes in the back of the head." Actually, awareness is only part of it; the other part involves communicating this ability to students. Teachers do so by continually watching for obstacles to learning and nipping problems in the bud before they interfere with the class as a whole. "Withit" teachers are constantly scanning the room and monitoring students' learning progress and behavior.

What is the opposite of a "withit" teacher? We've all seen teachers who talk to a student with their backs to the rest of the class, lecture to the ceiling while several individuals are daydreaming or talking to each other, or sit with paperwork at their desk while students who are supposed to be doing seatwork are going wild. Other problems include reprimanding the wrong student for misbehavior or correcting a less serious infraction while overlooking a more serious one. Some of us have probably been punished for retaliating after we have been poked, while the original perpetrator gets off free. Each of these examples suggests that the teacher is not aware of what is going on in the classroom—that is, isn't "withit."

Beyond the immediate variables it identified, Kounin's work strongly influenced the classroom management studies that followed. Earlier research had framed questions in terms of simple cause-and-effect relationships; that is, if the teacher reprimanded a student, for example, then the student either did or did not stop the misbehavior. Research following Kounin's work viewed classrooms as complex systems in which teacher actions determined only part of the flow. Philip Jackson's book *Life in Classrooms* (1968) also was influential in helping researchers understand the complex tasks that teachers face. In addition, researchers switched to more detailed observational systems that examined the ways that effective teachers orchestrated the complexities of their classrooms.

One of the problems researchers encountered was the near invisibility of an effective teacher's actions in a productive learning environment; they were so efficient that it was difficult to pinpoint specific actions that made a difference. In hindsight we see that this was one of the most important findings of this literature. Effective classroom management doesn't involve simple formulas or single actions. Rather, it's the interaction of multiple factors and strategies, many of which have been considered in advance. This leads us to the topic of planning for efficient management.

PLANNING FOR CLASSROOM MANAGEMENT

Few veteran teachers would think of getting up in front of a group of students without planning for what they were trying to accomplish. As we saw in Chapter 3, they write less on paper than they did when they began teaching, but they are very clear, nevertheless, about what they want to accomplish and how they will go about it.

The need to plan for classroom management is no less important, but beginning teachers often fail to consider plans for management (Weinstein, Woolfolk, Dittmeier, and Shankar, 1994). This oversight is a major mistake. Effective teachers plan and consider strategies for management with as much effort as they put into lessons. This proactive planning makes their interactions with students both easier and more enjoyable.

In planning for management, a long-term goal should be the development of students who assume responsibility for their own behavior. Research on learning (Bruning, Shraw, and Ronning, 1999) and motivation (Pintrich and Schunk, 1996) highlights the importance of students' belief in themselves as self-regulated and capable students. Let's see how teachers at different levels attempt to teach this.

Felicia Perez works with inner-city first graders. She describes her goals in this way: "I try to teach each student a sense of individual responsibility. We have choice time in the afternoon, when students get to select an activity or game and pursue it. They're on their own and I'm trying to get them to think about and take responsibility for their own behavior."

Jeff Thompson teaches middle school science. His management goals are "to develop in them the ability to manage their own learning. I purposefully give them free time to work on individual projects. I want them to experience freedom *and* responsibility. Labs are especially difficult for them because there is all that equipment to mess around with. But we talk about it beforehand and we work with it. I'll even leave the room for a minute or two and stand outside in the hall and listen. I want to give them the feeling that *they're* in charge. Does it always work? No, but we're making progress."

Individual responsibility and self-control don't just happen. They develop over time through the efforts of teachers who plan for and teach these goals. Your plans for management should consider three aspects of your classroom environment:

- The characteristics of your students
- The physical environment in your room
- Classroom rules and procedures

Your classroom's physical arrangement and your rules and procedures will depend on the characteristics of your students, so we consider this factor first.

Student Characteristics

Whom you teach determines how you teach, and this is also true for management. As we saw in Chapter 2, some students pose greater management challenges than do others. In studies of lower elementary classrooms, for example, researchers found high-achieving students to be on task almost twice as much of the time as low-achieving students (Levin, Libman, and Amaid, 1980; Shimron, 1976). In addition, low achievers were idle or involved in inappropriate activities almost three times as often as high achievers. Some children learn to discipline themselves and take responsibility even when they're young, whereas others don't, and this accounts for some of these differences. Other differences result from the quality of the instruction and its match with students' needs and abilities. Whatever the reason, different students pose different management problems, and rules and procedures must be adapted to these differences. For example, classes composed of mostly low achievers will need to be more highly structured than will classes composed of mostly high achievers.

The developmental age of the learner also influences the management plans a teacher makes (Charles, 1999). Children at different stages understand and interpret rules and procedures in different ways. Some of these differences are outlined in Table 6.1.

Although these differences between developmental stages and ability groups suggest different emphases and approaches, the same basic principles that work with one type of student work with others. All students—high or low achievers, cultural minority and nonminority, and high or low socioeconomic status—need understandable sets of rules and procedures that are consistently enforced. And research examining learners with exceptionalities who are mainstreamed into regular classrooms suggests they respond to the same supportive and structured approach (Hardman et al., 1999). In addition, all students require a management system that is systematic and comprehensive, begins on the first day of class, and is maintained throughout the school year.

The Physical Environment

"I can't see the board."

"I didn't get a worksheet. Kevin didn't pass them back."

"What did she say? I couldn't hear her!"

Table 6.1 DEVELOPMENTAL DIFFERENCES IN LEARNERS

Stage	Description
Stage 1: Lower primary	Students in the lower primary grades are generally compliant and oriented toward pleasing their teacher; their attention spans are short, and they tend to break rules more from simply forgetting or not fully understanding them than for other reasons. Rules must be carefully and explicitly taught, modeled, practiced, and frequently reviewed with students at this age. Role playing and positive reinforcement for compliance can help solidify the rules in students' minds.
Stage 2: Middle elementary	This level is characterized by children who understand the game of schooling and generally are still interested in pleasing the teacher. Many elementary teachers believe this age group is the easiest to teach and manage because of these characteristics. Rules are easier to (re)teach at this level, and the teacher's central management task becomes one of maintenance and monitoring.
Stage 3: Middle and junior high	This stage spans grades seven through about nine and includes the tempestuous period of adolescence. As students become more oriented toward their peers, authority is questioned more often, and more disruptions result from attention seeking, humorous remarks, horseplay, and testing of limits. Classroom management can be demanding at this stage. Motivating students and maintaining compliance with the rules are the teacher's major tasks.
Stage 4: High school	In the later high school years, students mature, becoming more personally adjusted and more oriented toward academic learning. Management becomes easier, and more time and energy can be devoted to instructional tasks.

The physical environment is a second planning consideration, and the question we're trying to answer is, "How can I arrange the room to maximize order and learning?"

Several guidelines aid our decisions. First, all students must be able to see the board, overhead projector screen, maps, and other instructional aids. Surprisingly, some teachers don't consider this factor. For example, they display information on an overhead, but the projector itself obstructs the view of several students. As a result, those who can't see crane their necks, bumping other students in the process (who protest out loud), or they shout from the back of the room that they can't see. In other cases, the material displayed on the overhead (or information written on the board) is too small to be seen clearly by all the students. Both management and learning suffer.

In addition, the room should be arranged so the teacher can move from one instructional aid to another, such as from the overhead to a map, without students having to turn their desks or, if possible, even to shift their bodies. Something as simple as rotating 90 degrees in a desk can disrupt the flow of an activity for a lively, rambunctious student.

Materials, such as paper and scissors, should be accessed with a minimal amount of disruption, and procedures for using the drinking fountain, sink, and pencil sharpener should be specified. Many teachers make their desks and storage areas off limits without permission.

Seat arrangements have been researched and, not surprisingly, researchers have found that the best arrangement depends on the learning situation. In some studies, rows have been found to be most effective (Bennett and Blundell, 1983), whereas clusters of four or five desks, or circle patterns, are more desirable in others (Rosenfield, Lambert, and Black, 1985). Teachers should try different arrangements and select the one that works the best for them. Consider the following problem encountered by a seventh-grade teacher.

Priscilla Lopez had 33 seventh graders in a room designed for a maximum of 27, and as a result the students were very close together. She tried arranging the desks in her room in a two-ring semicircle with the outer row behind the inner.

She soon moved the desks back to their original positions. She explained the move in this way, "They weren't trying to be disruptive," she told us. "But as they faced each other across the front of the room, they would inaudibly mouth questions like, 'What are you doing tonight?' or they would be pinching each other on the rear ends. They couldn't handle it, so I went back to a standard arrangement of rows. Interestingly, my advanced kids were okay. Once I told them, it was enough."

This example illustrates the need to consider both the physical arrangement of the room *and* the characteristics of the students as we plan for management. Priscilla experimented with different arrangements and found the one that was most effective for her students.

Where individual students should sit is another issue. Several factors affect this question. First, for students in the fourth or fifth through the eighth or ninth grades, the social aspects of schooling increase, and who sits next to whom becomes important. Second, research has identified an "action zone" in classrooms; students seated in the center or front of the classroom tend to interact more frequently with the teacher; the number of behavioral problems increases as students sit farther away (Adams and Biddle, 1970). Students in the back and corners of the room are more likely to be off task than those close to the front or the teacher's desk.

In response to these factors, some teachers change their room arrangement and student seating charts on a regular schedule, both for the sake of variety and to put different students at the front of the room. They use seat assignments strategically as a management tool to help students become involved and to maintain that involvement throughout the day. Many effective teachers begin the school year with arbitrary seat assignments, planning to make changes after they've had several weeks to observe the patterns of behavior that evolve.

Should students be allowed to sit where they want? If you are a new teacher, a bit anxious about management, or have had management problems in the past, this probably isn't desirable. Later, it can be used as a reward for good classroom behavior with the condition that the good behavior continue. In short, student choice is a privilege, not a right, and it may not be possible in the lower elementary grades, where self-control hasn't yet developed.

Classroom Rules: Establishing Standards for Behavior

Classroom rules *establish standards for acceptable student behavior.* The process of creating rules presents an opportunity to help learners think about their rights and responsibilities in your class. By establishing standards for behavior they help make the classroom predictable and eliminate uncertainty.

The value of rules is well documented. When they're clear, specific, and enforced, student behavior improves (Emmer, Evertson, Clements, and Worsham, 2000; Evertson, Emmer, Clements, and Worsham, 2000). As Kounin discovered, effective managers prevent misbehavior rather than eliminate problems after they occur. Rules, established in advance, are a cornerstone in this process.

Some ways of establishing rules are better than others. Guidelines are outlined in Figure 6.1 and discussed in the paragraphs that follow.

We see "student involvement" at the top of Figure 6.1. Involving students in the process is consistent with a responsibility model of management and has three important benefits:

- It promotes a sense of ownership, increasing the likelihood that students will follow the rules.
- It emphasizes student self-control and personal responsibility.
- It treats students as moral thinkers, helping them see the values, such as respect for others, behind rules.

As teachers have worked with their students, they've found it helpful to refer to the Golden Rule, emphasizing how rules establish broad guidelines for treating others in the same way we want to be treated.

Rules must be consistent with the policies of the school and district. This statement may be obvious, but we include it as a reminder to check these policies before you prepare your own classroom rules.

Your list of rules should be as short as possible. No specific number exists, but five is often cited as a guideline. The number of rules to follow should be short enough for students to remember. Interestingly, the most common reason students break rules is simply because they forget. This tendency is particularly true with young children, but it is often

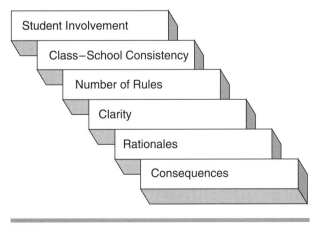

Figure 6.1 Guidelines for Developing Rules

the case with older students as well. For example, middle school and high school students are sometimes given legal-size sheets of paper with long lists of single-spaced rules, the rules are discussed on the first day of class, and they aren't referred to again until they're broken. Under these conditions, we all would forget. The solution is to identify a short list that you intend to enforce consistently. Some examples might include:

- Speak only when given permission by the teacher.
- Remain in your seat until given permission to leave.
- Bring all materials to every class.
- Keep hands and materials to yourself.
- Treat the teacher and your classmates with respect.

These rules pertain to most if not all classrooms. For example, researchers have found that up to 80 percent of classroom management problems involve students talking inappropriately, and much of the remaining 20 percent are related to students' being out of their seats without permission or failing to bring books, pencils, or notebook paper to class (Jones and Jones, 2001).

Teachers, particularly at the middle and junior high levels, also complain about students' tendencies to hit, poke, shove, grab, and "fiddle" with each other and each other's belongings. If the rules we identified were consistently enforced, most management problems would cease to exist.

In discussing rules with students, state them clearly and specifically. For example, compare the following rules:

a. Always come to school prepared.
b. Bring your book, notebook, paper, and pencil to every class.

Rule *b* is specific in describing the desired behavior; its meaning is clear. In contrast, rule *a* requires additional interpretation; interpretation adds to uncertainty, and, in extreme cases it can lead to misunderstanding and controversy. When rules are stated in more general terms, such as "Treat the teacher and your classmates with respect," explain and provide examples of obeying the rule and other examples that illustrate breaking the rule.

In presenting rules, carefully explain the *reasons* for them. Providing reasons for rules may be the most important guideline that exists. It demonstrates that rules aren't arbitrary, and as we emphasized earlier, it communicates that the world is a sensible and orderly place. This might be as simple as explaining why one person talking at a time is necessary for learning, or it could involve a longer discussion about the need to respect the rights of others. It's impossible to implement a "responsibility model" of management without explaining the reasons for rules, and we can't emphasize its importance too strongly.

Finally, plan consequences. Plan for what you will do when students break rules, and communicate these consequences to the students. Many teachers have difficulty with management because they're uncertain about how to respond when rules are broken. Planning helps eliminate much of this uncertainty.

In considering consequences, student characteristics are important. High school students may need only a simple reminder, and consequences may be unnecessary. On the other hand, with younger students you may have to consistently enforce rules with specific consequences until they're socialized into your classroom routines.

Table 6.2 SAMPLE CONSEQUENCES FOR BREAKING OR FOLLOWING RULES

Consequences for Breaking Rules

First infraction	Name on list
Second infraction	Check by name
Third infraction	Second check by name
Fourth infraction	Half hour of detention
Fifth infraction	Call to parents

Consequences for Following Rules

A check is removed for each day that no infractions occur. If only a name remains and no infractions occur, the name is removed.

All students without names on the list are given 45 minutes of free time Friday afternoons to do as they choose. The only restrictions are that they must stay in the classroom and must not disrupt the students who didn't earn the free time.

Source: L. and M. Canter (1992).

Assertive Discipline. In their very popular but controversial approach, *Assertive Discipline,* Lee and Marlene Canter (1992) advocate planning consequences for both breaking and following rules. The system describes specific reinforcers that are given for following the rules and punishers that are administered for breaking them. A sample set of reinforcers and punishers is illustrated in Table 6.2.

Plans can vary, of course, and the consequences you choose depend on your professional judgment. These differences aren't important. What is important from an assertive discipline perspective is the fact that teachers specifically plan consequences for each infraction.

Assertive discipline is controversial. Critics charge that it's punitive, pits teachers against students, and stresses obedience and conformity at the expense of learning and self-control (Curwin and Mendler, 1988; McLaughlin, 1994). Supporters disagree, contending that its emphasis on stated rules and positive reinforcement is proactive and effective (Canter, 1988).

Regardless of the controversy, the program has been widely used. It is difficult to find a school district in the country that hasn't had at least some exposure to assertive discipline; estimates suggest that more than 750,000 teachers have been trained in the program (Hill, 1990).

Procedures: Creating an Efficient Learning Environment

Procedures *establish the patterns that learners will follow in their daily activities.* As opposed to rules, which are few in number, the typical classroom will have procedures for all routine classroom activities. For instance, procedures will exist for putting materials in folders, passing in and returning work, bathroom passes, changing activities, going to lunch, and many other activities. With high school students, who understand the game of school, establishing procedures is quite simple and planning for them is fairly easy. In contrast, planning procedures for a kindergarten or first-grade class requires careful consideration. They must be taught, explained, and monitored carefully at the beginning of the school year.

As procedures become established, they become routines. This is your goal. Routines are invaluable to both teachers and students. They simplify teachers' days by reducing the number of decisions they must make and allowing them to devote their emotional and physical energies to instruction. They help students by communicating expectations and making the environment predictable. As a simple example, if students know they are to come in and get out their homework while the teacher checks attendance, the teacher doesn't have to spend time or energy reminding them.

Some general areas where procedures need to be considered are listed in Table 6.3. Planning for them is essential for the smooth functioning of your classroom.

To illustrate the amount of detail needed in considering procedures, we've broken down one area—beginning of class—into subareas (see Table 6.4). While the amount of detail may seem overwhelming, it is important to think about these factors, considering the ages of your students, and the school you teach in. Talking to other teachers can be invaluable here. Find out what procedures teachers in earlier grades and other classrooms use and build on this foundation. Don't feel obligated to follow other teachers' procedures, but when you deviate from those regularly used in your school, make sure you take the time to teach and explain these differences to your students.

As with planning rules and consequences, the specific procedures aren't essential; thinking about and planning for them in advance is.

Table 6.3 **AREAS FOR CONSIDERING CLASSROOM PROCEDURES**

Procedural Area	Concerns
1. Entering classroom/beginning of period	What should students do when they enter the classroom?
2. Large-group instruction	What are the rules for participation (e.g., should students raise their hands to respond)?
3. Individual/small-group instruction	What should students do when they need help? When they're done?
4. Materials and equipment	How are papers handed in and back? What about tape and scissors?
5. End of period	How do students leave the classroom (e.g., does the bell or the teacher signal permission to leave)?
6. Out-of-room policies	How do children receive permission to use the bathroom or go to the main office?

Table 6.4 SAMPLE BEGINNING-OF-CLASS PROCEDURES

Area	Questions
1. Entering class	Should students go directly to their seats when they enter the class? Can they talk? Can they walk around the room? Is there an assignment on the board?
2. Attendance	How will the teacher take attendance? What about tardies (e.g., do they go to the office to remove their names from the absentee list)?
3. Previous absences	Is a note from parents required? What about missed work (e.g., homework and quizzes)?
4. Logistics	What about lunch count? Milk money? Special schedule for the day (e.g., assemblies, PE, etc.)?

IMPLEMENTING MANAGEMENT PLANS

It is August 29, Yolanda's first day of kindergarten. She has been to the school before to see her brother in a play and to attend the Fall Carnival. She has heard about school from her brother and parents, but still she is not sure what to expect. Her dad walks her to school, and she feels good. The sun is warm, and she is excited. As she gets closer to school, she notices all the people and cars. Her dad helps her thread her way through the crowds to her classroom. She sees some familiar faces of neighborhood playmates, but most of the people are strangers. The teacher approaches her, smiles, welcomes her, and takes her to her desk just as the bell rings. She sits down, apprehensively, not sure what to do next.

Jim, too, is excited about his first day of school. He is in fifth grade and is looking forward to playing on the playground before school and seeing all of his old friends. When he arrives at school, the playground is just as he expected—chaos. He goes over to the baseball diamond where some of his friends are playing catch and half-heartedly trying to get a game going.

Soon the bell rings, and the students funnel into the school. Jim knows the name of his teacher and the location of the classroom. Reputation has it that he is strict but good. The teacher stands at the door and directs each student to find the desk with his or her name on it. As the teacher moves to the front of the room, Jim thinks, "I wonder what this year will be like."

Delia is beginning her junior year of high school. In addition to the rest of her schedule, she is taking advanced placement American history, even though she was in standard world history as a tenth grader. She is excited to be in school this first morning but somewhat anxious about the honors class. After the perfunctory homeroom discussions of pep rallies and other activities, the bell sends her to first period, where Mrs. Perez waits. As she enters the class, she notes a sign on the board: "Seat yourself and fill out the card on your desk." For better or for worse, she is in advanced placement American history.

These examples have two things in common. First, each involves students beginning the first day of school with expectations and apprehensions. The expectations result from past experience or descriptions of experiences from others, and the apprehensions result from uncertainty about what is expected.

Concern in response to uncertainty is universal. We all feel more comfortable when we know what is expected of us. Teachers address this need when they plan for classroom management and communicate these plans to students.

Second, each illustrates the beginning of school. This crucial period sets the stage for the remainder of the year.

Implementing Plans: The First 10 Days

The beginning of the year is crucial for classroom management. It sets the tone and lays the foundation for the rest of the year. A disorganized first two weeks communicates uncertainty to students and drains the energy and resolve of the teacher.

Suggestions from a number of studies can be summarized in one word—*simplify* (Emmer et al., 2000; Evertson et al., 2000)! Treat the first day as distinct and view it as the beginning of a long-term effort to teach your rules and procedures. Resist the urge to jump into content; instead, spend the necessary time organizing the class for the rest of the year.

Research offers some suggestions. They're illustrated in Figure 6.2 and discussed in the paragraphs that follow (based on work by Vasa, 1984).

Plan for Maximum Contact and Control. Plan instructional activities during the first two weeks of class with management concerns a high priority. Use whole-class instruction rather than small-group work, minimize work with individual students, and keep the number of transitions from one activity to another low. Stay in the classroom and don't allow yourself to become distracted by parents or new students.

Teach Rules and Procedures. We cannot overemphasize the importance of explicitly teaching rules and procedures. Teachers often simply "present" their rules, which is much like teaching a concept or principle in the abstract. Students construct understanding of

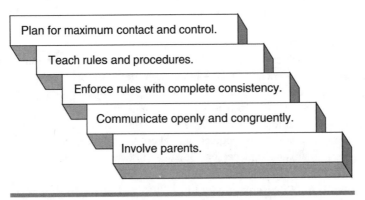

Figure 6.2 Guidelines for the First Day of Class

rules and procedures, just as they construct understanding of any concept, principle, or generalization. So just as you would provide examples to teach the concepts *arthropod* or *metaphor,* for example, you must provide examples to help your students understand rules and procedures.

Let's look at how one teacher does this.

A second-grade teacher begins her first day of class by having students write their full name on a card and taping the name tag to their shoulder with masking tape. Her instructions to her class begin.

Teacher: Now, everyone, when I teach I have some rules that are necessary. My first rule is that when we're having a discussion, it is very important to me that you wait and stay completely quiet until I call on you. I will call on each of you as we go along, so you must wait your turn. Now, what is the first rule, Sidney?

Sidney: . . . We don't talk until you call on us.

Teacher: Yes, exactly, Sidney. So if I call on Sharon and she is having a hard time answering the question, what do you do? Carlos?

Carlos: I . . . wait. I don't say anything.

Teacher: Yes, excellent, Carlos. And why do you suppose this rule is so important? Kim?

Kim: If . . . if we shout out answers, other kids can't hear.

Teacher: That's right, Kim. That's very important. And it's also important that we all get a chance to think about and practice on the ideas we're learning. So, we must wait our turn.

The teacher in this case actually "taught" students the rule, much in the same way she would teach any concept. She presented and explained it, followed with an example, and explained why the rule was important. Time and effort is well spent on this process. It eliminates problems before they begin and results in a more smoothly functioning classroom throughout the year.

Some teachers display the rules on a front bulletin board, a portion of the chalkboard, or some other prominent place. Others prefer to hand out rules on a sheet of paper and discuss them. How the rules are displayed isn't an important issue; the essential factor is that they are carefully taught, reviewed, and reinforced. Our goal is for all students to be aware of all our rules at all times.

Teaching procedures is similar to teaching rules. Researchers have found that effective primary teachers actually have young children practice "dry runs" on procedures like putting papers in folders at the front of the room and using and returning materials, such as scissors (McGreal, 1985). They do two or three dry runs each day for the first few days, and the patterns then become firmly established.

Some essential procedures that should be considered the first few days include:

- Entering and leaving the classroom
- Using materials and facilities, such as the pencil sharpener
- Using the bathroom
- Turning in assignments

Enforce Rules with Consistency. Monitor and enforce rules with complete consistency during this period. Your goal is to make the management environment completely predictable. You want all students to know what the rules are and that you will intervene immediately when a rule is broken. For instance:

The second day of class, Glen Stancil began reviewing problems for finding the area of rectangles with his sixth graders. He knew that they had covered the topic in fifth grade, but he wasn't sure of their understanding. He displayed a problem and began, "What's the first step in the solution? . . . Toni?"

" . . . "

"We multiply," Susan jumped in.

Glen turned directly to Susan and asked firmly but evenly, "Susan, what was the first rule we discussed?"

"We . . . don't talk until you call on us."

"Yes, exactly. Very good. Thanks, Susan. Now, what are we asked for in the problem, Toni?"

Despite a teacher's careful efforts to teach rules in the first few days, students will still break them, usually because they simply forget or slip up. Each time this happens, successful teachers take the time to stop and immediately remind the students of the rule and why it is important. This is what Glen did.

While most students comply with the rules when they are carefully taught and reviewed, some students test us; in these cases, it is even more important that rules are monitored thoroughly and consistently. We pass the test by dealing with the infraction before continuing on with our instruction.

Instruction may be disrupted by these management interventions during the first few days of the year. However, we cannot state too strongly how important it is to establish the patterns you expect for the remainder of the year during this period. Unfortunately, we've seen many examples of teachers near the end of the first or second grading period who are still trying to teach over students who are visiting with each other in the back of the room, goofing off, or even sitting with their backs to the teacher. Learning can't occur under these conditions. Time spent establishing desired patterns during the first two weeks will pay enormous dividends during the rest of the year.

Communicate Openly and Congruently. Communicate openly and congruently with your students. Notice, for example, that Glen intervened directly and firmly when Susan broke the rule. In Chapter 5, we discussed the need for congruent verbal and nonverbal behavior. This congruence is particularly important in dealing with management issues. Telling students to be quiet as we glance over our shoulders at them communicates a different message than moving toward them, facing them directly, looking in their eyes, and then telling them to stop talking.

There is, however, no place in the classroom for threats and ultimatums. They detract from a positive climate and reduce the teacher's credibility. Open and honest communication makes the teacher accessible and human without reducing authority. It enhances the dignity of both the students and the teacher.

Involve Parents. Research indicates that students benefit from home-school cooperation in several ways:

- More positive student attitudes toward school as evidenced by better attendance rates

- Higher academic achievement and greater willingness to do homework
- Increased understanding and support from parents

(Cameron and Lee, 1997; Lopez and Scribner, 1999)

One teacher's efforts to involve parents from the beginning of the year are illustrated in Figure 6.3. This communication serves at least three functions. First, the students' parents are made aware of important rules and procedures. As a result, when students leave the house in the morning, parents will be more inclined to say, "Do you have your homework with you?" or "Do you have paper?" Unfortunately, not all parents will be helpful or cooperative, but if the letter increases the support in only a few, you are ahead of where you would have been.

Second, the letter communicates that the teacher is accessible to parents. It also paves the way for further communication should the teacher need to call parents about some issue later in the year.

Finally, the signature at the bottom symbolizes a form of commitment to the rules and procedures on the part of both the student and their parents; it's a type of contract. As a result, serious infractions are less likely to take place.

Communication can be enhanced in other ways. A simple handwritten note sent home with a child who has been doing particularly well takes only a minute and can do much to promote a positive home-school partnership. Periodic phone calls, while admittedly time consuming, can help with both management and achievement problems. This pattern can also be established in the first two weeks. Getting a phone call during the first two weeks of school communicates that the teacher is on top of things and that he or she cares about the student. The most common parental complaint we hear is "Why weren't we told he was misbehaving?" or "We never knew he was having trouble in history." You are much more likely to have problems with parents by not communicating than you are by being a little overzealous at the beginning of the school year.

Learner Diversity: Challenges to Home-School Communication

Student diversity is an asset; it provides opportunities for students to learn about themselves and others. However, diversity can also present barriers to a teacher wanting to establish links between home and school. Some include:

- Economic barriers
- Cultural barriers
- Language barriers

Economic Barriers. Communication and the development of links between home and school take time. Parents working two jobs and struggling to make ends meet, for example, may not have the time or energy to become fully involved in their child's schooling (Ellis, Dowdy, Graham, and Jones, 1992). Child care and lack of transportation are other potential obstacles. Research indicates that parents *do* care about their children's education but that schools need to be flexible in working with them (Epstein, 1990).

Cultural Barriers. Many of our students' parents experienced a very different educational system than the one their children are in, and they may not understand our goals, rules, and procedures in the way we intend. For example, one study found that

September 30, 2001

Dear Parents and Students,

It was a pleasure meeting so many of you during our open house. Thank you for your cooperation and help in making this year the best one ever for your youngster.

I am looking forward to an exciting year in geography, and I hope you are too! In order for us to work together more effectively, some guidelines are necessary. They are listed below. Please read through the information carefully and sign the bottom of the page. If you have any questions or comments, please feel free to call Lakeside Junior High School (272-8160). I will return your call promptly. This sheet must be kept in your student's notebook and/or folder all year.

Sincerely,

Survival Guidelines

1. Treat your classmates and the teacher with respect.

2. Be in class, seated, and quiet when the bell rings.

3. Bring covered textbooks, notebook, and/or folder, paper, pen, and pencils to class every day.

4. Raise your hand for permission to speak or to leave your seat.

5. Keep hands, feet, and objects to yourself.

Homework Guidelines

1. Motto: I will always TRY, and I will NEVER give up!

2. I will complete all assignments. If the assignment is not finished or is not ready when called for, a zero will be given.

3. Head your paper properly---directions were given in class. Use pen or pencil---no red, orange, or pink ink. If you have questions, see Mrs. Barnhard.

4. Whenever you are absent, it is your responsibility to come in early in the morning (8:15-8:50) and make arrangements for makeup work. Class time will not be used for this activity. Tests are always assigned 3 to 5 days in advance. If you are absent the day before the test, you should come prepared to take the test as announced.

5. No extra credit work will be given. If you do all of the required work and study for the tests, there should be no need for extra credit.

_____ (student) _____ (parent)

Figure 6.3 Letter to Parents

Puerto Rican parents believed schools in the United States were too impersonal and that teachers didn't demonstrate that they cared for children enough (Harry, 1992).

Misinterpretation can occur in both directions. Asian and Latino parents often defer to the school and a teacher's authority in matters of discipline, believing schools are the proper place for handling management problems. Teachers sometimes view this deference as apathy, not realizing that parents care, but feel that the school's authority shouldn't be questioned (Harry, 1992). This again illustrates the need for open communication.

Language Barriers. Language can be another obstacle to home-school cooperation. Some parents speak only halting English, making communication through letters and phone calls difficult and making it hard for parents to help their children with homework (Delgado-Gaitan, 1992). The following are some strategies for overcoming language barriers:

- Ask other teachers or parents to translate letters into parents' native languages.
- Use older students in the school to help translate letters.
- Involve students in three way parent-student-teacher conferences.

Research consistently indicates that parents want to help and become involved (Hoover-Dempsy, Bassler, and Burow, 1995). Teachers need to capitalize on this desire by making every effort to open and maintain communication with parents.

The Relationship between Management and Instruction

At the beginning of the chapter we said that productive learning environments are orderly and focus on learning. We also said that it is virtually impossible to maintain an orderly classroom in the absence of good teaching and vice versa. We want to revisit this relationship now.

By establishing expectations, rules, and procedures early in the school year, we can devote more of the remaining time to instruction and to monitoring the rules and procedures we've created. An important measure of a productive learning environment is the extent to which it allows instruction to take place with as little disruption as possible. If instruction is effective, the need for management interventions sharply decrease.

We focus now on three instructional factors that help minimize the likelihood of management problems: *orchestration, momentum,* and *smoothness.*

Orchestration. **Orchestration** *refers to the teacher's ability to maintain the flow of a lesson while addressing human and management concerns.* A student blurting out, "Can I go to the bathroom?" or the teacher having to say, "Sarah, please turn around," can be disruptive to the lesson. Effective teachers accommodate these potential disruptions without losing the flow of the lesson.

Well-established procedures help orchestration. If a procedure for going to the bathroom has been taught and practiced, for example, a quick nod of the head to the one student and a quiet "Sarah, please turn around," can be smoothly integrated into the overall lesson.

Overlapping, *or the ability to monitor more than one variable at a time* (Kounin, 1970), is closely related to orchestration. It is especially important in elementary classrooms, where, for example, it is common for most of the students to be working at their desks individually while the teacher conducts a small reading group.

At the secondary level, teachers can lose the class while they're dealing with individual problems, such as students who were late or absent the day before. Effective teachers have procedures for dealing with these situations, and in cases where contingencies arise they give the class a task and quickly deal with the incident while simultaneously scanning the room. In short, they can do two things at once. This isn't easy, but with practice and effort it can be learned.

Momentum. **Momentum** *provides the lesson with strength and direction.* Lessons with momentum move at a brisk pace, fast enough to keep learners involved, but not so fast that they get lost. The questioning strategies we discussed in Chapter 5 are important tools teachers can use to help maintain momentum.

Momentum can be thought of as a vector—a line that indicates the strength and direction of a force. Just as forces have direction and strength, so do lessons. Some lesson vectors are weak, barely maintaining the teacher's interest, much less students'. Successful lessons actively involve students; they're swept along by the lesson's momentum.

Here we again see how management and instruction are interdependent. Students are much less likely to be disruptive when they're actively involved, and it's easier to involve students when the classroom is orderly.

Let's see how one teacher established and maintained lesson momentum with a potentially dry topic.

I was starting a lesson on the Crusades in my World History class, and I knew that it was deadly last year. The students could have cared less about that old stuff.

So I decided that I would try something different. I went into the room and said, "I have an announcement. The school administration has just decided that all extracurricular activities will be eliminated in the school. They decided that the benefits didn't warrant the cost, and the purpose of school is for learning, not extracurricular activities."

They, of course, were outraged. I let them talk for a few minutes and then I asked what we might do about it. Well, one thing led to another, and we finally decided that we would be on a "crusade" to get extracurricular activities back into the school. I used it as a framework, and we kept referring back to it as an analogy as we studied the real Crusades.

By involving students in the lesson and relating the content to students' own backgrounds and concerns, the teacher created a powerful lesson vector that carried through the whole unit.

Events that drain energy away from the thrust of a lesson detract from momentum. For example, a fire bell during a class in which the novel *Old Yeller* is being read orally and is coming to its heart-rending conclusion is an example of an out-of-class obstacle to momentum. Teacher-related sources are found in Table 6.5.

Smoothness. **Smoothness** *describes a lesson's continuity.* When teachers allow lessons to wander or spend too much time interrupting lessons to reprimand students, problems with smoothness occur. Smoothness relates closely to the concept *connected discourse,* which we discussed in Chapter 4. Some obstacles to smoothness are shown in Table 6.6.

Table 6.5 OBSTACLES TO MOMENTUM

Behavior	Example
Behavior overdwelling	Nagging or preaching. Continuing to talk about a misbehavior after it stopped. For example, "How many times do I have to tell you to stop that talking?" or "This is the third time today that I've told you to stop playing with your pencils."
Content overdwelling	Staying on task well after students have mastered it. For example, teaching the concept of odd numbers by having the class name *all* odd numbers up to 100.
Fragmentation	Having single students or small groups do work that the whole group could do. (If this is the case, why not do the activity as a whole and save time and effort?)

Source: Adapted from Kounin, 1977.

Table 6.6 OBSTACLES TO SMOOTHNESS

Behavior	Examples
Distractions	Calling attention to a piece of paper on the floor in the middle of explaining a math problem. (This *may* be important, but should it occur now?)
Intrusions	In the middle of a reading lesson, the teacher says, "I just noticed that Sally isn't here. Does anybody know why she's absent?" (The teacher should write a note to himself or herself and find out later.)
Flip-flops	Returning to an activity after it is done. After science books are put away and social studies has begun, the teacher says, "Oh, yeah, I just remembered one more thing about arthropods."

Source: Adapted from Kounin, 1977.

The keys to maintaining smoothness are well-planned lessons with aligned instruction together with a well-established system of rules and procedures that help maintain order.

In summary, orchestration, momentum, and smoothness help produce a productive learning environment. They contribute to learning and facilitate management.

Classroom Management: Situational Variables. Certain types of activities are intrinsically harder to manage than others. For example, researchers found that engagement rates were highest for teacher-led small groups and lowest for pupil presentations (Gump, 1967). In addition, engagement rates for whole-class activities, such as discussions and question-and-answer sessions, were higher than those during seatwork, and the more often seatwork was used, the lower engagement rates were (Burns, 1984).

Other studies have found similar patterns in favor of teacher-led work (Kounin and Sherman, 1979; Rosenshine, 1980).

Lesson momentum helps us understand these results. Brisk question-and-answer sessions, which are typical of whole-group activities, help maintain momentum, whereas students must establish their own pace and momentum during individual assignments and seatwork. These are reasons we suggested using whole-group instruction at the beginning of the school year.

This doesn't imply that only teacher-led strategies should be used, however. As students get used to your routines and the patterns for the year are established, you can gradually move to more student-centered lessons. As you plan for them, be aware that different types of activities put different management demands on teachers and different self-management requirements on students.

Also, be aware that beginnings of classes, transitions from one activity to another, and ends of classes are times when management problems are most likely to occur. Being aware of these possibilities helps you plan strategically for them.

MANAGEMENT INTERVENTIONS

The best laid plans of mice and men often go awry.

Robert Burns

Management interventions *are teacher actions designed to eliminate unwanted student behaviors.* In our discussion of management during the first 10 days of school, we briefly discussed the need for interventions when students break rules. The purpose in those interventions is to establish desired patterns of behavior early in the school year and reduce problems later on. This strategy works. Despite the teacher's best efforts, however, management incidents will inevitably occur. When this happens, teachers must intervene. These interventions are often as brief as "Jerry, pay attention please" and occur as frequently as 16 times per hour in the typical classroom (White, 1975). In learning environments that aren't productive, however, frequent interventions chew up valuable time, interrupt momentum, bother students, and wear out the teacher. In a reanalysis of his 1970 data, Kounin (1983) found that some teachers had engagement rates of only 25 percent and accumulated nearly 1,000 interventions in one day. Whew!

Defining Misbehavior

Interventions occur as a result of misbehavior. This isn't as simple as it appears on the surface, however, because what is viewed as misbehavior in one classroom can be acceptable in another. And the same behavior in two different contexts can result in different reactions from the teacher (Doyle, 1986). For example, a teacher is more likely to overlook students who are off task near the end of a lesson than at the beginning or middle. Also, some talking between students is generally accepted during transitions but not during the main part of a lesson. So how can teachers, much less students, understand what is meant by misbehavior?

Two factors are important—the context in which the behavior occurs and the impact of the behavior on learning (Charles, 1999; Jones and Jones, 2001). For example, talking during a transition is a different context than talking during a learning activity;

talking during the transition typically doesn't interfere with learning, unless it makes the transition so long that instructional time is lost.

Researchers have identified five broad categories of misbehavior that appear here in increasing order of seriousness:

- Private inattention and off-task behavior that doesn't bother others
- Talking or off-task behavior that bothers other members of the class
- Defying authority or refusing to obey the teacher
- Behaving immorally, such as cheating, lying, or stealing.
- Behaving aggressively, including verbal or physical attacks on the teacher or other students (Charles, 1999)

We examine interventions for these misbehaviors in the sections that follow.

An Intervention Continuum

Disruptions vary widely, from an isolated incident (such as a student briefly whispering to a neighbor during quiet time) to chronic infractions (such as someone repeatedly poking, tapping, or kicking other students). Because infractions vary, teachers' reactions should also vary. To maximize instructional time and minimize disruptions, our goal is to keep interventions as unobtrusive as possible. A continuum designed to reach this goal is illustrated in Figure 6.4 and discussed in the following sections.

Praising Desired Behavior. Teachers are commonly encouraged to "catch 'em being good," and since our goal in any classroom is to promote positive actions, "praising desired behavior" is a sensible beginning point, particularly as a method of preventing misbehavior. Elementary teachers praise openly and freely, and middle and secondary teachers often quietly comment to students after class, "I'm extremely pleased with your work this last week. You're getting better and better at this stuff. Keep it up."

Interestingly, praise for desirable behavior occurs less often than we might expect, probably because desired behavior is taken for granted, whereas misbehavior attracts attention. Making an effort to change these patterns and acknowledge desired behavior and good work can significantly contribute to a productive learning environment.

Ignoring Inappropriate Behavior. If an incident of misbehavior is brief, we're often better off simply ignoring than calling attention to it. This strategy is appropriate, for example, if

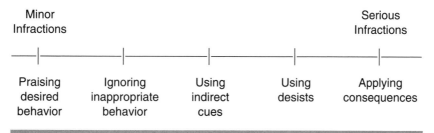

Figure 6.4 An Intervention Continuum

two students whisper to each other but soon stop. Combining praise and ignoring misbehavior can be very effective with minor disruptions (Charles, 1999; Jones and Jones, 2001).

Using Indirect Cues. Teachers can use **indirect cues,** such as *proximity, methods of redirecting attention, and praising other students,* when students are displaying behaviors that can't be ignored but can be stopped or diverted without addressing them directly. For example, suppose Chris has poked Tanya, and you hear her mutter, "Stop it, Chris." You can move near Chris and call on him, which is likely to bring him back into the lesson and eliminate his poking. Your *proximity* and question redirect his attention.

Praising other students can also be an effective management tool. Teachers, especially in the lower grades, use statements like, "I really like the way Armondo is working so quietly," which uses Armondo as an example for the rest of the students.

Using Desists. A **desist** *occurs when a teacher tells a student to stop a behavior* (Kounin, 1970). "Glenys, we don't leave our seat without permission," "Glenys!", a finger to the lips, or a stern facial expression are all desists, and they're the most common teacher reaction to misbehavior (Humphrey, 1979; Sieber, 1981).

Clarity and tone are important in the effectiveness of desists. For example, "Randy, what is the rule about touching other students in this class?" or, "Randy, how do you think that makes Willy feel?" are clearer than "Randy, stop that," because they link the behavior to a rule or the consequences of the behavior. Students react to these subtle differences, preferring rule and consequence reminders to teacher commands (Nucci, 1987).

The tone of desists should be firm but not angry. Research indicates that kindergarten students handled with rough desists actually became more disruptive and that older students felt uncomfortable in classes in which rough desists were used (Kounin, 1970). In contrast, gentle reprimands and the suggestion of alternative behaviors, combined with effective questioning techniques, reduced time off task by 20 minutes a day (Borg and Ascione, 1982). (Here again we see the interdependence of management and instruction.)

Clear communication (including congruence between verbal and nonverbal behavior), an awareness of what's happening in the classroom (withitness), and the characteristics of effective instruction are essential in effectively using desists to stop misbehavior. However, even when these important elements are used, desists alone sometimes don't work.

Applying Consequences. Careful planning and effective instruction will eliminate much misbehavior before it starts. Some minor incidents can be ignored, and simple desists will stop others. When these strategies don't stop disruptions, you must apply consequences.

Logical consequences are preferable because they treat misbehaviors as problems and demonstrate a link between the behavior and the consequence. Classrooms are busy places, however, and it isn't always possible to solve problems with logical consequences. In these instances, behavioral consequences are acceptable:

Damon is an active sixth grader. He loves to talk and seems to know just how far he can go before Mrs. Lopez gets exasperated with him. He understands the rules and the reasons for them, but his interest in talking takes precedence. Ignoring him isn't working. A call to his parents helped for a while, but soon he was back to his usual behavior—never quite enough to require a drastic response, but always a thorn in Mrs. Lopez's side.

Finally, she decides that she will give him one warning. At a second disruption, he is placed in timeout from regular instructional activities. She meets with Damon and explains the new rules. The next day, he begins to misbehave almost immediately.

"Damon," she warns, "you can't work while you're talking, and you're keeping others from finishing their work. Please get busy."

He stops, but 5 minutes later he's at it again. "Damon," she says quietly as she moves back to his desk, "I've warned you. Now please go back to the timeout area."

A week later, Damon is working quietly and comfortably with the rest of the class. (Adapted from Eggen and Kauchak, 2001)

Damon's behavior is common, particularly in elementary and middle schools, and this type of behavior is what drives teachers up the wall. Students like Damon cause more teacher stress and burnout than threats of violence and bodily harm. He is disruptive, so his behavior can't be ignored; praise for good work helps to a certain extent, but much of his reinforcement comes from his buddies. Desists work briefly, but teachers burn out constantly monitoring him. Mrs. Lopez had little choice but to apply consequences.

The key to handling students like Damon is consistency. He understands what he is doing, and he is capable of controlling himself. When he can—with absolute certainty—predict the consequences of his behavior, he'll quit. He knew that his second infraction would result in timeout and, when it did, he quickly changed his behavior. There was no argument, little time was used, and the class wasn't disrupted.

Dealing with Individual Problems

So far, we have approached classroom management primarily from a group perspective. Periodically, however, we will have one or more students who don't respond like the rest of the class, and concentrated individual action is warranted.

One approach to this problem is both humanistic and informational, based on the works of Gordon (1974) and Glasser (1969, 1977). These authors stress the importance of clear and open communication between teacher and students. Gordon emphasized active listening in which both teachers and students acknowledge each other's message by restating it to communicate understanding. Glasser (1977) emphasized helping students understand the roles and obligations of everyone in the classroom and outlined 10 sequential steps to dealing with behavior problems. The steps range from simple intervention to contact with an outside agency. The process stops as soon as the behavior improves. Since the procedure is labor intensive, it should primarily be used as a last resort. The steps are outlined as follows:

1. Identify the student and list typical responses (interventions) to his or her past behavior.
2. Look at the list, discard ineffective interventions and focus on those that are more productive.
3. Try to make the student feel accepted. Talk to the student, give him or her special responsibilities, and use extra encouragement.

4. If progress isn't made, discuss the problem with the student and require the student to describe the behavior in his or her own words. When you're satisfied that the student understands why the behavior is a problem, ask that he or she stop it.

5. Again, confer with the student and have the student describe the behavior and state whether or not it is against the rules. Ask the student what he or she should be doing instead.

6. Repeat step 5, but call attention to the fact that previous attempts haven't been successful. Require that a plan of action be drawn up that will solve the problem. This plan must include the student's commitment to the plan.

7. If the student doesn't follow the plan, take action. Isolate the student or use timeout procedures. During this time, the *student* is responsible for devising a reinstatement plan intended to solve the problem. The plan must be approved by the teacher.

8. Place the student in in-school suspension. Because the student has not been able to behave acceptably, the principal is called in. Return to the classroom is contingent upon following the rules.

9. If a student cannot be integrated back into the classroom, the parents are called in to discuss the problem and made aware that the student will be sent home. One-day home suspensions are used when students continue to ignore the rules.

10. If the student still does not respond, it may be necessary to refer him or her to another agency.

As you can see, the process is time consuming. When other approaches fail, however, teachers should look for alternate solutions such as these to problems that are both stressful and detract from productive learning environments.

The cooperation and participation of the principal is essential. Talk the problem over with your principal, and if his or her intervention is necessary, ask for it in advance. Also, recruit parents' assistance; most are eager to work with teachers in creating positive environments for their children.

Serious Management Problems: Violence and Aggression

Class is disrupted by a scuffle. You look up to see that Ron has left his seat and gone to Phil's desk, where he is punching and shouting at Phil. Phil is not so much fighting back as trying to protect himself. You don't know how this started, but you do know that Phil gets along well with other students and that Ron often starts fights and arguments without provocation. (Brophy and Rohrkemper, 1987, p. 60)

This morning several students excitedly tell you that on the way to school they saw Tom beating up Sam and taking his lunch money. Tom is the class bully and has done things like this many times. (Brophy and Rohrkemper, 1987, p. 53)

What would you do in these situations? What would be your immediate reaction? How would you follow through? What long-term strategies would you employ to try and prevent these problems from recurring? These questions were asked of teachers identified by their principals as effective in dealing with serious management problems

(Brophy and McCaslin, 1992). In this section, we consider their responses together with other research examining violence and aggression in schools.

Problems of violence and aggression require both immediate actions and long-term solutions. Let's look at them.

Immediate Actions. Immediate actions involve three steps: (1) Stop the incident (if possible), (2) protect the victim, and (3) get help. For instance, in the case of the classroom scuffle, a loud noise, such as shouting, clapping, or slamming a chair against the floor will often surprise the students enough so they'll stop. At that point, you can begin to talk to them, check to see if Phil is all right, and then take them to the administration where you can get help.

If your interventions don't stop the fight, immediately rush a student to the main office for help. Unless you're sure that you can separate the students without danger to yourself or them, attempting to do so is unwise.

You are legally required to intervene in the case of a fight. If you ignore a fight, even on the playground, parents can sue for *negligence,* on the grounds that you are failing to protect a student from injury. However, the law doesn't say that you're required to physically break up the fight; immediately reporting it to the administration is an acceptable form of intervention.

Long-Term Solutions. In the long term, students must first be helped to understand the severity of their actions, that aggression will not be allowed, and they're accountable for their behavior (Brophy, 1996; Limber et al., 1998). In the incident with the lunch money, for example, Tom must understand that his behavior was reported, it's unacceptable and won't be tolerated.

As a preventive strategy, students must learn how to control their tempers, cope with frustration, and negotiate and talk rather than fight. One approach uses problem-solving simulations to help aggressive youth understand the motives and intentions of other people. Research indicates that these youngsters often respond aggressively because they misperceive others' intentions as being hostile (Hudley, 1992). Following problem-solving sessions, aggressive students were less hostile in their interpretation of ambiguous situations and were rated as less aggressive by their teachers.

Other approaches to preventing aggression include teaching students to express anger verbally instead of physically and to solve conflicts through communication and negotiation rather than fighting (Burstyn and Stevens, 1999; Lee, Pulvino, and Perrone, 1998). One form of communication and negotiation is learning to make and defend a position—to argue effectively. Students taught to make effective arguments—emphasizing that arguing and verbal aggression are very different—become less combative when encountering others with whom they disagree. Learning to argue also has incidental benefits: People skilled at arguing are seen by their peers as intelligent and credible.

Experts also suggest the involvement of parents and other school personnel (Brophy, 1996; Moles, 1992). Research indicates that a large majority of parents (88%) want to be notified immediately if school problems occur (Harris, Kagay, and Ross, 1987). In addition, school counselors, school psychologists, social workers, and principals have all been trained to deal with these problems and can provide advice and assistance. Experienced teachers can also provide a wealth of information about how they've handled similar problems. No teacher should face persistent or serious problems of violence or aggression alone.

In conclusion, we want to put problems of school violence and aggression into perspective. Though they are possibilities—and you should understand options for dealing with them—the majority of your management problems will involve issues of cooperation and motivation. Many can be prevented, others can be dealt with quickly, and some require individual attention. We all hear about students carrying guns to school and incidents of assault on teachers in the news. Statistically, however, considering the huge numbers of students that pass through schools each day, these incidents remain infrequent.

Summary

The Importance of Classroom Management. The importance of classroom management is difficult to overstate. It is the number one concern of beginning teachers, and disruptive students are an important source of teacher stress. It has historically been a major concern of school policy makers, parents, and the public at large.

Effective management is strongly linked to achievement. Students learn more in environments that are orderly and safe.

Classroom Management: A Definition. Research has identified several important factors related to classroom management. First, classroom management and instruction are interdependent; one cannot exist without the other. Second, effective teachers prevent, rather than solve, most classroom management problems. Third, effective classroom management is hard to analyze because smoothly run classrooms mask the considerable time and effort needed to produce them.

Planning for Classroom Management. Planning for management is as essential as planning for instruction. Developmental differences in students and the physical environment both influence the ways teachers plan their management systems.

Rules and procedures are the threads that structure the social fabric of the classroom. Rules should be relatively few in number and provide standards for acceptable behavior. Procedures describe efficient ways of completing a myriad of classroom tasks. As procedures become established, they develop into routines that make the classroom operate smoothly.

Implementing Management Plans. The beginning of the school year is crucial for classroom management. Rules and procedures are established during this time, and teachers need to communicate and enforce their expectations clearly and consistently. These expectations often need to be explicitly taught and illustrated for younger students; older students, who have been socialized to schools may only need to be reminded.

Effective managers orchestrate their classrooms so that routines and procedures complement instruction. Lesson momentum creates a positive vector that pulls students into lessons and involves them in learning. Smoothness maintains the direction of the lesson while minimizing internal and external distractions.

Management Interventions. Misbehavior depends on both the context and the amount of disruption it causes. Teachers need to help students understand what constitutes misbehavior and how they're responsible for behaving appropriately.

In responding to misbehavior, the match between the problem and its consequences is important. Minor problems must be dealt with quickly and efficiently to minimize their effects on the lesson.

More serious or persistent breaches of conduct need to be dealt with firmly and directly. In dealing with problem students, expectations should be clearly defined and enforced in agreed-upon contracts. If this approach doesn't work, other adults, including principals and parents, need to be called in to ensure that the problem does not detract from learning.

Important Concepts

Classroom management
Classroom rules
Desists
Indirect cues
Logical consequences
Management interventions
Momentum
Obedience model of management

Orchestration
Overlapping
Procedures
Productive learning environment
Responsibility model
  of management
Smoothness
Withitness

Reflecting on Teaching and Learning

Selina Moreno sat at her desk during planning week, the week before students returned from summer vacation, and looked out the window.

"This year has got to be better than last year," she thought, and then with a half smile she mumbled audibly, "How could it be any worse?"

Selina had been hired in the middle of the school year to replace a fifth-grade teacher who left for "health reasons." Some of Selina's colleagues implied that the other teacher had quit because of frustration, and Selina soon found out why. The classroom was a mess, the previous teacher seemed to have no rules, and the students couldn't describe any routines that they were used to following. In addition to the lack of structure, the class had more than its share of "problem students," whom the other teachers nicknamed the "Wild Bunch." It didn't take Selina long to figure out who these students were, but it took her the rest of the school year to try to figure out what to do with them. This year was going to be different, she vowed, and she started making plans to ensure that it happened.

On the first day of class, she greeted her fifth graders with a stern but pleasant face. She told them that their names were on their assigned seats, and directed them to quickly find the seats and sit down quietly.

When they were settled, she began, "Good morning, class. My name is Miss Moreno and I'm glad to have you in my class this year. Every class needs rules and I've written some up here on this bulletin board. I'd like to go over them briefly. Who can read the first one? . . . Andrea?"

" . . . Talk only when called on by the teacher," Andrea read hesitantly.

"Good, Andrea. You need to be quiet unless you raise your hand and I call your name. Who can read the second one? . . . Javier?"

"Don't leave your seat without permission."

"Good, Javier. We can't just wander around the classroom. You need to stay in your seat unless I tell you you can leave it."

The discussion of rules continued until Selina summarized by saying, "Class, these rules are important. If you follow them we'll get along fine. If not, you're going to have trouble in here and you don't want that, do you?"

Selina then spent about 5 minutes on procedures. After that she outlined the schedule for the day and the week and launched into her first lesson of the year. Initially, the class was a little disorganized, but after a couple of weeks they were doing what Selina wanted.

About a month later, Selina was sitting in the faculty lunch room when her friend, Freddie, another second year teacher, came by.

"How's it going?" Freddie asked as she looked into her lunch bag. "Ugh, not yogurt and fruit again. This diet is getting real old."

"I know what you mean. My class is kind of like that."

"What do you mean?" replied Freddie with a puzzled look.

"Well, it's a lot better than last year. At least the kids aren't driving me nuts, but they don't seem very excited about coming to class."

"Why not?" prompted Freddie between spoonfuls of yogurt.

"Well, we're doing whole class instruction, just like the management books say to do at the beginning of the year, but the kids seemed bored. I tried to do some small-group work, but Tony, the class clown, spoiled it for everybody, so I told them we couldn't do small-group work anymore. That went over like a lead balloon."

Freddie nodded sympathetically.

"Then I tried a structured reward system for the class. Between you and me, the class didn't need it. It was designed to rein in Tony. So I told them that any day that we got through with any of the three tokens left over, we'd do learning centers at the back of the room for the last half hour of the day. They really like to play the math and word games. So true to form, Tony messes it up just about every other day and the class gets mad at him. I thought peer pressure would work, but Tony seems oblivious. Sometimes I think he even likes the negative attention. Needless to say, I'm a little bummed. Any suggestions?"

Freddie thought for a while before responding.

Questions for Analysis

1. Was Selina's class more obedience or responsibility oriented? What evidence do you have for your conclusion?

2. Analyze the way Selina established rules and procedures in her classroom. How could the process have been improved?

3. Comment on the effectiveness of Selina's strategies for teaching procedures. How might they be improved?

4. Comment on the relationship between Selina's instruction and management. How could this relationship be improved?

5. Analyze the effectiveness of Selina's structured reward system. How could it be improved?

Discussion Questions

1. How can a teacher tell if students have developed responsibility? How might the definition of responsibility change with grade level? What types of instructional and managerial strategies promote responsibility? What types discourage the development of responsibility?
2. How do the following factors influence the number of procedures that operate in a classroom?
   a. Grade level
   b. Subject matter
   c. Type of student (e.g., high versus low achiever)
   d. Type of instruction (e.g., large group versus small group)
3. What advantages are there to seeking student input on rules? Disadvantages? Is this practice more important with younger or older students? Why?
4. If you were a substitute teacher (or a student teacher) and were going to take over a class mid-year for the rest of the year, what kinds of things would you need to know and do in terms of classroom management?
5. Explain the statement "Misbehavior is contextual." Give a concrete example. Why might this idea be difficult to understand for some students? Why is it important that students understand it? What can teachers do to help students understand this idea?
6. What are the advantages and disadvantages of the following interventions?
   a. Praising desired behavior
   b. Ignoring inappropriate behavior
   c. Using indirect cues
   d. Using desists
   e. Applying consequences

Portfolio Activities

1. *Management: The Teacher's Perspective.* Interview a teacher to find out his or her views about management. The following questions might serve as a framework:
   a. What are your goals for classroom management?
   b. How have these changed over the years?
   c. How does the particular class that you teach right now influence either your management goals or how you implement your management plans?
   d. How do your management strategies change over the school year?
   e. What is the most difficult or challenging aspect of classroom management?
   Analyze these responses in terms of the contents of this chapter.
2. *Classroom Rules and Procedures.* Interview a teacher about the rules and procedures in his or her classroom.
   a. What are they?
   b. How are they communicated to students?

    c. What are the biggest problem areas?

    d. How have these changed over the years?

    e. What management advice does the teacher have for a beginning teacher?

    Analyze the teacher's responses in terms of the contents of this chapter.

3. *School Rules.* Observe students as they move and interact in the halls. Infer what the rules are in regard to dress, appropriate hall behavior, and tardiness and the bell. Discuss these topics with a teacher and compare your conclusions. What role will you play in enforcing school rules?

4. *Classroom Rules.* Interview two high- and two low-ability students in a class and record their answers to the following questions:

    a. What rules do you have in your class?

    b. Which ones are most important?

    c. Why do you have them?

    d. What happens if they are not followed?

    Compare the responses of the two groups of students. What do their responses suggest about working with different kinds of students?

5. *Classroom Procedures.* Observe a class for several sessions and try to identify the procedural rules which are functioning for the following activities:

    a. Entering the class

    b. Handing in papers

    c. Sharpening pencils and accessing materials

    d. Volunteering to answer a question

    e. Exiting class

    Discuss your findings with a student (or teacher) to check the accuracy of your findings. Which of these procedures would you use in your classroom?

6. *Interactive Management.* Tape and observe a classroom lesson. Identify places in the lesson where the teacher either verbally or nonverbally exhibited the following behaviors/characteristics:

    a. Withitness

    b. Overlapping

    c. Accountability

    d. Momentum

    e. Smoothness

    How did these contribute to the lesson's effectiveness?

Constructivist Approaches to Instruction

*I*n Chapter 4 we described the research base that describes effective teaching, and we summarized this research in a general model of instruction. Research indicates that teacher enthusiasm and high expectations, together with the ability to conduct effective reviews, provide focus and feedback, and reach meaningful closure at the end of a lesson increase learning in students of all ages. In Chapter 5 we focused on ways teachers can promote learning by actively involving students in learning activities, and in Chapter 6 we discussed the characteristics of productive learning environments, with special emphasis on classroom management. Those chapters described abilities that all teachers and classrooms—regardless of grade level, content area, or topic—should have.

This section of the book builds on the foundation we've developed, and we're now going to focus on teaching models that can be used to reach specific goals. In some cases the goals are primarily cognitive, whereas in others they're more oriented toward social development.

The framework we're using in this chapter is constructivism—a view of learning suggesting that learners create (construct) their own understanding of the topics they study rather than having that understanding delivered to them by teachers or written materials. When you've completed your study of this chapter, you should be able to meet the following goals:

- Describe the characteristics of constructivism.
- Identify the characteristics of constructivism in case studies of classroom instruction.
- Develop learning activities based on constructivist views of learning.
- Explain how groupwork can be used to enhance learning.

Lucy Zuniga, a sixth-grade teacher with 28 students in her class has been working on a unit on heat transfer. The students have been involved in activities on convection and radiation, and she now wants them to understand *conduction*. The students have also studied matter, the particles that make up matter, and the characteristics of solids, liquids, and gases.

On Monday evening Lucy is planning for the week's science activities as she thinks to herself, "I'll do this tomorrow . . . and also the wire and wax activity—that will give them one more way to think about conduction. . . . Yeah, let's see if I have everything."

She then glanced over to a shelf where she had a coffee maker with a glass coffee pot sitting on it. She got up, went over, and looked in a drawer for a long spoon, a piece of heavy copper wire, some wax, and an alcohol burner. Seeing the materials there, she went back to her planning.

At 10:59 on Tuesday morning, Lucy walked among her students as they finished their math assignment. She glanced at the clock and said, "All right, everyone, put your work in your folders. Those of you who haven't already completed your work, finish it tonight and put it in your folders as soon as you come in the room in the morning. Now let's get ready for science."

Several of the students got up, put their papers in their folders, and returned to their desks.

At 11:01 Lucy began, "Now . . . let's look at what we have here," and she brought down the coffee maker, pot, and spoon, as shown in the following drawing.

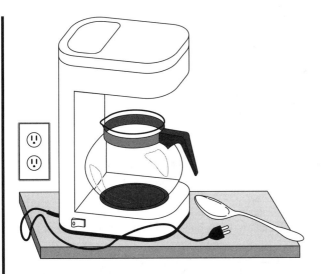

"Let's feel the coffee pot and the spoon," Lucy suggested. "C'mon up, Sarafina," she gestured to Sarafina, who was sitting near the front of the room.

"How do they feel?"

"Smooth."

"Okay, . . . how else do they feel?"

" . . . Cold."

"Okay, good. . . . Sarafina says that the spoon and coffee pot feel smooth and cold," Lucy turned to the rest of the class. "Now I'm going to pour some water in the coffee pot and put the spoon in it."

She filled the coffee pot about a third full, put the spoon in it, and plugged it in, so it appeared as follows:

"Now," Lucy continued, "Let's review for a few minutes while we watch the coffee pot. . . . We've been talking about heat and energy. What is one way that heat is transferred, Bharat?"

" . . . Radiation?"

"Yes, good, Bharat," Lucy smiled at Bharat. "Who can give us an example. . . . Bev?"

" . . . Well . . . like when you hold your hand over a hot burner on a stove, your hand gets warm."

"Good, Bev . . . and explain why that's an example . . . Dominique?"

" . . . Your hand gets warm, but . . . it's up above the burner, and . . . there's nothing between your hand . . . well, there's air between the burner and your hand, but it wouldn't matter. . . . Anyway, your hand gets warm because the waves go up and heat it."

"Yes, very good explanation," Lucy smiled. "How about another example? Jim?"

" . . . When we stand out in the sun, it warms us up."

"And what else do we know about radiation, Lakasha? . . . Think about what Dominique said."

" . . . It goes even if there's no air. . . . Like from the sun to the earth."

"Good, Lakasha," Lucy smiled. "Can you add a little more to that? What do we mean when we say 'no air'?"

" . . . Like . . . a vacuum?" Lakasha responded hesitantly.

"And what's that have to do with what Dominique said?"

" . . . She said there was no air . . . no . . . she said it wouldn't matter if there was no air."

"Yes, good, both of you."

" . . . It travels in waves," Ramon interjected, keying on what Dominique had said.

"Yes, Ramon, good. . . . Now remember, everyone, radiation is a form of heat energy that travels in waves, and it doesn't need any matter to travel through. We can't see the waves, but they move, such as going from the burner to our hand. We know the waves moved because our hand gets warm."

Lucy went through a similar process as she guided the students in a review of convection, in the process emphasizing that convection requires matter, such as gases and liquids, and the particles of the gas or liquid actually move from one place to another, such as a convection current in the ocean, and the movement of the air in a convection oven.

"Now let's look at this again," Lucy directed, pointing to the coffee pot. Now carefully come up and touch the top of the spoon," she directed to Sarafina, who came up and felt it.

"It's hot," Sarafina said quickly.

"It's hot!" Lucy repeated. "Now . . . that brings up a question. It was cold before, and now it's hot. . . . hmm? Now I want you to be very good observers and thinkers, and I want you to work with your partner and try to explain why the spoon got hot. . . . Now before we start, what do we know for sure?"

" . . . The coffee pot did it," Jeremy suggested, referring to the coffee pot and spoon.

"Sure, we know that heating up the coffee pot is important. . . . But we want to think about exactly *how* it did it. . . . And, what are you going to keep in mind as you work on our problem?

" . . . "

"What have we been discussing?"

" . . . Stuff about heat," Leeman volunteered.

"What about heat?"

" . . . Radiation and convection," Jessica added.

"Yes, very good . . . Keep radiation and convection in mind when you work on your explanation. . . . Now go ahead."

The students, who were seated next to their partner, slid their desks together and started talking. The room quickly became a buzz of voices as students worked. Lucy moved among them, sometimes listening to their comments and moving on, and at other times, stopping to make a comment or suggestion of her own. Several of the students got up, went and looked more closely at the coffee maker and spoon, and with warnings from Lucy about being careful with the hot pot, held their hands near the system, felt the end of the spoon, and talked briefly to each other.

Lucy allowed the students to continue working for about 5 minutes and then announced, "All right, everyone, I think you've been doing some good thinking, so let's share some of our ideas."

"I have a question, Mrs. Zuniga," Elizabeth asked. "When I put my hand near the burner, I could feel some heat. Is that radiation?"

"Good question, Elizabeth. Did everyone hear Elizabeth's question? What do you think . . . anyone?"

The students briefly discussed Elizabeth's question and concluded that it was indeed an example of radiation.

"This is the kind of thinking we're looking for," Lucy went on. "Elizabeth is relating what we're doing here to what we did yesterday. Excellent!"

"Okay, let's go on. . . . Which group wants to volunteer?"

"We think it's radiation," Jason volunteered. "The waves go up the spoon and make it hot, . . . like our hand over the burner."

"Go ahead, Sonja," Lucy encouraged, seeing her shaking her head.

" . . . No, I don't think so," Sonja said uncertainly.

"Why not?" Jason wondered.

"Radiation doesn't need something to travel through . . . like we said before . . . when we put our hand over the burner, there wasn't anything there."

"There was air there."

"Yeah, but radiation can go through air. It can't go through something hard . . . like a spoon."

"Jason asks a good question," Lucy commented. "How do we know that radiation can't go through solids, or at least doesn't go through them very well?"

" . . . "

Suppose you're out in the hot sun, and you move into the shade. . . . How do you feel?"

" . . . Cooler," Kathy offered after a few seconds.

"Why do you suppose?"

"The tree . . . or whatever blocked the sun."

"What's your reaction to that?" Lucy turned to Jason.

"I . . . guess so. . . . Yes, that's true."

The class discussed the possibility of radiation making the spoon hot for a couple more minutes, finally concluding that it probably wasn't radiation.

They turned to a discussion of convection and concluded that while convection could have heated the water in the pot, convection couldn't have heated the spoon, since the particles in the spoon couldn't move from one place to another.

Lucy displayed the following drawing on the overhead.

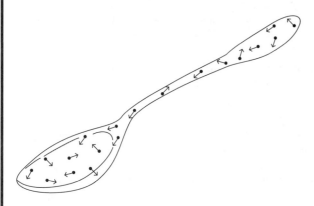

"Let's take a look at this drawing," Lucy directed. "What do you notice about it?"

" . . . There's a bunch of little dots with arrows on them in the spoon," Simone offered.

"And what do you suppose they're supposed to represent?" Lucy probed.

" . . . The particles of the spoon," Juanita suggested.

"Good, and how about the arrows?"

" . . . "

"What do you notice about the arrows? . . . Michael?"

"Some are long and some are short . . . and they're pointing in all different directions."

"Good, so what might they represent?"

"The particles moving?" Michael offered with a question in his voice.

"Sure," Lucy confirmed. "Remember, we used the dots and arrows to help us visualize the movement of air particles. . . . But there's an important difference here. . . . What is it?"

" . . . "

"What is an important difference between gases and solids?"

"Solids are heavy and gases aren't," Dennis noted.

"Okay, and what else? . . . What about the way they move?"

" . . . Air molecules move around, but solids don't," Toni responded, seeing Lucy look at her.

Lucy guided the students into noticing that the spoon was in contact with the pot.

Then she had eight of the students come up to the front of the room, blindfolded them, and told them to move around slowly. In the process, and with considerable laughter from the rest of the class, they bumped into each other a few times. She then directed them to move around more quickly, and as they did, they bumped into each other harder and more often. She then had them stop and return to their desks.

"Now," Lucy continued after the class had settled down, "what did you observe?"

"They ran into each other," Jenny commented.

"They ran into each other harder when they moved faster," Larry added.

Lucy continued her questioning, and through her guidance they concluded that the students represented particles of matter, and heated particles moved fast, "bumped" un-heated particles, and made them move fast as well.

"Now, what does all this have to do with the spoon?" Lucy asked. "Let's see if another example will help. I'd like everyone to look at this," Lucy continued, as she took out a piece of wire with three pieces of wax stuck on it.

"We're going to heat the wire with this burner," she continued, placing the unlit burner under one end of the wire, so it appeared as follows:

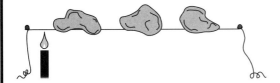

"What do you think will happen?" Lucy continued. Some of her students predicted the wire would get hot. Others said the wax would melt. Lucy prompted them by asking, "If the wax melts, which will melt first?" From students' quizzical looks she could tell they were thinking.

"Well, let's see. Watch carefully," she continued, lighting the burner and putting it under one end of the wire. As the wire heated, the piece of wax closest to the flame started to droop, then fall. The other two followed in order.

"What happened?" Lucy asked.

After students discussed the fact that the hot wax globs fell in sequence, Lucy encouraged them to compare this demonstration with the spoon example.

She then introduced the term *conduction* and through her prompting helped students conclude that conduction has the following characteristics:

1. It is a form of energy transfer.
2. It occurs by having molecules move and interact.

She closed the lesson by asking students as their homework assignment to predict what would happen if they replaced a piece of wood or a butter knife for the piece of wire.

To begin our discussion, let's think about Lucy's lesson in the context of the research base we summarized in Chapter 4 and our discussion of student involvement in Chapter 5. We see that she first *reviewed* radiation and convection, and then provided for *focus* by displaying her coffee maker and spoon and asking students to explain why the top of the spoon got hot. This attracted her students' attention and provided a framework for the rest of the lesson.

Lucy was well *organized*. First she showed the coffee maker and spoon, then turned to her review while they were heated, which allowed her to maximize her *instructional time*. She communicated clearly throughout the lesson, stayed focused on the topic, used clear language, and emphasized important points with repetition.

One of the most important aspects of her instruction was the way she represented her topic. The students saw a concrete demonstration—the coffee maker and spoon, a simulation where the blindfolded students illustrated bumping into each other, a model that helped them visualize a similar process in the spoon, and the demonstrations with the wire and wax. She also asked them to predict differences between the piece of wood and a butter knife.

Her students were highly involved throughout the lesson, both as they worked with their partners and in the whole-class discussion. She asked many questions, distributed them to a variety of students, and prompted where appropriate. She applied both the effective teaching research and strategies for involving students throughout the lesson.

In carefully examining Lucy's lesson, however, we see that a more detailed analysis is necessary to fully understand how she promoted learning in her classroom. This analysis is the topic of our chapter.

CONSTRUCTIVISM: A VIEW OF LEARNING

Over the past 25 years, a rapidly expanding literature has changed our views of the ways that students learn and develop (Eggen, 2001), and this understanding has moved the focus in teaching away from the teacher and toward the students (Bransford et al., 2000; Lambert and McCombs, 1998). This doesn't imply that teachers have less important roles in promoting student learning, however. In fact, their roles are even more important than they were once believed to be.

Let's see why this is the case. It is now widely believed that learners create their own understanding of the topics they study (Mayer, 1998; Phillips, 1997), and the term used to describe this process of creating understanding is **constructivism,** *a view of learning in which learners use their own experiences to create understanding that makes sense to them rather than having understanding delivered to them in already organized forms* (Eggen and Kauchak, 2001).

As a way of helping us clarify the idea of constructivism, think about a tape recorder. It captures the exact wording of a speaker, stores it, and plays it back in precisely the form in which it was spoken. As learners, we don't behave like tape recorders. Rather than recording and storing exact copies of what we hear or read, we modify the information so that it makes sense to us. So what we store in our memories is the result of our own efforts to understand what we've experienced. To illustrate this process, consider the following conclusions often held by students:

- Summer is warmer than winter [in the Northern Hemisphere] because we're closer to the sun in summer. (We are, in fact, slightly farther from the sun.)
- The forces forward on a car traveling at a steady speed of 50 miles per hour are greater than the forces backward. (The forces are equal.)
- All Muslims are Arabs. (Only about 18 percent of the world's Muslims are Arabs.)
- Geography is primarily a process of naming locations and making maps. (The study of geography includes the study of culture, economics, and politics, among many other topics.)

In addition, other conclusions that children form are not only inaccurate but also humorous:

- *Syntax* is all the money the church collects from sinners.
- *Trousers* is an uncommon noun because it's singular on the top and plural on the bottom.
- Most of the houses in France are made of plaster of Paris.

Obviously, no teacher wanted students to make these conclusions, nor did students "record" them from a teacher's description or book. The conclusions can only be explained by saying learners constructed them. No other theory of learning is able to offer an acceptable explanation for learner misconceptions such as these.

These examples help us see why we said earlier that teachers' roles are even more important than they were once believed to be. If students did indeed record understanding, teaching would be simple. Teachers would merely present information, students would record and store it in the form in which it was presented, and they would use it later when necessary.

Since students don't record information, however, learning is much more complex. Students' experiences, together with their existing background knowledge, strongly influence the understanding that they construct. For instance, we've all had the experience of holding our hands close to a candle or burner on a stove. The closer we are to the heat source, the hotter it feels. So, based on these experiences, concluding that we (in the Northern Hemisphere) are closer to the sun in the summer makes sense.

We can even see how kids can come up with some of the off-the-wall conclusions that they create. They make objects from plaster of Paris, for example, and they learn that Paris, the city, is in France. When we see these connections, we realize that the leap to the conclusion that houses in France are made of plaster of Paris is actually quite sensible for a young child.

This also helps us understand why teaching is much more complex than simply explaining information to students. For example, in addition to clearly explaining topics, we must ask them a large number of questions because their answers reveal their current understanding. When their answers indicate that their understanding is incomplete or invalid, we must intervene with additional questions and examples to try and help them construct more complete or valid ideas.

CHARACTERISTICS OF CONSTRUCTIVISM

While different constructivists disagree on some aspects of the knowledge construction process, most agree on the characteristics listed in Figure 7.1 (Eggen and Kauchak, 2001; Good and Brophy, 2000). Let's take a look at them.

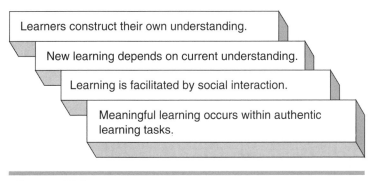

Figure 7.1 Characteristics of Constructivism

Learners Construct Understanding

The basic principle of constructivism is that learners construct (create), rather than record, their understanding, and this is the idea we discussed in the last section.

Let's look at some dialogue from Lucy's lesson to illustrate this process.

Jason: We think it's radiation. The waves go up the spoon and make it hot . . . like our hand over the burner.

Lucy: Go ahead, Sonja.

Sonja: No, I don't think so.

Jason: Why not?

Sonja: Radiation doesn't need something to travel through . . . like we said before . . . when we put our hand over the burner, there wasn't anything there.

Jason: There was air there.

Sonja: Yeah, but radiation can go through air. It can't go through something hard . . . like a spoon.

Lucy: Jason asks a good question. How do we know that radiation can't go through solids, or at least doesn't go through them very well?

"*. . .*"

Lucy: Suppose you're out in the hot sun, and you move into the shade. . . . How do you feel?

Kathy: Cooler.

Lucy: Why do you suppose?

Kathy: The tree . . . or whatever, blocked the sun.

Lucy: What's your reaction to that?

Jason: I . . . guess so. . . . Yes, that's true.

Jason initially thought radiation caused the spoon to get warm. As the lesson developed, his understanding gradually evolved to the point where he believed that something else caused the warming.

We can also see from students' comments that they didn't "receive understanding" from Lucy. Until Jason was faced with the example of being cooler in the shade, he was unwilling to give up his ideas about radiation. Until his ideas about radiation no longer made sense to him, he was unwilling to consider a different explanation. This process of individuals creating their own personal meaning is the core of constructivism.

Lucy played an essential role in the process. She could have simply explained the concept of *conduction,* and this is what teachers commonly do. But these verbal explanations often do little to help ideas "make sense," and learners frequently develop understandings that are immature and incomplete. Research supports this view:

> Cognitive research is revealing that even with what is taken to be good instruction, many students, including academically talented ones, understand less than we think they do. With determination, students taking an examination are commonly able to identify what they have been told or what they have read; careful probing, however, often shows that their understanding is limited or distorted, if not altogether wrong (Rutherford and Ahlgren, 1990, p. 185).

Lucy demonstrated a great deal of expertise as she guided students to an understanding of *conduction.* We examine her instruction in more detail later in the chapter.

New Learning Depends on Current Understanding

A second essential characteristic of constructivism is that all new learning depends upon previous learning. The importance of learners' background knowledge is both intuitively sensible and well documented by research (Bruning et al., 1999). Constructivists see new learning interpreted in the immediate *context* of students' current understanding, not learned first as isolated information that is later related to existing knowledge.

This aspect of constructivism is important for several reasons. First, it helps explain why some students learn faster or easier than others; they have more background knowledge. It also explains why reviews are effective at the beginning of lessons; it helps activate students' background knowledge. It also explains why teacher questioning is essential; it helps teachers assess students' background knowledge, allowing them to connect new information to what students already know.

We see the importance of background knowledge illustrated in Lucy's lesson. Jason interpreted the heating of the spoon in the context of his understanding of radiation; he didn't simply add new understanding to old. His understanding of radiation influenced his interpretation of the heating of the spoon, and different understanding would have resulted in a different interpretation. During the lesson Lucy's students, with her guidance, gradually developed a more mature understanding of heat transfer, based on their previous understandings. This is the foundation of knowledge construction.

Social Interaction Increases Learning

Lucy's lesson also illustrates the central role of social interaction in constructivist views of learning. **Social interaction** *in a constructivist context refers to content-focused discussions of the topic students are studying.* Constructivist teachers encourage students to verbalize their thinking and refine their ideas by comparing them with others. Social interaction was an important component of Lucy's lesson, both as students worked in their groups and when the class as a whole discussed the results. For example, when students worked in their groups, Jason and his partner concluded that radiation heated the spoon, and he retained this idea until it no longer made sense to him. His understanding changed as a result of interacting with other students.

Lucy played an essential role in facilitating the social interaction so that it resulted in student learning. For example, she offered the example of being in the hot sun and then moving into the shade, and she asked Jason what his reaction was to Kathy's comment about the tree blocking the sun. She provided enough guidance and support to help her students make progress, but not so much that she reduced their active role in the learning process. This is a sophisticated form of instruction requiring a great deal of teacher expertise (Brown, 1994).

Authentic Tasks Promote Understanding

A final characteristic of constructivism is that it engages students in realistic learning situations. Let's think about Lucy's lesson once more. Her goal was for students to understand the concept of *conduction,* and she helped her students reach the goal with concrete objects—a coffee maker, the pot, and the spoon, and the real-world problem of explaining why the handle of the spoon got hot. This problem illustrates an **authentic**

Table 7.1 **AUTHENTIC TASKS IN VARIOUS CONTENT AREAS**

Content Area	Example
Math	Students go to a supermarket as a source of comparison-shopping problems.
English	Students write persuasive essays for a school or class newspaper.
Algebra	Students write algebraic equations to help them make precise solutions composed of solids (chemicals) and liquids.
Geometry	Students solve for the dimensions of buildings, using similar triangles.
Biology	Students explain why some members of the class have attached earlobes, while others' earlobes are detached.
Geography	Students explain why some cities, such as San Francisco, Chicago, Seattle, and New York, are large and economically important, whereas Minot, North Dakota, and Oxford, Mississippi, remain relatively small.
History	Students examine the origins of their home town and relate them to the history of the region, state, and country at the time.
Art	Students create an original piece of art.
Technology	Students use technology to design or solve work problems.

task, *a learning activity that requires understanding similar to the understanding required in the real world* (Eggen and Kauchak, 2001; Needels and Knapp, 1994).

With some thought, many ideas can be made more realistic by embedding them in authentic tasks, as we see in Table 7.1.

Constructivist Learning Activities and Student Motivation

Constructivism also has important implications for student motivation. For instance, let's look again as some of the features of Lucy's lesson:

- Students were faced with a question—what caused the spoon to get hot?—which served as a focus for the lesson.
- Students were active throughout the lesson, both in their groups and in the whole-class discussion.
- Students were given the control and responsibility to work on their own.
- Students developed understandings that made sense to them.
- Students acquired understandings that can be applied in the everyday world.

Each of these factors contributes to motivation. Building lessons around problems and questions can stimulate curiosity, and curiosity is one of the characteristics of intrinsically motivating activities (Lepper and Hodell, 1989). Active involvement in learning activities is more motivating than being passive (Zahorik, 1996), and student control and responsibility are associated with increased motivation (Lepper and Hodell, 1989). Finally, developing understanding that is practical and makes sense increases students' sense of **self-efficacy,** *their belief in their capability of accomplishing specific tasks* (Pintrich and Schunk, 1996). Constructivism and learner motivation complement each other.

Misconceptions about Constructivist Learning Activities

While an enormous literature examining constructivism has evolved over the last 25 years, a number of misconceptions about classroom applications of constructivism have evolved (Eggen, 2001). The result is that constructivism is often misinterpreted and misapplied by classroom teachers (Airasian and Walsh, 1997; Osborne, 1997). Three of the most common misconceptions are outlined in Figure 7.2 and discussed in the following paragraphs.

Misconception 1: Since constructivist learning activities are student centered, clear goals and careful preparation are less important than they are with traditional instruction.

This is false. In reality, clear goals are even more important in planning lessons based on constructivist views of learning, because they provide teachers with a framework that guides both their choice of content representation and the kinds of questions they ask (Eggen, 2001). As students build on their current understanding, teachers may modify their goals, but clear goals are crucial nevertheless.

Misconception 2: If learners are involved in discussions and other forms of social interaction, learning automatically takes place.

This isn't necessarily true. Teachers need to carefully monitor discussions, and if students head down blind alleys or develop misunderstandings about the topic, teachers must intervene and redirect the discussion (Brown and Campione, 1994). Lucy, for example, carefully monitored both the groupwork and the whole-class discussion, intervening when she felt it was necessary in order to keep the students on track. Let's see how she did this by examining some of the dialogue that occurred after Jason and his partner concluded that radiation caused the handle of the spoon to get hot.

Lucy: Jason asks a good question. How do we know that radiation can't go through solids, or at least doesn't go through them very well?
" . . . "
Lucy: Suppose you're out in the hot sun, and you move into the shade. . . . How do you feel?
Kathy: Cooler.
Lucy: Why do you suppose?

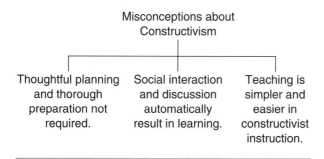

Misconceptions about Constructivism

| Thoughtful planning and thorough preparation not required. | Social interaction and discussion automatically result in learning. | Teaching is simpler and easier in constructivist instruction. |

Figure 7.2 Misconceptions about Constructivism

Kathy: The tree . . . or whatever, blocked the sun.
Lucy: What's your reaction to that?
Jason: I . . . guess so. . . . Yes, that's true.

Lucy's question, "Suppose you're out in the hot sun, and you move into the shade. How do you feel?" that led to Kathy's conclusion, "The tree . . . or whatever, blocked the sun," was essential. Without this intervention Jason would have continued to believe that the handle of the spoon was heated by radiation, and he would have constructed an inaccurate understanding of the concept *conduction*.

The professional judgment required to know when and how extensively to intervene is very sophisticated. Not enough intervention leaves students with incomplete or inaccurate understandings; too much intervention puts them in passive roles, which also decreases learning as well as motivation.

Misconception 3: Since teachers are not lecturing and explaining when teaching based on constructivism, their roles are less important than in traditional instruction.

As we just saw, teachers' roles are both *more* important and *more* difficult when teaching based on constructivist views of learning. Guiding students into genuine understanding is a sophisticated process; there are no rules that tell us when to intervene or how extensive the intervention should be. Teachers must make these decisions on their own based on their knowledge of the content and their past experiences.

Keeping these misconceptions in mind, let's turn now to planning for constructivist learning activities.

PLANNING FOR CONSTRUCTIVIST LEARNING ACTIVITIES

As we've seen, learning activities based on constructivist views of learning are student centered, and this shift in emphasis from the teacher to the students requires careful thought. The elements of the planning process are outlined in Table 7.2 and discussed in the sections that follow.

Identifying Clear and Precise Goals

In Chapter 5 we saw that clear and precise goals are essential for all forms of teaching. For grounding instruction in constructivist views of learning, they're even more important. In addition to guiding decisions about ways to represent content for learners, they provide the framework for the kinds of learning activities teachers plan and the questions they ask.

This point is crucial. As we've said repeatedly, grounding instruction in constructivist views of learning is very sophisticated and demanding. Monitoring student behavior for evidence of understanding, maintaining classroom order and the flow of the lesson, and forming and directing questions to students places an enormous demand on teachers' memories (Eggen and Kauchak, 2001). Monitoring students as they work in cooperative groups is little easier. Teachers often respond to this memory load by reducing instruction to lecture.

A much more effective way of reducing the memory load is to have very clear and precise goals in mind before beginning the lesson. With a precise goal, questioning be-

Table 7.2 CHARACTERISTICS OF STUDENT-CENTERED PLANNING

Planning Element	Rationale
Identifying clear and precise goals	Clear goals provide the framework for representations of content and questioning.
Multiple representations of content	Students construct understanding based on the representations of content.
	Content representations help accommodate student background differences.
Planning for social interaction	Social interaction provides feedback for teachers and students and helps students' individual constructions to converge.
Planning for productive learning environments	Constructing understanding requires learning environments that are safe, orderly, and learning focused.
Planning for assessment	To accommodate differences in student understanding assessment must be an integral part of the teaching-learning process.

comes clearly focused, which frees teachers' memories to monitor student behavior for evidence of understanding and to modify goals when evidence indicates that students aren't developing an understanding of the topic. So setting clear goals in advance is even more essential with constructivist approaches to teaching than it is with traditional views of instruction.

Multiple Representations of Content

We saw in Chapters 4 and 5 that one of the most important factors in promoting learning is the way teachers represent the topics they teach. This is true for teaching at all levels and in all content areas. Now, using constructivist views of learning as a framework, we can see *why* content representations are so important.

First, in the natural world, people have a great many specific experiences, and these experiences are what they use to construct their understanding of how the world works. As young children play together, for example, they gradually construct understandings of socially acceptable and socially unacceptable behavior based on their encounters with—and the responses of—their peers. The same basic experiential processes are at work in much of what both children and adults learn. Effective teachers facilitate this learning process by designing focused learning experiences that provide examples of the ideas being learned.

Second, modern theories of learning and development attribute a great deal of importance to learners' background knowledge. Direct physical experiences as well as books, movies, travel, and conversation all provide representations people use to construct the vast array of understandings that they develop. Learners who have a rich history of experience have been exposed to more representations that support their learning and development than those whose backgrounds are less rich. While constructivists may differ philosophically on issues such as the role of social interaction and the validity of the learners' constructions, all constructivists endorse the importance of these experiences.

In an ideal world, learners would be able to use these natural processes to construct functional understandings of their world. Since this isn't realistic and doesn't always occur, teachers can capitalize on these same processes by bringing representations of the world into the classroom for students.

Let's see how Lucy incorporated these ideas in her planning. Her representations of the concept *conduction* included:

- The coffee maker and spoon—a concrete example
- The model of the molecular motion in the spoon—a way of helping students visualize conduction
- The blindfolded students—a simulation that helped them see the way the particles in the spoon "bumped" each other
- The burner, wire, and wax, which combined the concrete representation with the models that further illustrated *conduction*
- Her assignment involving the piece of wood and metal knife

Each was intended to illustrate an aspect of conduction or represent conduction in a way that was slightly different from the others. In planning this way, Lucy attempted to capitalize on an idea called *multiple representations of content*. As learners construct understanding, each case or example adds different perspectives that others may have missed. For instance, the coffee maker and spoon will be meaningful to some students, whereas Lucy's model will be more meaningful to others. The same is true for the simulation and the wire with the wax pieces.

One way of visualizing multiple representations and their meaningfulness is to think of "criss-crossing" a conceptual landscape (Spiro et al., 1992). Each representation helps fill in pieces for the others. Providing an array of examples acknowledges the uniqueness of students and provides multiple paths for making ideas meaningful.

In Chapter 5 we also saw that effective content representations have one essential characteristic—*the information learners need to understand the topic exists in the representations*, and we see this characteristic illustrated in Lucy's examples. Regardless of their backgrounds, the combination of examples Lucy used contained sufficient information to allow all the students to acquire a meaningful understanding of *conduction*.

Using Technology to Represent Content: Databases. In Chapter 5 we saw that technology can be used to represent topics that are hard to otherwise illustrate. It has other applications as well. Let's look at an example.

Jan Harrison's high school social studies class was in the middle of a unit on factors influencing economic growth. Students in the class had divided up into groups of two or three and were doing in-depth research on a specific country. They were also bringing their results back to the class for discussion, trying to identify factors that contributed to economic growth. As students shared their information with each other, a lively debate ensued.

"I think it's population density. In the country we're studying, El Salvador, there are 671 people per square mile and the average income is only $700 per person," Hee-Won asserted.

"I'm not so sure," Simon replied. "We've got data from the old USSR and the population density was only 33 people per square mile and their per capita income was only $3,000 per person. But their defense budget was 17 percent of their total GNP."

"Good points, Hee-Won and Simon. Cassie, did you want to add something?" Jan interjected to acknowledge Cassie, who had been waving her hand.

"We found that literacy rate has a lot to do with it. We're studying India and it has a literacy rate of 36 percent and its average income per person is only $300."

"Also interesting data, Cassie. Class, what are we going to do with all this information we have? How can we organize it systematically so we can make sense of all this data?"

After considerable discussion the class decided that they needed to organize the information in some way so they could make cross-country comparisons. The class struggled for a while with key elements and finally decided that each group would provide the following information:

- Size of country
- Population
- Density
- Gross national product (GNP)
- Defense budget
- Average personal income
- Literacy rate

When they brought this information back to class, they struggled with how to organize it so that it made sense.

Further discussion resulted in the following table, which Jan helped them place into the database outlined in Table 7.3.

A **database** *is a computerized record-keeping system that organizes large amounts of information* (Forcier, 1996). In developing a database, students learn to organize information, and the analysis of the data gives them practice with critical thinking skills. For instance, Jan's students refined their vocabulary, conducted research, verified the accuracy of data, noted similarities and differences among data, and explored relationships (Forcier, 1996). Organizing and using databases is consistent with constructivist views of learning (Jonassen, 1996). Students are faced with meaningful tasks, and the process is facilitated by working with others.

Table 7.3 USING A DATABASE TO INVESTIGATE ECONOMIC GROWTH

Country	Size	Pop.	Density	GNP	Defense	Literacy	Average Income
El Salvador							
India							
USSR							

Source: Adapted from Jonassen, 1996.

Lucy, in her unit on different types of energy transfer, might have used the following database to help her students see relationships in their data.

	Examples	Explanation for Heat Transfer	Movement of Molecules
Radiation			
Convection			
Conduction			

The advantage of using a database in her lesson would be that all the information and experiences students had encountered over a number of days was organized and displayed in a single file. The relationships are made more apparent, which makes the information more accessible and meaningful.

As in designing any learning activities based on constructivist views of learning, teacher decision making is required at a number of points when using databases. Some questions that must be answered include:

- How much direction should the teacher provide?
- When and how should the basic idea of a database be introduced?
- Who should have responsibility for organizing and constructing the outline of the database?
- Who should take responsibility for analyzing the information in the database?

These decisions are a matter of judgment. Greater teacher direction provides faster lesson pace, but students' "learning to learn" on their own is reduced. Decreased teacher intervention gives students a greater chance to learn on their own, but lack of direction can cause frustration and boredom. A good source for helping you learn to incorporate databases into your instruction is Roblyer and Edwards (2000).

Planning for Social Interaction

The need for interaction between teacher and students and students with each other is widely accepted as important in helping learners construct understanding. This emphasis is valid for three reasons. First, constructing understanding is ultimately an individual process, and, because of background differences, emotional and cultural factors, and perceptions, individuals' constructions will vary. The only way teachers can determine the extent to which students are correctly interpreting the representations they use is to discuss them. Ultimately, we want individual learners' constructions to converge, and discussion is a major vehicle that ensures this convergence.

Second, discussion provides feedback for both teachers and students. It helps learners understand the extent to which their constructions are valid, and it provides them with additional information that helps them continue to construct and reconstruct their understanding. Discussion also provides teachers with information that allows them to assess the extent to which students are progressing toward their learning goals.

Third, interaction accommodates the limitations of learners' memories. If their memories become overloaded with information, it will be apparent to the teacher, who can immediately intervene.

Planning for interaction is essential, and this is why clear goals and effective representations of content are so important. Without them, the lesson lacks focus, and pseudolearning or "anything goes" constructivism can result.

Too often, planning for social interaction simply means "put the students into groups." It isn't that simple, however. If groupwork isn't carefully planned, it can result in confusion and wasted time. Effective groupwork requires specifying tasks clearly, teaching students how to work together effectively, and careful monitoring by the teacher.

In whole-group activities, social interaction is facilitated by teacher questioning. The questioning skills we discussed in Chapter 5 are essential. Without these, discussions tend to revert to minilectures, and the benefits of social interaction are lost.

The quality of the representations teachers use also influences student interaction. Effective representations provide students with the information they can use to construct understanding, so they give students focal points for discussing and exchanging ideas. This is why authentic learning tasks and multiple representations of content are so important. If the representations are ineffective, virtually no amount of teacher guidance will result in meaningful discussions.

Planning for Productive Learning Environments

In Chapter 6 we found that productive learning environments are safe, orderly, and learning focused. A productive learning environment is crucial if learning activities based on constructivism are to be successful. Constructivist learning requires that students feel free to offer conclusions, conjectures, and evidence without fear of criticism or embarrassment. It also requires students who are willing to listen to each other, wait their turn, and consider and reconsider their own ideas while others are talking. Students may not have these abilities or inclinations when constructivist instruction is first introduced, so teachers need to help them learn to take responsibility for their own behavior. Conscious planning helps identify the specific skills to be developed and the strategies, such as modeling, that will be used to teach them.

Planning for Assessment

Basing instruction on constructivism also has implications for assessing learning. Rather than answering questions about abstract and isolated problems, students demonstrate their understanding in real-world contexts. Lucy's students, for example, were asked to predict what would have happened if they had used a piece of wood or a butter knife instead of a wire for the demonstration with the burner and wax. In addition to assessing students' ability to apply the information they've learned, teachers can gather information about students' thinking in the process. (We discuss assessment in detail in Chapter 12.)

In summary, when teachers plan for learning activities based on constructivism, they identify goals, organize and sequence learning activities, and assess learning just as they would when using traditional approaches. Planning for constructivist activities, however, requires more care in the way content is represented, as well as conscious planning for social interaction and the learning environment. In addition, teachers need to be more flexible in their thinking, adapting goals and strategies as instruction unfolds.

CONDUCTING CONSTRUCTIVIST LEARNING ACTIVITIES

Having examined planning based on constructivism, let's turn now to the learning activities themselves. These processes are illustrated in Figure 7.3.

The model in Figure 7.3 helps us visualize four important aspects of lessons based on constructivism:

- Constructivist lessons typically begin with a problem or question that must be solved or answered.
- The lesson focuses on the solution to the problem or the answer to the question. The explanations and answers come from learners, not from teachers. The link in Figure 7.3 is from learners, to answers, to the question. There isn't a direct link from teachers, to answers, to questions.
- Explanations and answers derive from content representations and social interaction.
- Teachers help students construct understanding by guiding the social interaction and providing the content representations.

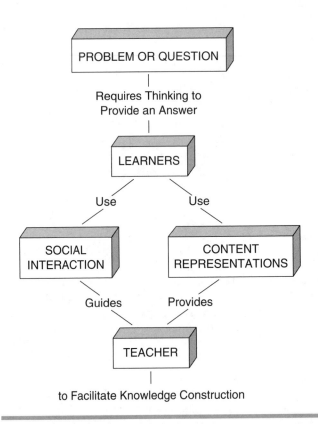

Figure 7.3 Conducting Constructivist Learning Activities

Let's look now at the way Lucy conducted her lesson. As we analyze it, we'll focus on her thinking, because some of what she did was subtle but important for promoting thorough understanding in her students. For example,

> *Lucy:* Now . . . let's look at what we have here (displaying the coffee maker, pot, and spoon). Let's feel the coffee pot and the spoon. C'mon up, Sarafina. . . . How do they feel?
>
> *Sarafina:* Smooth.
>
> *Lucy:* Okay . . . how else do they feel?
>
> *Sarafina:* Cold.
>
> *Lucy:* Okay, good. . . . Sarafina says that the spoon and coffee pot feel smooth and cold.

The dialogue you just read illustrates what we mean by "subtle but important." We saw earlier that lessons based on constructivism typically begin with a problem or question. Lucy, however, modified this procedure slightly. To understand *conduction*, the students needed to know that the spoon was initially cold. Lucy could have set up her demonstration in advance and simply told the students that the spoon was initially cold and then pose her question, but this would have been less meaningful. This is why the model in Figure 7.3 shows the link from the teacher to the content representation, and from the representation to the students, rather than directly from the teacher to the students—it was important for the students to see for themselves that the spoon was initially cold. This also illustrates the statement, "The explanations and answers come from learners, not from teachers." The teacher's role in constructivist-based lessons is to facilitate this explanation and meaning making.

Having set up her demonstration and asking Sarafina to confirm that the spoon was cold, Lucy then assessed the students' current understanding with additional questioning. Let's see how she did this.

> *Lucy:* Now let's review for a few minutes while we watch the coffee pot. . . . We've been talking about heat and energy. What is one way that heat is transferred, Bharat?
>
> *Bharat:* Radiation.
>
> *Lucy:* Yes, good, Bharat. Who can give us an example. . . . Bev?
>
> *Bev:* Well . . . like when you hold your hand over a hot burner on a stove, your hand gets warm.
>
> *Lucy:* Good, Bev . . . and explain why that's an example . . . Dominique?
>
> *Dominique:* Your hand gets warm, but . . . it's up above the burner, and . . . there's nothing between your hand . . . well, there's air between the burner and your hand, but it wouldn't matter. . . . Anyway, your hand gets warm because the waves go up and heat it.
>
> *Lucy:* Yes, very good explanation. How about another example? Jim?
>
> *Jim:* When we stand out in the sun, it warms us up.
>
> *Lucy:* And what else do we know about radiation, Lakasha? . . . Think about what Dominique said.
>
> *Lakasha:* It goes even if there's no air. . . . Like from the sun to the earth.
>
> *Lucy:* Good, Lakasha. . . . Can you add a little more to that? What do we mean when we say "no air"?

Lakasha: Like . . . a vacuum?

Lucy: And what's that have to do with what Dominique said?

Lakasha: She said there was no air . . . no . . . she said it wouldn't matter if there was no air.

Ramon: It travels in waves.

Lucy: Yes, Ramon, good. . . . Now remember everyone, radiation is a form of heat energy that travels in waves, and it doesn't need any matter to travel through. We can't see the waves, but they move, such as going from the burner to our hand. We know the waves moved because our hand gets warm.

Students' responses indicated they had a valid understanding of radiation, and Lucy also assessed their understanding of convection the same way.

Then Lucy used her demonstration to focus students' attention on her problem. Let's see how she did this.

Lucy: Now let's look at this again (*pointing to the coffee pot*). Now carefully come up and touch the top of the spoon (*directed to Sarafina, since she had confirmed that the spoon was initially cold*).

Sarafina: It's hot.

Lucy: It's hot! . . . Now that brings up a question. It was cold before, and now it's hot. . . . hmm? Now I want you to be very good observers and thinkers, and I want you to work with your partner and try to explain why the spoon got hot. . . . Now before we start, what do we know for sure?

Jeremy: The coffee pot did it (referring to the coffee pot and spoon).

Lucy: Sure, we know that heating up the coffee pot is important. . . . But we want to think about exactly *how* it did it. . . . And what are you going to keep in mind as you work on our problem?

" . . . "

Lucy: What have we been discussing?

Leeman: Stuff about heat.

Lucy: What about heat?

Jessica: Radiation and convection.

Lucy: Yes, very good. . . . Keep radiation and convection in mind when you work on your explanation. . . . Now go ahead.

This dialogue illustrates the point, "Constructivist lessons focus on explanations and answers to questions." Lucy posed the question of why the spoon got hot and reminded her students that they were trying to answer the question in the context of what they already understood—*radiation* and *convection*.

Reminding students that they should keep radiation and convection in mind is another "subtle but important" feature of Lucy's lesson. Students often think about topics in isolation, and when they later encounter topics they've previously studied, they fail to connect and often become confused. This could have been the case with Lucy's students. Had they not been reminded to keep radiation and convection in mind, they might have later confused them with conduction.

Jason's initial suggestion that radiation is what heated the spoon illustrates this potential confusion.

Jason: We think it's radiation. The waves go up the spoon and make it hot . . . like our hand over the burner.

Lucy: Go ahead, Sonja (*seeing Sonja shaking her head*).

Sonja: No, I don't think so.

Jason: Why not?

Sonja: Radiation doesn't need something to travel through . . . like we said before. . . .when we put our hand over the burner, there wasn't anything there.

Jason: There was air there.

Sonja: Yeah, but radiation can go through air. It can't go through something hard . . . like a spoon.

Lucy: Jason asks a good question. How do we know that radiation can't go through solids, or at least doesn't go through them very well?
   " . . . "

Lucy: Suppose you're out in the hot sun, and you move into the shade. . . . How do you feel?

Kathy: Cooler.

Lucy: Why do you suppose?

Kathy: The tree . . . or whatever blocked the sun.

Lucy: What's your reaction to that (turning to Jason)?

Jason: I . . . guess so. . . . Yes, that's true.

We've now seen four excerpts of dialogue from Lucy's lesson. They illustrate five important features of learning activities based on constructivism:

- Lesson focus
- The influence of existing understanding
- The role of social interaction
- Ongoing assessment

Let's look at them.

Lesson Focus

Lucy's entire lesson focused on her initial problem (why the spoon got hot), and it was based on her content representations (her demonstrations, model, and simulation). None of the discussion was conducted in the abstract. Her clear goal and her representations provided the framework that allowed her to guide students as they attempted to figure out why the examples worked as they did.

The Influence of Existing Understanding

We see the influence of existing understanding illustrated in Jason's attempt to use radiation as the explanation for why the spoon got hot. This is easy to understand. Lucy encouraged students to keep radiation and convection in mind, so his attempt to use one or the other as an explanatory framework is sensible. Lucy anticipated this possibility, and she was able to intervene as we saw in the dialogue. This helped eliminate Jason's initial confusion and helped all students relate the three methods of heat transfer to each other. Had Lucy not encouraged them to keep radiation and convection in mind, the likelihood of confusion later on would have been greater. This again illustrates the sophistication of Lucy's thinking as she planned and conducted the lesson.

The Role of Social Interaction

Each of the excerpts of the preceding dialogue illustrates why social interaction is so essential. While explaining ideas is potentially easier for teachers, it simply doesn't work very well for promoting deep understanding of the topics students study. This doesn't imply that teachers should never explain ideas to students; rather, it suggests that we should be skeptical of how much understanding is promoted through explanation alone. Interaction encourages students to form and revise their ideas as the lesson progresses.

Ongoing Assessment

Finally, we see that assessment in Lucy's lesson was ongoing. The students' answers to her questions gave her continual indicators of their understanding, which allowed her to intervene when necessary, as she did when Jason tried to use radiation as an explanation for the spoon getting hot.

Each of these features helps teachers make four ongoing decisions while conducting learning activities based on constructivism:

- *When* to intervene to guide the lesson in the direction of the goal
- *How* extensively to intervene
- *When* to provide additional representations of the topic
- *When* and *how* to bring the lesson to closure

We saw all four of these decisions illustrated in Lucy's lesson. With practice, you'll become better at making these decisions. As you develop, keep one essential question in mind as you interact with the students—"What is the goal?" This question will help you maintain the focus of the lesson, it will guide your questioning, and it will help you decide whether or not your initial goal should be modified.

Summary

Constructivism: A View of Learning. Constructivism views learning as an individual process in which learners develop their own understanding of the topics they study rather than receive understanding in an already organized form. New learning exists in the context of current understanding and is facilitated by social interaction as learners work with authentic tasks, problems, and questions. Constructivism is becoming increasingly influential in learning and teaching, influenced by research indicating that learners often fail to understand the topics they study in more than a superficial way.

Characteristics of Constructivism. Constructivist lessons have four characteristics. First, they emphasize active student construction of new ideas. Second, constructivists believe that all new learning is embedded in and dependent on current understanding. Third, learning is facilitated by social interaction, both between students and in whole group discussions. Finally, learning is enhanced when new content is embedded in realistic or lifelike learning activities.

Constructivist activities are motivating for students in several ways. Since they begin with a question or problem, they activate students' curiosity. Constructivist lessons actively involve students and use social interaction to examine and challenge ideas. In addition, because they focus on student learning and understanding, students' efforts during the lesson can increase students' sense of self-efficacy.

Planning Constructivist Learning Activities. Constructivist lessons require a clear content goal that acts as a cognitive compass for the teacher during the lesson. In addition to designing authentic learning tasks, teachers also need to design ways to represent abstract ideas in multiple ways to provide alternate perspectives to students. Another planning task is to provide opportunities for student interaction, which not only allows the teacher to assess current student understanding, but also enhances learning.

Conducting Constructivist Learning Activities. Constructivist learning activities begin with a question or problem that provides the focal point for the lesson. Learners utilize different content representations and social interaction to grapple with the question or problem. The teacher assists this process through strategic questions and timely additions of new examples that assist students in their attempts to develop new understanding.

Important Concepts

Authentic task	Self-efficacy
Constructivism	Social interaction
Database	

Reflecting on Teaching and Learning

As you've studied this chapter, you've seen how teachers can design and implement instruction based on constructivist views of learning. Read the following case study now and consider how effectively the teacher implemented the ideas discussed in the chapter.

Kelly Lang has her students involved in a unit on different kinds of poetry, she has examined several different forms of poetry, and she wants to have her students understand Haiku.

She began the class by saying, "We've been studying poetry for several days now, and I want us to look at another form. . . . Look up here at what I've displayed on the overhead," and she displayed the following:

Deep in a windless
wood, not one leaf dares to move . . .
Something is afraid.

Into a forest
I called . . . The voice in reply
was no voice I knew.

I called to the wind
"Who's there?" . . . Whoever it was
still knocks at my gate.

"Now go ahead and work with your partner for a few minutes, and I want the two of you to write down as many things as you can that these three excerpts have in common. When you're finished, we'll discuss them."

"Do we turn our papers in?" Omar wondered.

"Yes," Kelly smiled. "Remember, we said that you always turn your papers in, unless I tell you otherwise. . . . Okay . . . go ahead. You have 4 minutes."

The students, who were seated next to their partners, turned together, and a buzz of voices soon rose in the room. As the students worked, Kelly moved up and down the aisles glancing at what the students had written and making periodic comments, suggestions, and reminders about what they were supposed to do.

At the end of the 4 minutes, Kelly announced, "Okay, everyone, turn back this way. . . . Now . . . let's go ahead and see what we've come up with. . . . Tell us one thing you have written down. . . . Go ahead, Latasha."

" . . . Three lines in each one."

"Good. . . . Dale?"

"The middle line is longer than the top one and the bottom one."

"Toni?"

" . . . There's three little periods in each one."

"What are those little periods called?" Kelly queried, "and what do they mean? . . . Anyone?"

" . . . "

"No one? . . . Okay, I'll tell you. . . . They're called 'ellipses' and they're used to indicate that something is left out of the line. . . . See, you learned something new," she smiled. "Now, . . . back to what we're doing. What else? . . . Nita?"

"Everybody already took ours."

"Ohh, no," Kelly prompted. "Look a little more carefully. What are each of the examples about? . . . I mean what kind of a theme do they have?"

"They're like . . . I'm not sure what you mean."

"Well, what's the first one about?"

" . . . The woods?"

"Yes, each of the excerpts is about nature," Kelly waved. "Good, Nita.

"Now, if you look," she continued, "you'll see that they're also each expressing some form of emotion, . . . like in the first one it says that something is afraid. . . . The emotion may be unstated, but it's there, nevertheless.

"So, let's go on. . . . What else do you see in the examples? . . . Anyone?"

" . . . "

"How many syllables in the first line of each poem? . . . Look carefully. . . . How many?"

" . . . There's five in the first and second one, . . . and . . . six in the third one," Jamie said after studying the examples for several seconds.

"Not quite," Kelly smiled. "Actually, there's five in the third one as well. Maybe you thought 'called' has two syllables, but it's really just one. . . . Now . . . if you look at the third line, you'll see that it also has five syllables in it. . . . Everyone take a good look . . . Do you all see? . . . Very good. . . . Okay, let's take a look at the second line of each. How many syllables there? . . . Look carefully."

" . . . I think . . . seven," Noreen offered hesitantly.

"Excellent, Noreen! . . . Indeed it is seven. . . . So we have a pattern in the examples. . . . Go ahead and summarize it for us. . . . Somebody want to volunteer?"

" . . . I will," Tony waved. " . . . they have five syllables in the first line, . . . and . . . in the third line, and . . . seven in the middle line."

"Good, and can someone add to that . . . what are they about?"

" . . . Nature," Juan noted.

"All right, and one more part. . . . Someone?"

" . . . They tell about . . . some . . . emotional something," Donna added, "But I don't really get that. . . . I don't see it."

"It is a little hard to see," Kelly acknowledged. "It's sort of unstated, but if you look carefully, you can kind of see that it's there."

Kelly then went on, "Now, what I want you to do is get together again, and compose a poem similar to the ones we've been studying. . . . Then, we'll share them. . . . Okay? . . . Go ahead."

Questions for Analysis

Let's look at Kelly's lesson now based on the information in this chapter. In doing your analysis, you may want to consider the following questions. In each case, be specific and take information directly from the case study in completing your analysis.

1. The chapter focused on instruction based on constructivist views of learning. How effectively did Kelly apply the characteristics of constructivism in her lesson? If you believe her lesson could have been more constructivist, make specific suggestions for doing so.
2. Multiple representations of content are important when teaching based on constructivist views of learning. How effectively did Kelly implement the idea of multiple representations of content? Be specific in your response.
3. The ability to ask questions that guide learners' developing understanding is critical in constructivist approaches to instruction. How effective was Kelly's questioning? If you believe it could have been more effective, identify specific instances in the case study where it could have been improved.
4. As in many classes, Kelly's students had diverse backgrounds. How effectively did her lesson accommodate the background diversity of her students? Again, be specific in your response.

Discussion Questions

1. Think about your present beliefs about good teaching. Where did they come from? What kinds of experiences did you use to form those beliefs? What kinds of experiences are you finding most valuable in your teacher education program in terms of learning to teach? What do your answers to these questions tell you about constructivism as it applies to learning to teach?

2. Are all kinds of social interaction equally valuable? What factors influence the effectiveness of social interaction as a learning tool?

3. What types of authentic tasks do you encounter in your teacher education programs? What makes them authentic? How does their authenticity influence their effectiveness in promoting growth?

4. Should all learning tasks be authentic? Why or why not? What obstacles do teachers face in attempting to incorporate authentic tasks in their teaching?

5. What can teachers do to make the following teaching activities more constructivist and learner centered?

   a. lectures
   b. learning from text
   c. labs
   d. drill and practice

6. As technology becomes increasingly prominent in schools, will constructivism become more or less important? Why?

Portfolio Activities

1. *Constructivism in the Classroom.* Observe an interactive lesson in which a teacher is teaching a new idea or concept. To what extent does the lesson incorporate these components of constructivism:

   a. Learners construct their own understanding.
   b. New learning depends on current understanding.
   c. Learning is facilitated by social interaction.
   d. Authentic tasks promote learning.

   What could the teacher have done to make the lesson more constructivist?

2. *Constructivism: The Learner's Perspective.* Interview several students individually after observing a lesson. Ask:

   a. What did they learn (ask them to explain in their own words)?
   b. How is this idea or skill related to other ones?
   c. Why is it important?

   What do their responses tell you about what students take away from a lesson?

3. *Social Interaction.* Observe a class for several hours and note the number of opportunities students have to talk with each other. Are these opportunities structured or unstructured? Are they sanctioned by the teacher? Then interview the teacher. Some questions you might ask are:

   a. How important is student interaction for learning?
   b. How does it promote learning?
   c. What strategies does the teacher use to structure or encourage social interaction?
   d. What problems are encountered when using social interaction as a learning tool?

   How do you plan to use social interaction to promote learning in your classroom?

4. *Authentic Learning Tasks.* Examine a teacher's edition of a text in a content area that you are going to teach in. How adequately does the text translate abstract ideas into authentic tasks? How does the content area influence the kinds of authentic tasks used? How could the teacher supplement the text to make learning more constructivist?

5. *Constructivism: Planning.* Plan a lesson using the guidelines found in this chapter.

   a. How did you accommodate or include:
      ■ Student construction of understanding
      ■ Student background knowledge
      ■ Social interaction
      ■ Authentic learning tasks?
   b. How does the planning process differ from planning a different kind of lesson?
   c. What was the most difficult aspect of planning? The easiest? How is planning a constructivist activity different from other types of lessons?

6. *Constructivism: Implementation.* Teach the lesson that you planned for in activity 5 above.

   a. How did your role as a teacher change? Was it easier or harder?
   b. How did students respond to the lesson?
   c. What were the strengths and weaknesses of the lesson?
   d. What would you do differently next time?

8

Learning
and
Teaching
Concepts

■

*C*oncept learning represents an important part of the curriculum at all levels, including college. In fact, concept learning is a central focus of this text, as indicated by the fact that important concepts are given in **bold** type in the body of the chapters, and they're listed at the end of each.

Students use concepts to help them understand and organize their world, and teachers support the process by providing clear examples and helping students see how the examples illustrate the concept's characteristics. In this chapter, we examine concept learning and describe ways that teachers can help learners construct concepts that are meaningful to them. When you've completed your study of this chapter, you should be able to meet the following goals:

- Explain the role that concepts play in the school curriculum.
- Describe how examples contribute to concept learning.
- Identify the relationships between superordinate, coordinate, and subordinate concepts.
- Describe similarities and differences between inductive and deductive approaches to teaching concepts.
- Describe the relationships between principles, generalizations, and academic rules and how to teach each.

Terry Marsden, a high school social studies teacher, finished taking roll, hung the attendance sheet on the door and began:

"Class, let's continue our unit on research techniques in history. Remember, we're trying to understand where the content in our history books comes from, and what it is that historians do. To do that I'd like us to look at two headlines that might have appeared in 1770."

LONDON TIMES

Boston Mob Attacks British Soldiers. Five Killed and Eight Wounded by British Troops Attempting to Quell Riot.

BOSTON GLOBE

Massacre in Boston! British Troops Fire on Innocent People. Five Innocents Killed and Eight Wounded in Military Massacre.

Terry continued, "What's going on here? Jacinta?"

"We . . . we have two different versions of the same event."

"Which one is correct?" Terry asked. "Or perhaps more importantly for our purposes today, how could we find out? . . . Let's leave the Boston Massacre for a second and talk about two important ideas in historical research: . . . primary and secondary sources. Today we are going to learn the difference between these two." With that, she drew the diagram that appears in Figure 8.1 on the board.

She continued, "Primary data sources are original documents; the person describing the event was actually there. *Original* means firsthand and unchanged. For instance, take a look at this. What is it? . . . Duk?" and she then held up a piece of homework that one of the students had turned in the day before.

"It . . . looks like our homework."

"Yes, exactly, Duk?" Terry smiled. "It is your homework. And if someone wanted to do an analysis of the homework in this class, this would be a primary source. . . . It is an actual, unmodified piece of homework.

"An example of a primary source in our Boston Massacre situation could be a letter from someone who had actually witnessed the event, or a newspaper columnist who was there and wrote an article about it.

"A secondary source, by contrast, is a description by a person who was not there but who got information from someone who may or may not have directly observed the event.

"So what would be a secondary source in the case of our homework? . . . Kyung?"

"It would be like . . . like someone in the class describing the kind of homework that you usually give in here."

"Good, Kyung. . . . Now, let's write these definitions on the board so we won't forget them."

Terry wrote the definitions on the board and said, "Let's stop here for a second, and think about why the differences between the two types of sources is important. . . . Anyone? . . . Steve?"

"With . . . a primary source there's less of an opinion involved. A secondary source . . . has interpreted it . . . like the newspaper headlines."

"Good thinking, Steve. . . . We can think of a secondary source as a filter that the information has passed through. So distortion or inaccuracy increases when secondary sources are used. Let's see how this works by looking at some different types of data and see if we can tell whether they are primary or secondary. How about this one?" and she held up a small book.

"What is it?" Jed asked.

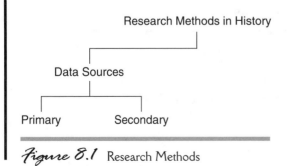

Figure 8.1 Research Methods

"Good question. . . . It's a diary. . . . So what do you think? . . . Yolando?"

"It's . . . a primary source."

"Why?" Terry probed.

" . . . Because it was written by the person himself."

"Good," Terry nodded smiling. "In fact, historians have used the diaries of historical figures extensively in their analysis of historical events. Let's label that one primary with a big *P*.

"How about another one? . . . This is Fawn Brody's biography of Thomas Jefferson." Terry held up the book. "Would that be a primary or secondary source? . . . Sarah?"

"Secondary . . . because she was a modern biographer and wasn't there at the time that it occurred."

"Good, let's put an *S* to indicate 'secondary' by it.

"Now, how about this one? . . . Let's pretend we're writing a history of the student government in our high school. Would the minutes of the student government meetings be primary or secondary? . . . Taeko?"

"I'm . . . not sure."

"Let's think about it," Terry continued. "Remember, one of the important ideas about primary sources is that the person writing them had to be there."

"Ohh . . . okay. The secretary taking the minutes would be there so it would be a primary source."

"Good. Let's write that up here. Now can any one give us an example of a secondary source using the same topic? . . . Bill?"

"How about a school newspaper article written from the minutes. The person who wrote the article wouldn't have been actually there."

They continued for several more minutes, with Terry giving some additional examples and also asking the students to supply some of their own. Then she returned to the Boston Massacre headlines and her outline of research methods in history.

UNDERSTANDING CONCEPTS

We have two goals when we teach concepts. The first is to have our students understand what the concept is. This is done through the use of examples that illustrate or contain the essential characteristics that define the concept. Terry helped her students understand primary and secondary data sources by presenting them with concrete examples of these concepts and analyzing these examples through interactive questioning. The second goal is to help students understand how the concept relates to other concepts. This prevents students from learning and remembering concepts as isolated categories. We want concepts to be connected to what students already know and to be differentiated from closely related concepts. Terry accomplished this second goal by linking primary and secondary sources to data sources and research methods in history and by comparing the two concepts to each other. When we accomplish these two goals, we have meaningful concept learning.

Think about some of the topics that you've studied in this book so far. Among many others, you examined *behaviorism* and *teacher-effectiveness* research in Chapter 1, *at-risk students* and *culture* in Chapter 2, *affective domain* and *objectives* in Chapter 3, and *academic learning time* and *modeling* in Chapter 4. Similar examples could be found in Chapters 5, 6, and 7.

Each of these topics is a *concept*. Forming concepts is one of the most important forms of learning that exists, both in and out of school. They're essential units of human thought; they guide our communication and help us understand our environment. For example, when we read a newspaper columnist and conclude he or she has a strong conservative bias, we are using the concepts *conservative* and *bias*. These concepts allow us to understand the author and help us communicate our understanding to others.

The next section looks at how concepts help us understand the world and communicate that understanding to others.

Concepts: Categories That Simplify the World

As we see from the preceding examples, concepts represent a major portion of the school curriculum, and much of teachers' efforts are directed at teaching them (Klausmeier, 1992). **Concepts** are *mental categories, or classes, of objects, events, or ideas, illustrated by examples and defined by common characteristics.* For example, if students saw the polygons in Figure 8.2, they would describe them all as squares, even though the shapes vary in size and orientation. *Square* represents a mental category or class into which all examples of squares can be placed.

Concepts help us simplify the world. The concept *square,* for example, allows people to think and talk about the examples in Figure 8.2 as a group instead of as specific objects. Having to remember each object separately would make learning impossibly complex and unwieldy.

Similarly, the concepts *primary source* and *secondary source* helped Terry's students simplify their study. For instance, rather than looking at George Washington's diary, a letter written at the time of the Boston Massacre, and a newspaper article written by an eyewitness, as documents to be studied and understood separately, students could classify all three as *primary sources,* making their study much easier and their understanding of the world more complete.

Additional examples of concepts in language arts, social studies, science, and math are listed in Table 8.1. This is only a brief list, and you can probably think of many more for each area. Students also study *major scale* and *tempo* in music, *perspective* and *balance* in

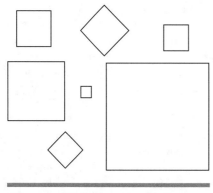

Figure 8.2 Squares

Table 8.1 CONCEPTS IN DIFFERENT CONTENT AREAS

Language Arts	Social Studies	Science	Math
Gerund	Culture	Acid	Composite number
Noun	Republican	Conifer	Equivalent fraction
Plot	Conservative	Compound	Square
Simile	Mercantilism	Force	Multiplication
Direct object	Gross national product	Momentum	Ellipse

art, and *aerobic exercise* and *isotonic exercise* in physical education. In addition, we teach many other concepts in school that don't neatly fit into a particular content area such as *honesty, justice, love, internal conflict,* and our previous example with *bias.*

From our discussion, we see that some concepts, such as *square* or *noun,* are simple and can be taught to young children, whereas others, like *mercantilism,* are more difficult, requiring more mature students.

Let's examine concepts a bit further. Consider the italicized words in each of the following sentences.

Anya *runs* very fast.

I *studied* for this test for four hours.

You *are reading* the information in this section.

Beena *drove* the ball out of the park.

Kathy *is* a good math student.

We see that the italicized words are quite dissimilar—their spellings are different, some indicate an event in the past while others are in the present, one involves two italicized words, and some suggest more energy than do others. However, despite their differences, they are similar in that they all *describe an action or a state of being.* Because of this common feature, we put them in a category that includes all words that indicate action or state of being. We have formed the concept *verb.* This illustrates one view of the way concepts are formed.

Theories of Concept Learning

Think again about the concept *verb,* and also think about concepts that we commonly hear on the news, such as *environmentalist, Republican,* and *lobbyist.* How did you learn those concepts and how do you use them?

Rule-Governed Theories of Concept Learning. Some concepts, such as *primary source* in Terry's lesson, or *verb* or *square,* have clear and precise **characteristics** (sometimes called *attributes* or *features*), *which are a concept's defining elements. Square,* for instance, has four characteristics—*closed, plane, equal sides,* and *equal angles,* and students can identify examples of squares based on the rule saying that squares must have these attributes. Other characteristics, such as size, color, or orientation, aren't essential, so students don't have to consider them in making their classifications. They don't alter the concept. Similarly, the concept *verb* has two characteristics: It either shows action or a state of being, and, as with square, students can classify parts of speech as verbs based on this rule. The individual word isn't important in the classification.

Early concept learning research (e.g., Bruner, Goodenow, and Austin, 1956) found that learners can quickly identify the essential characteristics of a concept and classify examples accordingly. Concepts are differentiated from one another on the basis of the rules for each. For example, learners differentiate a square from a rectangle based on the rule for squares, compared to one for rectangles, indicating that rectangles must be plane closed figures with equal angles but with opposite sides equal in length, rather than having all sides equal.

More recent research emphasizes the *constructive* nature of the process. As we saw in Chapter 7, learners construct—rather than record—their understanding of concept rules (Confrey, 1990; Greeno, Collins, and Resnick, 1996).

Prototype Theories of Concept Learning. An alternative to this rule-based view of concept learning emphasizes examples. To illustrate this perspective, let's look at another concept, such as *Republican*. What are its characteristics? Some might suggest that fiscal and social conservativism, lowering taxes, small government, and a pro-business orientation are important features. However, some Republican presidents have raised taxes and significantly increased the size of government through military spending. So what is the rule we follow for classifying people as Republicans?

Prototype theories of concept learning don't assume a classification system based on a strict rule for inclusion as a member of the concept (Wattenmaker, Dewey, Murphy, and Medin, 1986). Rather, learners construct a **prototype,** *which is the best representative of its category* (Busmeyer and Myung, 1988; Nosofsky, 1988; Schwartz and Reisberg, 1991). For example, George W. Bush might be a prototype for a Republican in this country. Or, in many instances, a prototype isn't a specific, physical example, such as George W. Bush. Rather, it is a mental composite constructed from encountering several examples which the learner combines in the mind. To illustrate this idea, think of the concept *bird*. The image that you generate is frequently a prototype based on previous examples you've encountered.

Representing Concepts: Examples and Nonexamples

Whatever your view of concept learning—rule governed or prototype—examples are essential for learning and understanding concepts. In Chapter 5 we said that effective representations of content were essential for promoting the involvement of students, and in Chapter 7 we again emphasized the role of representations in helping students construct understanding of the topics they study. This emphasis is equally important for concept learning, where specific **examples**—*typical members of the class*—and **nonexamples**—*nonmembers of the class*—are essential. Regardless of a concept's complexity, the key to concept learning is a carefully selected set of examples and nonexamples (Tennyson and Cocchiarella, 1986).

To illustrate the importance of examples, let's look at a simple illustration of learning a concept such as *dog*, as it occurs naturally. Children learn about dogs by encountering collies, terriers, poodles, chihuahuas, and other examples. Parents and other adults help with statements such as "Look, Anya, there's a dog!" As with the illustration of the concept *verb,* the collies, terriers, and others are dissimilar in many ways. Having been told that all are dogs, however, children identify similarities among them, and they begin to construct the concept.

The process is also aided by nonexamples such as cats and bears and, later, more closely related nonexamples such as coyotes, wolves, and foxes. In these instances, learners are told, "No, Matt, that's not a dog. It's a kitty. Listen to him meow," or, "No. It looks like a dog, but it's a wolf. It lives in the wild and not with people."

The examples tell us what a concept *is* by illustrating its essential characteristics or providing an effective prototype, and the nonexamples help us discriminate the concept from closely related concepts. Consider the following examples:

Sammy, the running back, was a freight train moving down the field.

As a running back, Sammy was like a freight train moving down the field.

Obviously, the two statements are closely related. However, they illustrate two different concepts. The first is a metaphor, which involves a nonliteral comparison, and the second is a simile, which also makes a nonliteral comparison but includes the word *like* or *as* in it. The essential characteristics of metaphors are illustrated in the first example, and a key discriminating characteristic is shown in the nonexample. As students learn the concept *metaphor,* nonexamples such as *similes* are crucial to prevent them from overgeneralizing and including inappropriate examples in the category. The same process occurs when we tell young children that foxes and wolves are not dogs.

From this discussion we see that concept learning as it occurs naturally and concept learning in formal school settings are similar. Learners encounters examples and nonexamples in either day-to-day experience—as in the case with dogs—or are presented examples and nonexamples—as demonstrated with *verbs, metaphors,* and *similes.* In both cases the concept is learned by identifying its essential characteristics and discriminating them from closely related concepts. What differentiates the two types of learning is the teacher's conscious effort to provide students with adequate examples.

Different Types of Examples. We know examples are the key to representing concepts effectively, but finding effective examples for our instruction can be difficult. For instance, how might you illustrate concepts such as *atom,* or *culture?* When teachers have difficulty finding or creating good examples, they often revert back to definitions alone, which students then memorize. The memorized definitions then exist in isolation, unconnected to other ideas they've learned or the real world in which they live.

Table 5.1 of Chapter 5 illustrated a variety of ways that content could be effectively represented. Two of the topics—*arthropod* and *mercantilism*—were concepts, and a real lobster and a vignette, respectively, were suggested as examples to illustrate them.

Table 8.2 includes some additional forms of examples that can be used to teach concepts.

The ideal in illustrating any concept is the real thing, and teachers should try to use actual objects and demonstrations whenever possible. Sometimes this is impractical, however, and other alternatives need to be used. A **model** *is a concrete representation to help us visualize what we cannot observe directly.* Models are especially useful in science for a variety of topics ranging from molecules to atomic structure.

Table 8.2 **TYPES AND ILLUSTRATIONS OF EXAMPLES**

Realia (the real thing)	A real heart from the butcher shop to be cut open and shown to students
	Paragraphs in which parts of speech are embedded
Models	A plastic model of the solar system with the order and sizes of planets represented
	A plastic heart illustrating the heart's structure
Pictures	Pictures of the Rockies and Appalachians to illustrate young and mature mountains
	Pictures of firefighters and postal workers to illustrate community helpers
Simulations	A mock trial to illustrate the judicial system at work
	A debate in which students are asked to take conservative and liberal positions on issues
Case studies	Written dialogue between two people, illustrating opinion versus fact
	The case studies that introduce the chapters of this book
	The case study illustrating *mercantilism* in Chapter 4

Just as models are useful in science, simulations are commonly used in social studies to illustrate concepts impossible to illustrate in other ways. Several social simulations are now available on video disk to help students understand complex processes. One, *Oregon Trail,* designed to illustrate the difficulties and complex decisions faced by pioneers, places students in the role of pioneers traveling across the plains, making decisions about supplies, trails, and mode of travel. Another, *Sim City,* allows students opportunities to construct a city, in the process investigating factors such as transportation and the placement of utilities.

The use of case studies is another powerful instructional tool that can be used to illustrate difficult concepts. We introduce each of the chapters of this text with case studies to illustrate the abstract concepts that help you understand learning and teaching. Without them, the content would be much less meaningful to you as developing professionals. Case studies form the backbone of much of the instruction in many teacher education programs as well as courses in business and law (Shulman, 1992).

Case studies are especially effective for illustrating many complex concepts taught in our schools today. As an example, consider the following:

Pedro is a boy living in a small Mexican village. Every day he rises early, for he must walk the 2 miles to his school. He has a breakfast of beans and bread made from ground corn, leaves the house, and begins his trek. He likes the walk because he can wave to his papa toiling daily in the cornfields that provide the food and income for the family.

When Pedro comes home from school, he often plays soccer with his friends in the village. After dinner, his mother usually plays songs on a guitar while Papa sings, but this evening she must go to a meeting of the town council, where they are trying to raise money for a new addition to the school. No decisions can be made without the approval of the council.

Ryoko is a young girl living in a city in Japan. Ryoko is up early and helps her mother with breakfast for her younger brothers and sisters. Ryoko loves the rice smothered in a sauce made from fish that she often eats in the morning.

Ryoko skips out the door, bowing to her father as she goes. He is preparing tools to go to the docks where he will meet his partner for their daily fishing expedition. He has been a fisherman for thirty years.

Ryoko comes home from school, finishes her work and then goes down the street to play ping pong with the rest of the neighborhood boys and girls. She is the best one in the area. Before bed, Ryoko listens to stories of the old days told by her grandfather, who lives with them.

These elementary social studies case studies illustrate the concept *culture* and provide a form of semiconcrete experience for students that they would not get otherwise. Often when we teach a concept such as *culture* to young children, we describe it verbally as consisting of factors such as the food, work, recreation, and music of a people. Rarely, however, do we actually *illustrate* these characteristics, and as a result the concept is less meaningful for learners. Case studies help learners build that meaning by illustrating the interplay of complex characteristics.

What Makes Concepts Easy or Hard to Learn?

The ease of learning a concept is directly related to the number of characteristics it has and how concrete they are (Tennyson and Cocchiarella, 1986). *Square* is easy to learn, for example, because it has few characteristics and they're concrete. *Liberal* or *conservative,* in contrast, are much harder. Their characteristics are more abstract, and there are many more of them. This helps us understand why many people have difficulty precisely describing what makes a conservative a conservative and how liberals and conservatives are different.

These differences are reflected in where concepts are placed in the school curriculum. Simple, concrete concepts, such as squares and other shapes, are taught in kindergarten or before, while many abstract concepts don't appear until the middle school years or later.

Concept Learning: Misconceptions and Conceptual Change

The effect of background knowledge on learning was a theme emphasized in Chapter 7 when we discussed instruction based on constructivist views of learning, and it is important for concept learning as well (Greeno, Collins, and Resnick, 1996). While learners construct understanding of concepts on the basis of examples and nonexamples, their background knowledge, expectations, beliefs, and emotions also influence their thinking (Dole and Sinatra, 1998). Learners develop many intuitive understandings of the topics they study and, once formed, these understandings are extremely resistant to change (Leander and Brown, 1999; Shuell, 1996). For instance, in science, students often confuse reptiles with amphibians and spiders with insects; in geography students have problems with longitude and latitude; and in language arts students have difficulty differentiating between figures of speech such as simile, metaphor, and personification.

To develop more valid understandings, researchers have found that learners must become uncomfortable with their present understanding, and a new conception must be understandable and more capable of explaining their experiences than their original ideas (Dole and Sinatra, 1998; Nissani and Hoefler-Nissani, 1992). This can only be accomplished if their intuitive (and often inaccurate) understandings are directly confronted (Chinn and Brewer, 1993). Let's look at an example of how teachers do this.

Elaine Madison has been working with her middle-school students on basic science concepts and has defined force as any push or pull and work as the combination of force and movement. She knows that students often incorrectly think that work is done if effort is expended, regardless of whether movement occurs.

To try to eliminate these misconceptions, she suggested, "Kari, stand up and hold up the chair."

Kari stood, lifted the chair that was at the side of the room, and remained standing motionless.

"Now," Elaine continued. "Is Kari doing any work?"

"Yes," Jared volunteered.

"What did we say the definition of work is?" Elaine probed.

"The combination of force and movement," Natalie offered.

"Okay, is Kari doing any work?" Elaine went on.

"If she stands there for a while, she'll get tired, and you get tired when you work," Jared persisted.

"But she's not moving," Kathy added. "For work to be done, there has to be movement."

"That doesn't make sense," Jared continued. "That means you can get tired without doing any work."

"What actually makes you tired?" Elaine queried.

"Holding up the chair."

"Sure. So, the effort of holding up the chair would make any of us tired. Effort is the force we're exerting, and exerting a force can make us tired."

The class continued to discuss the example, noting that Kari actually did do work when she first lifted the chair. They then discussed additional examples, noting that because of their day-to-day experience they tend to equate effort, work, and being tired. As a result of this discussion, Jared finally concluded that the idea that work requires movement made sense. (Eggen and Kauchak, 2001)

This example illustrates how difficult it is to change misconceptions. They exist because they make sense to us, and changing them requires reorganizing our existing understanding. It's also possible that a student like Jared will revert back to his earlier thinking—work equals effort—even though he accepted the definition; additional examples and discussion will be required for him to permanently restructure his ideas. Alert teachers are aware of this possibility and provide additional experiences.

Making Concepts Meaningful: Superordinate, Coordinate, and Subordinate Concepts

Rather than learning concepts in isolation, we want students to link or connect them to other concepts (Glover et al., 1990). For example, students learn that *metaphor* is a *figure of speech,* and that other figures of speech also exist, such as *simile, onomatopoeia, personification,* and *alliteration.* Students go even further to find that there are special kinds of metaphors.

We can summarize these connective links by using the idea of superordinate, coordinate, and subordinate concepts. **Superordinate concepts** *are larger categories into which the concept fits,* **coordinate concepts** *are "parallel" concepts that fit into the same superordinate category,* and **subordinate concepts** *are subsets of the concept we're focusing on.* These relationships are illustrated in Table 8.3.

Superordinate concepts serve two important functions. First, they provide a link to the concept being learned. What is a dog? A dog is a mammal. What is a metaphor? A metaphor is a figure of speech. *Mammal* and *figure of speech* are superordinate to *dog* and *metaphor.* If we understand the superordinate concept, it provides a mental hook to which the concept can be attached. Superordinate concepts help make a concept meaningful by providing associations between it and related concepts (Gage and Berliner, 1998).

Second, superordinate concepts allow us to make inferences about examples that we have not yet encountered. For instance, if we learn that kayaks and yawls are both boats, we can make some conclusions about their characteristics, even if we have no experience with them. We know, for example, that they are designed for travel on water, they're probably large enough to carry people, and they are watertight.

Understanding coordinate concepts is useful because they provide links to closely related concepts and can also be used as nonexamples. For instance, in looking at the coordinate concepts in Table 8.3 we see that metaphor, simile, personification, and alliteration are all coordinate to each other. They are all different kinds of figures of speech, making that concept richer or deeper for students. Examples of similes, alliteration, and personification can also be used as nonexamples for the concept of metaphor.

Similarly, subordinate concepts provide greater information about the concept we are teaching and can also help determine additional examples. For instance, *action verbs* and *linking verbs* are both subordinate to the concept *verb,* and the examples we choose when teaching should include cases of each.

Table 8.3 THE RELATIONSHIP BETWEEN SUPERORDINATE, COORDINATE, AND SUBORDINATE CONCEPTS

Concept	Superordinate Concept	Coordinate Concept	Subordinate Concept
Dog	Mammal	Dog, horse, cat	Beagle, collie
Verb	Part of speech	Noun, adjective	Action verb, linking verb
Square	Plane figure	Rectangle, triangle, circle	Large square, colored square
Conservative	Political philosophy	Liberal	Economic conservative, social conservative
Metaphor	Figure of speech	Simile, alliteration, personification	Types of metaphors

Defining Concepts. An efficient way of making a concept meaningful is to summarize it in a **definition,** *which is a statement relating the concept, a superordinate concept, and characteristics.* For instance we define *verb* as follows: "A verb is a part of speech that describes an action or state of being." *Verb* (the concept) is linked to *part of speech* (a superordinate concept) and *action or state of being* (characteristics).

Concept Name. As we introduced this section, we provided a list of concepts in Table 8.1. Technically, we provided a list of *labels* or *terms* we use to *name* concepts. This distinction is important because teachers sometimes tacitly assume that they're teaching a concept by simply using the name in a definition. For instance, how much do we learn about the concept *oxymoron* from the following description?

> An oxymoron is a statement that uses contradictory language or terms juxtaposed in the same sentence.

The answer is, typically, not much. Names are simply labels used for communication. When one person uses the term *metaphor,* for example, it communicates meaning to another person if they both understand the concept.

This is the key idea—*understanding* the concept—and this is the reason we are emphasizing the difference between the concept itself and the name of the concept. Understanding can only be achieved by studying examples and nonexamples. For instance, when learners see examples such as "The cruel kindness of an insincere kiss," or "The sweet pain of a remembered love," the concept *oxymoron* begins to become meaningful. This meaningfulness is impossible to achieve using a name and definition alone.

PLANNING FOR CONCEPT LEARNING AND TEACHING

In one sense, teaching concepts is actually quite simple; in another, it can be very difficult. Let's explain what we mean by that statement. Research indicates that concepts are learned most efficiently when students are provided with examples (and nonexamples) and a definition that identifies essential features and a superordinate concept (Tennyson and Cocchiarella, 1986). This makes sense. We know that when we teach concepts, we need to provide students with examples and either give or help them form a definition that identifies essential characteristics. The problem is that many concepts are hard to illustrate, and, as a result, they are hard to learn. This is not a problem for concepts like *square, noun,* or *mammal.* However, consider again the concepts *conservative* and *culture.* These concepts are difficult to illustrate. As other examples, consider the concepts *Republican* and *Democrat.* How many of us can precisely describe the differences between the two? Usually not many, and yet these concepts are at the foundation of our political system. One reason people have difficulty with these concepts is that they have loose boundaries and often have never been precisely illustrated or defined. Labels are commonly used instead, and they are often defined with abstract terms, but rarely are they well illustrated.

We have strongly emphasized the role of examples throughout this text, and we're continuing our emphasis here. Much of the work involved in effective concept teaching occurs before the lesson itself. During planning the teacher analyzes the concept to determine essential characteristics and the most appropriate way to link the concept to what students already know. Based on this analysis, the teacher prepares materials that allow students to make the connection between the world of abstractions and the world of students' reality. This connection is important from a learning perspective because research suggests that concept learning proceeds in stages, with the first step being the formation of an idealized image of the concept (Nosofsky, 1988; Schwartz and Reisberg, 1991). This image originates from concrete examples that the learner has encountered.

Try this yourself. What comes to mind when you think of these concepts: *democracy, love, good teaching*? When we have done this with our students, they report things like "the United States," "my husband or wife or boyfriend," and "the class from Mr. Henry, my high school English teacher," respectively. A natural tendency is to jump from the abstract to a concrete object that represents a prototype of the concept (Paivio, 1971).

The use of examples to illustrate concepts provides templates for this image. At a later stage of concept learning, people are able to describe their concepts in words like "A democracy is a form of government in which the governed have input into important decisions." Here, it is still important that the words used to describe a concept are meaningful (i.e., the students understand the relationship of the words to their experiences). The teacher ensures this through the use of examples.

Keeping these ideas in mind, planning for teaching concepts involves two essential steps: identifying a precise goal, and finding or preparing examples that will help students reach the goal.

Identifying Precise Goals

Clear goals are important for all effective teaching, and this is particularly true for teaching concepts. As with all forms of teaching, clear thinking is important. This thinking answers the question, "Exactly what do I want the students to know or understand about this concept?" Let's look at the seemingly simple concept *mammal*. What characteristics do we want the students to associate with mammals? Fur? Live birth? Warm blooded? Nurses young? Placental? Advanced nervous system? Highly adaptable? Four-chambered heart? Seven cervical vertebrae? Each is a characteristic of mammals, but trying to teach all of them, particularly in a single lesson, wouldn't be appropriate. With young children the teacher might decide to focus on *fur, warm blooded,* and *nurses young.* In contrast, a junior high teacher in a lesson on ecology might want to focus on mammals' ability to adapt to their environments.

The point here is that thinking about goals involves more than a vague notion like, "To understand mammals." We must decide exactly what we want our students to understand about them. The same is true for virtually any concept we plan to teach.

Goals and Examples

The reason precise goals are so essential is that they provide the basis for making decisions about the examples we select to illustrate the concept. For instance, if our goal is for young children to understand that mammals are warm blooded, nurse their young, and are furry, a child's pet (to illustrate warm and furry) combined with a videotape or even pictures of a dog nursing puppies or a cow nursing a calf would be excellent examples (Seeing a real dog nursing puppies would, of course, be better, but a video or pictures are reasonable compromises.)

However, if our goal is for students to understand that mammals are more adaptable than most other animals, the examples we just discussed would be totally ineffective. The adaptability of mammals might be illustrated with videos of animals in a variety of environments, such as musk ox in the arctic, rodents in the Sahara Desert, and jaguars in the jungles of South America.

Without a clear goal, creating or finding effective examples is impossible, because we're not sure what we want students to understand. Examples are what students use to construct understanding, so the examples we use must be consistent with our goal.

We saw that clear thinking about goals and examples is essential even when dealing with a simple concept, such as *mammal.* It is much more difficult with planning to teach concepts like *conservative, liberal, Republican, Democrat,* or *nationalism.* However, the thought processes for the teacher are the same as with *mammal;* they still attempt to answer the question, "Exactly what do I want the students to know about conservatives?" for instance.

Creating examples that illustrate what you want students to understand in the case of the concept *conservative,* for example, is also demanding. Examples (such as a child's pet in the case of *mammal*) don't readily exist, so teachers must create them. Here is where case studies and vignettes can be powerful. For instance, look back at our discussion of ways to represent topics in Chapter 5, and look particularly at the examples of the concept *mercantilism.* These vignettes provide clear and concrete representations of an important historical concept that is virtually impossible to illustrate in any other way. Writing vignettes, such as these, is initially difficult and demanding, but once they're written and stored in your computer, they can be easily revised and, once refined, can be used over and over.

TEACHING CONCEPTS: INVOLVING STUDENTS IN LEARNING

We teach concepts in one of two ways. One way is to present students with a definition and use the examples to illustrate it. This was the strategy Terry Marsden used when she taught the concepts *primary source* and *secondary source.* A second way to teach concepts is to present students with a series of examples and nonexamples and guide them to an understanding of the concept based on patterns they see in the examples. The first is called a deductive and the second an inductive instructional strategy. Each has advantages and disadvantages, and expert teachers are skilled in both. What is essential to each is that teachers involve students in analyzing the examples for essential characteristics. Let's begin our discussion of concept teaching by looking at a lesson where a concept is taught deductively.

Deductive Concept Teaching: A Teacher-Centered Approach

Al Lombana, a middle school Spanish teacher, wanted to help his students understand indirect objects.

As the class bell rang, he began by saying, "Class, in Spanish just like in English it's important to know how words work in a sentence so we know where to place them. For example, look up here at the board.

Mis padres me mandaron el libro.

"It says, 'My parents sent me the book,' " explained Al, writing it under the Spanish. "Who remembers what *parents* is? . . . Ajat?"

"I think it's the subject."

"Good, Ajat. And how about *book*? What part of speech is *book*? . . . Jacinta?"

"Umm, direct object?"

"Yes, Jacinta, *book* is the direct object because that's what the parents sent. Now we've got this other funny word—*me*. *Me* is an indirect object. It's important to know about indirect objects because in Spanish they go before the verb. Today we're going to learn about indirect objects. I've written a definition on the board."

He continued, "Read that definition for me, Karen."

Karen responded, "An indirect object of a verb tells to or from whom or to or from what something is done."

"Okay," Al smiled. "Let's look at the definition. First, we've been studying parts of speech all year. What is a verb? . . . Gabriella?"

"It's a word that shows action or a state of being."

"Good, Gabriella. Give me an example of an action verb. Steve?"

"*Hit.*"

"Fine, Steve. And how about a state of being verb—Joe?"

"*Is.*"

"Good everyone. Now what do we mean when we say direct object? . . . Baldemar?"

"I think they are words that receive the action of the verb," Baldemar responded. "Like, 'Bill hit the ball.' *Ball* is the direct object."

"Real fine, Baldemar," Al praised. "Now remember indirect objects tell to or for whom or to or for what something is done. Let's change Baldemar's sentence to read, 'He hit Ted the ball.' *Ball* is still the direct object, but *Ted* is the indirect object. It tells who Bill hit the ball to. Let's look at another example. See if you can identify the indirect object in this one (*writing it on the board*): 'Mom bought Jim the jacket.' Which is the indirect object and why? . . . Mario?"

"I think it's *Jim*, because it tells who Mom bought the jacket for."

"Excellent, Mario. Now let's try this one," and he wrote the following sentence on the board: 'He told the policeman the details of the accident.' Which is the indirect object? . . . Sally?"

"*Policeman*," Sally responded, "because it describes who received the details."

"Good! That's exactly correct. You've identified precisely why *the policeman* is the indirect object. Now how about this one? 'The student gave the teacher the homework.' What do you think? . . . Kim? Which is the indirect object?"

"Hmm, I think it's homework."

"Look again, Kim. What did the student give?"

"The homework."

"Okay," Al smiled. "So that's the direct object. Now, who did he give it to?"

"The teacher."

"Good, Kim. So what is *teacher*?"

"An indirect object."

"Good thinking, Kim!"

Then Al gave the students the example, 'Santa Claus brought the kids presents,' had them analyze it, and asked individual students to provide additional examples for analysis. After four different students had each given an example, Al passed out a worksheet with a series of sentences. The students were directed to circle the indirect object in each sentence. As he did this, he said, "Now we're going to see if you can find the indirect object in Spanish sentences."

Now compare this lesson with one where a concept is taught inductively.

Inductive Concept Teaching: A Learner-Centered Approach

As the students entered Maria Torrez's biology class, they found trays of plants and seeds at their lab stations. These were divided into two piles labeled *monocotyledon* and *dicotyledon*. In the monocotyledon pile were samples of grasses, onions, and a potted flowering daffodil plant. In addition, there were some soaked corn seeds that had just started to germinate and a picture of a corn plant showing the flowering part and the ears with tassels. In the dicotyledon pile were samples of pea and bean plants, a carrot, a rose flower, plus the hip (fruit) from an old rose flower. The students also had sprouting bean seeds to dissect.

The worksheet at each lab station asked them to list similarities within each group in terms of the following criteria:

a. Seeds
b. Root pattern
c. Leaf vein patterns
d. Vascular arrangements in stems
e. Flowers

After the students had time to analyze the specimens, write notes in their lab manuals, and discuss the findings in their groups, Maria brought the class together.

"Okay, everyone, let's talk about what we did in our lab today. But before that I want to review two key terms." With that she wrote *angiosperm* and *cotyledon* on the board.

"Who remembers what these mean? What's an angiosperm? . . . Angie?"

"It's a plant . . . a kind of plant where the seed is inside the fruit."

"Good, Angie. Can anyone give me an example of an angiosperm? . . . Moy?"

"How about a cherry?"

"Good, Moy. There definitely is a seed inside a cherry—it's the pit or stone that we don't eat and if we plant it, it'll grow into a tree. And what about cotyledon? Who remembers what a cotyledon is? . . . Ricardo?"

"It's like a baby plant inside the seed."

"Good, Ricardo. A cotyledon is an embryonic leaf enclosed within a seed. Now what did we find out today in our lab about monocotyledons and dicotyledons? Let's start with the seeds. How are the two types of seeds different? . . . Kim?"

"They're shaped differently. . . . Like the corn seed was different from the bean seed because it was in one part. But the bean seed split into two parts."

"Good, Kim. That's why we call them dicotyledons. *Di* means two; *mono* means one. Let's write these ideas down on the board." Then, writing as she spoke, she continued,

"The first one under Similarities is they both have seeds. Then, under Differences, we'll write monocots have one seed part and dicots have two.

"Let's compare the roots next. What did you find out about the roots of mono- and dicotyledons? . . . Carlos?"

"Well, they both have roots, but they're shaped different. . . ."

"How is that?" Maria probed. "Tell us how they're different."

"Well, the grass roots are wide and spread out and the roots of the carrots and bean roots go real deep and aren't spread out."

"Good comparison, Carlos. We call the deep root of the dicots a taproot and it's very good at extracting moisture and nutrients from deep in the soil. Now think for a moment. What would the grass root system be good for?"

The lesson continued with Maria comparing similarities and differences between monocots and dicots on the other essential characteristics—leaf patterns, vascular arrangement, and flowers—that she had targeted with her lab worksheet. When these features were identified, the class created a definition linking monocots and dicots to angiosperms.

A Comparison of Deductive and Inductive Approaches to Concept Teaching

Let's take a look at Al's and Maria's lessons now and see how they're similar and different. Three similarities are important.

1. Al and Maria both used a combination of examples and nonexamples to help students identify the essential characteristics of the concepts—*indirect objects* in Al's case and *monocotyledons* and *dicotyledons* in Maria's. This is consistent with research about how students effectively learn concepts.
2. The concepts were linked to superordinate concepts that helped establish their relationship to other concepts. Al helped the students link indirect objects to parts of speech and direct objects, and Maria helped her students link monocots and dicots to angiosperms. The importance of linking concepts to superordinate and coordinate concepts is also confirmed by research (Gage and Berliner, 1998).
3. Both lessons were highly interactive, and Al and Maria asked many questions to involve their students in the lesson. For example, when Kim gave an incorrect response (in Al's lesson), he prompted her until she understood the example. Maria also led her students through a comparison of the examples, helping them identify essential characteristics of monocots and dicots.

However, there were important differences between the two lessons. One was sequence. Al began his lesson with a definition and continued by linking characteristics to examples; Maria began with examples and used the examples and her questioning to guide the students as they gradually constructed understanding of the concepts.

Because of these different approaches, the teachers' and students' roles were different in each. Maria took on the role of instructional guide by displaying the examples and assisting students in analyzing the data to identify the concepts' characteristics; Al was more direct in helping the students link essential characteristics to examples.

These similarities and differences are summarized in Table 8.4 and analyzed in the sections that follow.

Table 8.4   INDUCTIVE AND DEDUCTIVE CONCEPT TEACHING

	Similarities	Sequence	Teacher Role	Student Role
I N D U C T I V E	Both use examples Concept is defined in terms of characteristics	Examples ↓ Definition	Present examples and help students analyze examples to extract essential characteristics	Analyze examples to define concept
D E D U C T I V E	Essential characteristics linked to example	Definition ↓ Example	Define concept and assist students to link definition with examples	Link definition to examples

Deductive Concept Teaching: A Closer Look.   In teaching concepts deductively, our primary goal is to help students understand the concept by linking the definition to real-world examples. The name of the concept, a superordinate concept, and a description of the concept's essential characteristics are included in the definition to help students understand what the concept is and how it relates to the examples.

Let's analyze again both Terry Marsden's and Al Lombana's lessons to see how they illustrate these ideas. Terry's lesson is a good illustration, and three important elements are illustrated in it. First, she presented the headlines. They acted as an attention getter and provided a framework for the concepts *primary source* and *secondary source*. Second, Terry drew a diagram on the board that put the concepts into a larger context—research methods in history. Third, Terry wrote the definitions on the board for ready reference throughout the lesson. This made the information available to all the students (including the ones who were dozing when she gave the definition) and helped in note taking.

The central feature of both Terry's and Al's lessons involved linking the definitions they presented to the examples. They did this directly at first; then they asked the students to categorize and explain examples; and finally, the students generated their own examples. This gradual shift of responsibility helped students develop a clear understanding of the concepts while ensuring a high rate of success.

One final comment should be made about the lessons. Both Terry and Al taught two coordinate concepts at the same time—*primary* and *secondary source* in Terry's case, and *indirect object* and *direct object* in Al's. This allowed the examples of one concept to serve as the nonexamples for the other. The curriculum offers many opportunities to teach concepts in this way, such as *adverb* and *adjective* in language arts, *old mountains* and *new mountains* in earth science, *longitude* and *latitude* in geography, and *positive* and *nega-*

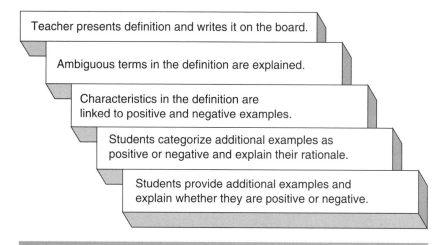

Figure 8.3 Steps in Deductive Concept Teaching

tive numbers in math. Research indicates that this is an effective way of teaching pairs of coordinate concepts (Tennyson and Cocchiarella, 1986).

The sequential steps in a deductive concept lesson are summarized in Figure 8.3.

Inductive Concept Teaching: Further Analysis. Inductive concept teaching is the counterpart to what we saw in Terry's and Al's lessons. When using this strategy, teachers present positive and negative examples and guide students as they look for patterns in the positive examples and compare them to the negative examples.

Let's analyze Maria's lesson as an illustration. First, Maria had displayed examples of monocots and dicots for the students as they came in the room. The examples were effective because the characteristics of the concepts were observable in them. Maria then guided the students' analysis of the examples until they identified the essential characteristics of each concept. The lesson was inductive because it began with examples which students were responsible for analyzing for essential characteristics.

The fact that Maria supplied the name of the concepts did not detract from the inductive aspects of the activity because the students were responsible (with Maria's guidance) for analyzing the examples and identifying the concepts' characteristics. Supplying the term merely provides a label for the concepts the students were constructing. The steps involved in teaching concepts inductively are summarized in Figure 8.4.

When they teach concepts inductively, teachers commonly have two goals. The first is to construct a valid understanding of the concept, and this is similar to the primary goal when using a deductive approach.

A second goal is for students to learn to analyze data and think critically. Research examining inductive and deductive teaching strategies indicates that inductive approaches help students become efficient at data analysis through such opportunities (Derry and Murphy, 1986). We reexamine the development of students' thinking skills in Chapter 10.

As we did in our analysis of deductive approaches to concept teaching, we need to make a final comment here. Throughout our discussion of inductive strategies for

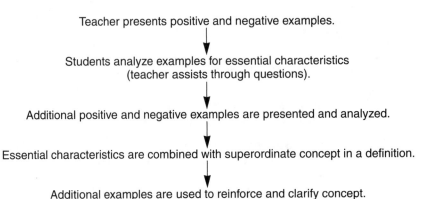

Teacher presents positive and negative examples.

Students analyze examples for essential characteristics
(teacher assists through questions).

Additional positive and negative examples are presented and analyzed.

Essential characteristics are combined with superordinate concept in a definition.

Additional examples are used to reinforce and clarify concept.

Figure 8.4 Steps in Inductive Concept Teaching

teaching concepts, we have emphasized the role of the teacher. Because Maria's approach was inductive and Al's deductive doesn't suggest in the least that her teaching role was less important than his. In many ways it was more important. Inductive strategies for teaching concepts are grounded in constructivist views of learning, and the misconceptions that exist in basing instruction on constructivism (such as tacitly believing that the teacher's role is less important, and believing that learning is occurring if students are active) apply here as well. Maria had to make the same kinds of decisions that we saw Lucy Zuniga make in the case study that introduced Chapter 7. In fact, Lucy was also teaching a concept—*conduction.* It was more abstract than *monocot* and *dicot,* but it is a concept nevertheless.

Research has examined the effects of teachers' guidance on learning, and it indicates that when teachers fail to provide adequate guidance, learning decreases (Hardiman, Pollatsek, and Weil, 1986; Schauble, 1990). Without sufficient guidance in the form of questions and prompts, students often become lost and frustrated, and this confusion can lead to misconceptions (Brown and Campione, 1994). Inductive approaches to concept teaching are sophisticated and demanding, and they require high levels of expertise, guidance, and teacher judgment.

Spontaneous Concept Teaching

Most of the concepts that we teach are planned, sequenced, and integrated into the total curriculum. However, spontaneous concept teaching opportunities occur daily. Let's look at an example:

Fey Shah's fourth-grade language arts class was reading a story about the pioneers' adventures as they traveled west. As they were reading, they ran across the word *crik.*

"What's a crik?" Jesse asked.

"It's a word the pioneers used for the word *creek,*" Fey smiled. "Like *creek* and *crik.* Does anyone know what a creek is? . . . No one? Well, what does the story tell us? . . . How is it used in the story?"

"When we come to the next crik, we'll stop to let the horses drink," Esteban responded.

"So we know it has water in it. Well, a creek is kind of like a river but it's smaller. Remember when we took our field trip to the Bennet Farm? . . . Remember that little stream that flowed out of the fish pond? . . . That's a creek. It's not as big as a river, but the water in it moves. That's one thing that makes it different from a lake or pond."

Then Fey remembered a cover of a *National Geographic* that showed a creek meandering through a meadow, brought it down from the shelf and showed it to the class.

Concepts pop up continually in classrooms, and their meanings are often unclear. Sometimes students will tell us that they do not understand a term; at others we have to infer it from frowns or blank looks. A quick question, such as "What is a (crik)?" or "What does (crik) mean?" can serve as the springboard for a minilesson on the confusing concept.

Table 8.5 outlines several instructional strategies teachers can use when opportunities for spontaneous concept teaching arise.

UNDERSTANDING RELATIONSHIPS AMONG CONCEPTS: GENERALIZATIONS, PRINCIPLES, AND ACADEMIC RULES

To introduce this section, let's think again about Terry Marsden's lesson at the beginning of this chapter. Terry's objective was for her students to understand the concepts of primary and secondary data sources. She then presented examples and guided her students toward a definition of these concepts. During the lesson the class concluded that "distortion or inaccuracy increases when secondary sources are used." This statement is a **generalization,** *a statement that relates two concepts for which there are known exceptions.* Like concepts, generalizations are useful because they help structure and simplify the world

Table 8.5 STRATEGIES FOR TEACHING CONCEPTS SPONTANEOUSLY

Strategy	Example
Link to superordinate example.	It's a *body of water.*
Provide an analogy or coordinate concept.	It's kind of like a river.
Present examples.	The stream by the Bennett Farm The picture in *National Geographic*
Present nonexamples.	A lake A pond
Identify characteristics.	It has water in it. It's smaller than a river. The water in it moves.
Provide context.	How is it used in the story?

around us. In using generalizations, however, we should remember that exceptions exist, so conclusions based on them can be inaccurate.

Some additional examples of generalizations include the following:

- Herbivores have longer legs than do carnivores.
- The earlier (historically) the musical piece, the fewer the instruments in the orchestra.
- Complementary colors balance each other, with the brighter ones standing out and darker ones receding.
- Teachers who are well organized have students who learn more than do disorganized teachers.

We can quickly identify exceptions to each of the statements. If a teacher is well organized but uses ineffective examples and puts learners in passive roles, for instance, students will likely learn less than they will in a class where the teacher is less well organized but uses effective examples and puts the learners in active roles. Most of what we know about learning and teaching exists as generalizations based upon research data.

A **principle** (or law) is a special kind of generalization *that describes a relationship between two or more concepts that is accepted as true for all cases.* Principles make up an important part of the school curriculum, particularly in science. The following are some examples.

- Objects at rest remain at rest and moving objects remain moving in a straight line unless a force acts on them (Newton's law of inertia).
- The farther from the equator, the longer the days in summer and the shorter the days in winter.
- The greater the force on an object, the greater its acceleration.

In each of these instances concepts are linked in a statement describing the way the world operates.

Finally, consider the following statements.

- Pronouns must agree with their antecedent in number and gender.
- In English, adjectives precede the noun they modify.
- In Spanish, adjectives follow the noun they modify.
- In rounding off numbers, round up if the last numeral is five or more, and round down if the last numeral is four or less.

Again, we see that the statements describe a relationship between two concepts, but these statements are **academic rules,** *which are relationships that have been arbitrarily developed by people.* The arbitrary nature of academic rules is illustrated by the fact that adjectives precede nouns in English but follow nouns in Spanish. As English evolved, it would have been equally valid to have the adjective follow the noun as it does in Spanish (and French). This is the case with all our rules of grammar, spelling, and punctuation. Rules are particularly important in language arts because they provide for consistency in communication.

While academic rules are most common in language arts, they exist in other areas as well, such as the example with rounding in math. As in grammar, spelling, and punctuation, this is an arbitrary rule or convention that we follow to make the process uniform.

TEACHING GENERALIZATIONS, PRINCIPLES, AND ACADEMIC RULES

How are generalizations and principles learned, and what implications does this have for the classroom? Like concepts, they are abstractions whose meaning depends on examples, and these examples can be taught either inductively or deductively. Generalizations are meaningful only if learners can relate the abstract statement to real-world events. This is especially true for young children whose capacity for abstract thought is hampered by limited vocabulary, verbal ability, and experience.

Planning for Teaching Generalizations, Principles, and Academic Rules

Planning for teaching generalizations, principles, and rules is similar to planning for teaching concepts. It involves:

- Identifying the topic
- Determining a clear and precise goal
- Preparing examples

The topic provides a content focus. For instance, in the case study that introduced Chapter 5, José Alvarez planned and implemented a lesson on *heat and expansion*. This was his topic. His goals were for the students to understand the principles, "Heat makes substances expand," and "Heat increases the movement of molecules." His goals were clear, and their clarity helped him find examples that clearly represented the topic. The kind of thinking José did was similar to Terry's, Al's, and Maria's thinking in this chapter. In each case the teacher was very clear about his or her goal, and they created (or found) examples that helped their students reach the goals.

As you can see, planning considerations for teaching generalizations, principles, and rules are nearly the same as those for teaching concepts. We want to provide experiences that will allow students to construct meaningful representations of the abstraction (the generalization, principle, or rule).

Implementing Lessons for Teaching Generalizations, Principles, and Academic Rules

Like concepts, generalizations, principles, and academic rules can be taught either inductively or deductively. When an inductive strategy is used, we first provide students with information and guide them to the generalization, principle, or rule, just as we do when using an inductive approach for teaching concepts. José's lesson in Chapter 5 is an example of an inductive approach for teaching the principles "Heat makes substances expand," and "Heat increases the movement of molecules." (He also taught the concept of *expansion* during the process. This was incidental to his central goal, which illustrates the opportunity inductive approaches provide for incidental learning.)

In a deductive approach, the generalization, principle, or rule is first stated, written on the board or overhead, terms within it are defined, and it is then related to examples. Had José chosen to use a deductive approach, he would have first stated the principles (and probably written them on the board or displayed them on an overhead), explained

Table 8.6 INDUCTIVE AND DEDUCTIVE STRATEGIES FOR TEACHING GENERALIZATIONS, PRINCIPLES, AND ACADEMIC RULES

Lesson Phase	Inductive Sequence	Deductive Sequence
Introduction	Examples are presented; students make observations	The abstraction (generalization, principle, or rule) is stated; concepts are clarified
Development	Teacher guides students as they search for patterns in the examples	Teacher presents examples and helps students link them to the abstraction
Closure	Teacher guides students to a statement of the generalization, principle, or rule (abstraction); students apply the abstraction to unique real-world situations	Students apply the abstraction to unique real-world situations

the concepts within them, and then applied the principles to examples. Differences between the two strategies are summarized in Table 8.6.

ACCOMMODATING DIVERSITY IN CONCEPT LEARNING AND TEACHING

As we approach the end of this chapter, we want to again consider the diversity of our students—one of the themes of this text. To do so, let's think back to Chapter 5 where we discussed differences in students' background knowledge. There we said that the content representations we use should have one essential characteristic: *The information learners need to understand the topic exists in the representations.* As an illustration, we suggested that a lobster would be a good example to teach *arthropod,* pointing out that regardless of background experience, gender, ethnicity, or socioeconomic status, learners can feel the hard shell and coldness of a lobster and see its jointed legs and body parts. *Arthropod* is a concept, and a lobster is an excellent way to illustrate it for *all* learners.

The same applies with principles, generalizations, and academic rules. Again, let's think back to José and the way he represented the principles, "Heat makes substances expand," and "Heat increases the movement of molecules." As with the concept *arthropod,* regardless of background his students could see the heated balloon expand and, again regardless of background, could visualize the spacing and movement of the molecules from his model of the bottles and balloons. It is representations of this sort that help accommodate learner diversity.

The same idea applies when teaching academic rules. For instance, consider the following passage.

Jefferson County has six *schools*—one high *school,* two middle schools, and three elementary schools. Five of the schools are in Brooksville, the largest *city* in Jefferson *county.* The city's schools and the schools in three other *counties* hold an annual scholastic and athletic competition, and students in the counties' schools met this year in Brooksville. In all, students from five *cities* were involved, and the cities' students did very well.

The two *women* advisors of Brooksville's debate teams were particularly proud because the women's teams won both of their debates. The members of Debate-1 swept the competition. The members of Debate-2 also squeaked out a win, and theirs was perhaps a greater accomplishment, since they haven't competed as long.

Four *girls* and three *boys* won both athletic and scholastic honors. The girls' accomplishments were noteworthy in math on the academic side and tennis on the athletic side. The boys' achievements were in writing and track. One *boy* set a new school record in the 100-meter dash.

Many *children* from the elementary schools participated as well, and the children's accomplishments were equally impressive. Several of the children wrote short *stories.* One *child* wrote a *story* involving a *woman* and the woman's struggle to keep her farm in the face of hardship. The child's story and the story's plot were very sophisticated. Several stories' plots and characters were interesting and well developed. The stories were put in a *display,* and three of the *displays* were photographed for the local newspaper. The displays' contents included the stories as well as some background information on the author. Lakesha Jefferson had her story published in the paper, and hers was the first of its type to be presented this way.

As in the other cases, all the information the students need to understand the rules for forming plural nouns is embedded in the passage. For instance, the passage contains, "three other *counties,*" "five *cities,*" "two *women,*" "four *girls,*" and "three *boys.*" Students aren't required to memorize the rule; they *see* it illustrated in the example. This is the essence of accommodating learner diversity while teaching concepts, principles, generalizations, and academic rules.

UTILIZING TECHNOLOGY IN CONCEPT LEARNING

It is midmorning when Lyn Chan, a teacher at Skyline Elementary School in South San Francisco, begins to talk about dinosaurs and ancient food chains. Millions of years ago, several types of dinosaurs roamed the earth, she tells her class of 30 fifth and sixth graders. There were meat eaters, plant eaters, and flying reptiles, she adds as she touches a button on a remote control. A picture of a brontosaurus appears on the video screen, followed by a pterodactyl. As the kids watch, they call out the names of the dinosaurs they recognize.

But one boy is curious. "How do we know how they lived back then?" he asks.

Chan is delighted. "I'm glad you asked that," she says. It is one of the moments that teachers live for, the look in a young person's eye that says, I'm interested! Tell me more! (Herber, 1990, p. 23)

Technology can play a powerful role in helping teachers represent abstract concepts for learners, bringing the far away and remote into the classroom. Videotape, computer simulations, and videodiscs all provide convenient ways to bring the outside world into the classroom. Videodiscs, with their capacity to store 108,000 razor-sharp images along with theater-quality sound, are especially powerful technological tools (Forcier, 1996).

For example, the *National Gallery of Art* videodisc by Videodisc Publishing contains a vast array of works by great artists, information that would be inaccessible in any other way. *Windows on Science,* a collection of still-life and moving images, allows science teachers to illustrate hard-to-imagine ideas and structures. One teacher shared this experience:

> In a unit on the human ear, for example, I begin by asking questions: "What is an ear?" "How does it work?" "What is vibration?" I hold up a plastic model of the ear and begin explaining how we hear. Then I stop for just a second to click on a slide of the ear from a life science videodisc, and my presentation comes alive. "Oh, that's how it works," says one boy. "It looks like a little snail shell," says another.
>
> By showing just this one slide from the many slides, diagrams, and film clips available on the videodisc, my students can actually *see* inside the ear. It's so much better than a text-book. The students are really attentive and in tune with the subject. (Weiland, 1990, p. 22)

An integrated multimedia package in social studies called *Grapevine* combines videodisc with a computer hypercard program. In it are contained snapshots as well as news footage of scenes from the Great Depression (Solomon, 1989). The package not only allows teachers to transport their students back in time but also provides opportunities for students to use these images in projects and reports.

These technology resources can provide powerful ways for representing concepts, principles, and generalizations when the actual materials are unavailable. Virtually all schools now have videotape players, and videodisc players are becoming more common as prices come down.

In each of these cases, we're trying to represent the topics we teach in ways that are as meaningful as possible. This means providing as much information as we can in the representations, and technology can be an important resource in helping us do that.

Summary

Understanding Concepts. Concepts form an important part of the curriculum. When we teach concepts, we want students to understand: (1) the concept's essential characteristics, (2) how these relate to positive and negative examples, and (3) the relationship of the concept to other ideas. This last function is accomplished by linking the concept to superordinate, coordinate, and subordinate concepts.

Planning for Concept Learning and Teaching. When we plan for concept teaching, our primary concern is providing examples that assist learners in identifying essential characteristics. This requires that teachers thoroughly understand the different dimensions of the concept, how it is related to other concepts, and how the concept can be illustrated with examples.

Teaching Concepts: Involving Students in Learning. Concepts are taught in two major ways. In deductive teaching, a definition is presented and linked to positive and negative examples. An inductive sequence presents students with examples and then asks students to analyze the examples to identify essential characteristics. Both types of concept lessons are interactive, to encourage student involvement and to allow the teacher to gauge whether students are understanding the concept.

Spontaneous concept teaching occurs when ambiguous concepts are encountered in the course of a lesson. The same essential components of effective concept teaching apply here: (1) positive and negative examples, (2) characteristics, (3) superordinate concept, and (4) coordinate concept.

Understanding Relationships among Concepts: Generalizations, Principles, and Academic Rules. Generalizations, principles, and academic rules connect concepts and describe patterns in the world. Like concepts, these abstractions can be taught both inductively and deductively. As with concepts, examples in the form of data are essential to help students link these abstractions to the real world.

Teaching Generalizations, Principles, and Academic Rules. As with teaching concepts, generalizations, principles, and academic rules can be taught inductively or deductively. In a deductive approach, the abstraction (generalization, principle, or rule) is stated and linked to examples. In an inductive sequence, teachers present students with examples and guide them to a statement of the abstraction.

Accommodating Diversity in Concept Learning and Teaching. To accommodate background differences when students are learning concepts, principles, generalizations, and academic rules, teachers try to provide representations that contain all the information students need to understand the topic being taught.

Utilizing Technology in Concept Learning. Technology is an important resource for representing topics when the real thing isn't available. As with other forms of instruction, it is a powerful tool for helping teachers represent concepts that are hard to illustrate in other ways. Computers, videodiscs, CD-ROMs, and videotape all can be utilized to illustrate concepts and the relationships among them.

Important Concepts

Academic rules	Model
Characteristics	Nonexample
Concept	Principle
Coordinate concept	Prototype
Definition	Subordinate concept
Example	Superordinate concept
Generalization	

Reflecting on Teaching and Learning

As you've studied this chapter, you've seen how teachers can design and implement instruction to help their students understand concepts, generalizations, principles, and academic rules. Read the following case study now and consider how effectively the teacher implemented the ideas discussed in the chapter.

Carl Ruiz has his art class involved in a study of the Impressionist school of art. He began his third-period class by saying, "Let's take a look at some paintings today done by Impressionists. This one is by Vincent Van Gogh. It's called *Seascape on Saintes Maries*. Since there are boats and water, that makes sense, doesn't it? The other is by Monet. What do you think it might be called? . . . Isabelle?"

" . . . How about 'Harbor Scene'?" Isabelle responded after gazing at the picture.

"That's a good idea. How about you, Tim?"

"Maybe . . . 'Sailboats'?"

"Actually you're both close. It's called *Bridge at Argenteuil*. Argenteuil must be the name of a harbor with a bridge that Monet painted. He has other paintings located here. Let's take a look at these paintings and talk about how the artist put them together. Let's focus on the Van Gogh first. What do we see in it? . . . Kyo?"

" . . . I see a bunch of boats on a choppy sea."

"OK, good," Carl smiled. "Anything else? . . . Yolando?"

" . . . They look like small fishing boats because they only have one mast."

"Good observation, Yolando. . . . How does the painting make you feel?"

" . . . Kind of like I'm right on the water."

"Why do you think it does that?"

"Well, I'm not quite sure. . . . You can see, almost feel, the waves in the front of the painting. They sort of look almost alive, if that makes any sense."

"That's an excellent description, Yolando!" Carl responded enthusiastically. "Keep what Yolando said in mind, everyone. Now, look over here. Does everyone see these waves here? Why do they stand out? . . . Gary."

"Got me," Gary shrugged.

"What color are they?" Carl prompted.

" . . . Yellow."

"OK, and what color is the background?"

"Blue-green."

"Okay. Does anything else in the painting stand out? . . . Jeremy?"

" . . . The sails on the boats. Hey, they're yellow, too."

"Good," Carl smiled in response to Jeremy's revelation. "Now notice the color of the sky surrounding these sails. What color would you call it? . . . Michelle?"

" . . . Mmm, purple, almost violet."

"Okay, let's keep those combinations in mind as we look at the next picture. This one is the Monet. And it's a water scene too. But look at the water. How is it different from Van Gogh's *Seascape*? . . . Duk?"

" . . . It's really calm. There are only little waves and not much is moving."

"Fine, Duk. Now, let's look at this painting more closely. What do we tend to focus on when we see it? . . . What does Monet want us to look at here? . . . Anyone? . . . Sam?"

" . . . I think it's the sailboat."

"Why do you think so?"

" . . . Well, for one thing it's in the center of the picture."

"Good, the position of an object pulls the viewer toward it. Why else are we drawn to the sailboat? Look at its mast. What does the mast do in this painting? . . . Suzanne?"

" . . . It really sticks out."

"Why do you think so?"

" . . . Well, I don't know. It just does."

"Think about our observations of Van Gogh's *Seascape on Saintes Maries.* How does our Monet compare to that picture?"

" . . . Well, they both have light colors next to dark," Suzanne responded, looking back and forth from one picture to the other.

"Excellent, Suzanne!"

"Now, I'd like you to look at this painting that I put together just this morning. What does it look like? . . . Fred?"

" . . . A bull's eye."

"Good, and what colors do we have here? . . . Jianna?"

"Red and green."

"Okay. What happens when we put these two colors together? What does it do to the painting? . . . Sonya?"

" . . . The red kind of jumps out at you and the green sort of fades."

"Good. Who remembers what we call color pairs like the ones we've been discussing? Let's write them up on the board." Carl then wrote:

Yellow-Violet

Orange-Blue

Red-Green

"George, do you remember?"

" . . . They're complementary colors."

"Excellent! Everyone, look at the color wheel. Note how the color pairs are at opposite sides of the color wheel. Now let's look back at the three paintings we've been discussing to see if we can make a statement about what happens when we put complementary colors next to each other. Think for a minute. . . . Give it a try Nancy."

" . . . I think they do two things. One is that they really make each other stand out. It's a really sharp contrast. The other is that the dark colors look like they sink," Nancy said hesitantly.

"Good ideas, Nancy. Did everyone hear them? Let's write them down here so everyone can see. . . . What did Nancy say? Janet?"

" . . . Complementary colors next to each other make each other stand out," Janet repeated.

"Excellent, Janet! That's a precise statement of the relationship we found. Now what else? . . . Suki?"

"The brighter color in the pair stands out and the darker one recedes," Steve responded confidently after hearing Janet's description.

"Okay! Good work, all of you. Now let's take a look at one more painting and I want everyone to see if these statements make sense. This one is called *The Dance,* and it's by Henri Matisse. Which colors stand out and which recede? . . . Tony?"

"The oranges really jump out and the greens and blues recede."

Carl continued, "Excellent! and why is that the case? . . . Ken?"

" . . . The orange is lighter, so it stands out, and the greens and blues are darker so they recede."

"Very good explanation, Ken, and good work everyone," Carl emphasized triumphantly with outstretched hands in the air. "Now let's see if we can apply these ideas to our own paintings. I've set up some still-lifes over here for us to paint. Let's try to use some of the complementary colors that we discussed to emphasize objects in our paintings."

The students went to work on their paintings and continued through the rest of the period.

Questions for Analysis

Let's look at Carl's lesson now based on the information in this chapter. In doing your analysis, you may want to consider the following questions. In each case, be specific and take information directly from the case study in completing your analysis.

1. What type of content was Carl Ruiz teaching? How good a job did he do in teaching these content forms? What else might he have done to improve his teaching of this type of content?
2. Was the lesson inductive or deductive? Why? How could it be changed to utilize the other strategy?
3. What strategies did Carl use to actively involve students in learning? How might this involvement be improved?
4. Comment on the quality of Carl's teaching. How might it be improved?
5. To what extent was Carl's lesson based on constructivist views of learning? Defend your answer using the characteristics of constructivism discussed in Chapter 7.

Discussion Questions

1. How does the importance of concepts in the curriculum vary with respect to:
   a. Grade level (e.g., Is there relatively more emphasis on concept learning in the first few grades than in high school or vice versa? How do the kinds of concepts change?)
   b. Ability level (e.g., Do lower-ability students need more or less emphasis on concepts?)
   c. Subject matter (How does the specific focus of a content area, like social studies or art, influence the emphasis on concepts?)
2. What are the implications of this chapter with respect to assessing for concept learning?
3. Some researchers in the area of concept learning have suggested that the optimal number of positive/negative examples to be used in teaching a concept is three. What factors might influence this number?
4. What advantages are there in asking students to generate their own examples and nonexamples of concepts, generalizations, principles, and academic rules? What disadvantages might exist?
5. What are the advantages and disadvantages of inductive and deductive approaches to concept teaching? How does your particular grade-level focus (elementary or secondary) influence the value of either? Content area?

6. What concepts have you encountered in your teacher education program? In the class you are in right now? How were they taught? Assessed? How could this instruction be made more effective?

Portfolio Activities

1. *Cognitive Goals.* Examine a school district's curriculum guide for a specific area of the curriculum (e.g., fourth-grade social studies or high school biology). What percentage of the goals involve concept learning? In your answer construct a list of the important concepts included. Do you think the emphasis on concept learning is appropriate? If not, how would you modify?

2. *Textbook Content Goals.* Analyze a chapter from a content-area textbook in your area (e.g., second-grade science or eighth-grade English). How much emphasis (pages or sections) is given to concepts? How are they organized? Is the organization apparent to students? How would you improve the presentation of concepts in this text?

3. *Concept Teaching in Textbooks.* Identify a specific concept being taught in a school text. Analyze the quality of the concept teaching in terms of the following criteria:

   a. Characteristics (clearly defined?)
   b. Examples and nonexamples (linked to characteristics?)
   c. Superordinate concept (familiar to students?)
   d. Coordinate concept (clearly differentiated from the target concept?)

   What could you as a teacher do to supplement the content of the text?

4. *Interactive Concept Teaching.* Observe a teacher teaching a concept (or teach one yourself) and critique the lesson in terms of the criteria in Portfolio Activity 3. What would you do differently next time?

5. *Interactive Teaching of Generalizations, Principles, or Rules.* Observe (or tape) a lesson in which one of these three forms of content is being taught.

   a. Identify the abstraction.
   b. What examples were used to illustrate the abstraction?
   c. Was the sequence inductive or deductive? Explain.
   d. Were students asked to apply the generalization? How?

   What suggestion do you have for making the lesson more effective?

6. *Concept Learning: The Students' Perspective.* Identify a concept that you feel is important. Interview several students, ideally some that are high and low in ability, asking them to explain the concept in terms of the following:

   a. Essential characteristics
   b. Examples
   c. Links to other concepts

   What do students' responses tell you about their understanding of the concept? What implications do their responses have for you as a teacher?

9

Capitalizing on Social Interaction

*A*s you've studied the content of this text, you've seen that student involvement is a critical part of the learning process, and when you studied constructivism in Chapter 7, you found that social interaction is an effective way to promote involvement and increase understanding. In this chapter we return to the topic of social interaction and examine cooperative learning, discussions, and peer tutoring, three instructional strategies that have social interaction as a core element. When you've completed your study of this chapter you should be able to meet the following goals:

- Explain how social interaction facilitates learning.
- Explain how group goals, individual accountability and equal opportunity for success contribute to the effectiveness of cooperative learning.
- Plan and implement different cooperative learning strategies.
- Describe how discussions can be used to attain both cognitive and affective goals.
- Describe how to plan for and implement peer tutoring lessons.

Maria Sanchez, a sixth-grade middle school teacher, was staring out the window of the teacher's lounge, when Terry Cummings, her friend and confidante, came up behind her.

"Hey, what's wrong?" Terry asked. "You look like you lost your dog or something."

"Not really," Maria replied with a wry smile. "I'm just a little discouraged. I've been teaching my tail off, but I can't seem to get the kids into it. I'm putting my whole self into it, or at least I think I am, and half the class isn't even listening. They seem bored, and I hate to admit it, but when they're that way, it drags me down. Any ideas?"

"Hmm . . . don't know . . . maybe . . . maybe you're trying too hard. Sounds like you're giving a hundred percent, but maybe it's in the wrong direction. I used to be 'Ringmaster Ned' too, but the rest of the circus wasn't with me," Terry replied with a sympathetic shrug.

"I'm not sure what you mean. . . . Say more. . . . I thought that's what good teaching was all about—being in front of them and giving it my all?"

"Well, it is . . . I mean, sure, we're giving our all, but . . . and yes, there are times when we need to stand up and explain and model things, but . . . if that's all you do, you know, I mean . . . if that's all *we* do, . . . no matter how enthusiastic we are, we'll lose 'em. My kids need to be doing stuff—talking, writing, working with each other. I've got some ideas if you're interested."

"Sure, can't hurt . . . I'm sort of desperate. I'll try anything."

When people think about teaching, they often picture a teacher at the front of the room explaining, writing on the board, and asking questions. This approach can be effective for learning certain types of content, such as concepts, generalizations, and academic rules, which you studied in Chapter 8, and for learning skills and organized bodies of knowledge, which you will study in Chapter 11.

Some goals, however, can't be effectively met by having a teacher standing in front of the room and explaining. We've all heard teachers say, or have even said ourselves, "The kid is capable. He just won't work." Often the problem is motivation, and motivation often suffers when teachers talk too much and students listen passively. This is one reason to use teaching strategies that employ social interaction. They are motivating to students (Zahorik, 1996). In other cases, students won't listen to each other. They appear narrow minded and are even rude to their classmates. These behaviors reflect students' attitudes, values, and interpersonal skills. Developing students' inclinations and abilities to listen, to work with their classmates on projects, and to cooperate in solving problems are important educational goals. For these goals, alternatives to whole-group, teacher-centered instruction are needed. This chapter describes instructional approaches designed to reach these goals.

SOCIAL INTERACTION: THEORETICAL PERSPECTIVES

Theories and research examining the way people learn should guide the way we teach. This is the conceptual foundation on which this text is based. In this section we describe research that examines the role that language and social interaction play in learning.

The powerful role that social interaction plays in learning can be explained from three theoretical perspectives. The first of these is the developmental theories of Jean Piaget and Lev Vygotsky. The second explanation for the effectiveness of social interaction in learning is elaboration theory. The third perspective on the effectiveness of learning theory comes from motivational theory. Let's examine each of these now.

Developmental Theories

Devon: Look at the bugs. (*Holding a beetle between his fingers and pointing at a spider.*)
Gino: Yech . . . Put that thing down. Besides, that's not a bug. It's a spider. (*Gesturing to the spider.*)
Devon: What do you mean? A bug is a bug. They look the same.
Gino: Nope. Bugs have six legs. See? (*Touching the legs of the beetle.*) He has eight legs. . . . Look. (*Pointing to the spider.*)
Devon: So, . . . bugs . . . have . . . six legs, and spiders have eight. (Eggen and Kauchak, 2001, p. 293)

From a developmental perspective, social interaction encourages learning because it encourages students to reevaluate their own views of the world.

Jean Piaget, the Swiss developmental psychologist, would interpret this episode by saying that Devon's equilibrium was disrupted by the discussion since he saw evidence that the beetle and spider were different, and he resolved the problem by reconstructing his thinking to accommodate the evidence (Berk, 1997; Byrnes, 2001). The same occurs when we share our political views with someone else and change our views in light of the conversation. In both instances, exposure to a different perspective caused people to reevaluate and change their beliefs.

Lev Vygotsky (1978) explains the importance of social interaction from a different perspective. He views development and learning as processes that begin on the outside and then are internalized. For example, let's see how social interaction helps a father teach his toddler how to get dressed.

"Okay, here we go. Let's get dressed so we can go visit Grandma. First, we take off your pajamas and put on your underwear. Wow, these pajamas are tight. Next we put on your shirt. There. Then your big boys, and now your pants. Look at those little doggies on the pants."

"Doggy?"

"Yes, those are doggies. Aren't they cute? Ruff, ruff! Grrr! Now we put on this sock. Then your shoe. Now you do the other one."

"Shoe?"

"Yes, that's a shoe. Wait a minute, though. What do we have to put on before the shoe? Look over here" (*pointing to the sock*). "That's right, first you put on your sock, then your shoe."

"Sock first?"

"Yeah, that's right. Put on your sock first, then your shoe. Atta boy!" (Eggen and Kauchak, 1999, p. 48)

Through interactive dialogue embedded in activity, the father helped his son learn how to dress himself. Social interaction plays a similar role in the classroom. It provides a forum for the exchange of ideas that are first discussed externally or orally and then internalized. As we use language to learn new concepts, our view of the word changes. For example, after we take an art or music history class, we see and hear things that we didn't know existed before. Language also allows us to share our thoughts with others, refining them in the process.

In both views of social interaction—Piaget's and Vygotsky's—social interaction facilitates learning by encouraging students to listen to the views and perspectives of others. Piaget views this social interaction as a catalyst for students to reevaluate their own beliefs about the world; Vygotsky sees social interaction as a vehicle for more knowledge about others to share their expertise with others. In both instances, students learn by talking and listening.

Elaboration Theory

Elaboration *makes information meaningful by forming additional links in existing knowledge.* Cognitive research on the way people learn suggests that one of the most effective ways to retain new information is to elaborate or restructure it and connect it to what we already know (Slavin, 1995; Ormrod, 2000). For example, effective note taking is most effective when we actively restructure the information in ways that are meaningful to us. In a similar way when we read, active note taking encourages us to elaborate on content and connect it to what we already know.

Social interaction facilitates elaboration in two ways. It forces us to organize our own ideas, restructuring them so they'll make sense to another person. Social interaction also encourages us to elaborate on the ideas of others, listening to them and connecting them to what we already know and believe.

Motivation Theory

A third explanation for the effectiveness of social interaction in the classroom relates to **motivation theory** (Slavin, 1995). In all too many classrooms, the primary mode of interaction is teacher-student, with students not only competing for the right to speak but also for the teacher's approval for a right answer. Since interaction is competitive, and one student's success decreases the chances that others will succeed, many drop out, failing to participate, or view participants as nerds or teacher's pets. Social interaction in the form of groupwork, when structured effectively, can encourage students to work together towards common learning goals.

A final thought—if social interaction is so good, why don't we just let students talk all the time? The answer is that what they talk about and how they talk about it are essential dimensions of effective group interaction. Ways of effectively structuring social interaction in the classroom through groupwork are discussed in the next section.

USING GROUPWORK TO FACILITATE LEARNING

A kindergarten teacher is teaching her students basic shapes. After explaining and illustrating each with cardboard shapes, she divides the class into groups of two and asks each group to find examples of circles, squares, and triangles in their own classroom. When the class comes back together, students share their examples.

A middle school math teacher is teaching how to solve word problems involving areas of different geometric shapes. She divides the class into teams of four students and asks each team to solve the next few problems. Students in each team take turns explaining their solutions to the problems. Later the teams take turns at the board explaining how they solved the different problems.

A senior high English teacher is reviewing literary devices like simile, metaphor, personification, and alliteration. He assigns a scene from Shakespeare's *Julius Caesar* and asks students in groups of two to identify as many of these devices as they can. The whole class compares their findings after 15 minutes.

Because of the nature of interaction in crowded classrooms, it is all too easy for quiet or less confident students to become uninvolved. Unfortunately, in classrooms of 25 to 30, students soon learn that the odds of being called on are small, and less attentive ones often drift off. To reduce some of this demand and elicit the participation of all students, teachers can use groupwork to enhance student learning. Student **groupwork** involves *"students working together in a group small enough so that everyone can participate on a task that has been clearly assigned"* (Cohen, 1986, pp. 1–2). The purpose of groupwork is to provide opportunities for each student to become actively involved in the thinking task at hand and increase his or her learning through social interaction.

To understand the process of student groupwork, consider again the teaching episodes at the beginning of this section. In each the teacher presented a cognitive task to students that built upon and reinforced lesson content. In each the teacher broke the class into manageable groups and required that each member become actively involved in discussing the learning task at hand. Finally, the teacher provided feedback by discussing the products of the groups. The combination of these elements—focus on lesson content, active interactive involvement and feedback—combine to make groupwork effective.

Let's examine more closely how teachers can design effective lessons using groupwork.

Organizing and Conducting Groupwork Activities

A major goal of groupwork is to provide opportunities for all students to become actively involved in the learning task. The assignment of the task by the teacher provides cognitive focus; the fact that the task is done within small groups of students provides opportunities for student interactions, which can be both instructionally and motivationally beneficial. Effective use of groupwork requires careful planning and organization to make sure that the task and the interactions contribute to learning. If the process isn't well organized, a great deal of instructional time can be lost in the transitions to and from groupwork. Goals and directions to students need to be very clear to prevent the activities from disintegrating into aimless "bull sessions."

Suggestions for planning and organizing effective groupwork activities include:

- Train students in groupwork with short, simple tasks. Have students practice moving into and out of the groups quickly.
- Seat group members together prior to the groupwork activity, so the transition from the whole-class activity to student groups and back again can be accomplished with a minimum of disruption.
- Give students a clear and specific task to accomplish in the groups.
- Specify the amount of time students are allowed to accomplish the task (and keep it short). Five minutes is usually the maximum and teachers should monitor learner progress carefully.
- Require that students produce a product as a result of the groupwork.

Effective use of student groups requires that all of these elements be employed. For instance, seating students together prevents loss of instructional time in transitions. Clear directions, a specific and short time allotment, a required written product, and monitoring all help keep students on task and academically focused.

The process of repeatedly moving back and forth from groupwork to whole-class responses requires considerable logistical planning. One way to manage the process is to provide a signal such as turning off the lights or a clacker that makes a noise loud enough for all to hear. Another is for the teacher to raise her or his hand as a signal to reconvene, and students are taught to raise their own hands and stop talking when they see this signal.

Working in Pairs: Introducing Groupwork

The simplest form of groupwork involves organizing students in pairs and giving each pair a task. This strategy, also called **think–pair–share,** encourages students to *think about content, compare their thoughts with their partner, and share their answer with the whole group* (Kagan, 1994). The elementary and high school teachers in the episodes at the beginning of this section used this strategy in their lessons.

Simple collaboration in pairs has several positive features:

- It is easy to implement; students can learn to work with one other person easier than with a larger group.
- Working in pairs encourages each member of the pair to contribute, and the likelihood of one or more members of a group being left out is less than it would be in groups of three or more.
- For purposes of equitable distribution, the class is effectively cut in half. Involvement is high when pairs are working, and teachers have to call on only half as many students as they would during a whole-class discussion, since each is speaking for a pair.

Another strategy that employs working with groups of two is called **pairs check** (Kagan, 1994). In this arrangement *pairs of students are provided with handouts containing problems with specific right and wrong answers* (e.g., math, capitalization, or punctuation problems in English), *which one member of the pair solves and the second member checks.* After every two questions or problems, each pair checks with another group to compare answers. The class can then discuss areas of disagreement or confusion after all the groups have had a chance to complete the assignment.

Working with Larger Groups

Collaboration in pairs is easiest to manage, and it is a good place to begin when you are first introducing your students to groupwork. There are times, however, when you may want students to work in groups of three, four, or five. Groups larger than five are unwieldy, and they are generally not recommended (Cohen, 1986).

The primary advantage in having students work in groups of three or more is the opportunity to promote collaboration and social skills, in addition to the cognitive goals of the lesson. The middle school math teacher used teams of four for her groupwork activities. An important difference between learning in and out of school is that in-school learning is primarily individual, while out-of-school learning is usually collaborative (Resnick, 1987). Giving students practice in collaborating while they work on cognitive tasks helps bridge this gap.

Combining Pairs

Combining pairs *is a groupwork strategy that retains the simplicity of a single pair yet promotes the social skill development of larger groups.* Our middle school math teacher employed this strategy when she had students first solve each problem individually, then share and explain their answer with a partner, and finally had partner teams compare their answers. It is effective for groupwork on comprehension- and application-level activities in either a seatwork or class discussion setting. We look at its implementation in a seatwork arrangement first.

Combining Pairs with Seatwork. The process is organized and implemented in the following steps.

1. Student pairs are formed.
2. Pairs are combined into groups of four. The groups of four can be seated together, as illustrated in Figure 9.1. In this arrangement, the pairs are seated side by side facing the opposite pairs.
3. Students are given a series of exercises with convergent answers, such as solving math problems, identifying parts of speech in sentences, or applying a grammar or spelling rule.
4. Individuals respond to an exercise.
5. Partners compare their answers.
6. In cases where the partners cannot agree on the correct answers, they confer with the other pair.

In classes not divisible by four, one or more groups of five can be arranged, and in those groups a pair and a trio will work together. Like all forms of groupwork, this arrangement requires careful monitoring to prevent some individuals from deferring to their partners or freeloading by merely copying their partners' answers.

Combining Pairs in Interactive Questioning. Combining pairs in interactive question-and-answer sessions is a groupwork process that can effectively promote learning in teacher-centered lessons. It is similar to combining pairs with seatwork.

The steps in organizing and implementing this instructional strategy are:

1. Groups of four are formed (with one or more groups of five).
2. The group members are assigned a number from one to four.
3. The teacher asks the class a question with a convergent answer, such as the solution to a problem, the longitude of a designated city, or the correct punctuation of a sentence.
4. The group members are responsible for seeing that all members of their group know the answer and are able to explain *why* that answer is correct, so that any member of the group can explain it to the whole class.

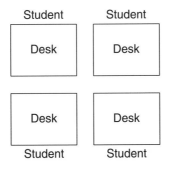

Figure 9.1 Seating Arrangement for Combined Pairs

The teacher then calls a number from one to four, and the students in the groups with those numbers raise their hands. The teacher calls on an individual to answer and *explain* why that is the answer.

A simple incentive system can also be implemented with this process. If the individual answers correctly, every student in his or her group gets a point. If the student provides an adequate explanation, each member gets an additional point.

The incentive system can be made more complex and competitive among groups if the teacher chooses to do so. For example, one group could be called on to answer the question, and a second could be asked to provide the explanation, which would allow two different groups to earn a point. If a group member was unable to answer or explain, a different group would have the opportunity to respond and earn the point.

This process is simple and promotes high levels of student involvement, even in large classes. For example, a class of 33 would have seven groups of four and one group of five. In a typical question-and-answer session, each group would have several opportunities to respond and earn points. Students of all ability levels are motivated because the whole group is rewarded if the individual called on is able to respond correctly. High achievers will explain and even tutor others in their group with less understanding, and the lower achievers experience success and the rewards of contributing to their group.

Groupwork with Higher-Level Tasks

Groupwork can also be used to involve students in higher-level learning tasks such as problem solving or inquiry. When this is done, however, the teacher needs to ensure that all members of the group participate; lower achievers or less aggressive members of the pairs often defer to the higher achievers or more aggressive partners, resulting in reduced involvement by less able students.

Although there is no simple answer to this problem, teachers can take several steps to encourage equal participation. First, require that students solve each problem individually before conferring with their partners, explaining the rationale for this action to students. Second, monitor the groups to be sure they are following your directions, encouraging equal participation as you circulate around the room. Third, strategically call on nonvolunteers in groups, reminding the class that all members of the group need to understand how to solve the problems.

We next examine cooperative learning, a structured instructional approach that uses social interaction to facilitate student growth and development.

COOPERATIVE LEARNING

To begin our discussion of cooperative learning, let's return to Maria Sanchez and her work with her sixth graders.

Maria began her Friday's language arts class by passing back the vocabulary and spelling quizzes from the previous day. As she circulated around the room she overheard the following comments,

"Uh oh, another D."

"I can't do this."

"I hate spelling."

A couple of students didn't say anything, instead looking at their papers, crumpling them up, and throwing them in their desks.

"I can't really blame them; over one-third failed the quiz," she acknowledged to herself. And it seemed as if it was the same third who had problems every week.

Recalling her conversations with Terry Cummings, she decided she would try something different. She called Terry on Saturday, and the two of them talked for an hour and a half. Based on Terry's suggestions, she went to work. Though it took most of her weekend, she felt she was ready on Monday.

With renewed enthusiasm, she began Monday's class by saying, "I know we've been having problems with our spelling and vocabulary quizzes, and I've decided it's time to try something different. I know you all can learn this information, so I've designed a different kind of activity to help you. We're going to help each other learn this information, and I'll show you how."

With that she broke the class into groups of four, explained how each group was a team, and how they were to work as a team and help each other learn. She had the teams move their desks together and gave each team 5 minutes to decide on a team name.

Maria went on to explain another new feature by saying, "We're going to have some competition in here, and it's the best kind of competition there is. You all are going to be competing with yourselves. If your quiz score this week is above your average, you are going to earn 'improvement points' that contribute to your team score. If your whole team improves, you will be eligible for additional rewards. You'll all see how it works when we get started."

Next she went over the spelling and vocabulary words as she normally did on Monday, explaining their definitions and helping students understand the structure of each word. Then she asked each student to take out a sheet of paper for a pretest, similar to the actual test they'd receive on Thursday. She explained that the pretest wasn't for a grade but was only designed to help all students find out what words they knew and which they didn't.

After they took the quiz, students exchanged papers and graded each other's. Then Maria passed out an envelope and four sets of different-colored flashcards to each group. She explained how each set was for a different student in the group and that each student was to write the definition and correct spelling of each word that they had missed to study in class on Tuesday.

She began Tuesday's language arts class by reminding the students of the new seating arrangement. Each student then chose a partner from within their group for that day and the next. As Maria circulated around the room, students took turns helping each other either spell the word or provide the definition. Maria reminded them that they were finished only when all the members of their teams knew the spellings and definitions perfectly. Some pairs did this very effectively, while others needed extra guidance from Maria on helping each other.

On Thursday they took the quiz as usual. She was struck by their comments as they left the class.

"Easy, Miss Sanchez. Piece of cake."

"Miss Sanchez, I think I got all of them right."

Even Randy, who pretended to dislike anything academic, admitted, "It was okay. I think I did all right."

At lunchtime, rather than joining the other teachers, she decided to score the papers to see how they did.

"Terrific?" she thought as she recorded the last score in her grade book. "No, not quite. Some of the students are still struggling, but over 90 percent of the class got a B or better and only two students failed."

Cooperative Learning: The Essential Components

Cooperative learning *is a set of instructional strategies used to help learners meet specific learning and interpersonal goals in structured groups.* Cooperative learning is more structured than *groupwork,* which we discussed earlier; otherwise the two are quite similar. A number of cooperative learning strategies exist, but research indicates that the most effective ones share the following characteristics (Slavin, 1995):

- Group goals
- Individual accountability
- Equal opportunity for success

Group Goals. Think about a team sport, such as soccer or basketball. Team members are of unequal ability, but they all contribute to the team effort, and winning a game rewards the entire team. Group goals in cooperative learning function similarly. **Group goals** *reward students of unequal achievement for working together and helping each other.*

Classroom activities and grading systems often do just the opposite, creating situations where students compete for the teacher's recognition and high grades. Less capable students learn that they can't compete, and often stop trying. Group goals, in contrast, motivate students to help each other and give them a stake in one another's success.

Maria implemented group goals when she divided students into teams of four and structured the activity so that each team member's score contributed to the team score.

Individual Accountability. **Individual accountability** *means that each team member is responsible for mastering the content, and each student is assessed individually.* This is an essential idea. Students involved in cooperative learning should understand that *everyone* is expected to learn and that cooperative activities will be followed by an assessment in which they all demonstrate that they understand the content. Maria Sanchez's Thursday quizzes illustrate this characteristic.

Equal Opportunity for Success. **Equal opportunity for success** *means that all students, regardless of past achievement, have similar chances to be rewarded for their effort.* This is accomplished by implementing a system of *improvement points,* which are bonus points earned for quiz scores that exceed a student's average. This means that students only compete with their past performance and not with each other. Increased effort will result in improvement, which in turn results in points that contribute to the team score. A low achiever who improves more than a high achiever will earn more improvement points and thereby contribute more to the team than does the high achiever. In this way, equal opportunity for success is accomplished.

Why Use Cooperative Learning? The simplest answer to this question is that it works. Cooperative learning is one of the better researched instructional strategies that exist, and the results of this research indicate that cooperative learning produces cognitive, affective, and interpersonal benefits (Johnson and Johnson, 1994; Slavin, 1995).

Implemented effectively, cooperative learning strategies can improve students' achievement more than traditional approaches to instruction, both on teacher-made and standardized tests (Slavin, 1995). These improvements result from increased student motivation, greater time on task, and active involvement.

Slavin (1995) also found that students' self-esteem increased, they felt more in control of their academic success, and they began to link success to their efforts, an important factor in motivation. Low achievers tend to attribute their success or failure to luck or other forces outside their control (Pintrich and Schunk, 1996), and cooperative learning helps change this pattern.

Cooperative Learning: Getting Started

"I don't get it. What are we supposed to do?"

"I can't hear, it's too noisy."

"Teacher, Ken won't share the materials."

Successful cooperative learning activities don't just happen. Instead, they are the result of thoughtful teacher planning and preparation. When students have had limited experience with these instructional strategies, the teacher needs to make a special effort in introducing cooperative learning to students.

Teachers implementing cooperative learning strategies in their classes identify the following potential problem areas:

1. Noise
2. Failure to get along
3. Misbehavior
4. Ineffective use of group time (Kagan, 1994; Slavin, 1995)

Let's see how the teacher can address each of these potential problem areas.

Noise. Noise is often a healthy by-product of productive student interaction. When implementing cooperative learning strategies, we should expect our classrooms to be slightly noisier because students are working and talking in small groups. Excessive noise, however, can interfere with group functioning, frazzle the teacher, and bother other classrooms.

The most common cause of noise in cooperative learning activities is student energy and enthusiasm. Students become so involved in their interactions with other team members that they don't realize that noise is becoming a problem.

Some teachers deal with the problem by discussing and modeling the social skill, "Using quiet voices," which encourages students to work together yet keep the noise level to a minimum. Other teachers use signals, such as flicking the light switch, as cues to remind students to lower the noise level.

Failure to Get Along. Learning to work together effectively doesn't automatically happen; this social skill needs to be developed. Remember that in many of their learning activities students sit quietly, isolated from each other. Cooperative learning requires them to talk, listen, and help each other learn. The process is often made more complicated by the heterogeneous nature of the group.

Teachers use the following cooperative team-building exercises to develop students' interactive skills (Slavin, 1995):

1. *Name learning:* Allocate some time at the beginning of group formation for students to learn each other's names. Make this a game and give an oral quiz where other team members have to name each of their partners.
2. *Interview:* Extend the name-learning exercise to one in which students interview each other about interests, hobbies, favorite foods, or something that no one else knows about them. Have students present these in a short introduction to the rest of the class.
3. *Team name or logo:* Encourage students to develop a name for their group. In doing this, stress broad participation, consensus building, and respect for individual rights.

Cases where a student is a social isolate or students protest being assigned together can be particular problems. To protect quiet students, you should have a classroom rule that requires students to treat each other with courtesy and respect, and *enforce the rule consistently.* An important goal for cooperative learning in particular, and school in general, is for students to learn to treat each other fairly. Breaking this rule should be the one cardinal sin in your class. With effort and persistence you can enforce this rule, and many of the problems associated with students wanting to work only with their friends will disappear.

Misbehavior. Cooperative learning strategies are designed to be interactive, and often the freedom and lack of structure results in increased student management problems. Solutions to this potential problem are specific task demands and agenda setting, accountability, and careful student monitoring.

As we saw in Chapter 6, many management problems occur because of unclear student roles and expectations (e.g., "What are we supposed to do?"). Before you break students into groups, make sure that all students know what they are expected to do. Don't just describe student tasks, directly model them with the same learning materials students will be using. Student accountability also helps create structure and minimize management problems. When students know there is a product expected or a quiz that will be given, their efforts become more focused on the learning task at hand.

Once students are in groups, monitor the groups by circulating around the room and helping individual groups. Public praise is a powerful tool to help other students understand effective and appropriate group behaviors (e.g., "Class, the Eagles group over here has gotten right down to work and are almost done with the first part.")

Ineffective Use of Group Time. Teacher monitoring, which we described as an effective tool against misbehavior, can also help combat wasted time. Stand back from time to time and observe the whole classroom. Which groups are working well? Which students are busy and which ones are dawdling or playing? Spend extra time with those groups that need extra help. Make sure that groups that do work effectively are rewarded with group recognition, and make a special effort to call the whole class's attention to the link between groupwork and group performance. This strategy works on the individual level and should also work at the group level.

Let's look now at three types of cooperative learning instructional strategies.

STAD: Student Teams–Achievement Divisions

One of the best known types of cooperative learning is called **student teams–achievement divisions (STAD)** which *uses four- or five-member teams to master basic skills.* Maria Sanchez used STAD to teach spelling and vocabulary. Teachers have used STAD to teach a range of topics, some of which are described in Table 9.1.

STAD: An Overview. When using STAD, teachers initially present the content or skill as they normally would. For example, if you're teaching the concepts *insect* and *arachnid,* you could use either an inductive or a deductive approach as discussed in Chapter 8. Then, rather than working on the concept or skill individually, such as an assignment asking students to identify additional examples or the essential characteristics of insects, students collaborate on the assignments in a structured setting. When they understand the content, an individual assessment is administered and scored by the teacher and the scores are used to calculate improvement points (which we'll discuss shortly). These are averaged for each team, and teams earning a specified number of improvement points are offered group rewards or recognitions (e.g., free time, pictures on the bulletin board, or certificates).

Planning STAD Activities. The teacher's actions in planning STAD activities are summarized in Table 9.2 and discussed in the sections that follow. As we see in Table 9.2,

Table 9.1 **APPLICATIONS OF STAD IN DIFFERENT CURRICULUM AREAS**

Subject Area	Examples of Topics
Language arts	Capitalization rules Rules for using apostrophes Punctuation rules
Math	Adding fractions Solving word problems Simplifying expressions
Science	Facts about the solar system Balancing chemical equations Understanding concepts, such as insect, crustacean, or arachnid
Social studies	State and national capitols Longitude and latitude problems Climate regions throughout the world
Health	Parts of body systems Characteristics of different drugs

Table 9.2 **STEPS IN PLANNING STAD LEARNING ACTIVITIES**

1. Identify content or skills to be mastered.

2. Plan large group presentation and seatwork materials similar to planning for any topic.

3. Plan for assigning students to groups.

4. Plan for improvement points.

5. Plan for group rewards.

planning for the instructional aspects of STAD activities is similar to planning for any instruction, as was discussed in Chapter 3. In addition, however, STAD requires planning for the cooperative elements of the process, together with designing a system for improvement points and group rewards.

Assigning Students to Groups. In organizing cooperative learning activities, the teacher attempts to place students in groups of four or five—more than five are unwieldy and less effective—that have an approximately equal mix of high, medium, and low achievers and are balanced in terms of gender and cultural backgrounds. This heterogeneity is important, and *students should not be allowed to select the members of their groups.*

Assigning students to heterogeneous groups is important for several reasons. One is the ability imbalances it creates; brighter students tend to select brighter students as members of their group, causing imbalances in the overall groups. Student self-selection also tends to create homogeneous groups in terms of gender and ethnicity, robbing students of valuable opportunities to learn about students different from themselves. Finally, allowing students to select their group partners can also lead to management problems that result from students talking and playing with friends rather than working.

Using averages from the last grading period, present averages (if you begin cooperative learning sometime after the beginning of the grading period), or use pretesting as a basis for balancing students in terms of achievement.

Planning for Improvement Points. An essential component of STAD is the use of improvement points, which helps provide equal opportunity for success. Improvement points are determined by comparing students' scores on a quiz to their averages—which are called *base scores*—at the present point in the grading period. If you're beginning cooperative learning at the beginning of the grading period, base scores can be calculated using their grades from the previous term. Table 9.3 outlines a simple conversion (Kagan, 1994; Slavin, 1995).

Improvement points can then be calculated using the base score. Table 9.4 outlines two options (Kagan, 1994; Slavin, 1995). You may choose one of these options or, depending on your students' motivation and history of achievement, some modification of either.

To reflect students' most recent quiz scores, base scores can be recalculated at any time. If you're using a computer program to help with figuring averages, this is a matter of only a few key strokes. Otherwise, you may choose to recalculate base scores after

Table 9.3 **DETERMINING INITIAL BASE SCORES**

A	90
A–/B+	85
B	80
B–/C+	75
C	70
C–/D+	65
F	60

Table 9.4 **OPTIONS FOR AWARDING IMPROVEMENT POINTS**

Improvement Points	Less Difficult	More Difficult
0	5 or more below base score	Equal to or below base score
10	4 below to 4 above base	1–9 above base
20	5–9 above base	10–14 above base
30	10 or more above base score or perfect score	15 or more above base score or perfect score

every second or third quiz, depending on what is most effective and efficient. Whatever you choose to do, it is important to explain your system to students. When students understand your reasons for making the process more challenging, they usually respond positively.

Planning for Group Rewards. While the use of reinforcers to motivate learners is somewhat controversial, teachers often offer rewards based upon improvement. This emphasis on improvement can be motivating for some students. Team scores are determined by averaging improvement points for the team, and awards are then given. Table 9.5 offers a sample reward system. As with the system for improvement points, the criteria for group rewards can be adapted according to your judgment.

Pros might receive congratulations, Stars an attractive certificate, and Superstars a larger certificate plus additional recognition, such as a photo displayed on the bulletin board, buttons to wear around school, newsletters to be sent home to parents, or special privileges. It is important to stress that teams are not competing with each other. If individuals improve, all teams can potentially become Superstars.

Team composition can be changed periodically, such as after four or five weeks, to allow students to work with other classmates and to give students on low-scoring teams a chance for increased success.

Table 9.5 **CRITERIA FOR GROUP AWARDS**

Criterion (Average improvement)	Award
10	Pros
15	Stars
20	Superstars

Implementing STAD Learning Activities. As we said earlier, initial instruction in STAD is designed to provide an informational base, which can be done in any number of ways. However, in place of independent practice, the students then become involved in *team study,* which allows students to interact and help each other.

Team Study. Slavin (1995) recommends the following steps in team study.

1. Prepare worksheets. Worksheets should require direct application of the concepts, principles, or skills taught in the lesson. Answers to the items on the work sheets must also be prepared to provide feedback to students.
2. Arrange the room so groups can work together. This can be done by having teammates move desks together or meet at team tables. During the first session, let students select a team name. Make sure students know how to talk with each other in quiet voices just above a whisper.
3. Within each team of four students, identify pairs (or in the case of a team of five, identify the pair and trio).
4. Hand out two worksheets per team. Only two are given to encourage students to work together. Each person individually works the problems or answers the questions and checks with his or her partner (or both partners for a trio). If they disagree, they should present their arguments and resolve the problem themselves. If they can't settle the disagreement, they confer with the other pair (or trio) on their team. If the entire team of four or five cannot resolve the disagreement, then—and only then—they can ask the teacher for help. (To emphasize that the worksheets are for studying and not merely to be filled out and handed in, Slavin (1995) recommends including answers with the worksheets. Teachers, however, report more success when the answers are not included.)
5. Emphasize that students are finished studying only when they are certain that everyone on their team understands and can explain each of the items on the worksheet.
6. Circulate among the teams, promoting cooperation and offering encouragement and praise.

Quizzes. After team study is completed, students are given a quiz that measures their understanding of the content. As we saw earlier, students take the quiz as individuals, and the quiz is scored as it normally would be. The quiz should parallel the worksheet, but identical items should be avoided to prevent students from merely memorizing the information. Improvement points are then calculated and team rewards are given.

Evaluation and Grading. When base scores are used, teachers often arrange for improvement to be reflected in the individual students' term grades. For instance, a student who averages 20 or more improvement points on tests might have his or her grade raised from a C to a C+ or perhaps even higher. The decision is yours, but students should see improvement reflected in their grades. This puts them in the position of competing only with their past performance, and it gives every student in the class a chance for success.

Jigsaw II

In addition to learning basic facts, skills, and concepts, cooperative learning strategies can also be adapted to help students learn organized bodies of knowledge. Jigsaw II, developed by Robert Slavin (1986), assigns students to groups and asks each student to become an "expert" on one aspect or part of an organized body of knowledge. These "experts" are then responsible for teaching other team members, all of whom are then held accountable for all the information covered by each member. Let's see how Jigsaw works in a middle school social studies class.

Tom Harris was passing back tests from a unit on Early Americans on the North American continent. As he finished, he noticed that there were still 5 minutes of class time so he called the class together, "Excellent job on this test! You all worked hard and I could tell, because it showed up on your scores. Class, we only have a few minutes but I'd like to say a few words about our next unit of study. The topic is early explorers and we'll be looking at the explorers from Europe who helped discover and explore not only our country, but other countries in North and South America. Who remembers one of these early explorers? Anyone? Think now, you've studied these before. . . . Sal?"

" . . . How about Christopher Columbus?"

"Good, Sal. Any others? . . . Sal, did you have something else you wanted to say?"

"Yeah. Do we have to study this stuff again? We've done it so many times and it's boring."

"I know you've studied this before . . . "

Just then the bell rang and Tom concluded by saying, "Let's continue this on Monday. Everybody have a good weekend. No homework. See you then!"

As Tom thought about this class during his planning period, he shook his head, thinking, "The kids are right . . . This chapter is a little dry. But they need to know it. How to get them involved and excited? . . . Hmmm?"

The next Monday Tom began his American History class by saying, "I thought quite a bit about our new unit over the weekend. . . . Sal, you'll be interested to know that I listened to you on Friday. You probably *have* studied this information before, but I'm not sure you learned it in an organized way. That's important because we're going to use this information later on when we study other topics.

"To learn this material we're going to try something different. We're going to form into teams of four and each team member is going to become an expert on one group of explorers. Then that student will teach the other team members to get them ready for the quiz. To help us organize the information, I've constructed the following sheets."

With that he passed out the following charts.

NAMES	PLACES	DATES	REASONS FOR EXPLORING	ACCOMPLISHMENTS
Spanish				
Portuguese				
English				
French				

"I've divided the class into different teams of four," he continued, "and each of you will be responsible for one of these groups of explorers. To help you put the information into the charts, I've gathered some other books that you can use. On Thursday the experts from each group will get together to check their information. That means all of the people studying the Spanish explorers will get together to review their findings. The same for the other groups. On Friday and Monday we'll go back to our groups and each of you will share you information with other team members—you'll be the expert and each of you will teach the other students. Then we'll take our quiz on Tuesday. . . . Questions? . . . Maria?"

"Who gets which topic in the group?"

"Good question. That's the first thing you need to decide when you get into groups. Now I'd like Group 1 to come up here and pull your seats together. That will be Xavier, Melissa, Brad, and Tanya. Group 2 . . . "

Jigsaw II *is a cooperative learning strategy that uses task specialization to make individual students "experts" on a particular area or topic.* It is similar to STAD in two respects. First, students work cooperatively and are held accountable for their learning with a quiz at the end of the unit of study. These quizzes are scored like STAD, using improvement points to provide equal opportunity for success. Second, students are mixed according to ability, gender, and cultural background as they are with STAD.

Jigsaw II differs from STAD in three ways, however. First, the goals of instruction are not specific facts, concepts, or skills, but rather students' understanding of the interconnections between ideas—organized bodies of knowledge. Second, the source of information is different. The teacher using STAD presents new information, whereas with Jigsaw II students rely primarily on texts and other books.

A final difference relates to the idea of task specialization, from which the strategy gets its name. Each member of a Jigsaw learning group becomes an expert on a particular topic and uses this expertise to teach other members. When groups work together, the different parts of the "jigsaw puzzle" fit together to make a coherent picture. This task specialization is important because it promotes interdependence; each student must depend on his or her partners to learn their information. For teams to do well on the quiz, individual students must work and pull together as a group. When this occurs, students can see tangible evidence of their cooperative efforts. The steps involved in using Jigsaw II in the classroom are summarized in Table 9.6.

Table 9.6 STEPS IN IMPLEMENTING JIGSAW II

Planning

1. Identify an area of study requiring students to understand interconnected or organized bodies of information that can be broken down into subtopics.

2. Divide the content area into three or four roughly equal subtopics that will allow different students to specialize in their study.

3. Locate resources (e.g., websites, textbooks, reference books, encyclopedias) that students can use to study the topic.

4. Develop expert worksheets or charts that structure students' study efforts and ensure that students will learn essential information.

5. Divide students into heterogeneous groups.

Implementation

1. Introduce and explain procedures and divide students into groups.

2. Hand out worksheets or charts and explain how they are to be used to guide individual study and group teaching.

3. Monitor study in the different groups.

4. Convene expert groups (use groups of six or smaller) to discuss and compare information.

5. Monitor students as they teach their topic to other members of the group.

Evaluation

1. Administer quiz or test as you normally would. Make sure quiz covers all topics and encourages students to interrelate information across topics.

2. Score, using improvement points.

3. Recognize team achievements and provide feedback about group performance.

A key to the effectiveness of Jigsaw II is the expert worksheets or charts that the students use. Typically, students—on their own—won't be able to identify key points of information. It is essential that the teacher organize and structure the content to guide the students' study and work with their peers. If the expert study guides are disorganized and disjointed, student learning suffers.

Group Investigation

Karen Selway was enjoying a good year with her third graders. Virtually all had made major progress on their basic skills and she felt good about the foundation she had laid in reading and math. She still wanted them to work on their writing and library skills and wanted to give them some experience in handling a large group project.

After their return from lunch on Monday afternoon, she began by saying, "Class, today we're going to begin a new unit of study. And this time, rather than everyone learning the same thing, each of you will have a chance to read and learn about something that you're specifically interested in. When I tried to think of a topic that we all could study, I

asked myself, What's something that every third grader in my class likes? Guess what I decided? Think for a minute while I put this word on the board."

PETS

She could tell from the wiggles and excited talking that she had guessed correctly. She
then proceeded to brainstorm with the group about different pet topics. After considerable
discussion the class agreed to pursue the following topics:

Dogs   Bunnies and Hamsters
Cats   Fish
Birds   Other Pets (Turtles, Hermit Crabs, Snakes)

Students decided which topic they wanted to investigate. Then Karen asked them to
list several kinds of pets they would be interested in learning more about and used this information to group them together into topic groups that night.

When the students came to class the next day, she had stacks of pet books from the
public library on tables at the back of the room. She also had the names of different students
divided into groups on the basis of their interest. There were two groups of four each for
both dogs and cats because of the high interest in these topics; other groups had between
three and five members. After a general overview of each group's responsibilities and procedures, she broke the class into groups and had them begin researching their topics.

As she circulated around the room, a number of questions surfaced.

"What do we do first?"

"Where do we find out about the pets?"

"Who is supposed to do what?"

Karen had anticipated most of these questions. When they seemed common to all the
groups, she called the class together and discussed them. Other questions like "Do we want
to report on all the different kinds of dogs?" were particular to an individual group. When
Karen encountered these, she sat down with each group to help them work through it.

For the next two weeks her students spent their time reading books, visiting the school
library, visiting pet stores, interviewing people who owned these pets, and compiling a report on the room's computers, complete with pictures and posters. On Pet Day they invited
parents and the principal to come in and visit the different groups who were set up in different places around the room. Each member of the team was assigned responsibility to
talk about one aspect of the report. On the next day Karen helped the class pull together all
the information by using the following chart.

PET	COST	CARE AND FEEDING	ADVANTAGES	DISADVANTAGES
Dogs				
Cats				
Birds				
Fish				
Other Pets				

Analyzing Group Investigation. This was an example of **group investigation,** *a cooperative learning strategy that promotes group planning and inquiry.* Like STAD and Jigsaw II, it places students into cooperative groups to learn about some topic, but it differs in that the focus is relatively less on content goals and more on inquiry skills.

Group investigation is less structured than the other strategies you've studied, and this lack of structure has advantages and disadvantages. Group investigations have the advantage of giving students the chance to wrestle with ill-structured tasks, which are the kinds of problems we face in real life. Seldom are we presented with situations where we are told what to learn and how to learn it. Instead we're required to first clarify and then structure problems before we solve them (Eggen and Kauchak, 2001).

This lack of structure is also a disadvantage, and some students get lost when they first encounter it. Karen dealt with this issue both individually and in whole-class discussions. Teachers using group investigation for the first time should anticipate these fits and starts.

One way to deal with these learning problems is to use some teacher-directed strategies. Modeling, thinkalouds, and the liberal use of examples can help students learn these skills. Some examples of these strategies applied to Karen's class can be found in Table 9.7.

Implementing Group Investigation. In implementing group investigation, the teacher's role changes from information disseminator to facilitator and resource person. As a facilitator, the teacher circulates around the room helping students in different groups work together. As a resource person, the teacher helps students understand and structure the learning task as well as helping them access resources available to them. The specific steps involved in planning and implementing group investigations can be found in Table 9.8.

Table 9.7 **TEACHING LEARNING STRATEGIES IN GROUP INVESTIGATION**

Teaching Strategy	Example
Modeling	"Class, I've had several students ask about how to outline your reports. Let's look up on the board and I'll show you how you might do it with the topic of horses."
Thinkalouds	"We're encountering some problems in finding our topics in the encyclopedia. Let's go over to the encyclopedia and brainstorm some words that might help us find our topics."
Examples	"There have been some questions about what kinds of pictures to put on your bulletin boards. Let me show you some examples of ones done last year. Remember, you don't have to do it just like these. They're just designed to give you some ideas."

Table 9.8 STEPS IN IMPLEMENTING GROUP INVESTIGATIONS

Planning

1. Identify a common topic that will serve as a focal point for the class as a whole.

2. Catalog or gather resources that students can use as they investigate the topic.

Implementation

1. Introduce the general topic to the class and have students identify specific subtopics that individual groups will investigate.

2. Divide students into study groups on the basis of student interest and heterogeneity.

3. Assist students in cooperative planning regarding goals, procedures, and products.

4. Monitor student progress, assisting students to work effectively in groups.

Evaluation

1. Use group presentations to share information gained.

2. Provide individual and group feedback about projects, presentations, and group effectiveness.

Computer-Mediated Communication: Using Technology to Facilitate Cooperative Learning

Technology is changing the way teachers teach and students learn. Perhaps no where is this change more dramatic than the Internet. The Internet is a network of computer networks that links computers worldwide. Through the Internet students are able not only to access information from a vast array of sources but also to interact with other students across the country and around the world.

Technology Facilitating Student Interaction. When we talk about student interaction, we typically think of learners talking face to face in cooperative learning or discussion groups. This face-to-face communication has definite advantages in terms of both ease of communication and motivation. However, computer-mediated communication through e-mail and the Internet provides opportunities for students to communicate and work with students thousands of miles away through electronic mail.

Students in one fifth-grade classroom are engaged in a research project on pets. As one source of data they interviewed their classmates about their pets. Then they put the information on a computer and shared this data with other students around the country. One class wrote back to another, "We would like to know more about your pet bear. . . . Where does the bear stay? How much food does the bear eat in a week?" (Julyan, 1989, p. 33)

In investigating the topic of pets through computer-mediated communication, students wrestled with the problem of definitions (Is an ant a pet?) and tried to answer questions like, "Do dog owners in warm climates have more short-haired dogs?" and "Do cat owners tend to have more pets than dog owners?" Through a computer network, students were able to gather data from other locations and experience the process of doing a real investigation in their own classrooms.

Computer-mediated communication through the Internet, an interconnected collection of more than 46,000 independent systems, allows students to interact with students, not only across the country, but around the world (Peha, 1995; Rottier, 1995). Through the Internet students

- Are provided access to remote data sources.
- Can collaborate on group projects with students at different locations.
- Can send their work to other students for evaluation or response.
  (Peha, 1995)

Teachers who have used computer-mediated communication in their teaching have found it to be both motivating and challenging.

One creative use of computer-mediated communication is ICONS, International Communications and Negotiations Simulation, a high school social studies simulation project (Rottier, 1995). Through the ICONS system, students from countries as far away as Germany, Korea, and Chile collaborate and negotiate in attempting to come up with mutually agreed-upon solutions to problems such as world health, human rights, and the spread of nuclear weapons technology. The problems are organized by the ICONS system; students are assigned to countries and are responsible for researching their country's position, formulating policy, and defining their roles as statespersons. For the first four weeks, they use the Internet to gather data; during the second four weeks students dialogue with their counterparts in other countries in an attempt to resolve differences and come up with a comprehensive, worldwide policy. During the final debriefing phase, students reflect on their activities and apply the information they learned to new, but similar problems.

Technology as an Information Source. Another way that technology can support cooperative learning is as an information source. One source of vast information resources on the Internet is the World Wide Web (WWW, or just "the Web"). The Web consists of millions of sites of information displayed in hypermedia format; it supports formatted text, graphics, animations, and even audio and video. Software programs called browsers allow students to navigate the Web, bookmark valuable sites, and control how web pages are displayed. Search engines, sites on the Internet that students can use to locate topics of interest, make the process of information access quick and efficient.

Technology can also be used to gather and share raw data. For example, in one project, NGS Kids Network, funded by the National Geographic Society, middle school students studied the problem of water pollution (Bradsher and Hagan, 1995). To do this, they gathered water samples from reservoirs near them and tested them for acidity and other water pollutants, using standard, predetermined procedures such as pH paper and nitrate test strips. Then they shared their data with other sites across the country, looking for patterns and asking questions about other sites' data. "In essence students and teachers explore science by doing what scientists do; they participate in a scientific community devoted to learning about the world" (Bradsher and Hagan, 1995, p. 41).

All three of the projects described here can be conducted using equipment found in many, if not most schools. For example, equipment required for the ICONS project include a computer, modem, printer, ordinary telephone line, and word processing and computer software. Through the use of commonly available technologies teachers can provide opportunities for students to interact with and learn about students from all over the country and the world as well as accessing up-to-date information on virtually any topic.

Using Cooperative Learning to Capitalize on Diversity

In addition to increasing achievement, cooperative learning can also be used to help students learn about each other and develop their interpersonal skills. When groups are mixed by ethnicity, sex, and ability, the strategy can result in improved attitudes toward different ethnic groups and increased interethnic friendships (Slavin, 1995). The same benefits can occur in helping students with exceptionalities integrate into the regular classroom (Hardman et al., 1999).

One teacher reported this success.

A special education student in the sixth grade was transferred to our classroom, a fifth/sixth grade. The classroom she was in has several special education students. The first—I'll call her Sara—was having behavior difficulties in her first classroom and was about to be expelled because of her unacceptable behavior with her peers. We offered her the opportunity to try our room with no special education students and with cooperative learning techniques being applied in various subjects along with TAI (cooperative learning) math. Sara was welcomed by her new classmates. We added her to one of the TAI math learning teams, and the students taught her the program's routine. Sara worked very steadily and methodically, trying to catch up academically and to fit in socially. She began to take more pride in her dress and grooming habits. I have been working with Sara on her basic facts in preparation for the weekly facts quizzes. Her attitude toward her schoolwork and her self-concept has blossomed within the length of time she has been in our classroom. (Nancy Chrest, fifth/sixth grade teacher, George C. Weimer Elementary School, St. Albans, WV, cited in Slavin, 1995, p. 58)

These are impressive results, especially when you consider that they were achieved with little additional teacher effort and without outside help. They are a testimony to the power of students helping students, in general, and cooperative learning in particular.

The positive effects of cooperative learning on interpersonal attitudes probably stem from several factors:

- Opportunities for different types of students to work together on joint projects
- Equal status roles for participants
- Opportunities for different types of students to learn about each other as individuals
- The teacher's implicit but unequivocal support for diverse students working together (Slavin, 1995)

Slavin speculates that cooperative learning's effects on intergroup relations may result from opportunities for friendships and blurring of intergroup boundaries. As students work together, they develop friendships across racial and ability groups, which tend to soften and blur well-defined peer group boundaries and lead to other cross-group friendships.

However, developing improved relationships requires careful planning. The following strategies can be effective.

- Grouping
- Specific tasks
- Training

To maximize cooperative learning's positive effects, students should be strategically grouped so that groups have equal numbers of high- and low-ability students, boys and girls, and students from different ethnic and SES groups. Specifically planning for the appropriate mix of group members has been stressed throughout our discussion of cooperative learning.

Learning tasks need to be structured so that they require cooperation and communication (Cohen, 1994; Good, McCaslin, and Reys, 1992). Teachers need to rotate student roles so everyone in the group has an opportunity to perform different tasks, such as presenting information and checking answers.

Training is required to develop effective group interaction skills (S. Kagan, 1994; Webb and Farivar, 1994), which include the following:

- *Listening.* Listening to each others' ideas and helping other students verbalize and express their ideas.
- *Checking for understanding.* Asking for clarification when answers are incomplete or unclear.
- *Emotional support.* Providing positive feedback for answers
- *Staying on task.* Maintaining focus on the specific learning task at hand.

Teacher discussion, modeling, and appropriate reinforcement are effective ways to teach and maintain these skills.

This completes our discussion of cooperative learning. We turn now to *discussions,* another strategy designed to capitalize on social interaction.

DISCUSSIONS

Shannon Wilson's sixth-grade language arts class had been reading *Sounder,* the story of a poor, African-American sharecropper family in the South during the Depression. The father, concerned about his family's diet and health, had taken to raiding rich people's smokehouses at night to put some meat on his family's table. Shannon's class was discussing the moral implications of his stealing.

"So where do you think the father goes at night when his wife can't find him?"

" . . . He's going out to get food for his family," Tammy replied.

"And where is he getting this food? . . . Ramon?"

" . . . From other people's smokehouses."

"Which other people? . . . Tanya?"

"From the rich, white folks who have big farms."

"Okay, we've got the facts of the story down. Now let's focus on the stealing itself. Was the father wrong to steal?. . . . Let's think about it. . . . What do you think? . . . Kareem?"

" . . . Well, . . . I . . . think maybe he was . . . like . . . because he's bound to get caught . . . eventually . . . and thrown in jail or something."

"Francisco?" Shannon nodded, seeing his raised hand.

" . . . I . . . agree. He shouldn't have done it . . . cuz . . . it's against the law."

" . . . I wanted to ask . . . what's he s'pposed to do . . . let his family starve?" Gabriela interjected.

"Gabriela asks a real good question, class. Anybody want to respond? . . . Kerry?"

" . . . I kinda think so, too. Even though it's bad to steal, he can't just . . . like . . . let his kids go hungry. It said right in the book that they weren't getting enough to eat."

"Hey . . . You can't just break the law any old time you please . . . even if you're hungry," Trang retorted.

"Now everyone, let's think about what we've been saying . . . " Shannon interjected.

The lesson continued as the class continued to wrestle with the moral dilemma raised by the book they were reading.

Using Discussions to Promote Student Growth

Discussions *are instructional strategies that use teacher-student and student-student interactions as the primary vehicle for learning.* They are characterized by decreased focus on the teacher, increased student-to-student interactions, and high levels of student involvement. Effectively used, discussions can stimulate thinking, challenge attitudes and beliefs, and develop interpersonal skills (Oser, 1986; Dillon, 1987). However, if not organized and managed properly, they can be boring for students, frustrating for the teacher, and a general waste of time.

In contrast with the strategies we've discussed earlier in this book—which focus primarily on cognitive goals—discussions are effective for dealing with both cognitive and affective topics. In addition, they can help develop students' communication and interpersonal skills. We briefly analyze these goals in the following sections.

Cognitive Goals. Discussions are useful when we want students to develop critical thinking abilities and investigate questions that don't have simple answers (Gall, 1987). Because they focus on areas where there isn't a single best answer, students feel comfortable contributing, knowing that they won't be "right" or "wrong," and involvement often increases. As students interact, their background knowledge increases, and social interaction helps students see problems and issues from different points of view.

Affective Goals. As we saw in Shannon's class, discussions can also be used to help students examine their attitudes and values. By focusing on specific issues, discussions can provide the intellectual grist that allows students to examine their own beliefs. Through teacher questioning and listening to the different opinions of their classmates, students can evaluate the adequacy of their own beliefs while comparing them to the beliefs of others. Research on discussions reveals that they can be an effective vehicle to clarify values and promote moral growth (Gall, 1987; Oser, 1986).

Communication Skills. Because discussions provide extended opportunities for students to talk and listen to each other, they are a powerful tool for developing students' communication and social skills. Developing these communication skills should be an integral goal for all discussions. Some of these social skills include:

- Expressing ideas and opinions clearly
- Justifying assertions

- Acknowledging and paraphrasing others' ideas
- Asking for clarification and elaboration when others' ideas aren't clear
- Sharing ideas equally and avoiding monopolizing discussions
- Inviting silent group members to participate

How can teachers use discussions to accomplish these diverse goals? We begin answering this question by discussing the planning and implementation of cognitively oriented discussions in the next section.

Promoting Cognitive Growth with Discussions: Planning

Planning for discussions is similar to planning for the use of any strategy. Teachers first identify a *topic* and specify a clear *goal*. In addition, considering *students' background knowledge* and the *physical arrangement* of the room are even more critical when discussions are used. Let's see why.

Identifying Discussion Topics. As noted earlier, discussions are effective strategies when topics are complex, open ended and don't have cut-and-dried answers. For example, topics such as solving word problems in math, identifying parts of speech in language arts, or describing characteristics of mammals in science would not be appropriate discussion topics. With them, there is little to discuss. Discussions are most effective in low-consensus areas like social studies and the humanities, where questions are likely to have multiple answers (Gage and Berliner, 1998).

Specifying Goals. Merely identifying a topic isn't enough, however. Teachers need to consider what they want students to take away from a discussion. Let's examine the importance of goals by comparing two lessons.

Paula Marsh had assigned the chapter on the beginnings of the Revolutionary War to be read as homework and began her American history class by saying:

"Today we begin our discussion of the Revolutionary War. We've been talking about all of the events that led up to the war. What were some of these? Lanal?"

"The Stamp Act."

"Good. Angelo?"

"The Tea Act and the Boston Tea Party."

"Fine, Angelo. Any others? Miguel?"

"The First Continental Congress."

"And when was that held? Does anyone remember? Go ahead, Miguel."

"In 1774 in Philadelphia."

"And what was the major outcome from this meeting?"

We leave this room and walk across the hall, where Jacinta Lopez's American history class is studying the same topic.

Jacinta began, "We've been studying the Revolutionary War, and you all know a lot about it. But," she continued, "some historians, reviewing all the facts about the War suggest that on paper the British 'should' have won. When they say this, they're not saying 'should' like 'ought' but rather that the British had important advantages but wasted them. I'd like for us to think about that notion today, and see if our conclusions agree with those of the historians. . . . What do you think? Take a little time to consider it while I put this statement on the board."

She wrote, "The British advantages during the Revolutionary War should have ensured victory," on the chalkboard.

"Okay," Jacinta went on, "now that you've had time to think, does anyone want to take a stab at this? Sharese?"

" . . . I basically agree with the statement," Sharese replied. "They had more soldiers, more guns, and better equipment, and should have won."

" . . . I think Sharese's right," Martina added. "They not only had more soldiers but the soldiers they did have were better trained. Also. . . ."

"If the British had treated the colonists decent, there wouldn't have been a war in the first place," Ramon interjected.

"That's an interesting point, Ramon," Jacinta smiled. "But given that there was a war, we're considering whether or not the British should have won. . . . Anything else, Martha?"

" . . . No . . . not really. I was just going to say that they had a physical advantage."

"Okay, Martha," she nodded. "Hank, you look like you were going to say something."

"Oh, I was just going to say that the British soldiers often weren't in the right place."

"I don't know what you mean, Hank," Jeff put in.

"Well, even though they had more soldiers, this wasn't always important. Like at Saratoga. One big part of Burgoyne's army captured Philadelphia instead of going to Albany like he should've. So those troops were wasted. It would be interesting to know what might've happened if Burgoyne had gone to Albany. Maybe we'd still be British."

"That's a very interesting thought, Hank. Jeremy, do you have something to add?"

" . . . Just that some of the troops the British had were mercenaries. They were just being paid to fight, so they didn't fight all that hard."

"So numbers might not be the only thing to think about when we talk about advantages and disadvantages. Is that what you're saying?"

" . . . I . . . guess so."

"Okay! Very good, everyone. Now, let's return to our question on the board. What other advantages or disadvantages did the British have that influenced the outcome of the war?"

Now let's compare the two episodes. While the *topic was the same* for both lessons and the teachers both focused students on the content through their questioning, their *goals were very different.* Paula Marsh was reviewing facts about events leading up to the Revolutionary War, while Jacinta Lopez was trying to get students to identify relationships and make applications. To meet these goals, questions from the upper levels of Bloom's taxonomy (1956) served as a conceptual framework and guide. For example, the following questions served as guides in Jacinta's lesson.

Analysis: What were the relative strengths and weaknesses of the American and British forces? How did the French influence the outcome of the war?

Synthesis: Design a strategy or plan that would have used Britain's sea power to greater advantage.

Evaluation: Was the American victory the result of a lucky chain of events or superior strategy? Take a position and defend it.

Jacinta's goals did not stop there, however. If they had, we might argue that the processes are little different from other instructional strategies. In addition to understanding an organized body of knowledge that focused on the Revolutionary War and developing their thinking, she also wanted them to develop other important skills, such as willingness to listen to another's point of view, cooperation, and the ability to take and defend a position. These are important goals for discussions. Because of these supplementary goals, discussions are much less driven by the content per se, instead providing opportunities for students to use this content as they develop discussion skills.

Students' Background Knowledge. When a teacher is considering using discussion as a strategy, student background knowledge is an essential factor in the decision. Unlike other strategies, where the content is taught as an integral part of the lesson, discussions require that students be thoroughly conversant with the information related to the topic *prior* to the lesson. This was clearly demonstrated in Jacinta Lopez's lesson. For instance, Sharese demonstrated her background knowledge by observing that the British had more soldiers, guns, and equipment. Martha's comment about the soldiers' training in response to Sharese reflected similar background knowledge. Hank's comment about the battle of Saratoga is perhaps more significant, because he demonstrated understanding of a cause-and-effect relationship in addition to a knowledge of facts.

The quality of the discussion would not have been possible if students' background knowledge had not been developed. Students must have something to discuss if a discussion is going to work, and the teacher must be sure that their background knowledge is extensive before using discussion as a strategy. If the students' background knowledge is inadequate or undeveloped, discussions can easily disintegrate into aimless bull sessions.

Arranging the Room for Discussions. A final planning task is to arrange the room to promote communication and involvement among participants. Research indicates that students are more likely to interact with each other if they are face to face (Gall, 1987).

To accomplish this, you might consider either circles or half-circles (Arends, 2001). These configurations allow everyone in the class to see each other and they position the teacher within the group. This communicates that the teacher is an equal among other participants and encourages students to take a more active role in participating in and structuring the lesson.

Promoting Cognitive Growth with Discussions: Implementation

In beginning discussion activities, we need to draw students into the lesson and help them understand the lesson's goal, refocusing them when necessary during the course of the lesson. Finally, teachers help students to reach closure by encouraging them to summarize the discussion at the end. These goals are accomplished through the following three steps:

- Agenda setting
- Refocusing students during the lesson
- Summarization

Agenda Setting. Jacinta began her lesson by saying, "Some historians, reviewing all the facts about the War suggest that on paper the British 'should' have won. . . . I'd like for us to think about that notion today, and see if our conclusions agree with those of the historians. . . . What do you think?" By introducing the topic in this way, she both clarified the goal and presented a question that attracted students' interest. Then she wrote the question on the board as a way of maintaining academic focus. Effective discussions begin with clear focusing events.

Refocusing Students during the Lesson. It's easy in a discussion to drift off the subject and begin dealing with issues that aren't relevant to the goal of the discussion. For instance, Ramon's comment, "If the British had treated the colonists decent, there wouldn't have been a war in the first place," though appropriate as a discussion issue in itself, was irrelevant to the issue of whether or not the British should have won the war. A less effective teacher might have allowed the discussion to drift in that direction, but Jacinta refocused the class by saying, "That's an interesting point, Ramon . . . But, given that there was a war, we're considering whether or not the British should have won. . . ." The ability to recognize irrelevant information is an important thinking skill, and Jacinta's comment helped the class recognize Ramon's comment as irrelevant. At the same time her own social skills and positive manner refocused the class without cutting Ramon off or admonishing him in any way. We examine this strategy further in the next section.

The Teacher's Role. In most classrooms teacher talk is the dominant element, and the teacher uses this talk to steer a lesson in a clear direction (Cazden, 1988). This pattern of teacher control can be effective when the goal is to learn facts, concepts, generalizations, or skills, such as Paula Marsh's lesson on facts about the Revolutionary War. However, this type of interaction is less effective when the goals are for students to learn discussion skills and productive ways of interacting with each other. In contrast with Paula's class, Jacinta Lopez's lesson involved more student-to-student talk, and her role changed from lecturer or knowledge source to facilitator of the discussion process.

Because the teacher's role in a discussion is less direct and often less apparent, it appears to be easier. In fact, it is just the opposite. During discussions a teacher must listen carefully to each student's response, avoid commenting when students are interacting appropriately, interject questions when ideas need to be stimulated, and refocus the discussion when the students drift off as Ramon did in Jacinta Lopez's lesson.

Effectively guiding a discussion requires more sophisticated skills than teacher-centered lessons because the teacher is not in direct control of the activity and a great deal of subtle judgment is required. A skilled discussion leader must do all of the following:

- *Focus the discussion.* A primary role for the teacher is to keep the class on track, without taking ownership of the discussion away from the students, as Jacinta Lopez managed to do so skillfully. Periods of silence characterized by student thought are typical (and potentially unnerving).
- *Encourage thoughtfulness.* In conducting discussions, the teacher must be skilled in using questions that solicit alternate points of view, relationships between ideas, and analysis of different points of view rather than convergent, focused answers.
- *Maintain momentum.* Discussion must be monitored constantly to ensure that momentum is maintained, and the teacher must intervene when necessary. This requires careful judgment. If teachers intervene too often, the discussion

reverts back to a teacher-directed activity; if they don't intervene when necessary, the discussion can meander and even disintegrate. The teacher should intervene under the following conditions:

- lesson digressions
- errors of fact
- logical fallacies
- a small number of students dominating the discussion
- when the lesson should be summarized and brought to closure

As a rule of thumb, cut a discussion off too soon instead of letting it go too long. To prevent teacher domination, some have advocated teachers refrain from questioning completely (Dillon, 1987). This isn't realistic, however, and in doing so, teachers abdicate important opportunities to stimulate thought and encourage connections. Teacher guidance is critical in effective discussions, as we saw in Jacinta Lopez's lesson. As teachers acquire expertise, they develop a feel for when intervention is and is not appropriate.

Affective Discussions: Promoting Ethical and Moral Growth

The proper place of values and moral education in the curriculum is also controversial. The controversy is less about whether or not it should be taught—most educators agree that it is needed—and more about the form that it should take (Wynne, 1997).

One position, called **character education,** *emphasizes the transmission of moral values, such as honesty and citizenship, and the translation of these values into behavior.* For example, the state of Georgia recently passed a law requiring character education programs to focus on 27 character traits including patriotism, respect for others, courtesy, and compassion (Jacobson, 1999). Instruction in character education emphasizes the study of values, practicing these values both in school and out, and rewarding displays of these values.

Moral education, by contrast, *is more value free, emphasizing instead the development of students' moral reasoning.* Moral education uses moral dilemmas and classroom discussions to teach problem solving and to bring about changes in the way learners think with respect to moral issues.

Critics of character education argue that it emphasizes indoctrination instead of education (Kohn, 1997); critics of moral education assert that it has a relativistic view of morals, with no right or wrong answers (Wynne, 1997).

The strength of character education is its willingness to identify and promote core values, such as honesty, caring, and respect for others. Few would argue that these values are inappropriate. However, emphasizing student thinking and decision making is important as well, and this is the focus of the moral education perspective.

For either moral or character education to work, there must be some public consensus about the values included in them. Does such consensus exist? A recent poll suggests that it does (Rose and Gallup, 1999). When asked whether the following values should be taught in public schools, the following percentages of a national sample replied affirmatively: honesty (97%), democracy (93%), acceptance of people of different races and ethnic backgrounds (93%), and caring for friends and family members (90%). At the other end of the continuum were acceptance of people with different sexual orientations—that is, homosexuals or bisexuals (55%)—and acceptance of the right of a woman to choose an abortion (48%). In considering which values to promote in their classrooms, teachers should be aware of public attitudes toward these values. This doesn't mean teachers should avoid discussing controversial topics or values; instead it suggests being aware of students' current values and beliefs and building upon them. This makes sense both pedagogically (Eggen and Kauchak, 2001; Ormrod, 2000) as well as politically. But integrating affective content into the curriculum without proselytizing or appearing heavy handed is a delicate balancing act.

This problem is important for all teachers, as value-related discussions are impossible to avoid. Sometimes affective concerns are explicit, such as when freedom of speech and individual rights are discussed in social studies classes. Health classes deal with sex education, and evolution versus creationism continues to be debated in science classes in different parts of the country.

Other instances of affective issues are more subtle, however, and teachers often address affective issues without realizing it. For example, teachers who say,

"Class, the civil rights movement was perhaps the most important event in twentieth-century America," or

"The effect of pollutants on our planet is the biggest problem facing modern man," or

"Julius Caesar wasn't just a play about ancient Rome. It was a play about politics and democracy and the potential for abuse by people in power."

are making value-laden statements that can lead to lively discussions.

Opportunities to examine values often occur as natural by-products of other lessons. For example, a discussion in biology might consider benefits of pesticides, such as increased productivity, with negative side effects, such as the impact on wildlife. A lesson on ethnic groups could focus on the internment of Japanese Americans during World War II, resulting in a discussion of the importance of individual rights versus perceived risks to national security. A literature class reading *Lord of the Flies* might consider individual responsibility versus peer pressure. A class focusing on career choices might list different occupations and use this as a springboard for a discussion of the values underlying different occupational choices. A conflict of values exists in each of these topics, with potential as a springboard for subsequent discussion.

Clarifying Values through Moral Dilemmas. Value-oriented discussions can also be started through moral dilemmas (Oser, 1986; Kruger, 1992). A **moral dilemma** *presents students with an everyday problem, the solution to which involves the resolution of a value conflict.* Shannon Wilson, in the teaching episode at the beginning of this section, used a moral dilemma as the focus for her lesson. Was it right for the father to steal to feed his children? This dilemma was embedded in the book the class was reading, which provided both background knowledge and motivation for her students.

Teachers can also construct their own moral dilemmas to stimulate moral thought. Consider the following:

John was working as a teacher's aid and ran across a copy of the final exam sitting on the teacher's desk. The exam was for a course that his best friend, Gary, was repeating for graduation. At lunch, Gary expressed concern that he wouldn't pass the course because his boss had made him work every night for the last two weeks, and the heavy schedule had prevented him from studying. Gary asked John to get him a copy of the test. If John didn't, Gary might not be able to graduate. John's refusal would almost certainly end their friendship. What should John do?

The conflicts here are honesty versus friendship. Some questions to encourage thinking about this conflict could include:

Which is more important, honesty or friendship?

What would happen if John steals a copy of the exam?

What if he doesn't?

What circumstances in the problem make a difference?

What other alternatives are there?

In leading a discussion involving a conflict of values, there are several guidelines to follow (Oser, 1986; Kruger, 1992). Students should be encouraged to take a personal position in terms of the dilemma (e.g., What would *you* do?). This encourages involvement and causes students to reflect on their own values. In doing this, an atmosphere of acceptance for various value positions should be established. Students should be encouraged to listen and respond to the views of others. One of the major advantages of discussing different value positions is each student's consideration of alternative views.

In dealing with any of these value-laden topics, the teacher's role is to help students understand the issues involved through strategic questions. These should establish what the problem is, what value positions are involved, and what alternatives exist. In addition, students should be encouraged to clarify and voice their own thoughts on the issues involved. Teachers should refrain from imposing their views on students, and students should not feel pressured to respond.

This concludes our examination of discussion strategies. In the next section we look at how peer tutoring can be used to facilitate learning in the classroom.

PEER TUTORING: STUDENTS AS RESOURCES

Effective teachers use all available resources, one of which is the students themselves. In this section, we discuss using students as peer tutors to enhance the learning of content while developing skills outside the cognitive domain.

Jim Corbin, a resource teacher for students with exceptionalities, and Maria Sandoval, a first-grade teacher, were talking in the teacher's lounge over lunch. Both were encountering problems in the area of reading.

"I just don't have enough time to spend with my slower students," Maria commented. "I know what they need . . . quality time in small groups where I can give them individual help and encouragement—but I've got 27 students in that class, and when I spend extra time with them, I feel guilty about slighting the others."

"I know how you feel," Jim replied, and after hesitating briefly he continued. "Numbers aren't my problem; it's motivation. I'm working with fourth and fifth graders who are really discouraged. They just don't think they can do it."

As Jim and Maria talked, they wondered if there was any way that they could help each other. They'd both heard of peer tutoring but had never heard of resource students acting as tutors for regular students. They both had their doubts, but they agreed to give it a try.

For the next week Jim prepared his students, teaching them to explain and demonstrate the reading skills they were teaching and showing them how to provide helpful praise and feedback. Maria helped by pulling together reading materials that would provide a concrete agenda for the tutoring sessions.

The next Monday Jim brought his nine resource students down to pick up the first graders. When they returned to the resource room, Jim circulated around the room, monitoring each pair's progress. As Jim had anticipated, some tutors did better than others, but all groups seemed to work reasonably well. Jim could tell it was working for his students by the way they entered his classroom and got ready for the tutoring sessions. Before, they dragged themselves in, and it was like pulling teeth to get them to work. Now, they arrived on time and appeared eager to work. He wondered how it was working for Maria's students.

Research on Peer Tutoring

Peer tutoring, as the term implies, *involves students teaching students.* Peer tutoring offers two specific benefits. First, because the sessions are one to one, instruction is individualized, which is effective for all teaching situations and especially for skill learning. Second, peer tutoring can be motivational, both for the tutor and the student being helped. Helping someone learn is intrinsically motivating for the tutors (Slavin, 1995), and the satisfaction that comes with increased understanding motivates those being helped.

The idea of students helping students is not new. The ancient Greeks and Romans used tutors, and in nineteenth-century England, where pupil-teacher ratios of 400 or 500 to one often existed, teachers coped by first teaching older monitors who then worked with younger students. Teachers in America's one-room schoolhouses dealt with the vast differences in grades one through eight by having older or more capable students help others.

Two primary peer tutoring arrangements exist. **Cross-age tutoring,** like the English system, *uses older students to help younger ones.* Cross-age tutoring benefits from the more mature tutor's knowledge and skills but is harder to manage logistically, because it is difficult because of scheduling and coordination problems. **Same-age peer tutoring** addresses this problem and *can be used in any heterogeneous class where students are at different levels of learning.*

As we saw in the introductory episode, peer tutoring has also been successfully used with students with exceptionalities. In one study, upper elementary special education students were trained to act as reading tutors for first graders (Top and Osguthorpe, 1987). After twelve weeks of tutoring, researchers found that both the tutors and first graders outperformed comparable control students on reading achievement tests. In addition, the special education tutors showed significant increases in their perceptions of their general academic ability as well as their ability in reading and spelling. Other research suggests that peer tutoring is effective in teaching content while also fostering social interaction and improved attitudes toward those with exceptionalities (Fuchs et al., 1997; Elbaum et al., 1999).

A Basic Peer Tutoring Model

Peer tutoring is most commonly used to supplement typical teacher-led instruction. We call this the *basic tutoring model* and examine it in this section.

The strategy has two phases: planning and implementation, each involving four steps, which are summarized in Table 9.9 and discussed in the sections that follow.

Planning for Peer Tutoring

Identify a Topic. One-to-one peer tutoring can be used in any subject where the topic includes convergent information with clear right and wrong answers. For example, math skills such as two-digit by one-digit multiplication, language arts concepts such as adjectives or proper nouns, finding the longitude and latitude of various locations, and a variety of grammar and spelling rules can all be taught using peer tutoring. Organized bodies of knowledge and thinking skills, with their complexity and divergence, are less applicable to peer tutoring activities.

Prepare Instructional Materials. Convergent topics allow the teacher to construct specific practice and feedback exercises that provide structure for the tutoring sessions. Tutors then focus on the problems and exercises in the materials. Maria Sandoval did this when she pulled learning materials together for Jim Corbin's students. These materials provide valuable practice and feedback for content taught during initial whole group activities.

Assign Students to Pairs. One peer tutoring arrangement is to pair a high with a low achiever and let the more advanced student do all the tutoring. A different option, called **reciprocal tutoring,** *pairs students of comparable ability, with students taking turns being the tutor.* In this arrangement, students usually slide into a pattern where they simply work together rather than having one formally designated as tutor for a period of time and then switching.

Train Students to be Effective Tutors. Like teachers, effective tutors are made, not born. Preparing both the tutors and the students being tutored is important for the effectiveness of the process (Fuchs et al., 1994; Slavin, 1995). Untrained tutors sometimes imitate

---

Table 9.9 **STEPS IN PLANNING AND IMPLEMENTING PEER TUTORING**

Planning	Implementing
1. Identify a topic.	**1.** Group presentation
2. Prepare instructional materials.	**2.** Break into peer-tutoring groups
3. Assign students to pairs.	**3.** Monitor progress
4. Train students to be effective tutors.	**4.** Evaluate tutoring pairs

the worst from their teachers, including punitiveness and a lack of helpful feedback. A list of effective training components includes the following:

- *Explaining objectives.* At the beginning of a session, the tutor should provide focus by explaining the major skill or concept to be learned. The teacher assists by putting this at the top of the tutoring worksheet.
- *Staying on task.* When an extraneous subject comes up, have tutors remind their partners of the objective and call their attention to the number of examples, pages, or steps left to do.
- *Providing emotional support.* Encourage tutors to make supportive comments for incorrect answers, such as, "Not quite. Let's look at it again. What is the first thing you did . . . ?"
- *Giving praise and other positive feedback.* Discuss the importance of positive feedback and provide examples of different forms of praise (e.g., "Good answer!" "Great, you're really getting this."). If possible, have the tutor link the praise to specific behaviors ("Good, you remembered to carry the three to the hundreds column."). At the end of the lesson, have the tutor state what was learned and relate this to the session objective.
- *Encouraging verbalization.* Instruct the tutor to encourage thinking out loud, both for himself or herself and his or her partner. This makes the cognitive operations being taught observable, providing a model for the partner and feedback for the tutor.

Implementing Peer Tutoring Activities

When implementing peer tutoring, teachers first present content as they typically would and then break students into groups, monitoring and evaluating them continually.

Group Presentation. Introduce and teach the content in the same way you normally would. This stage is important because it lays the conceptual foundation for tutoring that will follow by providing common understandings and vocabulary.

Break into Peer Tutoring Groups. Give students the worksheets designed to reinforce the content you've just presented. Specify the amount of time they have for the tutoring session, and clearly state your expectations.

Monitor Progress. Circulate around the room to answer questions and ensure that the tutoring is proceeding smoothly. To the extent possible, answer only procedural questions. Answer content questions only when the tutor is unable to do so. This places responsibility for learning on the peer teams. Check the exercise sheets at the end of the session for any error patterns that might suggest areas for reteaching.

Evaluate Tutoring Pairs. If a tutoring pair is not functioning, rearrange the students. One of the motivational advantages of peer tutoring is the fact that students are exposed to different teaching styles and personalities; to take advantage of this, reconstitute the tutoring pairs periodically.

Peer tutoring works because it places students in an active learning role and individualizes instruction. One of its advantages is that it can be easily combined with large group direct instruction. As such, it provides individualized practice and feedback.

Summary

Social Interaction: Theoretical Perspectives. Constructivist theories support the use of social interaction in the classroom by emphasizing the central role that dialogue and verbalization play in learning. Vygotsky, a Russian psychologist, viewed language as an important medium for both learning and development. Language provides a medium for students to conceptualize their own thoughts and refine these by comparing them to thoughts of others.

Using Groupwork to Facilitate Learning. Groupwork provides an effective strategy for promoting and maintaining high levels of student involvement by engaging students in tasks to be solved in a group. Combined with skilled questioning, it can also help students develop social skills and promote the development of higher-order thinking skills.

Cooperative Learning. Cooperative learning strategies place students on learning teams and reward group performance. Cooperative learning strategies can be used to teach both basic skills and other, higher level skills. To be effective, cooperative learning strategies should stress group goals, individual accountability, and provide equal opportunities for success.

Student teams–achievement divisions (STAD) has proven effective in teaching facts, concepts, and skills. Jigsaw techniques assign different students on a team to investigate different aspects of a larger body of knowledge. Subsequent sharing and quizzes or group projects make all students accountable for the information gained by the group. Group investigation places students in teams to attack a common problem from different perspectives. In all of these strategies, the development of social interaction skills and inquiry can be as important as content acquisition.

Discussions. Discussions are interactive instructional strategies that can be used to teach higher-level thinking skills, affective goals, and interpersonal communication skills. Content-oriented discussions invite students to use higher-level and critical thinking skills to refine and integrate previous information they have learned. Student content background is essential here. During discussions, the teacher's role is less directive and obtrusive, first framing the discussion with a question or problem and then monitoring its progress through questions and clarifying statements.

Affective discussions are designed to help students clarify their own values and beliefs through the dual processes of articulating their own views and listening to those of others. As with content-oriented discussions, the teacher acts as facilitator and clarifier rather than position taker.

Peer Tutoring: Students as Resources. Peer tutoring provides another student-centered approach to teaching content. Cross-age tutoring uses older students to help younger ones; same-age peer tutoring uses students in the same class to help each other. Structure is essential for effective peer tutoring; student worksheets provide a focused instructional agenda for both tutor and tutees.

Important Concepts

Character education

Combining peers

Cooperative learning

Cross-age peer tutoring

Discussions

Elaboration

Equal opportunity for success

Group investigation

Group goals

Groupwork

Individual accountability

Jigsaw II

Moral dilemma

Pairs check

Peer tutoring

Reciprocal tutoring

Same-age peer tutoring

Student teams–achievement divisions
  (STAD)

Think–pair–share

Reflecting on Teaching and Learning

Ken Johnson had been reading and hearing about cooperative learning. A number of his colleagues at Franklin Middle School had experienced some success with it, so Ken had been wanting to try it. As he looked over his language arts curriculum for the next few months, he saw that end-of-sentence punctuation was one of the topics he needed to cover. "Hmm, I wonder if cooperative learning would work here," he thought to himself.

As the day to begin the unit drew nearer, he made specific plans for the cooperative learning unit. He knew that students should be involved in helping each other out on teams but wasn't quite sure how to arrange this. He'd bring the topic up in the faculty lounge, but the explanations he received weren't clear. He couldn't quite understand the differences between STAD, Jigsaw, and Group Investigation. "Oh, well, probably the best way to learn is by trying it out," he thought as he looked through his teacher's edition of the language arts textbook that he was using.

On the first day of the unit, he began by saying, "Class, we're going to try something different. Instead of my teaching you everything, you're going to learn how to help each other. So the first thing we need to do is get into groups of three or four and these will be our cooperative learning teams. I thought of assigning you to teams but thought you might learn better with someone you know, so go ahead and find two or three other students that you want to work with and decide on a group name. I'll give you 5 minutes to do this."

As Ken circulated around the room, he worked at smoothing over group disputes. In some instances, teams of five arose and Ken was faced with the choice of breaking them up into smaller units or letting them go. He decided to let them go. He also encountered the problem of isolated students and students who couldn't find partners. He helped each of them find a potential partner.

When most of the students had found a group, he continued, "Here's how the activity will work. We're going to be learning about end-of-sentence punctuation. I know most of you know something about the topic, but I've been noticing on some of the writing that you've been handing in that we could use a little more work.

"So first I'd like everyone in the team to read pages 170 to 175 in your language arts text. Then I'd like each of you to write three sentences that are declarative, interrogatory, and imperative. Don't worry if you don't know what that means. You'll find out. Then share these with your partners and see if they can figure out which is which. We'll continue on with this tomorrow and I'll give each group a group quiz. Because we're using co-operative learning, I'll let you help each other and the grade you get for this assignment will be the same for everyone in the group. Any questions? Ryan?"

"What are we supposed to do in the groups? I'm not sure I understand."

"You're supposed to read pages 170–175 in your text. Here, I'll write them on the board. Then you make up one of each of the three kinds of sentences and share these with the other members of the team. Any other questions? Then let's get into our groups and start working."

As Ken circulated around the room, he helped students from different groups get going. He noticed that some groups, mostly his A and B students, got right to work while other groups were slow to start. As Ken worked with different groups, he repeated his directions. Finally, after about 10 minutes, most of the groups were working productively. "Hmm," he thought, "maybe this is going to work."

The next day he began class by saying, "Class, we did a good job yesterday learning about different kinds of sentences and how periods, question marks, and exclamation points can help the reader understand what we're trying to say. To help you practice for the quiz today, I've got an exercise that asks you to punctuate different kinds of sentences. This is exactly what you'll be doing on the group quiz at the end of our hour. So work hard and I'll be circulating around the room if you have any questions."

After Ken distributed the practice sheets to the different groups, he circulated around the room. He found that a number of groups had trouble deciding whether a sentence really warranted an exclamation point or just needed a period. Students felt that they didn't have enough background information to make a decision. While Ken half-heartedly agreed, he urged them to make a decision anyway.

Towards the end of the class, Ken asked all groups to look to the front of the room.

"Class, I've got your group quiz here. I'm only going to give one to each group and you have to work cooperatively at deciding the right answer. That's why this is called co-operative learning. When you're done, hand the quiz in with all of the members of your group's names on it and I'll grade them for tomorrow. Good luck."

As Ken passed out the quiz, he wandered around the room answering questions and making sure each of the groups was working okay. Some were and some weren't. He also noticed that in most groups the brightest students was given the job of secretary and tended to do most of the work.

"I wonder if this is working like it should," he thought. "They don't seem to be cooperating like they should."

Question for Analysis

1. What type of cooperative learning strategy should Ken Johnson have used? Why?
2. How effective was Ken in forming cooperative learning groups? What alternative might you suggest?
3. How effective was Ken's instruction in structuring the cooperative learning activity? What else might he have done?
4. Analyze Ken's cooperative learning activity in terms of the three essential components identified by research. How could he adjust his activity to be more effective?
5. Analyze the effectiveness of the learning materials Ken used. How could their effectiveness have been increased?

Discussion Questions

1. How would you respond to parents who raise concerns about their son or daughter being involved in peer tutoring, either as a tutor or student?

2. Which of the three cooperative learning strategies—STAD, Jigsaw II, and Group Investigation—are most appropriate for the lower grades? Upper grades? Why?

3. Are the three cooperative learning strategies more appropriate in some content areas than in others? Which and why?

4. Which of the three cooperative learning strategies would be most effective for fostering improved intergroup relations? Why?

5. What is the place of values in the curriculum? How would you respond to objections from people who contend that values don't belong in the curriculum? What advantages and disadvantages are there to character and moral education approaches to teaching values?

6. Which values should the schools try to develop? Examine the following values and rank order the five most important values from an educational perspective. Compare these with other people in the class.

Broadminded	Logical
Forgiving	Loving
Honest	Obedient
Imaginative	Polite
Independent	Responsible
Intellectual	Self-controlled

7. Are discussions more valuable in some areas of the curriculum than others? Which and why? How does the value of discussion vary with grade level? What is the lowest grade level that can still benefit from discussions?

Portfolio Activities

1. *Groupwork.* Plan and teach a lesson incorporating student groupwork.
   a. What kind of groupwork did you use? Was it appropriate for your goal?
   b. How well did you plan for logistical concerns such as transitions into and out of groupwork? What would you do differently next time?
   c. How did groupwork influence student motivation?
   d. How effective was the groupwork activity in promoting learning? How can you tell?

2. *Cooperative Learning.* Identify a classroom that is using cooperative learning. Observe the classroom and answer the following:
   a. What kind of cooperative learning strategy was being used?
   b. What kinds of content goals were targeted?
   c. How were the groups composed (teacher interview)?
   d. How did the teacher promote: (l) group goals, (2) individual accountability, and (3) equal opportunity for success?

   e. What special management strategies did the teacher use?

   f. How could the lesson be changed to improve learning?

3. *Affective Goals.* Examine a blank report card. What do the categories in the report card say about the affective goals in that school at that level? What areas are emphasized? What areas are missing? How could the report card be modified to help students develop in these areas?

4. *Discussions: Interaction Patterns.* The purpose of this exercise is to analyze the interaction patterns in a discussion. To do this, sketch out a seating chart of the participants before observing a class discussion. Mark the first person who talks with a 1, the second with a 2, and so on. After the session, analyze your data in terms of the following questions:

   a. How did the discussion begin?

   b. Was the prevalent interaction pattern T-S-T or S-S?

   c. What percentage of the students participated? What did the teacher do to influence this?

   d. What role did the teacher play?

   e. How did the teacher's questions guide the discussion?

   f. How did the discussion end?

   g. What suggestions do you have to make the discussion more effective?

5. *Discussions.* Identify an instructor at either the elementary or secondary level or the college level who is good at leading discussions and ask to sit in on one of his or her discussions.

   a. What instructional activities (e.g., readings or lecture) preceded the discussion?

   b. What kinds of interaction patterns developed?

   c. What kinds of questions seemed most effective in provoking thoughtful interaction?

   d. How was silence used?

   e. How appropriate would this discussion style be in your content area or level?

6. *Peer Tutoring.* Identify a classroom that is using peer tutoring. Observe a peer tutoring session and analyze it in terms of the following dimensions:

   a. Goals

   b. Instructional materials

   c. Type of peer tutoring (e.g., cross-age or reciprocal)

   d. Training (you will have to interview the teacher for this)

   e. Teacher monitoring

   f. Teacher's evaluation of the process (a short interview will be needed)

   g. Your suggestions for making peer tutoring more effective

10

Problem-Based Instruction

*T*o this point, you've seen how the general instructional model provides a framework for the strategies in this text, and you've studied both learner-centered and teacher-centered strategies designed to teach content, including concepts, skills, and organized bodies of knowledge.

In this chapter we examine problem-based instruction, a collection of teaching strategies that includes project-based instruction, problem solving, inquiry, case-based instruction, and anchored instruction.

When you've completed your study of this chapter, you should be able to meet the following goals:

- Describe characteristics of problem-based instruction.
- Implement project-based instruction.
- Implement strategies to help students learn to solve problems.
- Develop learning activities to promote inquiry strategies in learners.

PROBLEM-BASED INSTRUCTION

To introduce you to the topic of problem-based learning and instruction, let's look in on a classroom application.

Students at Bayview Middle School, on the banks of Chesapeake Bay, are actively involved in a debate about farm fertilizers, pesticides, and water pollution. Brad Evers, their social studies teacher, has been working with the other members of his teaching team to prepare students for this debate. Sonya Woodside, the science teacher, has been focusing on the chemical and biological aspects of pollution. Ted Barret, their English teacher, has been helping students use the Internet to gather information and write reports. Kim Starrow, the math teacher, has been focusing on graphing skills to help students integrate graphs into their presentations.

Kasha, a member of the environmental group, rises to speak. "Our group is in favor of House Bill 370. It prohibits farmers from using fertilizers and pesticides within 300 feet of any stream flowing into the Bay."

"We strongly disagree," replies Jacob, a member of the Farmer's Coalition. "This bill is unfair. It will put many farmers out of business and is unnecessary. Besides, fertilizer helps things grow. What evidence is there that fertilizer hurts anything?"

"But what about us? We make our living off of the fish and oysters in the Bay. Shouldn't our jobs be protected as well?" Jared counters as the moderator gives him the floor.

The debate continues with each group given opportunities to present their perspectives, using charts, graphs, and printed materials. (adapted from Slavin, Madden, Dolan, and Wasik, 1994, pp. 3–4)

Problem-Based Instruction: An Overview

Problem-based instruction *is a collection of integrative teaching strategies that use problems as the focus for direction, teaching problem-solving skills while developing self-directed learning*

(Krajcik, Blumenfeld, Marx, and Soloway, 1994). Problem-based instructional strategies typically have the following characteristics:

- Lessons begin with a problem or question, and solving the problem or answering the question becomes the focus of the lesson (T. Duffy and Cunningham, 1996; Grabinger, 1996).
- Students are actively involved in learning while investigating the problem, designing strategies, and finding solutions (Slavin, Madden, Dolan, and Wasik, 1994).
- The teacher's role in problem-based instruction is primarily facilitative. The teacher guides students' efforts through questioning and other forms of instructional scaffolding

(Maxwell, Bellisimo, and Mergendoller, 1999; Stepien and Gallagher, 1993).

Unlike other more content-oriented strategies, teachers use problem-based instruction to accomplish multiple goals. The goals of problem-based lessons are for students to (1) learn to investigate questions and problems systematically, (2) develop self-regulation and self-directed learning abilities, and (3) learn content. These goals were evident in Brad Evers's classroom. Students learned about pollution in the Chesapeake Bay while also developing their own abilities to conduct investigations into meaningful problems.

As the name implies, problem-based instructional strategies begin with a question or problem. In Brad Evers's class the problem involved the effects of pollution on the Chesapeake Bay. Later in the chapter you'll read about one classroom that attempts to find the area of an irregularly shaped room and another that tries to determine whether brand name or generic aspirins are better. These problems provide the focal point for students' investigatory efforts.

The primary goals for problem-based learning activities are the development of problem-solving abilities and self-directed learning; learning content is less prominent. If learning content is a primary goal, alternate strategies, such as direct instruction, lecture-discussion, or guided discovery, are probably more effective. However, some evidence indicates that content learned during problem-based lessons is retained longer and transfers better than content learned when other strategies are used (Duffy and Cunningham, 1996; Sternberg, 1998).

But what is self-directed learning, and how do problem-based strategies contribute to its development? **Self-directed learning** *develops when students are aware of and take control of their learning progress.* Self-directed learning is a form of metacognition, which involves knowing what we need to know, knowing what we know, knowing what we don't know, and devising strategies to bridge these gaps (Hmelo and Lin, 1998).

During problem-based instruction, students first assess what they know about the problem they are facing. On the basis of this assessment, students decide what additional information they need and develop plans to address these deficiencies. As they gather new information, they use this information to solve the problem they're encountering. If the information is sufficient and their goal met, the problem is solved. If not, students, on the basis of need, reformulate new learning strategies.

The teacher assists in the process by asking facilitative questions, such as:

What do you already know?

What additional information do you need?

Where can you find this information?

Questions such as these encourage students to think about the process they are going through, which helps them develop as self-directed learners. Unlike some of the other more content-oriented strategies that you've read about, in problem-based instruction the teacher's role is more facilitator and guide rather than information organizer and disseminator.

Problem-Based Instruction: Theoretical Foundations

Problem-based instruction is grounded in the philosophy of John Dewey, who advocated the use of experiential learning in classrooms, and constructivist views of learning. Let's look at these ideas in more detail.

Philosophical Underpinnings. John Dewey (1859–1952), probably the most influential educational philosopher in America, believed that children are socially active learners who learn by exploring their environments (Dewey, 1916). He believed schools should take advantage of children's natural curiosity by bringing the outside world into the classroom, making it the focus for study.

In studying the world, students should be active inquirers. Dewey proposed that this inquiry should be guided by the scientific method, which has the following characteristics:

- Learners are involved in authentic experiences that genuinely interest them.
- Learners examine problems that stimulate thinking and focus their efforts.
- As they solve problems, learners acquire information.
- Learners form tentative solutions that may solve the problem.
- Learners test the solutions by applying them to the problem. Applications help learners validate their knowledge.

We saw elements of these characteristics in Brad's classroom. Knowing that his students would be interested in the bay that they lived on, he designed a problem-based unit that allowed them to explore a problem that affected their lives and the lives of their parents. Dewey believed that the knowledge students learn shouldn't be some inert information found in books or delivered in lectures. Instead, knowledge becomes useful and alive when it is applied to the solution of some problem. Dewey's work had a major influence on the progressive education movement in the United States and continues to be felt in areas such as project-based learning, thematic units, and interdisciplinary teaching.

Constructivist Frameworks. As we've seen earlier in the text, constructivists believe that student learning is most effective when students actively construct knowledge, connecting it to what they already know. Problem-based learning encourages active knowledge construction by placing students in the middle of active learning situations. Students learn by actively trying to solve problems, such as investigating the effects of pollutants on our waterways.

One particular kind of constructivism, called *sociocultural learning theory,* stresses the importance of social interactions in learning. Based upon the work of the Russian psychologist Lev Vygotsky, sociocultural theory emphasizes that learning is inherently social and embedded within particular cultural settings (Cobb and Bowers, 1999). As learners within problem-based lessons interact with each other, they not only learn from each other but also create new knowledge for themselves.

From a sociocultural perspective, forming a community of learners is crucial. Teachers need to help students learn how to learn from each other. From this perspective the social interaction and group problem-solving skills that are learned are as important as other goals, such as learning content and higher-level analytical skills. Active listening, turn taking, building upon the ideas of others, and constructive disagreement, interaction skills that are so important in cooperative learning, are also essential in problem-based learning.

Because of the value of social interaction in problem-based learning, all of the strategies described in this chapter will be framed as group activities. However, many of these could be assigned as individual projects. For example, individual students could be asked to work on Brad Evers's problem and present their results individually. In organizing problem-based learning in this way, teachers miss valuable opportunities to take advantage of social learning.

In the next section we analyze project-based instruction, one of the most widely used problem-based learning teaching strategies.

PROJECT-BASED LEARNING

Project-based learning, *a comprehensive approach to classroom teaching and learning, involves students in projects: relatively long-term, problem-focused, and meaningful units of instruction that integrate concepts from a number of disciplines or fields of study.* During project-based learning, "students pursue solutions to authentic problems by asking and refining questions, debating ideas, making predictions, designing plans or experiments, collecting and analyzing data, drawing conclusions, communicating their ideas and findings to others, asking new questions, and creating products" (Good and Brophy, 2000, p. 242).

Essential Components

Project-based learning utilizes the following components:

- An authentic question or problem organizes and drives the activities.
- Collaboration provides opportunities for students to learn to work together toward a common goal.
- Activities include information gathering from a variety of sources that may involve interdisciplinary connections.
- Answers or solutions to the problem or question lead to a series of products that result in a final presentation project in a form (e.g., debate, report, videotape, presentation) that can be shared with others and critiqued.

Let's analyze these characteristics using Brad Evers's classroom as an example.

Authentic Question or Problem. Project-based learning begins with a question or problem that is real to students and that can serve as the focal point for student investigations. An effective problem

- Fulfills a specific purpose: It relates to important learning outcomes and connects to a teacher's goals.
- Presents an open-ended task to accomplish.

- Compels interest by challenging students.
- Connects student learning to real-world experience. (Gagnon and Collay, 2001)

This question or problem could be a social issue or problem, a topic encountered in the regular curriculum, or a topic that interests the students. Brad Evers used the topic of pollution in the Chesapeake Bay to focus his students' studies. The topic was authentic or real to them because they live along the bay and could relate their studies to their own lives and the lives of their parents, many of whom are farmers and fishermen.

In addition to being authentic, the problems should also be open ended and ill defined, posing a sense of mystery or puzzlement. This is important for several reasons. Ill-defined problems offer challenges to students, providing them with opportunities to wrestle with, understand, and frame the learning task ahead of them. This challenge is similar to the one students encounter when they write a more traditional term paper and can be the most educationally rewarding part of the process. In addition, an open-ended problem is motivating, providing students with both challenge and choice.

Additional examples of topics that could serve as focal points for project-based learning are found in Table 10.1. Each of these questions or problems could serve as the focus of a long-term investigation by students.

Collaboration with Other Students. As students work together on their projects, they develop valuable group interaction skills. They learn to form group goals collaboratively, to listen, to express their own ideas, and to compromise as conflicts occur. These are valuable skills in school as well as in real life.

Collaboration also has cognitive benefits as well (Eggen and Kauchak, 2001). The process of organizing ideas and putting them into words is a challenging task that promotes learning, as anyone who has had to write about something knows. In addition, listening to others' ideas and understanding them, incorporating them with our own, not only contributes to our own thinking but also helps create new ideas.

Information Gathering. Project-based learning activities involve students in a variety of information-gathering activities. These could include, but are not limited to, the following:

- Gathering information from printed sources
- Using the Internet

Table 10.1 PROJECT-BASED QUESTIONS OR PROBLEMS

Content Area	Question or Problem
High school social studies	What factors influence voter turnout in an election?
High school health	How healthy are the lunches that students eat at our school?
Elementary science	What kinds of plants and animals inhabit a nearby pond?
Middle school history	What is the history of the town or city that we live in?
Middle school social studies	Where do last names come from and what do they mean?
Elementary science/social studies	What are the advantages and disadvantages of different pets?

- Interviewing people
- Gathering specimens (e.g. plants and animals)

Students in Brad's classroom used books and magazines like *National Geographic* as well as the Internet to obtain basic information about the bay and the problems of pollution. They also interviewed a number of people, including farmers and fishermen as well as public officials such as water quality officials and wildlife conservation officers. They also collected and analyzed water samples from different sites along the bay.

Often the process of information gathering requires crossing disciplinary or content boundaries. Note that although all of the original questions in Table 10.1 were embedded in a particular content area or areas, they could potentially lead to interdisciplinary investigations. For example, the high school health project focusing on nutrition could incorporate science topics to frame the question, social studies to investigate issues of sampling, math to report results, and writing to present conclusions. In a similar way the elementary project on pets could involve a broad array of skills such as interviewing, using math to report findings, and reading and writing in the language arts curriculum. Project-based learning often serves as the focal point for interdisciplinary units that connect multiple content areas.

Products. The products of project-based learning are an important learning component and need to be shared with others. The creation of a product encourages students to integrate their new learning into some form of cohesive and coherent report. This is a demanding task that fosters learning. Producing a product also brings closure to the project, which carries with it motivational benefits (McCombs and Pope, 1994). Feedback from others also permits the learners to reflect on and extend their emerging knowledge and to revise their products if necessary.

Products can take a number of forms. The most obvious is some type of written report that can be shared with others. Other alternatives include:

- A letter to a politician or newspaper
- A multimedia presentation with an audience in mind
- A drama or short story
- A debate

Students should view the products they create not only as a worthwhile summary of their efforts but also as functional, designed to inform or persuade a specific audience.

Brad's students reported their findings in a number of ways. To encourage them to consider multiple perspectives on the problem, he assigned them to teams that focused on different aspects of the problem. Prior to the debate each team presented their findings to the whole class using different forms of technology, including videotapes, audio tapes, and PowerPoint. Students then used this information during the debate, in which they assumed different roles and perspectives.

Implementing Project-Based Instruction in the Classroom

Project-based learning is complex, both from a teacher and student perspective. For teachers, it requires a number of different roles, starting with planning and ending with assessment. It also requires students to assume different roles, and teachers need to assist students as they learn how to perform these new roles. In this section we describe how teachers can make project-based instruction work in their classrooms, starting with the process of planning.

Planning. All good teaching starts with a goal that then guides teachers' subsequent instructional efforts. Brad Evers had several goals. He wanted students to learn about pollution and how it affected the area in which they lived. He also wanted students to learn to work together cooperatively on projects and develop their abilities to direct their own learning in the future. These multiple goals are typical in project-based learning.

A second planning task is to identify a topic for study and then frame the topic in terms of a problem for students to investigate. Topics for project-based learning can come from several sources. The most obvious is the assigned curriculum. Though teachers are expected to teach a number of "assigned" topics, all it takes is a little creativity to transform these into the focal point of projects. For example, a unit on the Crusades can be converted into active investigations by students into the human efforts that went into the Crusades, including reports on recruitment efforts, songs, and battle strategies (Cohen, 1991). In a similar way, a social studies lesson on local political structures or a science lesson on pollution can be converted into project-based instruction on the politics of pollution on the Chesapeake Bay, as Brad Evers did.

Another teacher planning task during project-based learning is to organize resources, both in print and media formats. This task has been made much simpler with the advent of the Internet, but teachers still need to plan for access to computers and the availability of relevant websites as well as more mundane things like printing.

Implementing. The first step in implementing project-based learning in the classroom is to orient students to the problem. Let's see how Brad did this in his classroom.

"Class, I've got some pictures I'd like to show you. They're from a book called, *Then and Now: A Historical Look at Chesapeake Bay.* What do you notice about the first one? Seth?"

"That's Sassafras Creek. I can tell from the old pier that's still there. But there weren't any condos there then."

"Good, Seth. What else do you notice, class?"

Brad continues, sharing with his class both old and modern pictures of the bay, helping them see the changes that have occurred over time to the physical appearance of the bay. Then he shares with them some figures on the amount of oysters and fish that were harvested over the years and asks students to explain the decline. During the discussion, he asks if any of the students boat or fish in the bay and asks them to share their experiences. He asks them to go home that evening and ask their parents about their early memories of Chesapeake Bay and how it has changed over time.

An effective problem has several essential characteristics. First, it must be real or meaningful to students. In addition, it must be understandable and afford a starting point for students' investigative efforts. Finally, it must be complex and open ended so that it provides students with multiple options for their investigations.

After orienting students to the problem, teachers need to organize them into study teams. One of the easiest, but not necessarily the best, way to do this is by student choice. However, the same kinds of concerns raised in Chapter 9 about this method of comprising cooperative learning groups also apply here. Groups may not be balanced in terms of ability, ethnicity, or gender. Working with friends or in homogeneous groups often prevents students from learning about others and how to work with students who are different from them.

After students are organized into study teams, teachers need to structure the teams' efforts by establishing timelines, both for intermediate and final projects. Timelines provide concrete due dates for different groups to meet. Teachers can also assist with these timelines by meeting with the different groups on a periodic basis to facilitate each group's progress.

Major tasks each group will need to struggle with are data collection and analysis. For example, the students in Brad's class chose to interview a number of people connected to the bay. Before they did this, they needed to construct an interview protocol to structure their interviews. They also needed to decide whether the interviews should be audio- or video-recorded or whether notes should be taken. Brad helped in the process by asking groups to think ahead and consider what their final reports or products would look like.

The final products that result from project-based learning can and should take multiple forms. Students should take the audience into consideration in planning their reports and should be encouraged to employ a variety of media formats. Even if one of the products is a traditional paper, students should be encouraged to consider ways to make the information in it accessible and interesting. Doing this not only develops perspective taking, a valuable social skill (Berk, 2000), but also employs multiple learning tasks, a major way of addressing student diversity (Cohen, 1991). In addition, creating a consumer-oriented exhibit or report is a valuable skill in later life.

One way to think of these final learning products is in terms of exhibits. **Exhibits** *are presentations of student work that document learning.* Characteristics of effective exhibits include the following:

- Students produce the exhibit to document their accomplishment of a task.
- Students present their exhibit publicly and explain their thinking.
- Students respond to questions from their teacher or peers.
- Teachers use the exhibit to determine what learning has taken place.
- Teachers help students understand the learning that has occurred.
- Teachers align student explanations and thinking with requirements of state or national standards.

(Gagnon and Collay, 2001)

Exhibits provide a public forum where members of the learning community come together to discuss the learning that has taken place during project-based learning.

Assessment. Assessment should be an integral part of project-based learning and should occur in three phases. Before project-based instruction occurs, teachers should ascertain, either formally through a written preassessment or informally through questions, what students know about the topic. This can provide valuable information for organizing groups as well as gathering resources.

Assessment can also provide valuable information during project-based lessons. Checklists and rating scales can provide students with valuable feedback about their learning as well as the progress of their project. A rubric such as the one in Figure 10.1 can help students assess their own planning progress as well as provide the teacher with a concrete format to conference with students about their progress and accomplishments.

Project Goals	No Evidence		Partial Evidence		Clear Evidence
1. Topic clearly defined	1	2	3	4	5
2. Information-gathering procedures detailed	1	2	3	4	5
3. Data analysis procedures described	1	2	3	4	5
4. Final product planned	1	2	3	4	5

Figure 10.1 Rubric for Assessing Project-Based Learning

Assessment can also provide valuable information to students about their final project and how effective they were in presenting this to other students. Rubrics similar to the one in Figure 10.1 can be developed, shared with students, and used during presentations to provide feedback about strengths and weaknesses.

To help students develop self-direction in their learning they should be involved in the assessment process from the beginning (McCombs and Pope, 1994). Teachers should

- Inform students at the planning stage what is expected when their projects are completed.
- Use ongoing student conferences to discuss progress and provide feedback.
- Involve students in providing feedback to each other.
- Encourage students self-evaluations of their learning progress.

In assessing project-based learning, teachers should focus not only on the products produced but also the growth and changes that are occurring in students.

Research on Project-Based Learning

Research on project-based learning is encouraging. Research suggests that it is an effective vehicle to teach basic learning skills at the same time as content. Project-based learning also has motivational benefits. In addition, there is some evidence that this form of learning can help develop self-directed learning in students.

Project-based learning is an effective vehicle for teaching basic learning skills because these skills are an integral part of students' projects. In addition to developing reading and writing skills, project-based learning can also teach a number of valuable learning strategies, including teaching students to

- Prioritize learning objectives.
- Identify areas of knowledge deficit.
- Search for information broadly.
- Integrate information effectively.
- Present ideas clearly.

(Blumberg, 1998)

Because students are actively immersed in these processes in the pursuit of their projects, they can see why they're useful and appreciate their value.

Motivation and Project-based Instruction. Research also suggests that project-based learning is motivating. Motivational aspects of project-based work include:

- Authentic problems that are challenging
- Choice in deciding what and how to do it

- Varied and novel tasks
- Collaboration with peers
- Closure in the form of a final product

(Good and Brophy, 2000)

In one study of high school English projects, students identified voice and choice as significant factors in the effectiveness of their projects (Davis, 1998).

This choice is important because it provides opportunities for students to develop self-directed learning skills (Blumberg, 1998; van den Heuk, Wolfhagen, Dolmans, and van der Vleuten, 1998). Rather than sitting passively listening to a teacher's presentation, students involved in projects are constantly asking themselves questions such as:

- Why am I doing this?
- What are my goals and objectives?
- What do I know and need to find out?
- How can I present my findings to an audience?

Teachers can facilitate the development of self-directed learning by providing feedback to students as they progress through their projects.

However, research on problem-based learning in medicine raises some cautionary flags (Albanese and Mitchell, 1993). Though medical students using problem-based learning became better thinkers and more adept at clinical problem solving, they also scored lower on basic science examinations and viewed themselves as less prepared in terms of basic science knowledge. The message from this research is clear and reinforces a major theme of this text. There is no *one* best way to teach. Each strategy or approach has both strengths and weaknesses. Teachers need to have a clear vision of the overall goals in their curriculum and use different approaches to teaching strategically. If the goal is basic content acquisition, other strategies such as lecture discussion and direct instruction may be more appropriate. If, instead, teachers want to develop students' self-direct learning and thinking skills, problem-based learning may be valuable.

This concludes our discussion of project-based learning. In the next section we discuss problem solving, a second form of problem-based instruction.

PROBLEM SOLVING

- You're a sixth-grade middle school teacher, and many of your students come to class without their books, pencils, and other materials.
- You're planning on meeting some friends for dinner at a new restaurant, but you don't know how to get there, and your friends have already left.
- You're involved in a personal relationship with someone, but the relationship isn't as satisfying as you had originally hoped.

What do these examples have in common? While different in their orientation, each is a problem. A **problem** *exists when you're in a state different from a desired state, and there's some uncertainty about reaching the desired state* (Bransford and Stein, 1984). To solve a problem, we must figure out how to move from the state we're in to the desired state. Let's see what problem solving looks like in the classroom.

Laura Hunter, a fifth-grade teacher at Bennion Elementary, is trying to teach her students about area by involving them in a problem-solving lesson. The class has been introduced to the concepts of perimeter and area but is still struggling with them.

Identify the problem

↓

Represent the problem

↓

Select a strategy

↓

Carry out the strategy

↓

Evaluate results

Figure 10.2 Problem-Solving Model

Laura begins by posing the following problem: "The principal is planning to recarpet the classroom and needs to know how much carpeting to order." The complexity of the problem is increased by the fact that the room is irregularly shaped and that the linoleum part of the room, which is on the outside perimeter of the room under the computers, will not be carpeted.

To help students in their problem solving, Laura displays an overhead with the five-step problem-solving model shown in Figure 10.2. Breaking students into groups of four, she has each group identify what the problem is. After reporting back to the whole class, each group is then responsible for measuring a different part of the room with rulers, yard-sticks, and tape measures. They report back to a group that is coordinating measurements and constructing a diagram of the whole room.

Laura then asks each group to select a strategy to find the carpeted area of the room. As the different groups work on doing this, two strategies emerge. One is to find the total area of the room and subtract out the linoleum or noncarpeted parts of the room. The other is to compute the area of a rectangle within the carpeted area and then add on additional, irregularly shaped carpeted sections. As students discuss their strategies, they use the diagram they generated and hand-held computers to find the area.

After selecting and implementing their strategies, the groups report back to the whole class. The class discusses not only the different problem-solving strategies but also interpersonal problems within the groups.

In evaluating their results, the class finds that the answers generated by the different groups differ and the class discusses why. Laura asks for suggestions about ways to make the answers more accurate and students suggest starting with common numbers and using the same strategies. (adapted from Eggen and Kauchak, 2001, pp. 309–311)

How was this an example of problem solving? The state Laura's students were in was not knowing how much carpet was needed to carpet the room, and the desired state was determining that amount. Her instruction at one level was aimed at helping them figure out how to move to the desired state. At another level it was designed to help students become better problem solvers. In our other cases, the desired states are students bringing their materials, knowing how to get to the restaurant, and being in a satisfying relationship.

From these examples we see that problem solving is actually much broader than the way it is typically presented in schools. Problems like the ones Laura's students were studying are common, but in the past we probably haven't thought of not knowing how to get to a restaurant, for example, as a problem.

Adopting a more general view of problem solving helps us see that problems and how to solve them are very real parts of our everyday lives. The hope is that the problem-solving strategies that students learn in schools will transfer over into other dimensions of their lives. We examine these strategies later in this section when we discuss a general problem solving model.

Well-Defined and Ill-Defined Problems

All too often in classrooms students are given problems where the solution method is quite clear. This is unfortunate because it robs students of the opportunity to wrestle with problems that are more like the ones we encounter in real life. Problem-solving experts commonly distinguish well-defined from ill-defined problems (Eysenck and Keane, 1990). A **well-defined problem** *has only one correct solution and a certain method for finding it,* whereas an **ill-defined problem** *has more than one solution and no generally agreed upon strategy for reaching it* (Dunkle, Schraw, and Bendixon, 1995; Ormrod, 1999). Getting our students to bring their materials, finding a route to the restaurant, and being in an unsatisfactory relationship are all ill-defined problems. For example, in terms of the last problem, we want to be in one that is satisfying, but we're often not sure what "satisfying" means, and even if we did know, how to get there is uncertain.

The distinction between a well-defined and ill-defined problem often depends on the learners themselves. As an example, let's look again at Laura's lesson. Finding the amount of carpeting necessary appears to be well defined, and for an expert, it is: Simply determine the total area of the floor, and subtract the area covered by linoleum. Only one answer exists, and the solution is straightforward. For Laura's students, however, the problem was ill defined. Their understanding of the goal wasn't clear, some of them were uncertain about the difference between area and perimeter (as an interview after the lesson revealed), and they used a variety of strategies to reach the goal.

There are several advantages to using ill-defined problems in the classroom. The first is that they are more similar to problems learners encounter in the real world, so they provide practice in dealing with these realistic, everyday problems. Because they are more open ended, they can also be more motivating, encouraging students to be more creative in their solutions.

A Problem-Solving Model

Over the last 40 years or more, experts have tried to develop approaches to problem solving that can be applied in a variety of situations. One result of these efforts is the five-step problem solving model illustrated in Figure 10.2 and discussed here (Bransford and Stein, 1984).

Identifying the Problem. On the surface, it appears that identifying the problem should be simple. However, particularly with ill-defined problems and novice problem solvers, identifying the problem is one of the most demanding aspects of problem solving (Hayes, 1988).

Let's look at a classroom example:

Question: *There are 26 sheep and 10 goats on a ship. How old is the captain?*

Amazingly, in one study, 75 percent of the second graders who were asked this question answered 36 (cited in Prawat, 1989)! Obviously, they had difficulty understanding what the problem was asking.

Obstacles to identifying problems effectively include:

- Lack of experience with the process
- Lack of domain-specific knowledge
- The tendency to rush toward a solution before the problem has been clearly defined
- The tendency to think convergently (Bruning et al., 1999)

Let's see how these obstacles operate in a problem involving classroom teaching.

Paula Waites, a second-year teacher, is having classroom management problems. Her students are inattentive and disruptive, and in spite of clearly stated rules and an effort to enforce them consistently, the behaviors persist.

"I'm not sure what to do," Paula confided to her friend, Linda, an eight-year veteran. "I know that I'm supposed to be consistent, and I'm trying. I told them that I mean business, and I've written several referrals during the last week, but it isn't helping that much. I guess I'll just have to get tougher, but I hate coming down on them all the time. I've thought and thought about it, and that's all I can come up with."

"I'm not sure," Linda responded, "but maybe you ought to try something a little different."

"I don't know what you mean."

"Maybe try working up a few really nifty activities, even if it takes some extra work. If the kids like them, maybe they'll behave better. . . . Whenever my kids are acting up, the first thing I ask myself is if I'm doing a good job of teaching. I mean, that isn't always the case, but it's often a factor in their behavior."

"Gee, I guess I never actually thought about approaching it that way. I admit that most of what I do is sort of lead discussions about what they've read, or were supposed to read in the book."

A week later Paula reported that she had been working very hard, but that her students were behaving much better. (Eggen and Kauchak, 2001; p. 327)

Paula encountered two related obstacles when she tried to solve her management problem. The first was lack of experience in thinking about teaching problems; the second was a lack of domain-specific knowledge about management and motivation. She also thought convergently, rushing to the conclusion that her students' lack of attention was the result of something in the students rather than something that she was responsible for. Fortunately for Paula, her experienced friend, Linda, was able to help her redefine the problem in a more productive manner.

Even though she was working with a somewhat well-defined problem, Laura attempted to give her students some practice in problem finding by beginning with the general problem of carpeting. She did this by asking students in small groups to think about the problem. Let's see how she did this.

After the students worked together for several minutes, Laura had each of the groups report their results to the class.

"Fred, what did your team decide you were supposed to do?" Laura began.

"Measure the area."

"Okay. Grant, can you give me some more details?"

"We decided we should measure the perimeter around and about 2 feet from the computers and the linoleum and measure all around."

"I'm writing, 'Remember the linoleum,' so you remember to go through that process," Laura noted, writing on the overhead.

"Okay, have we identified all the parts of the problem? . . . Paige, do you want to add anything?"

"Ahh . . . we could make a drawing of the outside of the room. Like on the graph paper like we did yesterday. Write the measurements on the side," Paige continued.

"Okay, outside measurements," Laura repeated as she wrote down what Paige said.

"Okay, who else? . . . Jamison?"

"We decided we had to get the perimeter before we could get the area. Everything else is the same."

"Okay," Laura commented, "so now we know what the problem is." (Eggen and Kauchak, 2001, pp. 309–310)

After further discussion, Laura's students concluded that this was an area problem, allowing them to connect it to what they had been studying previously. In the real world, the process of identifying the problem can be the most important factor leading to a workable solution.

Representing the Problem. After the problem has been identified, the next step for students is to represent it in a meaningful way. This can be as simple as merely thinking about the problem, to as complex as using drawings, graphs, or tables to represent the problem. The limited amount of information we can hold in our conscious memory is one obstacle that all problem solvers face. Putting as much information as possible on paper helps reduce the amount we must remember. Concrete examples and drawings are particularly helpful, because they help us rethink the problem and perhaps use analogies as a strategy. Using something visual can be helpful because the load on our memory is reduced and the problem becomes linked to learners' backgrounds (Lovett and Anderson, 1994).

Laura helped her students represent the problem when she encouraged students to measure the room and construct a diagram of it that they could use in their subsequent problem solving efforts. This helped them focus on important aspects of the problem like the size and shape of the linoleum while ignoring other irrelevant aspects of the room, such as the windows and chairs.

Selecting a Strategy. Having identified and represented the problem, a strategy for solving needs to be selected. In solving more well-defined problems, an **algorithm,** *or spec-*

ified set of steps for solving problems, can be applied. When we solve algebraic equations, multiply whole numbers, or add fractions with unlike denominators, we are using algorithms. One algorithm that Laura's students used was "length times width equals area." However, her students had to modify this by adapting it to the irregularly shaped room they were working with.

Implementing the Strategy. Implementing the strategy is the fourth step in the process. Successful implementation depends on how clearly the problem has been defined and represented. If learners have trouble implementing a strategy, they need to go back to the earlier steps.

Evaluating the Results. Evaluating results, the final step in problem solving, is often very difficult for learners. We've all heard teachers complain that their students, particularly in solving math problems, all too often write down answers whether or not they make sense. For example,

> One boy, quite a good student, was working on the problem, "If you have six jugs, and you want to put two-thirds of a pint of lemonade into each jug, how much lemonade will you need?" His answer was 18 pints. I [Holt] said, "How much in each jug?" "Two-thirds of a pint." I said, "Is that more or less than a pint?" "Less." I said, "How many jugs are there?" "Six." I said, "But that doesn't make any sense." He shrugged his shoulders and said, "Well, that's the way the system worked out." (Holt, 1964, p. 18)

Getting an answer, regardless of whether or not it makes sense, is typically students' goal. Young children, in particular, have trouble at this stage, wanting to rush through, find an answer, and get on to the next problem to finish the assignment (Schunk, 1994).

When students learn to evaluate their results, their problem-solving abilities greatly improve (L. Baker, 1989; Zimmerman, 1990). Teachers can help in this process, particularly in math, by having students estimate answers before they begin. Estimates require thought, and when answers and estimates are far apart, questions are raised. The habit of estimating is an important disposition that teachers should try to help students develop.

Helping Learners Become Better Problem Solvers

Within the framework of this general problem-solving model, what specifically can teachers do to help learners become better problem solvers? Concrete suggestions are included in Figure 10.3 and discussed in the sections that follow (adapted from Eggen and Kauchak, 2001).

Present Problems in Meaningful Contexts. In looking at Laura's lesson again, we see she attempted to set the stage for area problems involving irregularly shaped figures by beginning with a carpeting problem involving her own classroom. Placing problems in concrete contexts such as this improves problem-solving ability by helping students see how problems relate to their own personal experience and background knowledge (Mayer, 1992).

Present a Variety of Examples. We saw in Chapter 8 how critical examples are for learning concepts, generalizations, principles, and academic rules, and it is true for problem

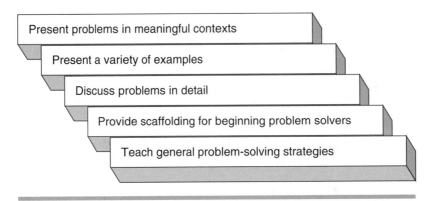

Figure 10.3   Helping Students Become Better Problem Solvers

solving as well. We will see in our discussion of heuristics that experience is important for developing problem-solving expertise, and another way of acquiring experience is to solve a wide variety of examples embedded in meaningful contexts (Reed, Willis, and Guarino, 1994). To develop expertise, Laura's students need to solve a variety of additional area problems.

Discuss Problems in Detail. One of the most common weaknesses in problem solving, particularly in math and science, is *students don't get enough practice in talking about the problems they are attempting to solve.* Wrestling with problem-related ideas and trying to put them into words are absolutely critical activities if students are to become better problem solvers. We all have difficulty in expressing our thoughts and ideas; this ability, as with most others, improves with practice.

In our earlier discussion of constructivism, we saw that social interaction contributes to understanding. In the case of problem solving, research suggests that having students discuss problems in detail during problem-solving activities increases their understanding of the problem (Perry et al., 1993; Stern, 1993). Laura implemented this research by having the students work in groups as they progressed through each of the problem-solving steps. Giving students a chance to dialogue, being patient as they struggle to express themselves, and holding back the tendency to provide more support than necessary all contribute to students' developing understanding.

Provide Scaffolding for Beginning Problem Solvers. We will discuss the concept of *scaffolding* in Chapter 11 when we discuss Vygotsky's work, and we will see that expert teachers provide only enough scaffolding to help their students progress and keep them on track. With problem solving, scaffolding is the support teachers provide as beginners attempt to solve specific problems.

Scaffolding is often misinterpreted, however, to suggest that teachers explain a solution while learners watch passively and then attempt it on their own, much as skills have been taught in the past. Effective scaffolding provides only enough support so that learners make progress *on their own.* As we will see in Chapter 11, a painter's scaffold supports the painter, but the painter does the painting; the teacher provides support, but the learner solves the problem. A major way that teachers help students learn to problem solve is through analyzing worked examples.

In typical problem-solving instruction, teachers usually display one or more problems, model solutions to them, and then have students try to solve them on their own. Students tend to memorize the steps involved, often with little understanding. In contrast, analyzing problems, discussing them in detail, and then relating solutions to them makes the entire process much more meaningful. Laura did this in her lesson through interactive questioning that encouraged students to compare similarities and differences in the various ways students solved the problem.

Research supports analyzing problem solving through worked examples; students using worked examples required less assistance from the teacher, developed more accurate solutions, and required less time than students involved in traditional instruction (Carroll, 1994). They even outperformed students receiving individualized instruction. In addition, using worked examples increases transfer and provides an understanding of the broader principles involved in the problem (Reed et al., 1994).

The combination of the worked examples *with discussion,* as Laura did in her lesson, promotes the most learning. Worked examples provide representations; the discussion makes the representations and the solution meaningful for students (Atkinson et al., 2000).

Teach General Problem-Solving Strategies. When we teach students to problem solve, we not only want them to learn how to solve the specific problems we're focusing on, we also want them to become better problem solvers in general. Emphasis on broader problem-solving strategies can increase problem-solving abilities by helping students understand the logic and utility of the processes they are using (Mayer, 1992; Resnick, 1987).

Heuristics *are general, widely applicable problem solving strategies* that can be helpful (Mayer, 1992). Some common heuristics are outlined in Table 10.2.

Each of the heuristics in Table 10.2 has advantages. Since experience is one of the most important factors in acquiring problem-solving expertise, trial and error, although inefficient, is valuable for beginning problem solvers. Since ambiguous desired states are characteristic of ill-defined problems, means-ends analysis helps people determine what the problem actually is, i.e., identify the problem. Working backward

Table 10.2 **HEURISTICS USED FOR PROBLEM SOLVING**

Heuristic	Description
Trial and error	Often used with unfamiliar problems, it amounts to picking a solution and seeing how it works. It can be valuable for giving learners experience with new problems.
Means-ends analysis	Effective for ill-defined problems, it involves breaking the problem into subgoals and working successively on each.
Working backward	Effective in cases where parameters are known, such as what time a class or meeting starts and how far away you are.
Drawing analogies	An attempt to attack unfamiliar problems, it compares them to familiar ones that have already been solved (Mayer, 1992).

can also be effective for well-defined problems that lack algorithms. If you know that you can spend $450 a month for rent, for example, working backward can help you make decisions about amenities and whether or not you'll need to look for a roommate. Finally, drawing analogies can be helpful for learners with experience in related problems. Teachers can teach these strategies through modeling and thinkalouds, much as they do with other cognitive skills.

Teachers can help students think in terms of general strategies by teaching the strategy and reminding students of the steps in the process. Laura did this by displaying the problem-solving model in an overhead and referring to it continuously during her lesson. The goal in teaching general problem-solving strategies is to help students develop the inclination to identify problems clearly, check to see if the strategies they choose will solve it, try to represent it visually, and evaluate their results.

Teachers can also help students develop these inclinations through questioning. For example, as students attempt to solve problems, the teacher can ask questions such as the following to help students develop an awareness of the process:

What (exactly) are you doing?

(Can you describe it precisely?)

Why are you doing it?

(How does it fit into the solution?)

How does it help you?

(What will you do with the outcome when you obtain it?)
(Schoenfield, 1989, p. 98)

Anchored Instruction: Technology as a Tool to Teach Problem Solving

One of the dilemmas teachers encounter when we try to teach our students how to problem solve is the difficulty of constructing realistic, complex problems for students to wrestle with. All too often when students encounter word problems in math, for example, the goal is clear, only those numbers needed to solve are included, and even the type of computation needed to solve the problem is suggested by the problem's placement in a particular chapter (Cognition and Technology Group at Vanderbilt, 1992). Unfortunately, these aren't the kind of problems most people encounter in their everyday lives. Real-life problems are messier and more complicated, with a number of viable routes providing alternate solutions. Technology provides one way to teach students how to solve these kinds of problems. For example,

> Jasper has just purchased a new boat and is planning to drive it home. The boat consumes 5 gallons of fuel per hour and travels at 8 mph. The gas tank holds 12 gallons of gas. The boat is currently located at mile marker 156. Jasper's home dock is at mile marker 132. There are two gas stations on the way home. One is at mile marker 140.3 and the other is at mile marker 133. They charge $1.10 and $1.25 per gallon, respectively. They don't take credit cards. Jasper started the day with $20. He bought 5 gallons of gas at $1.25 per gallon (not including a discount of 4 cents per gallon for paying cash) and paid $8.25 for repairs to his boat. It's 2:35. Sundown is at 7:52. Can Jasper make it home before sunset without running out of fuel? (Williams, Bareiss, and Reiser, 1996, p. 2)

This problem is part of a videodisc-based series called *The Adventures of Jasper Woodbury* designed to promote problem solving, reasoning, and effective communication. Each segment begins with a 15- or 20-minute adventure or story. The fuel problem described is actually a condensed version; the actual problem contains much more detail, including both relevant and irrelevant data that students must sift through for its relevance and value. At the end of each story the character or characters are faced with a challenge or problem that serves as the problem.

The problem is purposefully left open ended to provide opportunities for students to define, represent, and solve complex real-life problems. Each problem in the series has a number of viable solutions; each solution has both pros and cons. Students are encouraged to work in groups discussing and comparing their individual problem-solving strategies with other students. Each problem is designed to be solved in three or four days or more. The fact that the video is contained in a hypermedia computer program allows students to return to problem segments to extract data or reaffirm facts.

The creators of the Jasper Series call this problem-based approach to instruction **anchored instruction.** The *anchor* is the rich, interesting problem situation that provides a focus or reason for setting goals, planning, and using mathematical tools to solve problems. The goal of anchored instruction is to develop knowledge that is useful and flexible and that can be used to solve other problems.

The creators of the program claim that the research on the series has been positive. They report that middle school students using the Jasper series did as well as controls on basic math concepts but performed better on math verbal problems, were better at planning for problem solving and generating subgoals, and had more positive attitudes toward math (Cognition and Technology Group at Vanderbilt, 1992). The also cite teachers' comments to support their findings:

> "The kids would go home so excited and [the parents would say] 'I've got to find out about this Jasper. It is all my kid talks about . . . ' "

and

> "If you have any way of getting to my kids in high school, you'll find that they remember those four Jasper episodes. They may not remember anything else we did worked that year but they'll remember . . . those episodes because it did hit them and make an impact on them this year." (Cognition and Technology Group at Vanderbilt, 1992, p. 307)

More recent development efforts in this series attempt to make the problem-solving process more open ended by involving students in design problems. For example, in one problem called *Blueprint for Success* students apply geometry concepts in the design of a playground (Williams, Bareiss, and Reiser, 1996). Within physical and financial parameters established by a video, students measure lines and angles, do proportional reasoning, and create and read scale drawings. For additional information about the Jasper series, consult the World Wide Web site: http://peabody.vanderbilt.edu/projects/funded/jasper/preview/AdvJW.html

This completes our discussion of problem solving. In the next section we extend our discussion of problem-based learning as we discuss inquiry-based instruction.

INQUIRY STRATEGIES

Inquiry strategies, *another form of problem-based instruction, actively involve students in learning activities designed to answer questions about how the world operates.* The term *inquiry* probably seems somewhat distant from our everyday living, but that's not true. It is, in fact, very much a part of our lives. The question of how much high-cholesterol food is too much and how much exercise is required to provide aerobic benefit are inquiry problems. The conclusion that secondhand smoke is potentially harmful is the result of an inquiry investigation, and the now common ban on smoking in public places is an outcome of these results.

Many other examples exist. Congressional investigations, probes into alleged wrongdoing, and attempts to explain catastrophes such as airline crashes are all inquiry problems. The research studies cited throughout this text are all based on inquiry problems, which have attempted to answer questions such as, "Why do students in one kind of classroom learn more than those in another?"

Inquiry also occurs on a more personal level. An owner who compares her auto's gas mileage when she burns 85 octane gasoline to burning 91 octane is conducting an inquiry investigation.

Involving students in inquiry is an effective way to teach content, increase motivation, and help students develop their analytical thinking skills. Let's see how this can happen in the classroom.

Carlos Sanchez, a high school health teacher, is involved in a unit on drugs and drug use with his health students. In the process they've discussed how drugs influence the nervous system, the dangers of addictive drugs, and the possible overuse of prescription drugs, and now they have turned to over-the-counter medications.

"My dad takes two aspirin every night before he goes to bed," Jacinta offers during the discussion. "Do you think that's bad for him?"

"What kind of aspirin?" Jamie wondered out loud.

" . . . I dunno . . . I guess . . . Bayer. . . . Actually, yes, he makes jokes that Bayer is the best."

"Mr. Sanchez, is Bayer really the best?" asked Jacinta.

"That's an interesting idea," Carlos interjects. "Do we know if Bayer really is better? . . . Of course, the advertisers would have us believe that it's the only one that's any good, and way more Bayer is sold than any other brand."

"My mom takes the cheapest stuff she can find," Luanne shrugged. "We went to the drug store to get a prescription, and the guy . . . the prescription guy, said they're all alike."

"Really interesting!" Carlos smiled. "Let's see what we can find out about aspirin. . . . Let's think about it for a few minutes. How could we get a handle on whether or not Bayer really is better than another one, like maybe Norwich? . . . Go ahead and turn to the person next to you, take 3 minutes, and see if you can come up with some ways of answering that question. We'll brainstorm for a few minutes, and we'll go from there."

The students talked among themselves for the brief period. Carlos called them together, and they began to share their ideas.

"Go ahead, someone," Carlos encouraged.

" . . . We thought we could check the stuff in them . . . you know, look at the bottle to see if they have the same stuff in them . . . if one has more stuff, maybe it's better," Nina offered.

"Good idea," Carlos nodded smiling. "Who else? . . . Go ahead, Tamara."

" . . . We could check to see which one dissolved faster . . . 'cause they talk about how fast they're supposed to work . . . like if one dissolved faster than another one, maybe it works faster . . . so . . . maybe it's better."

"Also very good thinking," Carlos smiled, pleased with the responses.

"We could see which one made the pain go away faster," Jack added.

"That's also a good thought, Jack," Carlos responded. "We'll have to keep that one in mind to see how we might get at that information."

" . . . Maybe we could ask some people . . . You know like Luanne said her drug per-son . . . the pharmacist said they're all alike. Maybe we should ask a bunch of people and see what they say."

"That's excellent," Carlos shook his head and smiled. "That's really excellent thinking. . . . These are all good hypotheses—or best guesses about how to answer our questions. Let's go to work on them."

They decided, with some guidance from Carlos, that they wouldn't try to answer the question about which aspirin brand made the pain go away faster until they had gathered some information about the other questions.

With some additional guidance, the class organized themselves into teams, and the teams set out to gather information. They agreed that they would bring in at least three dif-ferent brands of aspirin, check the ingredients, conduct experiments to see which brand dissolved fastest, and interview their parents and pharmacists to gather their opinions.

Since this was Wednesday, the class agreed that they would have their interviews completed by the following Monday. They would gather their samples of aspirin by Friday and collect the rest of their data then.

Let's stop here and consider what Carlos did with his class. First, we see that his learning activity was a form of problem solving. The students were in a state (not knowing which aspirin was better) different from a desired state (knowing), and they had to devise a solution to move from the present to the desired state. We also see that they were dealing with an ill-defined problem, since the notion of "better" is some-what ambiguous.

The learning activity differed from typical problem solving, however, in that the so-lution to the problem involved gathering factual information, which would be used to answer a specific question. The specificity of the question and the extent to which data-gathering procedures are closely linked to the question distinguish inquiry from looser, more unstructured project-based learning. This attempt to answer a question through specific data-gathering procedures is the essence of an inquiry investigation. **Inquiry** *is a process that gathers facts and observations and uses them to answer questions.* Inquiry is par-ticularly valuable for giving students practice in defining informational questions, gath-ering data to solve those questions, and developing their abilities to analyze and evaluate data.

The basic steps in the inquiry process are outlined in Figure 10.4 and discussed in the sections that follow.

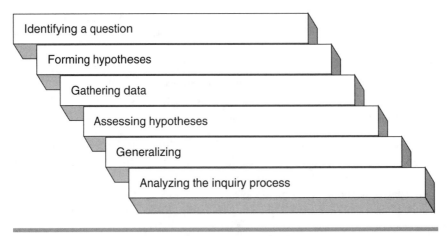

Figure 10.4 Steps in the Inquiry Process

Identifying a Question

The inquiry process begins by asking or identifying a question. The question for Carlos's students was determining which kind of aspirin is the best, or determining if Bayer is really better than other brands.

In many cases involving inquiry problems, an **operational definition,** or *a definition used for the purpose of the investigation,* is required. Carlos's students, for example, were operationally defining *better* as "dissolves faster," "has more effective ingredients," and "is endorsed by more people."

Operational definitions are also very much a part of our lives. For example, .1 percent blood alcohol level has been operationally defined in many states as the safe driving maximum. (In 1995 it was redefined in some states as .08 percent, which illustrates the fact that operational definitions are not absolute.) Borderline high blood pressure is operationally defined as 140 (systolic) over 90 (diastolic). Technically, death is operationally defined as absence of brain wave activity. If it were absolute or cut and dried, controversies about the removal of life support systems wouldn't exist. One of the benefits of inquiry activities is providing students experience in wrestling with operational definitions and how they work in our everyday lives.

For the teacher, the first step in planning for inquiry activities involves framing the content you would normally teach in ways that will allow students to gather and analyze data. Some examples of possible inquiry questions are offered in Table 10.3.

Forming Hypotheses

Once a question has been posed and analyzed, the class is ready to try to answer or address it. In framing the question in ways that information can be gathered to answer it, students are involved in the process of hypothesizing. An **hypothesis** *is a tentative solution to a problem that can be confirmed with facts or observations.* While Carlos's students didn't formally state hypotheses, they offered implicit hypotheses to their question with com-

Table 10.3 **INQUIRY PROBLEMS IN DIFFERENT CONTENT AREAS**

Content Area	Possible Question
English/Language arts	What factors influence the content of authors' works?
Science	How is plant growth affected by sunlight, water, or type of soil?
Social studies	What are the primary causes of wars and conflicts?
Building technology	What type of building material is best for different structures?
Health	What combinations of exercises is most effective for developing cardiovascular fitness?

ments such as, " . . . We thought we could check the stuff in them . . . you know, look at the bottle to see if they have the same stuff in them . . . if one has more stuff, maybe it's better," and " . . . like if one dissolved faster than another one, maybe it works faster . . . so . . . maybe it's better." They were tacitly hypothesizing that aspirin with more ingredients is better, as is aspirin that dissolves faster. Carlos moved the process forward by introducing the term *hypothesis* and defining it as a "best guess about how to answer our questions."

Gathering Data

Gathering data follows directly from the hypotheses generated. While seemingly straightforward, it requires guidance and direction from the teacher. To see how this works, let's return to Carlos's class and focus on one of the groups.

The students brought their aspirin samples to class on Friday and began their work in groups. First they wrote down the ingredients for each brand and then tried to measure how fast the samples dissolved.

"How are we going to do this?" Andrea wondered out loud to David and Lenita.

" . . . How about we drop them at the same time into the water, and watch them?" David suggested.

" . . . Good idea," Lenita confirmed.

The students poured some water from the tap into two plastic drink cups and dropped a Bayer in one and a Norwich in the second one.

"Sheesh, its hard to tell when it's dissolved," David noted after a few minutes.

Carlos, who had been watching the students' progress, stopped by the group and said, "Let's think about this for a minute. Look in the cups. What do you notice there?"

" . . . The . . . aspirins are . . . dissolved," Lenita said tentatively.

"Okay, and what else?"

"It was hard to tell," Andrea added.

"All right. . . . Anything else?"

" . . . "

"Look at the amount of water."

"Ahh," Lenita nodded with realization. "They're different."

"Dumb," David shrugged.

"Not at all," Carlos countered. "This is why we're doing this activity. See what you're learning from it? What do you notice about the aspirin in these two glasses, Lenita?"

"It looks like the aspirin in the glass with more water dissolved faster."

"Good, so what are two possible explanations for what happened? Andrea, give me one."

"This kind of aspirin (pointing to the one glass) dissolves faster."

"What's another one, David?"

"Hmm . . . or more water makes aspirin dissolve faster?"

"Now, what might you do?"

"Do it again and keep the amount of water the same," Andrea replied after some thought.

"Sure," Carlos encouraged. "And, as long as we're at it . . . what might you do about the fact that it's hard to tell when the aspirins are dissolved?" With some additional prompting, the students concluded that they would conduct several trials and could average the times to get the most accurate reading possible.

Carlos continued to move from group to group. Finally, as the period neared a close, he directed, "Turn in all your results to me on Monday *just before school,* and I'll have them on the board when our class begins. . . . Don't forget, *just before school on Monday.*"

From this episode, we see that teacher monitoring and appropriate intervention are important. Carlos watched the students as they worked, and he waited to intervene until they had considered the process and conducted a trial on their own. Had he intervened sooner, the opportunity and responsibility of doing their own thinking would have been taken away from them. In doing this, he demonstrated the essence of effective scaffolding.

As students acquire experience—with the teacher providing appropriate support—much can be learned about gathering accurate information. Andrea, David, and Lenita, for example, learned about controlling variables, conducting several trials to increase reliability, and averaging to summarize the information. Perhaps even more important than the actual results of the investigation, Carlos's students learned a great deal about the methods scientists use to gather and verify information. Many curriculum experts believe that experiencing these logical methods are among the most important goals in the classroom (Osborne, 1996).

Assessing Hypotheses

To examine this part of the process, let's look once more at Carlos's work with his students as he begins his class on Monday.

After completing his routines, he moved to the front of the room and said, "Now, everyone, we've had a lot of fun with this activity, but now we're at what is really the most important part of the whole process. . . . Just getting the information is one thing, but figuring out what it means is another. We're going to really learn a lot here today, so I want you to all be alert and think carefully about what we're doing."

He then turned to the board, where the ingredients for each brand were written, tables of dissolving times were displayed, and people's opinions were tallied.

"Let's see what we think all this means," Carlos directed. "What do you notice about the results?"

" . . . The ingredients are the same," Joanne observed.

"Not quite," Jeff countered. "Well, I guess they're almost the same."

"For the most part," Joanne confirmed.

"What do the rest of you think?" Carlos queried. The students discussed the ingredients for a few more minutes, concluded that essential ingredients were virtually the same, and decided that they couldn't conclude that one was better than another on the basis of the ingredients.

They then turned to the dissolving rates.

"Norwich dissolves faster than Bayer," Leroy offered.

"Not always," Kevin interjected.

"Its average is lower."

"True."

Again the class discussed the results. In the process, Dana wondered, "Because it dissolves faster, does that make it better?"

"Good point," Carlos smiled.

" . . . Yeah, but they advertise that it helps you fast. It has to dissolve to do that . . . doesn't it? . . . Sure it does. . . . a whole aspirin can't go into your bloodstream," Monica offered.

To chuckles from the class, Carlos wondered, "What do you think of Monica's argument?"

After a couple more minutes of discussion, Brad concluded with finality, " . . . It doesn't make sense to me, that dissolving slower . . . is better, since they tell us that . . . fast is good."

The class then turned to the opinion poll they had gathered, discussing the results in much the same way as they had done with the ingredients and dissolving times, and in the process they tentatively concluded that all aspirin are essentially the same.

"Now, we've tentatively concluded that all aspirin seem to be about the same," Carlos said, changing the direction of the discussion. "What does that suggest to us about other products, or does it suggest anything to us? What about McDonald's, Wendy's, and Burger King? Are they all the same? How about toothpaste . . . different brands of orange juice, milk . . . or even cars? Are there any conclusions that we can draw?"

The students offered a number of comments and, with Carlos's guidance, concluded that before they could make any sweeping conclusions they would have to know some things, such as: Are all the ingredients the same in different brands of toothpaste, for example, and are different cars equipped similarly? They also agreed to consider the opinion of "experts," such as *Consumers Report*.

"Before our time is all gone, I'd like us to think a little about what we did and why. How did we get started on this problem? Who remembers? Antonio?"

"Jacinta asked if Bayer was really the best."

"Good memory, Antonio. That's correct. Our inquiry started with a question. Then we had some tentative ideas or guesses. Who remembers what we call these tentative ideas? Shanda?"

"Hypotheses?"

"Fine, Shanda. Hypotheses are our best guesses about how the world works. And why was it important to use the same amount of water when we were trying to discover which kind of aspirin dissolved the quickest?"

Just then the bell rang. Carlos dismissed his class with a smile and, "Let's stop here. Good work, class. See you tomorrow."

The process of assessing hypotheses is arguably the most valuable part of inquiry lessons, and, as we saw in our earlier discussion of problem solving, social interaction and discussion are critical at this point. From their discussion Carlos's students acquired experience in several important aspects of the process. Among them were:

- Examining issues of reliability. For example, to what extent were the methods they used to measure dissolving rates reliable?
- Considering the appropriateness of peoples' opinions—and particularly the opinions of experts—in making conclusions about hypotheses.
- Using evidence (versus opinions, feelings, beliefs, or intuition) as a basis for forming conclusions.
- Developing tolerance for problems, questions, and issues that are somewhat ambiguous.

These are important life skills that arguably may contribute more to learners' educations than the content they learn.

Generalizing

That next step in an inquiry activity involves considering the generalizability of the results. Carlos initiated this discussion when he asked, "What does that suggest to us about other products, or does it suggest anything to us? What about McDonald's, Wendy's, and Burger King? Are they all the same? . . . Are there any conclusions that we can draw?"

In addition to assessing the results themselves, analyzing conclusions to see if they can be generalized to other situations is an important higher-order thinking skill.

Analyzing the Inquiry Process

In the final stage of the inquiry model, the teacher asks students to analyze and reflect upon the inquiry process. Carlos Sanchez initiated this stage when he said, "Before our time is all gone, I'd like us to think a little about what we did and why." In response to this request, students identified how inquiry began and how hypotheses guided the inquiry process. By talking about inquiry processes in the context of lessons, teachers make abstract ideas become real and help students see how inquiry plays out in real life.

Summary

Problem-Based Learning. Problem-based learning refers to a family of teaching strategies that use a problem or question as a focal point for student learning. They are designed to help students become self-directed learners as well as teach critical thinking skills and content. They are based on the philosophical foundations of John Dewey as well as the psychological underpinnings of constructivism.

Project-Based Learning. Project-based learning is an open-ended form of problem-based learning that allows students to investigate a question that is meaningful to them. Following the introduction of a question or problem, students work in groups to gather information to address the issue. The product of their efforts is some type of exhibit that serves as the focal point for a class discussion of the issues raised and content learned.

Problem Solving. Problems involve situations where individuals attempt to move from one state to another. Well-defined problems have clear goals and paths for reaching them, whereas ill-defined problems have vague goals without clear paths for reaching them.

Teachers can help learners become better problem solvers by presenting problems in meaningful contexts, discussing problems in detail, having learners practice defining problems, and scaffolding beginning problem solvers. Analyzing worked examples is one effective form of scaffolding.

Inquiry Strategies. Inquiry strategies give learners practice in defining problems, hypothesizing solutions, gathering data, and assessing hypotheses based on the data. Teachers can help students develop inquiry skills through multiple opportunities to practice them and by encouraging discussion of the process.

Important Concepts

Algorithm	Inquiry strategies
Anchored instruction	Operational definition
Exhibit	Problem
Heuristics	Problem-based instruction
Hypothesis	Project-based learning
Ill-defined problem	Self-directed learning
Inquiry	Well-defined problem

Reflecting on Teaching and Learning

As you've studied this chapter, you've seen how teachers can design and implement instruction to increase learners' problem-solving abilities. Please read the following case study now and consider how effectively the teacher implemented the ideas discussed in the chapter.

Leon Wilson has his high school American history students involved in a discussion of the events prior to the American Revolutionary War. He wants them to see how the cost of the conflicts between the British and French led to taxation of the American colonists, unrest, and ultimately to the Revolutionary War.

We join him as he begins his class.

"We made a beginning yesterday in trying to understand developments that led up to the Revolutionary War. Let's take a quick look at what we discussed," he began, after the bell had signaled the beginning of class and he completed his beginning-of-class routines.

"Where did we leave off? . . . Juan?"

". . . We started discussing how the French went into Canada and . . . the British . . . came here," Juan responded.

"Yes, good, Juan," Leon commented. "And what did we find out? Alberta?"

Alberta and a number of other students then described a series of events and their dates, such as Champlain creating Quebec City in 1608, and the fact that a number of cities, such as Detroit, St. Louis, New Orleans, and Des Moines were started by France—originally because of the fur traders, and forts were built there. They also noted that the British were originally east of the Appalachian Mountains, but gradually moved west.

They also observed that the French employed a seigniorial system, which offered settlers land if they would serve in the military; they had a better relationship with Native Americans than did the British; and the Iroquois nation was more powerful than either the French or the British.

As they responded, Leon wrote items of information on the board until finally they had a list:

FRENCH	BRITISH	CONFLICTS
Quebec 1608	Jamestown 1607	King William's War (1689–97)
Fur traders	Expanded west	Iroquois Nation dominant
Hudson Bay to Gulf of Mexico	New York—center of trade and commerce	Seven Years' War (1756–63)
Forts on Ohio-Mississippi Valley	Wars incredibly costly	Washington taken prisoner 1754
Influenced waned after 1763	Colonialists taxed	British naval blockades
80,000 population	Administrative difficulty in colonies	Quebec falls—1759
Wars incredibly costly	1,500,000 population	Treaty of Paris—1763
Related well to native Americans	Powerful navy	
Native Americans hurt by smallpox	Blockaded French in old and new world	
Seigniorial system		

"Now let's take a look at the information we have here," Leon continued. "Let's see if we can figure out, based on it, why some of the conflicts occurred," and he wrote on the board:

Why did conflicts occur between the French and the British?

"To help us get started, let's make some comparisons between the British and French."

". . . The British landed here . . . but the French went to Canada," Andrew volunteered.

"Okay," Leon responded. "What else? I haven't heard from you, Sue," smiling at her.

After Sue and several others offered additional comparisons, Leon refocused the class by saying, "Now let's think back to our question . . . why do you suppose the British and the French initially began to fight in these areas? . . . Sarah?"

" . . . The British were sort of fenced in by the mountains, so the French could do as they pleased. Then when the British went west, trouble started."

"Anyone else . . . How do you respond to Sarah's idea?"

After several more comments, the class generally agreed that Sarah's suggestion made sense.

"Now why do you suppose the French originally were more successful than the British? What do you think? . . . Dan?"

". . . Well . . . they had that signor . . . you know . . . system, so they were more motivated to fight, cuz of the land and stuff."

"Other thoughts? . . . Bette?"

". . . I think that the Native Americans were part of it. The French got along better with them, so they helped the French."

"Okay, but what about the British? . . . What advantages did they have? Stan?"

". . . Well, there were more British than French. There were more than a million British, and . . . well . . . also, the British came because of religion, and they brought their families. So they were really motivated to fight. The French were trappers . . . and you know . . . like . . . traders and they weren't as motivated."

"Good points, everyone. So then what happened to turn the tide against the French?"

". . . It cost too much. . . . See where it says that the British blockaded the French, and the wars were terrible costly."

"Very good thinking, everyone," Leon gestured and smiled. "Really good."

Leon continued guiding the students' analyses of the information they had listed as well as other information they recalled, and then he extended the discussion by asking the students to consider what the world might be like today if the outcome of the war had been different.

After several ideas and some disagreements, he said finally, "Now for tomorrow, I want you to consider a different question. . . . We know what happened in the French and Indian Wars, and we also know that the American Revolution followed in a matter of a few years. I want you to write one paragraph explaining how the French and British conflict caused, or at least contributed to, the American Revolutionary War. . . . Then we'll discuss them tomorrow. Be sure that you support your statements with information that we've read or discussed, just as we've been doing here in class."

Questions for Analysis

1. How effectively did Leon teach problem solving in his lesson? Describe what he might have done to make it more of a problem-solving activity.
2. Describe how Leon might have planned and implemented his lesson in an inquiry format.
3. In Chapter 9 you studied discussions as a teaching strategy. How well did Leon implement the characteristics of effective discussions in his lesson?
4. What kind of content—concept, generalization, principle, or organized body of knowledge—was Leon teaching? Explain.
5. As in most classes, Leon's students had diverse backgrounds. How effectively did his lesson accommodate the background differences of his students? Explain.

Discussion Questions

1. What are the major advantages of problem-based learning from a teacher's perspective? From a student's perspective?
2. Which form of problem-based instruction—project-based learning, problem solving, or inquiry—is most valuable for the content area or teaching level you'll find yourself at? Why?

3. Why do most of the problem-solving experiences that learners have in schools involve well-defined rather than ill-defined problems? What might teachers do to provide more experiences with ill-defined problems for learners?

4. Inquiry is infrequently used in schools. Why is this so? What could be done to increase the amount of inquiry conducted?

5. How constructivist were Carlos Sanchez and Leon Wilson in their lessons? Which of the two was the more constructivist? Why do you think so?

6. Some critics see the current emphasis on thinking skills as a fad. Others view the development of thinking skills as antagonistic to content acquisition (e.g., the idea of cultural literacy mentioned earlier). How would you respond to these critics?

7. Most teachers agree that teaching thinking skills is important. Since this is the case, why thinking so rarely taught? List several reasons. What might be done to overcome these obstacles?

Portfolio Activities

1. *Project-Based Learning.* Design and teach a unit based on project-based learning (or observe one taught by someone else). Analyze the unit afterwards using the following questions:

    a. Did the introductory question or problem serve as an effective focal point for students' investigative efforts?

    b. Were the teacher's grouping strategies effective?

    c. Did the teacher effectively use timelines to structure students' efforts?

    d. Did the teacher effectively monitor students?

    e. Did the learning exhibits reflect student learning?

    f. Did the teacher effectively use student exhibits as focal points for student learning?

    g. What suggestion do you have to improve the process?

2. *Problem Solving.* Plan and teach a problem-solving lesson (or observe one taught by someone else). Analyze the lesson afterwards using the following question.

    a. Was the problem well defined or ill defined? Why?

    b. How did the lesson encourage students to define the problem?

    c. How did students represent the problem?

    d. What type of strategies did students use to solve the problem? What heuristics were used?

    e. Were students encouraged to evaluate the results of their problem-solving efforts?

    f. What did the teacher do to help students become better problem solvers? What more could have been done?

3. *Inquiry.* Plan and teach an inquiry lesson (or observe one taught by someone else). Analyze and evaluate the lesson using the following questions.

    a. Was the question or problem well defined?

    b. Did students form a number of hypotheses?

    c. What kinds of data were gathered?

    d. How successful were students in assessing their hypotheses?

    e. Were students encouraged to generalize beyond their immediate problem?

    f. How could the lesson have been improved?

11

Teacher-Centered Instruction

*I*n this chapter we continue our study of teaching strategies and their effect on student learning. In earlier chapters we focused on learner-centered approaches to instruction as we described teaching based on constructivist views of learning, considered peer interaction models, and examined problem-based learning. In this chapter we turn to a detailed analysis of teacher-centered instruction.

Teacher-centered instruction has a long history in education (Cuban, 1986). Its usefulness is evidenced by its popularity and applicability to a wide range of teaching situations. In this chapter we analyze two of these applications. First we'll examine the use of direct instruction to teach concepts and skills at all grade levels, and then we'll look at ways to adapt lectures to make them meaningful for students. When you're through with your study of this chapter, you should be able to meet the following objectives:

- Identify areas of the curriculum that can be taught using teacher-centered instruction.
- Identify the major steps in teaching skills using direct instruction.
- Explain how lecture discussion can be used to involve students in learning.
- Describe different ways to organize content during lecture discussions.

Sean Barnett, a first-year second-grade teacher, is working with his students in a unit on addition. With his plan on his desk, Sean began math by saying, "Okay, kids, today we are going to go a step further with our work in addition so that we'll be able to solve problems like this," displaying the following on the overhead.

> *Jana and Patti are friends. They were saving special soda cans to get a free CD. They can get the CD if they save 35 cans. Jana had 15 cans and Patti had 12. How many did they have together?*

After pausing briefly to give students a chance to read the problem, Sean continued. "Now, why do you think it's important to know how many Jana and Patti have together?"

" . . . So they can know how much they get, like . . . so they can get their CD," Devon answered haltingly.

"Sure," Sean smiled. "If they know how many they have, they'll know how close they're coming to getting their CD. If they don't, they're stuck. That's why it's important. . . . We'll come back to the problem in a minute," he continued, "but before we do, let's review. Everyone take out your counter sticks and beans and do this problem."

Sean wrote the following numbers on the chalkboard and watched as students used their sticks and beans to demonstrate their answer.

$$\begin{array}{r} 8 \\ +7 \\ \hline \end{array}$$

"Very good," Sean smiled as most of the students laid a stick with 10 beans glued on it and 5 more beans on the centers of their desks. Others laid out 15 beans, and Sean showed them how they could exchange 10 of them for a stick with 10 glued on it.

Sean had the students do two more problems with their counters, then said, "Let's begin by looking at our problem again."

Turning on the overhead again, he said, "Everyone look up here. Good. Now what does the problem ask us? . . . Shalinda?"

"How many . . . they have together?" Shalinda responded hesitantly.

"And how many does Jana have? . . . Abdul?"

" . . . Fifteen?"

"Good, Abdul. And how many does Patti have? Celinda?"

"Twelve."

"Okay, so let's put the problem on the chalkboard like this." Sean wrote:

```
  15
+12
```

"Now I'd like everyone to show me how to make a 15 at your desk by using your sticks and beans."

Sean paused as the class worked at their desks.

"Does everyone's look like this?" Sean asked as he demonstrated at the flannel board.

They did the same with the 12, and Sean continued, "Now, watch what I do here. . . . When I add 5 and 2, what do I get? Hmm, let me think about that . . . 5 and 2 are 7. Let's put a 7 up on the chalkboard," he said as he walked to the chalkboard and added a 7.

```
  15
+12
   7
```

"Now show me that with your beans," and he watched as the students combined seven beans on their desks.

"Now we still have to add the 10s. What do we get when we add two 10s? Hmm, that should be easy. One 10 and one 10 is two 10s. Now look where I have to put the 2 up here. It is under the 10s column because the 2 means two 10s." With that, he wrote the following on the chalkboard.

```
  15
+12
  27
```

"So how many cans did Jana and Patti have together? . . . Alesha?"

" . . . 27?"

"Good, Alesha. They had 27 altogether. Now with your beans, what is this 7?" he asked, pointing to the 7 on the chalkboard. . . . Carol?"

" . . . It's this," she said, motioning to the seven beans on her desk.

"Good. Yes, it is. It's the seven individual beans. . . . Now . . . what is this 2? . . . Jeremy?" Sean went on, pointing to the numeral on the chalkboard.

"It's . . . these," Jeremy answered, holding up the two sticks with the beans glued on them.

"Now we saw that I added the 5 and the 2 before I added the two 1s. Why do you suppose I did that? . . . Anyone?"

"Maybe . . . you have to find out how many . . . ones you have to see if we can make a 10 . . . or something," Callie offered.

"That's excellent thinking, Callie. That's exactly right. We'll see why again tomorrow when we have some problems in which we'll have to regroup, and that will be just a little tougher, but for now let's remember what Callie said.

"Now who can describe in words for us one more time what the 2 means. . . . Leroy?"

"It's . . . two, ah, two . . . bunches or something like that of 10 beans."

"Yes, that's correct, Leroy. It's two groups of 10 beans or, in the case of Jana and Patti, it's two groups of 10 soda cans.

"So let's look again. There is an important difference between this 2," Sean points to the 10s column, "and this 2," pointing to the 2 in the 12. What is this difference? . . . Katrina?"

"That 2 . . . is two . . . groups of 10, and that one is just 2 . . . by itself."

"Yes, that's good thinking, Katrina. Good work, everyone. . . . Show me this 2," pointing to the 10s column.

The students held up two sticks with the beans glued on them.

"Good, and show me this 2," pointing to the 2 in the 12, and the students held up two beans.

"Great," Sean nodded. "Now let's try another one," he continued, displaying the following on the chalkboard.

$$\begin{array}{r} 23 \\ +12 \\ \hline \end{array}$$

Sean watched as students used their beans and sticks to make 35, and again they discussed the problem. They did two more, and then Sean gave the students an assignment of 10 more problems to do for homework (adapted from Eggen and Kauchak, 2001).

TEACHER-CENTERED AND LEARNER-CENTERED INSTRUCTION

A great deal has been written about the advantages of learner-centered compared to teacher-centered approaches to instruction (e.g., Lambert and McCombs, 1998; Shuell, 1996). This might lead some to conclude that the only appropriate approaches to instruction are learner centered, such as instruction based on constructivist views of learning, as we discussed it in Chapter 7, or the problem-based learning models we examined in Chapter 10.

This isn't true. For some goals teacher-centered approaches are more effective, and for others learner-centered approaches are superior (Shuell, 1996). Expert teachers are skilled with both. Helping you understand when teacher-centered instruction is effective and learning to plan and implement teacher-centered lessons are the goals of this chapter.

Teacher-centered instruction involves strategies "*in which the teacher's role is to present the knowledge to be learned and to direct, in a rather explicit manner, the learning process of the students*" (Shuell, 1996, p. 731). Research indicates that teacher-centered instruction is appropriate when content has one or more of the following characteristics (Eggen and Kauchak, 2001; Shuell, 1996):

- It is content that is specific and well defined. Adding one- and two-digit numbers, as Sean's students were doing, is an example.

- It is content that all students are expected to master. Sean's goal was for all his students to master the process of addition; it's a basic skill.
- It is content students would have difficulty obtaining on their own.

Making students responsible for constructing their own understanding of the procedure for adding two-digit numbers—as would be the case in instruction based on constructivism, for example—is inefficient and potentially confusing; for Sean's goals, a teacher-centered approach is more effective.

In looking back to earlier chapters, we can see that teacher-centered and learner-centered approaches are very compatible. For instance, the basic skills Sean's students mastered with his teacher centered approach are necessary for the problem-based learning models we discussed in Chapter 10. Sean's approach was teacher centered, and problem-based learning is more learner centered. Similarly, teachers might use a well-organized lecture discussion, a teacher-centered strategy, to help students acquire the background knowledge needed to carry on an effective discussion—a learner-centered process we discussed in Chapter 9.

Having identified goals for which teacher-centered approaches are appropriate, let's examine its characteristics.

CHARACTERISTICS OF TEACHER-CENTERED INSTRUCTION

To begin this section, let's look again at Sean's work with his second-graders. As we saw, Sean's goal was compatible with a teacher-centered approach; he was teaching well-defined content that all his students were expected to master. In addition, his instruction had the following characteristics:

- During planning, Sean identified specific objectives for the lesson and designed learning activities to help students meet the objectives.
- The lesson remained focused on the objectives.
- Sean took primary responsibility for guiding the learning by modeling and explaining a specific procedure for the skill.
- Students practiced the skill with the goal of developing automaticity.

TYPES OF TEACHER-CENTERED INSTRUCTION

Having identified content for which teacher-centered instruction is appropriate and having listed the characteristics of teacher-centered strategies, let's turn now to three teacher-centered approaches—direct instruction and two types of expository teaching, lectures, and lecture discussions.

DIRECT INSTRUCTION

At the beginning of the chapter we said that teacher-centered instruction involves well-defined content objectives and learning activities specified by the teacher, lessons that remain focused on the objectives, and teachers taking primary responsibility for guiding the learning. One teacher-centered approach, called **direct instruction,** *is a teacher-centered strategy designed to help students learn concepts and procedural skills.* Direct instruction is used when teachers want to ensure that all students master essential content (Gersten, Taylor, and Graves, 1999).

We discussed concepts and concept learning in detail in Chapter 8, so let's turn now to an examination of procedural skills.

Procedural Skills

Procedural skills have three essential characteristics:

- *They have a specific set of identifiable operations or procedures* (which is why they're called procedural skills).
- *They can be illustrated with a large and varied number of examples.*
- *They are developed through practice* (Doyle, 1983; Eggen and Kauchak, 2001).

Adding two-digit numbers, as we saw in Sean's lesson, is a procedural skill. The four basic operations—adding, subtracting, multiplying, and dividing—are procedural skills, as are simplifying expressions such as $9 + 3 \times 8 - 10/5$ or solving equations like $3(2x + 6) = 24$ in algebra. Solving algebraic equations obviously requires a more developed and sophisticated learner than do simple subtraction problems, but they are skills nevertheless.

Skills are not limited to math. Applying academic rules in any content area involves skills. For instance,

get   getting
jump   jumping
play   playing

The academic rule we follow for adding *ing* to words is "Double the ending consonant if it is preceded by a short vowel sound, but do not if it is preceded by another consonant or a long vowel sound." Applying this rule is a procedural skill, as are applying the rules for capitalization, punctuation, subject-verb agreement, and many others in the language arts curriculum.

Examples can also be found in other areas of the curriculum. When geography students use longitude and latitude to pinpoint locations, or when chemistry students balance equations, they are practicing procedural skills. They can be very basic, as in Sean's lesson, or very sophisticated, such as verifying identities in trigonometry; applying study skills such as summarizing in English; or using thinking skills such as recognizing irrelevant information in all curriculum areas.

Procedural skills are important because they apply in a variety of contexts. As a simple example, addition allows us to combine apples as well as dollars and cents. What we are adding doesn't matter; addition is an essential skill because it can be applied in a variety of situations. In a similar way, the ability to punctuate a sentence properly allows us to communicate in both school essays and love letters. Rosenshine (1983) called these abilities the "how to" of learning versus the who, what, where, or when. When students have learned a skill, they have an ability that will be useful in later learning.

Interestingly, recognizing the importance of procedural skills has occurred at the same time that technology has become a central component of American life and work. The need for people who can think and use technology in an intelligent manner has replaced the need for those who can simply remember large amounts of information (Jonassen, 1996).

Direct Instruction: The Research Base

A persuasive body of research exists suggesting that teacher-centered instruction is effective for helping students reach certain goals (Weinert and Helmke, 1995). This research comes from three primary sources:

- The teacher effectiveness literature
- Observational learning
- The work of Lev Vygotsky

The Teacher-Effectiveness Literature. The first source of support for the effectiveness of direct instruction can be found in the teacher effectiveness literature initially described in Chapter 1. These findings have been summarized as follows:

> Direct instruction can be characterized by the following features: (a) The teacher's classroom management is especially effective and the rate of student interruptive behaviors is very low; (b) the teacher maintains a strong academic focus and uses available instructional time intensively to initiate and facilitate students' learning activities; (c) the teacher ensures that as many students as possible achieve good learning progress by carefully choosing appropriate tasks, clearly presenting subject-matter information and solution strategies, continuously diagnosing each student's learning progress and learning difficulties, and providing effective help through remedial instruction.
>
> Many studies—both in the classroom and in the laboratory under experimental conditions—have shown that instruction in which the teacher actively presents information to students and supports individual learning processes is more effective than instruction in which the teacher's only role is to provide those external conditions that make individual or social learning success possible. (Weinert and Helmke, 1995, p. 138)

Observational Learning. The second source of support for direct instruction comes from a body of research on observational learning (Bandura, 1993, 1986). **Observational learning** *occurs when people acquire new attitudes, skills, and behaviors by watching and imitating the actions of others.* Modeling is one of the most important aspects of observational learning. **Modeling** *describes the tendency of people to imitate behaviors they observe in others,* and everyday examples are common. Teenagers imitate the fashion and hairstyles of athletes and celebrities, and young people imitate the behaviors of their parents. (Children are 10 times more likely to exercise if both their parents exercise than if neither exercises, for example.)

Students also imitate the behaviors of their teachers, and teachers take advantage of this tendency when they demonstrate positive attitudes such as tolerance and respect for other people. Teachers also use modeling to demonstrate complex skills such as writing and solving algebraic equations. Research indicates that teacher modeling is one of the most powerful vehicles available for teaching both attitudes and skills (Bandura, 1993).

Lev Vygotsky's Work: The Social Side of Skill Learning. Research on the social aspects of learning emphasizes the importance of verbal interaction in helping students acquire understanding and skills (Cohen and Lotan, 1997; Wertsch, 1991), and while direct instruction is teacher centered, much of its effectiveness results from the interaction between teachers and students.

Two concepts from the work of Lev Vygotsky, a Russian psychologist (1978), capitalize on this interaction. The first is **scaffolding,** which is *the instructional support teachers provide as students acquire skills.* Teachers can provide instructional scaffolding in a variety of ways, including breaking complex skills into subskills, asking questions and adjusting their difficulty, presenting examples, modeling the steps in solving problems, and providing prompts and cues.

The second is the **zone of proximal development,** which is *the state of learning in which a student cannot solve a problem or perform a skill alone but can be successful with the help of a teacher.* The zone of proximal development is instructional paydirt; it is within the zone that teachers are most effective in aiding learning. Outside the zone, students either don't need help (they have already mastered a new skill) or lack the prerequisite skills or background knowledge to benefit from instruction.

When using the direct instruction model, we attempt to implement lessons within students' zone of proximal development, using scaffolding as instructional support. For example, when Sean first introduced adding with two-digit numbers, many of his students were not able to perform this skill by themselves. By the end of the lesson, however, most of his students were able to perform the skill on their own. Sean had successfully helped his students move through the zone of proximal development by providing scaffolding in the form of questions, problems, and the bean counter sticks.

Goals of Direct Instruction

We have three goals when we use direct instruction to teach procedural skills—*understanding, automaticity,* and *transfer.* They are illustrated in Figure 11.1 and discussed in the sections that follow.

Understanding. The most fundamental of these goals is understanding, and, interestingly, this represents a change in thinking about teaching procedural skills. Historically, teaching skills typically consisted of three steps: (1) The teacher would describe the skill, (2) students memorized a series of steps and practiced the skill, and (3) teachers assessed the students' abilities to perform the skill. Little true understanding resulted; the teacher's goal was to teach students to follow the steps, *not* understand why the steps were necessary (Perkins and Blythe, 1994).

This has completely changed, and understanding is now strongly emphasized in direct instruction. Sean's lesson illustrates this emphasis. Let's look at some of his attempts to promote understanding. First, he presented the skill in the context of a real-world problem:

Jana and Patti are friends. They were saving special soda cans to get a free CD. They can get the CD if they save 35 cans. Jana had 15 cans and Patti had 12. How many did they have together?

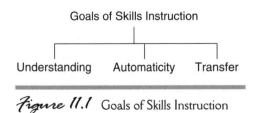

Goals of Skills Instruction

Understanding   Automaticity   Transfer

Figure 11.1 Goals of Skills Instruction

Then, after reviewing, he turned to an analysis of the problem. Let's examine some of the dialogue.

Sean: Everyone look up here. Good. Now what does the problem ask us? . . . Shalinda?
Shalinda: How many . . . they have together?
Sean: And how many does Jana have? . . . Abdul?
Abdul: Fifteen.
Sean: Good, Abdul. And how many does Patti have? Celinda?
Celinda: Twelve.
Sean: Okay, so let's put the problem on the chalkboard like this (*and he wrote the 15 plus 12 on the board*).

Sean then demonstrated adding the problem and returned to questioning.

Sean: Now show me that with your beans (*and he watched as the students combined seven beans on their desks*).
Sean: So how many cans did Jana and Patti have together? . . . Alesha?
Alesha: Twenty seven.
Sean: Good, Alesha. They had 27 altogether. Now, with your beans, what is this 7 (*pointing to the 7 on the chalkboard*). . . . Carol?"
Carol: It's this (*motioning to the seven beans on her desk*).
Sean: Good. Yes, it is. It's the seven individual beans. Now, what is this 2? . . . Jeremy (*again pointing to the numeral on the board*).
Jeremy: It's . . . these (*holding up the two sticks with the beans glued on them*).

Two aspects of Sean's teaching are important here. First, he did very little explaining; he helped students understand the skill primarily through questioning. This strategy not only placed them in active roles but also allowed Sean to monitor their understanding. Second, he had his students demonstrate the meaning of the numbers with concrete examples (such as having Jeremy demonstrate with the sticks and beans that the 2 in 27 was two groups of 10). He strongly stressed understanding and deemphasized memorization.

His emphasis on understanding was even more clearly demonstrated later in the lesson. Let's look at some more dialogue that illustrates Sean's attempt to help his students understand how the 2 in 12 is different from the 2 in 27.

Sean: So let's look again. There is an important difference between this 2 (*pointing to the 2 in 27*) and this 2 (*pointing to the 2 in the 12*). What is this difference? . . . Katrina?
Katrina: That 2 . . . is two groups of 10, and that one is just 2 by itself.
Sean: Yes, that's good thinking, Katrina. Good work, everyone. . . . Show me this 2 (*pointing to the 2 in 27, and seeing the students hold two sticks with the beans glued on them*).
Sean: Good, and show me this 2 (*pointing to the 2 in the 12, and seeing the students hold up two beans*).

Again, Sean focused on understanding by emphasizing the difference between the *units* place and the *tens* place, and he cleverly used the same numeral (2) to help make his point as clear as possible. His lesson clearly demonstrates the emphasis that is now placed on understanding in teaching procedural skills.

Automaticity. When we teach procedural skills, we want students to "overlearn" them to the point where they can use the skills effortlessly and virtually without conscious thought. We call this the point of automaticity. **Automaticity** *occurs when skills are overlearned to the point where they can be used with little mental effort.* Learning to drive a car is an example. Initially we clutch both hands to the wheel, devoting all of our attention to the process of driving. As automaticity develops, we can talk on cell phones, put on makeup, and even shave—as we see other people doing—while driving. Automatized skills are: (1) fast, (2) effortless, (3) consistent, and (4) free of the need for conscious control (Logan, 1988). These characteristics allow us to plug in the skills while we perform other cognitive operations.

This last point is a strong argument for overlearning (Weinert and Helmke, 1995). Our available working memory is limited, and automatized skills free memory space that can be devoted to more complex tasks. For example, in writing a paper, if we have learned word processing skills to the point of automaticity, we use them effortlessly, allowing us to concentrate on organization and development of the paper. Similarly, if students have overlearned basic math operations, they can focus their mental energy on the solutions to word problems. Research indicates that one of the reasons poor math students have difficulties with word problems is that performing the necessary procedural skill requires so much available memory that they have too little left to think about or solve the problem (Leinhardt, 1987).

Transfer. When we teach skills, we also want them to be used in a wide variety of settings and situations. **Transfer** *occurs when a concept or skill learned in one context can later be applied in a different context.* Transfer occurs, for example, when writing skills learned in English are applied in writing assignments in science and social studies. Transfer also occurs when a student learns map-reading skills in geography and uses those skills to help plan a family trip. Our ultimate goal in teaching procedural skills is to have them transfer both to other subject-matter areas and into the real world.

Accomplishing these goals requires careful planning. This is the topic of the next section.

Planning for Direct Instruction

Planning for direct instruction lessons involves three steps:

- Specifying a clear goal
- Identifying prerequisite knowledge
- Preparing examples

Specifying Clear Goals. As with effectively planning for any form of teaching, having a precise goal in mind when teaching procedural skills is essential. Sean, for example, had two goals:

- For students to be able to add two-column numbers when regrouping wasn't required.
- For students to explain the difference between the ones place and the 10s place in a two-column number.

As we saw during his lesson, while both goals were important, Sean put a great deal of emphasis on the second one. This emphasis was a result of his clear thinking about specific goals. To promote understanding in skills instruction, this kind of teacher thinking during planning is crucial.

Identifying Prerequisite Knowledge. The direct instructional model focuses on teaching and learning specific concepts or skills. However, research on learning indicates that all new learning depends on what students already know—their background knowledge (Eggen and Kauchak, 2001). Background knowledge provides hooks for new learning. In planning for direct instruction lessons, teachers need to consider how the concept or skill will be introduced and connected to what students already know.

Planning for accessing prerequisite knowledge is slightly different for teaching a concept as compared to teaching a skill. For concepts, the task usually involves identifying a superordinate concept to which the concept can be linked. Though the goal in direct instruction may be to understand a specific concept (or concepts), a broader goal is for students to understand how the concept relates to other ideas.

Identifying prerequisites for a skills lesson is slightly more complicated because it involves identifying subskills that lay the foundation for the new skill. **Task analysis,** or *the process of breaking a skill into its subparts,* which we discussed in Chapter 3, can be helpful here. Sean, for example, taught—and reviewed—one-column addition before he moved to two-column addition. And his students had to know basic math facts—additional prerequisites—before they could solve addition problems.

Selecting Examples and Problems. The final phase in planning for direct instruction lessons is selecting examples or problems. A strength of direct instruction is the opportunities it provides for practice, but this practice takes different forms with different kinds of content. In learning a concept, students can relate the definition to examples and can categorize examples themselves. In learning a skill, sample problems both help students understand the procedures and give them a chance to practice the skill on their own. In both instances—concept learning or skill learning—selecting concrete examples and problems is essential to the success of the lesson.

In teaching concepts with the direct instruction model, the teacher has two tasks—selecting and sequencing the examples. Examples are selected based on the extent to which they illustrate the concept's essential characteristics.

After selecting examples, the next task is to sequence them. Usually, the clearest and most obvious ones are presented first. For example, when teaching a simple concept, such as *mammal,* we would first use obvious examples like *dog, cat, cow,* or *horse* rather than *whale, seal,* or *bat.* Once learners begin to understand the concept, additional examples can be used to enrich their understanding.

The extent to which examples illustrate the essential characteristics is a second way to think about sequencing. Again in a lesson on mammals, *dog* and *cat* are good examples because they clearly illustrate characteristics such as being furry, warm blooded, and milk producers. Further, most students have had direct experiences with these mammals, which makes them more meaningful.

In selecting and sequencing examples and problems for skill acquisition, student success is important. One reason for using the direct instruction model is to help students acquire proficiency with the skill as efficiently as possible. This suggests that problems should be selected and sequenced so that students can develop both the skill and confidence through successful practice.

Sean helped accomplish this goal by providing the easiest problems first. He first used problems that involved single-digit addition and then moved to two-column addition. As his students' skills develop, he will move to two-column problems that require regrouping and then to problems with three columns or more. By sequencing from simple to complex, Sean provided instructional scaffolding that ensured high success rates and minimized frustration and confusion.

Having identified goals, determined prerequisite knowledge and skills, and selected and sequenced examples and problems, the teacher is ready to put these planning steps into action.

Implementing Direct Instruction Lessons

Implementing lessons using the direct instruction model occurs in four phases. They are illustrated in Table 11.1 and discussed in the sections that follow.

Phase 1: Introduction. The introduction phase in a direct instruction lesson performs several functions. First, it draws students into the activity; without student attention, the teacher's best efforts are wasted. In addition, the introduction provides an overview of the content to follow, allowing students to see where the lesson is going and how it relates to content already learned (Gersten et al., 1999). The introduction also provides opportunities for the teacher to motivate students, to explain how the new content will be beneficial to them in the future. Let's examine each of these functions.

FOCUS. In Chapter 4 we defined **focus** as *the process teachers use to attract and maintain students' attention during a learning activity.* It is important to draw students into any lesson

Table 11.1 PHASES IN DIRECT INSTRUCTION LESSONS

Step	Description	Example
Introduction	A lesson overview is provided and an attempt is made to motivate students.	Sean presented the problem of Jana and Patti wanting to buy a CD and had the students explain why it was important.
Presentation	The concept or skill is explained and illustrated.	Sean demonstrated addition of two-column numbers and had the students demonstrate their understanding with hands-on materials.
Guided practice	Students practice with the concept or skill under the guidance of the teacher.	Sean had his students demonstrate the solutions to problems while he monitored their progress.
Independent practice	Students practice on their own.	Sean gave his students 10 problems to do for homework.

and to focus their attention on the learning task. However, research indicates that teachers often neglect this important function; in one study of skills instruction, researchers found that only 5 percent of the teachers made a conscious attempt to draw students into the lesson (Anderson et al., 1984).

Sean used his soda can problem as a form of focus. It gave a context for the lesson and provided an umbrella for the skill that the students were learning.

As another example, let's look at a science teacher introducing the skill of controlling variables. He begins by referring students back to a concrete experience they had the previous day.

"We talked yesterday about experiments and how experiments help us learn about cause-and-effect relationships. We talked about manipulating or changing something, like in our gerbil food experiment. Today, we're going to talk about how to control variables to make our experiment more precise. Let's talk about the experiment we did yesterday."

Similarly, an art teacher who has been working on one-point perspective and is making the transition to two-point describes similarities and differences between drawing the two types of pictures. In each of these examples, the teacher links new material to old, ensuring that the new skill is integrated with familiar ones.

MOTIVATION. A second element in the introductory phase of the model addresses motivation. Research indicates that positive teacher expectations and student accountability contribute to student achievement (Good and Brophy, 2000). Teachers can address both of these variables by communicating that the skill is important and that they all can learn it if they work and persevere.

To illustrate, let's look at Sean's lesson again. He presented the problem, saying that Jana and Patti were saving soda cans to get a free CD and that Jana had saved 15 cans and Patti 12.

Sean: Now, why do you think it's important to know how many Jana and Patti have together?

Devon: So they can know how much they get, like . . . so they can get their CD.

Sean: Sure. If they know how many they have, they'll know how close they're coming to getting their CD. If they don't, they're stuck. That's why it's important.

This simple step took very little time or effort, and it increased the likelihood that the problem would be meaningful and that students would think it was important.

Having set the stage both cognitively and affectively, the teacher is ready to move to the next stage.

Phase 2: Presentation. In the second phase of the model, the teacher presents and demonstrates the skill or defines the concept. This part of the lesson is both the most crucial to skills instruction and the most difficult to implement (Duffy et al., 1985).

Teachers have two goals in explaining a skill. First, we want students to understand the skill and how it works; second, we want them to understand its usefulness and importance. Earlier, we saw how strongly Sean emphasized understanding in his lesson. He developed the presentation phase with questioning and he encouraged student involvement throughout the presentation phase.

To illustrate this emphasis again, we want to repeat a portion of the dialogue where Sean was attempting to help the students see the difference between the 2 in 12 and the 2 in 27.

Sean: So let's look again. There is an important difference between this 2 (*pointing to the 2 in 27*) and this 2 (*pointing to the 2 in the 12*). What is this difference? . . . Katrina?"

Katrina: That 2 . . . is two groups of 10, and that one is just 2 by itself.

Sean: Yes, that's good thinking, Katrina. Good work, everyone. . . . Show me this 2 (*pointing to the 2 in 27, and seeing the students hold two sticks with the beans glued on them*).

Sean: Good, and show me this 2 (*pointing to the 2 in the 12, and seeing the students hold up two beans*).

It is difficult to overemphasize the importance of this type of questioning and involvement for student learning. Without it, direct instruction becomes a teacher monologue, leaving students bored and disinterested.

Let's look at another example, in which Tanya Davis, an English teacher, wants her students to understand the proper use of semicolons.

Tanya: Class, today we're going to continue our discussion of different kinds of punctuation. Who remembers the different kinds of punctuation we've learned about so far? . . . Shelly?

Shelley: Commas and periods.

Tanya: Good, and who can tell us why we use punctuation in our writing? . . . Jon?

Jon: To help the reader understand what we're trying to say.

Tanya: Fine. Now we are moving on to semicolons. After today's lesson you'll be able to use semicolons to punctuate your sentences. Semicolons are a hybrid between commas and periods. They tell the reader, "There is a pause here—pause a little longer than a comma but not as long as a period." Because they're a hybrid, they look like this (*and Tanya writes ; on the board*). One use of a semicolon is between two independent clauses that are not joined by *and, but,* or *or.* They're useful for adding variety to our writing; they're an alternative to using conjunctions. For example, look at this sentence (*and Tanya displays, "The teacher was concerned about the quiz scores; he planned a special review session." on the overhead*). What are the two independent clauses here? Celeena?

Celeena: "The teacher was concerned about the test scores," and "he planned a special review session."

Tanya: Good. Notice how the ideas in the two clauses are related. That's why we don't use a period. Note, too, that the sentence could also be written this way (*and Tanya then displayed "The teacher was concerned about the quiz scores, so he planned a special review session." on the overhead*).

Tanya: In this case, we wouldn't need a semicolon. Let's take another sentence and see how a semicolon would work here (*displaying "We had to wait in line for hours but the rock concert was well worth the wait."*). What are the two independent clauses? . . . Gustavo?

Gustavo: "We had to wait in line for hours," and "the rock concert was worth the wait."
Tanya: Good. . . . So how would I write this using a semicolon? . . . Biela?
Biela: "We had to wait in line for hours," semicolon, and then "The rock concert was worth the wait."

Three aspects of Tanya's presentation are important:

- She described and explained the skill (using semicolons in writing).
- She provided clear examples of when and how the skill is used. (She gave examples of using semicolons in sentences.)
- She used questioning to involve the students throughout the presentation.

MODELING AND THINKALOUDS. The importance of examples in skills learning cannot be overemphasized. As we saw in Chapters 7 and 8, examples help students link abstractions such as concepts and generalizations to the real world. For skills, examples provide a concrete context in which the skill is performed. We saw earlier in the chapter that teachers model behaviors that they want their students to imitate; **thinkalouds** *are forms of modeling in which teachers describe their thinking while working with examples.* When teachers use thinkalouds, they want their students to imitate their thinking. Both Sean and Tanya used thinkalouds in the presentation phase of their lessons.

Extra care and effort in the presentation phase, as we saw in both Sean's and Tanya's lessons pay off in the next phase. Researchers have found that teachers who are effective in this phase provide many examples, give additional explanations when needed, check for student understanding, and involve their students throughout. In contrast, less effective teachers often spend little time in this phase, instead moving too quickly to student practice (Good, Grouws, and Ebmeier, 1983). Consequently, students are less successful, and the teacher often has to slow down or back up to help individual students correct problems and misconceptions. In extreme cases, unsuccessful students become frustrated, quit, and management problems occur.

Phase 3: Guided Practice. When the teacher feels that the class has a basic understanding of the skill, students are ready for guided practice. In this phase, the teacher provides additional examples and gives students only enough support to ensure that they can make progress on their own (scaffolding). As learners move through the zone of proximal development during this phase, they gradually accept more and more of the responsibility for demonstrating the skill.

Sean's students were involved in the guided practice phase when he gave them the problem of adding 23 and 12 and watched carefully to be sure they were able to demonstrate the solution with the beans and sticks. As their understanding increased, Sean would stop having them use the beans and sticks—using only the numerals instead—but his emphasis at this point was to ensure, as much as possible, that they truly understood the skill rather than simply memorizing the procedure.

Student answers and success rates are barometers of learning progress in this phase. As the phase begins, some uncertainty will exist; when it ends, learners should be 80–90 percent successful. Choosing appropriate examples, sequencing them from simple to complex, and eliciting correct answers and reasons as the students practice all influence learners' successes. Finally, this phase provides access to student errors, thus providing an opportunity to correct or "debug" common errors (Bruning et al., 1999). Let's see how this works with Sean and his students.

Sean's students have progressed to the point where they are now practicing subtraction where regrouping is required. This is a more demanding skill than just simple subtracting, so the likelihood of misunderstanding and errors is greater than it was with the simple two-column addition we saw earlier.

Let's see how Sean handles misunderstanding during the guided practice phase.

"Let's try one more," Sean directed. "Kim, Mario, Kevin, and Susan come up to the board and try this one. The rest of you work it at your seat and see if they get the right answer.

He then wrote the following on the board:

46
−8
───

As he watched the students at the board, he noticed that all had done the problem correctly except Kevin who was standing, staring at the board. He walked over to Kevin, put his hand on Kevin's shoulder and said, "Kim, can you explain what you did?"

" . . . "

"What did you do first, Kim?"

"I tried to subtract 8 from 6."

"And what happened?"

"I couldn't."

"Why not?"

"Because 8 is bigger than 6."

"So then what did you do?"

"I borrowed."

"Did everyone hear that?" Kevin asked turning to the class. "Kim tried to subtract 8 from 6 but she couldn't. So she had to borrow. Show us how you did that, Kim."

"Well, I went to the 4 and crossed it out and made it a 3."

"Now, what was this 4?" Sean probed, pointing to the 4.

" . . . "

"Was it four 10s, or was it four 1s?"

" . . . Four 10s."

"How do you know?"

" . . . It's here" (*pointing to the 4 to indicate that it is in the 10s column*).

"So when you crossed out the 4 and made it a three what were you doing?"

"Borrowing! Uh . . . I was borrowing 10 from the 40 and making it 30."

"Excellent, Kim. And where did that 10 go? Kevin do you know?"

"Did we add it to the 6?"

"Good thinking, Kevin. Now can you subtract the 8 from 16?"

"8?"

"Good, write it down. And how much is left in the 10s column?"

"3 . . . 1 . . . I mean 30."

"Write that down, too. So what is the correct answer, Kevin?"

"Thirty-eight."

"Good work, Kevin. Now let's try another one to be sure."

Two aspects of this process are important. First, as he did throughout the lesson, Sean emphasized understanding rather than merely performing the skill. Second, he helped Kevin—and the rest of the class—understand the process by questioning them rather than explaining the process to them. When students struggle to understand concepts and skills, our tendency is to try and solve the problem by explaining but, unfortunately, explaining—alone—often does little to increase understanding. The questioning skills Sean demonstrated are critical to developing understanding.

CHECKING FOR UNDERSTANDING. Student responses are essential for gauging learning progress. At least two aspects of effective interaction are important during this stage of the model (Rosenshine and Stevens, 1986). First, be sure to get information from as many students as possible. This ensures that *all* students understand the skill, not just ones who volunteer. One way to do so is to call on nonvolunteers as well as volunteers. (This is the equitable distribution we discussed in Chapter 5.) Other ways of assessing understanding are to ask for a simple show of hands or an unobtrusive thumbs up or thumbs down on the chest indicating those who got the problem right or have students work three or four problems and check the work by switching papers.

In this process, queries such as, "Are there any questions?" are generally not helpful. If there are questions, the students who have them usually won't admit it. (Think back on your own experience; none of us wants to admit that we don't understand something—everyone assumes he or she is the only one who is confused.)

Second, gauging the quality of student answers is important. Correct, quick, and firm answers indicate that students understand the skill, and the teacher can use general praise, such as a simple, "Good answer," in response (Rosenshine, 1983). This maintains a brisk lesson pace, allowing additional examples. Correct but hesitant answers suggest that students are not confident about the new skill, and the teacher can respond with appropriate supports such as interspersed explanations and encouraging feedback (e.g., "Yes, the apostrophe in this case indicates a contraction, not a possessive. We see there is no possession suggested in the sentence.")

Incorrect but careless answers also need to be differentiated from more serious problems. If the teacher thinks the student understands the process but got the answer wrong because of a rushed answer (e.g., a computational error), she can simply correct the error and move on. If, however, the mistake appears to indicate a misunderstanding of the skill, additional explanation and questioning will be needed to help correct the misconception. If a number of students are making errors, the material may need to be retaught.

THE MOTIVATIONAL BENEFITS OF EFFECTIVE FEEDBACK. As students wrestle with the new skill, teachers provide feedback. The quality of this feedback influences student motivation in two ways. First, information assists in the learning process, allowing students to learn the skill more efficiently. Seeing their own learning progress is a powerful form of student motivation (Pintrich and Schunk, 1996). Second, the content and tone of the feedback influences students' perceptions of their ability as learners.

Effective feedback increases student motivation by making the process of skill acquisition more efficient. Effective feedback has four essential characteristics:

- It is immediate.
- It is specific.

- It provides corrective information for the learner.
- It has a positive emotional tone.

(Brophy and Good, 1986; Rosenshine and Stevens, 1986)

As students try out the new skill, the teacher assists by pinpointing errors, suggesting correct alternatives and doing this in a positive and supportive manner.

A more subtle motivational aspect of feedback focuses on the implicit messages it gives about student competence and effort (Pintrich and Schunk, 1996). As students struggle to master a new skill, teacher comments about effort help reinforce the idea that effort results in achievement. Comments such as, "This is a tough idea but hang in there," and "I know your hard work will pay off," help focus students' attention on the critical link between effort and learning. These comments are especially useful for low ability students and students with learning problems.

However, as with all strategies, teacher sensitivity and judgment are essential. If teachers praise profusely when effort is minimal, for example, students tend to discredit the feedback and their own efforts and abilities as learners.

Phase 4: Independent Practice. Earlier in the chapter we said that one of the goals of direct instruction was to develop automaticity. This is the purpose of the independent practice phase. This practice typically occurs in two steps. In the first, students practice the skill as a seatwork assignment, so the teacher can give them some extra help if necessary and spot check their progress. In the second, students practice the skill as an out-of-class assignment, such as homework (Murphy et al., 1986).

An important transition occurs here. In previous stages student interactions were with the teacher, and the purpose of instruction was to help them understand the skill and how it should be performed. Now student interactions are primarily with materials—problems and examples—and the purpose of practicing is to develop mastery and automaticity.

EFFECTIVE INDEPENDENT PRACTICE. Research has identified several factors that can improve the quality of independent practice:

- Independent practice should always be preceded by careful presentation and guided practice to ensure understanding.
- Independent practice should be directly related to the content covered earlier in the lesson. This seems self-evident, but surprisingly seatwork, and particularly homework, is often unrelated to previous content (McGreal, 1985). Seatwork and homework do not teach; they reinforce earlier learning!
- Monitor students as they work alone. This increases on-task behavior and helps teachers assess learning progress. Research indicates that teachers who circulate during seatwork have engagement rates that are significantly higher than those who sit at their desks (Fisher et al., 1980).
- Use "response-to-need" questions and success rates as measures of effectiveness for independent practice (McGreal, 1985).

This last point needs further explanation. Response-to-need means that students are raising their hands because they need help and they are "responding to the need." While some teacher assistance is totally appropriate, if too many students are raising their hands or if the required explanations take too long (30 seconds or more), independent practice is not accomplishing its goal. If this happens, the teacher should move back to the guided practice or even the presentation phase before continuing. No rule exists to tell the teacher exactly how many response-to-need questions are too many, so judgment is again required.

Problem situations are often quite apparent. We have observed classes where the introduction and presentation phases were brief and somewhat cursory, guided practice was omitted entirely, and the teacher proceeded directly to independent practice. Students obviously had little idea of what they were supposed to do, so hands were up all over the room, and the teacher was running herself ragged trying to keep up with individual problems. Unconsciously, the teacher had—in effect—individualized instruction; each student had the skill explained to him or her individually. This is not only inefficient in terms of learning but also enormously demanding on the teacher. Predictably, classroom management problems also develop because students are unable to do the seatwork exercises, so they become frustrated and go off task.

As with guided practice, success rates during independent practice also help gauge its effectiveness. Students should be about 90 percent successful in their seatwork if it is effective (McGreal, 1985).

HOMEWORK. Homework is the logical extension of seatwork done in class, and it is a common strategy for increasing the amount of time students spend on a topic. Research on the effects of homework indicate that it generally increases learning (Corno and Xu, 1998; Cooper et al., 1998). An analysis of 15 studies comparing differing amounts of homework found an average effect large enough to move students from the 50th to the 65th percentile in achievement (Walberg et al., 1985).

For homework to be effective, it must be a logical extension of classroom work (Gage and Berliner, 1998), and success rates should be similar or even higher than those students experience during their seatwork. To provide focus and prevent confusion, assignments should be written on the board rather than given orally.

Homework assignments should be kept relatively short; researchers suggest that no assignment should take an elementary student longer than 20 minutes to complete (McGreal, 1985). You may disagree with this figure, but many homework assignments are excessive. If the presentation and guided practice phases are properly executed, students should be able to complete their assignments quickly and effectively. When this happens, performance improves and motivation increases.

Researchers have also found that in addition to amount, the frequency of homework is important; for example, 10 problems every night is more effective than 50 once a week (Walberg et al., 1985). Students should expect homework as one of their classroom routines, and it should be collected, scored, and returned. Alternatives for grading homework will be discussed in Chapter 12 when we examine assessment.

LECTURE DISCUSSIONS: TEACHER-CENTERED STRATEGIES FOR TEACHING ORGANIZED BODIES OF KNOWLEDGE

In the first part of the chapter we saw how teacher-centered instruction could be used to help students learn concepts and procedural skills. In this section we turn to lecture discussions and examine the types of learning for which they are most appropriate. Let's begin our study with a look at a social studies teacher using the strategy to help students understand political compromise.

Velda Houston is an American government teacher continuing a unit on the Constitution, including topics such as the electoral college, the branches of government, and the role and function of each branch.

As Velda planned the lesson, she sat and outlined her topic. In her notebook she sketched the information shown in Figure 11.2.

She put the information on a transparency and headed for her first-period class.

As the bell rang, Velda began, "Listen everyone. . . . To continue our work on the Constitution, I'd like to pose a problem to you. Mrs. Shah [another teacher in the school] has a special project she wants done, and she wants the smartest kid she can find to do it. Manolo wants the job and thinks he is qualified. He's a good writer and gets good grades on his essays. However, Jo also wants the job, and she thinks she is better qualified than Manolo. She's a whiz in math. What is Mrs. Shah going to do?"

"What are they supposed to do in the project?" Katy wondered.

"Well, a variety of things," Velda responded. "Mrs. Shah will have them doing things that involve math and some that involve writing."

"Boy, it's hard to tell," Ramon added. "How would you know?"

"Maybe take them both," Sue suggested. "Could she do that?"

"That's an excellent idea, Sue. Why not compromise and take them both? Think about that everyone?"

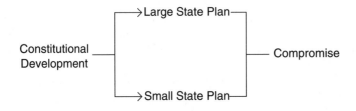

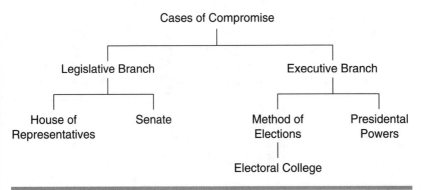

Figure 11.2 Organizational Scheme for Lesson on Constitutional Compromise

She paused a moment and then went on, "The situation we're going to discuss today is sort of an analogy to Mrs. Shah's problem. The makers of our country's Constitution were in a dilemma when it came to making a decision about how to elect our leaders. The compromises that had to be made are what we're going to discuss today."

Velda then strode across the front of the room and continued by saying, "I know I've said it before, but it's so important I'll have to repeat it again. The Constitution was a series of compromises between people like you and me. Just as Mrs. Shah could compromise and perhaps take both Manolo and Jo, the people who developed the Constitution had very different views of where this new country was heading. To arrive at something they could all agree on, they had to compromise.

"The forms of the compromise are diagrammed on the transparency you see," Velda said, displaying the information she had outlined on the overhead, and Velda displayed the information in Figure 11.2.

She continued, "The nature of this compromise process came out very clearly in the part of the Constitution having to do with the way we elect the members of Congress. Originally, when our forefathers were writing the Constitution, there was a lot of disagreement about how votes in the legislature should be allocated. States like Rhode Island wanted each state to have the same number of votes. Delaware felt the same way. On the other hand, New York and Pennsylvania wanted the votes to be determined by the number of people in the state. . . . Each idea seemed the most fair to the states who proposed them. The small states wanted them allocated by state; the large states wanted the votes to be distributed on the basis of population. Both of the ideas seemed fair, and neither side wanted to give in.

"So, as a compromise, they created a legislature with two bodies. The House of Representatives was based on population, and today we have 435 representatives. The most populous states, of course, have many more representatives than smaller ones. On the other hand, the Senate has two members from each state. So now we have 50 states times two equals 100 senators.

"Now let's analyze this process of compromise. How were the states supporting the two proposals different? . . . Miguel?"

" . . . New York was a large state, and Rhode Island was a very small state."

"Yes, good, Miguel," Velda smiled. "And what does that mean? . . . Jamie?"

" . . . Well, it was bigger," Jamie responded hesitantly.

"Bigger land area or bigger population or what?" Velda continued.

" . . . Both, I think," Jamie continued. "But probably the bigger population was most important."

"Yes, good, Jamie. Now why would the large states feel the way they did, and also why would the small states feel the way they did? What do you think? . . . Simao?"

" . . . It would relate to power," Simao answered. "If the representation was made on the basis of population, the large states would be more powerful than the small states."

"On the other hand, what would happen if representation were completely equal among the states?" Velda continued. "Toni?"

" . . . It would sort of throw the balance in the favor of the smaller states. It would mean a state like Wyoming with very little population could maybe stop a proposal from a big state like California."

"So as part of the process of compromise, what part of the legislature is based on population? . . . Camille?

"The . . . the House of Representatives?"

"Excellent, Camille. The total number of representatives is 435. The number of repre-sentatives from each state is determined by population. That would make populous states happy. And what part of the compromise made the smaller states happy? . . . Kareem?"

"The Senate?"

"Why, Kareem?"

"Because every state gets two, no matter how big or small they are."

"Excellent thinking everyone!" Velda commented energetically.

In earlier chapters, we asked you to think about specific strategies as they relate to the research base we discussed in Chapter 4. Now let's do the same with Velda's teach-ing. To what extent did she apply the research in her teaching, and where did she adapt? Let's take a look.

- She established *focus* by posing Mrs. Shah's dilemma in selecting a student and displaying her outline on the overhead.
- Her outline was also an effective *representation of content* for her lesson.
- She maintained high levels of *student involvement* with her questioning.
- She conducted the lesson with *enthusiasm* and *energy*.

Velda effectively applied several generic aspects of the research on effective teaching as she introduced, developed, and completed her lesson. But she also did a number of things that specifically addressed the kind of content she was teaching. Let's look at these content-specific strategies in more detail now.

Organized Bodies of Knowledge: Integrating Facts, Concepts, and Generalizations

To help us understand Velda's instruction, let's examine the content and her goals more closely. Her lesson focused on the general topic of *political compromise.* Within this broad area were facts, such as the number of representatives and senators in the House and Senate, as well as information about the relative sizes of different states. However, un-like the lessons described in Chapter 8, which focused on concepts, generalizations, principles, and academic rules, Velda's wasn't directed at any of these elements specifi-cally; rather it was aimed at the relationships among all these parts. Velda was teaching an **organized body of knowledge,** which is *a combination of facts, concepts, generaliza-tions (and principles and rules), integrated with each other.*

As another example, suppose you're comparing novels by twentieth-century Amer-ican writers. Your study would deal with the relationships among a number of facts; con-cepts like *plot, setting,* and *character;* and generalizations, such as "Writers' life experiences are reflected in their writing." It wouldn't focus on any of the elements separately.

Organized bodies of knowledge are an important part of the school curriculum. For example, geography students study the topography, climate, culture, and politics of one country and compare them to the same elements in other countries. In a study of immigration in the late nineteenth and early twentieth centuries, American history stu-dents examine reasons immigrants came to the United States, the difficulties they en-countered, and the ways they were assimilated into our culture. Chemistry students study the elements in the periodic table and the relationships among them. These are all organized bodies of knowledge.

One specialized subset of organized bodies of knowledge are **theories,** *which show precisely described relationships among the concepts and generalizations they are composed of.* In science, for example, we have the theory of evolution, molecular theory, and theories about the origins of the universe. In the social sciences, we have learning theories, such as behaviorism and constructivism; sociological theories, such as Durkheim's theory of suicide; and economic theories, such as supply-side economics. Each of these theories can be taught using a lecture discussion instructional strategy.

Using Lectures to Teach Organized Bodies of Knowledge

As we introduced the chapter, we said that teacher-centered instruction—in addition to teaching procedural skills—is appropriate for teaching content that would be difficult for students to obtain on their own. Velda's topic is an example. Finding and organizing all the historical information that led to the organization of our country's legislative branch, as it appears today, would be difficult for her students. Presenting this information in an interactive way so students can explore relationships, as Velda did, is an effective instructional strategy.

Traditional lectures are often used to teach organized bodies of knowledge. Lectures are the most common form of instruction in colleges and universities, and they remain firmly entrenched in many middle school, junior high, and high school classrooms (Cuban, 1984; Goodlad, 1984).

There are at least four reasons for their popularity:

- They are efficient; planning time is devoted to organizing the content. Less attention needs to be devoted to teaching strategy.
- They are flexible and can be adapted to a wide range of subjects.
- Most people can learn to lecture well enough to survive in a classroom; learning more sophisticated strategies is much more difficult.
- They require less energy from teachers. Simply telling students information helps teachers maintain control, and they don't have to do the thinking on their feet that guiding students with questioning requires.

Lectures have two serious flaws, however. First, research on learning indicates that learners must be actively involved if information is to be meaningfully encoded and retained (Eggen and Kauchak, 2001), and lectures permit—even encourage—students to be passive. At their worst, lectures are monologues in which the teacher talks and students listen. The teacher presents and explains the content, sometimes supplementing the information with charts, graphs, diagrams, and words on the chalkboard. The students' job is to understand and absorb what the teacher is trying to explain.

This arrangement can work for highly motivated, self-regulated high school and college students. College students pay for their education, and the decision to attend class is theirs. Successful high school students are also motivated, they are reinforced with good grades, and they've developed skills to learn from lectures. They understand the need to monitor their own attention; when they catch themselves drifting off, they pull themselves back. They actively take notes and use them later as a resource.

Poorly motivated high school students, typical junior high and middle school students, and virtually all elementary students lack these skills (Berk, 1997). If you talk longer than a couple minutes to first and second graders, they start fidgeting and looking out the window. Middle school, junior high, and high school students don't last much longer. They're bored; there's nothing to *do.*

A second flaw is that lectures don't provide a means for assessing student attention and understanding. While young children will openly yawn and fidget, high school students often hide their boredom, and glances at the clock are furtive and veiled (although even older students sometimes openly lay their heads down on desks, making no attempt to pay attention).

In addition to student boredom, lectures don't allow teachers to assess student understanding. It is *literally impossible* to determine whether or not students understand your examples and descriptions without interacting with them. This means you must *call on them* and have them describe what they are learning and how ideas are connected throughout your lessons.

Lecture is one of the great paradoxes of teaching. It is the least effective but most popular mode of instruction today.

Lecture Discussions: An Alternative to Standard Lectures

Lecture discussion *is a teaching strategy that combines short periods of teacher presentation with extensive teacher-student interaction.* This strategy combines the positive aspects of lecture—flexibility and economy of effort—with the benefits of interactive teaching. It is an instructional hybrid effectively suited to helping students understand organized bodies of knowledge. Velda Houston used lecture discussion to teach her students about political compromise. Let's see how she planned for her lesson.

Planning for Lecture Discussions

One of the first teaching tasks in planning for lecture discussions is to define and delimit the content to be taught.

When we discussed planning for teaching concepts, principles, generalizations, and academic rules, we identified three essential steps:

- Identifying the topic
- Determining a precise goal
- Preparing representations in the form of examples and data

In planning to teach an organized body of knowledge, you must identify a topic and your goal must also be clear, so the first two steps are similar to those when you plan to teach a concept or generalization.

The third step is different, however, and it's more complex. While finding good illustrations of concepts or generalizations can be difficult, the task is well defined. In teaching an organized body of knowledge, organizing and representing the content is more difficult.

This part of the planning process requires careful decision making. The following questions can be helpful:

- How does this topic relate to previous ones?
- What prerequisite ideas do students need to know?

- How can I organize the information so important ideas are interrelated?
- How should I present the organized information to the students?

Once you've answered the first two questions, the next step is to organize and represent the content you plan to teach. The following sections describe some different ways to do this.

Organization and Spatial Representations: A Picture Is Worth a Thousand Words. The term *organized* implies that the individual ideas in the body of knowledge are related and connected, and the graphic representation that teachers construct should make these connections clear.

Bodies of knowledge can be organized and represented in several different ways. Matrices, networks, hierarchies, and schematic diagrams provide sensory focus for students and illustrate conceptual relationships among ideas (Eggen and Kauchak, 2001).

Matrices. **Matrices** *are two-dimensional tables that illustrate similarities and differences in major ideas.* These can be simple tables for elementary students or detailed charts for older learners. Kathy Johnson, in the case study that introduced Chapter 4, used a matrix to organize her information on the northern and southern states. Figure 11.3 illustrates another simpler example from the area of elementary science.

Networks. **Networks** *are simple diagrams that link related ideas,* and they have proven effective in helping students learn from textbooks (Holley and Dansereau, 1984) and teacher presentations (Novak and Musonda, 1991). Networks, when shared on an overhead or blackboard, can help students see the interrelationship of ideas when a body of knowledge is being taught. A network from the area of physical education is illustrated in Figure 11.4.

Conceptual Hierarchies. Special types of network, **conceptual hierarchies,** *connect superordinate and subordinate ideas to each other.* For instance, in Figure 11.5 we see that nouns and pronouns are subsets of naming words, and adjectives and adverbs are subsets of modifying words. Hierarchies spatially illustrate these superordinate-subordinate relationships. Velda used a combination of a simple network and a conceptual hierarchy to help her students understand different aspects of political compromise in the Constitution.

	Examples	How They Grow
Fruit		
Vegetables		

Figure 11.3 Elementary Matrix Comparing Two Concepts

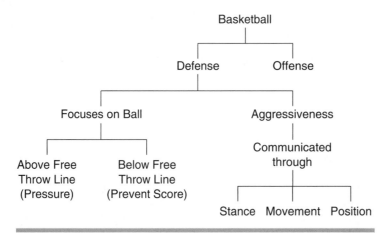

Figure 11.4 Network in Physical Education

Source: Adapted from Novak and Gowin, 1984.

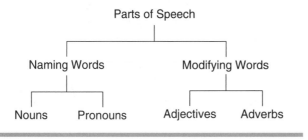

Figure 11.5 Conceptual Hierarchy for Parts of Speech

Spatially representing ideas within a body of knowledge helps both teachers and students (Winitzky, Kauchak, and Kelly, 1994). During planning, it helps the teacher break large amounts of content into manageable parts. As the lesson is implemented, it provides both focus and a form of conceptual organization for students. During study and review students can use these spatial organizers to connect and integrate ideas.

Your tasks in the planning process are to define the boundaries of the body of knowledge you plan to teach, link important ideas to each other, and organize and represent the information so these links can be identified. Once these are accomplished, you're ready to implement the lesson.

Implementing Lecture Discussion Lessons

Lecture discussions are implemented in four steps. They're outlined in Table 11.2 and discussed in the sections that follow.

Introduction. Done effectively, the content in lecture discussions is presented with a logical beginning and end, an understandable internal organization, and links to what

Table 11.2 **STEPS IN LECTURE DISCUSSION LESSONS**

Step	Description	Example
Introduction	Provide focus for the lesson	Mrs. Shah's problem in Velda's lesson
Presentation	Present students with background information	Velda provided historical information about the House of Representatives and Senate.
Comprehension Monitoring	Assess the extent to which students understand the information that has been presented	Velda asked Miguel to explain the different positions of large and small states.
Integration	Link information in different presentations to each other	Velda asked the students to relate power to the compromises they were discussing.

students already know. Done ineffectively, they're garbled sets of minilessons with no connecting theme. An effective introduction is essential to the success of lecture discussion lessons.

One effective way to introduce lecture discussions is to use **advance organizers** (Ausubel, 1978), *initial statements about the topic to be learned that provide a structure for the new information and relate it to information students already possess.*

Advance organizers can exist in a variety of forms. They can be a simple overview, such as:

> Yesterday we talked about the nomadic nature of the Native Americans who lived on the plains. We saw that they were hunters, and their lives were built around following herds of large animals—particularly the buffalo. Today we're going to see how the Spanish exploration of the New World changed Native Americans. We'll see how the horse revolutionized the way they lived, their economic base, the way they made war, their values, and even their relationships with their families. Keep these ideas in mind as we go through the lesson.

Advance organizers can also be a combination of a visual representation and a verbal description. For example, Velda introduced her lesson with her network and hierarchy together with the problem of how Mrs. Shah was trying to select a student for a special project.

Mrs. Shah's problem was an *analogy* for the problem of large-state and small-state representation in Congress. An **analogy** *describes a comparison between two ideas that are similar in some, but not all, respects.* Some additional examples of analogies that can be used as advance organizers include the following:

- A tree can be thought of as a city of cells in which each type of cell has a job to do and depends on the jobs of other cells.
- A learning schema is like a computer program; the content and the relations between the content are dependent upon the learner (programmer).
- Birds are reptiles with feathers; except for flight, their bodies work primarily the same way.

- Outer space is the last frontier. The same dangers and hardships faced by the pioneers are encountered by the astronauts.
- Red blood cells are our bodies' oxygen railroad.

In each example, a familiar frame of reference is used to present new and unfamiliar content. Analogies provide hooks for the new material; the more familiar the old material and the closer the fit of the analogy, the more learning is facilitated. Regardless of the form of the advance organizer, it is intended to provide focus and a conceptual framework for the content to follow.

Presentation. Once the topic is introduced, the teacher presents information in a mini-lecture. In her initial presentation, Velda described the conflict between large and small states, setting the stage for the importance of compromise. The purpose of this short presentation was to provide an information base for the discussion that followed.

Comprehension Monitoring. After some information has been presented, lecture discussions move to **comprehension monitoring,** *the process of questioning students to assess their understanding of the material.* To illustrate comprehension monitoring in Velda's lesson, let's return to her lesson:

Velda: Now let's analyze this process of compromise. How were the states supporting the two proposals different? Miguel?

Miguel: . . . New York was a large state, and Rhode Island was a very small state.

Velda: Yes, good, Miguel. And what does that mean? Jamie?

Jamie: . . . Well, it was bigger.

Velda: Bigger land area or bigger population or what?

Jamie: . . . Both, I think. But probably the bigger population was most important.

The comprehension-monitoring step of the cycle serves two functions. First, it makes the lesson interactive and draws students into the activity. When they know they will be questioned about material, they are more likely to listen to the presentation, and they're reinforced for doing so.

This illustrates the importance of expectations. If teachers expect all students to listen, learn, and participate, and hold them accountable through questioning, they are more likely to remain involved with the lesson. On the other hand, if teachers talk for extended periods or ask questions that are answered by only a few, the rest of the students are likely to tune out.

A second function of comprehension monitoring is feedback—for both the teacher and students. The quality of student responses helps teachers determine the extent to which they understand the material, and teachers can then adjust the presentation accordingly. If students are not understanding, there is no point in proceeding; teachers need to reteach misunderstood or confusing material.

Questions also provide students with feedback, and they encourage meaningful learning. Students' ability to answer the teacher's questions helps them gauge the extent to which they understand the content, and it also increases that understanding through active participation and listening to the ideas of others.

Integration. In the fourth step of a lecture discussion, teachers encourage **integration,** *the process of exploring relationships in the information, relating information in one presentation to another, and consolidating new information with previous understanding.*

Integration is a natural extension of comprehension monitoring. The difference between the two lies in the type of questions teachers ask. During integration, students are asked to establish cause-and-effect relationships, make predictions, and hypothesize. The exact type of question depends on the content being taught; the essential characteristic is that the questions cause students to search for links with other ideas in the lesson.

This process is supported by research (Cruikshank, 1985; Eggen and Kauchak, 2001) and makes intuitive sense. When parts of a lesson are interrelated, deeper understanding results. Links help ensure that the new content is being learned as a coherent and interconnected body.

To illustrate, let's look again at Velda's lesson:

Velda: Yes, good, Jamie. Now why would the large states feel the way they did, and also why would the small states feel the way they did? What do you think? . . . Simao?

Simao: . . . It would relate to power. If the representation was made on the basis of population, the large states would be much more powerful than the small states.

Velda: On the other hand, what would happen if representation were completely equal among the states? Toni?

Toni: . . . It would sort of throw the balance in the favor of the smaller states. It would mean a state like Wyoming with very little population could maybe stop a proposal from a very populated state like California.

In this short excerpt we see that Simao offered a cause-and-effect relationship between the population of states and power, and Toni hypothesized another relationship based on equal representation. Understanding these perspectives was essential to understanding the need for compromise, the central focus of this cycle. Combining integration with comprehension monitoring can result in a thorough understanding of the relationships in an organized body of knowledge.

Lecture Discussion Cycles: The Building Blocks of Lessons. What you saw illustrated in the preceding sections was one **lecture discussion cycle,** which is *a recurrent sequence of presenting information, monitoring comprehension, and integration,* and it is the core of lecture discussion as an instructional strategy. After one cycle is completed, a second occurs, then a third, and so on until the lesson is complete. Each cycle includes a brief *presentation,* followed by *comprehension monitoring,* and *integration.*

Integration is the essential link in lecture discussion cycles. Integration is broader and deeper with each cycle because the information in one cycle is integrated with content from earlier cycles.

Lecture discussion cycles are effective from a learning perspective because information is presented in relatively small chunks, and students are actively involved in the comprehension monitoring and integration phases.

These cycles also assist teachers as they attempt to help students understand complex organized bodies of knowledge. They allow teachers to break instruction into manageable parts, both during planning and in the lesson itself. This process helps

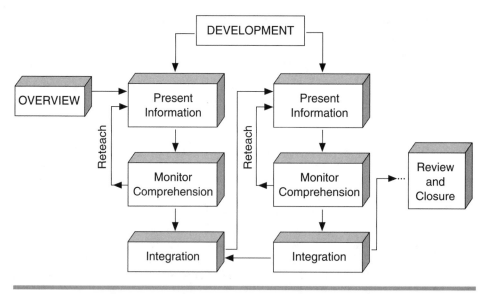

Figure 11.6 Lecture Discussion Cycles in the Total Lesson

teachers divide potentially overwhelming bodies of knowledge into parts that are teachable and comprehensible.

LINKING LECTURE DISCUSSION CYCLES. Each lecture discussion cycle takes only a few minutes. By stringing several of these cycles together, the teacher can consolidate the ideas in an organized body of knowledge into an effective lesson.

This process is outlined in Figure 11.6. Let's see how it's illustrated in Velda's lesson.

"Now that we understand how compromise produced the present form of our Congress, let's turn to the electoral college and see how the process of compromise shaped the way we elect our President. Note that on the overhead we just talked about the legislative branch," Velda said, pointing at the left side of the hierarchy on the overhead.

"Now we're turning to the presidential or executive branch. This is Article 2 of the Constitution. Let's see how our President is elected. Every four years, some time in December, 535 people in the Electoral College get together and cast their votes for the next President of the United States. When people vote for the President in the November elections, they are actually voting for the members of the Electoral College and not directly for the President.

"Let's think about this one. Why are there 535 members? Where did it come from? Where have we seen that number before? . . . Sherry?"

" . . . Well . . . we just learned that there are 435 members of the House and 100 members of the Senate. It must be the two combined?" she said with a question in her voice.

"Good, Sherry. And how are the members of the Senate distributed between the states? . . . Leroy?"

" . . . Two each."

"Okay, two per state times 50 states is 100. And what about the House? . . . Who re-members? . . . Terry?"

" . . . They're . . . based on population, I think . . . yeah, population. The states with the most people like California and New York have most, while those with not very many . . . like North Dakota, have only a couple or so."

"Good complete answer," Velda smiled at Terry. "So we see that there are 535 mem-bers, which are the combined numbers of the House and Senate. Using this information now, how is this another example of compromise? . . . Ajat?"

"Well . . . there were two views as to how the President should be elected. The small states wanted each state to have equal representation, while the big states wanted it done on the basis of population. Using both was a form of compromise."

"Now let's ask a big question that pulls this information together. Why was compro-mise necessary in designing the Electoral College? What difference does it make? . . . Ajat?"

" . . . The President is a big . . . powerful person who influences the country. If we had a President who liked the big states, the little ones would be upset. . . . And it could go the other way, too. If they elected a guy who only helped the little states, the others, the big ones, would be upset. So they had to have a . . . system that they all could live with."

"Good description, Ajat. That's an excellent analysis. Now let's examine a third com-promise dealing with why the President isn't elected directly, instead being chosen by an Electoral College. To do that, we need to know about a fellow by the name of Rousseau and his idea of an enlightened aristocracy."

Let's stop here and see how this second cycle was structured and how Velda con-nected the two. In the presentation step of the second cycle, she referred her students to the outline and talked about the Electoral College. Her outline, together with her statement, "Note that on the overhead we just talked about the legislative branch. . . . Now we're turning to the presidential or executive branch," provided a link between the first cycle and the second. Remember from Chapter 4 that transition signals are impor-tant communication skills that help students understand and construct connections be-tween related ideas.

In the comprehension-monitoring step of the second cycle, Velda checked to see if students remembered and understood the information about the structure of the legis-lature. She did this by asking questions such as:

Where have we seen that number before?

Where did it come from?

Having determined that students understood the link between the number in the electoral college and the structure of the two branches of the legislature, she then began to explore the implications of this connection by asking questions such as:

Why is that number significant?

How is this another example of compromise?

Why was compromise necessary in designing the Electoral College? What differ-ence does it make?

These questions linked the Electoral College, which was discussed in the second cycle, both to the number of representatives and senators—discussed in the first cycle—and to the concept of compromise, which was the theme of the lesson. Once these links are made, the next cycle was ready to begin with the presentation of new material. As teachers use questions such as these, students develop the inclination to look for these relationships on their own. This is a step toward self-regulated learning.

The lines between comprehension monitoring and integration and one cycle with another are often blurred and hard to identify. It isn't critical to identify precisely where one ends and the other begins. However, understanding the difference between comprehension monitoring and integration is important, because we want learners to do more than summarize, paraphrase, and identify similarities and differences; we want them to explain, identify causes and effects, and consider hypothetical relationships. All this is part of developing deep understanding of the topics they're studying.

RESEARCH AND THE LECTURE DISCUSSION CYCLE. Evidence supports the effectiveness of lecture discussion cycles. Research indicates that the amount learned from a lecture decreases as the length of the presentation increases (Gage and Berliner, 1998). Over time, student attention wanes and learning suffers. These results were obtained with college students, so we can safely predict the effects to be even greater with younger learners.

Further, researchers found that attention increases when a question is asked and decreases when a student is called on (Lemke, 1982). (Remember what was said in Chapter 5 about asking a question first and then calling on a student?) Student attention also improved during demonstrations, debates, and student-initiated questions, providing strong support for the idea of active student involvement.

Further support for the lecture discussion cycle comes from research on reading. Research indicates that questions interspersed in text material increase comprehension (Anderson and Armbruster, 1984), and the greater comprehension largely results from increased reader attention (Reynolds and Shirey, 1988). We've all had the experience of drifting off when we've been reading. Questions attract attention and help the reader focus on important material. Teacher questions during the comprehension monitoring and integration steps of lecture discussion cycles have the same effect.

How long is too long for presenting information without asking a question? As with most questions about effective instruction, the answer depends on the situation, but a ballpark figure is about 5 minutes. Shorter periods are necessary with younger, less academically talented, or poorly motivated students and with complex or abstract content. The specific answer to the question will develop from your own experience with students. Their nonverbal behaviors during the presentation step give clues about inattention, and student performance during the comprehension monitoring step provides additional data.

Closure. Closure, or bringing a lesson together at the end, is a characteristic of all good teaching, and it is particularly important in lecture discussion lessons, because the process of linking one cycle to earlier cycles is continuous, large and complex amounts of information are presented, and it's easy for students to lose track of the lesson's direction and the overall structure of the content. Effective closure helps to tie together ideas and to prevent this potential confusion.

A powerful way to conclude a lesson is to refer students back to the organizational scheme introduced at the beginning of the lesson. Visual representations such as hierarchies or matrices are again useful. Velda, for example, could bring her lesson to closure by referring students back to the overhead that began the lesson. The overhead, combined with summary statements by the students, provides an efficient and visual way of helping students remember the lesson's content. Research on the way learners process information supports the idea of combining statements of closure with visual summarizing devices (Schwartz, Ellsworth, Graham, and Knight, 1998; Willoughby, Porter, Belsito, and Yearsley, 1999).

This concludes our discussion of lecture discussions. The summary that follows is designed to help you integrate the ideas in the chapter.

Summary

Teacher-Centered and Learner-Centered Instruction. While a great deal of emphasis has been placed on learner-centered instruction, some goals are better met with teacher-centered approaches. When learners study well-defined content that all are expected to master or when students will have difficulty acquiring content on their own, teacher-centered instruction is desirable.

Characteristics of Teacher-Centered Instruction. Teacher-centered instruction typically involves lessons focused on specific objectives that have been determined in advance. In teacher-centered lessons, teachers take primary responsibility for modeling skills and guiding learning. All effective teacher-centered lessons actively involve learners through teacher questioning.

Direct instruction, lectures, and lecture discussions are three common types of teacher-centered instruction.

Direct Instruction. Direct instruction is a strategy typically used to teach procedural skills, which are forms of learning that have a specific set of operations, can be illustrated with large numbers of examples, and are developed through practice.

Direct instruction lessons begin with an introduction, which the teacher follows by presenting and modeling the skill and the students practice, first under the supervision of the teacher and then on their own. The goal in direct instruction lessons is to develop the skill to the point of automaticity so that it transfers to a variety of contexts.

Lecture Discussions: Teacher-Centered Strategies for Teaching Organized Bodies of Knowledge. Organized bodies of knowledge are interrelated connections of facts, concepts, generalizations, principles, and academic rules. Lecture discussions combine the flexibility and simplicity of lectures with the benefits of interactive teaching and are effective for teaching organized bodies of knowledge.

Effective lecture discussions begin with an introduction, which the teacher follows by presenting information in a minilecture. Comprehension monitoring and integration follow the presentation.

Lecture discussion lessons are developed when one cycle of presenting information, monitoring comprehension, and integration is linked to earlier cycles. With each succeeding cycle, the process of integration becomes broader and deeper.

Important Concepts

Advance organizer   Networks
Analogy   Observational learning
Automaticity   Organized body of knowledge
Comprehension monitoring   Procedural skills
Conceptual hierarchy   Scaffolding
Direct instruction   Task analysis
Focus   Teacher-centered instruction
Integration   Theory
Lecture discussion   Thinkaloud
Lecture discussion cycle   Transfer
Matrices   Zone of proximal development
Modeling

Reflecting on Teaching and Learning

Margaret Fontini looked over the year-long plans she had laid out for her sixth-grade language arts curriculum and saw the notes from her previous teacher year:

Students have trouble with summarization. Don't know where to start.

"I remember that unit. It was like pulling teeth. I just didn't know how to get the idea across. I've got to do better this time," she mumbled to herself as she opened several language arts teacher editions that she had on her bookshelf. On Monday, Margaret began her language arts class by saying, "Okay, class, please put your math away. If you haven't finished your problems, be sure to take them home and have them ready for class tomorrow."

After pausing for a few moments while students put their math books away, Margaret continued, "Today in language arts we're going to learn a new skill that will help us with our writing. It's called summarization. In addition, it should be helpful in other content areas as well. I'd like everyone to look up here on the overhead. I've got a definition for you."

A good summary restates the main idea of the passage, deletes unimportant and redundant information and, sometimes, involves superordination.

After pausing for a few moments to allow her students to read the definition, Margaret continued.

"Let's see what a good summary looks like. I'd like you to read this passage and then I'm going to show you two summaries. Your job is to see if you can tell me which summary for the paragraph is better. Here we go."

In the desert there are no clouds to stop the sun's burning rays. So the sun heats up the earth. As a result, it gets very hot, the temperature easily reaching 120 degrees. And rainfall is slight in the desert. Most deserts get less than 10 inches of rain per year. Years may pass between showers. Sometimes 5 or 10 years may go by without a drop of rain falling on the desert.

"Has everyone had a chance to read the paragraph? Now, let's look at two possible summaries that I've created. Look up on the overhead and tell me which is better."

1. The desert is a hot and dry place.
2. The sun in the desert is merciless.

"Who has an idea? Which do you think is better? Tanya?"

"I think number 1 is better. It . . . "

"Good Tanya, I agree with you. Number 1 is definitely better. Let's try another one. Again, read the paragraph and then I'll give you two possibilities to choose from."

> *The heat doesn't bother the seeds from plants and they can do without water for an extended period. After a rain, the seeds sprout and flowers bloom. Then the desert is covered with many brightly colored flowers. The desert is a beautiful place when there are red, yellow, orange, and blue flowers everywhere. But soon the ground begins to dry up. As the ground dries, the flowers produce new seeds and then die. These new seeds fall to the ground and wait for the next rainfall. When it rains, they grow, blossom, leave new seeds, and then die.*

"Has everyone had a chance to read this and think about a summary? Okay, then, which of these do you think is the better summary? Look up here on the overhead."

1. Desert flowers only bloom after a rain.
2. Seeds are perfectly suited to the desert.

"Ricardo, do you have an answer?"

"I think number 2 is better because the paragraph is more about seeds than flowers."

"Good, Ricardo. Does everyone agree? Any questions? If not, I have several more paragraphs about the desert that I'd like you to summarize on your own and we'll compare our answers tomorrow."

With that she handed out a piece of paper that had four paragraphs on it.

"Remember, class, you're supposed to write a summary for each of these paragraphs. Get busy, and I'll be around to help."

As students started on their assignment, Margaret circulated around the room. As she did this, a number of hands went up, asking for help. As she worked with each student, she noticed that they were all having trouble knowing where to start.

"Hmm, I guess I better do more work on getting started writing a summary. I'll do that first thing in class tomorrow."

Questions for Analysis

1. How effective was the introduction phase of the lesson? How could Margaret's introduction be improved?
2. How effective was the presentation phase of the lesson? How could it be improved?
3. How effective was the guided practice phase of the lesson? Explain, making direct reference to the case study in your assessment.
4. Analyze Margaret's examples during teacher-directed practice, using the concept of *scaffolding*.
5. Analyze the quality of the independent practice phase of the lesson. How could the independent practice phase of the lesson be improved?

Discussion Questions

1. How do the following factors influence the importance of procedural skills in the curriculum?

    a. Grade level
    b. Subject matter
    c. Ability level of students (i.e., high versus low)

2. Why is automaticity important to the following skills

    a. Learning to print in first grade?
    b. Learning to play a musical instrument?
    c. Learning a foreign language?

3. Teachers often have to make professional compromises: You've just begun a skills lesson and find out that because of a changed school schedule, you only have half as much time as you had planned. How will you adjust your teaching in terms of the four phases of the direct instruction model? Why?

    a. Introduction
    b. Explanation
    c. Guided practice
    d. Independent practice

4. How would you teach for transfer in the following lessons:

    a. Teaching map-reading skills to junior high students?
    b. Teaching punctuation skills to fifth graders?
    c. Teaching percentage word problems to high school basic math students?

5. Are organized bodies of knowledge more important at some grade levels or in some content areas than others? Which and why? How is the importance of organized bodies of information influenced by timing; that is, is this type of content more important at the beginning or end of a course or unit?

6. How do the following factors influence the optimal length of one lecture discussion cycle?

    a. Age of students
    b. Difficulty or complexity of material
    c. Background knowledge of students
    d. Student motivation
    e. The teacher's presentation skills

Portfolio Activities

1. *Skills and State and District Curriculum Guides.* Analyze an appropriate curriculum guide in your area or level and answer the following questions:

    a. What skills are identified?
    b. What suggestions or recommendations are given about how they should be taught?
    c. How are the skills sequenced?
    d. How is skill acquisition measured?

How helpful will guides such as this be for you as a teacher?

2. *Textbooks and Skills.* Examine a text in your area and answer the following questions:
   a. How much of the text is devoted to skills?
   b. How are the skills sequenced?
   c. What provision is there for practice and feedback?
   d. How does the text deal with long-term retention and transfer? How would you need to supplement this text to maximize skill learning in your classroom?

3. *Homework.* Interview a teacher or student and ask the following questions:
   a. How often is homework given?
   b. Is there any pattern to homework assignments (e.g., end-of-week or end-of-unit reviews)?
   c. Is homework graded and returned?
   d. How does it count toward the final grade in the course?
   e. How effective is it in promoting learning?
   How could homework be improved to increase learning in the classroom?

4. *Interactive Skills Teaching.* Observe and either audio- or videotape a skill-oriented lesson. Analyze it in terms of:
   a. Introduction
   b. Explanation
   c. Teacher-directed practice
   d. Independent practice
   e. Extended practice
   How could the lesson be improved to increase student learning?

5. *Interactive Skills Teaching: Trying It Out.* Plan for, teach, and tape a skills lesson using the basic skills model. Listen to or watch your tape and address the following questions:
   a. Was your introduction clear? Did it include the following?:
      (1) What the skill was
      (2) How it can be applied
      (3) Why it is useful
      (4) When it should be used
   b. Did you state a goal or objective for the lesson?
   c. Did you relate the skill to material previously covered?
   d. Did you think aloud while modeling the skill?
   e. What did student success rates during the following practices suggest about your pace?
      (1) Teacher-directed practice
      (2) Independent practice
      (3) Extended practice
   f. How did the amount of teacher talk vary throughout the lesson?
   g. What percentage of the class can perform the skill at an acceptable level? How do you know? Define what this level is and explain why this level is acceptable.
   What would you do differently next time?

6. *Organized Bodies of Knowledge: Textbooks.* Examine a chapter in a textbook in your teaching area that deals with an organized body of information. Analyze it in terms of the following (providing specific examples, if possible):

   a. Introduction/overview—Is there an introduction at the beginning that provides an overview of the content to follow?

   b. Organizational structure—Are there any aids (e.g., diagrams, outlines) that describe the organization of the content?

   c. Comprehension checks—Are there questions inserted in the text to check comprehension?

   d. Integrative links—Do questions or exercises encourage students to link ideas from one section to another?

   e. Summary

   What would you have to do as a teacher to supplement the text?

7. *Organized Bodies of Knowledge: Organizational Aids.* Take the content in the previous exercise and organize it using one (or more) of the following organizational aids:

   a. Outline

   b. Matrix

   c. Network

   d. Schematic diagram

   e. Conceptual hierarchy

   What other way(s) would there be to organize this content? What are the advantages and disadvantages of each?

8. *Interactive Teaching: Organization.* Observe (and audio or videotape, if possible) a lecture or lecture discussion. Take notes from the presentation. Organize the content in terms of one (or more) of the organizational aids discussed in this chapter. How could you use this type of organizational aid in your teaching?

9. *Lecture Discussion: Patterns of Interaction.* Observe a teacher (or professor) using a lecture discussion format (determine beforehand that the lesson will not be entirely lecture). Analyze the lesson in terms of:

   a. The length of each lecture discussion cycle (i.e., how long does the teacher talk before asking a question).

   b. What kinds of questions did the teacher ask? (Jot these questions down in order, with times attached to them. Later determine whether these were comprehension or integrative.) What could the instructor have done to make the lesson more effective?

10. *Lecture Discussion: Applying It in Your Classroom.* Plan, teach, and tape a lesson using the lecture discussion format. Analyze the taped lesson in terms of the following variables:

    a. Introduction/overview

    b. Organizational aids

    c. Average length of one lecture recitation cycle

    d. Comprehension checks in each cycle

    e. Integrative links in each cycle

    f. Summary

    In hindsight, what could you have done differently to make the lesson more effective?

12

Assessing Learner Understanding

*A*s you've studied the content of this book, you've seen how teacher actions in the form of careful planning, different instructional strategies, and classroom management all affect student learning. However, one important question remains unanswered: How do we know if students are actually learning what we intend? In this chapter we attempt to answer that question by examining traditional and alternative assessment, teachers' assessment practices, grading, homework, and communication with parents, all of which make up the topic of classroom assessment.

When you've completed your study of this chapter, you should be able to meet the following goals:

- Identify the functions of assessment.
- Describe the characteristics of effective assessment.
- Explain how effective teachers prepare students for, administer, and analyze assessment results.
- Design alternative assessments that can be used to measure performance and understanding.
- Describe ways of reducing bias in assessments.
- Explain how technology can be used to make assessment more effective and efficient.

Steve Vockel's fourth graders were working on applying rules for adding *-ing* to words. After putting several words on the board, Steve circulated among the students, making periodic comments.

"Check this one again, Nancy," he said when he saw that she had written *jumpping* on her paper. Later he commented at lunch, "My kids just can't seem to get the rule straight. Either they forget about the long vowel so they double the consonant on a word like *blow* or they forget about two consonants at the end of a word like *jump* and they double the *p*. What do you do about it? If I spend more time on it, we won't get other material covered."

Terry Graham gives her high school chemistry class a one- or two-problem quiz every other day. As she scored the students' answers to a problem in which the mass of an element in grams was converted to moles and number of atoms, she thought, "I need to do some more of these. They can convert moles to grams, but they can't go the other way."

Marianne Generette's middle school math class was passing their pre-algebra homework in to her. They had exchanged papers, scored the homework, and gone over problems causing difficulty.

"How many got all the problems right?" she asked the class.

"Good!" she responded to their show of hands. "You get this stuff. Remember that we have a test on this whole chapter on Friday, but for now we're going to move on to sub-traction of integers."

In each of these examples, the teacher was trying to gather information about his or her students' achievement and progress. A seatwork assignment for Steve, a quiz for Terry, and homework in Marianne's case provided information to make instructional decisions, such as moving to a new topic in Marianne's class. Periodically, even the conscientious gathering of data results in uncertainty, which was Steve's problem. He was caught in the dilemma of concluding that his students didn't understand the rule but at the same time feeling the need to move on.

CLASSROOM ASSESSMENT

The information-gathering and decision-making processes these three teachers were involved in, called **classroom assessment,** is the focus of this chapter. These processes include observing students as they work, listening to their answers in discussions, and examining the results of teacher-made and standardized tests. They also include **alternative assessments,** *which directly measure student performance through real-life tasks* (Worthen, 1993), such as having fourth graders write a letter, observing science students complete a lab activity, or seeing technology students design and use a spreadsheet. It involves decisions as well, such as assigning grades or choosing to reteach a difficult topic. When combined, *these elements make up a teacher's* **assessment system.**

Measurement and Evaluation

Two important processes are involved in assessment: **measurement,** *which includes all the information teachers gather as part of the assessment process,* and **evaluation,** *which refers to the decisions they make on the basis of the measurements.*

Effective teachers gather information—take measurements—from a variety of sources, including traditional paper-and-pencil tests, homework, answers in class, and alternative assessments, such as first graders' handwriting samples.

Assigning grades is the most common example of evaluation, and this is important, of course, but deciding when to give a quiz, what items will appear on it, and even when to move on to a new topic are also evaluation decisions.

Formal and Informal Measurement. Teachers gather information when they listen to students' answers, notice uncertain looks on their faces, and see that some aren't paying attention. These are **informal measurements,** *or measurements gathered in an incidental way.* **Formal measurement,** in comparison, *is the process of gathering information in a systematic way,* such as giving tests, quizzes, and homework to determine how much students have learned.

Both forms of measurement are important to teachers. Decisions about grading and reporting should be based on formal measurements, but many of the decisions teachers make on an everyday basis are based on informal measurements. Deciding to call on an inattentive student, for example, is based on observing the student's behavior—an informal measurement.

Functions of an Assessment System

Before we deal with the specifics of assessment, we need to understand the functions that an assessment system performs. These can be divided into two broad categories—instructional and institutional.

We assess students to promote learning, which is its most important instructional function (Airasian, 1997; Stiggins, 2001). The relationship between learning and assessment is clear and consistent. Students learn more in classes where assessment is a regular part of classroom routines, particularly when assessments are frequent and provide feedback to learners (Bangert-Drowns, Kulik, and Kulik, 1991; Kika, McLaughlin, and Dixon, 1992).

The reasons for this link are easy to understand. As we know from earlier chapters, practice and feedback are essential components of effective teaching, and assignments, quizzes, tests, and alternative assessments give students opportunities to demonstrate and receive feedback about their understanding. This feedback is helpful both to them and to other interested parties, such as their teachers, parents, and school and district administrators.

For teachers, assessments provide information about the effectiveness of their instruction. If students are not learning, teachers need to do something differently; if they are, teachers can move forward, building on this knowledge base.

Assessment results also provide valuable information for parents, allowing them to make decisions about homework, television, and a host of other school related issues. Research confirms what we intuitively know—a supportive home environment, including a commitment to homework and restriction of television, contribute to learning (Berk, 1997).

In addition to instructional functions, assessment fulfills institutional needs. Schools and districts need to know how their students perform compared to students in other schools, districts, and states. This information allows schools and school districts to adapt instructional practices to make them more effective.

Characteristics of Effective Assessment

Effective assessment in the real world of classroom teaching has three essential features: It must be *valid, reliable,* and *practical.* To be useful, while remaining professionally sound, the assessment system must possess all three features.

Validity. **Validity** *means that the assessment measures what it is supposed to measure.* It includes "the appropriateness of the interpretations made from test scores and other evaluation results" (Gronlund and Linn, 1995, p. 47).

One way of thinking about validity is to ask, "Is the assessment consistent with the specific goals being assessed?" The opposite is surprisingly common. We have all had teachers who taught one thing and then tested something else. This not only upsets students but also makes the test invalid.

Another way of thinking of validity is in terms of **instructional alignment** (Cohen, 1986). *This means that instruction is congruent with the teacher's goals and tests are congruent with both.* In the case studies at the beginning of the chapter, Steve's assignment would be aligned if one of his language arts goals was for students to learn how to add *ing* endings to words. In a similar way, the quizzes and assignments of the other two teachers would be aligned if they matched their goals and instruction. When a logical match exists between measurement procedures and what was intended and taught, we have validity.

Teachers should be aware of factors that can detract from validity. In Chapter 3, we saw that teachers plan, in part, to simplify their work. The same thing occurs in assessment. Teachers tend to assess students on the basis of characteristics that are easily measured, such as their behavior and the number of assignments they complete rather than the quality of the work, the difficulty of the assignment, or the appropriate weight of one assignment compared to another (Stiggins, 2001). Teachers also tend to fix on initial impressions of students, which may be based on inaccurate information, and then use additional information to corroborate their initial impressions (Good and Brophy, 2000). When this happens, validity suffers.

One way to guard against these tendencies is to design and implement a systematic assessment system, which leads us to the concept of *reliability.*

Reliability. Suppose we are teaching a concept and we ask students to give examples as we apply the concept to a new situation. A volunteer raises her hand and supplies an excellent example. We repeat the process with the same result. We do it once more, and again we get a very good example. We then conclude that the class understands the concept. However, we have heard from only three students, and further, they were volunteers. We have little idea about the class's overall understanding and particularly that of less able or more reluctant responders. Our conclusion could easily be invalid, because it was based on unreliable information.

Reliability *describes the extent to which measurements are consistent.* Because we didn't get information from all the students, consistency was impossible, so the results were unreliable. Unreliable measurements cannot be valid even if the measurements are consistent with the teacher's goals. A bathroom scale that gives a different reading each time we step on it (assuming our true weight doesn't change) would be an example of an unreliable instrument.

How common is the tendency for teachers to use unreliable assessments in their decision making? Research indicates that it is more common than we would expect. As teachers make the routine decisions necessary to keep a class or lesson moving, they tend to gather group data; that is, they tend to rely on the responses and nonverbal behavior of a subset of the class for feedback as the basis for deciding to repeat instruction or to move on to the next topic (Dahlof and Lundgren, 1970). A systematic attempt to gather assessment data from *all* students, and not just volunteers, makes the process more reliable and valid.

Practicality. In addition to being valid and reliable, an assessment system also needs to be practical. Assessment is one component of effective teaching, but it cannot take so much time and energy that other components are compromised. Elementary teachers are responsible for reading, math, science, social studies, spelling, language arts, and sometimes art, music, and physical education. Middle, junior high, and secondary teachers typically have five sections of 25 to 35 students a day, often with two or more preparations. Teachers are busy people and can't use assessment procedures that aren't efficient and practical.

The assessments that the teachers in our introductory case studies used were economical. Steve quickly wrote the words on the board and easily scored the responses. Terry only took minutes to prepare her chemistry problem, and Marianne had the students score their own papers. In each case, the assessment took little valuable instructional time and required minimal teacher energy.

Teachers' Assessment Patterns

How do effective assessment practices vary from grade level to grade level? Teachers of elementary students:

- Rely more heavily on performance assessments, where teachers gather and evaluate samples of students' work, such as samples of students' writing or solutions to problems.
- Depend heavily on commercially prepared and published tests, which help them simplify the demands on their time.
- Include affective goals, such as "Works and plays well with others." Typical kindergarten progress reports, for example, will have a third or more of the categories devoted to personal or social growth.

In the upper grades and high school, assessment patterns change:

- Teachers rely less on published tests, choosing instead to prepare their own.
- Teachers depend more heavily on tests than on performance measures for their assessments.
- Objective tests, such as multiple choice and fill-in-the-blanks, become more popular than subjective measures, such as essay tests.
- Emphasis on grades for cognitive performance increases, with correspondingly less emphasis given to affective goals.

Let's examine these patterns in more detail.

The lower elementary grades are characterized by considerable agreement about essential content and skills. Commercially prepared tests are useful because a high degree of consensus about the curriculum exists. Later, the curriculum becomes more differentiated and idiosyncratic. One history teacher's approach and emphasis will be different from another's, for example, so commercially prepared tests no longer meet each teacher's needs. As a result, teachers tend to customize the assessment process by preparing their own tests.

The press for simplification and time-efficient assessment is true for all teachers; teachers use assessment items that are easy and quick to score. Analysis of nearly 400 teacher-made tests encompassing thousands of test items found (Fleming and Chambers, 1983):

1. Just over 1 percent of all teacher-made test items were essay questions.
2. The most frequently used item format was short answer, such as:

   Which two planets in our solar system have orbits that overlap?

   What is the primary climate region in Spain?

3. Matching items were the next most commonly used by teachers.

4. Nearly 80 percent of all test items measured *knowledge* of facts, terms, rules, or principles, with few items measuring students' ability to apply this knowledge. Middle school and junior high school teachers were the worst offenders. Nearly 94 percent of their items were written at the knowledge level, compared to 69 percent for both elementary and senior high teachers.

5. Once items are constructed, teachers tend to reuse them without analysis and revision (Gullickson and Ellwein, 1985).

Why do these patterns exist? There are two primary reasons. The first is the need for efficiency and simplicity, and the second is a lack of knowledge about effective assessment procedures and feelings of inadequacy about their assessment capabilities (Plake and Impara, 1997).

With these factors in mind, the research findings are not surprising. Teachers write recall questions because it is easiest to write *and score* items at this level. When the efforts of constructing and scoring items are combined, the easiest formats to use are short answer and matching. Essay questions, while easy to construct, are extremely difficult to score, and teachers are notoriously inconsistent in comparing one student's essay to another's. Evidence indicates that even the physical attractiveness of the writer and penmanship can influence essay scoring (Bull and Stevens, 1979).

In contrast, multiple-choice items are easy to score, but good ones are difficult to construct; true-false questions, while appearing easy to prepare on the surface, are actually very demanding if prepared well. This, in combination with the widespread criticism of the format (i.e., the ease of guessing), explains why true-false is not widely used.

In addition to greater use of teacher-made tests, at the upper levels there is also greater emphasis on grades, accountability, and quality control. At the lower levels formal grades (e.g., A, B, C) are often replaced with descriptive statements (e.g., "Can print all the letters of the alphabet clearly," or "Can count from one to ten orally"). Later, more emphasis is placed on the accountability and comparison aspects of grading.

Measurement and evaluation differences also exist across subject-matter areas. Teachers in science and social studies tend to use more objective assessments, while those in the language arts—including reading, writing, and speaking—make greater use of performance assessments. It is easier to make up objective items in more convergent areas, whereas skill areas lend themselves more to performance assessments.

Having examined teachers' assessment patterns, we turn now to ways that both traditional and alternative assessments can be made more effective. We begin with traditional assessment.

USING TRADITIONAL ASSESSMENT PRACTICES TO PROMOTE LEARNING

In this section, we look at how teachers can make testing more effective by the way they prepare their students for tests, administer the tests, and analyze the results. As we will see, these strategies apply to any item format and content area as well as most grade levels. To begin, let's look at a seventh-grade social studies teacher preparing his class for a unit test. His goals for the unit were for students to understand the concept of culture, to apply it to various groups in Central America and Mexico, and to know basic facts about these countries.

Andy Robinson is finishing his unit on Mexico and Central America.

"Okay, everyone," Andy begins, "listen carefully, now. We finished with our study of Central America and its cultural traditions. I've reminded you since last Wednesday that we're having a test tomorrow."

"Oh, Mr. Robinson, do we have to?" Sheila groaned in mock protest.

"Too bad. Mean Mr. Robinson gives a test every week," Andy smiled back at Sheila. "Just think. We have it tomorrow, I'll give it back to you on Friday, and I'll even give you the weekend off."

"ALL RIGHT!" the class shouted.

Andy held up his hand to settle them down and continued, "Now, let's think about the test. First, let's talk about some individual items; then I'll give you an overview of the test. I'm going to ask you to think extra hard with some of the questions, but you've all been working hard, and I know you'll do well. Every time you've had a tough test, you've tried harder and done better."

He continued, "We've been comparing cultures, and I want you to get more practice in making those comparisons, plus I want you to keep working on writing clearly. Take a look at this," Andy said, displaying the following paragraphs on the overhead projector:

> Read the description, and identify (in the example) the characteristics of culture that were discussed in class.
>
> Jorgé (pronounced Hor-hay) is a small Mexican boy who is growing up on a farm in the mountains outside Mexico City. He rises early, goes to the small chapel in his home for his morning prayers, and then breakfasts on a large meal of beans and corn tortillas made from the products of the family farm. His mother always asks him if the Virgin Mary gave him her blessings, and Jorgé always says, "Yes," with a smile. Jorgé walks to school a mile down the dusty road. He leaves as his father goes out to cultivate the corn that is the primary source of income for the family. Jorgé's mother then milks the goats and turns the rich cream into delicious butter and cheese.
>
> In the early afternoon, Jorgé comes home from school, and the family talks quietly in their dialect, which is Spanish with some influence from the Aztecs. As the day cools, Jorgé often plays soccer with boys in the nearby village while his father strums his guitar and his mother hums the rhythmic Latin melodies they all love. They go to bed shortly after sunset to prepare for the next day.

"Read the example carefully, take out a piece of paper, and answer the question that is given in the directions," Andy continued after waiting for a few moments.

After about 10 minutes, Andy began, "Someone tell me what they wrote as a response."

"It says in the example that they eat beans and tortillas, and we discussed the food a group eats as part of their culture," Karim responded.

"Yes, good, Karim," Andy praised. "Notice, everyone, that Karim didn't just say 'food,' but instead identified the specific foods they eat in the example. This indicates that he is relating the information in the example to what we discussed in class."

The class went on, with students identifying the religion, type of work, and recreation in Jorgé's family.

"They're in good shape," Andy thought as he listened to their analysis. He went on, "That's all very good. Now, on the test tomorrow, you're going to have to do something like this. Remember, when you write your responses, you're going to have to relate the example to what we have discussed in class, just as we did with Jorgé and his family."

He continued, "You're also going to need to know different countries' climates, natural resources, and physical features as well as being able to locate them on a map and identify their capitals. For example, what country is this?" he asked, pointing to an outline map of Nicaragua. "Miguel?"

"Nicaragua!" Miguel responded instantly.

"Give us another example," the class requested.

"Okay," Andy smiled and displayed the following on the overhead:

> We are about 17 degrees north of the equator and are about in the middle of this country. We are in the most populous country in Central America. Most of the people here are of Indian or mixed European and Indian descent. This description best fits:
> a. Belize
> b. Guatemala
> c. Honduras
> d. Mexico

"What is the answer? Marinda?" Andy asked.

"It's Guatemala," Marinda said nervously after some hesitation.

"Yes, excellent, Marinda!" Andy encouraged, knowing that Marinda appeared to be genuinely nervous in anticipating tests and frequently missed them, the following day producing a note saying she had been sick. "Now tell us why it's Guatemala," Andy continued. "Sue?"

"First, 17 degrees only goes through sort of the middle of Guatemala and Belize," Sue responded.

"Also, Guatemala is the most populous country in Central America, and most of the people are of Indian descent," Martina added.

"Now, I'd like to share with you an outline that I used in preparing the test. It should give you a clear picture of how to spend your study time." With that, he displayed Figure 12.1 on an overhead.

"Will the essay question be like the one we practiced on, Mr. Robinson?" asked Antonio.

"Good question. Yes, the same format, but I'll give you different information to work with," Andy answered, concluding his review.

	Type of Item

Facts about Countries:
    Capitals
    Climate
    Natural Resources
    Physical Features
	Fill-in-the-blank
	Multiple choice
	25 questions × 1 = 25 points

Cultures of Countries	Short answer 3 questions × 5 = 15 points
Cultures of Countries	Essay 10 Points

Figure 12.1 Test Content Matrix

Let's look now at what Andy did and relate this to what research tells us about effective testing.

Preparing Students

As he prepared his students for the test, Andy did three things that helped his students achieve at their best: (1) he specified precisely what the test would cover; (2) he gave them a chance to practice the kinds of skills they would be expected to demonstrate when they took the actual test; and (3) he established positive expectations in his students as they prepared for the test. These factors work in combination with each other to ensure the best possible results. Let's look at each now.

Specifying test content offers security for students by providing a structured set of content and skills to be mastered (Carrier and Titus, 1981). Further, it can help reduce test anxiety (Everson, Tobias, Hartman, and Gourgey, 1991). Andy specified skills students would have to demonstrate when he said he wanted them to practice making comparisons, and provided structure when he said they would "need to know different countries' climate, natural resources, and physical features. . . ."

In addition, he shared *an overview of the test, including major content to be covered and the types of items to be expected.* This outline, called a **table of specifications,** serves two functions. First, it helps teachers systematically plan their tests. A cross grid with content on one axis and item type or level (e.g., high versus low or knowledge versus application) on the other ensures that the test accurately reflects the teacher's goals and instruction. Aligning the test with instruction increases validity.

Just describing what students need to know may not provide sufficient guidance for some students (particularly those in middle school or younger), so Andy did not stop at that point. In addition, he illustrated the description with sample exercises that paralleled those they would experience on the test. He offered a practice essay item and also provided practice with a multiple-choice format. Ensuring that students understand a particular format is important. When students take a test, two things are always being measured—their understanding of the content being covered on the test *and* their ability to respond to the format being used. If the second task interferes with the first, the validity of the test is reduced.

Practice with anticipated assessment formats can increase students' test-taking skills, which in turn reduces the impact of the format on students' performances. These positive effects have been confirmed with young children (Kalechstein, Kalechstein, and Doctor, 1981) and with cross-cultural groups (Dreisbach and Keogh, 1982).

Positive teacher attitudes and expectations about the test are also important. Andy established high expectations when he said, "I know you'll do well. Every time you've had a tough test, you've tried harder and done better." Research examining two decades of studies on the relationship between expectations and performance concluded that teacher expectations can positively influence student test performance (Good, 1987).

Reducing Test Anxiety. **Test anxiety** *is a relatively stable, unpleasant reaction to testing situations that lowers performance.* Experts suggest that test anxiety consists of two components (Pintrich and Schunk, 1996). The *emotional component* can include increased pulse rate, dry mouth, feelings of fright, and even "going blank." Its *cognitive or worry component* involves thoughts about failure, concerns about parents being upset, or being embarrassed by a low score. As they're taking a test, test-anxious students tend to be preoccupied with test difficulty, which interferes with their ability to focus on individual items.

Test anxiety increases when:

- Tests contain unfamiliar items or formats.
- High pressure to succeed exists.
- Time limits are imposed.
- Learners perceive the content or test as difficult (Wigfield and Eccles, 1989).

Unannounced tests and pop quizzes have an especially adverse effect on test anxiety (Saigh, 1984).

Teachers can help reduce test anxiety (Everson et al., 1991), and particularly the worry component (Pintrich and Schunk, 1996), if they

- Use criterion-referenced noncompetitive measures (we discuss criterion referencing later in the chapter).
- Avoid comparing students to each other, such as announcing test scores and grades.
- Increase the frequency of quizzes and tests.
- Teach students test-taking skills.
- Discuss test content and procedures prior to testing.
- Give clear directions and be sure students understand the test.
- Provide students with enough time to take tests.

Administering Tests

To illustrate effective test administration procedure, let's again join Andy and his students.

Andy came in the classroom before his students arrived, and even though his room is quite crowded, he moved the desks as far apart as possible and had them ready when students walked in. He opened a window and then changed his mind, reacting to the noise of a lawn mower outside.

As the class poured into the room, he directed them to their seats, asking for their attention. When everyone was looking at him, he instructed them to clear everything off their desks, as he passed out the tests.

"Tear the last sheet off the back of the test and write your name on it. Do that right now. Now as you take the test, put all your answers on this sheet. When you're finished, turn the test over, and I'll come around and pick it up. Then begin the assignment written on the board. It's due on Tuesday. If anyone gets too warm as you're working, raise your hand, and I'll turn on the fan," he continued, referring to the large floor fan at the front of the room.

"Work carefully on the test, now," he said with a smile. "You're all well prepared, and I know you will do your best. You have the whole period, so you should have plenty of time."

Andy stood in the front corner of the room, scanning the class as his students worked. As he watched, he noticed Marinda periodically looking out the window for several seconds at a time. Finally, he went over to her desk, looked at her paper, and whispered as he touched her shoulder, "It looks like you're moving along okay. Try and concentrate on the test a little harder now, and you'll do fine."

Suddenly the intercom broke into the silence. "Mr. Robinson," the voice said, "Mrs. Brown [the principal] needs to see you for a moment. Could you come down to the office?"

"I'll come down at the end of the period," Andy replied to the box. "I'm in the middle of a test right now."

"Thank you," the voice responded, as the intercom went silent.

As students finished their papers, Andy moved to their desks, picking up the tests and stacking them on a table in front of the room. Students then began the assignment Andy had referred to just before they began taking the test.

Now let's look at how Andy handled the administration of the test. He got to the room early and arranged the seating in advance to ensure as much distance as possible between the desks, and he arranged the overall physical environment to minimize distractions, such as the lawn mower outside. Distractions can affect test performance, especially for younger and low-ability students. Teachers administering standardized tests often deal with this problem by hanging a sign on the closed door.

Andy waited until he had everyone's attention and then gave specific directions for taking the test, collecting the papers, and doing an assignment after finishing. As students progressed with the test, Andy carefully monitored their behavior. When he noticed that Marinda seemed distracted, he went to her, offered encouragement, and urged her to increase her concentration.

As the test progressed, he stayed in the room and refused to go to the main office until after students were finished. Unfortunately, cheating is part of classroom reality, and some students will cheat if the opportunity presents itself. However, external factors, such as the teacher's leaving the room and the emotional climate of the class, contribute more to student cheating than the inherent characteristics of the students themselves (Blackburn and Miller, 1999).

Examining Results

To see how Andy Robinson dealt with the results of his test, let's return to his class once more.

Friday morning the students filed into the room and asked as they came in, "Do you have our tests finished yet?"

"You know I do," Andy responded. "I was up half the night scoring them."

"How did we do?"

"Mostly well, but there were a few problems, and I want to go over them this morning, so when you have another test it won't happen again," he replied quickly handing the students back their tests.

"What does this mean that you wrote on my paper, 'You identified *recreation* as a part of culture, but you didn't say what it was in the example'?" Sondra asked from the back of the room.

"Remember on Wednesday we said that you needed to identify both the characteristic and the example of it from the description, like soccer and music from the example with Jorgé that we analyzed," Andy responded. "Antonio swam, dived, and fished, and you needed to say that in your essay. We'll discuss the essay question in a bit, but let's start from the beginning of the test."

"A number of you had trouble with item 15," he continued. "Many of you took choice c. What is the correct answer? . . . Ann?"

Andy then discussed several of the items, in each case describing what was wrong with the incorrect choices. He discussed the essay question in detail and finally said, "I have placed two exceptionally good essay responses on the board for everyone to examine. We'll discuss these tomorrow. I will be here after school today and tomorrow morning before class. If you have any other questions, come and see me either time."

With that, he gathered up the tests, putting his original copy with notes for revising several of the items in a special file folder, and began his lesson for the day.

Let's turn now to Andy's actions after he administered the test. First, he scored and returned the test the following day; second, he discussed the test; and finally, he made positive comments about students' performance. All of these behaviors have positive effects on achievement.

Students need to receive feedback on their work, whether it be a test, quiz, or homework, and this feedback should occur as soon as possible. In discussing the test, Andy carefully reviewed the items the students had most commonly missed, providing corrective feedback in each case. In discussing objective items, the teacher should explain incorrect answers, if missed by a large number of students (Linn and Gronlund, 2000). Correct items can be skipped over unless the information is important for later study. This uses class time efficiently.

For the essay questions, Andy provided specific feedback in the cases of incorrect or incomplete answers. In addition, he displayed examples of excellent responses (with the students' names removed) for students to read. Finally, Andy made positive comments about the general performance of the class on the test.

Research on Classroom Testing: Implications for Teachers

Research on effective testing suggests several implications for teachers:

1. **Test thoroughly and often.** Be certain that as much information as possible is gathered about *each student*. Although they are sometimes controversial, paper-and-pencil tests, used properly, provide an important source of information for teachers (Worthen, 1993). While they should not be the only form of measurement, not using them on the grounds of potential damage to students simply has no support in the research literature (Stiggins, 2001).

2. Be certain that instruction and testing are aligned; the topics and content emphasized in class should be the same ones emphasized on the test.

3. During instruction and review sessions, give students a chance to practice on the kinds of items they will encounter on the test.

4. After you give a test, hand it back to students as soon as possible, carefully review commonly missed items, and then collect the copies again (Linn and Gronlund, 2000). Teachers don't have time to keep creating new test items; the learning derived from review of the test comes primarily from the discussion and not from the students' having the tests available for further review.

5. File a copy of the test, write notes on the copy, and revise the items that may have been misleading.

6. Choose an objective format, such as multiple choice, for outcomes that can be effectively measured with these items. Use essay items when you want to measure student ability to organize and present information or make and defend an argument. Keep essay items relatively short and describe clearly what the essay is to contain (Stiggins, 2001).

7. Establish positive expectations for students as they anticipate the test. Tests need to be constructed so that students have an opportunity to demonstrate what they've learned. The key is to establish positive expectations and then manage to have the class meet them, an outcome that in turn reinforces similar expectations for subsequent tests.

This concludes our discussion of effective use of traditional assessments. In the next section, we examine alternative assessments, which are being increasingly emphasized in our schools.

ALTERNATIVE ASSESSMENT

While traditional assessment formats remain popular, they are being increasingly criticized for the following reasons:

- Traditional testing focuses on knowledge and recall of information.
- Traditional tests provide little insight into the way learners are thinking.
- Traditional tests don't assess students' ability to apply their understanding to real world problems (Herman et al., 1992; Marzano et al., 1993).

In response to these criticisms, **alternative assessments** are being emphasized. These assessments *directly measure student performance through real-life tasks* (Herman et al., 1992; Worthen, 1993).

Some examples of alternative assessments include:

- Writing an editorial commentary for the school newspaper
- Compiling a portfolio of writing samples produced over the year with student evaluations of strengths and weaknesses
- Designing and constructing a study desk in a woodworking class
- Writing and illustrating a book for young readers

In addition to products, such as the editorial, the desk, or the book, teachers want to examine learners' thinking as they use alternative assessments (Gronlund, 1993).

Let's look at two forms of alternative assessments, *performance assessments* and *portfolios*.

Performance Assessment

A middle school science teacher notices that her students have difficulty designing and conducting simple science experiments (such as determining which brand of aspirin dissolves faster, as we saw in Chapter 10).

A health teacher reads in a professional journal that the biggest problem people have in applying first aid is not the mechanics per se, but knowing what to do when. In an attempt to address this problem, the teacher has a periodic unannounced "catastrophe" day. Students entering the classroom encounter a catastrophe victim with an unspecified injury. In each case, they must first diagnose the problem and then apply first aid interventions (Eggen and Kauchak, 2001, p. 609).

These teachers are using performance assessments to gather information about their students' thinking. **Performance assessments** *ask students to demonstrate their knowledge and skill by carrying out an activity or producing a product.*

Let's look now at the procedures teachers employ when they use performance assessments.

Designing Performance Assessments. Experts identify four steps in designing performance assessments (Gronlund, 1993): (1) specifying desired outcomes, (2) selecting the focus of evaluation, (3) structuring the evaluation setting, and (4) designing evaluation procedures.

SPECIFYING DESIRED OUTCOMES. The first step in designing any assessment is to develop a clear idea of what you're trying to measure. A clear description of the skill or process helps students understand what is required and assists the teacher in designing appropriate instruction. An example in the area of speech is outlined in Figure 12.2 (based on work by Gronlund, 1993).

SELECTING THE FOCUS OF EVALUATION. Having specified performance outcomes, teachers next decide whether the assessment will focus on processes or products. Processes are often the initial focus, with a shift to products after procedures are mastered (Gronlund, 1993). Examples of both processes and products as components of performance assessments are found in Table 12.1.

STRUCTURING THE EVALUATION SETTING. The value of performance assessments lies in their link to realistic tasks; ultimately, teachers want students to apply

Oral Presentation

_____ **1.** Stands naturally.
_____ **2.** Maintains eye contact.
_____ **3.** Uses gestures effectively.
_____ **4.** Uses clear language
_____ **5.** Has adequate volume.
_____ **6.** Speaks at an appropriate rate.
_____ **7.** Topics are well organized.
_____ **8.** Maintains interest of the group.

Figure 12.2 Performance Outcomes in Speech

Table 12.1 PROCESSES AND PRODUCTS AS COMPONENTS
OF PERFORMANCE

Content Area	Product	Process
Math	Correct answer	Problem-solving steps leading to the correct solution
Music	Performance of a work on an instrument	Correct fingering and breathing that produces the performance
English Composition	Essay, term paper, or composition	Preparation of drafts and thought processes that produce the product
Word Processing	Letter or copy of final draft	Proper stroking and techniques for presenting the paper
Science	Explanation for the outcomes of a demonstration	Thought processes involved in preparing the explanation

the skill in the real world. Time, expense, and safety may prevent realistic measurement procedures, however, and intermediate steps might be necessary.

For example, in driver education the goal is to produce safe drivers. However, putting students in heavy traffic to assess how well they function behind the wheel is both unrealistic and dangerous. Alternate assessment options exist that vary the amount or degree of realism. For example, at the low realism/high safety end of the continuum students can respond to written cases or use a simulator. At the high realism/low safety end of the performance continuum they can actually drive, first in parking lots and quiet roads and ultimately in rush hour city traffic.

DESIGNING EVALUATION PROCEDURES. The final step in creating performance assessments is to design evaluation procedures. Reliability is a primary concern. Well-defined criteria in the form of scoring rubrics, similar to those used with essay items, increase both reliability and validity (Mabry, 1999; Stiggins, 2001). Clearly written criteria provide models of excellence and performance targets for students (McTighe, 1996/1997). Effective criteria have four elements (Herman et al., 1992; Messick, 1994):

1. One or more dimensions that serve as a basis for assessing student performance
2. A description of each dimension
3. A scale of values on which each dimension is rated
4. Definitions of each value on the scale

Let's look now at three further alternate ways to evaluate learner performance: (5) systematic observation, (6) checklists, and (7) rating scales.

Systematic observations *involve describing learners' performances based on preset criteria.* For example, the science teacher attempting to teach her students inquiry skills might identify the following criteria.

a. Specified the problem
b. Stated hypotheses

    c. Identified variables

    d. Gathered, organized and displayed data

    e. Used data to assess the hypotheses

The teacher's notes as she observed students designing experiments would then be based on the criteria, increasing their reliability and providing feedback for students.

    Checklists *are written descriptions of dimensions that must be present in an acceptable performance* and extend systematic observation. When checklists are used, students' performances are simply checked off rather than described in notes. For example, the science teacher wanting to assess learners' inquiry abilities might prepare a checklist such as the one that appears in Figure 12.3. (Notes could be added if desired, which would then combine elements of both checklists and systematic observations.)

    Checklists are useful when behaviors either do or don't exist, such as item 3, "Identified controlled variables." In cases such as item 7, "Assesses hypotheses in written form," the results aren't merely present or absent; some assessments of hypotheses will be better than others. This leads us to rating scales.

    Rating scales *are written descriptions of dimensions and scales of values on which each dimension is rated.* They allow a better assessment of quality than is possible with checklists. A sample rating scale, based on the checklist in Figure 12.3, is illustrated in Figure 12.4.

    Although they are labor intensive to construct, rubrics that are used as a basis for making decisions should be constructed for each of the dimensions. For example, definitions

_____ **1.** Stated problem

_____ **2.** Stated hypotheses

_____ **3.** Identified controlled variables

_____ **4.** Identified independent and dependent variables

_____ **5.** Makes three measurements of dependent variables

_____ **6.** Organizes data in a chart or table

_____ **7.** Assesses hypotheses in written form

Figure 12.3 Checklist for Assessing Inquiry

Rate each item. A rating of 5 is excellent, and a rating of 1 is poor.

1. States problem clearly.   5 4 3 2 1

2. States hypotheses clearly.   5 4 3 2 1

3. Controls variables effectively.   5 4 3 2 1

4. Uses effective data gathering techniques.   5 4 3 2 1

5. Presents data effectively.   5 4 3 2 1

6. Draws appropriate conclusions.   5 4 3 2 1

Figure 12.4 Rating Scale for Assessing Inquiry

of values, such as the following, might be used to evaluate whether the problem was stated clearly.

Rating = 5	Problem is clear and complete. It indicates that students understand both the content and the importance of the problem. It provides a basis for hypothesizing solutions.
Rating = 4	Problem is reasonably clear. It is appropriate, but more significant problems exist with respect to the topic. A clear basis for hypothesizing solutions is provided.
Rating = 3	The problem is stated somewhat ambiguously. The basis for hypothesizing solutions isn't clear.
Rating = 2	The statement isn't in the form of a problem. Understanding of the problem and its significance isn't indicated in the statement.
Rating = 1	No problem stated.

Definitions for each of the other dimensions in the rating scale would be written in a form similar to those above. Using these descriptions, observers can achieve acceptable levels of reliability for both student performance and products (Herman et al., 1992).

Portfolio Assessment

The use of portfolios, another form of alternative assessment, has the additional advantage of involving students in the design, collection, and evaluation of learning products. **Portfolios** are *purposeful collections of student work that are reviewed against preset criteria* (Stiggins, 2001). Because they are cumulative, connected, and occur over a period of time, they can provide a motion picture of learning progress versus the snapshots provided by disconnected tests and quizzes (Ziomek, 1997). The physical portfolio or collection of students' products, such as essays, journal entries, artwork, and videotapes, is not the assessment; the portfolio assessment also includes the students' and teacher's judgments of learning progress based on these products.

Two features distinguish portfolios from other forms of assessment. First, portfolios collect work samples over time, reflecting developmental changes, and second, portfolios involve students in design, collection, and evaluation. Some examples of portfolio assessments could include:

- Pieces of art produced throughout the grading period or year.
- Samples of math papers including computation and problem solving.
- Drafts of different kinds of essays in language arts
- Drawings and written explanations for the results observed in demonstrations and hands-on activities in science

Portfolios should reflect learning progress. For example, different essays indicate changes that occur during a grading period, semester, or entire course. These samples can then be used in parent-teacher conferences and as feedback for the students themselves.

When using portfolios, students should be involved in deciding what will be included and how it will be evaluated. By involving students in these decisions, teachers help students become aware of options in assessing their own growth, which is another way of increasing learner self-regulation.

One lower elementary school student had this to say about the learning progress reflected in a year-long portfolio:

> Today I looked at my stories in my writing folder. I read some of my writing since September. I noticed that I've improved some stuff. Now I edit my stories and revise. Now I use periods, quotation marks. Sometimes my stories are longer. I used to misspelling words and now I look in a dictionary or ask a friend and now I write exciting and scary stories and now I have very good endings. Now I use capitals. I used to leave out words and write short simple stories. (Paulson et al., 1991, p. 63)

Through the process of self-analysis and evaluation students become more aware of their own growth as learners.

ACCOMMODATING DIVERSITY: REDUCING BIAS IN ASSESSMENT

As we've seen throughout this text, the diversity in our students influences our planning and the learning activities we conduct. This is true of assessment as well. We may have students, for example, who aren't familiar with the standard assessment practices of the school, such as multiple-choice or true-false formats. They may not understand the purposes of assessment, they may lack test-taking strategies, and may even have difficulties with the English language.

Teachers can respond to differences in students' assessment backgrounds in several ways:

- Provide practice with test taking
- Teach test-taking strategies
- Consider use of language in items
- Make provisions for nonnative English speakers

Provide Practice with Test Taking

For students who are unfamiliar with test-taking routines, providing practice with different items, as Andy Robinson did with his students, can be particularly effective. Clearly communicating the importance of assessments is essential because some students, such as Native Americans, may not understand how assessment influences learning (Deyhle, 1987). In addition, teaching specific test-taking strategies can be helpful.

Teach Test-Taking Strategies

Teaching test-taking strategies helps students improve their performance through awareness and understanding of test-taking demands. Some specific strategies include:

- Reacting to different testing formats
- Efficient use of time
- Carefully reading directions

For strategies to be most effective, teachers need to remind students about strategies as tests and individual items are discussed. For example, in multiple-choice items, one or two of the choices will often directly contradict the stem, and can therefore be eliminated. Reducing the choices to a plausible two is an effective strategy. When faced with essay items, preparing a brief outline is a simple strategy that can be used to increase the logic and organization of the response. Reminding students of these strategies and illustrating them can significantly improve learners' performance, particularly with young, low-ability, and minority students who have limited test-taking experience (Anastasi, 1988; Mehrens and Lehmann, 1987a).

Consider Use of Language in Items

With students from diverse cultural backgrounds, confusing or unfamiliar language is always a possibility. For example, students may have problems with items that take certain knowledge for granted, such as familiarity with American sports, common forms of transportation, historical figures, or music and other elements of U.S. culture (Cheng, 1987).

This problem has no easy solution, but being aware of and sensitive to the possibilities of unfamiliar content are beginning points. Also, encourage students to ask questions during tests, and give students opportunities to discuss the items on tests when they are handed back.

Make Provisions for Nonnative English Speakers

What if the next exam you take for one of your classes was written in Spanish? For most of us, this would be very difficult. Many of our students encounter a similar difficulty in our classrooms when tests are given in their nonnative language. As with other potential forms of bias in testing, easy solutions don't exist. However, some possibilities for accommodating nonnative English speakers include the following:

- Provide extra time to take the test. Allow students to take the test before or after school, using a translation dictionary.
- Translate the test into students' native languages until their English proficiency improves.
- If one is available, use an interpreter during tests.

Each of these suggestions is designed to ensure, as much as possible, that test scores reflect actual achievement and not learners' familiarity with common background knowledge or vocabulary. This increases validity and also provides the teacher with more accurate information about learning progress.

DESIGNING AN ASSESSMENT SYSTEM

While traditional tests and quizzes and alternative assessments are important, they don't represent the entire assessment system. In addition, an assessment system includes decisions about grading and reporting and communication with students, parents, and school officials. We examine the design of the total assessment system in this section.

Where to start? There are many decisions to make, such as the number of tests and quizzes, the kinds of assignments, the weight of each, and grading, that it is hard to know where to begin.

One way to begin is to analyze your teaching situation. What information are you expected to provide, and when is it due? Looking at a report card is a reasonable beginning point. In analyzing a report card, try to answer the following questions:

- What areas are evaluated?
- How is student performance described (e.g., letter grade, percentage, or descriptive statement)?
- How frequently do grades need to be given?
- How are affective dimensions like cooperation and following rules reported?
- How are tardiness and absences reported?

These may seem mundane, but we have encountered first-year teachers who were only weeks away from their first report cards and conferences with parents when they realized they were expected to give grades in penmanship and citizenship, and they had to scurry to gather the necessary information! Talking to other teachers can help clarify existing practices and avoid pitfalls, and your principal can be valuable in explaining the school's and district's expectations. When you're done designing your assessment system, you should be able to confidently defend the system to a parent or administrator (Loyd and Loyd, 1997).

Once you understand what is expected of you, and knowing that your assessments should be valid, reliable, frequent, and efficient, you can begin designing your own system.

Routines can be helpful in structuring your assessment system. The following represents one routine in elementary math:

Monday:	Review last week's work; introduce new concepts
Tuesday, Wednesday:	Develop concepts and skills with daily homework
Thursday:	Reinforce understanding; review for quiz
Friday:	Quiz

Teachers who use a system like this one report that students like the structure that the routine provided.

Grades and Grading

An essential part of assessment is some consideration of grades. You already know the form that these will take on report cards; your job now is to translate the various assignments, quizzes, tests, and alternative assessments into a comprehensive system. Two major ways of doing this are summarized in Table 12.2.

A point system is straightforward; the importance of each assignment and quiz is reflected in the points allocated. Then these are added up and grades are given. Weighted scores are slightly more complex. Let's see how one system, using Steve Vockel's spelling exercises on the board as an illustration, might work. Suppose Steve wrote 10 words on the board and then scored students' papers. Now imagine that he gave another short exercise of five items and a third of eight items. In scoring these items, teachers typically convert the raw scores to a percentage. A student who got 8 of 10 correct in the first case would have a score of 80 written in the gradebook; 2 of 5 in the second case would be a

Table 12.2 WEIGHTED SCORES AND POINT GRADING SYSTEMS

Point System		Weighted Scores	
Every graded assignment or quiz is given a point value. These are then added up to provide a total score.		Every assignment is given a letter grade and all grades are then weighted.	
Example:		*Example:*	
Assignments (20 × 10 pts.)	200	Assignments (20)	25%
Quizzes (8 × 25 pts.)	200	Quizzes (8)	25%
Tests (4 × 100 pts.)	400	Tests (4)	50%
Total possible points =	800	Total =	100%

Grade Range
  A 750–800
  B 700–750
  C 650–700
  D 600–650

score of 40; and 7 of 8 in the third case would be a score of 88. Teachers then typically find an average to arrive at the final score on which the student's grade is based. In this case, the student's average would be a 69, which in most grading systems is a D. In reality, however, the student responded to a total of 23 items, 17 of which he answered correctly. His actual percentage is 74—five points higher and a C in most grading systems. The problem with the system we just illustrated is that each of the exercises is given the same weight, even though the number of items is markedly different—10, 5, and 8, respectively.

If this system seems flawed, why is it so common? Two reasons are often given. First, it is simple, and as we have noted repeatedly, the need to simplify is powerful. Second, both students and parents tend to prefer the percentage system because it is simpler and easier to understand for them as well. We have talked to teachers who have used the raw scores, converting to a percentage only at the end of a marking period, and later went back to the percentage system throughout because of pressure from students.

Norm- and Criterion-Referenced Evaluation. In assigning grades within either system, teachers have two options. One, called **criterion-referenced evaluation,** *uses preestablished percentages or number totals for grades* (e.g., 90–100, A; 80–90, B; 70–80, C; etc.). The advantage of this approach is that it communicates grading standards clearly and is noncompetitive; students compete only against the criteria. The alternative, called **norm-referenced evaluation,** *compares students' performances to each other.* Grading on the curve is an example. Because it deemphasizes competition and focuses on content mastery, most experts favor criterion referencing, and it is also the most common system in place in classrooms (Crooks, 1988; Maehr, 1992).

Homework. Another major grading decision is how to handle homework. Research indicates that homework can have a positive impact on learning (Cooper, 1989), but it provides little guidance about how to integrate it into an assessment system.

A major issue here is accountability. Students should feel responsible for doing homework and should understand that homework is crucial to learning. They also need to be rewarded for conscientious efforts. Implementing a system that doesn't bury you under mounds of paperwork is the problem. Some options include:

1. Assign homework, grade it yourself, and record the scores. This is the best option for promoting learning, but it is demanding and time consuming. This option can be viable if you have an aide or a parent volunteer who can help with some of the routine work.
2. Assign homework, select samples from the assignment, have the students turn in those samples, and record the score on those problems. This is a compromise. The teacher scores the homework, but the amount is reduced. Students sometimes resent having done all the homework and getting credit for only part of it.
3. Have students grade their own papers in class, and score all the homework as a group. This saves teacher time and gives students immediate feedback. However, it takes class time, is subject to cheating, and doesn't work for written work and projects involving higher level outcomes.
4. Assign homework, give the students credit for having done the homework whether or not it is correct, and then use class time to cover material students found difficult. This option has the advantage of allowing students to correct their own mistakes. However, students often don't try as hard when homework isn't actually scored.
5. Assign homework, collect it at random intervals, and score and mark it. This option reduces the teacher's workload, but the homework must be collected regularly or students tend to stop doing it.
6. Do not grade homework, but give frequent short quizzes based on the material covered in the homework. This is effective with older and higher-achieving students, who understand the links between homework and achievement. It is ineffective with low achievers and poorly motivated students.

Which system should you adopt? We recommend that you talk to other teachers and experiment to find out what works best for you.

Communication

Communication is an integral part of an effective assessment system (Stiggins, 2001). At the beginning of the school year, you need to explain to students what is expected of them and share this information with parents. As information is gathered throughout the school year, it needs to be shared with both students and parents. Ways of doing this are the focus of this section.

We have seen throughout this text how expectations influence learning. For positive expectations to increase learning, both students and parents must know what your expectations are—this is why effective communication is critical in an effective assessment system. Further, researchers have documented the importance of the home-school partnership, and effective communication with parents is a critical dimension of this partnership (Epstein, 1990). Teachers use a variety of ways to communicate their expectations to parents and students.

Written Communication. In the primary grades, communication may be more directly with parents than with students. As children get older, the communication is directed to both. The letter in Figure 12.5 is used each year by a fifth-grade teacher to communicate expectations.

At the junior high and high school levels, parents and students often are interested in the content of the course and how student work will be graded. One algebra teacher sent home the document shown in Figure 12.6 at the beginning of the school year.

Dear Parents and Students,

I am looking forward to an exciting year in fifth grade, and I hope you are too! In order for us to work together most effectively, some guidelines are necessary. They are listed below. Please read through the information carefully and sign at the bottom of the page. Thank you for your cooperation and help in making this year the best one ever for your youngster.

Sincerely,
Mrs. Kathy Mease

Survival Guidelines

1. Follow directions the first time they are given.
2. Be in class, seated, and quiet when the bell rings.
3. Bring covered textbooks, notebook and/or folder, paper, pen, and pencils to class daily.
4. Raise your hand for permission to speak or to leave your seat.
5. Keep hands, feet, and objects to yourself.

Homework Guidelines

1. Motto---I will always TRY, and I will NEVER give up!
2. I will complete all assignments. If the assignment is not finished or is not ready when called for, a zero will be given.
3. Head your paper properly---directions were given in class. Use pen/pencil---no red, orange, or pink ink. If you have questions, see Mrs. Mease.
4. Whenever you are absent, it is your responsibility to come in early in the morning (7:30-8:00) and make arrangements for makeup work. Class time will not be used for this activity. Tests are always assigned three to five days in advance---if you are absent the day before the test, you should come prepared to take the test because you will be expected to take it.
5. No extra credit work will be given. If you do all the required work and study for the tests, there should be no need for extra credit.
6. A packet of papers is sent home with the children each Tuesday. Please look them over carefully. If you have any questions or comments, please feel free to call Lone Trail Elementary School (272-8160). I will return your call promptly.

Again, my best wishes for a terrific year.

_____ (student) _____ (parent)

Figure 12.5 Letter to Parents

Course Expectations

I.   Course Title: Algebra I

II. Course Description: This course explores basic algebraic concepts and applications, including a complete review of the number system. The main emphasis of the course is on solving linear and quadratic equations.

III. Course Objectives
   A. To understand the basic terms and symbols used in the study of algebra.
   B. To perform the basic operations with signed numbers.
   C. To solve simple linear equations and inequalities in one unknown.
   D. To understand the graphical properties of linear equations.
   E. To perform basic operations with polynomials.
   F. To solve quadratic equations using factoring.
   G. To perform fundamental operations with algebraic fractions.
   H. To solve quadratic equations using the quadratic formula.
   I. To apply equation solving techniques to story problems.

IV. Learning Activities
   A. Daily assignments   E. Peer tutoring
   B. Teacher demonstration   F. Reviews
   C. Class discussion   G. Student demonstration
   D. Note taking and writing projects

V.   Grading Procedure: Grades will be based on test performance, notebooks, daily assignments, and quizzes. Grades will be weighted as follows:
   Tests--40%   Quizzes--40%   Daily assignments--20%
   Final grades will be determined on the following scale:
   93-100% A   65-72% D
   85-92% B   0-64%   F
   73-84% C

VI. Materials
   A. Text: *Holt Algebra One,* Holt, Rinehart and Winston Publishers, 1996.
   B. Calculator: It is recommended that each student obtain a scientific calculator.
   C. Paper, pencil, and pen.
   D. Learning log.

VII. Student Expectations
   A. Students must come prepared to class each day with their book, notebook, pencil and paper, and assignments.
   B. School policy states that four unexcused absences will result in failure. Make-up tests must be taken within three days of return from absence. Make-up assignments must be turned in on the second day of return from absence. No make-up quizzes will be given. The low quiz in each grading period will be dropped.
   C. To facilitate roll taking and grading, students are expected to sit in the seats assigned to them.
   D. Cheating will not be tolerated. Anyone guilty of cheating will receive a zero on the test.
   E. Courtesy and respect are expected to be shown at all times. This includes not eating during class, listening to the lecture, and staying on task. Stereos and headsets are to be left in students' lockers.

I have read this document and understand the grading procedures and classroom rules. Please feel free to call the school at any time if you have questions or concerns (936-1148).

_____ Student _____ Parent

Figure 12.6 Course Expectations in Algebra

Note how the algebra teacher described (1) the content of the course, (2) instructional activities, (3) grading procedures and student requirements. These were addressed in a positive, businesslike manner and set the stage for a productive school year. We recommend a document like this at the beginning of the year. It is straightforward and informative and communicates not only positive expectations but also organization and competence.

Open House. Most school systems have a scheduled open house at a specified date early in the school year. Parents are invited to attend, and at the middle and high school levels they move through an abbreviated schedule of a typical day's activities. Teachers describe their policies and expectations and invite input from parents. The written expectations teachers have are often distributed in these sessions.

The image you project as a teacher is critical at this time. Because open house is often the only time you will see a parent during the year, the impression you make will be lasting. Proper dress, careful use of language and grammar, clear and neatly written communications, and a warm and pleasant but professional manner are all important in creating a good impression.

Parent-Teacher Conferences. An additional opportunity to communicate expectations, grading policies, and student progress is through conferences where parents and teachers meet face to face. Some teachers have experimented with inviting students to these conferences and have noted the benefits of students' being informed of and rewarded for their efforts in class. Suggestions for conducting successful parent-teacher conferences include:

1. Organize and prepare before the meeting. The files and records of each of your students should be readily available during the meeting.
2. Begin with a positive statement (e.g., "Mary is such a lively, energetic second grader"—despite the fact that she is about to drive you crazy.) This puts the parent at ease and sets the stage for later comments.
3. Be factual in your statements and use supporting documentation. At the elementary level, this might consist of samples of the student's work; at the secondary level, it should include scores and averages on assignments and tests.
4. Listen carefully to parents' questions and concerns. This shows you care, and it provides you with information about the student.
5. To end the session, summarize the discussion and end on an optimistic note (e.g., "Jim *can* learn math, and if we both encourage him on his homework, I'm sure we'll see a difference next report card.").

Phone Conferences. One of the most effective forms of communication is a simple phone call. They are effective for one important reason—they communicate that you care enough about a student to spend your personal time discussing problems or concerns about that individual in a one-to-one conference with a parent or caregiver. For this reason, a negative or defensive reaction by parents is rare, and the outcomes of these conversations are almost always productive. Even better, a periodic phone call to tell about improved work or behavior can pay big dividends. Parents are rarely called when their child does something *good,* so a call with positive feedback can be very effective in promoting a positive home-school partnership.

Communication: Report Cards. We have all had experience with report cards. While the form varies, report cards at a given level generally communicate similar information. An excerpt from a report sent to the parents of kindergarten children is shown in Figure 12.7.

KINDERGARTEN PROGRESS REPORT

2001-2002

Name: _____

Teacher: _____

School: _____

MARKING KEY

O - Outstanding
S - Satisfactory
I - Improvement Shown
N - Needs Improvement
Ø - Not Evaluated

Attendance	1	2	3	4	Total
Days Present					
Days Absent					
Days Tardy					

SOCIAL DEVELOPMENT AND WORK HABITS	1	2	3	4
Works and plays well with others				
Is kind and courteous				
Listens attentively				
Uses socially acceptable language				
Respects rules				
Accepts correction graciously				
Respects rights of others				

LANGUAGE READINESS	1	2	3	4
Recognizes colors: R O GR Y BL P BR BK WH				
Reads color words: R O GR Y BL P BR BK WH				
Identifies and uses opposites				
Knows rhyming sounds				
Know directions (up, down, left, right)				

MATHEMATICS	1	2	3	4
Recognizes shapes ○△□▭◇				
Counts objects 1, 2, 3, 4, 5, 6, 7, 8, 9, 10, 11, 12, 13, 14, 15, 16, 17, 18, 19, 20				
Correctly writes 0, 1, 2, 3, 4, 5, 6, 7, 8, 9, 10				
Recognizes 0, 1, 2, 3, 4, 5, 6, 7, 8, 9, 10, 11, 12, 13, 14, 15, 16, 17, 18, 19, 20				
Counts to _____				

MOTOR SKILLS	1	2	3	4
Demonstrates large muscle control (hop, skip, jump, throw, catch, run, balance)				
Demonstrates fine motor control:				
Forms letters and numbers correctly				
Holds pencil and crayon correctly				
Traces over lines				
Can cut out geometric shapes				

Figure 12.7 Kindergarten Progress Report

Notice that this report (1) includes affective and personal growth goals; (2) is based primarily on performance measures; and (3) uses an O, S, I, N scale versus an A, B, C, D scale for reporting. On a form like this, there also would be space for some short written comments.

Compare this kindergarten report to one used in the intermediate grades (Figure 12.8). We can see from this example that affective goals such as social behaviors and attitudes are still evaluated at the junior high level, but a separate scale is used. In addition, comparative information is provided in basic skills in the areas of absolute achievement, progress made during the quarter, and effort.

As students progress into high school, less emphasis is placed on affective considerations, and grades are often quantified in terms of percentages (see Figure 12.9). This latter point has strong implications for the kind of grading system the teacher designs, a point we made earlier.

Interim Progress Reports. Report cards are commonly sent home every 9 weeks. Typically, schools also report progress at midterm as well. In some cases students get interim progress reports only when a student is experiencing difficulty, while in others all students receive them. The purpose of the report is to provide feedback to both students and parents regarding progress, and they can be especially helpful if problems develop. Your school will have a form and a standard procedure for completing interim progress reports.

USING TECHNOLOGY IN ASSESSMENT

Because of its ability to store large amounts of data and process it quickly, technology is proving to be especially valuable in classroom assessment. Technology, and particularly computers, can serve three important and time-saving assessment functions (Newby et al., 2000; Roblyer and Edwards, 2000):

- Planning and constructing tests
- Analyzing test data, especially data gathered from objective tests
- Maintaining student records

One theme of this chapter has been the value of frequent classroom assessment. Computers provide an efficient way to store these data, analyze them, and present them to students in an understandable way. These functions are summarized in Table 12.3 and discussed in the paragraphs that follow.

Planning and Constructing Tests

As we saw in earlier sections, constructing effective test items can be a difficult and time-consuming task. The word processing capabilities of computers provide teachers with an effective tool for writing and revising individual items, and once items are written, computers are helpful for assembling them into a complete test. Initially, items focus on specific content or topics. Later, they can be grouped into similar item types and sequenced from easiest to hardest. This sequence helps reduce test anxiety by providing easy entry into a test.

STUDENT ID _____

BEHAVIOR AND ATTITUDES

BEHAVIOR AND ATTITUDES	Report Period			
	1	2	3	4
1. Accepts responsibility				
2. Follows directions				
3. Completes assignments on time				
4. Shows judgment in use and care of materials				
5. Displays creativity				
6. Is courteous and considerate of others				
7. Uses time well				
8. Works well in groups				
9. Abides by school rules				

BEHAVIOR AND ATTITUDES

These behaviors are important to success in school. These factors reflect attitude toward school, self, and others. They have a direct bearing on the progress being made in the basic skills.

E – Excellent

S – Satisfactory

NI – Needs Improvement

ACHIEVEMENT, PROGRESS, AND EFFORT	1			2			3			4		
	Achievement	Progress	Effort	Achievement	Progress	Effort	Achievement	Progress	Effort	Achievement	Progress	Effort
Reading												
Language Arts												
Handwriting												
Spelling												
Mathematics												
Health												
Science												
Social Studies												
Art* — Satisfactory Performance												
Art* — Needs Improvement												
Music* — Satisfactory Performance												
Music* — Needs Improvement												
Phys. Ed.* — Satisfactory Performance												
Phys. Ed.* — Needs Improvement												

* Letter grades are not given in these subject areas due to the difficulty of precise measurement of acquired skills.

Figure 12.8 Intermediate Grade Report Card

• REPORT CARD •

NAME	SCHOOL	STUDENT NUMBER	HOME ROOM	SCHOOL YEAR
ADDRESS		CITY	ZIP CODE	TELEPHONE

PERIOD FROM THRU	COURSE NAME	WGT	TEACHER NAME	TEA NO.	1ST GRD	1ST C	1ST ABS	2ND GRD	2ND C	2ND ABS	1ST SEM EXAM	2ND SEM AVG	3RD GRD	3RD C	3RD ABS	4TH GRD	4TH C	4TH ABS	2ND SEM EXAM	2ND SEM AVG	YR AVG	CREDIT EARNED
1	M/J LIFE SCI ADV			082	93A	0	0	90B	0	1		92B	90B	0	3	93A	0	2		92B	92B	
2	M/J BAND 4			129	97A	0	0	**A	0	2		99A	97A	0	3	95A	0	3		96A	97A	
3	ALGEBRA			029	96A	0	0	93A	0	1		95A	91BS		3	91BS		2		91B	93A	
4	POL. SCIENCE			053	92BS		1	91B	0	1		92B	93AS		2	94AS		2		94A	93A	
5	AM. LITERATURE			004	93AS		1	90B	0	1		92B	89BS		2	93AS		2		91B	91B	
6	M/J PHYS ED 2			101	96AS		0	97AS		1		97A	97AS		1	94AS		2		96A	96A	

PROMOTED

Figure 12.9 High School Report Form

Table 12.3 ASSESSMENT FUNCTIONS PERFORMED BY COMPUTERS

Function	Examples
Planning and construction	Preparing objectives Writing and storing items Creating tests Printing tests
Scoring and interpreting tests	Scoring tests Summarizing results Analyzing items
Maintaining student records	Developing a class summary Recording results Preparing grade reports Developing student profiles Reporting results to students

A number of commercially prepared software programs can assist in this process (e.g., *Create a Test, Exam Builder, Test Writer, Test IT! Deluxe, Tests-Made-Easy, Quick Quiz,* and *Test Generator*). They have the following capabilities:

- Develop a test file or item bank of multiple-choice, true-false, matching, and short-answer items that can be stored in the system. Within a file, items can be organized by topic, chapter, objective, or by difficulty.
- Select items from the created file bank either randomly, selectively, or by categories to generate multiple versions of a test.
- Modify items and integrate these into the total test.
- Produce student-ready copies and an answer key.

Analyzing Test Data

Once administered, tests need to be scored and analyzed. A high school teacher with five sections of 30 students and a 40-item exam faces a logistical challenge—$5 \times 30 \times 40 = 6,000$ individual items! Scoring and analyzing test data, converting scores to grades, and recording the grades can be enormously time consuming.

Most schools now have computers that can machine-score or scan teacher-made tests. To use this time-saving feature, test items need to be placed in formats that can be transferred to machine-scored answer sheets (i.e., multiple-choice, true-false, matching).

There are also a number of software programs available to machine-score tests (e.g., *Test Scorer, Quickscore,* and *Test Analysis*), and their average cost is around $200. These programs can:

- Score objective tests and provide descriptive statistics such as test mean, median and mode, range, and standard deviation.

- Generate a list of items showing difficulty level, the percentage of students who selected each response, the percentage of students who didn't respond to an item, and the correlation of each item with the total test.
- Sort student responses by score, grade/age, or gender.

A sample printout for a 15-item multiple-choice quiz given to a class of 35 students appears in Table 12.4. The printout identifies the item number, the number of students who selected each choice, the correct answer, the statistical average for the quiz (mean), a measure of the spread of scores (standard deviation), and the middle score (median).

The quiz was first machine scored, and the software program provided an immediate printout of the descriptive statistics and distribution of student responses. The distribution of responses is particularly useful in analyzing the quality of the items and possible student misconceptions.

Though most teachers use a criterion-referenced rather than a norm-referenced system for assigning their own grades, the descriptive statistics included with the analysis give an indication of the quiz's difficulty and class performance as a whole. For instance, a mean of 9.22 on a 15-item quiz suggests that the quiz was difficult for students, so some questions exist about (a) the students' understanding of the content, (b) the difficulty of the items, (c) the quality of some of the items, or all three. This type of analysis, together with teacher reflection and revision of test items, can improve the overall effectiveness of a teacher's assessment system.

Table 12.4 COMPUTER ANALYSIS OF TEST RESULTS

ITEM	1	2	3	4	5	6	7	8	9	10	11	12	13	14	15
A	34	0	0	0	0	30	1	0	4	0	0	0	8	1	1
B	0	0	0	1	7	4	0	0	8	19	13	1	0	0	6
C	1	2	30	27	3	1	11	34	4	11	21	16	10	28	3
D	0	33	5	7	5	0	13	1	17	2	0	18	17	6	17
E	0	0	0	0	20	0	10	0	2	3	0	0	0	0	7
Blank Responses	0	0	0	0	0	0	0	0	0	0	1	0	0	0	1
Correct Answer	A	D	C	C	E	A	C	C	D	C	C	D	D	C	C

Total number of students processed: 35

Statistical analysis

  Mean: 09.22

  Standard deviation: 2.084

  Median: 09.00

Maintaining Student Records

An effective assessment system frequently gathers information about student performance from a variety of sources. If this information is to be useful to the teacher, it must be stored so that it is easily accessible. In addition, students need to know where they stand in the course to make the best use of their time and resources. Computers provide an efficient way of storing, analyzing, and reporting student assessments.

One teacher commented:

> I keep my grades in an electronic gradebook. By entering my grades into an electronic gradebook as I grade papers, I always know how my students are progressing and exactly where my students stand in relation to each other. It does take a little time to enter the grades, but it makes my job easier during reporting periods. All I have to do is open my disk and record my students' grades on the grade sheet (Morrison et al., 1999, p. 355).

For teachers with some background in technology, general spreadsheet programs can be converted into individualized gradesheets (Forcier, 1999). Commercial software is available, and most of the programs designed to analyze individual test score data also have the following capabilities:

- Begin a new class file for each class or subject. These can be stored by name and/or student identification number.
- Average grades, create new grades, or change old ones, add extra credit.
- Compute descriptive statistics such as the mean, median, mode, and standard deviation for any test or set of scores.
- Translate numerical or raw scores into letter grades.
- Record the type of activity and the point value for each activity.
- Average grades on a quarterly, semester, and/or yearly basis.

The amount of time and energy saved and the increased decision-making capability make computers an invaluable asset in the assessment process.

This brings us to the end of this chapter and to the end of the text. We hope the information you have read and studied has been useful and practical. As we have seen, research has much to offer the classroom teacher, but only the teacher can translate this research into practice. We have seen how teacher judgment is a critical element in all the decisions teachers make. This should not be a matter of concern, for it is one of the characteristics that makes teaching a challenging profession. With sincere effort, you will make an important contribution to education—the most rewarding of professions. We hope this text contributes to your efforts.

Summary

Classroom Assessment. Classroom assessment includes the information teachers gather, called measurements, and the decisions they make about learning progress, which are termed evaluations.

The process of assessment has both instructional and institutional functions. Effective assessment increases learning and provides information for students, teachers, parents, and school and district administrators.

Effective assessments are valid when they are consistent with goals and learning activities. They should also be reliable, which means they're consistent, and they should be practical, meaning they're efficient and usable.

Using Traditional Assessment Practices to Promote Learning. Using traditional assessments effectively includes preparing students for tests, specifying what will be on the test, giving students a chance to practice with the content and format, and establishing positive expectations.

During testing, effective teachers create a comfortable environment, carefully monitor students, and provide specific directions for taking the test and spending time afterward.

Effective teachers also score and return tests promptly, discuss frequently missed items, and make generally positive comments about students' performance.

Assessment should be an ongoing part of instruction. Teachers should take great care in preparing items, should test thoroughly and often, and should revise defective items.

Alternative Assessment. Alternative assessments ask students to perform in ways similar to performances that would be required in the world outside the classroom. Systematic observation, checklists, and rating scales can all be used to provide assessments that have acceptable levels of reliability.

Portfolios—collections of students' work—which are then evaluated provide an additional form of alternative assessment. Portfolios have the additional advantage of allowing students' input into the selection and evaluation of materials included in the portfolio.

Accommodating Diversity: Reducing Bias in Assessment. Teachers can accommodate learner diversity by providing practice with test-taking skills, being sensitive to language and content that might be confusing to learners from different cultures, discussing test items after students have responded to them, and making special provisions for nonnative English speakers in administering and scoring tests.

Designing an Assessment System. An effective assessment system takes into account tests, quizzes, homework, and other sources of information about student progress. Talking to school leaders and other teachers can help in designing your system.

Communication needs to be an integral part of an effective assessment system. Positive and concrete expectations set the stage for future learning, and this information must be shared with both students and parents. Communication includes familiar practices, such as open house, parent-teacher conferences, report cards, and interim progress reports. One of the most effective is the simple practice of calling parents. It communicates commitment to students as individuals and a teacher's willingness to spend personal time to help students.

Using Technology in Assessment. Technology, and particularly computers, can help teachers reduce their workloads and use their time efficiently. Technology can be used in planning and constructing tests, analyzing test results, and storing and maintaining student records.

Important Concepts

Alternative assessment
Assessment system
Checklist
Classroom assessment
Criterion-referenced evaluation
Evaluation
Formal measurement
Informal measurement
Instructional alignment
Measurement

Norm-referenced evaluation
Performance assessment
Portfolio
Rating scale
Reliability
Systematic observation
Table of specifications
Test anxiety
Validity

Reflecting on Teaching and Learning

As you've studied this chapter, you've seen how effective teachers design and implement assessments that gather accurate information and increase learning. Read the following case study now and consider how effectively the teacher implemented the ideas discussed in the chapter.

Darren Wilson, an English teacher at Greenland Pines Middle School, teaches three sections of standard English and two sections of advanced English. We look in now as he begins a unit on singular and plural possessives with one of his standard English classes.

The tardy bell rings at 8:50 as Darren begins, "All right, listen, everyone. . . . We've had some practice in making nouns plural . . . and today, we're going to begin studying possessives . . . both singular and plural. Everybody turn to page 239 in your text. . . . We see at the top of the page that we're dealing with possessives. . . . This is very important in our writing. We want to be able to write well, and this is one of the places where people often get confused. . . . So when we're finished with our study here, you'll all be able to use possessives correctly in your writing."

He then wrote the following on the board:

Add an apostrophe s to singular nouns or plural nouns that don't end in s.

Add an apostrophe after the s if the plural noun doesn't end in s.

If a singular or plural pronoun is possessive, do not add an apostrophe.

"Let's review briefly," Darren continued. "Who can spell the plural form of *city* for me?"

"C-i-t-i-e-s," Horace volunteered.

"Okay, good . . . So what would be the possessive form of the word?"

" . . . Apostrophe after the s," Marvella offered.

"Yes," Darren smiled. "Good, now what is the plural form of child? . . . Juanita?"

" . . . Children."

"All right, make it possessive," Darren probed.

" . . . Ahh, s . . . no, . . . apostrophe s . . . yeah, it doesn't end in s."

"Good thinking," Darren smiled. He then presented and had students discuss two more examples, and as they finished, he said, "Now let's look at some more examples. . . . Look on the overhead."

Darren showed an overhead with 10 sentences including the following four:

1. Did you get the card that belonged to Esteban?
2. The plots of the stories were quite interesting.
3. Joe owns a new car; the car is red.
4. The breeze blew the hats of the women off.

"Now," Darren continued, "rewrite the sentences in their possessive form, correctly using apostrophes. . . . That's your homework for tomorrow. . . . If you jump on it, you should be finished by the end of the period."

On Tuesday, Darren first went over the exercises the students had completed for homework and then reviewed some additional examples where they had to create plural forms of nouns, make them possessive, and properly punctuate possessive pronouns.

Near the end of class Darren announced, "Class, tomorrow we're going to have a test on all of this stuff; singular nouns, plural nouns, pronouns . . . the whole works. You have your notes, so study hard . . . Are there any questions? . . . Okay, good. I expect you all to do well. I'll see you tomorrow."

On Wednesday morning the students filed into class. As the bell rang, Darren picked up the tests and, amid some groans and murmurs, asked, "Everybody ready?"

The test was composed of two parts. The first included 15 sentences that had to be rewritten, as the students had done with the homework exercises. They involved combinations of singular nouns, plural nouns, and pronouns that had to be punctuated properly. The second part of the test directed students to write a paragraph that included at least one example of each rule for forming possessives.

"Just a reminder," Darren interjected before the students started working. "For the second part of the test . . . remember that the paragraph has to make sense. It can't just be a bunch of sentences on the paper."

The students went to work and Darren watched, periodically walking up and down the aisles. Seeing that the period was half over and some of the students were only starting on their paragraphs, he announced, "You have 20 minutes left. Watch your time and work quickly. You need to finish by the end of the period."

He continued monitoring, again reminding them to work quickly when 10 minutes were left and again when 5 minutes were left.

Trang, Niksha, Nevella, and Rudy were hastily finishing the last few words of their paragraphs just as the bell rang. Nevella turned in her paper as Darren's third-period students were filing in the room.

"Here," Darren said. "This pass will get you into Mrs. Jeffrey's class if you're late. . . . How did you do?"

"Okay, I think," Nevella said over her shoulder as she scurried out of the room, "except for the last part. It was hard. I couldn't get started."

"I'll look at it," Darren said. "Get moving now."

On Thursday and Friday Darren moved on to punctuating different kinds of clauses and phrases. He scored the tests over the weekend and returned the papers on Monday. As he handed them back, he said, "Here are your papers. You did fine on the sentences, but your paragraphs need a lot of work. Why did you have so much trouble with them, when we had so much practice?"

"It was hard, Mr. Wilson."

"Not enough time."

"I hate to write."

Darren listened patiently and then said, "Be sure you write your scores in your note-books. . . . Okay. . . . You have them all written down? . . . Are there any questions?"

"Number 8," Enrique asked.

"Okay, let's look at 8," and he explained the item, finishing by saying, "Any others?"

A sprinkling of questions went around the room, and Darren responded, "We don't have time to go over all of them. I'll discuss three more."

He then responded to three students who seemed most urgent in waving their hands. He then collected their tests and moved on to the topic for the day.

Questions for Analysis

Let's look at Darren's lesson now based on the information in this chapter. In doing your analysis, consider the following questions. In each case, be specific and take information directly from the case study in doing your analysis.

1. Alternative assessment was discussed in the chapter. How effective was Darren's alternative assessment?
2. How well was Darren's instruction aligned? Explain specifically what could he have done to increase instructional alignment.
3. Preparing students for tests, administering tests, and analyzing results were discussed in the section on effective testing. How effectively did Darren conduct each part? If you believe one or more of the parts could have been conducted more effectively, describe specifically what he might have done.
4. Accommodating background diversity in learners is a theme of this text. How effectively did Darren's assessment accommodate the diversity in his students?
5. Identify the primary strengths and the primary weaknesses in Darren's teaching and assessment. Be specific in your analysis.

Discussion Questions

1. What advantages are there to establishing measurement routines? Are there any disadvantages to these routines?
2. Some have suggested that grades act as motivators. Do they work that way for you? What about the students you will teach? For what kinds of students will grades be the most motivating? The least motivating? How does age and grade level affect grades as motivators?
3. How does your specific teaching focus (e.g., subject matter or grade level) influence the kind of assessment instruments you will use?

4. Identify advantages and disadvantages of the following ways to assess student performance. How does the concept of validity affect the selection of one compared to the other?

   a. Essay
   b. Short answer
   c. Multiple choice
   d. True-false
   e. Performance assessment

5. Consider each of the options for collecting, scoring, and using homework that we presented in this chapter. What advantages and disadvantages does each have in addition to those we listed? How does the type of student (e.g., younger vs. older, high ability vs. low ability) influence the effectiveness of any option? What other options for handling homework exist?

6. What kind of grading system, norm- or criterion-referenced, do you prefer? Why? Do you think your choice is similar to the preferences of the students you will be teaching?

Portfolio Activities

1. *Analyzing an Assessment System.* Analyze the assessment system for the course in which you are using this book. Comment on the following dimensions:

   a. Type of evaluation instruments used (e.g., objective vs. performance assessment)
   b. Validity
   c. Frequency
   d. Course expectations
   e. Norm- or criterion-referenced grading

   How do each of these influence motivation and learning?

2. *Report cards.* Examine a report card.

   a. How are grades reported?
   b. How often are report cards given?
   c. In addition to content areas like social studies and science, what other areas (e.g., citizenship) are evaluated?

   What challenges does the report card present to you as a teacher?

3. *District Evaluation Policy.* Is there a document summarizing your district's or school's evaluation policy? If so, examine it and answer the following questions:

   a. Is there a statement of philosophy? If so, summarize the major points.
   b. How are parents involved in the process?˝
   c. What are each teacher's individual responsibilities?
   d. How do Ds and Fs influence promotion?
   e. What is the relationship of grades to extracurricular activities?
   f. How are unexcused absences and tardiness treated?

   What challenges will you encounter integrating these policies into your classroom assessment system?

4. *Test administration*. Observe a teacher administering a test or quiz. How did the teacher deal with the following issues:

   a. Expectations
   b. Directions
   c. Feedback
   d. Grades
   e. Makeups

   What suggestion do you have to make this process more effective?

5. *Homework*. Interview a teacher to see how the following are handled:

   a. Correcting
   b. Grades
   c. Late or missing
   d. Makeups for absences

   How do you plan to implement homework in your classroom?

6. *Record Keeping*. Interview a teacher at your grade level or in your subject matter area and find out what his or her responsibilities are in terms of the following:

   a. Individual attendance records
   b. Tardiness
   c. Report cards
   d. Cumulative folders

   What suggestions do they have for making the process more efficient? How will you handle these tasks in your classroom?

References

Abel, M., & Sewell, J. (1999). Stress and burnout in rural and urban secondary school teachers. *Journal of Educational Research, 92,* 287–294.

Adams, R., & Biddle, B. (1970). *Realities of teaching: Exploration with videotape.* New York: Holt, Rinehart and Winston.

Airasian, P. (1997). *Classroom assessment* (3rd ed.). New York: McGraw-Hill.

Airasian, P., & Walsh, M. (1997). Constructivist cautions. *Phi Delta Kappan, 78,* 444–449.

Albanese, M., & Mitchell, S. (1993). Problem-based learning: A review of literature on its outcomes and implementation issues. *Academic Medicine, 68,* 52–81.

Alexander, K., & McDill, E. (1976). Selection and allocation within schools: Some causes and consequences of curriculum placement. *American Sociological Review, 41,* 963–980.

American Association for the Advancement of Science (AAAS). (1993). *Benchmarks for science literacy.* Washington, DC: Author.

Anastasi, A. (1988). *Psychological testing* (6th ed.). New York: Macmillan.

Anastasiow, N., Bibley, S., Leonhardt, T., & Borish, G. (1970). A comparison of guided discovery, discovery, and didactic teaching of math to kindergarten poverty children. *American Educational Research Journal, 7,* 493–510.

Anderson, B. (1978). The effects of long wait-time on high school physics pupils' response length, classroom attitudes and achievement. *Dissertation Abstracts International, 39,* 349A (University Microfilms No. 78-23-871).

Anderson, L., Brubaker, N., Alleman-Brooks, J., & Duffy, G. (1984). *Making seatwork work (Research Series No. 142).* East Lansing: Michigan State University, Institute for Research on Teaching.

Anderson, R., Hiebert, E., Scott, J., & Wilkinson, I. (1985). *Becoming a nation of readers.* Washington, DC: National Institute of Education.

Anderson, T., & Armbruster, B. (1984). Studying. In D. Pearson (Ed.), *Handbook of reading research* (pp. 657–679). White Plains, NY: Longman.

Arends, R. (2001). *Learning to teach* (2nd ed). New York: Random House.

Armstrong, T. (1994). Multiple intelligences: Seven ways to approach curriculum. *Educational Leadership, 52*(3), 26–27.

Atkinson, R., Derry, S., Renkl, A., & Wortham, D. (2000). Learning from examples: Instructional principles from the worked examples research. *Review of Educational Research, 70*(2), 181–214.

Ausubel, D. (1978). In defense of advance organizers: A reply to the critics. *Review of Educational Research, 48,* 251–259.

Babad, E., Bernieri, F., & Rosenthal, R. (1991). Students as judges of teachers' verbal and nonverbal behavior. *American Educational Research Journal, 28*(1), 211–234.

Baker, L. (1989). Metacognition, comprehension monitoring, and the adult reader. *Educational Psychology Review,* 1, 3–38.

Bandura, A. (1986). *Social foundations of thought and action: A social cognitive theory.* Upper Saddle River, NJ: Prentice Hall.

Bandura, A. (1993). Perceived self-efficacy in cognitive development and functioning. *Educational Psychologist, 28*(2), 117–148.

Bangert-Drowns, R., Kulik, J., & Kulik, C. (1991). Effects of frequent classroom testing. *Journal of Educational Research, 85,* 89–99.

Banks, J. (2001). *Cultural diversity and education* (4th ed.). Boston: Allyn & Bacon.

Barab, S., & Landa, A. (1997). Designing effective interdisciplinary anchors. *Educational Leadership, 54,* 52–55.

Barr, R., & Parrett, W. (2001). *Hope fulfilled for at-risk youth.* Boston: Allyn & Bacon.

Baumrind, D. (1973). The development of instrumental competence through socialization. In A. Peck (Ed.), *Minnesota Symposium on Child Psychology, 7.* Minneapolis, MN: University of Minnesota Press.

Baumrind, D. (1991). The influence of parenting style on adolescent competence and substance use. *Journal of Early Adolescence, 11,* 56–95.

Beane, J. (1995). Curriculum integration and the disciplines of knowledge. *Phi Delta Kappan, 76*(8), 616–622.

Beane, J. (1997). *Curriculum integration: Designing the core of democratic education.* New York: Teachers College Press.

Becker, W. (1977). Teaching reading and language to the disadvantaged—what we have learned from field research. *Harvard Educational Review, 47,* 518–543.

Bennett, N., & Blundel, D. (1983). Quantity and quality of work in rows of classroom groups. *Educational Psychology, 3,* 93–105.

Berk, L. (1997). *Child development* (4th ed.). Boston: Allyn & Bacon.

Berk, L. (2000). *Child development* (5th ed.). Boston: Allyn & Bacon.

Berliner, D. (1984). *Making our schools more effective: Proceedings of three state conferences.* San Francisco: Far West Laboratory.

Berliner, D. (1987). Simple views of effective teaching and a simple theory of classroom instruction. In D. Berliner & B. Rosenshine (Eds.), *Talks to teachers* (pp. 93–110). New York: Random House.

Berliner, D. (1994). Expertise: The wonder of exemplary performances. In J. Mangieri & C. Collins (Eds.), *Creating powerful thinking in teachers and students* (pp. 161–186). Fort Worth, TX: Harcourt Brace.

Berliner, D. (2000). A personal response to those who bash education. *Journal of Teacher Education, 51,* 358–371.

Bernard, B. (1993). Fostering resilience in kids. *Educational Leadership, 51*(3), 44–48.

Blackburn, M., & Miller, R. (1999, April). *Intrinsic motivation for cheating and optimal challenge: Some sources and some consequences.* Paper presented at the Annual Meeting of the American Educational Research Association, Montreal.

Blair, J. (2000). Certification found valid for teachers. *Education Week, 20*(8), 1, 24–25.

Bloom, B. (1981). *All our children learning.* New York: McGraw-Hill.

Bloom, B., Englehart, M., Furst, E., Hill, W., & Krathwohl, O. (1956). *Taxonomy of educational objectives: The classification of educational goals: Handbook 1. The cognitive domain.* White Plains, NY: Longman.

Blumberg, P. (1998, April). *Evaluating the evidence that problem-based learners are self-directed learners: A review of the literature.* Paper presented at the annual meeting of the American Educational Research Association, San Diego.

Blumenfeld, P., Hicks, L., & Krajcik, J. (1996). Teaching educational psychology through instructional planning. *Educational Psychologist, 31*(1), 51–61.

Borg, W., & Ascione, F. (1982). Classroom management in elementary mainstreaming classrooms. *Journal of Educational Psychology, 74,* 85–95.

Borko, H., & Putnam, R. (1996). Learning to teach. In D. Berliner & R. Calfee (Eds.), *Handbook of educational psychology* (pp. 673–708). New York: Simon & Schuster.

Bowers, A. (1990.) *The effect of a multiple ability treatment on status and learning in the cooperative social studies classroom.* Unpublished doctoral dissertation. Stanford, CA: Stanford.

Bowie, R., & Bond, C. (1994). Influencing future teachers' attitudes toward Black English: Are we making a difference? *Journal of Teacher Education, 45*(2), 112–118.

Bradley, A. (1999). Science group finds middle school textbooks inadequate. *Education Week, 19*(6), 5.

Bradley, D. & Switlick, D. (1997) The past and future of special education. In D. Bradley, M. King-Sears, and D. Tessier-Switlick (Eds.), *Teaching students in inclusive settings* (pp. 1–20). Boston: Allyn & Bacon.

Bradsher, M., & Hagan, L. (1995). The kids network: Student-scientists pool resources. *Educational Leadership, 53*(2), 38–43.

Bransford, J., Brown, A., & Cocking, R. (Eds.). (2000). *How people learn: Brain, mind, experience, and school*. Washington, DC: National Academy Press.

Bransford, J., Goldman, S., & Vye, N. (1991). Making a difference in people's abilities to think: Reflections on a decade of work and some hopes for the future. In L. Okagaki & R. Sternberg (Eds.), *Directors of development* (pp. 147–180). Hillsdale, NJ: Erlbaum.

Bransford, J., & Stein, B. (1984). *The IDEAL problem solver*. New York: Freeman.

Brophy, J. (1986). Research linking teacher behavior to student achievement: Potential implications for instruction of Chapter 1 students. In B. Williams, P. Richmond, & B. Mason (Eds.), *Designs for Compensatory Education Conference proceedings and papers* (pp. IV-121–IV-179). Washington, DC: Research and Evaluation Associates.

Brophy, J. (1992). Probing the subtleties of subject-matter teaching. *Educational Leadership, 49*(7), 4–8.

Brophy, J. (1996). *Teaching problem students*. New York: Guilford Press.

Brophy, J., & Alleman, J. (1991). A caveat: Curriculum integration isn't always a good idea. *Educational Leadership, 49*, 66.

Brophy, J., & Good, T. (1986). Teacher behavior and student achievement. In M. Wittrock (Ed.), *Handbook of research on teaching* (3rd ed., pp. 328–375). New York: Macmillan.

Brophy, J., & McCaslin, M. (1992). Teachers' reports of how they perceive and cope with problem students. *Elementary School Journal, 93*(1), 3–68.

Brophy, J., & Rohrkemper, M. (1987). *Teachers' strategies for coping with hostile-aggressive students*. East Lansing: Michigan State University, Institute for Research on Teaching.

Brown, A. (1994). The advancement of learning. *Educational Researcher, 23*, 4–12.

Brown, A., & Campione, J. (1994). Guided discovery in a community of learners. In K. McGilly (Ed.), *Classroom lessons: Integrating cognitive theory and classroom practice* (pp. 229–270). Cambridge: MIT Press.

Brown, D. (1991). *The effects of state-mandated testing on elementary classroom instruction*. Unpublished doctoral dissertation. Knoxville, TN: University of Tennessee–Knoxville.

Bruner, J., Goodenow, J., & Austin, G. (1956). *A study of thinking*. New York: John Wiley.

Bruning, R., Schraw, G., & Ronning, R. (1999). *Cognitive psychology and instruction* (3rd ed.). Upper Saddle River, NJ: Prentice Hall.

Bryan, J., & Walbeck, N. (1970). Preaching and practicing generosity: Children's actions and reactions. *Child Development, 41*, 329–353.

Bull, R., & Stevens, J. (1979). The effects of attractiveness of writer and penmanship on essay grades. *Journal of Occupational Psychology, 52*, 53–59.

Bullock, A., & Hawk, P. (2001). *Developing a teaching portfolio*. Columbus, OH: Merrill.

Bullough, R. (1989). *First-year teacher*. New York: Teachers College Press.

Burns, R. (1984). How time is used in elementary schools: The activity structure of classrooms. In L. Anderson (Ed.), *Time and school learning: Theory, research, and practice*. London, England: Croom & Helm.

Burstyn, J., & Stevens, R. (1999, April). *Education in conflict resolution: Creating a whole school approach*. Paper presented at the annual meeting of the American Educational Research Association, Montreal.

Busmeyer, J., & Myung, I. (1988). A new method for investigating prototype learning. *Journal of Experimental Psychology: Learning, Memory & Cognition, 14*, 1292–1302.

Byrnes, J. (2001). *Cognitive development and learning* (2nd ed.). Boston: Allyn & Bacon.

Calderhead, J. (1996). Teachers: Beliefs and knowledge. In D. Berliner & R. Calfee (Eds.), *Handbook of educational psychology* (pp. 709–725). New York: Macmillan.

Cameron, C., & Lee, K. (1997). Bridging the gap between home and school with voice-mail technology. *Journal of Educational Research, 90*, 182–190.

Canter, L. (1988). Let the educator beware: A response to Curwin and Mendler. *Educational Leadership, 46*(2), 71–73.

Canter, L., & Canter, M. (1992). *Assertive discipline*. Santa Monica, CA: Lee Canter & Associates.

Carlsen, W. (1987, April). *Why do you ask? The effects of science teacher subject-matter knowledge on teacher questioning and classroom discourse*. Paper presented at the annual meeting of the American Educational Research Association, Washington, DC.

Carnine, D. (1990). New research on the brain: Implications for instruction. *Phi Delta Kappan, 71*, 372–377.

Carrier, C., & Titus, A. (1981). Effects of notetaking pretraining and text mode expectations on learning from lectures. *American Educational Research Journal, 18*, 385–397.

Carrol, W. (1994). Using worked examples as an instructional support in the algebra classroom. *Journal of Educational Psychology, 86*(3), 360–367.

Carter, C. (1997). Integrated middle school. Humanities: A process analysis. *Teacher Education Quarterly, 24*, 55–73.

Carter, C., & Mason, D. (1997, March). *Cognitive effects of integrated curriculum.* Paper presented at the annual conference of the American Educational Research Association, Chicago.

Carter, K. (1986). Test-wiseness for teachers and students. *Educational Measurement: Issues and Practice, 5*(6), 20–23.

Cazden, C. (1986). Classroom discourse. In M. Wittrock (Ed.), *Handbook of research on teaching* (3rd ed., pp. 432–464). New York: Macmillan.

Cazden, C. (1988). *Classroom discourse.* Portsmouth, NH: Heinemann.

Charles, C., (1996). *Building classroom discipline,* (5th ed). New York: Longman.

Chaskin, R., & Rauner, D. (1995). Youth and caring: An introduction. *Phi Delta Kappan, 76*, 667–674.

Chekles, K. (1997). The first seven . . . and the eighth. *Educational Leadership, 55*, 8–13.

Cheng, L. R. (1987). *Assessing Asian language performance.* Rockville, MD: Aspen.

Chewprecha, T., Gardner, M., & Sapianchai, X. (1980). Comparison of training methods in modifying questioning and wait-time behaviors of Thai high school chemistry teachers. *Journal of Research in Science Teaching, 17*, 191–200.

Chinn, C., & Brewer, W. (1993). The role of anomalous data in knowledge acquisition: A theoretical framework and implications for science instruction. *Review of Educational Research, 63*, 1–49.

Clandinin, J., & Connelly, M. (1996). Teacher as curriculum maker. In P. Jackson (Ed.), *Handbook of research on curriculum* (pp. 363–401). New York: Macmillan.

Clark, C., & Elmore, J. (1981). *Transforming curriculum in mathematics, science, and writing: A case study of teacher yearly planning* (Research Series no. 99). East Lansing, MI: Michigan State University Institute for Research on Teaching.

Clark, C., & Peterson, P. (1986). Teachers' thought processes. In M. Wittrock (Ed.), *Handbook of research on teaching* (3rd ed., pp. 255–296). New York: Macmillan.

Clark, C., & Yinger, R. (1979). *Three studies of teacher planning* (Research Series No. 55). East Lansing, MI: Michigan State University, Institute for Research on Teaching.

Cobb, P., & Bowers, J. (1999). Cognitive and situated learning: Perspectives in theory and practice. *Educational Researcher, 28*(2), 4–15.

Cochran-Smith, M. (2001). Editorial: Reforming teacher education's competing agendas. *Journal of Teacher Education, 52*(4), 263–265.

Cognition and Technology Group at Vanderbilt. (1992). The Jasper Series as an example of anchored instruction: Theory, program description, and assessment data. *Educational Psychologist, 27*(3), 291–315.

Cohen, E. (1986). *Designing groupwork: Strategies for the heterogeneous classroom.* New York: Teachers College Press.

Cohen, E. (1991). Strategies for creating a multiability classroom. *Cooperative Learning, 12*(1), 4–7.

Cohen, E. (1994). Restructuring the classroom: Conditions for productive small groups. *Review of Educational Research, 64*(1), 1–35.

Cohen, E., & Lotan, R. (Eds.). (1997). *Working for equity in heterogeneous classrooms: Sociological theory in practice.* New York: Teachers' College Press.

Coleman, J., Campbell, E., Hobson, D., McPortland, J., Mood, A., Weinfield, F., & York, R. (1966). *Equality of educational opportunity.* Washington, DC: U.S. Department of Health, Education and Welfare.

Collins, M. (1978). Effects of enthusiasm training on preservice elementary teachers. *Journal of Teacher Education, 24*, 53–57.

Confrey, J. (1990). A review of the research on student conceptions, in mathematics, science, and programming. In C. Cazden (Ed.), *Review of research in education,* Vol. 1 (pp. 3–56). Washington, DC: American Educational Research Association.

Connell, J., & Wellborn, J. (1990). Competence, autonomy, and relatedness: A motivational analysis of self-system processes. In M. Gunnar & L. Sroufe (Eds.), *The Minnesota Symposia on Child Psychology* (Vol. 22, pp. 43–77). Hillsdale, NJ: Erlbaum.

Cooper, H. (1989). Synthesis of research on homework. *Educational Leadership, 47*(3), 85–91.

Cooper, H., Lindsay, J., Nye, B., & Greathouse, S. (1998). Relationships among attitudes about homework, amount of homework assigned and completed, and student achievement. *Journal of Educational Psychology, 90*(1), 70–83.

Corno, L., & Xu, J. (1998, April). *Homework and personal responsibility.* Paper presented at the annual meeting of the American Educational Research Association, San Diego.

Crooks, T. (1988). The impact of classroom evaluation practices on students. *Review of Educational Research, 58*, 438–481.

Cruickshank, D. (1985). Applying research on teacher clarity. *Journal of Teacher Education, 35*(2), 44–48.

Cuban, L. (1984). *How teachers taught: Constancy and change in American classrooms:* 1890–1980. White Plains, NY: Longman.

Cuban, L. (1986). *Teachers and machine.* New York: Teachers College Press.

Curwin, R. (1992). *Rediscovering hope: Our greatest teaching strategy.* Bloomington, IN: National Education Service.

Curwin, R., & Mendler, A. (1988). Packaged discipline programs: Let the buyer beware. *Educational Leadership, 46*(2), 68–71.

Dahlof, U., & Lundgren, V. (1970). *Macro and micro approaches combined for curriculum process evaluation: A Swedish field project* (research report). Gotenberg, Sweden, University of Gotenberg, Institute of Education.

Darling-Hammond, L., & Cobbe, V. (1996). The changing context of teacher education. In F. Murray (Ed.), *The teacher educator's handbook* (pp. 14–62). San Francisco: Jossey-Bass.

Darling-Hammond, L., & Snyder, J. (1992). Reframing accountability: Creating learner-centered schools. In A. Liberman (Ed.), *The changing contexts of teaching* (pp. 3–17). Chicago: University of Chicago Press.

Davis, G., & Williams, B. (1992, April). *A field dependence/independence inventory and its relationship to left-right and creative thinking.* Paper presented at the annual meeting of the American Educational Research Association, San Francisco.

Davis, H. (1998). *Project-based learning.* Salt Lake City, Utah: Department of Educational Studies, University of Utah.

Delgado-Gaiton, C. (1992). School matters in the Mexican American home: Socializing children to education. *American Educational Research Journal, 29*(3), 495–516.

Delpit, L. (1995). *Other people's children: Cultural conflict in the classroom.* New York: New Press.

Derry, S., & Murphy, D. (1986). Designing systems that train learning ability: From theory to practice. *Review of Educational Research, 56,* 1–19.

Dewey, J. (1916). *Democracy and education.* New York: Macmillan.

Deyhle, D. (1987). Learning failure: Tests as gatekeepers and the culturally different child. In H. Trueba (Ed.), *Success or failure?* (pp. 85–108). Cambridge, MA: Newberry.

Diaz, R., & Berk, L. (1992, April). *Misguided assumptions of self-instructional training.* Paper presented at the annual meeting of the American Educational Research Association, San Francisco.

Diem, R. (1996). Using social studies as the catalyst for curriculum integration: The experience of a secondary school. *Social Education, 60,* 95–98.

Dillon, J. (1981). To question and not to question during discussions: 2. Non-questioning techniques. *Journal of Teacher Education, 32*(6), 15–20.

Dillon, J. (1987). *Questioning and discussion: A multidisciplinary study.* Norwood, NJ: Ablex.

Dole, J., & Sinatra, G. (1998). Reconceptualizing change in the cognitive construction of knowledge. *Educational Psychologist, 33*(2/3), 109–128.

Doyle, W. (1983). Academic work. *Review of Educational Research, 53,* 159–199.

Doyle, W. (1986). Classroom organization and management. In M. Wittrock (Ed.), *Handbook of research on teaching* (3rd ed., pp. 392–431). New York: Macmillan.

Dreisbach, M., & Keogh, B. (1982). Test-wiseness as a factor in readiness test performance of young Mexican American children. *Journal of Educational Psychology, 74,* 224–229.

Drexler, N., Harvey, G., & Kell, D. (1990). *Student and teacher success: The impact of computers in primary grades.* Paper presented at the annual meeting of the American Educational Research Association, Boston.

Duffy, T., & Cunningham, D. (1996). Constructivism: Implications for the design and delivery of instruction. In D. Jonassen (Ed.), *Handbook of Research for Educational Communications and Technology* (pp. 170–195). New York: Macmillan.

Duffy, G., Roehler, L., Meloth, M., & Vavrus, L. (1985, April). *Conceptualizing instructional explanation.* Paper presented at the annual meeting of the American Educational Research Association, Chicago.

Dunkin, M., & Biddle, B. (1974). *The study of teaching.* New York: Holt, Rinehart and Winston.

Dunkle, M., Schraw, G., & Bendixon, L. (1995, April). *Cognitive processes in well-defined and ill-defined problem solving.* Paper presented at the Annual Meeting of the American Educational Research Association, San Francisco.

Dunn, R., & Dunn, K. (1978). *Teaching students through their individual learning styles.* Reston, VA: Reston Publishing.

Dunn R., Dunn, K., & Price, G. (1985). *Learning style inventory.* Lawrence, KS: Price Systems.

Dunn, R., & Dunn, K. (1987). Dispelling outmoded beliefs about student learning. *Educational Leadership, 44*(6), 55–62.

Dykstra, D. (1996). Teaching introductory physics to college students. In C. Fosnot (Ed.), *Constructivism: Theory, perspective and practice* (pp. 182–204) New York: Teachers College Press.

Educational Testing Service. (1999). *Principles of learning and teaching test bulletin.* Princeton, NJ: Author.

Eggen, P. (1998, April). *A comparison of inner-city middle school teachers' classroom practices and their expressed beliefs about learning and effective instruction.* Paper presented at the annual meeting of the American Educational Research Association, San Diego.

Eggen, P. (2001, April). *Constructivism and the architecture of cognition: Implications for instruction.* Paper presented at the annual meeting of the American Educational Research Association, Seattle.

Eggen, P., & Kauchak, D. (1992). *Educational psychology.* Upper Saddle River, NJ: Prentice Hall.

Eggen, P., & Kauchak, D. (1999). *Educational psychology: Windows on classrooms* (4th ed.). Upper Saddle River, NJ: Prentice Hall.

Eggen, P., & Kauchak, D. (2001). *Educational psychology: Windows on classrooms* (5th ed.). Upper Saddle River, NJ: Prentice Hall.

Elam, S., & Rose, L. (1995). The 27th annual Phi Delta Kappa/Gallup poll. *Phi Delta Kappan, 77*(1), 41–49.

Elbaum, B.,Vaughn, S., Hughes, M., & Moody, S. (1999). Grouping practices and reading outcomes for students with disabilities. *Exceptional Children, 65*(3), 399–415.

Ellis, S., Dowdy, B., Graham, P., & Jones, R. (1992, April). *Parental support of planning skills in the context of homework and family demands.* Paper presented at the annual meeting of the American Educational Research Association, San Francisco.

Elwall, E., & Shanher, J. (1989). *Teaching reading in the elementary school* (2nd ed.). Columbus, OH: Merrill.

Emmer, E., Evertson, C., Clements, B., & Worsham, M. (2000). *Classroom management for secondary teachers* (5th ed.). Needham Heights, MA: Allyn & Bacon.

Epstein, J. (1990). School and family connections: Theory, research, and implications for integrating sociologies of education and family. In D. Unger & M. Sussman (Eds.), *Families in community settings: Interdisciplinary perspectives* (pp. 99–126). New York: Haworth Press.

Everson, H., Tobias, S., Hartman, H., & Gourgey, A. (1991, April). *Text anxiety in different curricular areas: An exploratory analysis of the role of subject matter.* Paper presented at the Annual Meeting of the American Educational Research Association, Chicago.

Evertson, C. (1980, April). *Differences in instructional activities in high- and low-achieving junior high classes.* Paper presented at the Annual Meeting of the American Educational Research Association, Boston.

Evertson, C., Emmer, E., Clements, B., & Worsham, M. (2000). *Classroom management for elementary teachers* (5th ed.). Needham Heights, MA: Allyn & Bacon.

Eysenck, M., & Keane, M. (1990). *Cognitive psychology: A student's handbook.* Hillsdale, NJ: Erlbaum.

Farr, C., & Moon, C. (1988, April). *New perspectives on intelligence: Examining field dependence/independence in light of Steinberg's Triarchic Theory of Intelligence.* Paper presented at the annual meeting of the American Educational Research Association, New Orleans.

Fatemi, E. (1999). Building the digital curriculum. *Education Week, 19*(4), 5–12.

Feldman, S. (2000). True merit pay. *Education Week, 19*(26), 21.

Fensham, P. (1992). Science & technology. In P. Jackson (Ed.), *Handbook of research on curriculum* (pp. 789–829). New York: Macmillan.

Fine, L. (2001). Studies examine racial disparities in special education. *Education Week, 19*(26), 6.

Fisher, C., Berliner, D., Filby, N., Marliave, R., Cohen, K., & Dishaw, M. (1980). Teaching behaviors, academic learning time, and student achievement: An overview. In C. Denham & A. Lieberman (Eds.), *Time to learn* (pp. 7–32). Washington, DC: National Institute of Education.

Fitzgerald, J. (1995). English-as-a-second-language learners' cognitive reading processes: A review of research in the United States. *Review of Educational Research, 65*(2), 145–190.

Fleming, M., & Chambers, B. (1983). Teacher-made tests: Windows on the classrooms. In W. Hathaway (Ed.), *Testing in the schools: New directions for testing and measurement* (No. 19). San Francisco: Jossey-Bass.

Forcier, R. (1996). *The computer as a productivity tool in education.* Columbus, OH: Merrill.

Forcier, R. (1999). *The computer as an educational tool* (2nd ed.). Columbus, OH: Merrill.

Frank, B. (1984). Effect of FID and study techniques and learning from a lecture. *American Educational Research Journal, 21,* 669–678.

Frederick, W. (1977). The use of classroom time in high schools above or below the median reading score. *Urban Education, 11,* 459–464.

Fuchs, L., Fuchs, D., Bentz, J., Phillips, N., & Hamlett, C. (1994). The nature of student interactions during peer tutoring with and without prior training and experience. *American Educational Research Journal, 31*(1), 75–103.

Fuchs, D., Fuchs, L., Mathes, P., & Simmons, D. (1997). Peer-assisted learning strategies: Making classrooms more responsive to diversity. *American Educational Research Journal, 34*(1), 174–206.

Furtado, L. (1997, November). *Interdisciplinary curriculum.* Paper presented at the annual meeting of the California Educational Research Association, Santa Barbara, CA.

Gage, N. (1985). *Hard gains in the soft sciences: The case of pedagogy.* Bloomington, IN: Phi Delta Kappa.

Gage, N., & Berliner, D. (1988). *Educational psychology* (4th ed.). Boston: Houghton Mifflin.

Gage, N., & Berliner, D. (1992). *Educational psychology* (5th ed.). Boston: Houghton Mifflin.

Gage, N., & Berliner, D. (1998). *Educational psychology* (6th ed.). Boston: Houghton Mifflin.

Gage, N., & Giaconia, R. (1981). *Teaching practices and student achievement: Causal connections.* New York University Education Quarterly, *12,* 2–9.

Gagnon, G., & Collay, M. (2001). *Designing for learning.* Thousand Oaks, CA: Corwin.

Gall, M. (1984). Synthesis of research on teachers' questioning. *Educational Leadership, 42*(3), 40–47.

Gall, M. (1987). Discussion methods. In M. Dunkin (Ed.), *International encyclopedia of teaching and teacher education* (pp. 232–236). Elmsford, NY: Pergamon Press.

Gall, M. (1984). Synthesis of research on teachers' questioning. *Educational Leadership, 42*(3), 40–47.

Gardner, H. (1983). *Frames of mind: The theory of multiple intelligences.* New York: Basic Books.

Gardner, H., & Hatch, T. (1989). Multiple intelligences go to school. *Educational Researcher, 18*(8), 4–10.

Gay, G. (2000). *Culturally responsive teaching; Theory, research and practice.* New York: Teachers College Press.

Gersten, R., Taylor, R., & Graves, A. (1999). Direct instruction and diversity. In R. Stevens (Ed.), *Teaching in American schools* (pp. 81–106). Upper Saddle River, NJ: Merrill/Prentice Hall.

Gersten, R., & Woodward, J. (1995). A longitudinal study of transitional and immersion bilingual education programs in one district. *Elementary School Journal, 95*(3), 223–239.

Gladney, L., & Greene, B. (1997, March). *Descriptions of motivation among African American high school students for their favorite and least favorite classes.* Paper presented at the Annual Meeting of the American Educational Research Association, Chicago.

Glasser, W. (1969). *Schools without failure.* New York: Harper & Row.

Glasser, W. (1977). Ten steps in good discipline. *Today's Education, 66,* 61–63.

Glickman, C. (1990). *Supervision of instruction* (2nd ed.). Boston: Allyn & Bacon.

Glover, J., Ronning, R., & Bruning, R. (1990). *Cognitive psychology for teachers.* New York: Macmillan.

Golden, N., Gersten, R., & Woodward, J. (1990). Effectiveness of guided practice during remedial reading instruction: An application of computer-managed instruction. *Elementary School Journal, 90*(3), 290–304.

Gollnick, D., & Chinn, P. (2002). *Multi-cultural education in a pluralistic society* (6th ed.). New York: Merrill/Macmillan.

Good, T. (1987). Two decades of research on teacher expectations: Findings and future directions. *Journal of Teacher Education, 37*(4), 32–47.

Good, T. (1996). Teaching effects and teacher evaluation. In J. Sikula (Ed.), *Handbook of research on teacher education* (2nd ed., pp. 617–665). New York: Macmillan.

Good, T., Biddle, B., & Brophy, J. (1975). *Teachers make a difference.* New York: Holt, Rinehart and Winston.

Good, T., & Brophy, J. (2000). *Looking in classrooms* (8th ed.). New York: HarperCollins.

Good T., Grouws, D., & Ebmeier, J. (1983). *Active mathematics teaching.* New York: Longman.

Good, T., McCaslin, M., & Reys, B. (1992). Investigating work groups to promote problem solving in mathematics. In J. Brophy (Ed.), *Advances in research on teaching* (Vol. 3, pp. 115–160). Greenwich, CT: JAI Press.

Goodenow, C. (1992). Strengthening the links between educational psychology and the study of social contexts. *Educational Psychologist, 27*(2), 177–196.

Goodenow, C. (1993). Classroom belonging among early adolescent students. Relationships to motivation and achievement. *Journal of Early Adolescence, 13,* 21–43.

Goodlad, J. (1984). *A place called school.* New York: McGraw-Hill.

Gordon, T. (1974). *Teacher effectiveness training.* New York: Wyden.

Grabinger, R. (1996). Rich environments for active learning. In D. Jonassen (Ed.), *Handbook of research for educational communications and technology* (pp. 665–692). New York: Macmillan.

Graham, S., & Johnson, L. (1989). Teaching reading to learning disabled students: A review of research-supported procedures. *Focus on Exceptional Children, 21*(6), 1–9.

Greeno, J., Collins, A., & Resnick, L. (1996). Cognition and learning. In D. Berliner & R. Calfee (Eds.), *Handbook of educational psychology* (pp. 15–46). New York: Macmillan.

Gronlund, N. (1993). *How to make achievement tests and assessments.* Needham Heights, MA: Allyn & Bacon.

Gronlund, N. (1995). *How to write and use instructional objectives* (5th ed.). Upper Saddle River, NJ: Merrill/Prentice Hall.

Gronlund, N., & Linn, R. (1995). *Measurement and evaluation in teaching* (7th ed.). Upper Saddle River, NJ: Prentice Hall.

Gullickson, A., & Ellwein, M. (1985). Post hoc analysis of teacher-made tests: The goodness-of-fit between prescription and practice. *Educational Measurement: Issues and Practice, 4*(1), 15–18.

Gump, P. (1967). *The classroom behavior setting: Its nature and relation to student behavior* (Final Report). Washington, DC: U.S. Office of Education, Bureau of Research (ED 015 515).

Guskey, T., & Gates, S. (1986). Synthesis of research on mastery learning. *Educational Leadership, 43,* 73–81.

Guthrie, L., & Richardson, S. (1996). Turned on to language arts: Computer literacy in the primary grades. *Educational Leadership, 53*(2), 14–18.

Guzetti, B., & Hynd, C. (1998, April). *The influence of text structures on males' and females' conceptual change in science.* Paper presented at the annual meeting of the American Educational Research Association, San Diego.

Hallahan, D., & Kauffman, J. (2000). *Exceptional children* (8th ed.). Needham Heights, MA: Allyn & Bacon.

Hallinan, M. (1984). Summary and implications. In P. Peterson, L. Wilkinson, & M. Hallinan (Eds.), *The social context of instruction: Group organization and group processes* (pp. 229–240). San Diego: Academic Press.

Hamilton, R., & Brady, M. (1991). Individual and classwide patterns of teachers' questioning in mainstreamed social studies and science classes. *Teaching & Teacher Education, 7*(3), 253–262.

Hardiman, P., Pollatsek, A., & Weil, A. (1986). Learning to understand the balance beam. *Cognition and Instruction, 3,* 1–30.

Hardman, M., Drew, C., & Egan, W. (1996). *Human exceptionality* (5th ed.). Needham Heights, MA: Allyn & Bacon.

Hardman, M., Drew, C., & Egan, W. (1999). *Human exceptionality* (6th ed.). Needham Heights, MA: Allyn & Bacon.

Harris, L., Kagay, M., & Ross, J. (1987). *The Metropolitan Life survey of the American teacher: Strengthening links between home and school.* New York: Louis Harris & Associates.

Harrow, A. (1972). *A taxonomy of the psychomotor domain: A guide for developing behavioral objectives.* New York: McKay.

Harry, B. (1992). An ethnographic study of cross-cultural communication with Puerto Rican American families in the special education system. *American Educational Research Journal, 29*(3), 471–488.

Haschak, J. (1992). It happens in the huddle. In J. Lounsbury (Ed.), *Connecting the curriculum through interdisciplinary instruction.* Columbus, OH: National Middle School Association. (ERIC Document Reproduction Service No. ED 362-262).

Hativa, N. (1988). Computer-based drill and practice in arithmetic: Widening the gap between high- and low-achieving students. *American Educational Research Journal, 25*(3), 366–397.

Hayes, J. (1988). *The complete problem solver* (2nd ed.). Hillsdale, NJ: Erlbaum.

Haynes, N., & Comer, J. (1995, March). *The School Development Program (SDP): Lessons from the past.* Paper presented at the Annual Meeting of the American Educational Research Association, San Francisco.

Heath, S. (1983). *Ways with words: Language, life, and work in communities and classrooms.* New York: Cambridge University Press.

Henderson, J., Winitzky, N., & Kauchak, D. (1996). *Effective teaching in advanced placement classrooms. Journal of Classroom Interaction, 31*(1), 29–35.

Herber, P. (1990). Helping kids get the picture. *Principal, 69*(2), 14–15.

Herman, J., Aschbacher, P., & Winters, L. (1992). *A practical guide to alternative assessment.* Alexandria, VA: Association for Supervision and Curriculum Development.

Heward, W. (1996). *Exceptional children* (5th ed.). Upper Saddle River, NJ: Merrill/Prentice Hall.

Hill, D. (1990). Order in the classroom. *Teacher, 1*(7), 70–77.

Hill, J., Yinger, R., & Robbins, D. (1981, April). *Instructional planning in a developmental preschool.* Paper presented at the annual meeting of the American Educational Research Association, Los Angeles.

Hines, C., Cruickshank, D., & Kennedy, J. (1985). Teacher clarity and its relationship to student achievement and satisfaction. *American Educational Research Journal, 22,* 87–99.

Hmelo, C., & Lin, X. (1998). Becoming self-directed learners: Strategy development in problem-based learning. In D. Evensen, & C. Hmelo (Eds.), *Problem-based learning: A research perspective on learning interaction.* Mahwah, NJ: Erlbaum.

Holley, C., & Dansereau, D. (1984). *Spatial learning strategies.* New York: Academic Press.

Holt, J. (1964). *How children fail.* New York: Putnam.

Hoover-Dempsey, K., Bassler, O., & Burow, R. (1995). Parents' reported involvement in students' homework: Strategies and practices. *Elementary School Journal, 95*(5), 435–449.

Hudley, C. (1998). *Urban minority adolescents' perceptions of classroom climate.* Paper presented at the Annual Meeting of the American Educational Research Association, San Diego.

Hudley, C. (1992, April). *The reduction of peer-directed aggression among highly aggressive African American boys.* Paper presented at the annual meeting of the American Educational Research Association, San Francisco.

Humphrey, F. (1979). *"Shh!" A sociolinguistic study of teachers' turn-taking sanctions in primary school lessons.* Unpublished doctoral dissertation, Georgetown University, Washington, DC.

Individuals with Disabilities Education Act Amendments, Pub.L. No.105-17,1. (1975).

Interstate New Teacher Assessment and Support Consortium (INTASC), 1993. *Model standards for beginning teacher licensing and development: A resource for state dialogues.* Washington, DC: Council of Chief State School Officers.

Jackson, P. (1968). *Life in classrooms.* New York: Holt, Rinehart and Winston.

Jacobs, H. (1989). *Interdisciplinary curriculum: Design and Implementation.* Alexandria, VA: ASCD.

Jacobsen, D., Eggen, P., & Kauchak, D. (2002). *Methods for teachers: A skills approach* (6th ed.). New York: Macmillan.

Jacobson, L. (1999). A kinder, gentler student body. *Education Week, 18*(42), 1, 22–23.

Jensen, A. (1987). Individual differences in mental ability. In J. Glover & R. Ronning (Eds.), *Historical foundations of educational psychology.* New York: Plenum Press.

Johnson, D., & Johnson, R. (1994). *Learning together and alone: Cooperation, competition, and individualization* (4th ed.). Needham Heights, MA: Allyn & Bacon.

Jonassen, D. (1996). *The computer as a productivity tool in education.* Columbus, OH: Merrill.

Jones V., & Jones, L. (1990). *Comprehensive classroom management: Motivating and managing students* (3rd ed.). Boston: Allyn & Bacon.

Jones, V. & Jones, L. (2001). *Comprehensive classroom management* (6th ed.). Boston: Allyn & Bacon.

Julyan, C. (1989). National Geographic kids network: Real science in the elementary classroom. *Classroom Computer Learning, 10*(2), 30–41.

Kagan, D. (1992). Implications of research on teacher belief. *Educational Psychologist, 27,* 65–90.

Kagan, J., Pearson, L., & Welch, L. (1966). Conceptual impulsivity and inductive reasoning. *Child Development, 37,* 123–130.

Kagan, S. (1994). *Cooperative learning.* San Juan Capistrano, CA: Resources for Teachers.

Kalechstein, P., Kalechstein, M., & Doctor, R. (1981). The effects of instruction on test-taking skills in second-grade Black children. *Measurement and Evaluation in Guidance, 13,* 198–202.

Karweit, N. (1989). Time & Learning: A review. In R. Slavin (Ed.), *School and classroom organization.* Hillsdale, NJ: Erlbaum.

Kauchak, D., & Peterson, K. (1987). *Teachers' thoughts on the assessment of their teaching.* Washington, DC: AERA.

Kerman, S. (1979). Teacher expectations and student achievement. *Phi Delta Kappan, 60,* 70–72.

Kika, F., McLaughlin, T., & Dixon, J. (1992). Effects of frequent testing of secondary algebra students. *Journal of Educational Research, 85,* 159–162.

Klausmeier, H. (1992). Concept learning and concept thinking. *Educational Psychologist, 27,* 267–286.

Knight, C., Halpen, G., & Halpen, G. (1992, April). *The effects of learning environment accommodations on the achievement of second graders.* Paper presented at the Annual Meeting of the American Educational Research Association: San Francisco.

Kohn, A. (1997). How not to teach values. *Phi Delta Kappan, 78*(6), 429–439.

Kounin, J. (1970). *Discipline and group management in classrooms.* New York: Holt, Rinehart and Winston.

Kounin, J. (1983). *Classrooms: Individuals or behavior settings* (Monographs in Teaching and Learning No. 1). Bloomington: Indiana University, School of Education.

Kounin, J., & Sherman, L. (1979). School environments as behavior settings. *Theory into Practice, 18,* 145–151.

Krajcik, J., Blumenfeld, P., Marx, R., & Soloway, E. (1994). A collaborative model for helping middle grade science teachers learn project-based instruction. *Elementary School Journal, 94*(5), 483–497.

Krathwohl, D., Bloom, B., & Masia, B. (1964). *Taxonomy of educational objectives: The classification of educational goals. Handbook 2. Affective domain.* New York: McKay.

Kruger, A. (1992). The effect of peer and adult-child transactive discussions on moral reasoning. *Merrill-Palmer Quarterly, 38*(2), 191–211.

Labov, W. (1972). *Language in the inner city: Studies in the "Black" English vernacular.* Philadelphia: University of Pennsylvania Press.

Lambert, N., & McCombs, B. (1998). Introduction: Learner-centered schools and classrooms as a direction for school reform. In N. Lambert & B. McCombs (Eds.), *How students learn: Reforming schools through learner-centered education* (pp. 1–22). Washington, DC: American Psychological Association.

Langer, J., Bartolome, L., Vasquez, O., & Lucas, T. (1990). Meaning construction in school literacy tasks: A study of bilingual students. *American Educational Research Journal, 27,* 427–471.

Lankes, A. (1995). Electronic portfolios: A new idea in assessment. *ERIC Digest.* (EDO-IR-95-9).

Larrivee, B., Semmel, M., & Gerber, M. (1997). Case studies of six schools varying in effectiveness for students with learning disabilities. *Elementary School Journal, 98*(1), 27–50.

Leander, K., & Brown, D. (1999). "You understand, but you don't believe it": Tracing the stabilities and instabilities of interaction in a physics classroom through a multidimensional framework. *Cognition and Instruction, 17*(1), 93–135.

Lee, J., Pulvino, C., & Perrone, P. (1998). *Restoring harmony: A guide for managing conflicts in schools.* Upper Saddle River, NJ: Merrill/Prentice Hall.

Lee, V., & Smith, J. (1999). Social support and achievement for young adolescents in Chicago: The role of school academic press. *American Educational Research Journal, 36*(4), 907–946.

Leinhardt, G. (1987). *Situated knowledge: An example from teaching.* Washington, DC: AERA.

Leinhardt, G., & Greeno, J. (1986). The cognitive skill of teaching. *Journal of Educational Psychology, 78*(2), 75–95.

Lemke, J. (1982, April). *Classroom communication of science* (Final report to NSF/RISE). Washington, DC: National Science Foundation. (ERIC Document Reproduction Service No. ED 222 346).

Lepper, M., & Hodell, M. (1989). Intrinsic motivation in the classroom. In C. Ames & R. Ames (Eds.), *Research on motivation in education* (Vol. 3, pp. 73–105). San Diego: Academic Press.

Levine, D., & Lezotte, L. (1995). Effective schools research. In J. Banks (Ed.), *Handbook of research on multicultural education* (pp. 525–547). New York: Macmillan.

Levin, H. (1988, March). *Structuring schools for greater effectiveness with educationally disadvantaged or at-risk students.* Paper presented at the Annual Meeting of the American Educational Research Association, San Francisco.

Levin, T., Libman, Z., & Amiad, R. (1980). Behavior patterns of students under an individualized learning strategy. *Instructional Science, 5,* 391–401.

Lewis, R. & Doorlag, D. (1999). *Teaching special students in general education classrooms.* Columbus, OH: Merrill.

Limber, S., Flerx, V., Nation, M., & Melton, G. (1998). Bullying among school children in the United States. In M. Watts (Ed.), *Cross-cultural perspectives on youth and violence.* Stamford, CT: J. I. Press.

Linn, R., & Gronlund, N. (2000). *Measurement and assessment in teaching* (8th ed.). Columbus, OH: Merrill.

Logan, G. (1988). Automaticity, resources, and memory: Theoretical controversies and practical implications. *Human Factors, 30,* 583–598.

López, G., & Scribner, J. (1999, April). *Discourses of involvement: A critical review of parent involvement research.* Paper presented at the annual meeting of the American Educational Research Association, Montreal.

Lovett, M., & Anderson, J. (1994). Effects of solving related proofs on memory and transfer in geometry problem solving. *Journal of Experimental Psychology, 20*(2), 366–378.

Loyd, B., & Loyd, D. (1997). Kindergarten through grade 12 standards: A philosophy of grading. In G. Phye (Ed.), *Handbook of classroom assessment* (pp. 481–490). San Diego: Academic Press.

Mabry, L. (1999). Writing to the rubric. *Phi Delta Kappan, 80*(9), 673–679.

Macionis, J. (2000). *Sociology* (6th ed.). Upper Saddle River, NJ: Prentice Hall.

Maddox, H., & Hoole, E. (1975). Performance decrement in the lecture. *Educational Review, 28,* 17–30.

Maehr, M. (1992, April). *Transforming the school culture to enhance motivation.* Paper presented at the Annual Meeting of the American Educational Research Association, San Francisco.

Mager, R. (1962). *Preparing instructional objectives.* Palo Alto, CA: Fearon.

Male, M. (1994). *Technology for inclusion* (2nd ed.). Boston, MA: Allyn & Bacon.

Manno, B. (1995). The new school wars: Battles over outcome-based education. *Phi Delta Kappan, 76*(4), 522–529.

Manzo, K. (2000). Algebra textbooks come up short in Project 2061 review. *Education Week, 19*(34), 5.

Marshall, H. (1992). Seeing, redefining, and supporting student learning. In H. Marshall (Ed.), *Redefining student learning: Roots of educational change* (pp. 1–32). Norwood, NJ: Ablex.

Martin, D. (1999). *The portfolio planner: Making professional portfolios work for you.* Upper Saddle River, NJ: Prentice Hall.

Marzano, R. (1992). *A different kind of classroom.* Alexandria, VA: Association for Supervision and Curriculum Development.

Marzano, R., Peckering, D., & McTighe, J. (1993). *Assessing students' outcomes.* Alexandria, VA: ASCD.

Maxwell, N., Bellisimo, Y., & Mergendoller, J. (1999, April). *Matching the strategy to the students: Why we modified the medical school problem-based learning for high school economics.* Paper presented at the Annual Meeting of the American Educational Research Association, Montreal.

Mayer, R. (1983). Can you repeat this? Qualitative effects of repetition and advance organizers from science prose. *Journal of Educational Psychology, 75,* 40–49.

Mayer, R. (1992). *Thinking, problem solving, cognition* (2nd ed.). New York: Freeman.

Mayer, R. (1996). Learners as information processors: Legacies and limitations of educational psychology's second metaphor. *Educational Psychologist, 31*(4), 151–161.

Mayer, R. (1998). Cognitive theory for education: What teachers need to know. In N. Lambert & B. McCombs (Eds.), *How students learn: Reforming schools through learner-centered instruction* (pp. 353–378). Washington, DC: American Psychological Association.

McCarthy, J. (1991). *Classroom environments which facilitate innovative strategies for teaching and learning.* Paper presented at the annual meeting of the American Educational Research Association, Chicago.

McCarthy, S. (1994). Authors, text, and talk: The internalization of dialogue from social interaction during writing. *Reading Research Quarterly, 29,* 201–231.

McCaslin, M., & Good, T. (1992). Compliant cognition: The misalliance of management and instructional goals in current school reform. *Educational Researcher, 21*(3), 4–17.

McCombs, B. (1998). Integrating metacognition, affect, and motivation in improving teacher education. In N. Lambert & B. McCombs (Eds.), *How students learn: Reforming schools through learner-centered education* (pp. 379–408). Washington, DC: American Psychological Association.

McCombs, B., & Pope, J. (1994). *Motivating hard to reach students.* Washington, DC: American Psychological Association.

McCormick, C., & Pressley, M. (1997). *Educational psychology.* New York: Longman.

McCutcheon, G. (1982). How do elementary school teachers plan? The nature of planning and influences on it. In W. Doyle & T. Good (Eds.), *Focus on teaching.* Chicago: University of Chicago Press.

McDaniel-Hine, L., & Willower, D. (1988). Elementary school teachers' work behavior. *Journal of Educational Research, 81,* 274–281.

McGreal, T. (1985, November). *Characteristics of effective teaching.* Paper presented at the first annual Intensive Training Symposium, Clearwater, FL.

McLaughlin, H. J. (1994). From negation to negotiation: Moving away from the management metaphor. *Action in Teacher Education, 16*(1), 75–84.

McTighe, J. (1996/97). What happens between assessments? *Educational Leadership, 54*(4), 6–12.

Means, B., & Knapp, M. (1991). Introduction: Rethinking teaching for disadvantaged students. In B. Means, C. Chelemer, & M. Knapp (Eds.), *Teaching advanced skills to at-risk students* (pp. 1–27). San Francisco: Jossey-Bass.

Medley, D. (1979). The effectiveness of teachers. In P. Peterson & H. Walbert (Eds.), *Research on teaching: Concepts, findings, and interpretations* (pp. 11–27). Berkeley, CA: McCutchan.

Mehrens, W., & Lehmann, I. (1987). *Using standardized tests in education* (4th ed.). White Plains, NY: Longman.

Meichenbaum, D. (1986). Cognitive behavior modification. In F. Kanfer & A. Goldstein (Eds.), *Helping people change: A textbook of methods* (3rd ed., pp. 346–380). New York: Pergamon Press.

Meng, K., & Patty, D. (1991). Field dependence and contextual organizers. *Journal of Educational Research, 84*(3), 183–190.

Mercer, C., & Mercer, A. (1993). *Teaching students with learning problems* (3rd ed.). New York: Macmillan.

Mercer, J. (1973). *Labeling the mentally retarded.* Berkeley: University of California Press.

Messick, S. (1994a). *Standards of validity and the validity of standards in performance assessment* (RM-94–17). Princeton, NJ: ETS.

Messick, S. (1994b). The matter of style: Manifestations of personality in cognition, learning, and teaching. *Educational Psychologist, 29,* 121–136.

Miller, S., Leinhardt, G., & Zigmond, N. (1988). Influencing engagement through accommodation: An ethnographic study of at-risk students. *American Educational Research Journal, 25,* 465–487.

Missouri Department of Elementary and Secondary Education (1995). *The show-me standards.* Columbus, MO: Author.

Mitchell, M. (1993). Situational interest: Its multifaceted structure in the secondry school mathematics classroom. *Journal of Educational Psychology, 85,* 424–436.

Moles, O. (1992, April). *Parental contacts about classroom behavior problems.* Paper presented at the Annual Meeting of the American Educational Research Association, San Francisco.

More families in poverty. (1993). *Executive Educator, 15,* 9–10.

Morine-Dershimer, G. (1979). *Teacher plans and classroom reality: The South Bay study: Part 4* (Research Series No. 60). East Lansing, MI: Michigan State University Institute for Research on Teaching.

Morine-Dershimer, G., & Reeve, P. (1994). Prospective teachers' images of management. *Action in Teacher Education, 16*(1), 29–40.

Morine-Dershimer, G., & Vallance, C. (1976). *Teacher planning* (Beginning Teacher Evaluation Study, Special Report C). San Francisco: Far West Laboratory.

Morrison, G., Lowther, D., & DeMuelle, L. (1999). *Integrating computer technology into the classroom.* Columbus, OH: Merrill.

Murnane, R., & Tyler, J. (2000). The increasing role of the GED in American education. *Education Week, 19*(34), 64, 48.

Murphy, J., Weil, M., & McGreal, T. (1986). The basic practice model of instruction. *Elementary School Journal, 87,* 83–95.

Murray, F. (1986, May). *Necessity: The developmental component in reasoning.* Paper presented at the sixteenth annual meeting, Jean Piaget Society, Philadelphia.

National Council of Teachers of Mathematics (NCTM). (1989). *Curriculum and evaluation standards for school mathematics.* Reston, VA: Author.

National Council of Teachers of Mathematics. (1991). *Professional standards for teaching mathematics.* Reston, VA: Author.

National Council of Teachers of Mathematics. (2000). *Principles and standards for school mathematics.* Reston, VA: Author.

National Commission on Excellence in Education. (1983). *A nation at risk: The imperative for educational reform.* Washington, DC: Government Printing Office.

Neale, D., Pace, A., & Case, A. (1983, April). *The influence of training, experience, and organizational environment on teachers' use of the systematic planning model.* Paper presented at the annual meeting of the American Educational Research Association, New Orleans.

Needels, M., & Knapp, M. (1994). Teaching writing to children who are underserved. *Journal of Educational Psychology, 86*(3), 339–349.

Newby, T., Stepich, D., Lehman, J., & Russell, J. (2000). *Instructional technology and teaching and learning* (2nd ed.). Columbus, OH: Merrill.

Nickerson, R. (1988). On improving thinking through instruction. In E. Rothkopf (Ed.), *Review of research in education* (pp. 3–57). Washington, DC: American Educational Research Association.

Nissani, M., & Hoefler-Nissani, D. (1992). Experimental studies of belief dependence of observations and of resistance to conceptual change. *Cognition and Instruction, 9,* 97–111.

Noblit, G., Rogers, D., & McCadden, B. (1995). In the meantime: The possibilities of caring. *Phi Delta Kappan, 76,* 680–685.

Nosofsky, R. (1988). Similarity, frequency, and category representations. *Journal of Experimental Psychology: Learning, Memory & Cognition, 14,* 54–65.

Novak, J., & Gowin, B. (1984). *Learning how to learn.* New York: Cambridge University Press.

Nucci, L. (1987). Synthesis of research on moral development. *Educational Leadership, 44*(5), 86–92.

Nucci, L. (1989). Knowledge of the learner: The development of children's concepts of self, morality & society convention. In M. Reynolds (Ed.), *Knowledge base for the beginning teacher* (pp. 117–129). New York: Pergamon.

Nystrand, M., & Gamoran, A. (1989, March). *Instructional discourse and student engagement.* Paper presented at the Annual Meeting of the American Educational Research Association, San Francisco.

Oakes, J. (1992). Can tracking research inform practice? *Educational Researcher, 21*(4), 12–21.

Office of Bilingual Education and Minority Affairs. (1999). *Facts about limited English proficiency students.* Washington, DC: U.S. Department of Education. (http://www.ed.gov/offices/OBEMLA/rileyfact.html)

Olsen, D. (1999, April). *Pedagogy that promotes student thinking in constructivist classrooms.* Paper presented at the annual conference of the American Educational Research Association, Montreal.

Olson, L. (2000). Finding and keeping competent teachers. *Education Week, 19*(18), 12–18.

Oregon Department of Education. (1996). *Grade level common curriculum goals, grades 6–8 content and performance standards.* Salem, OR: Author.

Orlich, D., Harder, R., & Callahan, R. (2001). *Teaching strategies* (6th ed.). Lexington, MA: Heath.

Ormrod, J. (1999). *Human learning* (3rd ed). Columbus, OH: Merrill.

Ormrod, J. (2000). *Educational psychology* (3rd ed). Columbus, OH: Merrill.

Osborne, J. (1996). Beyond constructivism. *Science Education, 80,* 53–81.

Oser, F. (1986). Moral education and values education: The discourse perspective. In M. Wittrock (Ed.), *Handbook of research on teaching* (3rd ed., pp. 917–941). New York: Macmillan.

Paivio, A. (1971). *Imagery and verbal processes.* New York: Holt, Rinehart and Winston.

Paulson, F., Paulson, P., & Meyers, C. (1991). What makes a portfolio a portfolio? *Educational Leadership, 48*(5), 63.

Peha, J. (1995). How K–12 teachers are using computer networks. *Educational Leadership, 53*(2), 18–25.

Peregoy, S., & Boyle, O. (2001). *Reading, writing, and learning in ESL* (3rd ed.). New York: Longman.

Perkins, D., & Blythe, T. (1994). Putting understanding up front. *Educational Leadership, 51,* 4–7.

Perry, M., Vanderstoep, S., & Yu, S. (1993). Asking questions in first-grade mathematics classes: Potential influences on mathematical thought. *Journal of Educational Psychology, 85*(1), 31–40.

Perry, R. (1985). Instructor expressiveness: Implications for improving teaching. In J. Donald & A. Sullivan (Eds.), *Using research to improve teaching* (pp. 35–49). San Francisco: Jossey-Bass.

Perry, R., Magnusson, J., Parsonson, K., & Dickens, W. (1986). Perceived control in the college classroom: Limitations in instructor expressiveness due to noncontingent feedback and lecture content. *Journal of Educational Psychology, 78,* 96–107.

Peterson, P. (1986). Selecting students and services for compensatory education: Lessons from aptitude-treatment interaction research. In B. Williams, P. Richmond, & B. Mason (Eds.), *Designs for Compensatory Education Conference: Proceedings and papers.* Washington, DC: Research and Evaluation Associates.

Peterson, P., Marx, A., & Clark, C. (1978). Teacher planning, teacher behavior, and student achievement. *American Educational Research Journal, 15,* 417–432.

Phillips, D. (1997). How, why, what, when, and where: Perspectives on constructivism in psychology and education. *Issues in Education, 3,* 151–194.

Philips, S. (1972). Participant structures and communicative competence: Warm Springs children in community and classroom. In C. Cazden,

V. John, & D. Hymes (Eds.), *Functions of language in the classroom* (pp. 370–394). New York: Teachers College Press.

Pintrich, P., & Schunk, D. (1996). *Motivation in education: Theory, research, and applications.* Upper Saddle River, NJ: Prentice Hall.

Plake, B., & Impara, J. (1997). Teacher assessment literacy: What do teachers know about assessment? In G. Phye (Ed.), *Handbook of classroom assessment* (pp. 54–70). San Diego: Academic Press.

Pogrow, S. (1990). Challenging at-risk students: Findings from the HOTS Program. *Phi Delta Kappan, 71*(5), 389–397.

Poole, M., Okeafor, K., & Sloan, E. (1989, April). *Teachers' interactions, personal efficacy, and change implementation.* Paper presented at the Annual Meeting of the American Educational Research Association, San Francisco.

Portner, J. (2000). Maryland study finds benefits in "Integrated Instruction" method. *Education Week, 19*(37), 10.

Prawat, R. (1989). Promoting access to knowledge, strategy, and disposition in students: A research synthesis. *Review of Educational Research, 59,* 1–41.

Presidential Task Force on Psychology in Education. (1993). *Learner-centered psychological principles: Guidelines for school redesign and reform.* Washington, DC: American Psychological Association.

Presseisen, B. (1986). *Thinking skills: Research and practice.* Washington, DC: National Education Association.

Ravetta, M., & Brunn, M. (1995, April). *Language learning, literacy, and cultural background: Second-language acquisition in a mainstreamed classroom.* Paper presented at the Annual Meeting of the American Educational Research Association, San Francisco.

Redfield, D., & Rousseau, E. (1981). A meta-analysis of experimental research on teacher questioning behavior. *Review of Educational Research, 51,* 237–245.

Reed, S., Willis, D., & Guarino, J. (1994). Selecting examples for solving word problems. *Journal of Educational Psychology, 86*(3), 380–388.

Resnick, L. (1987). *Education and learning to think.* Washington, DC: National Academy Press.

Resnick, L., & Klopfer, L. (1989). Toward the thinking curriculum: An overview. In L. Resnick & L. Klopfer (Eds.), *Toward the thinking curriculum: Current cognitive research* (pp. 1–18). Alexandria, VA: Association for Supervision and Curriculum Development.

Reynolds, R., & Shirey, L. (1988). The role of attention in studying and learning. In C. Weinstein, E. Goetz, & P. Alexander (Eds.), *Learning and study strategies* (pp. 77–110). New York: Academic Press.

Reynolds, R., Sinatra, G., & Jetton, T. (1996). Views of knowledge acquisition and representation: A continuum from experience-centered to mind-centered. *Educational Psychologist, 31,* 93–194.

Rickford, J. (1997). Suite for Ebony and phonics. *Discover, 18*(12), 82–87.

Rist, R. (1973). *The urban school: A factory for failure.* Cambridge, MA: Massachusetts Institute of Technology Press.

Roblyer, M., & Edwards, J. (2000). *Integrating educational technology into teaching* (2nd ed.). Upper Saddle River, NJ: Prentice Hall.

Rose, L., & Gallup, A. (1999). The 31st annual Phi Delta Kappa/Gallup Poll of the public's attitudes toward the public schools. *Phi Delta Kappan, 81,* 41–56.

Rosen, L., O'Leary, S., Joyce, S., Conway, G., & Pfiffer, L. (1984). The importance of prudent negative consequences for maintaining the appropriate behavior of hyperactive students. *Journal of Abnormal Child Psychology, 12,* 581–604.

Rosenfield, P., Lambert, S., & Black, R. (1985). Desk arrangement effects on pupil classroom behavior. *Journal of Educational Psychology, 77,* 101–108.

Rosenshine, B. (1971). *Teaching behaviors and student achievement.* London: National Foundation for Educational Research.

Rosenshine, B. (1979). Content, time, and direct instruction. In P. Peterson & H. Walberg (Eds.), *Research on teaching: Concepts, findings, and implications* (pp. 28–56). Berkeley, CA: McCutchan.

Rosenshine, B. (1980). How time is spent in elementary classrooms. In C. Denham & A. Lieberman (Eds.), *Time to learn.* Washington, DC: National Institute of Education.

Rosenshine, B. (1983). Teaching functions in instructional programs. *Elementary School Journal, 83,* 335–351.

Rosenshine, B., & Furst, N. (1973). The use of direct observation to study teaching. In R. Travers (Ed.), *Second handbook of research on teaching.* Chicago: Rand McNally.

Rosenshine, B., & Stevens, R. (1986). Teaching functions. In M. Wittrock (Ed.), *Handbook of research on teaching* (3rd ed., pp. 376–391). New York: Macmillan.

Ross, J. (1995). Strategies for enhancing teachers' beliefs in their effectiveness: Research on a school improvement hypothesis. *Teachers College Record, 97*(2), 227–251.

Roth, K. (1994). Second thoughts about interdisciplinary studies. *American Educator, 18,* 44–48.

Rothman, R. (1991). Schools stress speeding up, not slowing down. *Education Week, 9*(1), 11, 15.

Rottier, K. (1995). If kids ruled the world: Icons. *Educational Leadership, 53*(2), 51–53.

Rowe, M. (1974). Relation of wait-time and rewards to the development of language, logic, and fate control: Part 1. Wait-time. *Journal of Research in Science Teaching, 11,* 81–94.

Rowe, M. (1975). Help denied to those in need. *Science and Children, 12*(6), 23–25.

Rowe, M. (1986). Wait-time: Slowing down may be a way of speeding up. *Journal of Teacher Education, 37*(1), 43–50.

Rusnock, M., & Brandler, N. (1979, April). *Time off-task: Implications for learning.* Paper presented at the annual meeting of the American Educational Research Association, San Francisco.

Rutherford, F., & Algren, A. (1990). *Science for all Americans.* New York: Oxford University Press.

Saigh, P. (1984). Unscheduled assessment: Test anxiety, academic achievement, and social validity. *Educational Research Quarterly, 9*(4), 6–11.

Saracho, O. (1990). The match and mismatch of teachers' and students' cognitive styles. *Early Child Development and Care, 54,* 99–109.

Sardo, D. (1982, October). *Teacher planning styles in the middle school.* Paper presented at the Annual Meeting of the Eastern Educational Research Association, Ellenville, NY.

Sattler, J. (1992). *Assessment of children* (3rd ed.). San Diego: Jerome Sattler.

Schauble, L. (1990). Belief revision in children: The role of prior knowledge and strategies for generating evidence. *Journal of Experimental Child Psychology, 49,* 31–57.

Schmidt, P. (1992). Gap cited in awareness of students' home languages. *Education Week, 11*(32), 11.

Schnaiberg, L. (1999a). Arizona looks to its neighbor in crafting plan to take to voters. *Education Week, 18*(38), 9.

Schnaiberg, L. (1999b). Calif's year on the bilingual battleground. *Education Week, 18*(38), 1, 9, 10.

Schoenfeld, A. (1989). Teaching mathematical thinking and problem solving. In L. Resnick & L. Klopfer (Eds.), *Toward the thinking curriculum: Current cognitive research* (pp. 83–103). Alexandria, VA: Association for Supervision and Curriculum Development.

Schramm, S. (1997, March). *Related webs of meaning between the disciplines: Perceptions of secondary students who experienced an integrated curriculum.* Paper presented at the annual meeting of the American Educational Research Association, Chicago.

Schrum, L., & Fitzgerald, M. (1996). *Educators & information technologies: What will it take for adoption & implementation?* Paper presented at the annual meeting of the American Educational Research Association, New York.

Schunk, D. (1994, April). *Goal and self-evaluative influences during children's mathematical skill acquisition.*

Paper presented at the Annual Meeting of the American Educational Research Association, New Orleans.

Schwartz, B., & Reisberg, D. (1991). *Learning and memory.* New York: Norton.

Schwartz, N., Ellsworth, L., Graham, L., & Knight, B. (1998). Accessing prior knowledge to remember text: A comparison of advance organizers and maps. *Contemporary Educational Psychology, 23,* 65–89.

Senftleber, R. & Eggen, P. (1999, April). *A comparison of achievement and attitudes in a three-year integrated versus traditional middle-school science program.* Paper presented at the annual meeting of the American Educational Research Association, Montreal.

Sewall, G. (2000). History 2000: Why the older textbooks may be better than the new. *Education Week, 19*(38), 36, 52.

Shields, P., & Shaver, D. (1990, April). The *mismatch between the school and home cultures of academically at-risk students.* Paper presented at the Annual Meeting of the American Educational Research Association, Boston.

Shimron, J. (1976). Learning activities in individually prescribed instruction. *Instructional Science, 5,* 11–14.

Shipman, S., & Shipman, V. (1985). Cognitive styles: Some conceptual, methodological, and applied issues. In E. Gordon (Ed.), *Review of research in education* (12). Washington, DC: American Educational Research Association.

Shuell, T. (1996). Teaching and learning in a classroom context. In D. Berliner & R. Calfee (Eds.), *Handbook of educational psychology* (pp. 726–764). New York: Simon & Schuster.

Shulman, J. (Ed.). (1992). *Case methods in teacher education.* New York: Teachers College Press.

Shulman, L. (1986). Those who understand: Knowledge growth in teaching. *Educational Researcher, 15*(2), 4–14.

Shulman, L. (1987). Knowledge and teaching: Foundations of the new reform. *Harvard Educational Review, 57,* 1–22.

Shumow, L., & Harris, W. (1998, April). *Teachers' thinking about home-school relations in low-income urban communities.* Paper presented at the Annual Meeting of the American Educational Research Association, San Diego.

Sieber, R. (1981). Socialization implications of school discipline, or how first graders are taught to "listen." In R. Sieber & A. Gordon (Eds.), *Children and their organizations: Investigations in American culture* (pp. 18–43). Boston: G. K. Hall.

Sikula, J. (Ed.) (1996). *Handbook of research on teacher education* (2nd ed) New York: Macmillan.

Skinner, E., & Belmont, M. (1993). Motivation in the classroom: Reciprocal effects of teacher behavior and student engagement across the school year. *Journal of Educational Psychology, 85,* 571–581.

Slavin, R. (1985). Team-assisted individualization: A cooperative learning solution for adaptive instruction in mathematics. In M. Wang & H. Walberg (Eds.), *Adapting instruction to individual differences.* Berkeley, CA: McCutchan.

Slavin, R. (1986). *Using student team learning* (3rd ed.). Baltimore, MD: The Johns Hopkins University, Center for Research on Elementary and Middle School.

Slavin, R. (1987). Ability grouping and student achievement in elementary schools: A best-evidence synthesis. *Review of Educational Research, 57,* 293–336.

Slavin, R. (1989). PET and the pendulum: Faddism in education & how to stop it. *Phi Delta Kappan, 70*(10), 252–258.

Slavin, R. (1995). *Cooperative learning* (2nd ed.). Needham Heights, MA: Allyn & Bacon.

Slavin, R., Karweit, N., & Madden, N. (Eds.). (1989). *Effective programs for students at risk.* Needham Heights, MA: Allyn & Bacon.

Slavin, R., Madden, N., Dolan, L., & Wasik, B. (1994). Roots and wings: Inspiring academic excellence. *Educational Leadership, 52,* 10–14.

Smith, D., & Luckason, R. (1992). *Introduction to special education.* Boston, MA: Allyn & Bacon.

Smith, J., & Land, M. (1981). Low-inference verbal behaviors related to teacher clarity. *Journal of Classroom Interaction, 17,* 37–41.

Smith, L., & Cotten, M. (1980). Effect of lesson vagueness and discontinuity on student achievement and attitude. *Journal of Educational Psychology, 72,* 670–675.

Smyth, J. (1979). *An ecological analysis of pupil use of acadmic learing time.* Unpublished doctoral dissertation, University of Alberta.

Snider, V. (1990). What we know about learning styles from research in special education. *Educational Leadership, 48,* 53.

Snow, R., Corno, L., & Jackson III, D. (1996). Individual differences in affective and conative functions. In D. Berliner & R. Calfee (Eds.), *Handbook of educational psychology* (pp. 243–310). New York: Simon & Schuster/Macmillan.

Snyder, S., Bushur, L., Hoeksema, P., Olson, M., Clark, S., & Snyder, J. (1991, April). *The effect of instructional clarity and concept structure on students' achievement and perception.* Paper presented at the Annual Meeting of the American Educational Research Association, Chicago.

Snyderman, M., & Rothman, S. (1987). Survey of expert opinion on intelligence and aptitude testing. *American Psychologist, 42,* 137–144.

Solomon, G. (1989). Heard it, read it, and saw it on the grapevine. *Electronic Learning, 9*(7), 18–20.

Speidel, G. (1987). Conversation and language learning in the classroom. In K. Nelson & A. Van Kleeck (Eds.), *Children's language* (Vol. 6, pp. 99–135). Hillsdale, NJ: Erlbaum.

Spencer, D. (1988). Transitional bilingual education and the socialization of immigrants. *Harvard Educational Review, 58*(2), 133–153.

Spiro, R., Feltovich, P., Jacobson, M., & Coulson, R. (1992). Knowledge representation, content specification, and the development of skill in situation-specific knowledge assembly: Some constructivist issues as they relate to cognitive flexibility theory and hypertext. In T. Duffy & D. Jonassen (Eds.), *Constructivism and the technology of instruction: A conversation* (pp. 121–127). Hillsdale, NJ: Erlbaum.

Stallings, J. (1975). Implementation and child effects of teaching practices in Follow Through classrooms. *Monographs of the Society for Research in Child Development, 40*(7–8).

Stallings, J. (1980). Allocated academic learning time revisited, or beyond time on task. *Educational Researcher, 9*(11), 11–16.

Stepien, W., & Gallagher, S. (1993). Problem-based learning: As authentic as it gets. *Educational Leadership, 50*(7), 25–28.

Stern, E. (1993). What makes certain arithmetic word problems involving the comparison of sets so difficult for children? *Journal of Educational Psychology, 85*(1), 7–23.

Sternberg, R. (1986). *Intelligence applied: Understanding and increasing your intellectual skills.* San Diego, CA: Harcourt Brace Jovanovich.

Sternberg, R. (1998). Principles of teaching for successful intelligence. *Educational Psychologist, 33*(2/3), 65–72.

Stiggins, R. (2001). *Student-centered classroom assessment* (3rd ed.). Upper Saddle River, NJ: Prentice Hall.

Stipek, D. (1996). Motivation and instruction. In D. Berliner & R. Calfee (Eds.), *Handbook of Educational Psychology* (pp. 85–113). New York: Macmillan.

Stipek, D. (1998). *Motivation to learn* (3rd ed.). Needham Heights, MA: Allyn & Bacon.

Stoddart, T. (1999, April). *Language acquisition through science inquiry.* Symposium presented at the Annual Meeting of the American Educational Research Association, Montreal.

Stoddart, T., Connell, M., Stofflett, R., & Peck, D. (1993). Reconstructing elementary teacher candidates' understanding of mathematics and science content. *Teaching and Teacher Education, 9,* 229–241.

Sund, R., Adams, D., Hackett, J., & Moyer, R. (1985). *Accent on science, level 3.* Columbus, OH: Merrill.

Taylor, J. (1983). Influence of speech variety on teachers' evaluation of reading comprehension. *Journal of Educational Psychology, 75,* 662–667.

Taylor, P. (1970). *How teachers plan their courses.* Slough, Berkshire, UK: National Foundation for Educational Research.

Teachers and technology (1995). Washington, DC: U.S. Government Printing Office.

Teddlie, C., & Reynolds, D. (Eds.) (1998). *Research on school effectiveness.* Levittown, PA: Falmer.

Tennyson, R., & Cocchiarella, M. (1986). An empirically based instructional design theory for teaching concepts. *Review of Educational Research, 56,* 40–71.

Tierney, R., & Readence, J. (2000). *Reading strategies and practices* (5th ed.). Boston: Allyn & Bacon.

Tishman, S., Perkins, D., & Jay, E. (1995). *The thinking classroom: Creating a culture of thinking.* Needham Heights, MA: Allyn & Bacon.

Tobin, K. (1983). Management of time in classrooms. In B. Fraser (Ed.), *Classroom management* (pp. 22–35). Perth, Australia: WAIT Press.

Tobin, K. (1987). Role of wait-time in higher cognitive level learning. *Review of Educational Research, 57*(1), 69–95.

Tobin, K., & Capie, W. (1982). Relationships between classroom process variables and middle school science achievement. *Journal of Educational Psychology, 14,* 441–454.

Top, B., & Osgthorpe, R. (1987). Reverse-role tutoring: The effects of handicapped students tutoring regular class students. *Elementary School Journal, 87*(4), 413–423.

Turnbull, A., Turnbull, H. R., Shank, M., & Leal, D. (1999). *Exceptional lives.* (2nd ed.) Upper Saddle River, NJ: Prentice Hall.

Tyler, R. (1949). *Basic principles of curriculum and instruction.* Chicago: University of Chicago Press.

U.S. Census Bureau. (1996). *Statistics.* Washington, DC: Author.

U.S. Census Bureau. (1998a). Money, Income in the United States: 1998. *Current population survey.* World Wide Web http://www.census.gov/hhes/income95/inmed2.htmL.

U.S. Census Bureau. (1998b). *Statistics.* Washington, DC: Author.

U.S. Department of Education. (1998). *Advanced telecommunications in U.S.: Public school survey.* Washington, DC: National Center for Educational Statistics.

U.S. Department of Education. (2000). *Twenty-second annual report to Congress on the implementation of the Individuals With Disabilities Act.* Washington, DC: Government Printing Office.

U.S. Department of Education. (2001). *Twenty-third annual report to Congress on the implementation of the Individuals With Disabilities Act.* Washington, DC: Government Printing Office.

van den Heuk, M., Wolfhagen, K., Dolmans, D., & van der Vleuten, C. (1998, April). *The impact of student-generated learning issues on individual study time and academic achievement.* Paper presented at the annual meeting of the American Educational Research Association, San Diego.

Vars, G. (1996). The effects of interdisciplinary curriculum and instruction. In P. Hlebowitsh, & R. Wraga (Eds.), *Annual review of research for school leaders* (pp. 147–164). Reston, VA: National Association of Secondary School Principals.

Vasa, S. (1984). Classroom management: A selected review of the literature. In R. Egbert & M. Kluender (Eds.), *Using research to improve education* (pp. 64–73). Washington, DC: AACTE.

Veenman, S. (1984). Perceived problems of beginning teachers. *Review of Educational Research, 54*(2), 143–178.

Villegas, A. (1991). *Culturally responsive pedagogy for the 1990s and beyond.* Princeton, NJ: Educational Testing Service.

Virginia Board of Education. (1995). *United States history and social science standards of learning.* Richmond, VA: Author.

Vygotsky, L. (1978). *Mind in society: The development of higher psychological processes* (M. Cole, V. John-Steiner, S. Scribner, & E. Souberman, Eds. & Trans.). Cambridge, MA: Harvard University Press.

Walberg, H., Paschal, R., & Weinstein, T. (1985). Homework's powerful effects on learning. *Educational Leadership, 42*(7), 76–79.

Walczyk, J., & Hall, V. (1989). Is the failure to monitor comprehension an instance of cognitive impulsivity? *Journal of Educational Psychology, 81,* 294–298.

Wang, M., Haertel, G., & Walberg, H. (1993). Toward a knowledge base for school learning. *Review of Educational Research, 63*(3), 249–294.

Wang, M., Haertel, G., & Walberg, H. (1995, April). *Educational resilience: An emerging construct.* Paper presented at the Annual Meeting of the American Educational Research Association, San Francisco.

Washington, V., & Miller-Jones, D. (1989). Teacher interactions with non-Standard-English speakers during reading instruction. *Contemporary Child Psychology, 14,* 280–312.

Wattenmaker, W., Dewey, G., Murphy, T., & Medin, D. (1986). Linear separability and concept learning: Context, relational properties, and concept naturalness. *Cognitive Psychology, 18,* 158–194.

Waxman, H., Huang, S., Anderson, L., & Weinstein, T. (1997). Classroom process differences in inner-city elementary schools. *Journal of Educational Research, 91*(1), 49–59.

Weaver, L. & Padron, Y. (1997, March). *Mainstream classroom teachers' observations of ESL teachers' instruction.* Paper presented at the Annual Meeting of the American Educational Research Association, Chicago.

Webb, N., Farivar, S. (1994). Promoting helping behavior in cooperative small groups in middle school mathematics, *American Educational Research Journal, 31*(2), 369–395.

Weiland, B. (1990). Disc-over visual learning. *Science and Children, 28,* 22–23.

Weinert, F., & Helmke, A. (1995). Learning from wise mother nature or big brother instructor: The wrong choice as seen from an educational perspective. *Educational Psychologist, 30*(3), 135–142.

Weinstein, C., & Mignano, A. (1993). *Elementary classroom management.* New York: McGraw-Hill.

Weinstein, C., Woolfolk, A., Dittmeier, L., & Shankar, U. (1994). Protector or prison guard? Using metaphors and media to explore student teachers' thinking about classroom management. *Action in Teacher Education, 16*(1), 41–54.

Weinstein, R. (1998). Promoting positive expectations in schooling. In N. Lambert & B. McCombs (Eds.), *How students learn: Reforming schools through learner-centered education* (pp. 81–111). Washington, DC: American Psychological Association.

Wertsch, J. (1991). *Voices of the mind: A sociocultural approach to mediated action.* Cambridge, MA: Harvard University Press.

White, B., & Williams, H. (1996). *Construction in action: From understanding to pedagogy.* Paper presented at the Annual Meeting of the American Educational Research Association, New York.

White, M. (1975). Natural rates of teacher approval and disapproval in the classroom. *Journal of Applied Behavior Analysis, 8,* 367–372.

Wigfield, A., & Eccles, J. (1989). Test anxiety in elementary and secondary school students. *Educational Psychologist, 24,* 159–183.

Wiley, D., & Harnischfeger, A. (1974). Explosion of a myth: Quantity of schooling and exposure to instruction, major education vehicles. *Educational Researcher, 3,* 7–12.

Williams, S., Bareiss, R., & Reiser, B. (1996). *ASK Jasper: A multimedia publishing and performance support environment for design.* Paper presented at the Annual Meeting of the American Educational Research Association, New York.

Willoughby, T., Porter, L., Belsito, L., & Yearsley, T. (1999). Use of elaboration strategies by students in grades two, four, and six. *Elementary School Journal, 99*(3), 221–232.

Wilson, S., Shulman, L., & Richert, A. (1987). 150 different ways of knowing: Representations of knowledge in teaching. In J. Calderhead (Ed.), *Exploring teacher thinking* (pp. 104–124). London: Cassel.

Winitzky, N. (1998). Multicultural and mainstreamed classrooms. In R. Arends, *Learning to teach* (4th ed., pp. 132–170). New York: McGraw-Hill.

Winitzky, N., Kauchak, D., & Kelly, M. (1994). Measuring teachers' structural knowledge. *Teaching and Teacher Education, 10*(2), 125–139.

Winne, P. (1979). Experiments relating teachers' use of higher cognitive questions to student achievement. *Review of Educational Research, 49,* 13–50.

Wirth, A. (1993). Education and work: The choices we face. *Phi Delta Kappan, 74,* 361–366.

Witkin, H., Moore, C., Goodenough, D., & Cox, P. (1977). Field dependent and field independent cognitive styles and their educational implications. *Review of Educational Research, 47,* 1–64.

Wlodkowski, R. (1987, October). *The relationship between teacher motivation and student motivation—a dynamic relationship.* Paper presented at the Near East South Asia Council for Overseas Schools, Nairobi, Kenya.

Worthen, B. (1993). Critical issues that will determine the future of alternative assessment. *Phi Delta Kappan, 74,* 444–454.

Wynne, E. (1997, March). *Moral education and character education: A comparison/contrast.* Paper presented at the Annual Meeting of the American Educational Research Association, Chicago.

Yinger, R. (1977). *A study of teacher planning: Description and theory development using ethnographic and information processing methods.* Unpublished doctoral dissertation, Michigan State University, East Lansing, MI.

Young, B., & Smith, T. (1999). *The condition of education, 1996: Issues in focus: The social context of education.* Washington, DC: U.S. Department of Education. http://NCES.ed.gov/pubs/ce/c9700.html

Zahorik, J. (1975, April). *Teachers' planning models.* Paper presented at the Annual Meeting of the American Educational Research Association, Washington, DC.

Zahorik, J. (1996a). Elementary & secondary teachers' beliefs in their effectiveness: Research on a school improvement hypothesis. *Teachers College Record, 97*(2), 227–251.

Zahorik, J. (1996b). Elementary and secondary teachers' reports of how they make learning interesting. *The Elementary School Journal, 96*(5), 551–564.

Zimmerman, B. (1990). Self-regulated academic learning and achievement: The emergence of a social cognitive perspective. *Educational Psychology Review, 2,* 173–201.

Zimmerman, B., & Blotner, R. (1979). Effects of model persistence and success on children's problem solving. *Journal of Educational Psychology, 71,* 508–513.

Zimmerman, B., & Ringle, J. (1981). Effects of model persistence and statements of confidence on chil-dren's self-efficacy and problem solving. *Journal of Educational Psychology, 73,* 485–493.

Ziomek, R. (1997, March). *The concurrent validity of ACT's Passport Portfolio program: Initial validity results.* Paper presented at the Annual Meeting of the National Educational Research Association, Chicago.

Author Index

Subject Index